Section of a 1914 panoramic view of the 101 Ranch headquarters, with the White House at far right.

from the Terry Griffith collection

THE REAL WILD WEST

OTHER BOOKS BY MICHAEL WALLIS

Oil Man: The Story of Frank Phillips and the Birth of Phillips Petroleum

Route 66: The Mother Road

Pretty Boy: The Life and Times of Charles Arthur Floyd

Way Down Yonder in the Indian Nation: Writings from America's Heartland

Mankiller: A Chief and Her People
(with Wilma Mankiller)

En Divina Luz: The Penitente Moradas of New Mexico

Beyond the Hills: The Journey of Waite Phillips

Songdog Diary: 66 Stories from the Road
(with Suzanne Fitzgerald Wallis)

Oklahoma Crossroads

THE REAL WILD WEST

The 101 Ranch and the Creation of the American West

MICHAEL WALLIS

ST. MARTIN'S PRESS
New York

THE REAL WILD WEST

Dust jacket art: A 1914 Miller Brothers & Arlington 101 Ranch Real Wild West show poster. The three figures in the foreground are *(from left)* Zack Miller, Joe Miller, and George Miller. *(Jerry and Ruth Murphey Collection)*

Title page: A 1920s movie still, 101 Ranch. *(Frank Phillips Foundation, Inc.)*

For more information, please visit http://www.therealwildwest.com.

Book Design by Fritz Metsch

Library of Congress Cataloging-in-Publication Data

Wallis, Michael.
The real wild west : the 101 Ranch and the creation of the American West / Michael Wallis.—1st U.S. ed.
p. cm.
ISBN 0-312-19286-X
1. 101 Ranch Historic District (Okla.)—History. 2. 101 Ranch Historic District (Okla.)—Biography. 3. Ranch life—Oklahoma—Ponca City Region—History. 4. Ranchers—Oklahoma—Ponca City Region—Biography. 5. Miller family. 6. Ponca City Region (Okla.)—Biography. I. Title.
F704.A15W34 1999 98-50522
976.6'24—dc21 CIP

First Edition: April 1999

10 9 8 7 6 5 4 3 2

FOR

SUZANNE FITZGERALD WALLIS

The woman I will always love

FOR

BERT DORSEY

The grandfather I never knew

FOR

JERRY AND RUTH MURPHEY

The finest guardians who ever drew breath

AND FOR

ALL THOSE WHO EVER RODE
FOR THE HUNDRED AND ONE

So they will never be forgotten

As for man, his days are as grass:
as a flower of the field, so he flourisheth.
For the wind passeth over it, and it is gone;
and the place thereof shall know it no more.

—Psalms 103:15–16

Make Me a Cowboy Again for a Day

Thunder of hoofs on the range as you ride,
Hissing of iron and sizzling of hide,
Bellows of cattle and snort of cayuse,
Longhorns from Texas as wild as the deuce.
Mid-nite stampedes and milling of herds,
Yells of the Cow-men too angry for words,
Right in the thick of it all would I stay,
Make me a Cowboy again for a day.

Under the star-studded Canopy vast,
Camp-fire and coffee and comfort at last,
Bacon that sizzles and crisps in the pan,
After the round-up smells good to a man.
Stories of ranchers and rustlers retold,
Over the Pipe as the embers grow cold,
Those are the times that old memories play,
Make me a Cowboy again for a day.[1]

—Anonymous

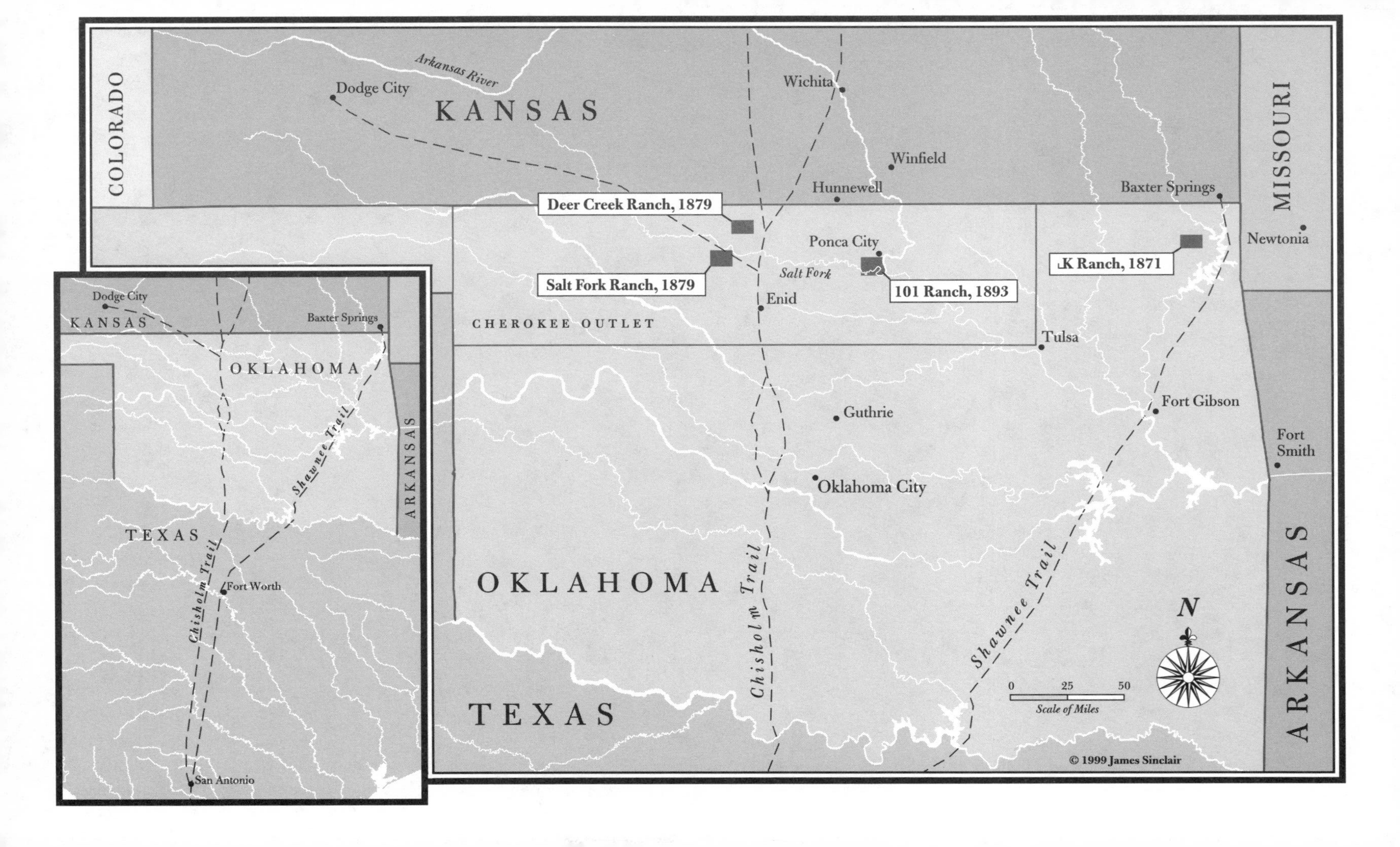
COLORADO
KANSAS
Dodge City
Arkansas River
Wichita
Winfield
Hunnewell
Baxter Springs
MISSOURI
Newtonia
Deer Creek Ranch, 1879
Salt Fork Ranch, 1879
Ponca City
Salt Fork
101 Ranch, 1893
Enid
⅃K Ranch, 1871
CHEROKEE OUTLET
Tulsa
Fort Gibson
Guthrie
Fort Smith
Oklahoma City
OKLAHOMA
Chisholm Trail
Shawnee Trail
TEXAS
ARKANSAS
N
0
25
50
Scale of Miles
© 1999 James Sinclair
Dodge City
KANSAS
Baxter Springs
OKLAHOMA
ARKANSAS
Shawnee Trail
TEXAS
Chisholm Trail
Fort Worth
San Antonio

CONTENTS

PROLOGUE

IT was a raw and damp October evening in Ponca City, in north-central Oklahoma. I was making the rounds, trying to reach as many old-timers as possible who could tell me everything they could recall about the 101 Ranch, the legendary Wild West empire created by the Miller family in the twilight of the nineteenth century.

After checking in at the motel, I found I had some time before my next appointment, and I went to the cocktail lounge to enjoy a taste of cheer. I reflected on the day, spent chasing ghosts and cottonwood leaves south of town at the site of one of the most important and influential ranches of the old American West.

The lounge was quiet. A nondescript couple sat huddled over drinks at a table on the far side of the room, whispering out of earshot. Radio music droned in the background. I took a seat at the bar and asked for a tequila neat. The barkeep, a handsome woman I judged to be about forty-five, obliged me with a wink and a smile.

"Say, don't I know you?" she asked. "Aren't you the fella that wrote that book about Route 66 and the one about 'Pretty Boy' Floyd?"

I acknowledged that I was that person.

"What brings ya up here? Workin' on another book?"

I told her I was at work on a volume about the 101 Ranch.

"Oh, that's nice," she said wiping the bar with a rag. "Was that a ranch around here someplace?"

I grinned and sipped some tequila. The woman was putting me on. Surely everyone in Oklahoma and certainly anyone from Ponca City knew damn good and well about the Hundred and One.

The woman looked at me with a blank stare.

"Was it a ranch around here?" she asked again. "Guess I never heard of it."

I almost dropped the glass. Seeing my surprise, the woman quickly added, "But see, I'm from Oklahoma City. I've only lived here about six years or so."

I was too stunned to speak.

"Is the ranch still going?" she asked. "Is it still in operation?"

I could see she was serious.

"No," I finally managed to answer. "It's gone. It's long gone."

Introduction

THE HUNDRED AND ONE

ONCE upon a time, in the far reaches of north-central Oklahoma, not far from the Kansas border, was a ranch empire of cattle, bucking horses, oil fields, and grasslands.

The ranch—which at its zenith encompassed 110,000 acres in the Ponca Indian country—was the wildest, woolliest, and most unusual operation of its kind in the history of the American West. It became known far and wide as the Miller Brothers' 101 Ranch. As a 101 Ranch publication from 1910 boasts, "The 101 Ranch, of Bliss, Okla., owned by the three Miller Brothers, is the wonderspot and the show place of all the great southwest. Here is ranching in all its old-time picturesqueness. Here are the thousands of cattle and horses, the unblocked trails and the cattle pastures, the unchanged cowboys and the wild west girls, the round-up camps, the corrals and many tribes of primitive Indians, living undisturbed in wigwam, lodge, or rough house."[1]

Everything about the place was done on a grand scale. As Glenn Shirley, in the foreword of Ellsworth Collings and Alma Miller England's book, *The 101 Ranch*, wrote, "Great Reputations have been given to a score of big cattle ranches that once covered the western United States from Mexico to Canada. But the Miller Brothers' 101 Ranch of Oklahoma was the most fabulous. It survived longer than most and reached its peak after the other big outfits had disintegrated. None ever duplicated its spectacle. It can never be repeated."[2]

The owners of the 101 Ranch operated their own trains, including a string of 150 freight cars and Pullmans. They grew far more food than they needed. After oil was discovered on the ranch in 1911, they ran every engine on the premises with fuel pumped from beneath the ranch's sod. The 101's holdings included thousands of acres devoted to wheat, corn, oats, and forage. The ranch's immensity contained schools and churches and miles of roads used by inhabitants and the public. A telephone system linked the ranch headquarters to every foreman on the distant range. Mounted riders delivered daily mail to all sections of the ranch.

The 101 Ranch orchards produced countless bushels of apples, cherries, and peaches. The ranch had grape arbors, a cider mill, a cannery, a tannery, packing plants, poultry farms, a dude ranch, novelty shops, an electric power plant, an oil refinery, blacksmith forges, an ice plant, a dairy machine and woodworking shops, a laundry, and a cafe. The Hundred and One, as it was called by those who lived and worked there, eventually sprawled over parts of four counties.

At the formidable two-story 101 Ranch Store, shoppers could buy everything from "a needle to a Ford car." Combining a department store with a trading post, it catered primarily to ranch employees but also attracted customers from a radius of more than one hundred miles. Hired hands were paid with printed "101" folding scrip and with coins stamped from copper and brass. The money was used to purchase clothing and groceries at the store, to buy food and drinks at the concession stands, and even to help pay off gambling debts.

This remarkable spread, now long vanished, remains the stuff of legends. Salty cowboys, who spent lifetimes chasing calves and sleeping in drafty bunkhouses, loved this ranch better than any other place. Cowgirls who could ride, rope, and shoot with the best of them called it home. They all believed the ranch would go on forever. Some argued that this was the land where the souls of sagebrush heroes and the most audacious saddle tramps were summoned to rest. Although this almost mythical domain has been broken up and scattered to the winds, a few old grizzled veterans still contend that the ranch remains a cowboy and cowgirl's Valhalla.

On this immense cattle ranch, launched in the 1890s, thrived a rollicking company of buckaroos, wranglers, ropers, trick shooters, and wild-horse riders. Guests from around the globe who ventured into the wide meadows of tall grass could have expected to see vast herds of grazing cattle and fleet cow ponies. They also might have encountered camels, elephants, and dancing mules. Oil tycoons and cigar-chewing politicians came to the ranch to sip whiskey, munch roasted buffalo, and wager huge sums of money—not on sleek horses but on turtles that raced at a gala event dubbed the National Terrapin Derby. Even finicky easterners could not help but feel like children again when they set foot on the 101 and shed their Yankee proprieties.

Will Rogers, before his days of fame, twirled a rope and sang cowboy songs all night long when he came calling at the ranch, and Lucille Mulhall—America's first "cowgirl"—rode with the 101 for a time. Geronimo, the Apache warrior, was brought there by U. S. Army guards so he could shoot and skin a buffalo for the benefit of a horde of ogling white folks. Bandleader John Philip Sousa became an honorary member of the Ponca tribe during a visit. Admiral Richard Byrd, after he had explored the North Pole, rode an elephant over the 101 Ranch empire. The nation's premier horticulturist, Luther Burbank, studied the records of crops grown on the ranch. So did entire classes of university students, craving agricultural knowledge they could not find anywhere else but at the Hundred and One.

Theodore Roosevelt and perennial presidential candidate William Jennings Bryan were guests at the ranch. So were Warren G. Harding, Jess Willard, John D. Rockefeller, General John Pershing, Pawnee Bill Lillie, and William S. Hart, the great early western film star. Others who came to the 101 Ranch included writers Mary Roberts Rinehart and Edna Ferber, boxing champion Jack Dempsey, publisher William Randolph Hearst, and one of the most mythologized western figures of all—William F. "Buffalo Bill" Cody, who spent some of his last days riding under the 101 name. Most of the guests sat down to tender beefsteaks bigger than saddlebags, served at the imposing stucco ranch headquarters, dubbed the White House, not far from the meandering Salt Fork River.

During the first three decades of the twentieth century, the 101 Ranch Real Wild West Show was known halfway around the globe. It featured as many as one thousand performers—cowboys and cowgirls, Indian warriors in bright paint and flowing feathers, clowns, sharpshooters, bucking horses, fancy Russian cossacks, equestrian acrobats, brave bull riders, trained buffalo, and musicians. Many of the 101 Ranch alumni were rough-and-tumble stars and luminaries whose names became household words. In 1929, *Time* magazine wrote

> To thousands of U. S. citizens the 101 Ranch Wild West Show represented the embodiment, the incarnation of that vanished West in which cowboys had not become associated with drugstores and Indians were not graduates of Carlisle. Many a European, too, saw the 101 Ranch Show, doubtless gained from it the impression that travelers in the western portion of the U. S. trembled before the tomahawk and the six-shooter. Begun informally, casually, when the Millers permitted some of their cowboys to perform at a local fair, the 101 Ranch Show grew into a circus that netted the Millers a million dollars a year. Sideshows it had, and freaks, and many a Bearded Lady and Human Skeleton vacationed during the winter in the

> elegant quarters on the Miller's [sic] luxurious ranch at Marland, Okla. But it was essentially a Wild West Show, with buffaloes and cattle, cowmen and cow-girls, pistols and scalping knives, and the sure-fire big scene of the Attack on the Stage Coach, with round-eyed, heart-pounding spectators writhing on the edges of pine-board seats.[3]

Kings and queens, matinée idols and millionaires, and hundreds of thousands of ordinary working folks cheered themselves hoarse when the nimble 101 Ranch riders performed at rodeo grounds, stadiums, and exhibition halls across the nation and in Europe, Mexico, and Canada. Indeed, the spectators, no matter their social standing, adored the 101. Striking images of the ranch, such as the 101's pet bear guzzling bottle after bottle of soda pop outside the ranch store, remained embedded decades later in the memories of adults. The costumed figures pictured on the 101 Ranch show posters, which came to life on movie screens and during shows at hundreds of hometown arenas, helped to create an American consciousness of the West that would be manifested in early Hollywood films.

The men and women of the 101 were a flamboyant bunch. Bandits and lawmen with notched six-guns who spent most of their lives riding the range traveled with the ranch's Wild West circuit. So did a multitude of Native American people. Eastern dudes and kids from all around the countryside ran away from home to hook up with the 101 and fulfill their dreams of becoming genuine cowboys or cowgirls. Sometimes their timing was impeccable; a few of them made the leap from real life to film just as the western motion-picture business was being created at the 101. Tom Mix, Hoot Gibson, Buck Jones, Ken Maynard, and others saddled cow ponies and drew wages from the 101 paymaster before they became famous film stars. Bill Pickett, the fabled black cowboy who invented the rodeo sport of bulldogging, proudly rode for the 101 until the day he died.

During the ranch's glory years, which extended from about 1905 to 1925, movie crews moved freely around the property among working cowboys. On Sundays, free rodeos were held. What was not so well known, especially abroad, was that the show and performers originated from an authentic working ranch that truly rivaled all the other great cattle operations featured in the folklore of the West. On this ranch, the West of imagination collided and merged with the West of reality—a spectacle that can never be duplicated.

But that was all a long time ago.

PART ONE

The Dark and Bloody Ground

The traveler can behold the great broad uncertain rivers which bore pioneers to the west, a wild and treacherous ocean coast, and cloven in between, the dark tumbled peaks and ridges of the Cumberland. It is, all of it, bloodied ground indeed. The conquest of its wilderness by a violent and often outcast people cast a torrent of blood.[1]

—Mary Bolté
Dark and Bloodied Ground

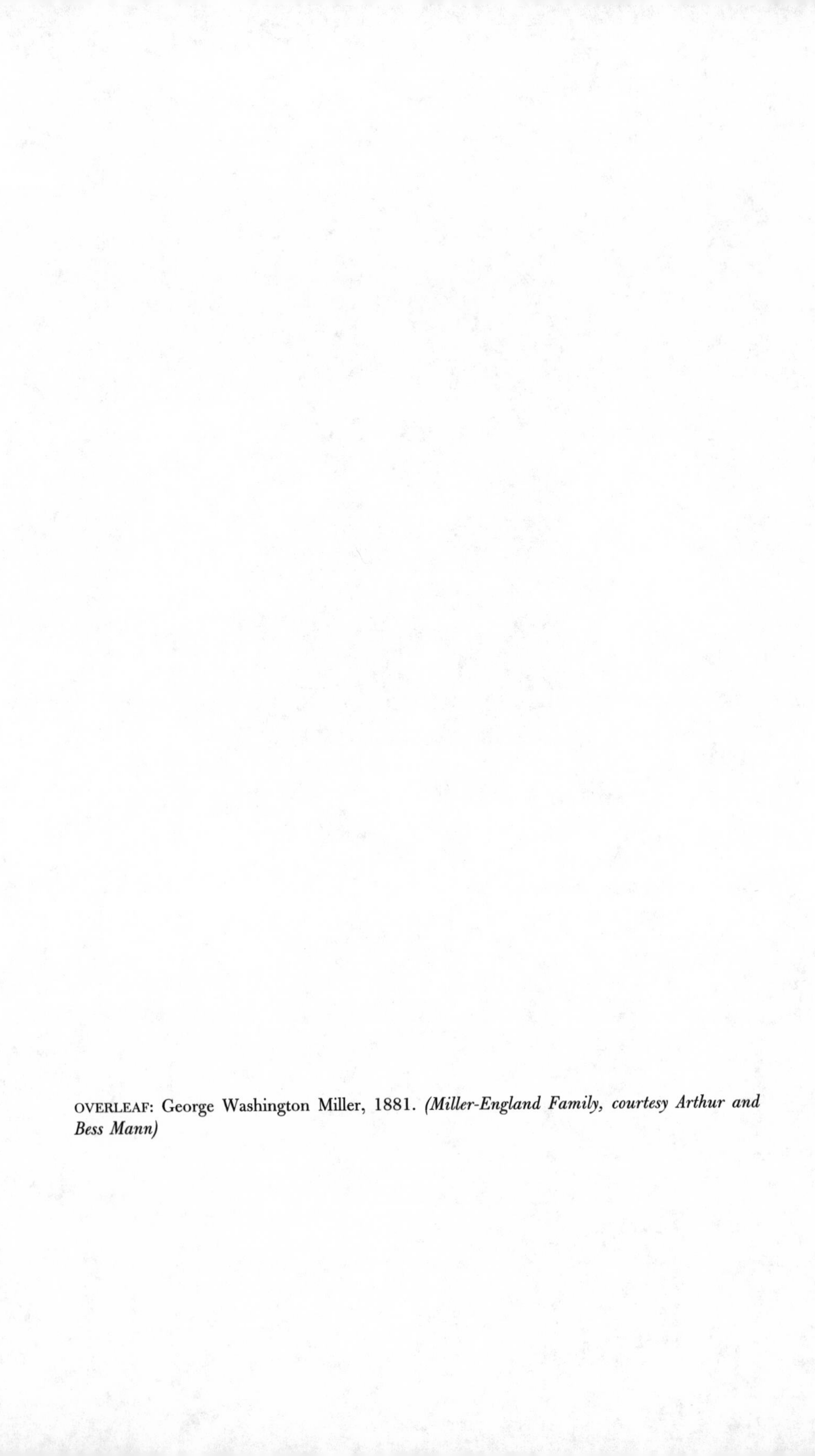

OVERLEAF: George Washington Miller, 1881. *(Miller-England Family, courtesy Arthur and Bess Mann)*

Chapter 1

KENTUCKY HOME

Stand at Cumberland Gap and watch the
procession of civilization, marching single file—
the buffalo following the trail to the salt springs,
the Indian, the fur-trader and hunter,
the cattle-raiser, the pioneer farmer—
and the frontier has passed by.[1]
—Frederick Jackson Turner

THE story of the 101 Ranch began in Kentucky in the early 1840s with the birth of George Washington Miller. Destined to be patriarch of the Miller family, he would rival the flamboyant William F. "Buffalo Bill" Cody as the originator of the world's very first Wild West show and rodeo.

It is altogether fitting that the genesis of the 101 empire was Kentucky. Only the fifteenth state to enter the Union, in 1792, it was the first state beyond the Alleghenies and a pioneer land that yielded early frontier legends such as Daniel Boone and Kit Carson. Many Indians and the English and Scotch-Irish settlers who hailed from Virginia and the Carolinas referred to the Kentucky country as the "hunting ground" because of the abundance of game. Later, in the era of fierce battles between Indians and white intruders, the region became known as the "dark and bloody ground."

"So rich was the soil, so plentiful were the fish and game and various the beauties of Kentucky, that its original inhabitants, including Shawnee and Cherokee, fought continuously over tribal boundaries and called it 'the dark and bloody ground,' " wrote Darcy O'Brien in his book *A Dark and Bloody Ground.* "The phrase, from which the name Kentucky derives, gained currency during the period of white settlement, when Daniel Boone and others wrote of the new land as a Garden of Eden well worth bloodshed."[2]

Despite its raw natural beauty, Kentucky was not a land for the citified or the weak. This became clear to the whites and Indians alike when their cultures collided and the region channeled more and more settlers into the Mississippi Valley and the lands beyond. White frontiersmen—rugged trail-blazers and hunters—who ventured into Kentucky in the 1700s became known as "long hunters" because they made extended trips over the mountains in search of game. Together, they helped to shape the most persistent myths of frontier America, recounting vivid tales that fueled the imagination of future generations of pioneers born in the middle of the nineteenth century.

Born on February 22, 1842, to George and Almira Fish Miller, George Washington Miller was a true son of the South. Although some records give his birth year as 1841, Miller's birthdate of February 22 was never in dispute, and it provided his parents with an obvious choice for his name. The baby arrived at his father's ancestral home in Lincoln County, near the town of Crab Orchard, in central Kentucky. The Miller residence was near Hanging Fork Creek. According to local legend, the tributary was named in early settlement days when two desperadoes who had escaped from Virginia authorities were captured and summarily hanged from a tall tree at the fork of a stream.

For reasons unknown, George Washington Miller's paternal grandfather, Armstead Milner, had changed the family surname from Milner to Miller. A farmer, he is listed in early Lincoln County records as both Milner and Miller in the late 1700s and early 1800s. A 1795 tax roll lists him as "a white male over 21 with 2 horses, 3 cattle."

Well into his eighties when he died, Armstead Miller was laid to rest in a small family burial ground near the old homesite. Over the years, the graveyard fell into ruin and was left unattended, protected only by a crumbling stone wall. Some graves were unmarked, and the few headstones, including that of Armstead Miller, eventually were worn smooth by the elements and no longer could be read. One discernible stone was at the grave of James Feland. Born in 1793, he was wounded severely as a soldier at the Battle of the Thames in the War of 1812, before marrying Armstead Miller's daughter Sallie. Feland died in 1828. Just a year later, another Miller daughter, Eliza Rout, died at age twenty-four, in her third year of marriage. She was buried in the family cemetery, with a marker bearing the somber epitaph, "Remember friends as you pass by, As you are now Wounce [sic] was I. As I am now so you must be. Prepare for death and eternity."

Little is known of Armstead Miller's son George or what became of him other than that he married Almira Fish in Lincoln County on June 8, 1831, fathered at least two sons, and drank to excess. His drunkenness and resulting foul behavior finally convinced Almira to end her stormy marriage not long after the birth of their son George Washington. Even before his parents' divorce became final, the youngster and his mother went to live with her parents, John and Mary Fish, born in 1788 and 1792, respectively.

There was ample room for Almira and her children at the Fish residence on a flourishing plantation a few miles east of Crab Orchard in central Kentucky, near the mouth of Copper Creek. This was the same comfortable home where Almira had been born on November 14, 1816, and she considered it a sanctuary. Soon after returning to her parents' home, Almira received the sad but inevitable news that alcohol finally had taken its toll; her former husband, George Miller, was dead.

George Washington Miller grew up not really knowing much about his father and the Milner/Miller family. His grandfather John Fish primarily raised him. George and his brother Walter, born in 1837, spent their formative years at the Fish homestead where, according to family records, "everything was done in a grand manner." Early on, his surroundings in Lincoln County influenced George greatly. Formed in 1780 as one of Kentucky's oldest and largest counties, it was named for Massachusetts native Benjamin Lincoln, a distinguished general in the American Revolution in charge of the Continental forces waging war against the British in the South.[3] George Miller was taught that his home county claimed many firsts in Kentucky history, including the first brick house, first mill, first circular race track, first white child's birth, and first Kentucky governor.

From his grandfather and other old-timers, the boy heard tales of the scalpings and skirmishes on the "dark and bloody ground." He learned that much of the murder and mayhem took place along the pioneer trail known as "the Road to Caintuck," "the Great Western Road," or "the Kentucky Path," but most often called "the Wilderness Road." The well-worn path ran right through Lincoln County and Crab Orchard.[4]

Young George Miller also heard of the acts of God that had left their marks, such as the great hailstorm of 1781 that showered stones nine inches in circumference over the land, destroying entire crops and leaving hundreds of wild and domestic animals dead in its wake. He heard in the distance the peculiar call of a conch shell that had been turned up from a field beside a nearby creek sixty years before his birth and still was used to summon field hands to meals. He learned to hunt and fish in the dense forests and along the never-dry streams and tributaries of the Kentucky, Cumberland, and Green Rivers—streams such as Hawkins Branch, Boone, Knob Lick, and others, named mostly for pioneers who had staked their claims long before.[5] He was spoon-fed endless accounts of his ancestors and others who endured uncertainties and faced "hostile savages" to carve a living out of the rich Kentucky soil.

They were the types of stories passed on by Lewis Collins in his 1877 book *History of Kentucky*:

> In the year 1781 or 2, near the Crab Orchard, in Lincoln County, a very singular adventure occurred at the house of a Mr. Woods. One morning he left his family, consisting of a wife, a daughter not yet grown, and a lame negro [sic] man, and rode off to the station near by, not expecting to return till night. Mrs. Woods being a short distance from her cabin, was alarmed by discovering several Indians advancing towards it. She instantly screamed loudly in order to give the alarm, and ran with her utmost speed, in hope of reaching the house before them. In this she succeeded, but before she could close the door, the foremost Indian had forced his way into the house. He was instantly seized by the lame negro man, and after a short scuffle, they both fell with violence, the negro underneath. Mrs. Woods was too busily engaged in keeping the door closed against the party without, to attend to the combatants; but the lame negro, holding the Indian tightly in his arms, called to the young girl to take the axe from under the bed and dispatch him with a blow on the head. She immediately attempted it; but the first attempt was a failure. She repeated the blow and killed him. The other Indians were at the door, endeavoring to force it open with their tomahawks. The negro rose and proposed to Mrs. Woods to let in another, and they would soon dispose of the whole of them in the same way. The cabin was but a short distance from the station, the occupants of which having discovered the perilous situation of the family, fired on the Indians and killed another, when the remainder made their escape.[6]

Stories of such conflicts instilled a deep sense of pioneer pride in George Washington Miller, whose early years in Kentucky established in him firm principles of courage, honor, and perseverance. These pioneer tales set the stage for a drama that George Washington Miller's three sons replayed until the final curtain fell more than ninety years after their father's birth.

DANIEL BOONE:
America's First "Cowboy"

PERHAPS THERE WAS no greater influence on young George W. Miller than the stories of Daniel Boone. Like his fellow Kentuckians, Miller grew up hearing tales about the legendary frontiersman. So revered was Boone that some folks considered him a latter-day Moses who had led his people—waves of white settlers—into the so-called promised land of "Ken-tucke."

But Boone—a diminutive man whose exploits elevated him to near-mythic stature in his lifetime—was a "cowboy" long before he made a name for himself as a frontiersman. Born in 1734 into a Pennsylvania Quaker family, Boone later recalled that his fondest childhood memory was his time spent tending cattle and listening to his mother as she churned and sang before a roaring fire. His "love for the wilderness and hunter's life," said Boone, started with his "being a herdsman and thus being so much in the woods."[1]

Within a few years, young Boone, who hated plowing fields as much as he loved tending cows, took up a rifle and began to build his reputation as a trailblazer, scout, and one of the "long hunters" who traversed the backwoods of the Appalachians in the 1760s.

Exaggerated accounts of Boone's exploits, especially at Cumberland Gap and on the new Wilderness Road that ran north through the fertile blue-grass countryside, inspired three future American heroes—Davy Crockett, Kit Carson (perhaps a distant relative of Boone and of Mary Anne Carson, G. W. Miller's wife, according to incomplete Carson family records), and William F. "Buffalo Bill" Cody. Destined to become the standard for a multitude of other western legends, Boone served as the model for the hunter-heroes in James Fenimore Cooper's adventure novels. Even English poet Lord Byron paid tribute to Boone in the romantic epic *Don Juan:*

> *"Of the great names which in our faces stare,*
> *The General Boon, back-woodsman of Kentucky,*
> *Was happiest amongst mortals anywhere. . . ."*

Contrary to popular myths, Boone never wore a coonskin cap but opted instead for the wide-brimmed beaver hat favored by his fellow Quakers. Although tales abound of his skills as an "Injun fighter," Boone—unlike some of his contemporaries—found no pleasure in violence and preferred solitude over the folklore and legend that overshadowed him. "I never killed but three," Boone often told visitors who found their way to his home in Missouri, anxious to learn how many Indians he had dispatched during his long life. "I am very sorry to say that I ever killed any for they have always been kinder to me than the whites."[2]

At about the turn of the nineteenth century, Boone moved to Missouri, where the Spanish had given him a land grant. As a magistrate, he held court beneath a towering elm known as the Judgment Tree. He always remained restless, however, and as an old man, he continued to roam, perhaps as far west as the Platte River and into the Yellowstone country.[3] In 1820, just a few weeks short of his eighty-sixth birthday, the old hunter died at his son's limestone home near Defiance, Missouri. Having felt hemmed in by the growing number of settlers moving farther west, he had been planning yet another move on the eve of his death. Laid out in the custom-designed cherry-wood coffin he had kept for years under his feather bed, Boone was buried near his beloved wife, Rebecca, on a knoll overlooking the Missouri River.

George Miller was a three-year-old boy in 1845 when Kentucky officials supposedly dug up the bones of Boone and his wife and brought them back to a site above the state capitol, in Frankfort. But there are those in Missouri who claim the wrong body was sent.[4] They believe the remains of a slave, and not of Boone, rest in Kentucky. Even in death, the Boone legends have persisted, and have helped to shape the national myths of the frontier.

Chapter 2

REBEL CHILD

The sun shines bright in the old Kentucky home;
'Tis summer, the darkeys are gay,
The corn-top's ripe and the meadow's in the bloom,
While the birds make music all the day.[1]

—Stephen C. Foster
"My Old Kentucky Home"

THE terrible collapse of his parents' marriage permanently affected young George Washington Miller, and he immersed himself in the rich history, culture, and folklore of mid-nineteenth-century Kentucky in his new life in his grandfather's home. In time, he readily came to accept the life of the ruling class and his place among the landed gentry on a busy Kentucky that depended on slave labor. Although Kentucky was a border state and did not maintain vast plantations such as those in the Deep South, slavery remained a venerated institution. As late as 1860, Kentucky had 38,645 slaveowners, surpassed only by Georgia and Virginia.[2]

Like the Millers and others of high social standing in the bluegrass region of antebellum Kentucky, the Fish family owned numerous slaves. They used them not only for domestic chores but also to toil on the hundreds of acres devoted to grain and grazing pasture for livestock, as well as to the important cash crops of burley tobacco and hemp.

George Washington Miller, or G.W., as he came to be called, was essentially raised by Fish family slaves who catered to his every whim. Older women servants, usually known as "Aunty" or "Mammy," served as affectionate second mothers to "Massa" Fish's grandson. Old "Uncles," the southern nickname for elderly black men, helped watch over the lad. In the vast fields, a gang of pitiful "wenches" and "buck niggers," in the pejorative slang of that time and place, prayed to Jesus for the chance to leave their backbreaking labor for a more comfortable position in the big house. Few made the transition.

Kentucky served as a sort of regional slavery clearinghouse, and caravans of blacks in ankle irons became common sights in Lexington and other human marketplaces. Undoubtedly, G.W. attended public slave sales or auctions—cruel transactions of human flesh at which whole families were sold as chattel like mules or horses. Often, husbands and wives were separated from their children, and babies simply were sold by the pound.[3]

As he grew up, G.W. learned about the busy farm that was his home by working closely with overseers hired by his grandfather to manage daily operations—planting, tilling, harvesting, and slave discipline. Long after the abolition of slavery, the Miller and Fish families were remembered as slave owners who had worked "their slaves and hired hands to their limits" and "whose tempers were never to be dealt with in a joking manner."[4] Still, although most Kentuckians generally considered themselves to be the most compassionate of slaveholders, there is little evidence that the Miller and Fish families treated their slaves any worse or any better than did others in Kentucky.

As John Fish indoctrinated his grandson in the use of slaves to work the crops and do his bidding, he also taught the boy to be proud and self-reliant. He instilled in him a devotion to family and land, and—in a region where gentlemen considered their honor sacred and often settled their differences with dueling pistols—a respect for the pledged word. The old man also steeped the boy in the manly pursuits of their social class, such as hunting in the forests of oak, hickory, and tulip trees, and riding at breakneck speed after hounds across lush meadows.

Like his grandfather, young George became a lover of livestock, and particularly of horseflesh—Kentucky thoroughbreds descended from fine horses brought from Virginia, noted for speed, strength, and stamina. Besides teaching him to appreciate sleek horses, Fish also shared with his grandson his knowledge of mules.[5]

By the time he reached his teenage years, George Miller had become a competent mule trader, at ease in the company of much older men and seasoned dealers who came to the Fish barns to appraise young mules. While developing the ability to work with mules, he discovered that a mule trader had to be a shrewd judge of men as well as of beasts.

The young Kentucky gentleman learned how to look for mules with clear, expressive eyes. He ran his hands down the mule's straight legs, feeling the bones and looking for swollen joints or sores. He pulled back their lips to check for missing teeth. He looked for a wide stance, black hooves, shiny coats, muscular chests, round rumps. He spoke to the animals, ever mindful that like humans, even mules craved attention.

After watching mules work day after day beneath the blazing sun, G.W. concluded that mules probably were smarter than horses. He noticed that if a horse and mule were paired, the mule always would invent a way to put most of the work on the horse. And at the feed trough, mules invariably walked away when they had had their fill, while horses ate until they foundered.[6] Perhaps George Miller respected mules because he realized that like them, he too was rebellious and stubborn. He further reasoned that mules, like slaves, carried grudges. If they were handled cruelly, they never forgot who had "done them wrong." That rage burned within them until they died or got even. George Miller had enough formal schooling to get along at barbecues and parties and to speak with assured knowledge of politics and the tobacco market. But he picked up his real education by haggling in the mule barn and by observing his grandfather hold forth over a tumbler of sour-mash bourbon and a plate of smoked country ham.

On June 13, 1857—four months after George Miller's fifteenth birthday—life changed at the Fish plantation. His mother, Almira, almost forty-one and fully prepared to give matrimony a second chance, wed Judge John Evans Carson, a prominent Kentucky jurist ten years her senior. In later years, family legend would have it that Judge Carson was a distant kinsman of Kentucky native Christopher "Kit" Carson, the illiterate trapper, Indian fighter, and guide who evolved into one of the most legendary figures in the American West.[7] Although no confirmation of that relationship has surfaced, ample documentation of Judge Carson's ancestry exists. His Irish forebears came from County Down, Ireland, to Pennsylvania in the early 1700s. Succeeding generations of Carsons settled in Virginia. Some fought under Colonel George Washington in the French and Indian War and in the American Revolution.[8]

Born to Joseph and Mary Evans Carson in Rockcastle County, Kentucky, in 1806, Judge Carson was no stranger to the Fish family. His first wife had been Almira's first cousin Marinda Fish, born in 1813 to James and Sarah Fish. Judge Carson had married Marinda in 1839. She bore him eight children before her death in 1853—Sarah Elizabeth, James Fish, Joseph, Zack T., Thomas, Mary Anne, George W., and John Evans Jr.[9]

After his mother's marriage to Judge Carson, George Miller stayed on at the Fish plantation and continued to work alongside his grandfather. However, he managed to spend some time with the Carson brood, which soon grew larger. In 1860, Almira gave birth to Hiatt Fish Carson, followed by her last child, a son she and her husband named David Carson. Tragedy struck when Hiatt became ill and died at only eleven months. He was buried in the Fish family cemetery.[10]

Unlike many fractious stepchildren relationships, George Miller and the Carson children got along. Indeed, several of the stepbrothers became close pals. One of the younger boys, George W. Carson—who family records assert was given the middle name William after one of Kit Carson's grandfathers—eventually moved west with Miller and served as one of his first cowboys on the Texas cattle trails.

Still, there was little doubt about which of the Carsons drew most of George Miller's attention. When she was just a young girl chasing about the porches and rooms of the Fish plantation, his attractive stepsister and second cousin Mary Anne Carson caught George Miller's eye. Born on August 26, 1846, at her father's plantation in Rockcastle County, Mary Anne, who was called Polly, Molly, or Mollie by friends and family, was two weeks shy of her seventh birthday when her mother, Marinda, died. The girl was almost eleven years old when her father married Almira, George Miller's mother. A gracious and loving woman, Almira filled an immense void in the lives of Mary Anne and the other Carson siblings.

The combined Carson-Miller family enjoyed periodic excursions to distant Louisville and more frequent visits to the villages of Stanford and nearby Crab Orchard Springs. The seat of Lincoln County and a pioneer station on the old Wilderness Road, Crab Orchard Springs was named for a large grove of crab-apple trees that grew there—or, in another version, in honor of Isaac Crabtree, one of the storied "long hunters" of Kentucky.[11]

Known for its soothing mineral springs and comfortable hotel, Crab Orchard, the "Saratoga of the South," attracted guests from all over the country as early as 1827. They came to "take the waters," play cards, and watch fleet horses run. The watering season stretched through the summer months. By the 1850s, the Crab Orchard Springs Hotel was in its heyday, hosting society's upper echelon from Kentucky, Louisiana, Mississippi, and Arkansas. Numerous northern gentlemen and their ladies—wealthy sugarcane and cotton planters accompanied by families and servants, anxious to escape the dreaded yellow fever—also journeyed to the spa to rub shoulders with the elite from the Deep South.

Music and dancing at masquerade and fancy-dress balls, hunting and horseback riding, and relaxing on spacious verandas made for idyllic days and nights for Kentuckians such as George Miller and his extended family.

Ironically, within a decade, many of the men who had danced with their wives at Crab Orchard would be fighting one another in the bloodiest combat that has occurred on American soil. Indeed, just as Miller reached his twenties, those halcyon times came to an abrupt halt for the entire South. Danger permeated the air, as thick as the cloying aroma of honeysuckle. War clouds loomed up and down the Mason-Dixon Line. There would be parties and horse races and good times again—but not for a very long time.

P. T. BARNUM INVENTS THE WILD WEST

PHINEAS TAYLOR BARNUM—who introduced to the American public General Tom Thumb, a popular dwarf; soprano Jenny Lind, "the Swedish Nightingale"; Chang and Eng, famed Siamese twins; Jumbo, the giant elephant; and a tent circus that became known as "The Greatest Show on Earth"—was no stranger to Kentucky. He brought his first traveling show there as early as 1837.[1]

Barnum, often accompanied by some of his human oddities, returned to Kentucky several times during his long career as a showman, including a lecture stop in 1867. At the same time, William F. Cody was earning his famous moniker by slaughtering buffalo to feed Kansas Pacific Railroad workers.[2] In 1872, the aging Barnum again returned to Kentucky, where robbers took a diamond ring and three hundred dollars in cash from him on a train near Louisville. By that time, George W. Miller had packed up his young family and fled Kentucky for greener pastures to the west, in Missouri.

It is not known if Miller, as a boy or man, ever saw one of Barnum's shows or if he heard him speak during one of his visits to the Bluegrass State. What is known is that at least forty years before G. W. Miller sponsored a cowboy roundup or Buffalo Bill Cody staged his first Wild West show, P. T. Barnum realized the untapped show-business potential of the American West. Evidence traces this development to June 1843, during an anniversary celebration at the site of the Battle of Bunker Hill near Boston. While Daniel Webster delivered an impressive oration, Barnum peeked inside an old canvas tent and discovered a herd of fifteen young buffalo, which he immediately bought for seven hundred dollars. Barnum promptly shipped the docile animals to New York and then transported them to a barn near Hoboken, New Jersey. He hired C. D. French, the herd's former owner, to care for them because "French understood the lasso."[3]

Newspapers soon heralded Barnum's buffalo, reportedly captured in the Rocky Mountains, and suggested that a buffalo chase be staged so curious easterners could see an expert use his lariat on the supposedly ferocious beasts. Handbills, posters, and advertisements appeared all over the city, announcing, "Grand Buffalo Hunt, Free of Charge—At Hoboken, on Thursday, August 31, at 3, 4, and 5 o'clock p.m. Mr. C. D. French, one of the most daring and experienced hunters of the West, has arrived thus far on his way to Europe with a Herd of Buffaloes, captured by himself, near Santa Fé. . . . Every man, woman, and child can here witness *the wild sports of the Western Prairies*, as the exhibition is to be free to all, and will take place on the extensive grounds and Race Course of Messrs. Stevens, within a few rods of the Hoboken Ferry."[4]

New Yorkers were ecstatic over the prospects of viewing such a spectacle, even if they were mystified about the identity of the anonymous patron willing to provide a free show. Little did anyone suspect that P. T. Barnum (called, among other names, "the prince of humbugs") owned the buffalo. Barnum also had purchased rights to receipts of all who paid to ride the ferryboats between New York and Hoboken for August 31, 1843, to witness the big Wild West exhibition. And for good measure, he also controlled all the food and drink concessions.

On that day, more than twenty-four thousand people went to Hoboken to see the buffalo, paying six and a quarter cents each way on the crowded ferries. Finally, the "wild" buffalo appeared, looking timid and thin despite the extra rations of oats they had been fed for the previous several days. C. D. French also showed up, costumed and painted like an Indian. "Mounted on a Prairie Horse and Mexican saddle," French poked and goaded the huge creatures but could persuade them to do nothing more than trot around the arena floor. The resulting laughter and shouting so terrified the buffalo that they fled for the refuge of a nearby swamp. During the commotion, one spectator was killed when he fell out of a tree. French finally roped one of the buffalo and entertained the crowd for the rest of the day and into the evening with an exhibition of lassoing from horseback. The last of the weary but satisfied fans got home from Hoboken well past midnight, and Barnum pocketed a hefty thirty-five hundred dollars in ferry revenue.[5]

Barnum did not stop with this exhibition. On the heels of his successful "Great Buffalo Hunt," he presented the first Wild West show in New York, featuring a band of Indians from Iowa, the state where Bill Cody was born in 1848. Still captivated by what he considered to be the Wild West, Barnum formed a partnership in 1860 with the crusty James C. "Grizzly" Adams and his California menagerie—twenty bears, an assortment of wolves, lions, buffalo, and elk, and a gigantic sea lion named Old Neptune. In one New York parade, the buckskin-clad Adams—who eventually died from wounds sustained from repeated maulings by bears—rode down Broadway astride a grizzly named General Frémont.[6]

A few years later, in 1864, after President Abraham Lincoln had received a delegation of Indian leaders at the White House, Barnum bribed their interpreter to bring the proud chiefs to his New York museum. Unknown to the Indians, who believed Barnum was paying them tribute by bringing crowds of people to see them, they were part of a mocking public exhibition.

"This little Indian, ladies and gentlemen, is Yellow Bear, chief of the Kiowas," Barnum would explain. "He has killed, no doubt, scores of white persons, and he is probably the meanest, black-hearted rascal that lives in the Far West. If the blood-thirsty little villain understood what I was saying, he would kill me in a moment; but, as he thinks I am complimenting him, I can safely state the truth to you, that he is a lying, thieving, treacherous, murdering monster. He has tortured to death poor, unprotected women, murdered their husbands, brained their helpless children; and he would gladly do the same to you or to me if he thought he could escape punishment."[7] Then Barnum gave the chief a condescending pat on the head and listened to the howls of laughter from the audience. When the Indian leaders finally figured out that their deceitful host was charging admission for visitors to gawk at them, they felt insulted and immediately returned to Washington. It was not the first or, sadly, the last time that white men would ridicule Indians. This patronizing attitude became engrained in the Wild West shows of the late 1800s and early 1900s, influencing the images millions of people formed of Indians.

Chapter 3

HEAR THE WIND BLOW

Down in the valley, the valley so low,
Hang your head over, hear the wind blow.
Hear the wind blow, dear, hear the wind blow,
Hang your head over, hear the wind blow.
—Old Kentucky folk lyric

WHEN the Civil War erupted, George Washington Miller's Kentucky, more than most states of the imperiled union, was torn asunder by opposing loyalties. Drawn to the South through family, cultural, and historical ties, Kentuckians also maintained an alliance with the North, continuing to nurture their strong commercial relationships and solid commitment to the Union.

Officially a neutral state, Kentucky sent one hundred thousand troops to fight for the North, including twenty-nine thousand black soldiers. It also sent forty thousand boys and men to the cause of the South. Of all the thousands who fought on each side, one-third of them never came home.

Coincidentally, Abraham Lincoln, just elected United States president, and Confederate President Jefferson Davis were both born in Kentucky, one year and one hundred miles apart. Mary Todd Lincoln, the president's wife, also was a Kentucky native and a genuine southern belle. Three of her sisters were married to Confederate officers, and two Todd brothers also took up the cause against the Union. One of them, Lieutenant David P. Todd, was charged with brutality to Yankee prisoners at Richmond, Virginia. The other, Dr. George Todd, served as a Confederate surgeon and opined once that his eminent brother-in-law Abe Lincoln was "one of the greatest scoundrels unhung."[1]

Nowhere else in the nation was the term *brother against brother* more meaningful than in Kentucky. Henry Clay, "the Great Compromiser," three-time unsuccessful presidential candidate, and powerful Kentucky statesman, recognized by many historians as one of the greatest United States senators in history, saw seven of his grandsons ride off to battle—three for the Union, four for the Confederacy. Similarly, Kentucky Senator George B. Crittenden drew great pride from his two sons who became major generals, one for each side.[2]

Although Kentucky tried to avoid the war by declaring itself neutral and maintaining the capital at Frankfort, Confederate supporters established a rival capital at Bowling Green. Strategically located, the border state became the scene for more than three hundred skirmishes and battles. Even after battle lines were drawn, loyalties remained deeply divided between the North and South in many parts of Kentucky. There was no question, however, at the Fish plantation or at the home of Judge John E. Carson. The Millers and Carsons and their kin had no doubts about their allegiance, for they were slave owners. They would unquestionably fight for their beloved Dixie. Their sense of chivalry and honor allowed no other course of action.

Family members recalled that in his later years, George Miller winced whenever he heard the words *Civil War*. Like most dyed-in-the-wool Rebels, he thought of the four-year struggle not as a civil insurrection but as "the War to Suppress Yankee Arrogance," "the War against Northern Aggression," or "the Second American Revolution."[3]

According to family history, several of the Carsons and Millers took up arms for the Confederacy, including Judge Carson, just turned fifty-five when the war started, and his stepson George Miller, an imposing twenty-year-old.[4] Little is known of G. W. Miller's war record, but his familiarity with ritualized and recreational violence such as cockfighting and dueling—combined with a love of firearms and fast horses—made him ideal for the cavalry. Family stories that have survived are as vague and incomplete as the archival records, which list seven George, G.W., or George W. Millers as Confederate soldiers from Kentucky.[5] Of those seven Millers found in official documents, the most likely to be the George W. Miller of 101 Ranch fame was a private who appeared on the rolls of Company E, one of the largest outfits of the Eleventh Regiment Cavalry, Kentucky Volunteers of the Confederate States Army. If so, it is likely that Miller fought at the Battle of Perryville on October 8, 1862, the largest and bloodiest battle in the state. Elsewhere the fighting continued, but the Battle of Perryville proved to be what some historians have described as the "Battle for Kentucky," and ensured that the state would remain Union territory for the rest of the war.[6]

Not all Kentucky rebels—especially not those from more established Confederate families—proved charitable or gracious when it came to accepting defeat and the ensuing collapse of the traditional southern way of life; too many comrades had been lost in battle or had succumbed to disease. The fact that Confederate soldiers were imprisoned by Union armies and sometimes simply vanished rankled southerners. As the tide of the war turned in 1863 and 1864, several cavalrymen from Company E, for example, ended up on the Eleventh Regiment rolls as "missing," and others were reported wounded or killed in various bloody actions in Kentucky and Tennessee. Records further bear out that some Company E soldiers died in 1863 and 1864 at Camp Douglas, a Yankee prison in Illinois which some survivors claimed was as atrocious as the Confederate's shameful Andersonville prison, in Georgia.[7]

By 1864, many Kentuckians, particularly in the southern and eastern counties, were so outraged by the federal government's efforts to free the slaves and by the recruitment of black troops for the Union army that President Lincoln placed the state under martial law. This only alienated the citizens even more. Other problems abounded. When General William Tecumseh Sherman ordered regular Union troops to join his notorious Georgia campaign in 1864, the poorly disciplined and ill-equipped members of the Home Guard who were left behind in Kentucky tormented defiant citizens and pillaged the homes and property of suspected southern sympathizers.[8] This led to the formation of bands of Rebel guerrillas and bushwhackers—relentless partisan fighters who retaliated against the Yankees with a vengeance.

Often, the civilian population was caught in the ensuing crossfire. Kentucky became a haven for vicious cutthroats and bandits. Among them was William Clarke Quantrill, notorious Confederate guerrilla of the Missouri and Kansas borderlands, who was wounded fatally in Spencer County, Kentucky, in May 1865. By then, so much violence and anarchy had erupted in Kentucky that General Sherman noted in correspondence, "It does appear that in Kentucky you are such a bundle of inexplicable family and State factions, that the veriest murderer, and horsethief, and dirty dog, if arrested can forthwith present credentials of respectability that I could not establish or you either."[9]

In Lincoln County, troops and irregulars from both sides, including

John Hunt Morgan and his horsemen, moved across the countryside throughout the war in constant search of fresh mounts. Smallpox and measles took a heavy toll on soldiers and civilians alike. Union forces confiscated Crab Orchard Baptist Church, with its balcony for slave parishioners. The Union army converted the brick building into a military hospital, and some of the soldiers who died there were laid to rest in the burial ground at the rear of the property. The Yankee soldiers left the church in ruins—they used pews for kindling and tore gaping holes in the plaster walls. It took decades for most folks to recover fully from the war, but the residents of Crab Orchard never forgot the Confederate soldiers who fought and died in those parts. Not all of them were Kentuckians; some were men and boys from Tennessee, Georgia, and Texas. Twenty-six of the Rebels were buried in a circle around a monument in Crab Orchard Cemetery.

George Washington Miller journeyed frequently to Crab Orchard and undoubtedly stood at that monument for the Confederate dead. Like so many men of his generation, he perceived that a way of life had disappeared. He thought of the uncertain future he faced in a decimated land that never would be the same. Pondering his future, he looked to the pioneers of his past, specifically frontiersmen such as the great Kentuckian Daniel Boone. Miller's journey to the West, at least in his mind, already had begun.

UNDER THE BLACK FLAG

If George Washington Miller had caught someone snooping around the Fish plantation, especially the mule barns and horse stables, the young Kentucky hothead would have shot the rascal, with no questions asked. It would not have mattered if the intruder was a Rebel or a Yank—the consequence would have been the same. To Miller, a thief was a thief, regardless of stripe.[1]

Not above acts of lawlessness himself later in his life, Miller was usually able to justify his conduct if laws had to be bent or even broken. After departing Kentucky, Miller and his family encountered their share of entanglements with legal and civil authorities. In one five-year period between 1897 and 1902, members of the Miller family, including G.W., faced criminal charges ranging from cattle theft and passing counterfeit money to cold-blooded murder.[2]

The lawless acts carried out by the Millers later on, in the Indian Nations, found their precedent in the reckless period that followed the Civil War and the ensuing era of Reconstruction. By the late 1860s, G. W. Miller already had begun to question authority. The land he loved so fervently had fallen under the rule of "Carpetbaggers," the epithet conservative southern whites used to describe corrupt northern Republicans who controlled political matters in the border and southern states after the war. To Miller and like-minded Rebels, the only rapscallions worse than Carpetbaggers were "scalawags"—white southern Republicans who consorted with "uppity niggers" and helped to implement Reconstruction in the decimated South.[3] Sometimes these southerners resorted to swift vigilante action or a night visit from a posse of hooded Ku Klux Klansmen to "set things straight." As long as his own family and property—especially his valuable mules and horses—were not at risk, Miller likely would have sympathized with the ruffians and bushwhackers who challenged Yankee authority.

Lawbreakers in border states such as Kentucky and Missouri became legendary folk heroes, cheered on by admirers who believed the corrupt Establishment had driven the brigands to lives of crime. Accounts of vigilantes such as the murderous Harpe brothers, who terrorized the Tennessee and Kentucky backcountry after the American Revolution, were told in country taverns and around hunters' fires, blended with reports of a different breed of criminal—gallant highwaymen and felons with hearts of gold and Robin Hood's sense of justice. Seemingly decent citizens such as George Miller bought into the myths, rationalizing that most of those who took to the outlaw trail after the war were persecuted former Johnny Rebs sharing their ill-gotten spoils with folks in need. These heroic criminals would come to be described as "social bandits" who preyed on the rich as a form of social and political protest.[4]

The single figure most responsible for the creation of this posse-style criminal dynasty, which lasted for more than seventy years and became the basis for popular outlaw legends of the Old West that the Miller family would later embellish themselves, was William Clarke Quantrill.

The feared Rebel guerrilla chieftain, only twenty-seven years old when he was shot and killed in Kentucky in 1865, left a legacy of lawlessness cloaked in the guise of patriotism and social injustice. Quantrill spawned the James-Younger gang and a string of other outlaw bands and lone-wolf marauders that stretched all the way to the Great Depression of the 1930s—the heyday of popular Oklahoma bandit Charles "Pretty Boy" Floyd.[5]

Quantrill, a former Ohio schoolteacher, led a band of mostly teenage farm boys on a rampage of hatred and murder along Union border strongholds in Kansas and Missouri during the Civil War. They left indelible impressions in Arkansas, Texas, and Kentucky. "At night and when we were in camp we played like schoolboys," was how Frank James, the Missouri-bred outlaw whose family celebrated its Kentucky roots, remembered his service with Quantrill's Raiders. "Some of the play was as rough as football. The truth was we were nothing but great big boys anyhow."[6]

The populace of Lawrence, Kansas, recalled "the boys" without affection. On the morning of August 21, 1863, the abolitionist town became the site of Quantrill's most infamous act. As dawn broke, Quantrill and 450 well-armed marauders swept down on Lawrence. They rode under the ominous black flag which, according to myth, was Quantrill's standard, a banner intended to show that no quarter would be given. The raiders stayed busy for four hours, pillaging and burning homes and businesses, leaving at least 150 citizens dead in the bloody streets.[7]

As the war raged on, Quantrill and others such as William "Bloody Bill" Anderson taught their young followers the tactics of advance scouting and surprise attack. The James and Younger brothers were among Quantrill's most able students. They honed survival skills that served them well in their future outlaw days.

Quantrill, mortally wounded during a skirmish with Union troops on a farm near Taylorsville, Kentucky, on May 10, 1865, was carried by wagon to a military-prison infirmary in Louisville. There he converted to Catholicism and finally died on June 6, 1865. Bequeathing money from his booty to a lady friend—which she used to finance a fancy Saint Louis whorehouse—Quantrill also had part of his blood money sent to a Catholic priest to purchase a plot and headstone in a Louisville graveyard.[8] The legacy created by the schoolteacher turned outlaw would continue to appeal to G. W. Miller as he began to create his own family empire in the West.

Chapter 4

KENTUCKY FAREWELL

Weep no more, my lady,
Oh! weep no more today!
We will sing one song for the old Kentucky home,
For the old Kentucky home, far away.[1]

—Stephen C. Foster
"My Old Kentucky Home"

BY the end of the war, in 1865, George Washington Miller had determined to marry his second cousin and stepsister Mary Anne Carson. The beguiling young lady had attracted him long before he mustered the courage to pursue her, perhaps as far back as childhood, just after her father wed George's mother. Miller firmly believed that there could be no other woman in his life except Miss Mary Anne. He confided to others in the family that he loved sweet Polly, or Molly, as most folks called her, "more than heaven."[2]

With "the War against Northern Aggression" lost, the confident Miller began to put all his energy into planning for the future—a future contingent on winning Molly's hand. He first had to take stock of his own resources to be certain he could take on a bride and start a family. He knew he had his work cut out for him. Before the war had officially ended, Miller had come home to find some of the countryside ravaged and burned, but the Fish plantation had escaped almost unscathed. Never one to linger or rest too long, Miller quickly rolled up his sleeves. By the time Robert E. Lee surrendered to Ulysses Grant, the enterprising young Miller had made a fair amount of money by trading government mules and horses.[3]

With part of the money he had earned from trading mules and horses, the young "colonel," as prominent southern white men of the time were called, purchased part of his Grandfather Fish's plantation. Soon afterward, Miller announced to his mother and John Carson his intention to wed

Molly, and he received their blessing. Next, while word of the betrothal spread quicker than gossip among a wide circle of family and friends, Miller formally proposed to Mary Anne Carson, and she accepted without hesitation.[4]

"Grandfather and Grandmother were step-brother and sister," Alice Miller Harth, a granddaughter of the Millers, wrote many years later. "They belonged to one of those families in which there are 'your children,' 'my children,' and 'our children.' While there was no blood relationship [sic], their parents approved the marriage."[5] On January 9, 1866, Colonel George Washington Miller and Mary Anne Carson were married in Louisville. Miller, already known as "something of a go-getter," was seven weeks away from his twenty-fifth birthday.[6] His bride was a vivacious nineteen-year-old southern belle with skin the color of moonlight.

In a book published in 1937, *The 101 Ranch*, Alma Miller England, the Millers' only daughter, described her parents as being "perfectly matched." She went on to write in a doting daughter's exuberant terms about how the young married couple started a life together that would take them from Kentucky to Oklahoma Territory. "She, too, was reared in the traditions of the Old South, which provided the foundations of hospitality, graciousness, and executive ability she possessed so abundantly in later life," Alma wrote of her mother. "He was a rugged Kentuckian of tall and powerful frame—every inch of him pure American. She was a wholesome motherly woman, handsome, and the perfect complement of such a man. He was good natured but of a volcanic temper while she was genial and jolly."[7]

Immediately after their nuptials, G.W. and Molly returned to Lincoln County. Miller's elderly grandfather John Fish had retired. It was time for the newlyweds to assume complete management of the Fish plantation—a difficult task in the new era of Reconstruction. Even though Kentucky officially had been a Union state, it suffered under the same conditions and problems imposed on the lower South, which included martial law.

The impact of the war was tremendous, leaving the South and border states impoverished and in turmoil. Although much of Kentucky's land escaped complete ruin, the romantic southern ideals that had shaped the lives of George Miller and his fellow plantation owners had disappeared, along with the slaves who had toiled to support the whites' lifestyle.

With the Emancipation Proclamation, Miller's human labor force vanished. It became necessary for him to find and employ freedmen as wage workers, or else turn to sharecroppers, most of whom were former slaves.

Neither choice held any appeal for Miller. The absence of slaves and the restrictive rules imposed by the federal government exacted a heavy toll on Miller and other landowners. Some, still loyal to Confederate values, fought back.

Vigilante groups and self-styled regulators clashed regularly with state militia and federal troops stationed in Kentucky. The Ku Klux Klan gained in strength and numbers as whites came to feel threatened by large numbers of blacks who no longer behaved like subordinates. Lynchings, burnings, rapes, and beatings against blacks and pro-Union whites were common.

The perpetrators "were not bandits or impoverished farmers, but well-known citizens of the gentry and yeomanry. They were men who saw in the postwar confusion profound threats to their accustomed status and power, men of property who saw all around them threats to their modest affluence, ordinary conservative men driven to violence as a way of restoring the traditional shape and behavior of their communities. Terrorism was a cheap, quick, dramatic way to achieve those goals," wrote Steven A. Channing in his book *Kentucky*.[8]

Despite the many troubles that plagued the young Miller couple, a spark of hope arrived on October 18, 1866—nine months after George and Mary Anne's marriage—when their first child was born, at the plantation. Miller was pleased that the baby was a boy. He already had picked out a name and was anxious to bestow it on his firstborn. Mary Anne had nothing to say in the matter. Miller insisted their son be named Wilkes Booth Miller. It was an unabashed tribute to John Wilkes Booth, the unbalanced Shakespearean actor and Confederate sympathizer who had shot Abraham Lincoln on Good Friday, April 14, 1865, five days after General Lee's surrender at Appomattox Court House, Virginia.

The naming of his first child for a crazed presidential assassin provides stunning insight into the mind of "Colonel" George Washington Miller during the bitter aftermath of the Civil War.[9] Like other Confederates who had marched off to war promising their sweethearts they would bring back a lock of Lincoln's hair, G. W. Miller had despised the Republican president. That hatred steadily increased, especially after Lincoln signed the Emancipation Proclamation. Miller considered Lincoln a tyrannical villain, even in death.[10] Perhaps Miller had read that after shooting Lincoln, Booth had shouted, "Sic semper tyrannis! The South is avenged!"[11]

The assassin's namesake in Kentucky quite predictably became the focus of his father's affections. Wilkes Booth Miller was only seventeen months old when his mother gave birth to a second son, on March 12, 1868. She and George named the baby Joseph Carson Miller after one of Mary Anne's older brothers. Sadly, the infant's arrival was eclipsed by great family tragedy.

In an unfortunate twist of fate, death also visited the family on the day the second Miller son was born. George Miller's mother, Almira Fish Carson, died, four months after her fifty-first birthday. Tragically, the family was already in mourning. Just one week before Almira's death, John Fish, the old ruler of the plantation, had passed away, two months before his eightieth birthday. Almira was laid to rest in the Fish family cemetery, not far from the fresh grave of John Fish. Within a week, George Miller had welcomed a new son but had lost his mother and grandfather.

Joy over the birth of baby Joseph Miller commingled with sadness at the family's sudden losses, and G. W. Miller steeled himself. His young wife provided comfort, and he turned inward for strength. As always, he also hoped his hectic work schedule at the plantation would ease his pain. It had little effect.

Growing bitter and disgusted during this difficult period, Miller became increasingly depressed. Economic constraints and the lack of a work force meant he could not operate the plantation on the same scale as John Fish had. After learning that postwar federal restrictions prevented him from becoming sole owner of the family plantation, G.W. began to consider relocation as a viable alternative.

He was not alone; large numbers of people were fleeing Kentucky. The exodus included freed slaves anxious to escape lynchings, cross burnings, and retribution. Former Confederates, fearful of their future in the Reconstruction South, also looked for better opportunities, as far away as South America and Mexico. By the late 1860s, thousands of freedmen and whites had turned westward. Other emigrants, caught up in what became known as "Texas fever," headed to the Lone Star State for a fresh start in the postwar cattle industry.

In 1869, Miller, discouraged in body and spirit but still determined to achieve his enormous aspirations, made the painful decision to leave his beloved Kentucky. He sold off his share in the Fish plantation, packed up his family and belongings, and paid his respects to his mother, grandfather, and other kinfolk buried in the cemetery surrounded by a wrought-iron fence.

George Washington Miller focused on the American West—the vastness that beckoned far beyond the woodlands and pastures of Kentucky. By establishing a mammoth livestock operation, Miller hoped to recover a way of life that had been lost. His intended destination was even farther west than the wide-open spaces of Texas. When folks asked where he planned to take his family to start over again, Miller never hesitated with an answer. California, he told them. The Millers were going as far west as they could go, to escape the bitter memories of a life destroyed by the war.

THE SOUTH'S AVENGING ANGEL

Like George Washington Miller, the strikingly handsome John Wilkes Booth committed himself to the Confederate cause and the steadfast tenet that slavery was a noble institution. Because of these shared convictions, both men possessed a deep hatred of Abraham Lincoln. They were among many southerners who viewed him as having been most responsible for freeing the slaves.

Miller no doubt would have enjoyed the drunken reception hosted by a prominent Kentucky judge and Rebel sympathizer to commemorate Lincoln's murder. William Quantrill and his guerrillas were in attendance when a celebrant raised his glass and proposed a toast: "Here's to the death of Abe Lincoln, hoping that his bones may serve in hell as a gridiron to fry Yankees on."[1]

Unlike Quantrill and his bloody raiders or Booth and his band of thugs, deserters, and mental defects, Colonel Miller did not obsess over his beliefs to the point that he was driven to fanatical violence. Instead, he remained content to cheer Booth's insane conduct from the sidelines and then proudly name his firstborn son after the assassin.

For the rest of his life, G. W. Miller held onto his Old South convictions and instilled many of them in his offspring, especially his sons. Miller carried those beliefs with his family when they left Kentucky. Rumors about the eldest Miller son's namesake—John Wilkes Booth—also followed the family to the West.

Twelve days after shooting Lincoln at Ford's Theater, Booth was allegedly slain by Union troops who found him hiding in a tobacco barn near Bowling Green, Virginia. The soldiers set fire to the building. Booth either killed himself or was shot in an ensuing gunbattle by Boston Corbett, an army sergeant and religious fanatic. But because Booth's body never was identified positively, a myth circulated for many years that he had escaped his captors.[2]

The Booth legend that persisted the longest came from the Oklahoma Territory town of Enid, just west of the immense domain created in the late 1800s by G. W. Miller and his sons. This Booth story began in Enid on January 13, 1903, with the demise of David E. George, an itinerant house painter nearly sixty years old who swallowed strychnine and died after having told several folks that he was John Wilkes Booth—the killer of Lincoln.[3]

Gossip about David George's death likely reached Colonel Miller at his nearby ranch before he himself died, three months later. Miller must have wondered if the bizarre tale had any shred of truth.

The story of David George did not cease with his death. His corpse was taken to an Enid undertaker for embalming, but because of questions about his identity, local authorities requested that burial be delayed until their investigation was completed. Apparently, that probe quickly fell apart, and everyone eventually lost interest in the case and forgot about the body, which languished for many years on a storage-room shelf.[4]

Enid old-timers could recall that when they were boys, they would sneak into the funeral parlor to take a peek at "John Wilkes Booth." Some Enid boosters planned to ship the body, entombed in a glass case, to the 1933 Chicago World's Fair as part of Oklahoma's exhibit. Not surprisingly, the world's fair officials rejected that proposal.[5]

The "Booth mummy" wound up in the possession of carnival exhibitors and went out on the road. By the late 1930s, the mummy was reported to be on the carnival circuit. It survived a train wreck, thieves, debt collectors, and enraged veterans of the Grand Army of the Republic who threatened to hang the cadaver.[6]

In 1938, a tattooed man from a circus bought the Booth mummy—by then known only as "John"—for several thousand dollars. He and his wife lugged the body around the country in a trailer that doubled as their home and a portable exhibit hall. When the tattooed man ran into financial problems, a report surfaced that "John" was seized in lieu of overdue loan payments.

Folks in Enid who tried to track the mummy through the years said that by the 1960s, they heard that "John" was on exhibit somewhere in Ohio. That was the last reported sighting of the remains of the man who once said he was John Wilkes Booth.[7]

Then in 1995, a Maryland schoolteacher and history buff petitioned a court to exhume the remains of John Wilkes Booth, whom most credible historians contend was buried in 1865 in a Baltimore cemetery. The teacher believed Booth really had escaped the burning barn and gone to Enid. He wanted to have tests conducted on the remains to prove his theory. The judge refused the request, finding no good reason to disturb the grave.

But in Oklahoma, stories still circulate about the mummy. So does another tale of Boston Corbett, the soldier who allegedly killed Booth.

After collecting a cash bounty for his deed, Corbett reportedly developed severe mental problems which led to his castrating himself as a radical form of penance for past promiscuities. By 1887, he had found a job as a doorkeeper for the Kansas legislature. His service was brief but memorable. Angered by a legislative chaplain's prayer which Corbett considered sacrilegious, he brandished two pistols and terrorized the entire chamber. Declared insane, Corbett escaped from Kansas State Hospital in Topeka in 1888, vanishing in the mists of history and time.

More than a century later, another story about Corbett has surfaced. It tells of his escaping to Oklahoma Territory, where he took an assumed name. It was said he found a town out in the cattle country that he liked, and he stayed there until the day he died. The name of the town was Enid.[8]

PART TWO

Go West, Young Man

If you have no family or friends to aid you, and no prospect opened to you there, turn your face to the great West, and there build up a home and fortune.[1]

—Horace Greeley

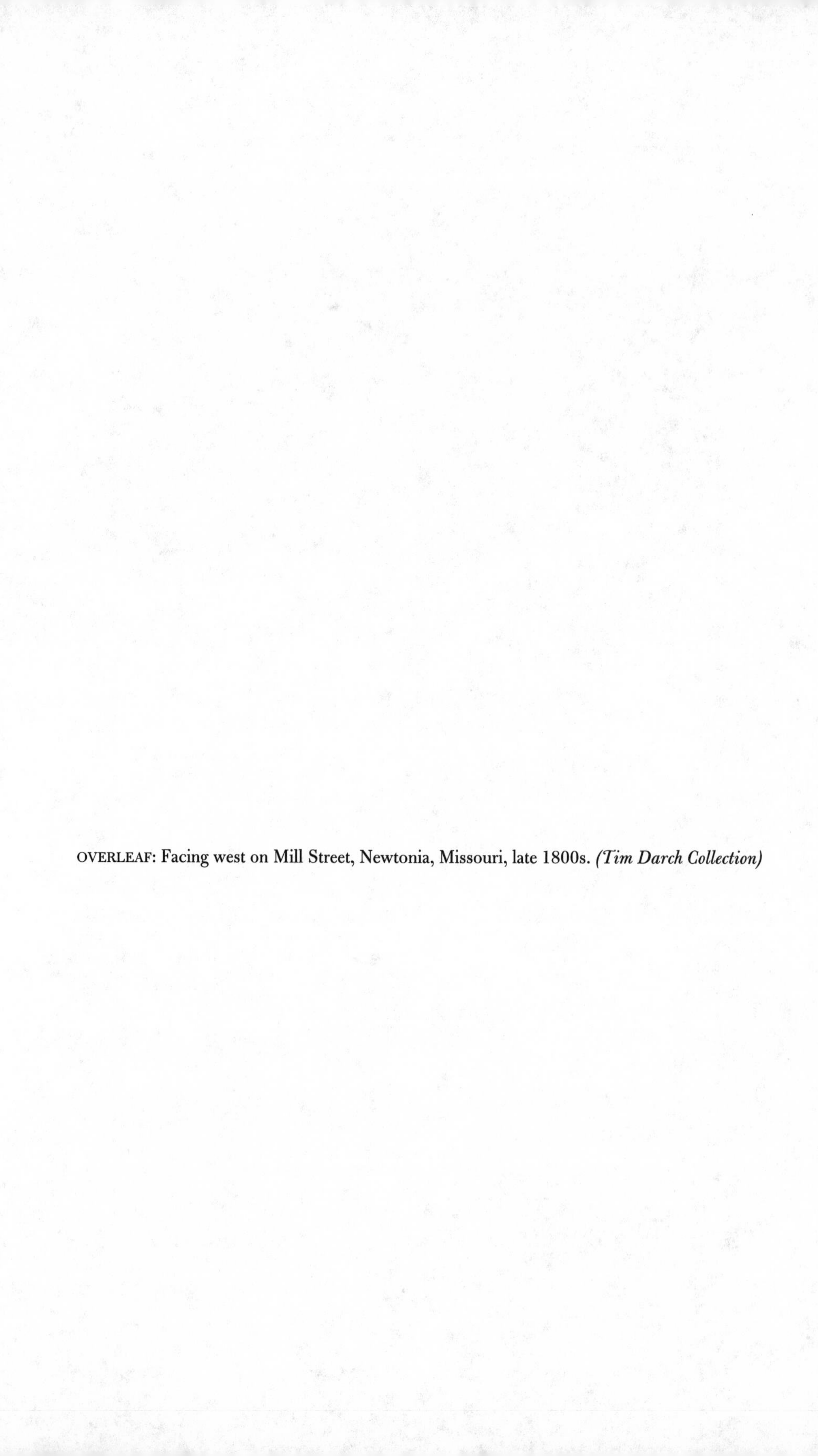

OVERLEAF: Facing west on Mill Street, Newtonia, Missouri, late 1800s. *(Tim Darch Collection)*

Chapter 5

CALIFORNIA BOUND

"Ho! for California! Excursion Party!"[1]
—1870 Advertisement

LEAVING his Kentucky plantation, G. W. Miller struck out for the great American West, accompanied by Molly, pregnant with their third child; Wilkes Booth, three years old; and Joseph, not quite two. They were on the road by New Year's Day 1870.

More than seventy years later, Joseph Miller's daughter, Alice Miller Harth, wrote of the family's journey in her memoirs.

"Grandfather . . . to further assert his independence, set out with grandmother to make a home in a new country. Their effects were meager and their departure unheralded. However, for the benefit of all who would listen, Grandfather made the statement that he, George W. Miller, intended someday to return to Crab Orchard, Kentucky, and drive Molly down the streets of town in 'the finest carriage drawn by the finest team of horses that money can buy.' Everything that Grandfather did is easier to understand in the light of this statement."[2]

Besides Molly and their young sons, Miller also brought along George W. Carson, his wife's twenty-year-old brother, and a former slave named Perry Britton, also twenty.[3] Miller figured he would need help shepherding his brood across the great prairies on the long journey. He also would have at least two able-bodied men with him when he established a cattle ranch in California.

Although the Civil War had devastated much of the nation, it had not had much impact on California. Miller and throngs of others, especially hundreds of Confederates fleeing ruined homes, wanted to move there to seek new opportunities. California gleamed like the proverbial pot of gold at the end of the rainbow. In the early 1870s, land was particularly cheap after several years of droughts. Much of the alfalfa pasturelands had dried up, and sizable herds of cattle and horses had perished. At the low point of the economy in 1865, most of the once great Mexican ranchos had become tax delinquent and fallen into the hands of land speculators. In some places, speculators sold pasturelands for only a dime an acre and cows for thirty-five cents a head. Millions of acres of grazing land could be bought for a very low price, leading to the first genuine California land boom. Wagon trains often brought five hundred people at a time along the Old Spanish Trail from Mississippi to southern California's cow country.

Prospective settlers organized excursion parties in various locales back east. To stimulate interest in joining these groups, transcontinental railroad companies hired lecturers to extol the virtues of the good life in southern California.[4] G. W. Miller may have attended one of those talks in Louisville or at the popular resort hotel in Crab Orchard.

People who signed up for an excursion train could count on at least five nights and days of travel to make the journey from the Missouri River to southern California. The early transcontinental trains carried dining cars only as far west as Chicago. Beyond the wide Missouri, it was necessary to pause at roadside stations for meals. "Railroad travel," wrote historical novelist Stewart Edward White, "across the plains was still a good deal of adventure, not to be lightly undertaken. People settled down for a week. They got acquainted with everybody else on the train, and visited back and forth, and even got up charades and entertainments. Every party had an elaborate hamper with tin compartments in which was a great store of bread and rolls and chicken."[5]

During the exhausting trek to California, trains loaded with settlers would stop, usually in the middle of nowhere, so passengers could stretch their legs and suck in some fresh air. Some travelers brought along guns and took potshots at buffalo as the tremendous herds moved before the trains. Nearly every train carried a preacher to conduct Sunday services and "a young man with a violin or a young lady with a guitar and a sweet voice" to entertain weary passengers.[6] Train seats folded into beds, and stoves were used for heating water, brewing coffee, and boiling diapers.

With dreams of a California ranch in mind, Colonel Miller and his party traveled directly from Kentucky to Saint Louis, the lively rail and commercial hub on the banks of the Mississippi just below its confluence with the Missouri and Illinois Rivers. Earlier Kentuckians were no strangers to Missouri, which long before had attracted Daniel Boone and his family; some had brought their southern lifestyle with them, including slavery and strong political and cultural traditions.

As the state where the Santa Fe and Oregon Trails and the short-lived Pony Express had originated, Missouri was generally known as the "Mother of the West." The state's largest city, Saint Louis, was the historic launching point for the Lewis and Clark expedition and for legions of fur trappers, soldiers, adventurers, and sodbusters. It had evolved from a fur-trading village founded by French settlers in 1764 to become, by the early 1870s, the bustling "Gateway to the West."

Saint Louis, tempered by political upheaval, social conflict, cholera epidemics, waterfront fires, and war, was the largest city Colonel Miller ever had seen. When he arrived there in early 1870, the city, grown prosperous on war supplies, boasted a population of more than three hundred thousand, making it the nation's third largest, after New York and Philadelphia.[7] Mindful of their city's pivotal role in westward expansion, local business leaders liked to boast to visitors that "the world passes through Saint Louis."

The Saint Louis that G. W. Miller and his party found was congested, and thick coal smoke enveloped the city day and night. At the old Soulard Market, where generations of Saint Louisans shopped for food, the Millers saw farmers and peddlers showing off pyramids of fruits and vegetables, caged fowl and rabbits, dressed opossums, skinned raccoons, goose and duck eggs, mounds of almonds, jars of pickles, and bins of pretzels. Gangs of workers harvested ice from the Mississippi to chill barrels brimming with raw oysters, shipped from New Orleans for such stellar eating establishments as Tony Faust's Oyster House Saloon, known as the "Delmonico's of the West."

The city had stately mansions, slum dwellings, flour mills, factories, shops, beer gardens, bawdy houses, schools, theaters, and parks. Acclaimed thespian Edwin Booth, brother of Lincoln's assassin, appeared on Saint Louis stages three times in the 1870s, always to sell-out audiences at DeBar's Grand Opera House, and always to poor reviews.[8] Although an ordinance had been passed prohibiting prostitutes from attending the theater, there was no way to stop the hundreds of homeless children—"street Arabs"—from sleeping in doorways throughout the city.[9] German accents and Irish brogues peppered conversations overheard on the streets. The aroma of commerce filled the air, pouring from breweries, bakeries, and foundries—and the distinct smell of manure wafted from stockyards. The city long had been a great cattle market. Even before the Civil War, many cattle, some shipped from as far as Texas and the Cherokee Nation, in Indian Territory, were fattened and slaughtered in Saint Louis.

Besides the continuous discussion of the business boom, much of the talk in Saint Louis in 1870 concerned activity along the Mississippi River. For three years, an engineer named Captain James Buchanan Eads had been spanning the river with the world's first steel truss bridge, still four years from completion. But the main talk along the levee concerned the twelve-hundred-mile steamboat race from New Orleans to Saint Louis to be held in June, pitting the *Natchez* against the *Robert E. Lee*. It promised to be the most exciting event in the history of the river. That summer, long after he had left the city, Miller learned that the *Lee*, named for his beloved Confederate leader, had won in three days, eighteen hours, fourteen minutes. Thousands of cheering supporters lining the levee greeted the winner as it steamed into port at Saint Louis on the Fourth of July.[10]

Despite all the clamor over racing steamboats, the Missouri River trade was dying and Mississippi River commerce was in a fast decline by 1870. The railroads, many of which relied on Saint Louis as a major terminal, had moved to the forefront as the most efficient means of transportation in the United States.

Although the newfangled transcontinental railroad was alluring, Colonel Miller elected not to take one of the popular excursion trains. Instead, he decided to transport his party and their goods westward on an overland route, a journey that could take as long as five months. Miller wanted to see something of the country, and he figured there was no better way to do that than by traversing the vast land in a covered wagon. After buying a pair of sturdy Missouri mules and an "outfit," Miller and his band of Kentuckians departed Saint Louis and struck out across open country, bound for the promised land of California.[11] The Miller family's grand adventure was under way.

NED BUNTLINE

JUST AS G. W. Miller and his family were proceeding west, a pudgy alcoholic rambler named Edward Zane Carroll Judson was busily assembling romantic symbols and fanciful icons that would create an enduring image of the Wild West.

Judson formed the public's image of the West by shamelessly blending large helpings of myth with ample doses of reality. He accomplished this alchemy and reached a wide and eager audience by churning out a raft of sensational dime novels and thrilling theatrical productions—each a vivid reconstruction very loosely based on events that the American public accepted as fact.

Although many of the particulars of his own checkered life are obscure, Judson clearly was, among other things, prone to stretching the truth out of all proportion. Somewhat of a contradiction, the notorious womanizer and drunk made a living from time to time by delivering fiery temperance lectures. But like P. T. Barnum, this rascal also had his hand on the pulse of America.

Born in upstate New York in 1823, Judson ran away to sea as a boy and later served in the U.S. Navy. He finagled a midshipman's commission after saving the crew of a ship that capsized in New York's East River. Soon he began to write stories, publishing some in *Knickerbocker Magazine* under his preferred pen name of Ned Buntline, the handle he used for the rest of his life.[1]

He left the navy and started a sensational newspaper, *Ned Buntline's Own*, at Nashville, Tennessee, but had to give it up in 1846 when he shot and killed a man who had accused Buntline of stealing his wife. Wounded by the dead man's brother, Buntline was pursued by an angry mob bent on lynching him. He escaped, but vigilantes dragged him out of jail and strung him up from the nearest awning post. A kindhearted bystander cut down Buntline, saving his life. He was taken back to his cell, but after a grand jury failed to return an indictment, Buntline was released; wisely, he slipped out of town.[2]

In 1849, he was back in New York, leading an anti-immigrant mob in a mêlée that left thirty-four people dead and 141 injured. After serving a year in prison, Buntline was released and given a hero's parade by his friends. He eventually became active in the Know-Nothing Party, an anti-immigrant, anti-Catholic political alliance popular in the 1850s. It took its name from party members who replied, when asked about their intentions, "I know nothing."[3] As a party leader, Buntline was indicted for inciting race riots in Saint Louis, but he escaped punishment by jumping bail.

Buntline continued to write, even during the Civil War, while he spent much of his time assigned to the Invalid Reserves or as a deserter. But his glory days came after the war, when Buntline stumbled across a young Iowa native named William Frederick Cody, born in 1846, who changed the way generations of Americans would view the West.

Buntline transformed Cody into Buffalo Bill, often touted as the world's greatest showman and the quintessential westerner.[4] Their first encounter—like everything else about the pair, apt to be greatly exaggerated and sensationalized—took place in 1869, at the time Colonel George W. Miller of Kentucky was planning to move west.

Although Buntline did not invent his frontier hero's famous sobriquet, he did produce four novels about Buffalo Bill, as well as a story, "Buffalo Bill, the King of the Border Men," which was turned into a play, set during Cody's first sojourn to New York. The commotion surrounding Cody's first visit to New York, in 1872, inspired Buntline to write—supposedly in less than four hours, with some liquid inspiration, in his room at Chicago's Palmer House—*The Scouts of the Prairie*, a melodrama in which Cody would play himself.[5]

In December 1872, the play opened in Chicago, starring Buffalo Bill Cody and Texas Jack Omohundro, his pal and a legendary army scout, as themselves. Buntline also cast himself in the play and enticed a talented Italian actress to accept the role of the Indian maiden called Dove Eye. He recruited a dozen tramps off the streets, dressed them in costumes, and splashed war paint on them to portray the "genuine Pawnee chiefs" promised in the advance billing.[6]

"On the whole it is not probable that Chicago will ever look upon the like again," wrote the *Chicago Times* critic on witnessing the drama at Nixon's Amphitheater. "Such a combination of incongruous drama, execrable acting, renowned performers, mixed audience, intolerable stench, scalping, blood and thunder is not likely to be vouchsafed to a city for a second time—even Chicago."[7]

Despite poor notices, the play became a huge hit. As noted historians

William H. Goetzmann and his son William N. Goetzmann point out, *The Scouts of the Prairie* was not educational or factual but instead "played solely upon the fanciful imagination and the evolving mythology about the frontier. In doing so, Buntline's new show founded all of the archetypal features we now associate with the Western novel, the Western film and the Western television series: brave heroes fighting against overwhelming odds, using their skills at gunplay and roping to subdue the Indians and save the beautiful maidens."[8]

The success of Buntline's landmark drama sparked twenty-six-year-old Cody's show-business career, which took off like prairie fire. But Cody soon wanted to cash in on his own dreams of adventure and excitement in the Great West. He broke his ties with Buntline and went on to remarkable fame and glory around the globe as an entertainer, years later spending some of his last days as a performer with the sons of George Washington Miller.[9]

Buntline continued his sensational writing but vanished from the limelight. He died in Stamford, Connecticut, on July 16, 1886. If there is a fitting epitaph for Buntline—this father of the frontier romance story who convinced others that the American West was a wild place populated by savages and beasts locked in mortal combat with noble white knights dressed in buckskin—it comes from Luther Standing Bear. A chief of the Sioux Nation, Standing Bear performed with Buffalo Bill's Wild West extravaganza beginning in 1902 and toured abroad with Cody in 1905. Standing Bear knew both worlds—that of his own people and the one which white men such as Ned Buntline had created:

"Only to the white man was nature a 'wilderness' and only to him was the land 'infested' with 'wild' animals and 'savage' people," wrote Standing Bear in *Land of the Spotted Eagle*, in 1933. "To us it was tame. Earth was bountiful and we were surrounded with the blessings of the Great Mystery. Not until the hairy man from the east came and with brutal frenzy heaped injustices upon us and the families that we loved was it 'wild' for us. When the very animals of the forest began fleeing from his approach, then it was that for us the 'Wild West' began."[10]

Standing Bear's words rang clear and true, even as white men continued to invent the Wild West.

Chapter 6

HOME ON THE RANGE

Oh, give me a home where the buffalo roam,
Where the deer and the antelope play,
Where seldom is heard a discouraging word
And the skies are not cloudy all day.[1]
—"Home on the Range," 1873

G. W. Miller had no time for Ned Buntline, reading dime novels, or listening to tall tales about frontier dandies decked out in fancy, fringed buckskin suits. He was resolved to guide his family safely to California. As the wagon, drawn by a pair of trusty mules, departed Saint Louis in early 1870 and made its way southwesterly through the Missouri Ozarks, Miller focused on the surrounding forests and the long road ahead.

Sometimes, by the evening campfire, he found a spare moment to seek sage wisdom from the well-worn pages of the *The Prairie Traveler,* a standard reference for wayfarers since before the Civil War.[2] Written by Captain Randolph Barnes Marcy, the prairie manual provided sound practical advice about gun safety, selecting campsites, treating venomous snakebites, hunting bears and panthers, managing mules and horses, and fording streams—one of the greatest dangers travelers faced. Much of Marcy's guidebook also dealt with Indians, including interpretation of smoke signals, communication by hand signs, and defending against war parties and surprise attacks on white settlements.

Miller was not overly concerned about hostile Indians, and he did not require any more information about mule behavior and horse ailments—he knew those animals well. What most interested Miller was which westward routes to follow beyond Missouri. Marcy's guide proved to be invaluable; it included a superb assortment of detailed road notes covering thirty-four significant overland routes.

Colonel Miller intended to follow the trail separating western Arkansas and Indian Territory to the gathering point of Fort Smith. He then would cross the Arkansas River and head out on the old California Road, a route through Indian Territory which first became popular with emigrants from southern states during the gold rush. Miller planned to stay on this southern route to the ancient city of Santa Fe, snug in the foothills of the Sangre de Cristo Mountains, then continue to Albuquerque, and finally make the long and difficult passage across the desert and mountains to California and the roaring Pacific.[3]

To reach Fort Smith, Miller's course in Missouri cut diagonally from Saint Louis down the rolling plateau separating the valleys of the Meramec and Bourbeuse Rivers to the high plains southwest of Springfield.[4] It followed the path of a stage line that the United States government had created twenty years before the Civil War. The road had become a critical military thoroughfare for Union and Confederate troops. Federals had erected a telegraph line along the route, with key stations at Saint Louis, Rolla, Lebanon, and Springfield. It became known as the Old Wire Road, and Rebel soldiers took great pains to keep the wires cut. By the time the Millers' wagon rolled down the road, the weathered poles stood wireless and tilting like ghostly gray totems.[5]

Each evening, the Miller party stopped to make camp. They found limestone caves and deep caverns, and plenty of firewood and fresh water from the Gasconade and Little Piney Rivers and the many cold streams and creeks. Snuggled under heavy quilts with her two small sons and with an unborn child stirring inside her, Molly Miller must have felt safe despite the night cries of wolves and the sad winter wind.

During the long days of travel, Miller kept close watch over the wagon carrying his sons and Molly, uncomfortable in her pregnancy. Periodically, young George Carson and Perry Britton, the former slave, rode ahead on saddle horses to scout the countryside, densely wooded with oak, hickory, hawthorn, and ash, and thickets of persimmon, sumac, and honey locust. Both Colonel Miller and his brother-in-law were crack shots. Each carried a brace of pistols for sidearms, and several rifles and shotguns were within easy reach in the wagon.[6] Miller remained watchful because Missouri was still true outlaw country. Remnants of Quantrill's Raiders, a mélange of renegades and brigands, and outlaw gangs such as those led by Jesse and Frank James and Cole Younger operated throughout the western half of the state.

"My grandfather brought his wife and children into Missouri and then Indian Territory at the same time all those outlaws were raising hell, but he wasn't really worried about any of them bothering him," said Zack T. Miller Jr., basing his account on family stories passed down by his father and uncles. "Remember, old G. W. Miller was a real Rebel and so were most of those outlaws. Why would he have been afraid of those men? They were after the rich Yankee bankers."[7]

As Colonel Miller's grandson correctly pointed out, many of the outlaws posed no threat to Miller because, like him, they were former Confederates. They were interested in robbing banks and trains, not waylaying a southern family looking for a new start. Some Missourians who retained southern sympathies cheered on the James gang in its audacious crimes. John Newman Edwards, a hero of the Confederacy and editor of the *Kansas City Times*, wrote impassioned editorial tributes to Jesse James and his band of robbers, comparing them to those who might have sat with King Arthur at his Round Table and ridden into tournaments with Sir Lancelot.[8]

Indeed, the outlaws often saw themselves as being on a noble mission, and they bristled at charges of thievery. A letter published in the *Kansas City Times* in 1872, attributed to Jesse James, constituted something of a political statement:

> Some editors call us thieves. We are not thieves—we are bold robbers. It hurts me to be called a thief. It makes me feel like they are trying to put me on a par with Grant and his party. We are bold robbers and I am proud of the name, for Alexander the Great was a bold robber, and Julius Caesar, and Napoleon Bonaparte, and Sir William Wallace. . . . Please rank me with these and not with the Grantites. Grant's partly has no respect for anyone. They rob the poor and rich, and we rob the rich and give to the poor. As to the author of this letter, the public will never know. I will close by hoping that Horace Greeley will defeat Grant, and then I can make an honest living, and then I will not have to rob, as taxes will not be so heavy.[9]

After several days of generally uneventful travel through outlaw territory, the Miller party reached the northern edge of the Missouri Ozark highlands in early 1870. They paused at Springfield, which by that year had grown to a population of 5,555. Always the consummate trader and entrepreneur, Miller not only kept a lookout for hazards and fresh game for the cook pot, but he also scanned the surrounding landscape for business possibilities. Just a couple of days' journey beyond Springfield, an ideal opportunity appeared on the prairie's horizon.

Deep in southwestern Missouri, not far from the Indian Territory border, Miller came upon Newtonia. This small village had been obliterated during the Civil War, and in 1868—the year it was incorporated—it was almost destroyed by a ferocious fire.[10] Some of the buildings still remained charred ruins. Yet Miller immediately liked the place and the people living there—most of them of good southern stock. Miller saw they were busily rebuilding the town, which served as a frontier outfitting point.

With the brunt of winter still ahead and a pivotal business possibility in the back of his mind, Miller decided to stay in Newtonia until spring. The Millers pitched camp on the edge of town, unsuspecting that this prairie hamlet would be their home for the next ten years and would serve as the first base for their ranching empire.

"WILD BILL"

IN 1870, WHEN G. W. Miller and his family traversed Missouri's Old Wire Road and paused for a brief rest at Springfield, street talk mostly concerned Reconstruction politics, land speculators' shenanigans, and the fight to get the railroad extended to the city. But some of the conversations at tonsorial parlors and taverns focused on a picturesque character still remembered around town, even after an absence of five years.

His real name was James Butler Hickok.[1] History would brand this former wagon boss, civilian army scout, and Union spy, distinguished by his shoulder-length auburn tresses and drooping straw-colored mustache, with an unforgettable nickname—"Wild Bill."

The origin of his illustrious handle is unclear, but that was what people were calling Hickok when he operated out of Springfield as a professional gambler at the end of the Civil War. So enduring was Hickok's mark that folks in the town still talk, 130 years later, about one of his most deadly altercations.[2] Trouble arose when Dave Tutt, a gambling companion of Hickok's, clashed with "Wild Bill" over the affections of a local woman. The situation was not helped by the fact that Hickok had been raised in a staunch abolitionist family in Illinois and was a steadfast Republican, while Tutt had served the Confederacy and was a Democrat.[3] Politics and affairs of the heart aside, their relationship further deteriorated when they quarreled over a wager during a card game at the Lyon House. Tempers flared and harsh words were exchanged, and a showdown followed the next evening, July 21, 1865.

"Wild Bill" and Tutt faced off on the downtown square for their duel. When they were about seventy-five yards apart, Hickok yelled at Tutt not to come any closer. Tutt responded by drawing a pistol from the holster on his leg. He took aim and fired, but the shot missed its mark. Simultaneously, Hickok lifted his single-action Colt revolver, cocked back the hammer, steadied himself, and returned fire. His bullet struck true. As one eyewitness noted, "Tutt was shot directly through the heart."[4] Tutt pitched forward, stone-dead before his body hit the street.

Hickok turned himself in, and John S. Phelps, later elected Missouri governor, defended him skillfully. A jury acquitted Hickok on a reduced charge of manslaughter, and he was released. His standing as a "shootist," or "man-killer," remained secure for the rest of his life, a reputation enhanced by scores of journalists and dime novelists and by Hickok himself.[5] No less a journalist than Henry M. Stanley (who later, in Africa, uttered the famous greeting, "Doctor Livingstone, I presume") tracked down Hickok to get his story.[6]

Some Old West historians insist that the Hickok-Tutt duel in Springfield was the first classic western showdown.[7] Similar confrontations, with conspicuous theatrical liberties, were incorporated into the repertoires of Wild West shows later produced by Colonel G. W. Miller's sons, "Buffalo Bill" Cody, Gordon W. "Pawnee Bill" Lillie, retired outlaws Frank James and Cole Younger, and many others.[8] But Wild West shows mostly featured violent spectacles and circus-style romps—recreations of large-scale historical events involving wagon trains, bands of Indians, companies of cowboys, and dashing calvarymen.

The "showdown," honed and perfected by novelists and screenwriters, became the staple of the western motion pictures that began to appear twenty-five years after Hickok's death (he was shot from behind during a poker game in 1876). In films, the climactic "shoot-out" between good guy and bad guy usually took place on the town's main street, with store clerks and housewives peeking from windows. This became the invariable conclusion of many rudimentary western movies—including a few spawned by the Millers in their Bison 101 films in the early 1900s—and, years later, scores of B movies and big-screen masterpieces such as *High Noon* and *Shane*.[9]

In reality, few differences of opinion in the West were settled by a ritualistic face-to-face confrontation between armed parties on a dusty street. Even in the fleeting heyday of the storied Kansas cattle towns frequented by boisterous Miller cowhands and charismatic shootists such as "Wild Bill" Hickok and Wyatt Earp, not many bona fide gun duels took place.[10] However, those shoot-outs became the stuff of legends for generations of Americans yet unborn.

Chapter 7

PRAIRIE CITY

The spirit of the South still lives in Missouri . . . [1]
—Floyd C. Shoemaker

IT was hogs—a bounty of hogs—that first attracted G. W. Miller to the village of Newtonia, snug on the vast prairies of extreme southwestern Missouri. Hogs gave him the inspiration to halt his family's arduous journey to California. It was not that Miller abruptly changed his mind and decided to become a hog farmer—far from it. He simply saw pigs as a means to an end. It proved to be a fortuitous decision.

Once Miller discovered that much of the economy in Newtonia depended on the raising of hogs and trade with residents of nearby Indian Territory, he realized he had an excellent opportunity. Planning to capture a substantial portion of the local hog market, he would use pork to trade for beef cattle in Texas. Through conversations with some of the locals and with drovers fresh off cattle trails, he learned of vast herds of longhorns deep in Texas. Those steers could be brought up the trails and fattened on sweet grass en route to northern markets. According to trail riders, steer prices were very cheap. In some instances, fifty pounds of bacon could be swapped for a healthy full-grown longhorn steer.[2] Miller realized that settlers had plenty of beef down in Texas, but they could use more bacon and good smoked hams.

Miller had found a way to build up his own herds of cattle and begin the ranching empire he wanted so badly to create. There was no need to go all the way to California when he could realize his dream in Newtonia. The family's winter camp thus became a permanent home.

Miller's son Zack T. Miller recalled in 1935, "He [G. W. Miller] was a born trader and an opportunist, the kind of man who would go to town on Saturday with a buckboard and a pair of colts and return home with a spring wagon, a mare, and a couple of cows. There were settlers scattered not distant from the little village of Newtonia who had hogs they wished to dispose of, and Colonel Miller soon began to trade various possessions for hogs."[3]

Before he could procure a stock of hogs, convert them into hams and bacon, and head south to Texas, Colonel Miller had to prepare a comfortable home for his wife and sons. Compared with the Great Plains and beyond, Missouri had abundant timber, clear flowing water, and plenty of grazing land. Settlers could erect a solid log home in only a few days, and an ample supply of game and fish lay close at hand. Pigeons, wild turkeys, and deer were plentiful, and cattle and hogs could feed on nuts and bluestem grass.

With money from selling his share in the Fish plantation, Miller acquired a sizable tract of land for a residence and pasture, although most livestock ran on the open range. He had enough acreage of rich sandy mulatto loam to raise corn, a staple for man and beast; tobacco; and wheat for bread and biscuits. Miller sowed the rest of the land in oats, barley, feed sorghum, and other forage crops for livestock.

Late in that winter of 1870, with the help of his brother-in-law, the former slave from Kentucky, and townsmen in Newtonia, Colonel Miller built a comfortable dwelling for Molly and the Miller sons.[4] Before long, they had to tack on extra rooms.

On April 20, 1870, Molly gave birth to her third son. She and George named him John Fish Miller, for G.W.'s beloved late grandfather and for Molly's father, John E. Carson. The rolls of the Newton County census, recorded in May 1870, listed the entire family, including one-month-old John, the first Miller in several generations to be born outside Kentucky.[5] Also registered on the census with the five Millers were Molly's brother, George Carson, and the young black man, Perry Britton.

The Millers' new home was in a region known as "the country of the Six Bulls." The name was attributed to Edmund Jennings, a native North Carolinian who had left Tennessee in the early 1800s and was said to have been the first white man to traverse southwestern Missouri. According to local legend, Jennings had spent so many years in the Missouri outback hunting, trapping, and living among various Indian tribes that when he finally went back to Jackson County, Tennessee, he scarcely could speak English. People there heard about the strange man dressed like an Indian and gathered around to hear his astounding stories of adventures in what he called "the country of the Six Boils," a reference to the six great springs which fed Indian Creek, Shoal Creek, Centre Creek, Spring River, and

North Fork. But Jennings' pronunciation of "Six Boils" sounded like "Six Bulls," the name that stuck for many years.[6]

The "Six Bulls" country lay in the foothills of the Ozark Mountains, which beckoned to white settlers who followed the adventurous Jennings. Newtonia was in Newton County, named in 1838 in honor of a Revolutionary War soldier.[7] Bounding it on the east were Lawrence and Jasper Counties, on the south McDonald County, and on the west Kansas and Indian Territory.

On the rich land of Oliver's Prairie, named for the area's first white settlers, was Newtonia, also known for many years as Prairie City. In the early 1830s, long before Newtonia was founded, a constant stream of settlers arrived from Kentucky, the Carolinas, and other southern states. They established farms and built homes, mills, churches, and schools in the nearby county seat of Neosho and at Sarcoxie, Granby, and other small towns scattered throughout the area. The settlers had to be ever watchful. Bands of Osage Indians raided some of the settlements, seizing hogs, corn, and other property.

By 1870, feelings about the Civil War still ran strong on both sides, and many survivors of the two battles fought at Newtonia shared George Miller's antipathy toward the North. He and his wife heard about the first engagement, when Newtonia was attacked on the morning of September 30, 1862. A strong Yankee force composed of several thousand Missouri, Kansas, and Wisconsin troops, along with mixed-blood Cherokees, sometimes called Pin Indians because they wore two crossed pins under their coat lapels or on their hunting shirts to signify that they were pro-Union.[8] The daylight assault was intended to be a surprise, but the Confederates had been alerted. Many of them were well entrenched behind stone walls and tucked inside the barn near the brick home built by slaves in 1840 for Matthew H. Ritchie, founder of Newtonia. He had settled in the county in 1832 and laid out the town of Newtonia in 1857.[9]

Following an hour-long artillery duel, the Wisconsin bluecoats advanced and drove the Texans from the perimeter into the heart of town. The fight became stubborn and deadly when some Missouri Rebels arrived to help their Texas allies.[10] Years later, veterans claimed they still could hear the war songs and fierce whoops of the Indian soldiers from both sides. There were reports of scalpings and hand-to-hand combat as Rebel troops fought with Bowie knives and the larger D-guard knives, customarily known as "Arkansas toothpicks."[11] The fight finally turned in late afternoon when Rebels charged the Union line, forcing a disorderly retreat. The soldiers hastily built rail pens to keep rooting hogs from mutilating corpses scattered over the ground.[12]

In that engagement and in a second battle, on October 28, 1864, the townspeople of Newtonia suffered. They often found themselves caught in the lethal crossfire of mountain howitzers and showers of bullets. Citizens endured indignities and atrocities throughout the war. They lived in constant fear of bushwhackers and raiding parties, and saw both Union and Confederate flags fly over their village.

It was into this postwar atmosphere that the Millers arrived. Newtonia was recovering slowly from battles and constant troop movements. The stalwart population tried to hide the scars, but constant reminders of the rancor and suffering kept old wounds festering.

Long after the war had ended, local boys hunting rabbits and squirrels for supper came across decomposed remains of soldiers in thickets and fields close to town. While removing the remains of one Yankee that had gone undetected for several years, a lucky farmer found in the soldier's pockets ninety-four dollars in gold and ten dollars in silver.[13] Local children, eventually including the Miller boys, dug bullets from the thick hides of trees and the walls of sagging barns. Each spring, like clockwork, plows turned up cannonballs, bayonets, and other relics of war.

In November 1868, more than a year before the Millers' arrival, another catastrophe had visited Newtonia, as if to complete the ruin of war. Almost the entire village was wiped out by a fire that spread from building to building. All the town's gristmill machinery and most of the business houses were destroyed.

In 1869, led by the Ritchies, who rebuilt their mills, storehouse, and furniture shops, Newtonians worked hard to mend their town. By early 1870, several businesses had reopened and the town's population was about six hundred.[14] The Newtonia that the Millers moved into sported four dry-goods stores; a drugstore; stores for furniture, stoves, and tin; millinery shops; two hotels; two wagon shops; three blacksmiths; a saddlery; a stable; a large sawmill; and one of the largest grist and flouring mills in that section of the state. At Newtonia High School, 150 students attended classes, presided over by five teachers.[15]

In the summer of 1870, a new Newtonia concern opened for business, a general store and grocery with a sign hanging out front bearing the names of the partners—Miller & Carson.[16] Colonel Miller reasoned that the store would create another source of income while he built up his cattle enterprise. He also figured the grocery would act as a kind of "company store" to provide his proposed ranch with needed supplies. Molly Miller and her brother George Carson managed the store while Colonel Miller was off buying hogs or scouting Indian Territory for possible sites for his ranch.[17] The Millers later enticed other family members and Kentucky friends to take jobs at the store.

As the summer progressed, Colonel Miller must have felt somewhat satisfied. In less than a year, he had relocated his family, built a new home and business, and come within reach of what he yearned for most—a big cattle spread. But just when everything appeared to be in order, disaster struck, leaving the Millers devastated as they struggled to find a place for themselves in their new town.

THE BANDIT QUEEN

NEWTONIA WITNESSED THE comings and goings of all sorts of characters before G. W. Miller and his family established a home and store there. William Clarke Quantrill and his mounted guerrilla fighters found their way to the little town on Oliver's Prairie and left indelible prints. So did Union and Confederate generals, Texas cavalrymen, Indian warriors, fiery Old Testament preachers, an assortment of man-killers and shootists, stumping politicians, renegades headed for the safety of Indian Territory, war refugees, and westward-bound settlers pausing at what they thought was the brink of civilized America.

Newtonia's most infamous visitor—perhaps even more so than Quantrill—was a teenage girl who spent only one evening in town but created quite a stir before her departure. Born February 5, 1848, at Carthage, Missouri, Myra Maebelle Shirley was the daughter of transplanted Kentuckians.[1] She studied literature, Greek, Latin, Hebrew, art, and deportment at Carthage Female Academy. She also became an accomplished pianist and was said to have entertained guests with musical interludes at her father's popular hotel on the Carthage town square.[2]

Myra adored her older brother, John Allison Shirley—better known as Bud—as much as she appreciated good horses.[3] The young lady with Kentucky bloodlines could ride like the wind, and she and her brother roamed the Missouri hills on horseback. Bud also taught his sister how to handle firearms. When she reached her teens, Myra Shirley was a fearless rider and a crack shot, capable of shooting a bumblebee off a thistle at thirty yards with her pistol.[4]

Despite her classical education and her family's efforts to turn out a genteel southern maiden, Miss Myra had other notions about her future. She became a convicted horse thief and a constant companion of killers and renegades. History, with help from pulp writers, would remember this spirited woman not as Myra Shirley but by the name she used for the last nine years of her troubled life—Belle Starr.

As the Civil War drew closer, the Shirleys' hotel and tavern became a gathering place for southern sympathizers. Rebel chieftain Quantrill went there to recruit some of his followers, including Bud Shirley. Tales abound that Quantrill was smitten with Myra and that she served as a spy or informant for the Confederates operating throughout southwestern Missouri.

A popular story that G. W. Miller and others liked to tell was that the young woman, later called "the bandit queen," had been held captive in Newtonia in 1863.[5] It all started when Myra was visiting friends in Newtonia, and the Union commander caught wind of her presence and heard she had helped her brother Bud sneak home to see his folks at Carthage. The Yankee officer ordered Myra placed under arrest, and sent troops to Carthage to seize her brother.

According to the legend, the Yankees brought Myra to the Ritchie family home, a local landmark. The imposing brick house served as headquarters for both Union and Confederate leaders during the war. In time, it was also used as a military hospital. In an upstairs chamber known as the "black room," wartime bloodstains could not be removed, causing the owners to paint the walls pitch-black.[6] Quantrill had spent a night in the residence with some of his men. Despite the Union sympathies of the owner, Quantrill spared the building from the torch because of the cordial treatment he had received.[7] But Quantrill was nowhere in sight the evening Myra was brought to the mansion under duress.

Despite her rough treatment, the clever Myra quickly took stock of the situation, relying on wits and talent she had learned as a little girl. The beguiling young woman charmed the officers and guards by playing the piano for them all night. The following morning, after Myra's marathon recital, the Yankees released her. Apparently they believed she was harmless and did not have enough time to return home and warn her Rebel brother, Bud.[8]

But the bluecoats underestimated Miss Shirley's riding prowess and her knowledge of the territory. Vowing that she would beat the soldiers to Carthage, she shunned the regular route from Newtonia to Carthage, taking every shortcut she knew, riding at breakneck speed through thirty-five miles of backcountry woods and fields. Myra arrived at her family's home before the detachment of soldiers. She alerted Bud, who escaped.

The next year, however, Bud Shirley's luck ran out. Union militia gunned him down at Sarcoxie, Missouri, an act that some people said caused Myra Maebelle Shirley to embark on the outlaw trail.

Like so many other romanticized outlaw tales, the account of "Belle Starr" banging away on the keyboard for Yankees at the Ritchie house made a cold winter's night a little more pleasurable, especially if a bit of brandy or fresh whiskey freed the storyteller's imagination.

In reality, Myra Shirley never robbed a train or bank and probably never killed anyone. She had a lust for adventure and a soft spot for desperate men such as Jim Reed, Cole Younger, July Johnson, and Sam Starr. Horse theft was the only crime she ever was convicted of. Judge Isaac Parker, the "hanging judge" of Fort Smith, Arkansas, sent her to a federal house of corrections in Detroit, Michigan, in 1883. She served nine months of a twelve-month sentence.[9] Belle's chaotic life ended on February 3, 1889, when an unknown assailant shot her from behind with a charge of buckshot, not far from her Indian Territory home on the Canadian River, where she hosted her lawless pals. It was two days before Belle's forty-first birthday.[10] After her death, dime novelists spun tales far more gory than anything she had lived.

Inspiration for some of the Wild West acts and western motion pictures later produced by the Miller family came from characters such as Belle Starr. In a curious way, she became the prototype for all cowgirls to come, whichever side of the law they rode on. Like Jesse James and "Wild Bill" Hickok, Belle Starr was a figure born of the Millers' early years in Missouri, Kansas, and Indian Territory—when Colonel Miller was shaping the foundation for the future 101 Ranch empire.

Chapter 8

GONE TO TEXAS

There were three waves of migration on this continent and the second was always the cattlemen. Ahead went the trappers and the Indian traders. . . . Behind the cattle came the farmers. . . . There were always cattle out ahead of the plows. And for a simplest reason. Beef and pork and mutton were the only crops in that land without roads which could take themselves to market. . . . Cattle made the first frontier where white men lived. And grass made cattle.[1]

—Archibald MacLeish
Green River

THE angel of death, no stranger in the outlaw-infested borderlands of the Missouri frontier, came calling at the Miller household in the summer of 1870. It was just after the sultry dog days, when Sirius, the Dog Star, brightest in the sky, rose and set with the sun and, according to folklore, added to the stifling heat.

The dark angel, as frontier families referred to death, took one of the Miller boys—Wilkes Booth, the cherished firstborn. A pure Rebel love child born nine months after his parents' marriage, he had always been a sickly lad.[2] On August 27, 1870, after a brief illness, the little boy, feverish and frail, died in his mother's arms. He was two months from his fourth birthday.

The Millers wanted their son to be buried beneath the bluegrass of Kentucky, where he had been born. They washed their boy's body and, because of the summer heat, laid it in a coffin packed with ice for the journey home to Lincoln County. They took a train from Springfield to Saint Louis, from there to Louisville, and finally to the old family place near Crab Orchard.[3] Wilkes Booth Miller was laid to rest in the Fish burial ground near kinfolk he never had known. Colonel Miller ordered a headstone placed over the grave with the boy's name and dates of birth and death, along with two simple words—"Going Home."[4] The family found comfort in knowing that the graves of little Wilkes Booth's grandmother, great-grandfather, and other loved ones were nearby.

The death of Wilkes Booth devasted G.W. and Molly, but in the tradition of pioneer folks, they steeled themselves and persevered. Both of them understood that their surviving sons, two-year-old Joseph and four-month-old John, still needed a great deal of care and attention. Back in Newtonia, the Millers threw themselves into their work. Molly stayed busy with her two small boys, home chores, and management of the Miller & Carson Store. Colonel Miller scoured the land, buying choice swine and gathering half-wild hogs that foraged on the open range.

Once the hogs were fattened, Miller had them slaughtered and cut into hams, thick strips for bacon, and salted fatback. He pickled some of the pork, using a mixture of ground alum, saltpeter, brown sugar, potash, and water to make brine. After the hams had been soaked in a tub of pickling solution for six weeks, they were dried, smoked, and rubbed with salt.[5] Miller packed away the meat until he had stockpiled enough to ride the trails south to Texas and trade for longhorn steers.

Anxious to make that first trek, Miller bided his time during the autumn and early winter of 1870. Besides gathering and processing as many hogs as possible, Miller busied himself with community activities and soon earned the respect of many local citizens. The one incident that ingrained Colonel Miller into the collective consciousness of Newtonia took place that autumn. Fifty-six years later, C. H. Miller—not related to G. W. Miller—had no trouble recollecting the occasion, which reflected the hooliganism and lawlessness that prevailed on the postwar Missouri frontier.[6]

Recalling the mêlée, C. H. Miller, son of a Presbyterian minister, noted, "The first time I ever saw Mr. Miller [G. W. Miller] was at the savage fist fight between Jim Lamraux, the Printer's Pride, and Jim Wilson, the Irish Wonder, who had been trying to pull off a fight with Lamraux for some time." A boy at the time, C. H. Miller noted, "Lamraux was not a man who courted trouble, and therefore peace and quiet had reigned in Newtonia. But it was not destined to remain so, for pretty soon the lid blew off. As usual the trouble was over a woman. It seems that Jim Lamraux was in love with one of twin girls. Wilson tried to pay court to the other one but she repulsed him coldly as she did not care for his type of man. Finally in desperation the Irish Wonder exclaimed, 'A woman doesn't think much of herself who will go with Jim Lamraux!' "

When the insult got back to Lamraux, he sent word to Wilson to retract his words or take a licking. Wilson took up the challenge, and friends of the two men arranged a meeting place about half a mile from town. The entire male population of Newtonia anxiously awaited the big fight.

To ensure that everything was fair and square, Colonel G. W. Miller was appointed as referee. As the big crowd of men and boys lined up against a stone wall and rail fence, Miller scratched a wide circle in the dirt with a stick to represent the ring. Then he demanded that the rivals state the cause of the combat. Everyone present thought the two were evenly matched, but Wilson was more confident—he weighed in at 225 pounds, and Lamraux at 180. Wilson, however, was a heavy eater, and activity at the supper table was the most exercise he received. Lamraux, on the other hand, was in the pink of condition, and got a good workout at the newspaper where he operated the handpress (and where C. H. Miller served as printer's devil).

Just before he signaled the start of the fight, G. W. Miller picked up a fence rail about five feet long and walked to the center of the circle. A hush fell over the gathering when Miller laid down his rules, emphasizing that it would be a fair fight. If anyone tried to interfere before one of the pugilists said "Enough," Miller would brain him with a rail. G. W. summoned the two shirtless men into the circle, and the battle commenced. C. H. Miller recalled,

> From the very beginning, Wilson crowded matters for he was determined to beat Lamraux by main strength. Lamraux side stepped the Irish Wonder's rushes and at the same time landed on Wilson's ribs, until soon he had him blowing like a porpoise. Only once was Lamraux touched, and that was due to a surprise blow of Wilson's, who, running away as if licked, turned back and struck Lamraux over the right eye. Lamraux then caught hold of Wilson's long hair with his right hand, and with his mighty left he planted blow after blow upon Wilson's unprotected face. In less than sixty seconds after this unmerciful beating began, Wilson cried "enough" and the fight was over. The Irish Wonder quickly sank to the ground, beaten and disgraced, for instead of licking Lamraux, he emerged from the battle totally disabled. In a few days Wilson left Newtonia for good, never to return.
>
> It has been a good many years since this affair, but the oldest inhabitant of Newtonia will remember always how George Miller appeared as he pranced around the battling men, flourishing that rail in his hands.

Just a few months later, the Millers, still grieving the loss of Wilkes Booth, observed their first Christmas in Missouri. As C. H. Miller recalled, this time it was Molly Miller who left an impression on the community.[7] The Presbyterian church needed a new roof. C.H.'s father, the Reverend W. L. Miller, and the church trustees appealed to the Ladies Aid Society for help with fund-raising. The ladies offered to sponsor a feast between Christmas and New Year's. In addition, a contest would be held to determine the most beautiful young lady and the most beautiful married lady in Newtonia.[8]

On the night of the church dinner, an even bigger crowd than had attended the fistfight turned out to cast ballots for the favorite beauties, nominating two ladies—one from the east side of town and the other from the west side. Molly Miller, a comely twenty-four-year-old, was the choice of the east siders, and the wife of Dan Weems, a local merchant and Miller's business rival, represented the west side. Ten cents would buy a vote, and the woman receiving the largest number was to be declared the most beautiful in Newtonia.

Conducted like an ordinary livestock sale with a popular auctioneer in control, the voting took place on a night charged with emotion. Just a few days before, during a Christmas Eve celebration on the town square, a fiery fight had erupted. G. W. Miller and some of his followers sparred with Weems and his chief ally, George Rice, the town's druggist, using Roman candles from a yuletide display as weapons. Before the fracas was over, Colonel Miller and Rice had sustained severe burns on their hands and arms. On the evening of the fund-raiser, each man showed up heavily bandaged but determined to see the lady of his choice take home the honors.

"The animosity that had been caused by the contest on Christmas Eve soon showed itself, and the forces of Miller and of Weems were both determined to win," remembered C. H. Miller. "The auctioneer became greatly elated as the money kept pouring in. Mounted on a big table, he would cry, 'One hundred votes for Mrs. Miller! Rally, Weems, rally!' Then, 'Two hundred votes for Mrs. Weems! Rally, Miller rally!' "

Finally, the pastor and church officers intervened when they learned that both Miller and Weems "declared that they would go broke before their wives should be defeated." Displaying the wisdom of Solomon, the Reverend Miller halted the voting and thanked all present for their enthusiastic participation. Noting that the contest seemed to be a stalemate, he recommended that a tie be declared. Both sides readily approved his suggestion. The second contest, for the town's most beautiful unmarried girl, also ended in a draw. By night's end, the church not only had collected enough money for a new roof, but also had funds for a fresh coat of paint and many other improvements.

C. H. Miller never forgot Molly, whom he described as a "charming woman . . . one of the most prominent members of our church, active and zealous in all good things and a leader 'of the quality' in Newtonia." The printer's devil formed a somewhat different impression of Colonel Miller, especially when the latter began to make trips to Texas to acquire longhorns. "I can bear witness to the fact that he was always a most generous man, ever ready to give to the church and to every good cause, and he was honored and respected by all who knew him . . . but on Sunday [G.W.] generally had some cattle to brand and so took the 'absent treatment' as far as church services were concerned. However, on Thanksgiving or Christmas or any time whenever there were big feasts, he was 'Johnny on the spot.' "

Early in 1871, George Miller began that "absent treatment" in earnest when he acquired what he believed was sufficient hog meat—more than twenty thousand pounds—to make his first journey to Texas.[9] The momentous journey commenced on February 16, 1871—"a very pretty winter day," one of Miller's hired hands scribbled in his diary.[10] Early that morning, as the sun started its ascent in the frosty heavens, Colonel Miller kissed Molly and his two young sons good-bye. He left them in Newtonia under the protection of some of his wife's younger brothers, summoned from Kentucky.[11] Then G.W. went to the barn, saddled his best horse, and set out for Texas.

"Gone to Texas," sometimes abbreviated to just "G.T.T," had become a popular phrase during the 1800s, often appearing on a sign tacked to a front door or carved in the bark of a shade tree, left behind by folks wanting to escape the law or bad debts or just get a fresh start.[12] That winter morning, G. W. Miller was "G.T.T." But unlike most people who left those initials behind, Miller planned to return. He was going to hunt up some wild Texas cattle and come right back home, up the dusty trail to Molly and his boys.

JESSE CHISHOLM'S TRAIL

THROUGHOUT 1870, COLONEL George Washington Miller—diligent as a new deacon—readied himself for his first journey from Missouri to the cow country of Texas. He gathered as much information as he could about life on the various cattle trails and which routes were the best.

Much of Miller's information came from travelers who had ridden the early cattle drives in the late 1860s, when farmers were worried about disease spread by cattle. He also gained insight from crusty muleskinners and bullwhackers who drove oxen teams across the plains. Another good source proved to be buffalo hunters, headed west lugging heavy guns such as the Henry and .50-caliber Sharps—dubbed the "Big Fifty"—or, a bit later, tried-and-true Winchester rifles, to supply tons of meat for railroad crews.

Miller especially liked to pick the brains of seasoned drovers and cattlemen he encountered during his frequent scouting trips into Indian Territory for additional grazing ground.[1] Those men were his best teachers. He quickly found that there was much to absorb, and he sopped it up quicker than a sourdough biscuit dipped in skillet gravy.

He listened to old-timers' warnings about "savages," as most whites then called Indians, even though Miller sometimes thought whites were the ones who deserved that derogatory name.[2] Colonel Miller was fascinated by bits of trail wisdom that later served him well when he found himself hundred of miles from home with an outfit of bachelors and motherless boys, herding hundreds of Texas steers through blinding dust and rain and across swollen streams and hostile territory.

Perhaps one of the greatest influences on Miller and others embarking on cattle trails was Jesse Chisholm. Born in Tennessee in 1805 of Scottish and Cherokee descent, Chisholm came to Indian Territory in the 1820s. For more than four decades, he labored as a trader, government interpreter, and trailblazer throughout the southern plains. Even many years later, when most people heard the name Chisholm, they thought of the famous cattle trail beaten out by millions of Texas longhorns driven to Kansas railroad towns and northern markets in the twenty-five years after the Civil War.

The name Chisholm became so popular that it often was used indiscriminately for all cattle trails out of Texas.[3] Ironically, Jesse Chisholm, remembered as a modest and impeccably honest man, was not even a cattleman and more than likely never owned a single cow.[4]

As early as 1832, Chisholm helped to create a wagon road from Fort Smith into Indian Territory. A few years later, hoping to locate a legendary gold mine, he guided an exploratory party up the Arkansas River to a site that eventually became Wichita, Kansas.[5] Even though he did not find a trace of gold, Chisholm liked the country so well that he later established his headquarters in the area.

In the spring of 1865, the mixed-blood trader, who bartered with Comanches, Kiowas, and other tribes during the war, started southward with several wagonloads of goods from his Kansas base toward the old Indian agency at Fort Cobb, on the Washita River.[6] Chisholm followed the faint traces of a trail that had been made nearly four years before by retreating Yankee troops after they had abandoned their Indian Territory military posts at the outbreak of the war.[7]

This trail, expanded later from south Texas to Abilene, Kansas, proved to be the most feasible route for cattle drivers looking for fresh water and good grazing for northbound herds. Prior to the opening of the Chisholm Trail, Texas herds had followed the Old Shawnee Trail through the eastern half of Indian Territory into a corner of southeastern Kansas and southwestern Missouri. Problems arose in those areas, however, when farmers and local citizens became fearful of cattle contaminated with the dreaded "Texas fever."

During the first season on the Chisholm Trail, in 1867, more than thirty-five thousand head of cattle were driven across Indian Territory from Texas ranges to shipping pens built by Illinois cattle feeder Joseph G. McCoy at Abilene, Kansas, on the Kansas Pacific Railroad. The next year, the season's drive was seventy-five thousand head; in 1869, the number doubled, as it did in 1870. After 1871, the number of cattle driven to Kansas averaged a half-million head each year.[8]

As an 1871 advertisement pointed out, that route was shorter than others and the streams encountered were "narrow and more easily forded than other trails . . . and as the trail is through thinly settled country, drovers are not subject to molestation by settlers, have no taxes to pay, and . . . no ferriage is necessary."[9]

The name for the trail was a logical development. Because Chisholm spent so much of his time hauling provisions along the trail, it was natural for drovers to use his name as a route designation. Still, it did not become a commonly used name until about 1870, at the time G. W. Miller was launching his business, two years after Chisholm had died in Indian Territory. While visiting Arapaho friends, he unknowingly had eaten contaminated bear grease from a brass cooking pot.[10] The old trader—admired and trusted by all who ever met him—was wrapped in a blanket and buffalo skin and buried on a low sand knoll overlooking the North Canadian River. Many years later, some Chisholm devotees, guessing at the location of his grave, erected a plain stone with the inscription: "No One Ever Left His Home Cold or Hungry."[11]

For twenty years, beginning in 1871, George Washington Miller traveled several cattle routes to and from Texas, including both the Old Shawnee and West Shawnee Trails. But the path named for Jesse Chisholm was the one Miller used most often. He rode up and down the Chisholm Trail so many times that he eventually wore down to the metal the wooden stock of the saddle rifle—an 1873 Winchester carbine—that he always held across his leg.[12]

"Come along, boys, and listen to my tale,
I'll tell you of my troubles on the old Chisholm Trail.
Coma ti yi youpy, youpy ya, youpy ya!
Coma ti yi youpy, youpy ya!"[13]

—"The Old Chisholm Trail"

Chapter 9

TRAILS SOUTH

When I die, I may not go to heaven.
I don't know if they let cowboys in.
If they don't, just let me go to Texas.
Texas is as close as I've been.[1]
—Country and western song

COLONEL George Washington Miller was six days away from his twenty-ninth birthday on the morning of February 16, 1871, when he started on his first overland trip to Texas cow country. He did not go alone.

Perry Britton, the twenty-one-year-old former slave, drove a camp wagon full to bursting with food staples, a water barrel, utensils, tools, bedding, medicines, and a little grain for draft animals. Also accompanying Miller were his brother-in-law, George W. Carson; George Van Hook, a Kentuckian who had followed the Millers to Newtonia from Crab Orchard; and hired hands Frank Kellogg, Luke Hatcher, and James D. Rainwater, a native of the hilly country near Fayetteville, Arkansas.[2] Like his boss, Rainwater was going to have a birthday during the long Texas journey. The slim boy, who rode a trained pony as well as any grown man, soon would turn fifteen.[3]

Rainwater typified the very young men and boys who went on cattle drives. As John Rolfe Burroughs explained in *Where the Old West Stayed Young*, "Few operators could afford to pay the twenty-five or thirty dollars a month which was the going wage for a grown man. Consequently a large number of the herders employed on the long cattle drives were boys twelve to fifteen years of age, who could be hired for as little as five dollars a month and found. It was this circumstance that added the common noun *cowboy* to our vocabulary."[4]

Rainwater kept a diary in 1871 in which he described many of the things that happened to the Miller party on its first Texas trek. Prior to November 1933, when he died in Saint Louis at age seventy-seven, Rainwater corresponded with Miller family members and shared with them his account of those days so long before.[5]

Miller also enlisted, in addition to his small band of horsemen, hearty teamsters to man ten large wagons loaded with twenty thousand pounds of cured hog meat to swap for lively longhorn steers when the party reached Texas.[6]

The going was predictably slow. That first day out, the Miller party arrived only at Rocky Point, on the southern boundary of Newton County, in time to have noon dinner. At nightfall, they camped at Keysville, near the Arkansas border, still 120 miles north of Fort Smith. At first light, everyone was saddled up and the wagons were rolling southward into Arkansas. The trip that afternoon took the Miller bunch along Sugar Creek and the site of a Confederate defeat at the Pea Ridge battleground.[7] There the riders spied trees still standing that had been shattered by cannon fire on March 7–8, 1862, during the Battle of Pea Ridge, also known as Elkhorn Tavern, one of the few major Civil War engagements west of the Mississippi.[8]

As they rode beneath broken limbs, Rainwater later noted in his journal, Colonel Miller doffed his hat. Perhaps G.W. thought of the damaged trees as mute remembrances of the thousands of men, especially those in gray, who had fought and died in two days of fierce combat on that scarred plateau in the northwestern corner of Arkansas.

The caravan proceeded south. The riders forded uncounted streams and creeks, camped at Nubbin Ridge, and by their first Sabbath on the trail, reached Rainwater's hometown, Fayetteville. Formerly a stop on the old Butterfield Overland Stage Route, it would become the home of the University of Arkansas, which opened the following year as Arkansas Industrial University.[9] Miller made sure his drovers enjoyed a hearty Sunday meal just south of town before they pressed on. That afternoon, they forded the west branch of the White River at least a dozen times before they collapsed for a night's rest on the river's banks in the shadow of the Boston Mountains.[10]

The next day, the caravan took until high noon to climb the steep mountains and reach the summit, prompting Rainwater to observe, "The world sure looks big when you are on top of a mountain."[11] The journey down the mountain went much faster, but Rainwater pointed out that they still had to splash across Lee's Creek sixteen times before the party reached the outskirts of Van Buren, on the north bank of the Arkansas River. "We heard frogs holler," wrote Rainwater while he doctored saddle sores by the evening fire.[12]

On February 20, four days after their departure, the mounted Miller escorts and the procession of ten wagons bearing heaps of smoked meat ferried the broad Arkansas River near its junction with the Poteau River and entered the town of Fort Smith, on the Arkansas side of the border with Indian Territory.[13] Once a small military outpost established to keep peace between the Osages and Cherokees, Fort Smith had grown into a supply terminal and departure point for travelers headed west.

For several years after the Civil War, Fort Smith continued to play an important role in commerce and as a military post for troops patrolling the countryside in search of guerrilla bands and helping to relocate refugees displaced by the war. But in early 1871, just about the time Colonel Miller and his party arrived, the townspeople learned that one of their major sources of income—the United States Army—had plans to depart.[14] The government decided that the military post had outlived its usefulness. The frontier was moving farther west, and the post no longer could function as an efficient provisions depot.

By July 1871, most of the garrison troops were due to evacuate, leaving only a small detachment to guard the government buildings until the United States marshal took charge of the old post that autumn.[15] The marshal was necessary because great numbers of lawless individuals and outlaw bands swarmed the town and countryside, especially in Indian Territory. Because of treaty rights, fugitives from justice could operate and live there outside the reach of the law.

"Into this sanctuary [Indian Territory] came horse thieves, bandits, murderers, gunfighters, gamblers, renegades, prostitutes, hoodlums, rustlers, and desperadoes of every description," William J. Butler wrote in *Fort Smith, Past and Present*. "They used Indian Territory as their home base for raiding banks, trains, and stage coaches throughout the immediate areas and all the surrounding states.

"Indian tribal law officers and a few United States deputy marshals did their best to maintain order but it was simply too great an undertaking for them to handle. The criminal population of the territory continued to increase, and murder, rape and robbery became everyday events."[16]

Terrified by this wave of crime, tribal leaders and white settlers alike from throughout Indian Territory and Fort Smith beseeched the federal government to rescue them from the robbers, rapists, and cold-blooded killers in their midst. Just a few weeks after Colonel Miller left Fort Smith on his Texas journey, Congress responded to the pleas by transferring a federal district court to Fort Smith with jurisdiction over Indian Territory.[17] It was not until 1875, however, that law-abiding folks got any substantial relief. That was when ardent Republican jurist Isaac Charles Parker, known as the "hanging judge," came to town to administer swift justice, in his courtroom and at the gallows, where a sign read, "The Gates of Hell."[18]

Judge Parker, along with his dour Bavarian hangman, George Maledon, and two hundred deputies sometimes called "the men who rode for Parker," had not yet arrived in Fort Smith that winter morning when Miller and his dauntless bunch crossed into the unknown. Despite the area's reputation, Colonel Miller, never cowardly, could not be discouraged from reaching Texas cow country. He ordered the procession of wagons and men to move forward. Leaving Arkansas, they forded the Poteau River, Indian Territory's only north-flowing major stream, and stopped alongside a tributary creek so Perry Britton could cook a hot supper and they could spend the night.[19] Colonel Miller broke out a jug of spirits that evening, perhaps to celebrate their safe passage. In his diary entry for the day, Rainwater wrote about Miller passing the bottle around the fire, the young drover's only mention of the consumption of strong drink on the trip to Texas. Even fourteen-year-old Rainwater got a sip of the potent beverage. The drink was not to his liking and he quickly spit it out, for which the other riders heckled him for the remainder of the trip.[20]

If the lack of journal entries is any indication, Colonel Miller's party must have had a run of good luck. Rainwater had little comment about the trip through Indian Territory, a route that took them between the Sans Bois and Jack Fork Mountains. They generally followed the east-west California Road to a point called Cross Roads on the heavily traveled Texas Road. In 1870, James J. McAlester, a white Confederate veteran from Arkansas with a Chickasaw wife, had opened a tent store there.[21] From this settlement, which eventually was named McAlester, the Miller party proceeded at a southward angle through the Choctaw Nation down the Texas Road—a historic path used for many years by white explorers, hunters, trappers, traders, military detachments, emigrants to Texas, and cattlemen.[22]

The wagons and riders passed near Kiowa Hill, east of the Pine Mountains; Stringtown, a stage stop on the old Butterfield Overland Route that sliced across Indian Territory; and Atoka, a trade center founded only a few years before and named for a Choctaw subchief.[23] They stopped briefly at Boggy Depot, located at the junction of the Texas Road and the Butterfield Overland Stage Route. Just ahead lay the Red River. Fed by the Washita, Blue and Kiamichi Rivers, this major stream formed the southern border, more than five hundred miles long, separating Indian Territory from Texas.

Miller's outfit crossed the Red River at Colbert's Ferry, named for Benjamin Franklin Colbert, who had come from Mississippi with the Chickasaws in 1846.[24] In exchange for maintaining the road leading to the ferry, the tribe allowed Colbert to charge $1.25 for every four-horse team, wagon, or stagecoach that used the crossing.[25] Colbert became a rich man as a result. George W. Miller's crossing of the tempestous Red River marked his first entrance into Texas. At last, he was nearing the domain of the longhorn.

Just a dozen miles south of the Red River, the Miller party reached Sherman, Texas, and then traveled to Fort Worth. At the junction of the West and Clear Forks of the Trinity River, the town of Fort Worth then had fewer than five hundred citizens, but was fast on its way to becoming a popular provisioning center on the Chisholm Trail. The Miller group pressed on to the southwest. The next settlement of any size was Comanche, where young Rainwater scribbled in his journal that he saw "the greatest tract of red sandy land" in his memory.[26]

Between Comanche and Brownwood, a settlement of native sandstone homes, Colonel Miller and his men met up with twenty to thirty riders, all armed with Winchester rifles and pistols, and two men bound hand and foot, riding in a wagon. The leader of the posse told Miller that the prisoners were accused killers and the first men to be arrested in Brownwood since the end of the Civil War. The posse was escorting them to the Brazos River valley town of Waco, sometimes called "Six-shooter Junction," to be tried for murder.[27]

Rainwater recorded the encounter and then wrote, "We camped that night on Jim Ned Creek," named for a wary old Indian spy known for tracking the movements of white intruders. The Miller party spent the next night in Brownwood. "We were offered all the land we might wish in that vicinity at $1.25 an acre," wrote Rainwater. "That beautiful wild land was covered with mesquite brush and mesquite green grass, a stretch of rich, black soil."[28]

Despite the low prices, neither Colonel Miller nor any of his men bought any land. They were after cows. Weary of eating trail dust and eager for Perry Britton to replenish his dwindling food supplies, they realized that their destination for the first half of their long journey was at hand.

From Brownwood, they traveled south into San Saba County, in central Texas.[29] George Miller's Kentucky blood boiled with excitement. He was in a land of Comanche and Kiowa raiders, Confederate exiles from Kentucky, wild mustangs, companies of Texas Rangers who called themselves "minutemen," and rolling hills dotted with cedar, mesquite, and hackberry. Best of all, Miller knew that San Saba was a cowman's paradise. He hoped and prayed that everyone there had a healthy appetite for smoked ham.

THE HANGING JUDGE, FRONTIER VIGILANTES, AND STONE-COLD KILLERS

Although G. W. Miller left his wife and children under the protection of kinfolk and friends in Newtonia, he constantly fretted about their safety during his frequent trips away from home. His anxiety intensified during the long cattle drives, which often kept him on the trail for three or four months at a time.

Miller's concern was justified; his family lived on the brink of Indian Territory, a huge sanctuary for the lawless. Thieves, killers, rapists, and robbers who had found refuge in Indian Territory regularly raided trains, banks, stagecoaches, and even homesteads in Missouri and other neighboring states. They stole horses and cattle from Texas ranches and snatched hogs and cows off Missouri farms, driving the livestock into Indian Territory and selling to unscrupulous dealers who never questioned bogus bills of sale or improper brand registrations.[1]

Law-abiding Indian Territory citizens were not spared the outrages. Neither the companies of Indian lighthorsemen, which guarded the borders against the importation of diseased cattle and helped to quell tribal squabbles, nor the Chickasaw and Choctaw vigilantes could quell the rising tide of lawbreakers.[2] For each horse thief or homicidal maniac captured and lynched, a half-dozen more appeared to take his place. Indian Territory became known as the consummate "robbers' roost," and its sinister reputation spread across the country. A popular slogan claimed, "There's no Sunday west of Saint Louis—no God west of Fort Smith."[3]

Colonel Miller must have breathed at least a partial sigh of relief in 1871, when his party reached Fort Smith and he learned that the federal government was stepping in to bring order to the troubled region. Even the "damn Yankee" government, which Miller mistrusted, might exterminate some of the evildoers who preyed on Missouri, Kansas, Arkansas, Texas, and Indian Territory. Still, it would be some time before any semblance of justice prevailed. A series of incompetent and corrupt judges continued in office for several years. "Notorious ruffians, desperadoes and outlaws have been sufficiently abundant in this region to give the whole community a bad reputation,"[4] wrote a *New York Tribune* reporter who visited Fort Smith in 1873.

To bring order to the lands between the Kansas border and Red River—the largest jurisdiction in the world—Judge Isaac C. Parker hired two hundred officers to track down lawbreakers.[5] These United States deputy marshals patroled a territory roughly the size of New England in search of ruthless killers and robbers. Any culprits caught operating in Indian Territory and surrounding states were hauled to Parker's courtroom at Fort Smith. It was a difficult and dangerous task, and one-third of Parker's deputies died in the line of duty.[6]

During the twenty-one years he served on the federal bench at Fort Smith, Judge Parker disposed of 13,500 cases, of which most were criminal.[7] More than nine thousand defendants pleaded guilty or were convicted, and Parker sentenced 160 to die on the gallows. Many of the condemned died in prison before the executions could be carried out, or they were killed in escape attempts. Some were pardoned or their terms were commuted. Of the seventy-nine who were hanged, sixty swung at the end of one of George Maledon's handwoven hemp ropes, oil soaked to prevent the hangman's knot, with its thirteen wraps, from slipping.[8]

But despite the best efforts of "Hanging Judge" Parker and the army of hired gunmen he sent into Indian Territory, frontier life for the Millers and other families remained dangerous, with plenty of peril and peculiar incidents that left permanent scars on the land and the people. During the twenty years after the Civil War, Missouri became known as "the Bandit State" or "the Outlaw State" because of national attention showered on the many desperadoes, particularly the James gang.[9]

In addition to outlaws, frightened citizens made the situation much worse when they formed vigilante groups. Driven by ignorance and paranoia, fueled by blatant racism and moral indignation, these self-righteous, self-styled crusaders pursued suspected thieves and lawbreakers, "loose females," "uppity free niggers," and anyone else who did not meet with their own moral ideals and social standards.[10] Punishment ranged from banishment or lashes with a hickory switch to tar and feathers or even lynching.

Many names were used to describe these self-appointed posses. Some called themselves the Ku Klux Klan, Honest Men's Leagues, Regulators, Law and Order Committees, and Anti–Horse Thief Associations. In the mountains of southwestern Missouri, not far from Newton County, a notorious group of violent vigilantes sprang up called the Bald Knobbers.[11]

Mostly former Union soldiers and conservative Republicans, the Bald Knobbers roamed through the Ozarks in the 1880s, many of them wearing hooded masks their wives had made. Bald Knobbers had no compunction about sidestepping the law and committing violence to preserve and protect their property. They considered it their absolute right, traced back to the Founding Fathers of the American Constitutional Convention.[12]

In September 1875, several prominent Newtonians joined a newly organized vigilante group called the Newton County Protective Society.[13] Colonel Miller and his kinsmen declined membership. They had better things to do. Still, for many years, outlaw tales and horror stories were dragged out and retold at every wedding, wake, baptism, and social gathering. While her husband tended to his cattle, Molly Miller continuously heard accounts of scalpings, raids, rapes, and executions.

One of the most popular stories during the decade the Millers lived in Newtonia—a favorite of old men whittling and spitting tobacco—was about a local citizen who shot and killed a Confederate prisoner who had killed the young man's father. After slaying his father's killer, the young man scalped him and sliced off his head and ears. It was said that when he took the grisly relics home, his wife was so shocked that she gave birth to a child without ears.[14]

Bizarre tales of accidental deaths, murders, omens, ghosts, and night riders were passed around supper tables along with platters of fried meat and bowls of beans. The stories helped while away a winter's eve for some people, but did little to calm a young mother trying to raise children while her husband rode cattle trails far from home.

Chapter 10

SAN SABA COUNTRY

"I can see the cattle grazing o'er the hills at early morn;
I can see the campfires smoking at the breakfast of the dawn;
I can hear the broncos neighing; I can hear the cowboys sing;
I'd like to be in Texas for the roundup in the spring."[1]
—Chorus, "I'd Like to Be in Texas"

AFTER many trying weeks on the trails leading from Missouri through Arkansas and Indian Territory, Colonel Miller and his road-weary men finally reached their destination—San Saba County, Texas. Finding themselves near the geographic center of Texas, the Miller party frequently encountered hardened cowboys, many of them Confederate veterans. In the midst of heated battles with cow thieves and Indians, or afterwards, during victory celebrations, those cowboys often shrieked the high-pitched "Texas yell," a blood-chilling scream appropriated from the Comanches.[2] The cowboys pulled on mule-eared boots,[3] knotted cotton bandannas twice as big as dinner napkins around their necks, and wore wide-brimmed hats to protect against the burning sun. They carried Bowie knives, rifles, and pistols, and were so skilled with their lariats that they bragged they could lasso the horns of the moon.

The local cowboys hailed from strong and healthy southern families that had settled the area years before San Saba County was organized, in 1856. These early white pioneers and their black slaves came by the wagonload to what became the Lone Star State from Alabama, Tennessee, Mississippi, and Kentucky.

As one pioneer family recounted, "Through the wilds, they moved determinedly toward the heart of the West—San Saba County. Where the hills flared with signal fires and cedar brakes offered secure retreats, where the pioneer settler's cows came home at night bristling with gaily feathered arrows, horses were stolen in droves and cattle killed at will, where crime stalked red-handed, and the Indians took full toll of human life, combating the frontiersman's rights to home and land."[4]

The settlers of San Saba sent sons and grandsons, brothers and uncles off to fight with Sam Houston for Texan independence in the Mexican War of 1846 and to ride as Rebel cavalrymen in the War against Yankee Aggression. They hacked out homes for themselves in the thickets along streams and rivers and throughout the valley of the San Saba, where there was plenty of sweet water and tall grass. They "lived in the unprotected frontier, with no shelter but the crude log cabins where winds whistled, Indians yelled, and wolves howled and mobs roared," as settlers later recalled.[5]

Many of the settlers joined companies of Texas Rangers to guard homes and livestock from marauding Comanches and cattle thieves and to break up feuds. Temporarily disbanded during Reconstruction, the Rangers reached the peak of their power between 1874 and 1880, when lawlessness became rampant and the last of the Indian raids occurred in the San Saba country.

Local cattlemen warned Colonel Miller shortly after he arrived that the much-feared Comanches lived just west of San Saba, Comanche, and Bosque Counties. But although he regarded the Comanches as "troublesome," Miller and his men experienced no real difficulties with Indians.[6] Miller must have realized that he shared crucial traits with the Comanches. They were a nomadic people and they wanted no one to encroach on their lands. For the Comanches, the choice was between freedom or death; Miller felt exactly the same way.

"It was the custom of the Comanches," Jim Rainwater related in his diary, "to leave their camps and ride into San Saba and the counties east just at the time the moon would be getting full. Then, when the moon was full, they would return to their homes, frequently killing settlers as they went and taking with them horses and other property."[7]

Upon arriving in San Saba cattle country, after washing off layers of dirt and sweat in the San Saba River, Miller sought out Riley Harkey, a member of one of the county's pioneer Anglo families and the cattle agent for the county.[8] Harkey's ancestors came from the bluegrass region of Kentucky, and his heritage impressed Colonel Miller.[9] With his parents and brothers, Harkey had moved to San Saba County from Arkansas in 1855 and settled in the area around Wallace Creek. During the "Lost Cause," Harkey rode with a company of Texas Rangers, or "minutemen," whose job was to protect settlers' cattle and horses from raids by Comanches and whites.[10]

After the war, Harkey prospered in the cattle business and as a breeder of fine horses.

Harkey also was known throughout the San Saba cattle country for driving a hard bargain when he bought or sold mustangs or steers. But Colonel G. W. Miller, too, had years of experience in haggling over everything from human flesh to champion mules, and he knew his ten wagonloads of smoked ham and bacon were worth their weight in gold. Much to his surprise, Miller not only negotiated a satisfactory deal, but also got twice as many head of cattle as he had expected, swapping fifty pounds of hog meat for every steer.[11] Harkey took a band of cowboys up the San Saba River and rounded up a great herd of cattle. Colonel Miller and his brother-in-law George Carson culled out the best of the bunch to form a herd of four hundred snorting and bellowing longhorns.[12]

In his diary, young Rainwater wrote of the considerable "red tape" Colonel Miller had to cut through with Harkey before the final deal was made. Miller's men and the San Saba cowboys then drove the cattle from a huge holding corral and walked them single file through a chute so the county treasurer could note the age and trail brand on each steer.[13]

With bill of sale in hand, Colonel Miller and his trail herders—reinforced by some freshly hired San Saba riders—and Perry Britton began the long trip north with the mess wagon replenished. Strong and willing, most of the new hands were horse breakers, called bronco busters, who knew how to handle spirited Texas cow ponies.

One San Saba cowboy, John P. Robbins, recalled such cattle drives. "Three to four months were spent in taking the cattle up the trail; food and clothing being carried in the grub wagon, drawn by two yoke of oxen. From daybreak to about an hour by sun the herd moved about ten miles, camp was pitched about sundown, and the cattle were left to bed for the night. A regular camp cook drove the grub wagon and cooked for the gang. After supper the Indians would often come into camp and get something to eat; very hostile Indians were found on the trail."[14]

The journey up the trail was grueling for men and beasts. Daily rations of greasy bacon, brown beans, flour bread, and stout coffee—called by some drovers "coffin varnish"—were the only things to look forward to at the close of a day spent in the saddle. In his handwritten journal, Jim Rainwater left a faithful account of Colonel Miller's first northbound cattle drive.

"We are going to have one hell of a storm," Rainwater wrote, quoting the prediction of a San Saba trail foreman identified only as Sanders. The thunderstorm brewed in the evening heavens that Easter Sunday of 1871 as the herd neared Fort Worth, and Sanders told each cowhand how to react if the herd became spooked.[15]

When the storm finally erupted, the longhorns stampeded. Throughout the ordeal, Rainwater rode with Miller, helping to maintain order despite lightning and thunder and torrents of rain. "That morning," Rainwater wrote, "Col. Miller had given me a $5 raise per month in wages, placing me on an equal scale with the rest of the men." As the herd stampeded, most of the horses ran with them, carrying their riders away. Miller, George Carson, and Rainwater, astride his trained pony, managed to control their mounts and hold the herd together. They worked with the runaway steers until late in the evening, not daring to pause for even a moment of rest until all the cattle had finally quieted down.[16]

As dawn broke, Colonel Miller rode out to count the cattle as they left their beds to feed on grass along the trail. To his delight, he discovered that not one was missing. At that night's supper fire, G.W. called up Rainwater, just turned fifteen years old, to stand before the others. For Rainwater's courage in the face of the storm, Miller gave him a black-and-white two-year-old steer which he could sell at market value when the party reached home.[17]

A few days later, the herd reached Sherman, just before the much-anticipated Red River crossing. Miller rode into town to fetch supplies, and at the general store, he purchased a slicker overcoat and a pair of pants for Rainwater.[18] "This was the greatest treat of my life up to that time," noted Rainwater. "It was the first time in my life that anyone, who wasn't any kin to me, had given me anything." But Rainwater did not have much time to savor his new outfit. Indian Territory loomed ahead, just across the Red River.

Even more than they feared renegade thieves and Indian raids, Miller and his crew dreaded violent storms and dangerous river crossings a half-mile wide, some of which involved quicksand. The Red and Canadian Rivers were especially treacherous. The patches of quicksand often snared slow-moving cows. Cattle could get caught in swift waters or step into sinkholes and drown. A crossing rarely went without a hitch.

In fording the Red River on that first northbound trip, Miller got lucky and lost only a lone two-year-old steer.[19] As Rainwater recounted the incident, the steer broke away from the herd and moved up a canyon on the Texas side. When it became clear that he could not head off the runaway and return it to the herd, Rainwater pulled his rifle from the saddle scabbard, aimed, and shot the animal. He and other cowboys skinned and butchered the steer, and Rainwater rode into camp on the Indian Territory side of the Red with a quarter of beef tied to his saddle. Once more, Miller had nothing but praise for the young cowboy's quick thinking. It was far better to have fresh beef to eat or to give to a party of Indians that might come calling than to allow the steer to escape.

The next major stop for the cowboys and their cattle was the Indian Territory town of Okmulgee, named for the Creek word for "bubbling water."[20] A small settlement with a few stores, a blacksmith, and a doctor, Okmulgee had served as the capital of the Creek Nation since 1869.[21] Miller and his trail hands found Okmulgee's muddy streets filled with Indian lighthorsemen, hunters, drifters, bootleggers, and Creek freedmen.

Several large cattle and horse ranches, owned by Creeks or by adopted tribesmen, operated in the area.[22] Most of the herds, like Miller's, had been purchased from Texas ranchers in the spring and brought into Indian Territory to be fattened in rich pasturelands before they were shipped north to market in the autumn. Few cattle were wintered in Indian Territory; when they were, ranchers fed them seed from cotton gins or let them eat stalks left in fields along creek banks.[23]

Besides cattlemen and visiting trail herds, the town and surrounding countryside also drew its share of whiskey peddlers, shady characters, and undesirables trying to elude warrants for their arrest, sworn out at the federal court in Fort Smith. These unsavory types often preyed on the ranchers and settlers in the remote areas surrounding Okmulgee; as pioneer Minda Geer Hardin recalled, "If a man would ride up to my door, draw a gun on me and tell me to get him something to eat, well, I did it and asked no questions. They were well behaved if no questions were asked."[24]

Rainwater's journal does not mention any encounters with outlaws, and at last the journey neared its end. Soon the herd crossed the broad Arkansas River at Childers' Ferry. Within a few days, the Miller party forded the meandering Neosho, the Osage word for "clear water," then Cabin Creek and Rock Creek, and entered the corner of southeastern Kansas. The cowboys drove the longhorns into pens near the railroad tracks in unruly Baxter Springs, "the first cowtown in Kansas."[25] From there, they would be shipped to slaughterhouses in Kansas City, Saint Louis, and Chicago.

Rainwater and the other cowboys were not sorry to end a trip spent herding ornery steers, eating trail grub, and sleeping through cold midnight rain. Their rest would be brief, however; soon there would be another big drove of longhorns to handle, and the cycle would start once again.[26] The young Texans and Missourians drew their wages from Colonel Miller and made a beeline for the old Corner Saloon to celebrate. After four grueling months, the cattle drive was completed.

Once his paperwork was in order and he had collected the earnings from the cattle sale, G. W. Miller saddled his tired cow pony. Hardly stopping, he rode straightway to Newtonia, where Molly and his sons waited.

G.W. yearned to hold his wife in his arms. He could not wait to see how much his boys had grown. He was anxious to tell all of them that at long last, the Miller family was in the cattle business.

COWBOYS

STARTING WITH HIS first trip to Texas, Colonel George Miller spent his life in the company of cattlemen, bronco busters, and drovers. He quickly became associated with certain of the so-called cattle barons and prominent ranchers of the time, including the Harkey family and others from San Saba County, the renowned Abel Head "Shanghai" Pierce, and Lee Kokernut, a noted Texan who became Miller's first ranching partner.

Literally thousands of cowboys eventually would draw wages from Colonel Miller or would ride and rope for his sons on the sprawling 101 Ranch. But it was the cowhands from those early years—the men and boys of the rugged cattle trails and feisty cow towns—who served as models for all future 101 cowboys and cowgirls. The later cowboys and cowgirls were often men and women who never branded a calf or slept a single night wrapped in a bedroll under the stars, but instead worked as flashy entertainers for the Millers' Wild West show or became motion-picture heroes and heroines. Their lives were far different from those of the men who inspired the name "cowboy" many years earlier.

Some historians claim the word *cow-boy* first was used in medieval Ireland to describe boys who tended cattle, but others say the name was bantered about in colonial America, when youngsters such as Daniel Boone herded cows.[1] Even so, only after the Civil War did the term *cowboy* come into common use.[2]

The heyday of genuine cowboys was brief, starting in 1865, when Texans returned home after serving the Confederacy, poor in cash but rich in rangelands teeming with ubiquitous longhorns. Prior to the war, those who had trailed cattle across the country usually were known as drovers. In the late 1860s, Texas ranchers used the term *cowboy* more and more as they gathered tens of thousands of unbranded wild longhorns during roundups at first called "cowhunts."[3] To herd cattle up the trails to northern railheads and markets, ranchers hired youngsters whom, by about 1870, they generally referred to as cowboys.

Some, like Jim Rainwater, were only twelve to sixteen years old. Some of them were hardly big enough to climb into a saddle, let alone combat stampedes, swollen rivers, lightning storms, and marauding Indians. Not everyone approved of such work. "Parents, do not allow your boys to load themselves down with Mexican spurs, six shooters and pipes," warned a reporter for the *Denton* (Texas) *Monitor*.[4] "Keep them off the prairies as professional cow hunters. There, in that occupation, who knows but they may forget that there is a distinction between 'mine' and 'thine'? Send them to school, teach them a trade, or keep them at home."

For those who made their living on the cattle trails from the late 1860s until about the mid-1880s, there was nothing glamorous or romantic about being a cowboy. Certainly, the early cowboys received scant praise from the popular press.

As the *Topeka Commonwealth* of August 15, 1871, put it,

> The Texas cattle herder is a character, the like of which can be found nowhere else on earth. Of course he is unlearned and illiterate, but with few wants and meager ambition. His diet is principally navy plug and whiskey and the occupation dearest to his heart is gambling. His dress consists of a flannel shirt with a handkerchief encircling his neck, butternut pants and a pair of long boots, in which are always the legs of his pants. His head is covered by a sombrero, which is a Mexican hat with a high crown and a brim of enormous dimensions. He generally wears a revolver on each side of his person, which he will use with as little hesitation on a man as on a wild animal. Such a character is dangerous and desperate and each one has generally killed his man.[5]

Many years later, Walter Prescott Webb, a native Texan and one of America's most distinguished historians, took exception with earlier descriptions of cowboys, especially in reference to firearms. "Cowboy life is very different from the ideas given by a Wild West Show or the 'movies,' " wrote Webb. "It is against Texas law to carry a pistol and the sale is unlawful. . . . Occasionally a rider will carry a Winchester on his saddle for coyotes or Lobo wolves, but in the seventeen years the writer has been intimate with range life he has never seen a cowboy carry a pistol hung about him, and few instances where one was carried concealed. There is always a gun of some sort with the outfit carried in the wagon."[6]

Like the writer for the *Topeka Commonwealth*, western author Ramon F. Adams sought not to glamorize or romanticize the cowboy. "The real cowhand's typical day was anything but romantic," he explained in his own folksy style. "There was no romance in gettin' up at four o'clock in the mornin', eatin' dust behind a trail herd, swimmin' muddy and turbulent rivers, nor in doctorin' screw worms, pullin' stupid cows from bog holes, sweatin' in the heat of summer and freezin' in the cold of winter."[7]

An unrealistic notion of ranch and trail life was not the only misconception propagated about cowboys. Contrary to the popular belief that all cowboys were young white men, they ranged in age from grizzled old Rebels to awkward adolescents and came from an assortment of ethnic backgrounds and social classes. Many were black or brown. Some were from southern stock of Scotch-Irish descent, but there were also numerous greenhorn immigrant lads, Indians, blacks, Mexicans, and mestizo cowboys, especially in Indian Territory and Texas.[8] Because blatant racism was rampant in nineteenth-century America, the white Texans and Anglo ranchers of Indian Territory referred to such cowboys as "Micks," "Meskins," "Greasers," "niggers," "Injuns," "savages," and "breeds."[9] Mexican vaqueros, some of the most expert ropers and horsemen ever to ride the plains, made a tremendous contribution to the ranching industry in Texas.[10] So did black cowboys, some of whom had been slaves who tended herds before the Civil War. On the great cattle drives of the late 1800s, when about eight million to ten million longhorns were trailed north from Texas, approximately one of every six cowboys was black.[11]

G. W. Miller, an unbending Rebel given to racial prejudice throughout his life, did not live to see Bill Pickett, arguably the single most talented cowboy who ever rode for the Miller family.[12] Pickett, who was black, was not only a skilled working cowboy and one of the best rodeo performers of all time.[13] He could work cows from dawn to dusk, but he also knew how to entertain big crowds and even was in a few motion pictures.

Pickett was born in Texas in 1871, just about the time Colonel Miller made his first trip to the San Saba country to buy cattle.[14] Remembered most for having invented the rodeo sport of bulldogging, Pickett joined up with the Miller brothers in 1905, two years after G. W. Miller's death. Through good times and bad, Pickett stayed with the Miller family—he was right there until the bitter end. Had he still been alive, even an old Kentucky bigot such as G. W. Miller would have had to admit that Pickett was a real cowboy.

Chapter 11

THE COWBOY'S DREAM

Last night, as I lay on the prairie,
And looked at the stars in the sky,
I wondered if ever a cowboy
Would drift to that sweet by and by.[1]
—"The Cowboy's Dream,"
old trail song

AS his success mounted, George Washington Miller boasted to his family and friends that he knew cows "front, back, and sideways."[2] In little time, Miller also became quite rich from his cattle exploits.

Indeed, the year 1871 was lucrative for all those who scoured the Texas plains and herded range cattle to Kansas railheads. Rising prices reflected a growing demand for beef at the Chicago market and at Denver, where yearlings brought ten dollars a head; two-year-olds, fifteen dollars; cows and calves, twenty-one to twenty-three dollars; and beef steers, ready to be fattened for slaughter after a couple of seasons on succulent bluestem grass, twenty-five to thirty dollars.[3]

Colonel Miller poured his year's profits into his first real cattle ranch, a spread established in 1871 a few miles south of Baxter Springs, Kansas, on Indian Territory acreage leased from the Quapaw tribe. Miller's partner in the venture was Lee Kokernut, whose family controlled a sizable ranch near Gonzales, in the Guadalupe River country east of San Antonio. Kokernut bossed men who were said to be as tough as nickel steak, cowhands liable to work so hard they might drown in their own sweat.

The Miller and Kokernut operation was called the L K Ranch. Some of Kokernut's most savvy horse wranglers and cowpunchers came from Texas to work the longhorn stock pastured there.[4] For a base of operations, the Millers decided to keep their family residence and maintain the general store in nearby Newtonia, Missouri.

On March 6, 1872, Colonel Miller and a party of his cowboys departed on a second cattle-buying trip to San Saba County, Texas.[5] It was a difficult decision for Miller to leave because only five days earlier, his grandmother Mary Fish had died in Kentucky. She was almost eighty years old.[6] Word of her death had reached Miller just as he was making final preparations for the cattle drive. In addition, Miller was somewhat anxious because his youngest son, John Fish Miller, not quite two years old, was ill with fever. Molly assured her husband that he could do nothing for the little boy by staying home and pacing the floor. Miller finally agreed, and he and his cowboys set out for Texas. Because he could not return to Crab Orchard, Miller did his grieving from the saddle while his grandmother was laid to rest beside her husband at the plantation's old burial ground.[7]

Included in the band of trail drivers once again was James Rainwater, the young Newtonian who had chronicled Miller's first Texas journey. Rainwater brought along the well-worn diary and hastily jotted down impressions along the way, but not as often as before. Most of the notations of the trip through Indian Territory were routine, such as his mention of fording the Arkansas River near Muskogee and crossing the Red River above Sherman, Texas.[8]

This time, moving due south through Indian Territory to Texas, Miller's party had no procession of creaky wagons filled with smoked pork and hams to fret over. Instead of hog meat, Colonel Miller carried saddlebags crammed with gold.[9] He had learned from his first visit that Texas ranchers had no use for paper money because most of them had been paid in worthless Confederate scrip after the war. Gold coins were more to their liking. Miller was pleased because gold was easier to transport than thousands of pounds of ham and bacon. Best of all, only three dollars' worth of gold fetched a steer priced at six dollars.

A few days into the journey, after Colonel Miller unsuccessfully attempted to buy cattle at Fort Worth, the cowboys rode far to the south to Kimble Bend in Brazos County, where they had to shell out a whole dollar for each bushel of corn to feed their horses.[10] "There are no farms west of this point," observed Rainwater in his diary as the Miller cowboys rode westward into Bosque County. He wrote that they did not come across "a town or village in the county, and I guess they didn't have any." Colonel Miller encountered trouble in Bosque County, where he discovered that one of his trail hands had stolen two thousands dollars in gold.[11]

Rainwater wrote,

> Miller showed one of the boys that much money in gold, and also he showed this same man where he hid it. Two days afterward when Miller looked for the money it was gone. We went on to San Saba, got our cattle and on the way back we again camped at the same spot where the money was stolen. The next morning we had a trial, the hats of all the boys were placed on the ground near a sack of shelled corn. All the boys were sent away from camp, each with a grain of corn, and returning he was to place the grain in the hat of the man he thought guilty. The result was that all the corn was put in one man's hat—we all suspected the same fellow. This man picked up his hat, looked at the corn, shook it out, put on his hat, got on his horse and rode away, and I presume he is riding yet.[12]

Rainwater described another noteworthy incident which occurred as Colonel Miller and the cowboys herded the longhorns farther north. One afternoon, the outfit was camped on the south bank of the North Canadian River, waiting for high water to subside so the herd could cross. Two young Indians rode into camp and asked Miller if he was interested in buying a couple of ponies. When he told them he was, they rode away. The next morning they returned, leading a pair of ponies as promised.

Rainwater recorded the incident:

> About two hours afterward, twenty or thirty light horse [sic] police came into camp and asked where we got the two ponies. We told them of the trade with the two Indians, one of whom was about twenty years old, the other twenty-five. The police explained the two ponies were stolen the night before, but told us to keep them and they could get the thieves. About twenty miles distant they caught up with the two boys and brought them back to our camp.
>
> The trial of the two young Indians was held the next morning within our camp, with our boys called as witnesses. The two were declared guilty. Their hands were tied behind them, their feet roped together and a rail placed between their legs. A rope was thrown over a limb, thus making the bodies of the prisoners stand up straight. The penalty consisted of lashes on their bare backs. One Indian was given fifty lashes, as this was his first offence [sic], and the blood ran down to his heels. It was the other's second offence [sic]. He was given 100 lashes and notified that under the Indian law, if he were convicted a third time, he would be shot

to death. When the whipping was over the police put a handful of salt in a pan of water, washed the backs of the two prisoners and turned them loose.[13]

The Indians' harsh attitude toward crime and punishment may have confounded some of Miller's young cowboys, especially having seen how mercifully he had treated the drover suspected of stealing his gold. Still, there was no time to ponder the punishment of Indians—the cattle trail beckoned.

Waiting for the swollen waters of the North Canadian to recede, the Miller party drove the herd across the first bridge built across the Canadian in Indian Territory. Only about two dozen head had made it across when the new bridge, perhaps already weakened by floodwater, collapsed under the great weight, sending cattle and cowboys into the water below. No serious injuries occurred, and by late in the day, all the cattle had swum back to rejoin the remainder of the herd on the south bank. After a few more days of waiting, the cowboys forded the entire bunch across the river. They headed straight for Okmulgee, then to the Arkansas River crossing at Childers' Ferry before tackling the short, final leg of the drive. After they turned some cattle loose in the pastures of the L K Ranch, the tired crew herded the rest to Baxter Springs, at trail's end.

When Colonel Miller reached his home in Newtonia, one glance at Molly's grim face told him tragedy had visited their family once again. On March 29, a little more than three weeks after he had left for Texas, the couple's youngest son, John Fish Miller, had died.[14] The boy's death had occurred just a month shy of his second birthday, following a brief illness. Molly and some of her brothers had taken his body back to Crab Orchard and buried him near his brother, Wilkes Booth Miller.[15] Four-year-old Joseph was the Millers' sole surviving child.

George Miller once again turned to work to relieve his deep sorrow, and he plunged into his cattle business with a vengeance. Working as much as twenty hours a day, he and Kokernut burned the L K brand into the hides and horns of thousands of beeves, thus initiating their odyssey to the slaughterhouse. As always, the relentless grind of hard labor among his cowboys proved to be Miller's best medicine.

Miller also possessed a well of inspiration and comfort he could tap when he needed support. Even though he usually avoided going to church, family members felt he had a strong spiritual source down deep.[16] Indeed, old-time cowboys who worked for the Miller family during the Newtonia years recalled that on that very first trail drive from Texas to Baxter Springs, Colonel Miller assembled his cowboys one Sunday morning at a camp on the banks of the Red River.[17] He climbed into the branches of a cottonwood tree and preached them a strong Sabbath sermon. They said it was a typical Miller thing to do.[18] This faith in God and in himself enabled Miller to remain confident, despite hardships and family deaths, that his cattle empire would grow.

STANDING BEAR:
Chief of the Poncas

IT WAS IMPORTANT to G. W. Miller that his dead sons were laid to rest among kinfolk in Kentucky. But Colonel Miller was not the only one concerned with burial in his family's homeland. Another father who desired that his son be returned to native soil was Standing Bear, a respected chief of the Ponca Indians.[1] Ultimately, the lives of the Millers and of Standing Bear's Ponca tribe—to all appearances as different as midnight and noon—would become unalterably entwined.

The poignant story of Standing Bear began far to the north of Indian Territory, near the confluence of the Niobrara and Missouri Rivers in the vicinity of northeastern Nebraska and Dakota Territory. That was where the Poncas, a tribe of about seven hundred farmers and hunters, maintained earth-lodge villages.[2] It was the only property ceded to them by the United States government in 1858, after the Poncas signed a treaty giving up most of their lands.

The ensuing years brought additional treaties and a flurry of paperwork and red tape, and the Poncas had to relinquish even more of their holdings to other tribes.[3] After years of stripping the Poncas of their land, the federal government decided in 1876 to acquire the rest of the land for the neighboring Sioux, a much larger tribe which resented the Poncas' presence on what they claimed was part of the permanent Sioux reservation.[4]

The U.S. Interior Department thus ordered the Poncas to relocate to Indian Territory, the federal government's convenient dumping ground for scores of tribes.[5] At first, the Poncas refused even to discuss the request, but under mounting pressure, tribal leaders at last met with government officials. After patiently listening to the white men, the assembled Ponca leaders decided that Standing Bear, a fifty-eight-year-old chief and elder, should act as official spokesman for the tribe. His message was clear. "We do not wish to sell our land," Standing Bear told the officials, "and we think no man has a right to take it from us. Here we will live, and here we will die."[6] The chief's simple message, although eloquent, was futile.

Finally, in early 1877, U.S. officials persuaded Standing Bear and nine other Ponca leaders to accompany them to Indian Territory and inspect the lands set aside for the tribe.[7] The Ponca chiefs did not like the site the government had selected and asked to be taken home.[8] When the officials refused this request, Standing Bear and the others began to walk northward toward their old villages on Dakota lands. After fifty difficult days with only meager rations, the Poncas made it as far as the Otoe agency in southern Nebraska, where they received provisions and ponies.[9]

Several days later, at the Omaha reservation, white officials convinced Standing Bear to seek help from President Rutherford B. Hayes, the purported Great Father. Standing Bear sent a telegram to Hayes explaining the Poncas' plight.[10] As a result, federal officials returned to the Ponca agency for yet another hearing with tribal leaders. Standing Bear again told the white men why the tribe did not wish to move to Indian Territory.

"This is my land," Standing Bear told the impatient bureaucrats. "The Great Father did not give it to me. My people were here and owned this land before there was any Great Father. We sold him some land, but we never sold this. This is mine. God gave it to me. When I want to sell it I will let you know. You are a rascal and liar, and I want you to go off my land. If you were treating a white man the way you are treating me, he would kill you, and everybody would say he did right. I will not do that. I will harm no white man, but this is my land, and I intend to stay here and make a good living for my wife and children. You can go."[11]

Standing Bear's words only angered the inflexible officials. The next morning, he was arrested and jailed for refusing to obey government orders, but after a military tribunal, he was eventually released. Yet the recalcitrant Office of Indian Affairs bureaucrats still would not budge from their decision, and finally commanded that the Ponca tribe be relocated on a sliver of Quapaw agency lands in the northeastern corner of Indian Territory.[12] The tribe was to remain there for a few years until the government designated a permanent home.

Although their leaders continued to oppose the move, the Ponca people's forced migration began in 1877, under extremely difficult conditions.[13] The Poncas' Trail of Tears was marked by disasters, including torrential rainstorms, a tornado, and an epidemic of malaria. Desperate to save his people, Standing Bear journeyed to Washington, D.C., and met with President Hayes to see about returning the tribe to its northern lands. The effort was unsuccessful.[14]

Every day, more Poncas perished from starvation or disease before reaching Indian Territory. In December 1878, Standing Bear's son died of malaria.[15] The chief, who had watched several other family members and close friends die, could take no more. He decided to defy the government edict and go home. Despite a fierce blizzard, Standing Bear placed his son's remains in a trunk, loaded it into an old wagon drawn by a pair of emaciated horses and, with thirty other Poncas, started the long and difficult journey north. He was determined to bury his son in Dakota ground near the Niobrara.[16]

Infuriated by what he termed Standing Bear's "escape," Secretary of the Interior Carl Schurz wired General George Crook to arrest the chief and his followers and return them to Indian Territory.[17] Crook's soldiers took the wayward Poncas into custody on the Omaha reservation in eastern Nebraska, where Chief Iron Eyes had given them asylum.[18]

During the trip south to Indian Territory, the Indian prisoners and their army guards camped near the city of Omaha, where Thomas H. Tibbles, a crusading assistant editor for the *Omaha Daily Herald*, rallied public support for Standing Bear and the destitute Poncas.[19] Tibbles made impassioned speeches to the Omaha people, circulated petitions, and raised funds for prominent attorneys to take the matter to court and seek Standing Bear's release on a writ of habeas corpus.[20]

When the landmark case went to trial in federal district court at Omaha, in 1879, the government lawyers argued that because "an Indian is not a person within the meaning of the law," Standing Bear was not entitled to the same protection as white citizens under the United States Constitution.[21] During the trial in the packed courtroom, white sympathizers sat spellbound as Standing Bear spoke on his own behalf. It was immediately obvious that he had been exposed to the influences of Christian missionaries.[22] Among other things, he said, "There is one God, and he made both Indians and white men. We were all made out of the dust of the earth. I once believed differently. I believed there was plenty of game, and plenty to eat, no sickness, no death and no pain. The best of the Indians would go to these happy hunting grounds. I thought that those who were bad would never live any more; that when they died that was the end of them.

"But I have learned that these things are not so, and that God wishes us to love Him and obey His commandments, follow the narrow road, work for Him on earth, and we shall have happiness after we die."[23]

Tibbles reported in his newspaper that when Standing Bear—attired in the full dress of a Ponca chief, including red-and-blue blanket, beaded belt, and bear-claw necklace—completed his speech, only sobs could be heard in the courtroom. Even General Crook and federal Judge Elmer S. Dundy, the presiding magistrate, were said to be in tears.

A few days later, Judge Dundy issued his famous ruling, a historic decision in American jurisprudence, which found that an Indian is indeed a human being the same as a white man, and as such, is entitled to the same rights. For the first time, Indian people were recognized as individuals, not just wards of the state.[24]

Standing Bear and his followers were released in May 1879. Eventually, he continued his journey to the ancestral grounds on the river bluffs and buried his son's remains with full tribal honors. Except for a brief and temporary move to Indian Territory to visit relatives, Standing Bear and his small band—about one-fourth of the Ponca tribe—stayed on the Dakota reservation. The old chief died there in obscurity in 1908.[25]

By that time, the Ponca tribe and the Miller family had been acquainted for almost thirty years. Because the L K Ranch was comprised of leased Quapaw lands, Colonel Miller and his first ranching partner, Lee Kokernut, came to know various beleaguered Poncas as soon as the tribe arrived in Indian Territory.[26]

Starting in the mid-1870s, G.W.'s son, Joseph Carson Miller, often accompanied his father to the ranch, and he struck up friendships with Indian youngsters. When he was still a small boy, Joe mastered their Siouan language and was as fluent as a full-blood in the Ponca dialect.[27] Joe Miller also became proficient in the universal sign language of the Plains Indians. He knew that drawing the first finger across the throat in a cutting motion was the sign for "Head-cutters," an old name that certain tribes bestowed on the Poncas because of their custom of scalping enemies killed in battle and then cutting off their heads and throwing them away.[28]

The interest and, more important, the sympathy which Colonel Miller and his young son showed those first Ponca Indians they met on the Quapaw lands would yield the Miller family big dividends in years to come.

PART THREE

The Cattleman's Last Frontier

In the decade following the Civil War, interrelated factors—pacification of the Indians, construction of the railroads, and decimation of the buffalo—opened the vast grasslands of the Great Plains to ever-growing herds of domestic cattle. . . . The cattleman's domain spread north from the Rio Grande to the Canadian border; soon, grass became scarce. It was perhaps inevitable that ranchers should turn their attention to the virgin ranges of Indian Territory. The region was to become the cattleman's last frontier.[1]

—William W. Savage Jr.
The Cherokee Strip Live Stock Association

OVERLEAF: A gang of Miller cowboys after a roundup near Hunnewell, Kansas, September 24, 1890. Joe Miller, with six-gun on his hip, is standing at the far left. *(Fred Strickland Collection)*

Chapter 12

THE FIRST COW TOWN IN KANSAS

Without Kansas the cowboy as we know him *would never have come into existence. The cattle were in Texas, but the cow towns were in Kansas.*[1]

—Jim Hoy

Cowboys and Kansas: Stories from the Tallgrass Prairie

THROUGHOUT the 1870s, George Washington Miller drastically advanced his family's cattle operation. Even when he was far from his loved ones, Miller, as bold as a bigamist, never felt that he was going it alone. Molly was always there for him; every step of the way, through the deaths of two young sons, endless cattle drives, and years spent living on the fringes of civilization with few comforts, Molly Carson Miller stuck with her obstinate husband. Likewise, G.W. did his best to make sure Molly stayed content. When her husband was off on cattle trails, Molly found that periodic trips to Crab Orchard and Lincoln County kept her spirits up. But too often, the journeys to her homeland acted only as bitter reminders that Kentucky was still the "dark and bloody ground."

The cycle of violence in Kentucky seemed never to end. On April 23, 1875, Molly's revered father, Judge John Evans Carson, was shot and killed on the church steps in Crab Orchard.[2] In a strange way, he was a belated victim of the Civil War. A longtime adversary who still quarreled with Judge Carson because of Carson's fervent pro-Confederate stance apparently ambushed him "over war talk," as one witness put it.[3] Accompanied by her younger brothers who lived in Newtonia, Molly went back to Crab Orchard to bury her father, but she could not stay long because she was seven months pregnant.

On June 21, 1875, Molly Miller delivered her fourth child. This time she had a daughter, whom she and G.W. named Alma, a popular name for girls for many years after the Battle of the Alma River, in 1854, during the Crimean War.[4] As the Millers' only daughter grew older, they would find that the name Alma, which meant "learned" in Arabic, was appropriate. The young woman would take to the academic life much better than her brothers did and would acquire more formal education than anyone else in the family. Alma was educated by tutors; attended Miss Nold's Seminary for Young Ladies, a private school in Louisville, Kentucky; and graduated from Vassar College, the distinguished liberal-arts school for women founded in 1861 in Poughkeepsie, New York.[5]

Joseph Miller, a tough little seven-year-old cowboy when Alma was born, was curious about the baby girl and learned to look out for her, but he missed having brothers. Colonel Miller doted on his new little southern belle, but like Joe, he wanted more boys to ride with him in search of cattle and high times on the prairies. On April 26, 1878, the thirteenth anniversary of the death of John Wilkes Booth, another son was born to the Millers at their Newtonia home.[6] They named him Zachary Taylor Miller, for one of Molly's brothers and for "Old Rough and Ready," the Indian fighter and former United States president who had owned slaves and planted cotton.[7]

The day the baby arrived, Colonel Miller put up a barrel of blackberry wine. "Molly," G.W. supposedly told his wife, "we'll open this barrel the day young Zachary here is twenty-one. We'll open it again the day he marries and a third time when his first son is born. That ought to kill off the bulk of it. The balance, his friends can finish at his wake!"[8]

By the year of Zack's birth, Colonel Miller had begun to scale back his holdings in Missouri. He kept only three horses, fewer than ten cows—mostly for fresh dairy products—and about twenty hogs at his Newtonia headquarters.[9] As if to indicate that he chose not to remain in Newtonia, Miller did not join the new Stock Breeders' Association that had been organized in Newton County in April 1877.[10] He concentrated his energies instead on the cattle trails. To avoid conflict with Missouri farmers who feared that cattle herds would trample their fields and spread the dreaded livestock disease known as "Texas fever," Colonel Miller stayed clear of the trails leading into southwestern Missouri. His cattle crews used the old Shawnee Trail and the Texas Road. In time, as they drove more and more herds northward, they found that trails to the west, such as the Chisholm, were better suited to their needs. The area had less timbered land to cross and fewer rivers to ford than eastern Indian Territory and southwestern

Missouri. Moreover, railroads were reaching more towns in Kansas, and Miller recognized the need to shift westward.

In only a few years, G. W. Miller had parlayed his first herd—four hundred longhorns purchased for twenty thousand pounds of ham and bacon—into a fairly large cattle operation. He had the ranch in Indian Territory and more leased pastures farther west, and he was driving as many as twenty-five thousand head of cattle over trails each year.[11] There was not much to recommend Miller's staying in Missouri any longer.

In the autumn of 1880, Colonel Miller sold the family home and his interest in the general store at Newtonia.[12] He uprooted his base of operations from Missouri and moved the entire family west to a new headquarters at Baxter Springs, Kansas, just north of the L K Ranch which he and Lee Kokernut operated in Indian Territory.[13] The move also put Miller closer to additional grazing pastures he had leased on his own in 1879 from the federal government, farther west in Indian Territory, south of Hunnewell, Kansas.

The Miller family's new home was in a thriving area. *Kansas: A Guide to the Sunflower State*, published many years later, described booming Baxter Springs: "In the 1860's Texas cattlemen drove thousands of longhorns to the fine pasture land around Baxter Springs. Especially large drives in 1867 and 1868 boomed the town. When the railroad was built in 1870 Baxter Springs became a wide-open cow town and shipping point so crowded with be-pistoled cowboys and cattlemen that it was called 'the toughest town on earth.' "[14] Located in the southeastern corner of Kansas only six miles from the Missouri line and about one-and-a-half miles north of Indian Territory, Baxter Springs and the adjacent grazing pastures reminded the Millers of the bluegrass country of their native Kentucky.[15]

Long before the Millers or any other white cattlemen were drawn to the area, its natural mineral springs were well known among many Indian tribes for their medicinal value.[16] En route to northern campgrounds, the Osages made regular stops at the springs on the trail blazed by Osage Chief Black Dog and named for him. In 1825, the United States government drafted a treaty with the Osages in which the tribe ceded all its lands in Arkansas and Missouri in exchange for land west of Missouri, in what became southeastern Kansas. The area was to serve as a barrier between the Osages and Missouri settlers, and it soon became known as the "Neutral Lands."[17]

The Neutral Lands had been granted to the Cherokee Nation in the Treaty of 1835. After the Treaty of 1866, the tribe ceded the Neutral

Lands in trust to the federal government to be sold. Parcels of land went up for sale, and large groups of settlers began to stake claims and establish small farms and ranches. The first white settler in the area was John Baxter, who came from Missouri in 1849 with his family, staked a claim near Spring River, and built a home, trading post, general store, and inn.[18]

During the Civil War, the Kansas town and its environs provided the stage for heated border fighting, and the area teemed with guerrillas, outlaws, and bushwhackers. From the first day he rode into Baxter Springs, in the early 1870s, several years before he moved his family there, Colonel Miller was regaled with stories of battles in the region and of the horror of a bleak autumn day when William C. Quantrill came calling.[19] Known by locals as "the Baxter Springs Massacre," the bloodbath occurred only six weeks after Quantrill and his guerrillas had laid waste to Lawrence, Kansas. The carnage at Baxter Springs took place on October 6, 1863, when Quantrill and several hundred of his followers attacked Fort Blair, a small Union outpost on the Military Road, and later slaughtered troops under the command of Major General James G. Blunt as they approached the fort from the north.[20] Blunt's troops consisted mostly of cavalry soldiers escorting the general and unprepared military bandsmen sporting brand-new uniforms. Of the 125 Union troops surprised in Quantrill's attack, ninety-three were shot and killed.[21] The dead included a twelve-year-old boy, a journalist, and fourteen frightened musicians who had waved white handkerchiefs as flags of surrender but were gunned down nonetheless. The corpses were subsequently burned.[22]

The deep wounds inflicted by Quantrill and the war remained sensitive in Baxter Springs even when G. W. Miller and his family moved there in 1880. Although the town prospered and grew because of the Texas cattle trade, local citizens remained fearful of tick fever and mostly resented the cowboys, many of whom had served as Confederates or came from southern families. Residents also grew weary of lawlessness as Baxter Springs boomed and became the first frontier cattle town on the southern border of Kansas.

Just as he heard old-timers speak of Quantrill's bloody deeds, Colonel Miller assuredly was told of the day in May 1876 when Jesse James and an accomplice thought to be Cole Younger boldly robbed the Baxter Springs Bank.[23] The two supposedly rode into town at about noon, tied their mounts to a corncrib, and strolled into the bank, where James asked the cashier to change a five-dollar bill. When the cashier turned back to the teller's window, he was looking at a pair of drawn guns and was given a sack to fill with money. After having robbed the bank of two thousand dollars, the outlaws made a run to the Indian Nations, with a citizen posse in hot pursuit.

About seven miles south of Baxter Springs, well into Indian Territory, the bandits stopped at a blacksmith shop to have their horses shod. They took up strategic positions inside the stable. When the members of the posse rode up, James and Younger disarmed them and broke their guns on rocks. The embarrassed citizens were ordered to return to Kansas, which they did without delay.[24]

Such colorful exploits made for good stories at saloon gatherings but did little to instill confidence among merchants. Although they enjoyed the prosperity brought by the demand for beef, townspeople had to put up with the cowboys, gamblers, whores, and ruffians who infested every cattle town. "During this time, human life was cheap in Baxter Springs; public hangings were a common event and gun fights drew very little attention," according to *The Baxter Springs Story*, published in 1958. "Everyone carried a gun for self-protection. Saloons and bawdy houses of the most virulent character were numerous, and the town was in one continuous state of uproar night and day, especially during the season when the cattle were being driven."[25]

The Shawnee Trail through Baxter Springs offered cattle drivers the shortest distance from Texas ranches to northern markets. By the time the Millers took up residence in Baxter Springs, the best of the cattle-boom days—from about 1868 to 1872—were over.[26] But in those early years, just as George Miller and Lee Kokernut were establishing their L K Ranch a few miles south of town, Baxter Springs boasted an active Stock Yards and Drovers Association organized for buying and selling cattle.[27] Stout corrals built to contain as many as twenty thousand head of cattle included ample grazing grounds and an abundance of pure water. These facilities removed the need for night herders, and thus relieved drovers of much work and anxiety.[28] Baxter Springs and their nearby ranch afforded Miller and Kokernut the perfect settings to fatten large numbers of cattle for further drives or for shipment to Kansas City.

The many trips from the Texas cow country to the L K Ranch usually took about 100 to 110 days, at an average of ten to fifteen miles a day.[29] Each herd would string out over the prairie for two or more miles, with the Miller cowboys riding along with either side of the line. As many as fifteen or twenty cowboys rode with each of Colonel Miller's herds, and a chuck wagon—the heart of every trail outfit—was drawn by a yoke of oxen.[30] The range cook, usually nicknamed Cookie, Coosie, Dough-Belly, or Sallie, was as important as any other member of the crew. He prepared the meals, known as chuck, or grub, and dispensed them—along with medicine, mail, and free advice—from the back of the wagon.[31] Dutch ovens (large cast-iron skillets with heavy lids) were used to make everything from bread and biscuits to a popular cowboy dish known as "son-of-a-bitch stew," a concoction that called for lots of beef guts—liver, heart, brains, sweetbreads, kidneys, and even marrow gut.[32]

Nearly every meal included Irish or sweet potatoes, beans, dried fruit, salt bacon, and onions, also known as "skunk eggs."[33] Sometimes the point men out front, who worked to keep the stock moving in the proper direction, or the drag rider, who rode behind the herd and breathed in clouds of dust, had time to chew down only a handful of beef jerky and some dried prunes. They had to sustain themselves with the knowledge that they could stretch out that evening with their Bull Durham tobacco and "bible"—cowboy slang for rolling papers—and enjoy quantities of hot coffee, the trail rider's mainstay. No trail cook who was interested in staying alive, let alone keeping his job, ever skimped on coffee.[34]

The standard recipe for a cup of passable cowboy coffee was a handful of grounds and a cup of water. Some of the seasoned hands contended that eggshells tossed into the pot helped to settle the brew, but eggs were rare on the trail, as were milk and sugar. Coffee was served "without," or "barefoot." Before they departed for Texas, Colonel Miller always made sure his cooks had packed away hundred-pound sacks of green coffee beans to parch in Dutch ovens. The best commercial brand of the day came from the Arbuckle Brothers of Pittsburgh.[35] It was so popular that Arbuckle's became the generic name for all coffee served in cowboy camps and ranch kitchens.[36]

Out on the trail at night as the cattle grazed, cowboys knew a big pot of Arbuckle's simmered over the cook fire. Trail hands, in relays of two hours each, kept vigil over the stock to prevent theft and to react to even the hint of a stampede. Just striking a match off a boot sole might cause the herd to scatter.

Cowboys learned that singing calmed the nervous beasts and prevented stampedes. The favorite tunes were old soldier songs and hymns. Sometimes they sang "Old Dan Tucker," "The Texas Lullaby," "Nearer My God to Thee," "In the Sweet By and By," or "Jesus, Lover of My Soul."[37] The main object was for the song to be restful. Once the cattle were bedded down, the cowboys riding night herd sang their songs. They sang calmly and quietly to soothe the big herds—and maybe to bring a bit of comfort to themselves.

All day long on the prairies I ride,
Not even a dog to trot by my side;
My fire I kindle with chips gathered round,
My coffee I boil without being ground.

I wash in a pool and wipe on a sack;
I carry my wardrobe all on my back;
For want of an oven I cook bread in a pot,
And sleep on the ground for the want of a cot.

My ceiling is the sky, my floor is the grass,
My music is the lowing of the herds as they pass;
My books are the brooks, my sermons the stones,
My parson is a wolf on his pulpit of bones.[38]

—"The Cowboy," trail song

MISS MOLLY:
The Kentucky Connection

"MISS MOLLY" CARSON Miller was plantation bred to be a proper Kentucky belle, in the traditions and stereotypes of the Old South, but like other genteel ladies who hailed from below the Mason-Dixon line, she was, as the saying went, a true steel magnolia.

"Although she died before I was born, I understood from my father and uncles that my grandmother was a genuine lady through and through but, if push came to shove, she was brave enough to charge hell with a bucket of ice water," reminisced Zack Miller Jr.[1] "I would suspect, knowing the places my grandfather took her and the life they had to lead, especially in those years when their children were young, that bravery would have been a reasonably important quality for any woman to possess. I would expect my grandmother had more than her share."

Another Miller grandson, who knew her well, agreed. "She was a grand dame, I'll tell you," Joseph Miller Jr. fondly recalled when he was about ninety.[2] "Her children idolized her and they always respected her wishes. She was a real asset to our family."

Alice Miller Harth, older sister of Joseph Miller Jr., also maintained a lasting respect for their grandmother and vivid memories of her personality. "Grandmother Miller had been a typical pioneer wife. She was a healthy, large and robust woman who didn't hesitate to put her shoulder to the wheel whenever such an effort seemed necessary."[3]

Harth also recalled that Molly Miller "had her strong points. In fact, she was a very strong person, strong to the point of being domineering. I feel she masterminded some business ventures entered into by Grandfather and their sons. I know that as long as she lived, her opinions counted."[4] Molly's influence ranged from convincing her rough-and-tumble husband eventually to shave off his Civil War–era mustache and beard to holding sway in key business decisions that affected the Millers' cattle operations.[5]

Molly Miller was not a stoic "Madonna of the Prairie." Neither was she the banal "squaw" wife content to cook, sew, bear children, and remain a drudge, or a "helpless damsel" cringing in constant fear of violation at the hands of deranged outlaws or "savage Injuns."[6] Miller did not fit the standard profile of the pioneer wife as portrayed by many historians and writers, most of whom have been men. Emerson Hough, author of *The Passing of the Frontier*, typifies the males who created one of the most prevalent images of the idealized western woman—the sunbonnet myth. "The chief figure of the American West, the figure of the ages," wrote Hough, "is not the long-haired, fringed-legged man riding a rawboned pony, but the gaunt and sad-faced woman sitting on the front seat of the wagon, following her lord where he might lead, her face hidden in the same ragged sunbonnet which had crossed the Appalachians and the Missouri long before. That was America, my brethren! There was the seed of America's wealth. There was the great romance of all America—the woman in the sunbonnet; and not, after all, the hero with the rifle across his saddle horn."[7]

Although some women did accompany herds on dangerous cattle trails and even worked as drovers, the ladylike but determined Molly would not have been comfortable in that role.[8] One of Miss Molly's chief contributions to the Miller family dynasty arose out of her role as a dogged—and mostly unsung—recruiter of cowboys and farmhands. As good a judge of hard workers as anyone in the Miller clan, Molly had an opportunity to look over the crop of potential employees at least once a year, when she took her children to Kentucky to visit their kin.

Between luxurious sessions at the Crab Orchard spa and mint-julep parties with old family friends, Molly interviewed young men—and sometimes women—interested in moving west to earn wages working for her husband. Throughout Lincoln County, from about 1870 through the 1890s, this Miller tie to the old homeland became known as "the Kentucky connection."[9] Some of the best Miller cowboys who ever rode the Shawnee and Chisholm Trails had been chosen by the matriarch of the Miller family. Some of them were related to Molly or G. W. Miller. The youngsters Molly enlisted came with excellent work references. Most were seasoned tobacco workers or had grown up on bluegrass farms around thoroughbred horses. They worked for the Millers in the spring and summer, then returned to Kentucky each autumn after the cattle roundups had ended and crops were harvested.[10] A few of the Kentucky recruits went on to become active in the Millers' Wild West shows, spawned in the glory years of the 101 Ranch during the early 1900s. One of those was Jesse Briscoe.[11]

Born on April 18, 1877, near Hustonville, Kentucky, Briscoe went to work for the Millers in 1898. In 1904, he married Midgie Cowger, another Miller employee.[12] When the Millers started their Wild West shows, the Briscoes went on the road as performers. They were still riding for the Millers when their Wild West show broke up in 1914, in England.[13]

Jesse, a capable livestock wrangler, became a skilled stuntman and movie extra. He worked with Hoot Gibson, another 101 Ranch cowboy, fabled stuntman Yakima Canutt, and many other western film greats. Midgie blossomed as an actress. In 1919, she earned the female lead opposite Harry Carey in *The Three Godfathers*, the third movie directed by Sean Aloysius O'Feeney, better known as John Ford.[14]

Jesse Briscoe was killed in a horse fall in 1922 while working on the Paramount studio lot. Midgie died in Phoenix in 1976, not having forgotten the start Molly Miller had given to her husband at the beginning of the century.[15] Briscoe was one of the many people who launched a lifelong career thanks to "Miss Molly" and her ties to Kentucky.

Chapter 13

THE SALT FORK OF THE ARKANSAS

Way down yonder in the Indian Nation,
I rode my pony on the reservation,
In those Oklahoma Hills where I was born.
Way down yonder in the Indian Nation,
A cowboy's life is my occupation,
In those Oklahoma Hills where I was born.[1]

—Woody Guthrie and Jack Guthrie
"Oklahoma Hills"

IN 1879, the year before Colonel George Miller moved his family from Newtonia to Baxter Springs, he significantly expanded his cattle holdings by leasing sixty thousand acres of raw grazing pastures in the Cherokee Outlet, in Indian Territory.[2]

Covering six-and-a-half-million acres of lush prairie grassland sixty miles wide and 180 miles long on the southern border of Kansas, the Cherokee Outlet was created by United States treaty after the federal government forcibly moved the Cherokee tribe to Indian Territory.[3] The outlet reached west, from the ninety-sixth to the one hundredth meridians, and gave the Cherokees a perpetual passage to the hunting grounds of the western plains.[4] People sometimes became confused because of the similarly named Cherokee Strip, a band of land just north of the Kansas line, only two-and-a-half miles wide, that extended west for 276 miles and ran north to the thirty-seventh parallel.[5] Many cattlemen and cowboys erroneously referred to the Cherokee Outlet as the Cherokee Strip. But the "strip" was in fact just a segment of the Cherokee Outlet overlapping into Kansas that early survey errors had created in 1837 and 1854. In 1866, the Cherokee Nation ceded the strip to Kansas and it eventually was sold to settlers; the proceeds went to the tribe.[6]

The 1866 treaty also provided that the federal government could relocate "friendly" Indian tribes to the Cherokee Outlet at a price agreeable to the Cherokees and to the purchasers. A few white settlers also attempted to enter the outlet and establish homesteads, but roving army patrols expelled them quickly. It was permissible for cattlemen to pay for grazing rights on Indian land, but no stipulations allowed whites to settle in the outlet. It appeared, however, that rules and treaties concerning Indians were made to be broken. Starting in the early 1870s, Kansas journalists wrote stirring editorials arguing that Indian lands belonged to the United States and therefore lay in the public domain and were eligible for homesteading.[7]

George W. Miller definitely was one of those interested in penetrating what he considered the cattleman's last frontier. Resolved to acquire ranging rights in the Cherokee Outlet from the Cherokee Nation, Miller left the L K Ranch near Baxter Springs in 1879 with a wagon and a few cowboys to look over the country and select his range.[8]

Miller's eldest son, Joseph, accompanied the party. Eleven years old but already a stellar horseman, Joe Miller knew as much as anyone about the ways of the trail.[9] He spoke nearly perfect Ponca Indian dialect, could build a branding fire with wet wood and a single match, and could track a whisper in a big wind.[10] Cowboys four times his age bragged that the Miller kid had more guts than they could hang on a fence.

At the time of their trip to the Cherokee Outlet, Colonel Miller and his son were aware that the United States government was trying to secure a large tract from the Cherokees for the Poncas, as compensation for the lands taken from them in Dakota Territory.[11] The Millers had been in Baxter Springs when the Poncas were brought to the nearby Quapaw agency to reside temporarily while awaiting a permanent home in Indian Territory. They saw the dissatisfaction among the Poncas, especially those who followed Standing Bear, one of the most respected tribal leaders.[12]

Like Standing Bear, White Eagle was a prominent Ponca chief who did not favor the move. He was especially alarmed by the great amount of sickness and death in the tribe, which he attributed to unfavorable climate in Indian Territory.[13] Many Poncas starved to death during the nearly two years they resided on Quapaw lands, and outbreaks of smallpox, typhoid, and malaria reduced the tribe's population further.

Colonel Miller and his son struck up a friendship with White Eagle and many of the starving Ponca people, sold beef to them, and sympathized with them in their misfortunes.[14] Undoubtedly, Miller sensed an opportunity—he knew the Poncas were to be relocated farther west, in the Cherokee Outlet, on land that would be ideal for grazing Texas cattle. Whatever his motives for befriending White Eagle, it is clear that Colonel Miller advised the Ponca leader frequently about tribal affairs, beginning a Miller family relationship with Indian tribes that would extend well into the twentieth century.

In their travels through the Cherokee Outlet in 1879, Colonel Miller and his son discussed the plight of the Poncas as they searched for the land which the federal government intended to transfer to the tribe.[15] When the Miller party reached the proposed Ponca lands and established a camp, Miller was impressed with what they found—plenty of tall grass and flowing streams. He believed that if White Eagle visited the locale, he would accept the government's invitation to relocate the tribe.[16]

But Miller also was aware that the date was drawing near for White Eagle to depart for Washington, D.C., to meet with federal officials. White Eagle had told Miller before he and his cowboys departed that for the good of the Ponca people, he planned to reject the government's offer. Clinging to a last bit of hope, Chief White Eagle would try once more to persuade the white officials to allow the Poncas to return to their homeland in the north.[17]

Miller realized that he had to act quickly. Without abandoning his trip, he must get immediate word to White Eagle that the fertile prairies in the Cherokee Outlet would be suitable for the Poncas' new home. Miller, perhaps believing that the pristine grazing lands he found in the outlet were slipping from his grasp, turned to his son for help.

The Millers' 1916 show magazine dramatically chronicled the eleven-year-old boy's daring ride through the Cherokee Outlet and across the Osage country back to the camp of White Eagle. In Joe Miller's words:

> Most fathers would have hesitated sending a mere boy on such a trip, but the lad had been a constant companion of his father and was fully competent to care for himself under all conditions to be met in the open. The boy possessed other qualifications which made him better fixed for the mission than any man in the party. At Baxter Springs Joe had spent much of his time with Indian boys of his own age and was known to all members of the tribe. He even then spoke the Indian language with considerable fluency. As he had accompanied his father in his examination of the coun-

try and listened to his comments, he was thoroughly familiar with the favorable features which his father desired to be brought to the attention of the Indians.

If the boy felt any hesitancy in starting upon the long ride to White Eagle's camp it was not in evidence when he rode away from his father's camp, with a boyish smile on his face and a parting wave of the hand.[18]

Joe Miller rode day and night, almost without stopping, and reined his cow pony at the Ponca camp sooner than his father had expected. As it turned out, Joe was just in time—White Eagle was ready to leave for Washington, D.C., the following morning.[19] The evening of Joe's arrival, White Eagle gathered all the chiefs and headmen of the Poncas in his tepee. For the first time in the memory of the tribe, a white boy sat on the buffalo robes in the center of the council circle and answered questions in their own language. Joe Miller would remember it for the rest of his life. Far into the night, the tribal elders smoked their pipes and talked.[20]

Thirty-seven years later, Joe Miller described the episode for those who produced the Millers' show magazine.

> The boy, hesitating at times as he searched his memory for the best word to use, answered their questions with a frankness and directness which convinced them of the truthfulness of his answers. . . . With a stick the boy drew upon the dirt floor of the tepee a rough map. He showed them where the Chikaskia met the Salt Fork and where that river ran into the Arkansas; where the valleys widened and where the high prairie was to be found. He told them of the horse high blue stem in the valleys and the heavy hanging vines of wild grape in the timbered bends; of the tall pecan and the thickets of plums; of the prairie chickens which flew from under the ponys' [sic] feet, and of the deer and turkey which ranged through the timber. Of the red bluffs of the Salt Fork, and the streams of water where a pony could always drink; they heard him tell, and they wondered when he told them how the sand bars in summer whitened with salt; to the Poncas, homesick and famished, stricken with fever and with no land to call their own, the picture made in their minds by the story of the boy was that of the Promised Land.[21]

After Joe completed his description, he sat quietly while the chiefs smoked and pondered everything he had told them. White Eagle looked at each of the elders before knocking the ashes from his pipe to signify that the council was ended. Then White Eagle turned to Joe Miller.[22]

"We have listened to you because you speak the words of your father," the chief told the boy. "Your message is good and we know him for our friend. Tomorrow I will ride with you and we will see this country of which you speak. I hope that we will find a home for our people. You have ridden far to bring us this word and the Poncas do not forget. Now you shall sleep."[23]

At daybreak, White Eagle and some of his men left with Joe Miller to see the Cherokee Outlet. When they saw that everything the boy had said was true, the Poncas decided to move there. White Eagle returned to tell his people of their new home and advise the federal government that its offer was acceptable.

Meanwhile, Colonel Miller had continued his journey up the Salt Fork and selected a location for what would become his second ranch. The land was outside the Ponca allotment; he would have to lease it from the Cherokee Nation.[24] Miller's 1879 lease, more than sixty thousand acres in the Cherokee Outlet, was divided into two separate pastures.[25] One was on Deer Creek, a tributary of the Salt Fork of the Arkansas River, about twenty miles south of Hunnewell, Kansas.[26] This operation, which Miller called the Deer Creek Ranch, included a fairly large cowboy camp. He dubbed the other operation the Salt Fork Ranch. It was near the future site of Lamont, south of Deer Creek along the Salt Fork of the Arkansas, the snow-fed stream born in the Colorado Rockies.[27] The Arkansas crossed half of Kansas before entering Indian Territory, where it ran southeasterly and gathered in the waters of the Salt Fork, the Chikaskia, the Cimarron, the Verdigris, the Grand, and the Illinois.

Miller built his main headquarters at the Salt Fork Ranch, including a three-room log cabin with a dirt roof, horse corrals, a branding pen and chute, storage for feed corn, and a horse barn with a hay roof.[28] For grazing rights to the two pastures, the lease called for an annual payment of two cents per acre to the Cherokee agency.[29] Almost instantly, as his drovers delivered herd after herd of longhorns to be fattened for market, Colonel Miller started to make large sums of money. The hours were long, the weather uncompromising, and the working conditions appalling at best, but the payoff made everything worthwhile. G. W. Miller was never averse to hard work.

Colonel Miller's efforts did not go unnoticed by the Poncas. Like their friend, the tribe began to prosper. The Poncas were so pleased with their new home on the Salt Fork and so grateful for the Millers' advice that they came up with yet another name for Colonel Miller. Observing that the Millers maintained an abiding interest in cattle, the tribe's elders knew exactly what to call Miller. They named their white friend *Tesca-nu-da-hunga*.[30] The name fit him perfectly; it meant "Big Cow Chief."

BOOMER SOONER

THE MAMMOTH CHEROKEE Outlet was removed considerably from the domain of the Cherokees, whose farms and homes were in northeastern Indian Territory.[1] Although federal law prohibited the Cherokees from residing in the outlet, they recognized that the region was choice grazing land for the Texas longhorns that G. W. Miller, Lee Kokernut, and other white cattlemen drove up the Chisholm Trail.[2]

Starting in the late 1860s, the Cherokees, to earn revenues from the sprawling pastures and to pressure the federal government to purchase the outlet lands, passed tax levies and began to collect fees for grazing rights.[3] Colonel Miller did not mind paying to graze stock on the pastures at his Deer Creek and Salt Fork Ranches, and he viewed the Cherokees' levies as simply another operating expense.[4]

Not every cattle operator shared Miller's attitude. Some disliked the grazing tax and tried everything possible to avoid paying the fees to the Cherokees.[5] In fact, Miller put up with Kansas stockmen who overgrazed the outlet by deliberately allowing their cattle to drift over the boundary into Indian Territory. Timber thieves rode out of Kansas to cut and steal stands of valuable cedar trees, and bands of scoundrels raided cattle herds feeding on bluestem.[6]

Kansas also had many farmers who wanted to move into the Cherokee Outlet and turn the prairies into crop fields. They complained of being excluded unfairly from Indian Territory while cattlemen made big profits off the outlet's grazing lands.[7] Many of the sodbusters protested that the time was long overdue for Indian Territory, and especially the Cherokee Outlet, to be opened for settlement.

The loudest of those protestors were called "Boomers," tenacious and aggressive professional promoters who urged, or "boomed," the concept of homesteading on Indian lands.[8] Newspaper stories and reams of propaganda pamphlets "booming" the virtues of the Cherokee Outlet and the Unassigned Lands in central Indian Territory—but carefully avoiding any mention of frontier hardships—flooded surrounding states. "Oklahoma! Well watered, well timbered, rich in soil, a most enchanting clime, may in the near future be your home," suggested one of the Boomer publications. Another implied that Indian Territory was ideal for vineyards "not excelled by California . . . where the next generation will see the Canadian and Red River country as the Rhine of America."[9] Railroad builders, bankers, newspaper publishers, and business and political leaders form the states neighboring Indian Territory, especially Kansas and Arkansas, aided and abetted the Boomers.[10] One of the early propagandists in the Boomer movement was Elias Cornelius Boudinot (prominent mixed-blood son of a Cherokee Treaty Party leader), a controversial lawyer who represented railroad interests.[11] In an editorial published in a Chicago newspaper, the highly acculturated Boudinot broke with his tribe's leaders and argued that Indian Territory was public domain and should be opened to homesteaders.[12]

Many Cherokees believed that Boudinot, whose father had been killed by tribesmen in 1839 after he and others transferred eastern Cherokee lands to the federal government for lands in Indian Territory, was still bent on revenge and out to destroy the Cherokee Nation.[13] E. C. Boudinot's article and his many public speeches, coupled with the extensive distribution of Boomer literature describing the Unassigned Lands of Indian Territory as a Garden of Eden, had the desired effect.

In 1879, while Colonel Miller was establishing ranches on Cherokee lands at Deer Creek and the Salt Fork River, the Boomers organized three "Oklahoma colonies," at Topeka, Kansas City, and in north Texas. At about this time, a dominant Boomer movement leader also emerged—Captain David L. Payne, a native of Indiana and a former Yankee soldier whom Boudinot's writings had inspired and encouraged.[14]

From 1879 until his death in a Wellington, Kansas, hotel room in 1884, Payne, a greatly romanticized figure in Oklahoma history, made his living leading several unsuccessful Boomer raids, or colonizing expeditions, into Indian Territory.[15] Each time, federal troops escorted Payne and his land-hungry Boomers out of Indian Territory. After Payne's death, his lieutenants not only staged more Boomer invasions but also continued to publicize the attractions of Indian Territory.[16] They pressed the United States Congress to remove tribal title to the lands so homesteaders could enter legally. Finally, the federal government yielded, and in 1889, President Benjamin Harrison issued the proclamation opening the Unassigned Lands, in the central portion of Indian Territory, to white settlers.[17]

On April 22, 1889, fifty thousand eager homeseekers rushed into the Unassigned Lands, the two-million-acre tract lying just below the Cherokee Outlet, to stake claims.[18] By sunset, they had staked nearly every homestead claim and several townsites. It was just the beginning—the first of five "land openings," or "runs," in the next several years, including the mammoth opening of the Cherokee Outlet, in 1893.[19]

With each of the runs, thousands of settlers chose not to wait for the official signal but tried to sneak into the territory sooner than anyone else. Many of the "Sooners," as they were known, were evicted, but some grabbed hunks of land and stayed put. Although *Sooner* began as yet another moniker for a thief, the nickname gradually replaced *Boomer* and became more acceptable.[20]

After statehood, in 1907, Oklahoma became known as the Sooner State and the University of Oklahoma took the name Sooner for its athletic teams. The university even adopted a fight song that became popular throughout the Sooner State, called "Boomer Sooner." Ironically, the song itself was "stolen"—the melody is the same as "Yale Boola," the fight song of Yale University.[21] E. C. Boudinot, David Payne, and all those early Boomers and Sooners no doubt would have thought it fitting.

Chapter 14

"101"

We'll brand 101 this time.[1]
—George Washington Miller, 1881

"I AM a southern gentleman; born in southern Kansas," George L. Miller always replied with a laugh when asked about his birth.[2] The last of the children born to Molly and G. W. Miller, the baby arrived at the Millers' home in Baxter Springs on September 9, 1881—a date that fell between the shooting death of the legendary Billy the Kid and the famous twenty-eight-second gun battle which erupted near the OK Corral in Tombstone, Arizona Territory.[3]

Named George Lee Kokernut Miller, the baby bore the first name of his father and the full name of G.W.'s ranching partner, Lee Kokernut.[4] Family and friends called the boy George, and eventually the youngster dropped Kokernut and went by George Lee or George L. Miller.[5] With George's birth, the Miller family was complete. There were four surviving children, Alma, a spirited and clever daughter, and Joe, Zack, and George—the three sons destined to rise as crown princes of the empire their father created on the cattleman's final frontier.

The year 1881 was a time of transition for the nation as well as for the Miller family. America was still primarily an agrarian society, but strains between the burgeoning urban sector and the farmers were already present. The Millers may have been largely unaware of these tensions, so intent were they on their westward moves. In addition to the birth of the last Miller child, 1881 also saw the Millers' departure from Baxter Springs. They moved farther west again, to the Kansas town of Winfield, the seat of Cowley County.[6]

The county, southwest of Wichita, comprised part of the border area between the Cherokee Strip in Kansas and the Cherokee Outlet to the south. Colonel Miller thought the move to Cowley County made perfect sense. In 1880, Miller had bought out Lee Kokernut's livestock and equipment at their L K Ranch on leased Quapaw lands, which meant Miller had no more interest in that part of Indian Territory.[7] As a result, he had no reason to stay in Baxter Springs, which had fallen on hard times when the longhorn cattle drives shifted westward.[8] A home in Winfield put Miller much closer to his new Deer Creek and Salt Fork Ranches.

Colonel Miller began to search Winfield for a residence in the spring of 1881, while Molly, pregnant with George Lee, traveled with the children to Crab Orchard.[9] Such visits afforded Molly an annual pilgrimage to see her family and to make important "Kentucky connections" with prospective bluegrass cowboys hoping to work for her husband. Molly returned to Baxter Springs that summer and remained there until George Lee's birth.[10] Soon after the baby arrived, Colonel Miller moved his family to a comfortable residence at 602 Manning, a tree-shaded Winfield street.[11]

Although he wanted only the best living accommodations for his wife and children, Colonel Miller was not well suited to town life. He spent most of his time on the trail in Texas or with his cowboys at his two big grazing pastures in the Cherokee Outlet. It was on those Indian lands in that pivotal year of 1881, after he had moved his family to Winfield, that Colonel Miller came up with the three numerals that would be associated forever with his family's name.[12] After severing his business ties with Kokernut, it was necessary for Miller to develop a new brand for his herds of longhorn steers. Although he and Kokernut remained friends, Miller no longer would use the L K mark—he needed a brand all his own.[13]

"Each ranch and range had its own brand or brands," explained Joseph B. Thoburn and Muriel H. Wright in their history of Oklahoma. "The brand was a device chosen by the owner of the ranch for the marking of the cattle and horses belonging thereto. The form of this device might take any style suggested by the fancy of the owner, so long as it conformed to one requirement, namely, that it should be distinctive and not subject to confusion with the brand of some other ranch or range."[14]

From the beginning, stories of how Colonel Miller ultimately selected his brand varied greatly. Many of the stories were at least partly correct, but some proved to be outright lies or outrageous yarns undoubtedly dreamed up by cowpokes hunkered around an evening fire while they enjoyed a liquid supper. What is known for sure is that by the autumn of 1881, Miller had settled on his own distinctive brand and had begun to use it, and that by the early 1880s, his brand was being burned into the horns and eventually the hides of all his cattle.[15]

Some of the ranchers and cowboys of the Cherokee Outlet claimed that Miller chose the 101 brand to represent the size of his ranch—101,000 acres.[16] But that yarn was wrong; when Miller began to use the brand, his spread covered only sixty thousand acres of leased lands. As his son Zack Miller later pointed out, "Our ranch took in that much land, owned and leased, by coincidence. We'd already been using the brand for years."[17] Others maintained that Colonel Miller purchased the brand from another cattle outfit named the 101 Ranch Company, operating far to the west in what was known as "No Man's Land" (the Oklahoma Panhandle).[18] That theory had a seed of truth in it; indeed, there was another 101 Ranch, organized in about 1881 near where New Mexico Territory, Colorado, and the Panhandle of present Oklahoma met.[19] Colonel Miller did buy up the remnants of the herd from the ranch when it relocated to Amarillo, Texas, in 1891.[20] But by then, Miller had been using 101 as his brand for at least twelve years and had no need to buy out the other ranch just to take the 101 name.

Yet the most reasonable, and by far the most colorful, explanation of how Colonel Miller came up with 101 as a cattle brand was offered by the Millers themselves, especially Joe and Zack.[21] Both men always swore the story was true, and Joe claimed he was present when his father got the idea to use the three numbers as his cattle brand.[22] The idea came in San Antonio, Texas, in 1881, when Colonel Miller, young Joe, and some of their best hands were gathering another herd of longhorns to drive north to their grazing lands.

Since its founding as a Spanish presidio in the eighteenth century, San Antonio had evolved into a bustling city where enterprising Texas cattlemen gathered millions of wild longhorns that had proliferated from stock left by the conquistadores.[23] No longer just a sleepy army garrison, San Antonio had become, near the end of the nineteenth century, the largest city in Texas. It also was a notable cow town that attracted young men eager to sign on for long drives on the Chisholm, Shawnee, and Western Trails to Kansas railheads. Many of them hired on with the Millers.[24]

As recounted in the book *The San Antonio Story*, "This driving of longhorns 'up the trail' changed San Antonio from a struggling little town into a 'wild and wooly' [sic] one, like any frontier town you see in the movies. . . . The cowboys brought lots of 'color.' They rode their horses right up into such places as the old Buckhorn . . . where the proprietor, Albert Friedrich, 'parked' their guns for them to keep them out of trouble. They celebrated by shooting up the town. They lost their pay gambling at faro. They danced with pretty *senoritas* in the open-air *fandangos* [dances] on the plazas. . . . When they came to town they 'turned loose. . . .' San Antonio was the Paris of the wilderness. Its bright lights were a beacon that shone across the chaparral. It was brightest after dark."[25]

In those years, when the Millers and their cowboys were regular visitors, San Antonio attracted many colorful characters, such as Roy Bean. A Kentucky native and notorious saloon keeper, Bean later, as a Texas justice of the peace, proclaimed himself to be "the law West of the Pecos." Bean and his Mexican wife lived in the San Antonio neighborhood known as Beanville, where he made a questionable living as a peddler of stolen firewood and beef and by running a slip-shod dairy. Angry customers reportedly claimed that they found minnows swimming in their milk.[26]

Colonel Miller no doubt met many of the former Confederate soldiers residing in the city, since he preferred to enlist battle-hardened Rebels as drovers. Defeated in war, some of these men had marched off to Mexico to fight for Emperor Maximilian, but they returned to Texas after the Mexican army captured and executed the idealistic Austrian archduke with grandiose plans for a French puppet state.[27] These brassy Texans cut loose like Comanches with their Rebel cries, called "cowboy yells" or "bad men yells," that echoed off saloon walls and through the streets, markets, and plazas of old San Antonio.[28]

Menacing man-killers and desperadoes also congregated in San Antonio in that heyday of the cattle trails, including the likes of Ben Thompson, John King Fisher, and John Wesley Hardin, who was said to have killed at least forty men and earned a law degree. A police constable eventually blew Hardin's brains out over a dice game at the Acme Saloon, on San Antonio Street in El Paso.[29]

Colonel Miller and other cattlemen passing through San Antonio tried to stay clear of its "Fatal Corner" on Commerce Street and other questionable haunts where many shootings erupted. They knew fights could erupt instantly over a bad debt, an unkind word, a soiled dove, or even an accidentally spilled glass of two-bit rotgut whiskey.[30] Sometimes quarrels escalated to the point that cowboys pulled six-guns from holsters in anger. When that happened, usually one or more wound up disabled or, worse, stretched out, cold as an ex-lover's heart, at the nearest undertaking establishment. Losing able-bodied cowboys to senseless gunplay or whorehouse brawls was not good business, so Miller encouraged his cattle crews to follow his example and avoid the more notorious pleasure palaces and dens of iniquity.[31]

It took Colonel Miller only a few trips to Texas before he discovered that his young cowboys found it nearly impossible to evade the temptations of city life. He knew his trail hands had more on their minds than prayer meetings or picnics along the San Antonio River. Miller, like many cattlemen and trail bosses, tended to stick close to the Menger Hotel, built in 1859 on Alamo Plaza.[32]

The Menger had perhaps the best culinary reputation in the city. The menu featured succulent bear steak, potted antelope, wild turkey stuffed with chestnuts, dried buffalo tongue, soup made from softshell turtles caught in the nearby San Antonio River, and for dessert, mango ice cream that remained a staple of the hotel for more than a century.[33] Everyone from Robert E. Lee to Oscar Wilde, including William T. Sherman, stayed at the opulent Menger.

Unlike Colonel Miller, who could afford expensive hotel rooms, the drovers chose more modest digs and found their pleasure elsewhere. Known across the Southwest as "the gay capital of the mesquite and chapparal [sic]," San Antonio offered a wide variety of diversions, all of which could turn even the most forthright cowboy's head.[34] There were cockfights, fiestas, and gambling lairs galore. Mexican, Anglo, and Negro strumpets sold their favors from cribs and bordellos scattered throughout the city.[35] On the plazas, town boys trapped wild pigeons; gangs of rats, bold enough to fight dogs and kill cats, hunted their next meal; and the odor of fresh horse manure mixed with the aroma of roasting kid goat. Here, under the glow of gaslights, the city's famous "chili queens" ladled out bowls brimming with pungent chili con carne, made of fiery peppers and chunks of tough longhorn meat, cooked for hours in huge iron kettles over mesquite fires.[36]

Within a few months, cowhands would have their fill of beef and cows in general. By the time they reached the end of the line in Kansas, they would crave everything but meat and instead would order oysters, shipped north by rail, or call for platters piled with eggs. Better yet, if there was a decent Chinese cook in town, the drovers demanded chop suey. But at the start of the trail ride in San Antonio, while their boss took care of paperwork and put the herd together, cowboys were still in the mood for beefsteak, German sausage, meat tamales, and as much chili con carne as they could stomach.

After such ample repasts, a cowboy extinguished the inferno in his throat with schooners of cold beer. San Antonio was noted for drinking establishments where, for only a nickel, a thirsty drover received a big urn of Saint Louis–brewed beer drawn from an ice-covered keg.[37] By 1877, the *San Antonio City Directory* listed sixty-two saloons, but unquestionably, even more were doing business as beer gardens, variety theaters, or billiard parlors.[38] The saloons' names were classics—the Alamo, the Bull's Head, the Parlor, the White Elephant, the Red Light, the Western Star, the Barrel House, Professor's, and the Workingman's Hall.[39] Some of the fancier joints stocked wines, brandies, and imported beers such as Löwenbrau or even Guinness, which made every Irish cowboy long for the "Old Sod." For cowboys who could not face another bowl of chili or were not rich enough to dine on turtle soup and porpoise steaks, some saloons laid out the proverbial "free lunch." Tables laden with rye bread, spicy sausages, sliced pork, crackers, pretzels, and cheese were open to all comers. Of course, the food was salted heavily to make sure beer sales stayed steady.

One of the San Antonio saloons the cowboys seemed to favor was a cafe at 101 East Second Street.[40] The owner chose not to invest much time in picking a name for his establishment, and merely appropriated the street address, calling his saloon "The Hundred and One." A large board sign bearing the name was nailed up over the door.[41] It was there, on an evening in 1881, that Colonel Miller, his son Joe, and Gid Guthrie, the Millers' trail boss, gathered with their cowherds for a final meal before leaving on the long journey to the Cherokee Outlet. A farewell supper at "The Hundred and One" had become a tradition for the Millers and their roundup party, but unlike previous routine visits, this meal would go down in ranching history as one of the most unforgettable.

Many years later, O. A. Cargill, a noted Oklahoma attorney and former mayor of Oklahoma City, recalled a get-together in the 1920s at his office with the Miller brothers and their friends Major Gordon W. "Pawnee Bill" Lillie and rancher Zack Mulhall.[42] Joe Miller told the story of how his father had chosen the 101 brand for his cattle herds.[43] Cargill wrote in 1965:

> Miller told me it came about in this manner. When he was a boy, his father took him on one of his trips to Texas to buy longhorn steers near San Antonio. They would buy several hundred head of two to four year old steers to drive north on the old Chisholm Trail. . . . Miller, his son and the cowboys would always eat at the same place in San Antonio. It

> was designated the 101 East Second Street. . . . One night Miller, his son, and all the cowboys were having their last meal. . . . Some of the cowboys had a little too much to drink, and were ordered out of the place by the owner. In the melee, as the cowboys left the cafe, one of them pulled the sign from over the door . . . carried it off, and hung it over the backend of the chuck wagon. . . . After their return home, the cowboys then took the "101" sign off the chuck wagon and nailed it over the ranch house cook shack, and this is how the Ranch came to be named "101."[44]

Although the Millers started to use 101 as a road brand in 1881, it would be years before they used it as a name for their ranch. That exception notwithstanding, Cargill's version of the 101 brand story complemented the much more graphic rendering provided in the 1940s by Zack Miller, who as an old man used to say, "The name really came from a saloon in San Antonio."[45]

Zack related his rendition to Fred Gipson, who included it in his down-home book about Zack, *The Fabulous Empire*. Gipson wrote:

> Gid Guthrie was Miller's trail boss that year. They'd made their buy in South Texas, and on the way north, they laid over in San Antonio one night to let the hands romp and stomp and paw up a little sand before taking the long trail into Kansas. The hands didn't need any urging; they made up as tough a trail crew as ever looked a cow brute in the rump. They located a honkytonk downtown called "The Hundred and One," which made a brag of having the wildest women, the rawest whiskey, and the worst gamblers in that old Mexican town. The boys wanted to investigate; this outfit might be bluffing.
>
> They sampled the whiskey. They tried out the women. They matched wits with the gamblers and then fist-whipped for cheats and swindlers. Before daylight, they were prizing up hell and propping it with a chunk. Some were down and the rest were staggering. It took four trips and half the town police for Miller to get the crew out of the wrecked place and back out to where the cattle were bedded down.[46]

When dawn broke, Colonel Miller met with the proprietor and paid for all the damages without hesitation or complaint. He said nothing to his men, who nursed hangovers, split lips, and knots on their heads for days. But the next time the Miller cowboys had to herd a bunch of Texas beef up the trail and Gid Guthrie asked about a road brand, Colonel Miller did not hesitate for a second.

"We'll forget the Lee Kokernut brand we've been using," Colonel Miller supposedly told Guthrie. "I've bought out that iron. We'll brand 101 this time. Before I'm done, I aim to make this tough crew so sick of the sight of them figures they'll ride a ten-mile circle around town to keep from reading that honkytonk signboard."[47]

Ranch lore had it that not a single working stiff who rode for Colonel Miller and his sons ever again mentioned the San Antonio establishment which bore three numerals for a name. As Glenn Shirley later related, " 'They never forgot the lesson,' " said Zack, " 'after those numbers had shimmered before their eyes day in and out while pushing two thousand longhorns north under a blistering sun into Indian Territory.' "[48]

They might have managed to forget that wicked saloon, but the numbers 101 were emblazoned in their minds and hearts forever.

DEVIL'S ROPE

If George Washington Miller was not the first cattlemen to build a barbed-wire fence in the Cherokee Outlet, as some folks suggested, he was one of the earliest ranchers to string wire around his big grazing pastures.[1]

Just about the time he decided to use 101 as a road brand for his cattle, Colonel Miller ordered some of his cowboys to erect a barbed-wire fence on his Deer Creek Ranch.[2] It was a courageous and controversial move, as were so many of the Miller family's actions in the late 1800s, when they put together their cattle kingdom.

To many westerners of that time, especially some uncompromising cowboys brought up in wide-open spaces, *any* kind of fence—hedge, stone, or rail—was a threat to their open-range culture and way of life. But something was distinctively sinister about barbed wire, or "bob wahr," as most Texas and Indian Territory range riders pronounced it.[3] Some critics, highly opposed to the use of barbed wire, came up with other names for the prickly strands.

When barbed wire first appeared in the 1870s, it was called devil's rope, a derogatory name used by religious groups and others concerned that the sharp steel barbs cut and injured too many cattle, horses, and men.[4] To those folks, barbed wire appeared to be the work of the devil himself. They found curious allies in the veteran drovers who also hated to see the rangeland fenced, but not for the same reasons.

The cowboys cursed barbed wire because it was restrictive and made them feel more like dirt farmers than range riders. Fences prevented cowboys and their herds from entering open grazing pastures and getting to water, and meant that a man had to spend a good portion of his time off his dependable cow pony and on foot. A frequent saying around cow camps was that a man on foot was no man at all. Fences did not make sense to many of the working men on the range. As one writer expressed it, a large number of cowboys frowned on the use of barbed wire because fences did not fit harmoniously with the land.[5] That was why cowboys, like preachers and pious firebrands, also called barbed wire devil's rope, devil's necklace, or sometimes devil's hat band.[6] Trail riders, including some of the Millers' hands, liked to sing a catchy ditty throughout the 1880s and into the 1890s:

They say that heaven is a free range land,
Good-bye, Good-bye, O fare you well;
But it's barbed wire fence for the devil's hat band
And barbed wire blankets down in hell![7]

Fences were not altogether new in the 1870s and 1880s; in colonial times, settlers had relied on stone, board, and split-log fences to control wayward livestock. But in the nineteenth century, the great throngs of white settlers pushing westward found that material for fencing, particularly wood, was limited. Indeed, the shortage of wood was surpassed only by the scarcity of water as a factor in the settlement of the American West.[8]

Beginning in the late 1860s and throughout the next decade, even after barbed wire started to make inroads, settlers revived the use of thorny hedges as fences across prairie states and territories.[9] Depending on locale and climate, different types of briers and plants were used for "living fences," including rose bushes, mesquite, cactus, honey locust, and pomegranate. Of all of them, the most popular hedge for controlling stock was the hardy and spiny bois d'arc, a small tree that was easily cultivated, tougher than hickory, and stronger than oak.[10]

A member of the mulberry family, the bois d'arc, or "wood of the bow" in French, was named by explorers who saw how the Osages and other tribes prized the yellow wood for making bows and arrows.[11] In Missouri, Kansas, and Indian Territory, the tree often was called the Osage orange because it yielded a large, inedible green fruit with a rough, pebbly skin. Other people knew the hedge as the "bodark," hedge apple, or horse apple.

It was said that in 1866 the illustrious Charles Goodnight, an early cattle herder from the Lone Star State and pioneer of the Goodnight-Loving Trail, built the first chuck wagon, from durable bois d'arc wood.[12] Because the wood was highly resistant to decay, bois d'arc was ideal for fence posts and other uses. Ranchers and farmers eventually found that a wire fence might be effective at holding cattle, but unlike bois d'arc hedges, it was worthless as a windbreak against strong prairie gales.

Starting in the 1870s, all sorts of designs were patented for barbed wire. Joseph Glidden, an enterprising Illinois farmer who was granted a patent in 1874, emerged out of the crowd of manufacturers as the chief producer.[13] Still, barbed wire remained a difficult sell until a brassy twenty-one-year-old drummer from Illinois named John Warne Gates headed to Texas in 1876 and demonstrated for even the most stubborn cattlemen the merits of Glidden's new wire.[14] Gates later would be known as "Bet-a-Million," after he placed big wagers with other salesmen on the speed of raindrops sliding down the window of a train car.[15]

When Gates arrived in the trading center of San Antonio in 1876, he had his work cut out for him. Sales of barbed wire were scarce, perhaps because many ranchers and Texas cowboys were former Confederates who suspected that wire fencing might be just another Yankee scheme to benefit northern industrialists at southerners' expense. Gates was lucky if any of the cattlemen he encountered at fancy hotels or in lively saloons gave him so much as a glance, much less an order for wire.[16] As far as they were concerned, a thief was presumed innocent until proved guilty, but a man like Gates, with a starched collar, had to prove himself.

After watching an old snake-oil quack work his magic and win over a bunch of skeptical Texans, Gates came up with a solution. He would try the same approach and put on a show for citizens, ranchers, and visiting cattle bosses.[17] After gaining permission from local officials to build a corral on the Military Plaza, right on the spot where San Antonio's city hall would stand later, Gates ordered his workmen to erect an eight-strand barbed-wire fence.[18] Next, the smooth talker issued his famous challenge: "This is the finest fence in the world. Light as air. Stronger than whiskey. Cheaper than dirt. All steel, and miles long. The cattle ain't been born that can get through it. Bring on your steers, gentlemen!"[19]

Many varied accounts exist about what happened next. The most popular version recounted that Gates hired some cowboys to drive a couple of dozen of the meanest longhorns they could find into the wire enclosure and turn them loose.[20] The steers, seeing nothing between them and freedom but a few strands of wire, charged the fence. They were repulsed quickly by the sharp barbs. Time and again, the cattle snorted and pawed the dust and ran at the fence, only to be turned back. After a while, the longhorns gave up and settled down. The barbed wire had held. The crowd of cowboys and townsfolk in the plaza stopped jeering, and their guffaws turned to cheers.[21] By sundown, so the tale went, Gates had sold hundreds of miles of barbed wire. Devil's rope was an idea whose time had come.[22]

Ignoring critics who longed to keep the ranges open, Colonel George Miller wished only to protect the ranges from outsiders and to prevent cattle from drifting. By erecting wire fences, Colonel Miller could reduce the size of his payroll because he would require fewer armed lineman riding pastures to confine herds and prevent cattle theft. The fencing of Miller's grasslands in the Cherokee Outlet also made life easier for Cherokee tax collectors, Miller's landlords—they no longer would have to search vast acreages to tally roving herds of livestock.[23]

Even if it meant his cowboys had to take on additional duties and carry pliers, hammers, and spades along with lariats and branding irons, Miller realized that fencing his pastures was an economic necessity. He also knew that with the advent of barbed-wire fences, other compromises would have to be made as more change swept across the Cherokee Outlet. Some of the challenges ahead would be formidable, and to get the job done, a man needed to be savvy and courageous. Bargaining with a cattle buyer or the Indian tax man had to be carried out without conceding too much. A man had to be decisive and stand by his convictions. Maybe that was the most important lesson Miller learned in those turbulent times in the outlet—never straddle a fence.

Chapter 15

WHERE THE COYOTES HOWL

Where the dewdrops fall and the butterfly rests,
The wild rose blooms on the prairie's crest,
Where the coyotes howl and the wind sports free,*
They laid him there on the lone prairie.[1]
—"The Dying Cowboy," bygone lament
**[emphasis added]*

IN the 1880s, the Millers' 101 brand flashed like rolling prairie flames throughout the Cherokee Outlet. The brand made a name for itself even beyond the land that would become Oklahoma.

Colonel George Miller and his boys continued to pasture Texas cattle and sell them to northern markets and in the rowdy Kansas rail towns of Dodge City, Newton, Wichita, and Caldwell. Then, as railroads were built southward toward the outlet, the Miller cowboys also became well acquainted with the loading pens at Arkansas City, Kiowa, and especially the feisty town of Hunnewell.

Several authors and historical sources, including some of the Miller family's promotional publications from the early 1900s, mistakenly perpetuated the tale that the 101 Ranch was founded in 1879, when Colonel Miller sojourned into the far reaches of the outlet and eventually created his Deer Creek and Salt Fork Ranches. That was not the case. It was not until 1892 that the Millers would begin efforts to establish their third ranch on the Salt Fork in the Ponca country; they named it the 101 Ranch the following year.[2]

Although the Miller family may have started to use the 101 numerals as a stock brand in 1881 on their Cherokee Outlet pastures, 101 was not branded on *all* the Millers' cattle and horses until the late 1880s.[3] From 1881 to 1887, the Millers identified their cattle with 101 burned on the left horn and with a large N O brand on the left side.[4] During those early years in the outlet, they continued to use the old L K brand on the left shoulder of all their horses. Several other brands and combinations of marks, such as 101 on the left hip of cows, were used on both horses and cattle until 1888, when the brand on the horn was eliminated. By then, all the cattle and horses were burned with 101 on the left hip. The L K and N O brands were not used after that time and the other markings also were dropped.[5]

The first public notice of the new 101 brand did not appear until November 21, 1883, when a brief mention of the Millers' brand transition was published in the *Arkansas City* (Kansas) *Traveler*. "George Miller, of Winfield, recently rounded up and branded 5,400 head of cattle at his ranch on Salt Fork, south of Hunnewell. He has changed his old brand of L K to 101 on hip and horn."[6]

No doubt some of the other brands noted in the Cherokee Strip Live Stock Association's *Brand Book*, published in 1882, referred to other cattle outfits Colonel Miller acquired as he was adding acreage to his Salt Fork and Deer Creek Ranches.[7] One such acquisition was the Bar-O-Bar, a small cattle ranch not far from the Salt Fork. The former owner used an iron which left the mark –O– burned into the left horn. Colonel Miller immediately recognized that the bars could be turned upright easily to form his signature 101.[8]

Before his death in 1936, Will A. Brooks, one of Colonel Miller's nephews, who came from Crab Orchard, Kentucky, in the late 1880s as a youth to work on his uncle's ranches, recalled the story of the Bar-O-Bar and another humorous incident of branding-iron alteration.[9] According to Brooks, his uncle mortgaged some cattle to Charles De Roberts, an early banker popularly known as "Dee." To mark the cattle properly, Colonel Miller had the branding iron altered so his 101 brand read I O D. A few days later, another cattleman who knew about the mortgage remarked to Miller, "Well, I see you're telling the world those cattle are mortgaged." Miller asked what the man meant. "I see you have them marked 'I Owe Dee,' " he answered. Colonel Miller thought it was a good joke and told several friends. Until those mortgaged cattle were sold and the loan paid, that group of steers was known as the "I Owe Dee" cattle.[10]

W. T. Melton of Diamond Tail Ranch once helped deliver to the 101 Ranch one thousand three-year-old steers from a cattle drive. He recalled the ranch and Miller's branding methods: "The houses were made of cottonwood logs. Miller didn't brand his cattle like the southern men did. His irons were only about two inches long, and curved just enough to fit around the base of the horn. The brand was placed on the back of the horn. The boys from the Diamond Tail Ranch made fun of Miller's way of branding, but they helped to do the branding."[11] Later, the Millers burned their brand into the animals' hides.

Although various stories exist about the origins of the 101 brand, Miller family tradition always maintained that a young cowpuncher named John M. Hiatt, said to be one of Colonel Miller's nephews, built the first branding fire, in 1881, to burn 101 onto the horns of some Miller steers, on Miller's grazing lands in the Cherokee Outlet.[12]

Hiatt, who spent a good portion of his life in the area of Hunnewell, Kansas, was a nineteen-year-old cowboy working on the branding crew when the order came down from Colonel Miller to use the new 101 brand.[13] Hiatt gathered a large pile of squaw wood, some cow chips (which the cowboys called "surface coal") and a bit of dried brush.[14] Then, with the swipe of a single match, young Hiatt ignited a blaze. Once the fire was roaring, the cowboy allowed the flames to peak and burn to a fiery glow. When branding, the iron could not be too hot or too cold. While Hiatt tended the fire, other cowboys brought in the cattle and castrated the male calves. They tossed the severed testicles, called "prairie oysters," into a pile for the camp cook to fry up as a suppertime treat. Along with a plate laden with a wad of beans, greasy fried potatoes, and a hunk of tough beef, all washed down with a tin cup of scalding brown coffee, the mouth-watering calf fries were a delicious culinary reward after a long day of hot and dirty work.[15]

When he thought the fire was just right and the irons—big enough to leave brands that drovers could read in the moonlight—were ready, Hiatt cried out, "Hot iron!" Then, as the fire tender pulled the glowing branding iron, or "scorcher," from the fiery coals, the real work began. Everyone on the crew took the time-honored ritual seriously because branding stock was one of the most important tasks in cow country.[16] Colonel Miller's brand signified more than just ownership. It identified his animals and his workers and served as a sort of coat of arms, or trademark.

"A man's brand is his own special mark," is how cowboy poet and singer Red Steagall explains it. "It says this is mine, leave it alone. You hire out to a man, you ride for his brand, and protect it like it was your own."[17]

This identification was crucial because Miller was not a lone wolf operating in the Cherokee Outlet. Plenty of other entrepreneurs had aspirations just as bold as those of the Kentucky colonel. Some of the cowmen had no intentions of lingering in the territory but were just passing through, usually on their way to a railhead in Kansas. Two of the most notable transients were Richard King and Mifflin Kenedy, of the illustrious King Ranch in Texas. King and Kenedy trailed herds of spirited horses, branded on jaw and shoulder with a K, through the Cherokee Outlet into southern Kansas in 1881, four years before King's death.[18] Another Texan who came to know the outlet passages was Abel Head "Shanghai" Pierce, an outlandish cattlemen who eventually would have his share of business dealings and some very heated personal disagreements with the equally contentious G. W. Miller.[19]

At first, the Cherokee Nation charged ranchmen only twenty-five cents a head on cattle brought into the outlet.[20] But even at that low rate, some stockmen evaded the tax. When the tribe complained, white ranch owners attempted to smooth things over by hiring Cherokee foremen.[21] That ploy had little effect. The ranchers' concerns about their situation in the outlet persisted because of the lack of any policy or understanding between Cherokee authorities and the federal government about leasing rights.[22]

In 1880, the Cherokee Nation levied a heftier tax of one dollar per head on outlet cattle grazed through the season, but cattlemen protested loudly and refused to pay.[23] The Cherokees initially threatened to expel the rebellious cowmen, but finally, in December 1880, the tribal council voted to reduce the head tax to forty cents on each grown cow and twenty-five cents on each yearling.[24] Still, the unrest in the Cherokee Outlet persisted.

The ranchers—a few of them so obstinate they would not move camp for a prairie fire—recalled that in 1879, Cherokee tax collectors had gathered approximately eleven hundred dollars in grazing fees from about twenty-five cattlemen, less that half the estimated number using outlet grasslands to feed their huge herds.[25] Those grazing fees increased to more than seventy-six hundred dollars in 1880, then to twenty-one thousand dollars in 1881, and to more than forty-one thousand dollars by 1882.[26] By that time, the ranchers had organized to protect their interests. The die was cast by 1881 when the wisest of the cowmen, including Colonel Miller, recognized the inescapable changes rising on the ranges of the Cherokee Outlet.

Many years later, W. J. Nicholson, a Cherokee Outlet cowpuncher, recalled the conflict between cattlemen and Boomers in the outlet:

> The only people in the country [Cherokee Outlet] in the early 80's were the cowmen, soldiers, Indians and a few of Captain Payne's Boomers. The law was for the soldiers to destroy any permanent improvements made on

> any ranch and thus run the Boomers out. I have seen the Ninth Cavalry, on their line of bay horses with their negro [sic] soldiers dressed in blue suits and brass buttons, line up in front of a Boomer's ranch-house, take his supplies out, pour on coal-oil and leave the green logs to smoulder. The order was that cattlemen would only be allowed to use tents. . . . The cowpunchers did not like the Boomer. They [the Boomers] plowed up good grass.[27]

The movement for the organization of Cherokee Outlet cattlemen who wished to defend their interests began in early 1881.[28] The first meeting, attended by Colonel Miller, was held at Caldwell, Kansas, on March 16, just a dozen days after James A. Garfield had been inaugurated as the twentieth U.S. president. (His term would end only six months later when he was shot and killed.[29]) Texas cattleman S. S. Birchfield was chosen as chairman of the meeting and R. F. Crawford was secretary. Perhaps the most important piece of business was arranging for the registration of cattle brands used in the outlet.[30]

But in March 1882, at the second meeting, held once again at Caldwell, the cattlemen—more confident than ever because of their early success in organizing—determined that they would erect wire fences to protect their investments in the outlet.[31] Although the federal government did not authorize "improvements," cowmen such as G. W. Miller believed that as long as they had to pay taxes to the Cherokees, they were justified in fencing the grazing lands with devil's rope.

Certain that they had strength in numbers, the cattle bosses were willing to take their chances with the Cherokee landlords and the federal government. They believed fences not only would cut down on the number of hired hands needed but also would discourage cattle and timber thieves and impede pesty Boomers and open-range cattlemen who refused to pay taxes.[32]

Besides Colonel Miller, one of the first cattlemen to approach the Cherokees about fencing pastures was Major Andrew Drumm, another prominent stockman and one of the first to graze his herds in the outlet.[33] A native of Ohio, Drumm had mined for gold in California, where he amassed a modest fortune.[34] As Miller had done in his early years out west, Drumm raised and slaughtered hogs before he entered the cattle business. He established a substantial ranch in the Cherokee Outlet between the Medicine River and the Salt Fork of the Arkansas, north of present Cherokee, Oklahoma.[35]

Although there were complaints about barbed-wire enclosures and formal permission for "cattlemen to fence the Outlet pasture was not immediately forthcoming from tribal officials," the delay had no impact on the cattlemen's fence-building activities.[36] Finally, on March 16, 1883, Secretary of the Interior Henry M. Teller issued an order for Cherokee Outlet ranchers to remove all fences, dwellings, and corrals. If they refused, federal soldiers would be dispatched to do the job for them.[37] The cowmen fired off letters of protest to Teller, arguing that without basic improvements, the range-cattle industry would perish. The ranchers also were taking even more decisive action.

The cattle owners had met once again at Caldwell. On March 6, 1883, they appointed nine directors, including Major Drumm, to draft a constitution, bylaws, and charter of incorporation for a new organization.[38] Within forty-eight hours, the Cherokee Strip Live Stock Association was born.

Practically every cattleman operating in the outlet paid the annual dues of ten dollars to join the association. Its headquarters were in Caldwell, one of the finest cow towns in Kansas and a place where ranch owners could ship surplus stock to market.[39] Chartered under state law as a Kansas corporation, the association had no capital stock or stockholders but boasted an active membership of several hundred ranchers and partnerships, including brokers and stockholders of large corporations.[40]

Four months after the incorporation, the directors leased from the Cherokee Nation more than six million acres in the outlet at a cost of a half million dollars for five years, with the stipulation that one hundred thousand dollars be paid in advance.[41] This came to less than two cents an acre in annual rent. Members subleased the land, and in return the association collected rents, fixed individual boundaries, arranged cattle roundups, recorded brands, and offered rewards for the capture of cow thieves.[42]

The organization wielded great influence in Indian Territory. For several years—until the opening of the Oklahoma country to white homesteaders—Colonel Miller and other ranchers with foresight took advantage of the situation. During what later must have seemed like only a fleeting speck of time, they roamed that land, secretly knowing it never would be theirs to keep. But sometimes, after a day riding fence lines and tending herds, they had time to rest beneath a full hunter's moon, time to listen to the chorus of the coyotes, songdogs of the prairie. Their voices echoed like an everlasting benediction over the ranges of bluestem and buffalo grass and the creeks flowing with good water.

RIDE 'EM, COWBOY

WHILE RIDING HERD in the Cherokee Outlet, the Millers also made time for recreation. In fact, Colonel Miller and his three lively sons steadfastly contended that they staged the very first *commercial* rodeo ever held.[1] That inaugural rodeo—which the Millers called a roundup—took place in autumn 1882 in Winfield, Kansas, a year or so after G.W. and his family had settled there.[2]

Although other cow outfits and several towns scattered across the West still dispute the Millers' boast, it would be impossible to prove otherwise. Some of the most zealous claims emanated from the Lone Star State. According to legend, folks in Texas wagered on horse races and cheered bronc riders and fancy ropers during "cowhunts" in the 1830s and 1840s.[3] One of the more noteworthy of those early "rodeos" occurred in 1844 when Major Jack Hays, a Texas Ranger, helped to organize a contest to demonstrate the riding and shooting skills of Comanche warriors, Texas Rangers, and Mexican rancheros on a prairie just west of San Pedro Creek in San Antonio.[4] When that contest—featuring wild-horse riders and crack target shooters—concluded and the dust settled, the judges presented Spanish blankets, Bowie knives, and pistols to the victorious contestants. The first-place winner was John McMullin, a young Texas Ranger. Long Quirt, a Comanche participant, came in second.[5] Despite the claims of die-hard Texan rodeo lovers, most historians would agree that instead of an authentic rodeo, as such a sporting event eventually became known, the 1844 San Antonio contest more closely resembled a Wild West show such as the 1843 buffalo chase sponsored by P. T. Barnum at Hoboken, New Jersey.[6]

Still other tales about early rodeos could be traced to New Mexico Territory, although some folks argued that those affairs were more like fiestas than anything else. After witnessing a June 1847 calf branding at the ancient city of Santa Fe, an American army officer offered the following description: "At this time of year the cowmen have what is called the round-up, when the calves are branded and the fat beasts selected to be driven to a fair hundreds of miles away. This round-up is a great time for the cowhands, a Donneybrook [sic] fair it is indeed. They contest with each other for the best roping and throwing, and there are horse races and whiskey and wines. At night in the clear moonlight there is much dancing in the streets."[7]

A few old-time cowboys swore that the first true rodeo took place at Deer Trail, in Colorado Territory, on July 4, 1869, when cowpunchers from the rival Mill Iron, Camp Stool, and Hashknife Ranches met on a trail drive.[8] Ground rules were laid down, wagers were made, and the best horses and toughest men from the three ranches were pitted against one another in a competition intended to bring relief from the rigors of herding longhorns.[9] Independence Day eventually became a popular date for many competitions. A July 4, 1883, cowboy contest was staged in Pecos, in the far reaches of west Texas. The famous "Old Glory Blowout" of Buffalo Bill Cody in North Platte, Nebraska, was held on Independence Day 1882. The first Prescott Frontier Days Celebration, a commercial rodeo in Arizona Territory, took place on July 4, 1888.[10]

Both the Pecos and Prescott contests were after G. W. Miller's cowboys held their roundup at Winfield, Kansas. Buffalo Bill's highly touted "Old Glory Blowout"—which occurred just a few months before the Millers' big roundup—was not so much a rodeo competition as an outdoor extravaganza featuring cowboys as entertainers.[11] This successful event provided the flashy showman with the impetus to package and launch his "Buffalo Bill's Wild West" (Cody never used the word *show*, even though that is precisely what it was) the following year in Omaha, Nebraska.[12]

Undoubtedly, the origins of rodeo will remain obscure, and the battle for bragging rights over where and when the first "rodeo" was held will never be settled to everyone's satisfaction. Thus, the Millers' claim that they were responsible for organizing the first commercial rodeo is as valid as any of the many others.[13]

By the early 1880s, many cities and towns in the western territories and states held annual events, including cowboy roundups, as gestures of civic pride and as suitable entertainment for local citizens. The Cowley County town of Winfield, Kansas, was no exception. In the 1870s, before the town was incorporated, citizens marked holidays with picnics, speeches, and games.[14] Sometimes they attended decorous community dances, at which men wore stiff paper collars and trimmed whiskers. As one early chronicler of Winfield history put it, "there were never any wallflowers, no red liquor, or disorder."[15]

During the first half of the 1870s, prairie fires, drought, and grasshopper plagues took a heavy toll on the country's croplands.[16] In 1880, another round of natural disasters struck the land, bringing more crop failures and a dramatic decline in population. But recovery began the following year, just as the Millers were establishing their first home in Winfield. By 1882, the county's farms and ranches already showed a substantial gain.[17] That summer, about the time Bill Cody was organizing his "Old Glory Blowout" in Nebraska, civic leaders in Winfield decided to stage an autumn agricultural fair to salute their town's new-found prosperity and to celebrate the harvest season.[18]

When the town fathers determined that some sort of major entertainment was needed to help draw crowds to the fair, they turned to Colonel Miller.[19] Although he just had returned to Winfield after one of his journeys up the Chisholm Trail, Miller met with the fair officials. Still as dirty as a drover's blanket after weeks on the dusty trail, he listened to the delegation and agreed to come to the rescue by putting on a public exhibition of riding and roping.[20]

G.W. sent one of his boys to the Hunnewell camp, just above the Cherokee Outlet line, to summon his seasoned hands. They were independent men and boys as good as their nerves who drew dollar-a-day wages to outthink cows. Every one of them was tough, and even the younger drovers—macho as stud bulls—had faces creased like old boots from too many seasons in the sun, wind, and rain.

The Miller cowboys showed up in Winfield riding stout ponies, clean-limbed and powerful, which could run faster than scalded cats. They brought along a collection of horses that had never been ridden, or at least not successfully. These wild, growling stallions, mean as the devil, bucked and snorted and arched their backs like mules in a hailstorm as they kicked up boiling clouds of dust.

After the cowboys and stock were assembled at the Winfield fairgrounds, G.W. saw to all the details to guarantee that the roundup would be a success. His efforts paid off.

"The cowboys, who had come up over the Chisholm Trail with the Miller herd, built an arena at Winfield. With their cow ponies and wild steers, selected from the Texas herd, they put on a program chiefly of roping and riding. It proved to be the money-getting entertainment that the fair boosters wanted," wrote Corb Sarchet, a Miller family friend, many years later.[21]

One of the stars of the 1882 Winfield Roundup was a sinewy fourteen-year-old cowboy—Joseph Carson Miller, the eldest of Colonel Miller's three sons, in his first public performance as a roper and rider.[22]

Although their cowboys continued to put on ranch roundups for their own enjoyment, it would be twenty-two years before the Millers attempted another public roundup for entertainment purposes.[23] But when the Millers finally decided to enter show business early in the new century, they did it with an authenticity that no one else ever duplicated. As the Miller brothers later proclaimed in splashy promotional literature from the early 1900s touting their Wild West shows, "Our brand stands for stern honesty wherever it is stamped. It ensures fulfillment with every promise. We will make you feel the life-giving atmosphere of the prairie, for we are 'The Real Thing.' "[24]

Chapter 16

RIDING THE HOME RANGE

During his long and lonely expeditions through the Indian Territory, George Miller picked his own trails, and the one he oftenest followed lay along the Arkansas River where the grass was long and juicy. This afterward became the reservation of the Ponca, Otoe and Missouri Indians. Mr. Miller had determined to own it some day. He settled in Kansas near Winfield, but the Ponca lands were ever in his mind.[1]

—Early 101 Wild West show program

BY the mid- to late 1880s, after the passage of strict livestock-quarantine regulations in Kansas, the great cattle drives began to diminish, leading to a financial decline intensified by catastrophic droughts and blizzards across the West.[2]

Yet the Millers continued to prosper, much as they had in the early 1880s. While overseeing his large ranching operations, Colonel Miller did not neglect the welfare of his family. He made sure Molly and Alma lived in comfort in the family residence at Winfield, Kansas, and that the three young Miller sons got an education in the ways of cattle. Miller wanted to be sure his boys knew cows front, back, and sideways, just as he did.

G.W. also kept his family's future land holdings and grazing pastures secure by further endearing his family to the various tribes residing in Indian Territory, especially the Poncas and Otoes.

As early as the autumn of 1883—less than a year after he had busted broncs during the Millers' successful Winfield Roundup—Joseph Miller, just fifteen years old, was given another "man-sized" assignment.[3] This time he would have to show his moxie in Alabama. Hearing of the roundup's success, the officials of the Alabama State Fair wished to make their 1883 agricultural fair a crowd pleaser and asked the Millers if they would provide entertainment for fairgoers in Birmingham.[4] Colonel Miller immediately seized on the opportunity. Busy shipping thousands of head of cattle to eastern markets, he sent his son Joe to handle the formidable task.

The teenager, a capable cowboy, was more than up to the task. Indeed, in 1879, when Joe was only eleven years old, his father had chosen him to ride alone through the Cherokee Outlet and across Osage country to the Ponca camp at Baxter Springs to alert White Eagle and other tribal leaders that the prairie land the government had selected for them would make a good home.

Joe Miller's ability to negotiate had long been evident. His daughter Alice Miller Harth later wrote, "Once, when Grandfather came home to Winfield the year Father was twelve, he called Father to him and said, 'Take this roll of bills and go to Texas and bring back a carload of cattle.' I think this was the end of Father's formal education and the beginning of a business career because every year he continued regularly to bring back from Texas and Louisiana, not only one carload of cattle, but many carloads which he, in company with a band of cowboys, drove up the old Chisholm Trail to Indian Territory."[5]

For the big Alabama event in September 1883, young Joe would not thrill audiences by riding rank or hard-to-handle mustangs, as he had at the Winfield Roundup. Instead, he and White Eagle would lead a delegation of fifty to one hundred Poncas to the state fairgrounds, where they would re-create an Indian village, with painted canvas tepees and an area for performing traditional dances.[6] The Poncas were to be used as exotic lures to attract large crowds. Decked out in their best moccasins, leggings, breechcloths, buckskin shirts, robes, eagle-feather warbonnets, and otter-skin headdresses, the Poncas would be put on display—just like prize livestock, award-winning pies and jams, and such freaks of nature as two-headed snakes and miniature ponies.

The payoff was promising. Every person who walked through the gate to see the costumed Poncas carrying wands and shaking gourd rattles as they danced to the beat of the big drums first had to present Joe Miller a hefty admission fee of twenty-five cents.[7] Joe told an Oklahoma City newspaper reporter more than forty-three years later,

> It was while we were giving our exhibitions on the fair grounds that the invitation came to White Eagle to speak at the First Baptist church, as I now remember it after such a period of years. It was our custom to introduce several of the chiefs outside the village, tell who they were, what they did at home and invite the crowds to come inside the village to see them.
>
> White Eagle was the tribal chief and, as such, was the one who preached to his own people in regard to their centuries-old religious beliefs. It was

> in this way that I was accustomed to introduce White Eagle to the crowds on the Alabama State Fair grounds. One afternoon, after I had introduced the chief, I was approached by a gentleman who introduced himself as pastor of the First Baptist Church.[8]

The pastor asked Joe if White Eagle would consider preaching at his church the following Sunday morning. When Joe relayed the request, the Ponca chief agreed.

"I have seen lots of crowds, but I have never seen anything to equal that which assembled to hear White Eagle preach," recalled Joe. "It was necessary for the police of Birmingham to attend in squads to handle the crowd, thousands of which could not even get inside the church. The daily papers on Saturday and again on Sunday morning had told of the fact that the Indian would preach and it looked like everyone wanted to hear him."

White Eagle emerged from his tepee early that Sabbath, attired in the "full regalia of his office"—a flowing blanket, long head feathers, and elegant beaded moccasins. Swarms of curiosity seekers who had read about his scheduled appearance in one of the city's largest churches were gathering at the fairgrounds. White Eagle asked Joe, who was fluent in the Ponca language, to act as interpreter because, at the last minute, the Ponca interpreter "got cold feet when he saw the immense crowd."[9]

White Eagle and Joe Miller were driven from the fairgrounds to the church in a deluxe horse-drawn cab. Police officers separated gawkers so the boy and the chief could enter the building. Inside, the preacher accompanied White Eagle and Joe through the buzzing swarm of parishioners to chairs on the altar.

"The size and attention of that crowd was [sic] enough to make any man quail, but White Eagle never flinched," Joe related. "After the opening service, the minister announced his pleasure at having White Eagle present and he would now speak. Drawing his blanket around him and holding it in place with his left hand, the chief spoke slowly and deliberately, using his right arm frequently for gestures. He would talk a while, then I would interpret."[10]

Standing tall in the pulpit with Joe at his side, the unflappable chief mesmerized the white southerners. Facing the vast audience seated before him, the chief explained his people's religious beliefs, telling them that "Indians have but one church, whereas the white people, even down in Oklahoma, have many churches, one on every corner and each declaring his own way the only true way, whereas the others face eternal hell fire."[11]

The Miller family home in Newtonia, Missouri, in the 1870s. *(Frank Phillips Foundation, Inc.)*

Decoration Day, 1883, Baxter Springs, Kansas. G. W. Miller established his home and headquarters in this early cattle town in the fall of 1880. *(Baxter Springs Heritage Center and Museum)*

In 1881, the Millers moved to Winfield, Kansas. In 1888, they purchased an impressive home at 508 West Ninth Street which remained the family's primary residence until 1903. *(Frank Phillips Foundation, Inc.)*

A group of Miller cowboys fresh off the Texas cattle trail at Winfield, Kansas, June 1887. *(Frank Phillips Foundation, Inc.)*

One of the first dugouts at the 101 Ranch headquarters, south of the Salt Fork River in Oklahoma Territory, 1893. *(Frank Phillips Foundation, Inc.)*

Wranglers and guests visit corrals near the first headquarters of the 101 Ranch, 1893. *(Frank Phillips Foundation, Inc.)*

Photograph by William S. Prettyman of the land run into the Cherokee Outlet, a few seconds past noon, September 16, 1893. *(Michael Wallis Collection)*

Colonel George Washington Miller—known by his friends as G.W.—pioneer cattleman and founder of the 101 Ranch, circa 1893. *(Frank Phillips Foundation, Inc.)*

Mary Anne Carson Miller, circa 1893, a Kentucky belle who moved west with her husband. Family records and documents spell her nickname as Molly and Mollie. In later years, she was fondly referred to as Mother Miller. *(Miller-England family, courtesy Arthur and Bess Mann)*

Mother Miller, matriarch of the Hundred and One empire, circa 1915. *(Miller-England family, courtesy Arthur and Bess Mann)*

Joseph Carson Miller, circa 1912. *(Frank Phillips Foundation, Inc.)*

Zachary Taylor Miller, circa 1915. *(Michael Wallis Collection)*

George Lee Miller, circa 1915. *(Michael Wallis Collection)*

Alma Miller England, circa 1903. *(Frank Phillips Foundation, Inc.)*

A Miller family gathering, 1902. Standing (*left to right*): A relative (unidentified), Mother Miller, G.W. holding George W. (Joe's son), Lizzie, Joe, and George L. Front (*left to right*): Alma, Alice (Joe's daughter), and Zack. *(Miller-England family, courtesy Arthur and Bess Mann)*

On the porch of the White House, circa 1912. Back row (*left to right*): Joe Jr., Mother Miller, Marianne England, Alma, Alice, "Uncle Doc" (*standing*), and Lizzie. Front row: George W. Miller (*left*) and Billy England. *(Courtesy The Glass Negative, Ponca City, Oklahoma)*

White Eagle, chief of the Ponca tribe and longtime friend of the Millers. *(Frank Phillips Foundation, Inc.)*

Early Miller cowhands branding calves on the Salt Fork ranges. *(Bethel Freeman Collection, courtesy The Glass Negative, Ponca City, Oklahoma)*

The 101 Ranch Cowboy Band at Hutchinson, Kansas, 1904. Shadowy figure, sitting fifth from left, is Ralph Hale, a cornet player from Hunnewell, Kansas. *(Fred Strickland Collection)*

Omar W. Coffelt with his pet buffalo at the 101 Ranch. Some cowboys claimed Coffelt acted as a hired gun for the Millers, disposing of persons who got in the family's way. *(Michael Wallis Collection, courtesy Steve H. Bunch)*

Part of the crowd of more than 65,000 people, many of them from the National Editorial Association, who flocked to the 101 Ranch on June 11, 1905, billed by the Millers as Oklahoma's Gala Day. *(Jerry and Ruth Murphey Collection)*

Famous photograph by Bennie Kent of Geronimo posing in a top hat behind the wheel of a Locomobile during the June 11, 1905, roundup at the 101 Ranch. To his left is Edward Le Clair Sr., a Ponca. When Geronimo admired his companion's beaded vest, Le Clair presented it to him. In 1909, when the celebrated Apache warrior died, he was buried in it. *(Frank Phillips Foundation, Inc.)*

Apache warrior Geronimo skins a bison he had just shot with a Winchester rifle from the front seat of a motorcar at the 101 Ranch, June 11, 1905. Although the Millers claimed it was the last bison Geronimo killed, in truth it was his first. *(Frank Phillips Foundation, Inc.)*

The Cherokee Kid—Will Rogers—performed alongside the Millers in the early 1900s and remained their close friend long after his name had become a household word. *(Will Rogers Memorial and Library)*

Major Gordon W. "Pawnee Bill" Lillie (*left*) and William F. "Buffalo Bill" Cody, photographed circa 1887, later became friendly competitors with the Millers. Cody joined the 101 Ranch Wild West Show in 1916, the year before his death. *(Jerry and Ruth Murphey Collection)*

Tom Mix on the 101 Ranch, circa 1906. *(Jack Keathly Collection)*

Bill Pickett, the inventor of bulldogging, in action on the Hundred and One, early 1900s. *(J.D. and Maxine Welch Collection)*

Summer camp on the 101 Ranch, August 1908. Mother Miller is seated in the buggy beneath the tree. *(From Jane Woodend's photo album/Jerry and Ruth Murphey Collection)*

Crack rifle and pistol shot Princess Wenona—a star attraction with the Millers' Wild West shows—and one of her canine pals, early 1900s. *(Jerry and Ruth Murphey Collection)*

Cowgirl Edith Tantlinger, who with her husband, Vern, appeared with the Millers' Wild West shows for many years, demonstrates her skill with a lariat, early 1900s. *(Jerry and Ruth Murphey Collection)*

Cowgirls on the 101 Ranch. In the far right background is the Millers' original White House, which burned to the ground in 1909. *(Frank Phillips Foundation, Inc.)*

Scene from the 101 Ranch Wild West Show, 1911. Lucille Mulhall, "America's first cowgirl," holds the reins; Tom Mix rides behind her on top of the stagecoach. *(From Jane Woodend's photo album/Jerry and Ruth Murphey Collection)*

Donato La Banca (*second row center*), one of the Millers' most celebrated bandleaders, strikes a formal pose with his musicians, circa 1911. *(Courtesy Mrs. Donald La Banca)*

The Miller brothers, along with wildcatter E. W. Marland, launched oil and gas operations in Oklahoma as early as 1909. *(Jerry and Ruth Murphey Collection)*

Spectators watch as a band of the Millers' show Indians attacks a wagon train during the filming of a movie at Inceville, near Santa Ynez Canyon in southern California, 1913. *(Frank Phillips Foundation, Inc.)*

A 101 Ranch crew in action at Inceville in front of a painted movie backdrop during filming of a cannon salute to Spanish-American War veterans, 1913. *(Frank Phillips Foundation, Inc.)*

Bennie Kent (*in derby*) and Vince Dillon (*far left*) take a break from filming on the 101 Ranch, May 18, 1914. *(Courtesy The Glass Negative, Ponca City, Oklahoma)*

Miller Brothers Wild West Show entertainers aboard ship en route to performances in England, 1914. *(Ruth and Jerry Murphey Collection, courtesy Zack Miller Jr.)*

Iron Tail, an Oglala Sioux war chief who had appeared with both Buffalo Bill and Pawnee Bill, became a featured entertainer for the Millers at the start of the 1913 show season. The Millers boasted that Iron Tail's likeness in profile appeared on the famous "Indian head-buffalo" nickels, first issued by the U.S. Treasury the same year. *(Jerry and Ruth Murphey Collection)*

Hundred and One Ranch Wild West show cowgirls, July 1915. Standing (*left to right*): unknown, Dolly, Bea Kirnan, Martha Allen Schultz, Vera Schultz, Tillie Baldwin, Alice Lee, Prairie Rose Henderson. Seated (*left to right*): Bessie Herberg, Jane Woodend, Jackie McFarlin, Tina Binder, unknown, Mabel Strickland. *(From Jane Woodend's photo album/Jerry and Ruth Murphey Collection)*

White Eagle further explained that his people did not accept the concept of hell. Instead, they believed that people made their own hell on earth and "that when an Indian does wrong it makes his heart hurt and he is sorely troubled, sometimes for a long time, and in this way he experiences his hell."

When White Eagle completed his remarks and Joe finished interpreting, they took their seats and the Baptist minister delivered a brief sermon. The chief's appearance before a congregation of white southerners was a masterful public-relations ploy which undoubtedly paid off in huge dividends at the fairgrounds. "Altogether I still remember it as one of the momentous occasions in an entire lifetime," Joe declared when he was almost fifty-nine years old, during the 1927 interview with the *Daily Oklahoman*.[12]

Joe Miller's early association with the Ponca tribe, including his experience in Alabama with White Eagle, served the entire Miller family well. A decade later, in 1893, the Cherokee Outlet was opened to white settlement, and the Ponca leaders offered to lease tribal lands to Colonel Miller so he could continue to graze his great herds of cattle.

Throughout the 1880s, Colonel Miller schooled Joe and the younger boys in the ways of cattlemen. G.W. also insisted that his children endure as much academic training as possible. Contrary to popular lore and even family opinion, all of the three Miller boys received a fair amount of formal schooling. This was especially true of Joe Miller.

In the autumn of 1883, immediately after the conclusion of the Alabama State Fair, Joe returned to the campus of Central University in Richmond, Kentucky, to continue his stint as a college student.[13] Joe first had enrolled at Central in the academic year of 1882–1883, at the age of fourteen, two years after he had helped direct a herd of snorting longhorns from Texas up the Chisholm Trail.[14] The university was a logical choice for the eldest Miller son. An important market for fine livestock and tobacco, Richmond was the seat of Madison County, where the bluegrass met the foothills of the Appalachians, just to the north of the Miller family's old stomping grounds of Lincoln and Rockcastle Counties. Daniel Boone had blazed trails through the area, and the mythologized western folk hero and Indian killer Christopher "Kit" Carson, reputedly a kinsman of Molly Carson Miller, was a native of Madison County.[15]

Founded by the Presbyterian Church as "an institution of learning of high order," Central University opened on September 22, 1874, with 224 students attending classes in one newly built classroom building.[16] Plagued almost from the outset by financial problems, Central boasted an enrollment of 235 students by the time Joe Miller arrived.[17] Although that number included a student from Turkey and one from the Sandwich Islands, most of the young men at Central were from southern states, chiefly Kentucky, with 176 enrollees.[18] The College of Philosophy, Letters, and Science, at Richmond, accounted for 163 students, and the other seventy-two were enrolled in the College of Medicine, in Louisville. Joe Miller was one of only two students from Kansas attending Central and the lone Kansan on the Richmond campus.[19]

When he arrived in Richmond—a pleasant town of three hundred inhabitants who were known to "open their homes to students, and thus throw around them the restraints of the family circle and the influences of the Christian household"—Joe immediately reported to the offices of the chancellor and the president of the faculty.[20] Like all other incoming students, Joe was required to present a certificate of good moral character before gaining formal admission.[21] Joe and his fellow students were obliged to participate in daily morning prayers in the university chapel and to attend public divine services in a local church "at least once on each Sabbath."[22]

The institution offered a wide assortment of courses, including astronomy, algebra, chemistry, calculus, ethics, geology, German, Greek, Latin, logic, physics, psychology, political economy, and rhetoric.[23] Joe Miller took only two academic courses during his first year at Central.[24] Like other freshmen, he was required to take a semester of algebra followed by a semester of geometry, along with a course in English analysis and elementary exercises in composition.[25] When Joe returned to Kentucky for his sophomore year in the autumn of 1883, after his appearance with White Eagle at the Alabama State Fair, he again took English and mathematics and added a course in bookkeeping.[26] By the summer of 1884, Joe had had his fill of academic life and the Presbyterian atmosphere at Central University.[27] He was weary of rules and regulations, and he longed for the freedom of life on the cattle ranges of Indian Territory and Kansas.[28]

G. W. and Molly Miller tried to convince Joe to return to Richmond and earn a college degree, but he would not be budged. Later, however, he supplemented his education during a brief and undistinguished spell at Spaulding's Business College in Kansas City, Missouri.[29]

Once he was thoroughly convinced that Joe's higher education was over, Colonel Miller decided to give him a chance to show his competency as a boss in the cattle business. To make sure Joe got off to an auspicious start, Miller presented his son in the mid-1880s with a sizable grubstake of ten thousand dollars.[30]

Joe Miller thanked his father and shook his hand. Then he kissed his mother good-bye. He saddled up a cow pony and rode out of Winfield, headed due south for Indian Territory. With the generous bankroll from his father tucked safely away, Joe soon lit out for Texas and never once looked back until he had crossed the Red River.[31]

After he reached Texas, Joe wisely stashed his money in a bank and found temporary employment in a mercantile establishment, where he put his bookkeeping skills to use.[32] It did not take long for him to discover that neither city life nor formal employment was for him. Like a loose mare always looking for a new pasture, he headed to extreme west Texas and the cowboy country in the vast, mountainous Big Bend area just north of the Río Grande.[33]

Joe found many familiar cowboy faces waiting for him in the tiny railroad town of Murphyville, founded just a few years before his arrival.[34] The original town name dated to 1882, when the Southern Pacific Railroad came into the area. T. C. Murphy, owner of the only water for miles around, bargained with railroad officials to supply water for the railroad if they would name the station for him. The railroad brass did not object to the name, but apparently some local citizens did. Eventually, Murphyville became known as Alpine, seat of Brewster County, the largest county in the state.[35]

The coveted water supply which Murphy owned was named Kokernut Springs, after the family that had been such an important part of the Millers' business life when G.W. moved to Missouri.[36] Joe Miller had heard that Lee Kokernut, his father's former cattle partner, was in the area, gathering a sizable herd of cows to herd to the far north. Joe sought out Kokernut to see if he might have work for a good cowhand.[37]

Instead of landing a job with Kokernut's cattle outfit, Joe found his father's old friend gravely ill and unable to lead the huge herd of four- and five-year-old steers up the trail to the ultimate delivery point, in the rangelands of Montana.[38] Joe realized he had found a prized opportunity, and he proposed that he buy the herd from Kokernut and lead it northward. The savvy Texan knew of Joe's early experiences on the trails and felt confident that the teenager was up to the challenge. They struck a deal.

For cash payment of four dollars a head and the promise to pay Kokernut the balance of the purchase price, Joe found himself the owner of twenty-five hundred steers, 136 saddle horses, a chuck wagon, and a team of mules.[39] Kokernut scratched out a note for Joe to take to the foreman, explaining that young Miller now owned the herd and would take the longhorns to market in Kansas instead of Montana. Kokernut also left instructions that the foreman, camp cook, and fourteen cowhands were to answer to nineteen-year-old Joe Miller.[40]

As Joe's sister, Alma Miller England, and Ellsworth Collings later wrote, "The cowboys were soldiers of fortune and served the man who paid and fed them. The herd was being held on grazing ground forty miles south of Alpine, trail branded, supplies in the wagon and the cowboys anxious to be on the trail. The morning after Joe arrived at the outfit he sat on one of his newly acquired saddle ponies and watched his herd take shape into a long column of shuffling hoofs and rattling horns and swing its head north. His first drive as owner had begun."[41]

After many weeks of enduring the dangers and hardships of the trail, Joe and his crew of hardened Texans finally made it to his father's rangelands south of Hunnewell, Kansas. Colonel Miller carefully inspected the steers and told his son he had made a good deal with Kokernut. Once the paperwork was completed, Joe was pleased to find that he had more than doubled his money.[42]

Joe Miller's trek up the trail with the herd he bought from Kokernut took place in 1887, when rangelands throughout the West, especially those in the far north, still were reeling from the shock of the "Big Die-Up" blizzards. The following year, Joe pulled off a similar deal and drove another big herd back to his father's ranch.[43]

Joe and his father stayed busy riding the home range, often bunking with their cowhands at Hunnewell, where they kept cattle pens and broke horses, or at cow camps in the big Miller pastures of the Cherokee Outlet. The rest of the family remained at home in Winfield, except during school holidays and summer, when the two other Miller sons joined their father and big brother on the range.

In 1888, Colonel Miller sold the family's residence at 602 Manning Street and, for the princely sum of ten thousand dollars, purchased a larger abode—an impressive Italianate Victorian brick-and-limestone home at 508 West Ninth Street, built in 1879–1882.[44]

The Millers were delighted with the spacious parlors, full-length windows, breezy porches with ornate railings, and gaslight fixtures in every room from garret to cellar.[45] Curved-top front doors nine feet tall opened into a foyer with a stained-glass window and the foot of a spiral stairway, graced by a carved walnut rail that wound up three floors.[46] A first-floor parlor on the south side featured another stained-glass window and a hand-carved oak fireplace, ideal for frigid Kansas winters. Beyond sliding doors, another fireplace warmed the library, on the north side, and a dining room extended the full width of the house. It had a well-outfitted kitchen and a servants' dining room and quarters. A second stairway, also with walnut rail, wound from the back hall to the second floor. The upper floors were reserved for family and guest bedrooms—one for each of the Millers—including a master bedroom with fireplace, a bathroom, and a large "clothes room."[47]

The thick brick walls contained a built-in ventilation system with ornate cast-iron grillwork that could be opened or closed to control air movement. Outside the house were limestone sidewalks, and a smooth wire fence enclosed the yard, planted with flower beds, gardens, and shade trees.[48] In the northwest corner of the property was a brick carriage house where G.W. kept an elegant surrey, a pair of prancing bays, and a gentle mare for Molly's use.[49] A cadre of servants handled all household chores, and gardeners pruned trees and shrubs and tended the garden. When he was home, G.W.—more than likely at his wife's suggestion—"always would attend church with his family, dressed in formal clothing, including a silk hat and gold-headed walking stick."[50]

As the Millers' daughter, Alma, pointed out almost fifty years later with coauthor Ellsworth Collings in their largely sanitized book about the 101 Ranch, it was in Winfield that "George Miller had at last begun to realize the ambitions he had formed as a boy on a Kentucky plantation. Thousands of cattle roamed over the vast ranges of his ranch across the Kansas-Oklahoma line. In Winfield he and his wife were in the forefront of society and cowboys coming up the trails were charmed with the open southern hospitality of the Miller home."[51]

The book did not mention the fact that the Miller's reputed "southern hospitality" extended only to white cowboys and not to those of color who rode for the 101 brand in those early years, even though as many as one in four cowboys who participated in the cattle drives through Texas was African-American.[52] G.W. and his wife never turned their back on their southern roots, and they never attempted to rid themselves of the deep racial prejudices instilled in them from birth as slave owners in antebellum Kentucky.

Shortly before his death, Jim North, a lifelong black resident of Winfield who once worked for G. W. Miller, recollected his early memories of the Miller family.[53] "There used to be a lot of fruit trees in the yard of the Miller home and a group of us kids would go in there and play," North recalled. "Mrs. Miller had a dog and a parrot that sat in the yard and that parrot could tell if I was a white boy or a black boy. He'd yell 'Mamma, so and so in the yard—sic 'em Shep,' and Mrs. Miller would come out and I'd have to leave."[54] North did not relate just how the Millers' parrot learned to distinguish between races, and unfortunately, he offered no opinion of people who would threaten to unleash a dog on a child simply because he was black.

Surely it annoyed a former slave master like G. W. Miller that Kansas had become such a haven for blacks—an increasing number of them moved into the western frontier in the late 1800s. At first, blacks came as United States Army troopers (dubbed "buffalo soldiers" by the Cheyennes and other tribes because their hair appeared similar to that of the buffalo), then as scouts and cowboys, and eventually as homesteaders eager to settle on free government land.[55]

During the Millers' years in Kansas, several African-American towns were organized, especially when Benjamin "Pap" Singleton, a former slave from Tennessee, helped stir the "exodus" of 1879–1880, when an estimated twenty thousand African-Americans—called "Exodusters"—left the South for the free lands of Kansas.[56] Known as the "Black Moses," Singleton organized an all-black town named for him, five miles north of Baxter Springs. Singleton also helped to settle Nicodemus, one of several other towns established in Kansas by black pioneers and used as a model of black independence in the West.[57]

In keeping with his concerns about the great numbers of blacks who flocked to Kansas, G. W. Miller vehemently opposed his offspring associating with black children.[58] Although Miller and his wife appreciated the cultural and social activities of Winfield, they kept their children out of local schools. Instead, the Millers employed private tutors who came to the home to teach Alma, Zack, and little George.[59]

By the close of the 1880s, on winter evenings after the servants had disappeared and the children were tucked into their feather beds upstairs, G.W. and Molly relished their brief moments together. These two, who represented a curious mixture of old southern traditions and new western ambitions, could sit before a smoldering fire and almost read the future in the pale wood smoke that climbed up the tall chimney and vanished into the heavens. The Millers saw prosperity in their future. They realized they were regaining the wealth and security they had once known in the blue-grass country of Kentucky.

THE BIG DIE-UP

THE LUXURIES OF the Miller home notwithstanding, there was nothing romantic about a cowpuncher's life.[1] Colonel G. W. Miller knew that from his first days as a cattleman. So did his three sons, long before they reached their teens and faced untold dangers and challenges on the range.[2]

Beyond stampedes, perilous river crossings, and rustlers, cowboys and drovers endured drought, torrential rain, hail and snowstorms, stinging sleet, mud and quicksand, tornadoes, range fires, venomous snakes, mosquitoes, and ticks. Nature struck heavy blows at man and beast throughout the West, and the Miller family and others in the cattle business unquestionably realized that each season on the trails and rangelands held its own terrors.

The scorching summer sun, choking clouds of dust, hailstones the size of quail eggs, and violent thunderstorms ranked high on any cowboy's list of miseries. Indeed, lightning was one of the most common causes of death for a cowboy in the late 1800s.[3] One cowboy on the Salt Fork in Kansas remembered lightning that "would hit the side of those hills and gouge out great holes in the earth like a bomb had struck them, and it killed seven or eight cattle in the herd back of us."[4] Still, many of the veteran cowhands argued that winter was the worst time of the year.

Icy blizzards struck the prairies with astonishing fury, and particularly wicked north winds, known as "blue northers," or "blue whistlers," quickly dropped temperatures to well below freezing.[5] "To one who, when ridin' far out on the wide plains, experienced the sudden blizzard out of the north sweepin' in fury across the land, it was an experience he never forgot," wrote Ramon F. Adams, salty chronicler on the West. "The howlin', freezin' wind drivin', swirlin', blindin' sheets of knifelike sleet and powdery snow that stung your face and seemed to smother you as it blotted out the rest of the world left you with a sense of absolute desolation and helplessness."[6]

Often, the most severe storms did not observe the calender and struck in late autumn or early spring. Whenever blizzards occurred, the more seasoned cowboys understood that blowing snow could blind them and the cattle. Riders wrapped up their heads and worked hard to keep herds on the move and away from fences and ravines so cattle would not stack up and perish. By the end of a long day in the saddle, booted feet sometimes were frozen so stiff the cowboys could not walk.

Frostbite could leave a man crippled or even dead. Pneumonia also took a heavy toll. Those who made their living as cowboys sometimes relied on "saddlebag doctors," often called "sawbones," who rode the range and carried medicines and surgical instruments in saddlebags.[7] Yet many cowboys were skeptical of frontier physicians and preferred to use their own trail remedies. To relieve stomach cramps caused by drinking alkali water, Tom White, a 101 Ranch cowboy in the 1880s, ingested a bit of Jamaica ginger, an herb he always carried with him on the trail.[8] A common remedy for frostbite was scraping a raw Irish potato and applying it to fingers, feet, and ears. Some cowboys fought off chills by wearing nutmeg on a string around their necks.[9] Some cowhands adopted the more accepted medical practices of the day, such as the treatment for frostbite from a popular home manual published in 1889: "Never permit warm water, warm air, or a fire anywhere near the parts frozen until the natural temperature is nearly restored, and then the utmost care must be used to avert serious consequences. Rub the frozen part with snow—the patient being in a cold room—and apply ice-water. The circulation should be restored very slowly. When reaction comes on, warm milk containing a little stimulant of some kind should be given."[10]

But during the winter of 1886–1887, even an ocean of the most powerful stimulants could not have fended off the winter blasts that descended on cow country across the American West.[11] That devastating winter brought blizzards that swept the Great Plains from the Canadian border to Texas like a serial killer and left millions of head of livestock dead, many ranchers ruined, and the entire cattle industry changed forever.[12] Because of the enormous losses, especially on the northern cattle ranges, that long winter came to be called the "Great Die-Up," or the "Big Die-Up."[13] That terrible season destroyed perhaps as much as 90 percent of the range animals and put a stop to fresh beef on the nation's dinner tables for years.[14]

Early in the winter of 1886, just before the snows began and temperatures dropped, eighteen-year-old Joe Miller—well on his way to becoming a ranching partner with his father—rode into Tulsa, a Creek settlement on the Arkansas River in Indian Territory, still affectionately called Tulsey Town by some Indian and white settlers.[15] There Joe purchased eleven hundred three-year-old steers at eleven dollars a head.[16]

After the roundup, Joe and his cowboys drove the herd to the Miller grazing pastures in the Cherokee Outlet, where they fed the cattle wagonloads of corn purchased from Kansas farmers.[17] Feed was at a premium because of an especially dry summer. To eliminate waste, Joe had asked the farmers to break each ear of corn in two by hitting it over a wagon sideboard so the steers would have bite-sized pieces. Yet even this shrewd tactic was not enough.

In the end, after all the expenses were tallied, the herd failed to earn the Millers a dime of profit.[18] But by that time, the wind was blowing hard and snow was falling as never before. The Millers and every other cattle outfit knew they were in for a long, mean season.

For several years, disaster had loomed. Overstocking of Texas ranges, combined with lack of moisture, had hurt the cattle industry as early as 1883. By the following year, prices had started to drop.[19] Although later boom times occurred, decline generally continued as wire fences went up and free range disappeared. The years from 1885 to 1890 were about as bad as any for most range cattlemen.[20]

Another sign of impending doom that alerted some cattleman prior to that disastrous winter of 1886 was the severe drought of the preceding summer. It left throats parched, grasslands withered, and streams and water holes dried up.[21] Nearly all of cow country was seared brown as tobacco, drier than the heart of a haystack; old-timers experiencing the dust bowl fifty years later could compare their misery with the conditions of the summer of 1886. Up in the Dakotas, a rancher named Lincoln Lang noted that "like a huge, sullen, glowing ball, the sun arose each morning through a cloud of haze that seemed to have settled upon the country. . . . Temperatures ranging up to 120 degrees in the shade was [sic] common."[22]

Throughout Kansas and Indian Territory that summer, cowhands spit cotton and rode through veils of smoke and ash as they stamped out prairie fires and listened to their bosses moan about the shortage of feed and the steadily falling price of beef in Chicago.[23] The cattle that managed to survive that brutal summer were already thin and weak and made good buzzard bait when snowstorms and subzero temperatures hit.

The historic winter of 1886–1887 struck particularly hard on the northern plains, where geese and ducks flew south more than a month early, muskrat fur was thicker than ever before and, for the first time in a generation, white arctic owls made an appearance.[24] Storm after storm swept across the countryside from Canada to Mexico, leaving snowdrifts one hundred feet high in some places, while temperatures plummeted to record lows. In parts of the plains, it snowed every day except three in February 1887.[25] Cows aborted entire calf crops, and desperate herds of starved cattle chewed tarpaper from the walls of ranch houses and ate wool off the carcasses of sheep.

So complete was the destruction that some men quit ranching and moved off the range after spring thaws came and they viewed piles of decaying animal bodies and rivers clogged with dead cattle. "A business that had been fascinating to me before, suddenly became distasteful," Granville Stuart, a Montana cattle baron, wrote years after the Big Die-Up. "I wanted no more of it. I never wanted to own again an animal that I could not feed and shelter."[26]

Stuart's son-in-law, E. C. "Teddy Blue" Abbott, also remembered that dreary time when many larger ranches went bankrupt and gave cowboys their walking papers. "The cowpunchers worked like slaves," Abbott wrote. "Think of riding all day in a blinding snowstorm, the temperature fifty and sixty below zero, and no dinner. . . . The horses' feet were cut and bleeding from the heavy crust, and the cattle had the hair and hide wore [sic] off their legs to the knees and backs. It was surely hell to see big four-year-old steers just able to stagger along. It was the same all over Wyoming, Montana, and Colorado, western Nebraska, and western Kansas."[27]

Although the winter was perhaps less severe in parts of Kansas and in Indian Territory, thousands of head of cattle starved or froze to death, some of them standing like statues.[28] Ten thousand cattle lay dead on the Kansas prairie between Garden City and Punished Woman Creek.[29] Entire families of sodbusters died from the cold, huddled in their dugouts and wooden huts. The smell of death overwhelmed the aroma of spring flowers on the prairies. Enterprising homesteaders earned a bit of money to see them through tight times by gathering animal bones and selling them to markets back east for fertilizer. Skeletons of some of the victims of the Big Die-Up still were being discovered in fields and ravines twenty years later.[30]

Even before the last thaws alleviated the immediate despair, buzzards and wolves dined on rotting carcasses. But when predators increased and threatened their small number of new calves, Colonel Miller and the other ranchers of the Cherokee Strip Live Stock Association offered a bounty of twenty dollars each for wolf pelts and $1.50 for coyotes.[31] Perhaps the killing of prairie wolves took some of the sting out of the hard times and gave Miller and the others a chance to punch back at nature.

But even as he sent out wolf hunters and parties of cowboys to skin dead steers lying in grasslands and river bottoms, G. W. Miller also had to face the hard truth. Although he had not suffered as badly as other cattlemen during the die-ups of the 1880s, Miller knew that the range never would be the same. It was the end of an era.

Chapter 17

LAND OF THE FAIR GOD

Miller fattened his cattle on the Strip [sic], *drove them to the nearest railroad points, and shipped to Chicago markets. The profits piled up; Miller expanded operations. He was building up a cattle empire and making it a big one. . . . But the thing was too good to last. . . . Then came the Man with the Hoe, the sod-busting nester who couldn't rest till he'd stuck a plow into the rich brown earth of that Strip. He wanted to own the land outright. And he meant to get it.*[1]

—Fred Gipson
Fabulous Empire

THE ferocious storms of the Big Die-Up did not last forever. Eventually the snowdrifts and ice melted. Muddy skies, brimming with frozen death, again turned clear and blue. Yet the awful winter of 1886–1887 was never forgotten. The impact devastated the cattle industry and left deep scars carved on the land and on a generation of ranchers, especially those operating on northern ranges.

Luckier cow outfits and cattlemen such as the Millers, who ran livestock in the Cherokee Outlet just before the land runs opened the future Oklahoma to white settlement, survived the savage storms that lashed across the plains. They kept at least part of their great herds of cattle alive. As his cowhands finished the grisly chore of skinning out the last of the dead and dying steers bearing the 101 brand and nursed wobbly calves to their feet, Colonel Miller and his fellow ranchers learned hard lessons from nature's wrath.[2]

"The tragic blizzards of 1886–1887 proved that cattle could not just be turned loose upon the High Plains to care for themselves," as Laurence Ivan Seidman wrote years later. "Ranchers would have to buy land from the government, fence it in, and provide feed for the winter if the cattle were to survive. Stockmen would have to share the land with farmers moving west in response to free and cheap government and railroad-promoted land."[3]

Despite the persistent perils of natural catastrophe, the Millers and other ranchers and their range riders learned to harden themselves and blunt their sensibilities. After a strong blizzard, cowboys who rode out into the grazing lands to salvage at least some part of a steer's value found it easier to cut the throats of dying animals and skin them while they were still warm than to try to skin a frozen-stiff critter.[4] This was just one of many violent aspects of the cowboy's work life, from branding and castrating cattle to the often traumatic experience of breaking green ponies, when bronc busters beat in the lesson that defiance brought instant retribution.

Cowboys formed an adversarial relationship with nature and were apt to consider almost all forms of untamed animal life as potential dangers or as competition for cattle. Life was cheap and retaliation was instantaneous. Any stray dog was considered a threat or nuisance to cattle and was usually shot on sight.[5] So were skunks, the animal most likely to carry rabies. Small animals, birds, snakes, and turtles made convenient targets for shooting contests during lulls in cowhands' often monotonous work schedule. Sometimes a bored cowhand was known to take a potshot at a fly on the bunkhouse ceiling. After an eighteen-hour day of riding fence lines and tending herds, cowhands took pleasure in setting loose packs of hounds to run down predators and varmints.

When a wolf or coyote den was located, a favorite ploy was to have a wiry cowboy squeeze through the narrow tunnel with a candle in one hand and a pistol in the other.[6] When the candle's glow reflected in the pups' eyes, the cowboy blasted away. During one such episode, veteran 101 Ranch cowboy Charles Orr almost met his match in a wolf den when his shot missed its mark. The frantic mother wolf scrambled to escape and wedged herself on Orr's back. After clawing off most of the screaming man's skin, the wolf burst from the tunnel only to be shot by another cowboy waiting outside. Orr had to be dug out of the ground like a wounded gopher and have his injuries doctored.[7]

The cowboys were often remarkably cruel to the cattle as well.[8] To make a headstrong cow budge, some punchers rubbed sand in its eyes or twisted the tail until the bone snapped.[9] "Anyone who's taken part in a gathering, roping, branding, dehorning, castrating, ear notching, wattle clipping, or winching a calf from its mother knows how mean and tough and brutal it can be," wrote twentieth-century social critic Edward Abbey. "And if the cowboy's mind and sensibilities have not been permanently deformed by that kind of work, he'll admit it. Brutal work tends to bring out the brutality in all of us."[10]

Generally, the men who paid cowboys' wages condoned such behavior. Bosses demanded that hired hands do whatever it took to get the job done. Sometimes that meant breaking the law. As Texas writer J. Frank Dobie put it, "The distinction between 'mine' and 'thine' . . . became so loose that perhaps a majority of ranch people followed the custom of killing only other people's cattle for beef."[11]

Working cowboys had to be double-backboned, in the vernacular of that time, and capable of committing acts of larceny and even murder, if it would benefit their cattle outfit. They faced blue northers and dust storms, tamed mustangs, scared off squatters, and chased cow thieves without giving quarter. Just to survive in the Oklahoma country, which one territorial newspaperman called the "Land of the Fair God," men had to be resilient and resourceful.[12] If they had a touch of felon's blood in their veins, so much the better. This was the breed of man that George Washington Miller and his family hired to ride for their 101 brand. And they were the kind of men the Millers sought as friends and allies, even after the passing of the trails.

By the late 1880s, with the coming of the Santa Fe Railway to the Cherokee Outlet, the glory days of countless cattle drives over trails from the Lone Star state neared an end.[13] Since 1871, Colonel Miller had stocked his Indian Territory ranches with longhorns driven up the dusty Texas trails, but by 1888, he relied more on the railroad for shipping cattle to his grazing lands during spring.[14] After the herds grew fat on lush grass, Miller packed them off by train to northern markets for slaughter in late summer and early autumn.

Joseph Miller, by then a strapping young man of twenty years, continued to use the old Texas cow trails for a few more years. He also took over increasing responsibility in the Millers' operations in the Cherokee Outlet and at Hunnewell, Kansas. In 1885, G. W. Miller had purchased six outlots totaling about ninety-three acres from the Town Company.[15] The Millers used the land for shelters, feed storage, and cattle pens. They also kept a crew of bronc busters and wranglers there, working year-round to turn green horses into saddle mounts that eventually made their way into the outfits' remudas.[16]

In those turbulent years just prior to the Oklahoma land runs in 1889 and later, some of the Millers' best hired hands worked out of Hunnewell. Named for a railroad official, the town had been established in 1880 on a four-hundred-acre site at the southern edge of the Cherokee Strip in Kansas, adjacent to the Cherokee Outlet.[17]

Those were heady times for the Miller cowboys, especially after payday. Marshals and a police judge hired by the railroad had all they could do just to keep order. A popular haunt for most of the cowboys around Hunnewell was the Red Light, a combination tavern and brothel, but many other establishments were equally notorious.[18] Eventually, the east side of town—lined with gambling dens, saloons, and dance halls—became known as "Smoky Row."[19] Sometimes cowpunchers' fistfights and arguments over women and cards spilled into the streets and gunfire erupted. When the old Hale Hotel (formerly called the Hunnewell House and Santa Fe Hotel) was razed in 1939, more than seventy pounds of lead was recovered from the white pine boards, tangible evidence of the many gun battles that took place inside and outside the establishment. The rowdy hotel was even immortalized in a song, by H. H. Halsell:

> *"The trail outfit is entering Hunnewell;*
> *The candles are lit in the Hale Hotel.*
> *There will be music and dancing all through the night,*
> *Courting and loving until broad daylight."*[20]

But Hunnewell was not just a place for cowpunchers to let off steam. Colonel Miller and other area ranchers who used the little railroad town for a shipping point could not let things get too far out of hand. In 1889 alone, 749 loads of cattle were shipped via the Frisco out of Hunnewell, while the Santa Fe shipped 762 loads of bellowing beeves to market.[21] This staggering productivity required excellent workers, and some of the best cowboys ever to rope and ride hired on with the Miller family during this period, including Charles Orr and Charles W. Hannah.[22] Several of the older hands had ridden with G.W. since that first cattle drive, in the winter of 1871. Jim Rainwater, who as a youth had kept a diary during the Millers' first trail drives, still worked as one of the outfit's head cowboys. So did George Van Hook, known for years as "the dean of Oklahoma cowboys."[23] Van Hook, who had come from Kentucky to Newtonia, was considered the Millers' right-hand man when the 101 brand first was used in the Cherokee Outlet. Van Hook eventually would spend fifty-three years as a cowboy, twenty-eight of which were in the Millers' employ.[24]

George Miller hired Jimmy Moore at Hunnewell in 1880.[25] Dublin born and "stoop-shouldered, with eyes bright as a squirrel's," the tough little Irishman took a special shine to Zack Miller. When Zack was old enough to join his father and brother Joe out on the range, Jimmy Moore already had taught the youngster how to handle a lariat by roping chickens, goats, and every fence post in sight.[26]

By the time he was twelve, Zack had his own hired hand, a youngster named Bert Colby.[27] Bert was barely eight years old when G.W. hired him to look after a herd of goats he had acquired for Zack. The Colby boy herded Zack's goats along the Walnut River at Winfield at the wage of fifty cents a day for twelve hours' work. Destined to become one of Zack's best friends for life, Colby worked his way up through the ranks, and after a few years joined the Miller cowboys on the cattle ranges.[28]

Some of the cowhands riding for the Millers were kinfolk, such as John Hiatt, nephew of Colonel Miller and the one always remembered for having ignited the first 101 branding fire, and W. A. Brooks, a cousin from Kentucky, who stayed with the Millers for many years. Walter T. "Uncle Doc" Miller, G.W.'s brother, was also a familiar figure around the horse pens at Hunnewell and at the Miller ranchlands in the Cherokee Outlet.[29]

"Uncle Doc was a medium-sized, brown-haired man who hung out at the ranch as if he was hiding from somebody," wrote Fred Gipson in *Fabulous Empire*. "He never went to town; he never went anywhere. He just stayed out at the ranch headquarters, spending most of his time cooking. . . . A time or two, Zack got the idea that it was a woman Uncle Doc was dodging; he never did know. But Uncle Doc was always powerful bitter about women for some reason or another."[30]

Known as somewhat of a prude, a teetotaler, and a Bible thumper, Doc Miller later became an ardent supporter of Carry Nation, the militant reformer and hatchet-wielding prohibitionist.[31] Family members recalled how, out on the range, Uncle Doc usually ended up in heated arguments with Irishman Jimmy Moore who, like most profane cowpunchers, was particularly fond of strong drink and mischief. Between squabbles with Moore, Doc frequently became embroiled in furious disagreements with his brother G.W.[32] Most of the disputes were over Colonel Miller's belief in the value of smooth sipping whiskey and his steadfast admiration of cowboys "with the hair on"—men such as Jimmy Moore who could drink, gamble, cuss, and howl at the moon, but knew when to draw the line and avoid getting into too much trouble.[33]

When Uncle Doc was not instigating a "hell and damnation" quarrel with his brother or convincing some youngster not to throw away his meager wages in the sinful dens of Hunnewell's Smoky Row, he did his fair share of range cooking for the outfit.[34] Yet despite any culinary skills he might have possessed, Uncle Doc was by no means the most famous of the cowboy chefs who bossed chuck wagons for Colonel Miller and his boys. That honor went to Oscar E. Brewster, who put in nine years as a cook on the range and trail, mostly for the Millers, before he quit cowboy life to become a schoolteacher.[35]

During those years leading up to the 1893 land run, which opened the millions of acres of the Cherokee Outlet to hordes of white settlers, cowhands riding for the Millers spent weeks at a time on the open range branding calves and working cattle. To a man, they always claimed the tastiest meals were served up at Oscar Brewster's chuck wagon.[36] Brewster, the men recalled, slung hash like a man possessed. In 1890, he set the open-prairie record of cooking three meals a day for forty-five to eighty-five hands during a twenty-one-day period at one of the Millers' annual roundups east of the Salt Fork of the Arkansas River.[37]

Brewster recollected when he was an old man, during a conversation with historian J. Frank Dobie,

> When they offered me the job, they said they would pay me a dollar and a half a day and furnish me a helper, or give me two and a half a day if I wanted to do the work without a helper. I took the two and a half. At first the men were coming in to eat at all times of the night. Joe Miller got after them and told me not to keep open all night long. I could generally get to bed by ten o'clock and would sleep till three.
>
> The noon meal, when they ate like starved bears, was apt to be the most rushed. I've cooked many a dinner with the horses standing in the harness. I would drive up to water, trying also to get close to wood, somewhere in the vicinity of where the noon roundup was to be. The first thing after jumping down from the wagon I'd shovel me a trench, lay wood in it and then, as soon as the coals were ready, would have the meat on—some of it roasting, some stewing in a pot. That time when I was feeding forty-five men at a single meal, I cooked a calf or a yearling every day, with plenty of beans and potatoes besides.[38]

Brewster turned out magnificent piecrust with a rolling pin he had fashioned from a walnut tree on the Canadian River. He also was a master with a Dutch oven, and made sure cowboys always had plenty of hot bread and sourdough biscuits at every meal, and oceans of scalding coffee.[39]

"There was a big fellow in the country named Theo Baughman," Brewster remembered. "He pretended to be a trail guide, but he never knew much. He was a kind of commission agent too, representing traders in Caldwell, Kansas, or other cow towns. He weighed three hundred pounds.

One day when I had coffee and dinner all ready for my outfit of thirteen men, here rode Baughman into camp. I asked him to take a drink of coffee, and believe me or not, he picked up a gallon coffee pot off the fire, boiling hot and full too, and drank it dry."[40]

Brewster's favorite roundup boss remained Joe Miller, who was particularly popular with many of the cowboys in the Cherokee Outlet.[41] He was still in his early twenties when he was made a captain of the eastern division of his family's holdings, in charge of an area that reached from the Rock Island Railroad to the Arkansas River and accounted for one-third of the Millers' range operations.[42] In 1890 alone, Joe Miller's cowboy crews rounded up more than twenty-eight thousand head of cattle.[43] But by then, Joe, like his astute father, was quite aware that time was running out for ranchers trying to make a living in the Cherokee Outlet.

It was impossible for the Millers to avoid the parade of white home-seekers known as Boomers who continued to gather on the Kansas border and made repeated attempts to colonize the unoccupied Indian land, or "Unassigned Lands," just below the Cherokee Outlet, that became known as the "Oklahoma country." Even though soldiers continued to remove the invaders, the Boomers pressed their cause and won over powerful political allies in Washington, D.C.[44] Soon public opinion turned in favor of the would-be homesteaders, poised to burst out of Kansas like hungry locusts.

Conditions were ripe for the lands to be opened. In 1887, Congress passed the Dawes Severalty Act.[45] This landmark legislation stipulated that all the Indians in Indian Territory, with the exception of the Five Tribes (or, as most people condescendingly called them, the Five Civilized Tribes), should be persuaded to accept individual land allotments and that the remainder of tribal property be opened to white settlers.[46] The Dawes Act became the official policy of the federal government, and commissions were formed to visit the Indian lands in Indian Territory.

Their appetites whetted, the Boomers and other advocates of opening territorial lands soon pressed for more congressional action. Their success finally came on March 3, 1889, when a rider called the Springer Amendment was attached to the Indian Appropriations Bill providing for the opening of the Unassigned Lands—about two million acres in the center of Indian Territory—to white settlement.[47] In March 1889, President Benjamin Harrison, in his third week of office, issued a proclamation for settling the territory.[48]

Like most other cattlemen, George Miller vehemently opposed the legislation because it authorized the appointment of a commission to negotiate with the Cherokees for the eventual purchase of the Cherokee Outlet.[49] Such opposition, however, could not stop the inevitable. At high noon on April 22, 1889—a clear, bright Monday—fifty thousand homeseekers gathered along the borders of the Unassigned Lands. They waited for the bugle blast, the pistol shots, and the wave of the flag signaling the first Oklahoma land run or, as many people called it, "the Harrison Horse Race."[50]

Settlers used any available means of transportation as they raced to stake their claims.[51] Thousands spilled across the plains on horseback and in racing sulkies, farm wagons, and fringe-topped surreys. Others came by steam engine and bicycles, and a few even ran on foot. By nightfall, settlers had staked out the towns of Guthrie, Oklahoma City, Kingfisher, El Reno, Stillwater, and Norman.[52]

As the Millers and their cowboys watched silently from horseback on their cattle ranges, thousands of homesteaders rushed through the outlet to the Unassigned Lands. Before the dust had settled and the newcomers had slapped together the last of the tent towns and crude shacks, G.W. and his son Joe realized there would be no stopping others who wanted to grab pieces of real estate. For the past decade, all the Millers had heard were the cries, "On to Oklahoma!" The increasing clamor would be for the lands of the Cherokee Outlet, and they knew nothing could stop the roar.

SHANGHAI PIERCE

DESPITE THE POPULAR mythology, G. W. Miller never believed there was anything romantic or glamorous about cows or cowboys.[1] Miller's primary goal was to make money in cattle. He did not give a hoot about creating legends or "winning the West." Primarily a hardheaded businessman, Miller never could be accused of being a purveyor of myth, such as Buffalo Bill Cody, nor did he ever resemble the capricious frontier characters created by dime novelists of that era.[2]

Through his long years on cattle trails and ranges, Colonel Miller became acquainted with like-minded men. Most of them were tough and spirited ranchers and cowmen operating out of Texas, the Cherokee Outlet, Kansas, and elsewhere in the West during the prime years of the cattle trails.

Some of them, such as Texan Lee Kokernut, were partners with Miller at one time or another.[3] But even if he did not know them personally, Colonel Miller undoubtedly was well aware of the reputations—both good and bad—of the most illustrious figures associated with the cattle industry. Although not in the same league as some of the cowmen when it came to the size and scope of their ranches, Miller was just as self-reliant and headstrong as the larger operators. A few of them created dynasties that they believed would last through the ages.[4] Known as cattle barons or cattle kings—both disparaging terms—these men took on an almost legendary status, despite their no-nonsense attitude toward business.[5]

Included in their ranks was Captain Richard King, son of Irish immigrants and founder of the King Ranch empire. Charles Goodnight, with Oliver Loving, blazed the famous Goodnight-Loving Trail from Texas to Kansas and was credited with having invented the chuck wagon. Samuel A. Maverick was the Texan responsible for the name *maverick*, applied to all unbranded range cattle. John T. Lytle, a trail driver, had property in Kansas, Colorado, and Montana which ended up worth almost ten million dollars.[6]

But out of the whole bunch, there was never much debate that the most flamboyant and iron willed of all the cattle-empire builders was "Shanghai"

Pierce.[7] George Washington Miller and the irrepressible Pierce were very familiar with each other and carried on an often tempestuous relationship for almost twenty years.[8]

Just a few years Miller's senior, Abel Head Pierce was born in 1834 in Rhode Island to industrious, conservative parents.[9] Tired of arguing with his straitlaced father, free-spirited Pierce left home at an early age. He eventually ended up in Texas, where he and his brother, Jonathan—a pair of transplanted Yankees—enlisted in the Confederate Army.[10]

In the Lone Star State, Pierce learned about cowboying and cattle and picked up his unusual moniker of Shanghai, which stuck for the rest of his life.[11] Several explanations have been given for how the colorful nickname came about, but six-feet-four-inch Pierce claimed it was because the large rowels, or wheels, on his custom-made spurs made him look like a fancy Shanghai rooster.[12]

Eager to make a fortune in the cattle business, Shanghai and his brother established a ranch near the Texas Gulf coast. Jonathan ran the operation while Shanghai and his cowboys rode out on the prairies and built up substantial herds by rustling, or "mavericking"—rounding up free-roving strays, branding them, and bringing them to market.[13]

But while he was building his cattle kingdom, Shanghai did all he could to discourage others, including fellow mavericker whom he and his men captured and lynched in Matagorda County, Texas, in 1871.[14] This act of ruthlessness occurred at about the time Pierce supposedly cheated a United States Army receiving agent out of 118 head of cattle by falsifying the count on a herd of government beeves.[15] It was not the first or the last time Shanghai Pierce would find himself a fugitive from justice.

Once the stray cattle were rounded up, Shanghai developed a solid line of credit with bankers and became a cattle buyer. He assembled huge herds and drove them to Cheyenne, Denver, New Orleans, or Kansas. He also became involved in various partnerships and business dealings in banks, railroads, and shipping, but the cattle trade remained his primary focus.[16]

Before long, Shanghai's exploits on the range began to take on mythic qualities. He was a skilled self-promoter and perhaps as big a braggart as ever emerged from Texas. Shang—as friends and business associates such as G. W. Miller called him—lived up to his colorful image as he gathered herds of mossbacked longhorns called "sea lions" because of their swimming prowess.[17] Hundreds of old-time cowhands remembered Shang and the roar of his foghorn voice. He left a lasting impression, riding into cattle camps, always accompanied by his black servant, Neptune Holmes, astride a pack mule laden with saddlebags crammed with enough gold coin to buy entire herds.[18]

At about the time George Miller started to trail cattle out of Texas, he began to hear tales of Shanghai Pierce. Likewise, Pierce started to hear about Miller. During one of Miller's early sojourns with a swarm of cow-hunters in Texas, he ventured into Brazos County, where he encountered a successful cattle buyer and merchant named H. B. English.[19] Because Miller and his brother-in-law George Carson had established a thriving store at Newtonia, Missouri, it seemed expedient to become partners with English in a mercantile operation in Texas. They reached agreement, and soon the firm of Miller and English was turning quite a profit.[20]

The partners captured part of the cowboy market both coming and going. English sold supplies to drovers headed north up the trail, and Miller restocked the cattlemen for their return. Pierce, who had been buying cattle from English, began to use Miller and English as his chief source of supplies.[21]

Even after Miller and his family got out of the mercantile industry, Shanghai and G.W. continued to do business in the cattle trade and developed a friendship. It was said that whenever G. W. Miller and Shanghai Pierce got together—whether at Pierce's ranch, on the trail, or in a drinking establishment at Hunnewell—to share a jug of strong drink, the two cattlemen roared like range bulls at rutting time.[22] Their mutual esteem, however, did not last. About the time the government was getting ready to open the Cherokee Outlet for white settlement, the relationship between Colonel Miller and Shanghai Pierce started to erode.[23] Their tangles over cattle deals resulted in disagreements that could not be patched up.

Again, like a pair of bellowing bulls, it seemed there was room for only one of them in the pasture. Neither of the proud and stubborn cowmen would bend. They became bitter enemies and traded accusations and threats. They even tried to kill each other, and when that failed, they did their level best to ruin each other's reputation.[24] They remained in that impasse for the rest of their lives.

Chapter 18

THE RUN OF '93

The year 1893 was momentous not only for the country but it was mighty damn important for the Miller family. It was a time marked by an extraordinary world's fair and a devastating economic depression. Then on September 16, 1893, millions of acres of Indian lands in the Cherokee Outlet were opened. And on that very same date, the Hundred and One Ranch was officially born.[1]

—Zack T. Miller Jr., 1988

ONCE the great Oklahoma land runs commenced, the veteran cattlemen, more comfortable on old cow trails guzzling creek-water coffee than at home with their families, acknowledged that their lives never would be the same. The time of the drover had come to an abrupt and rather unceremonious conclusion.

Out on the boundless grasslands, savvy range riders with plenty of horse sense felt the pulse of the land quicken. Even tenderfeet—cowhands still green enough not to know manure from wild honey—realized that the enormous white wave of anxious sodbusters, Boomers, and homesteaders never could be stemmed.

After Congress passed the Organic Act in 1890, which divided Indian Territory into two parts and established an Oklahoma Territory government with a capital at Guthrie, it was clear as a preacher's piss that the settlers would keep coming.[2] The land run of 1889 was just the beginning. That frantic stampede of land-hungry white pilgrims was the first of five runs; other Indian lands eventually were opened to white settlement by lottery and sealed bids. Most everyone's attention turned toward the Cherokee Outlet, where some of the most desirable land made the nesters' mouths water.[3]

G. W. Miller and his son Joe sensed the change approaching on the prairie winds. So did their bronc breakers at Hunnewell, Kansas, and the cow bosses who oversaw the two big Miller spreads in the Cherokee Outlet. All of them recognized that the improbable covenant between the Indians and the cattlemen who leased grazing pastures was about to end.[4]

The harsh realization must have been more sobering to G. W. Miller than one of Uncle Doc's biting temperance lectures, delivered in a cold autumn rain after a night spent sipping snake-head whisky. And whether it was in a saloon on Hunnewell's Smoky Row or after supper with some of his men at a remote line camp, G.W. did not have to hunt far to find an excuse to take a bracing snort or two. There was little to offer any encouragement in the 1890s for any cattleman in the Cherokee Outlet.[5]

Colonel Miller and other members of the Cherokee Strip Live Stock Association still were smarting over the federal government's voiding of their five-year renewal lease that the Cherokees had approved in 1888 at an annual fee of two hundred thousand dollars, double the original rental price.[6] The government had broken its word to white men as well as to Indians. Pressured by homesteaders and by farm and railroad interests, federal officials declared that because the Cherokees had failed to use the outlet as an easement, they had no right to lease the lands to cattle operators.[7]

Then President Benjamin Harrison, bolstered by an opinion from the attorney general, issued a proclamation forbidding any further grazing in the Cherokee Outlet and ordering all cattle to be removed by October 1, 1890.[8] Even though that deadline was extended to December 1, the results were the same. Harrison's proclamation doomed the last remaining hopes of the Cherokee Strip Live Stock Association, disrupted Indians living in the region, and created total chaos in the livestock industry when as many as 250,000 head of cattle were removed from the outlet.[9]

The association was well on its way to disbanding, although it took until about the time of the outlet's opening in 1893 for that actually to occur. Beginning in 1889, demoralized association members were forced to sell off as many of their cattle as possible and search for new pasturelands for their remaining stock.[10] Most of the ranchers and cattle companies sustained heavy financial losses, and some went bankrupt. Although under pressure and feeling the strain, the Millers were not among them.

Colonel Miller thumbed his nose at the government and rolled the dice. He and his boys refused to leave their two big pastures, the Deer Creek and the Salt Fork, which they had leased from the Indians for years. Instead of heeding President Harrison's orders to depart, the Miller outfits stayed in the outlet for more than two years beyond the deadline.[11] Miller felt that he had no choice. As Fred Gipson later wrote, "The backbone to all of

G.W.'s fast-building fortunes was the grassland he controlled on the Strip [Cherokee Outlet]. The big cowman bawled his wrath at government interference till he could be heard half across Kansas; then he rode down to the Salt Fork to talk it over with Jimmy Moore."[12]

G.W. told Moore and the other cowboys to take down the barbed-wire fences and roll them up. Miller's compliance with the government decree stopped there. He instructed Moore and the other foremen to keep the herds grazing on the two outlet spreads. They also posted riders as lookouts so the cattle could be moved at the first sight of mounted army patrols, assigned to enforce the ban on cattle.[13] When black troopers, known as buffalo soldiers, rode into the Salt Fork pasture in pursuit of the Miller cowboys, they were decoyed easily toward the river.[14] Usually the soldiers, unwitting of the danger, plunged their horses up to their bellies in quicksand bogs. Before panic set in, the Miller cowhands appeared from out of nowhere. They threw ropes to the trapped men, pulled them to safety, and led the bedraggled soldiers to a line camp for hot grub and some rest by a warm fire. The standard story the Miller cowhands told the troopers was that the herd of cattle was being trailed out of Texas and was bound for Kansas.[15]

Ordinarily, the ploy worked, but if the cowboys' hospitality was not enough to win over the soldiers, Jimmy Moore presented the highest-ranking man with the gift of a sturdy Indian pony or slipped him a few twenty-dollar gold pieces. For Colonel Miller, the payment of bribes to meddlesome soldiers was simply another necessary business expense, much like the rent he had paid to the Cherokees for years.[16] Yet despite his success at deceiving soldiers, Miller knew his illegal grazing on outlet lands could not last forever.

Meanwhile, the Cherokees became aware that that they too were fighting a losing battle with the federal government as well as with outlet cattlemen who no longer forked over lease fees to the tribe. A congressional commission appointed to work with the Cherokees and negotiate the sale of the outlet finally made an offer, which the tribe had no choice but to accept.[17] Late in 1891, the Cherokees gave up their rights to the outlet lands for $8,595,736.12, less than half what the tribe had been offered years earlier by the syndicate of cattlemen.[18]

As preparations began for the big land opening and government surveyors began to divide the Cherokee Outlet into 160-acre homesteads, G. W. Miller met with Joe and some of the most trusted foremen. They decided to give up their Deer Creek and Salt Fork Ranches. Immediately, they turned to their old friends the Poncas for help.[19]

Joe Miller, using his Ponca language skills, led negotiations for leasing lands with White Eagle and the other Ponca leaders. Many years later, Fred Gipson discussed Joe's role in the establishment of the 101 Ranch: "G.W. had to have grass located for his herds before the opening of the Strip [sic] that was to come in the fall of 1893; so in the spring of '92 he sent his oldest son Joe down to the Ponca Reservation [sic] to make a trade for grazing rights on the Ponca lands. Joe had no trouble carrying out the mission. White Eagle, head chief of the Poncas, hadn't forgotten how Joe and G.W. had helped to find land for him and his people when they were homeless. The Millers and the Poncas had been friends ever since and now White Eagle was glad for a chance to return a favor."[20]

At White Eagle's recommendation, the government agent for the Poncas agreed that the Miller family eventually could lease tens of thousands of acres at the annual rate of one cent per acre. Although it took years for the Millers to acquire that much leased acreage and obtain title to some of the land, White Eagle and the other chieftains promised that the lease would remain renewable forever. Eventually, the Millers negotiated a similar contract with the Otoe tribe.[21]

Throughout late 1892, as G.W.'s cowboys herded cattle from the outlet pastures to the new range on the banks of the Salt Fork River in Ponca and Otoe country, preparations were under way for the official opening of the Cherokee Outlet.[22] Interest in those lands increased in May 1893 when a business panic rocked the nation, triggering a massive depression that lasted for four years.[23] Banks failed and unemployment soared. As a result, the proposed opening of the Cherokee Outlet, which was being touted across the nation, attracted an even greater number of farmers and potential homeseekers.[24]

On August 19, 1893, President Grover Cleveland issued a proclamation which set the date for the opening of the Cherokee Outlet and the surplus lands of the Tonkawa and Pawnee Indians at high noon on September 16.[25] The Miller family was ready. By that time, Joe had been made a full partner in the family livestock business. His name was printed alongside G.W.'s on the Millers' official letterhead. which bore the image of a Texas longhorn steer.[26]

Joe was prepared to grab his share of the outlet for himself and his family. So was a multitude of others. For weeks before the land opening, men and women gathered along the southern boundary of Kansas, just above the outlet. As with the run of 1889, they came in wagons, carts, buggies, bicycles, and on horseback. Some walked.[27] The ones most anxious to claim a prime piece of real estate went first to the Dakotas, Montana, or Wyoming to procure and train western-bred broncos, known for speed and endurance. One fellow journeyed all the way to Idaho and spent three months driving a herd of horses back to the edge of the Cherokee Outlet.[28]

True to his heritage, Joe Miller chose a pure-blooded steed from the Bluegrass State. Many years later, an account of his participation in the Cherokee Outlet land rush was included in promotional material used by the Miller brothers in their Wild West shows.[29] Joe's exciting ride on a sleek Kentucky bay read better than fact—it was the stuff of dime novels.

A Miller publication of 1908 read, "In the course of time Oklahoma was opened to white settlement, and a youth sat at noon on a thoroughbred Kentucky racehorse, near the Chilocco Indian school, a few miles south of Arkansas City, Kansas. Surrounding him were thousands of home-hungry persons, in naked wagons, ahorse and afoot, all feverishly intent on making the race into the new land for a homestead. The richest prizes lay along the river courses, and speed and endurance were the essentials. Many looked with envy upon the blooded racer and his exuberant rider. . . . As the sun reached the meridian, a United States Army officer raised his pistol and fired. His troopers sprang aside and loosed the great army of homeseekers."[30]

Out of the throng of homesteaders and adventurers leaped the Kentucky bay, bound straight south for the promised land. Joe, perched on his fine mount, and a line of other people gathered near Chilocco Indian School charged across the boundary eight minutes early when an excited soldier accidentally fired his gun.[31] A hundred thousand people rushed from scores of other points along the border. They headed for tracts surveyed into homesteads, counties, townships, sections, and quarter sections, with townsites staked at convenient distances. From the second the crack of gunfire echoed across the plains, Joe and his fleet horse kept the lead and soon disappeared over the horizon.[32]

It was a ride of forty miles, but before sunset, Joe had reached a bend in the Salt Fork of the Arkansas River on the edge of the Ponca lands.[33] He reined the horse, slipped from the saddle, and planted a flag in the ground. The horse, strained and spent from the race across the outlet, sank to its knees and died. Joe, also completely exhausted, dropped to the ground beside the animal and fell fast asleep.[34]

Although the Millers had been in the area for some time, the staking of land for a proper headquarters marked the formal establishment of a new Miller ranch. This ranch would bear the name of the famous stock brand the family had used proudly for several years—the 101.[35] A new era had begun for the Miller family.

THE GREAT WHITE CITY

In many ways, 1893 proved to be the most pivotal year of all for Colonel G. W. Miller and his family. With the official founding of the 101 Ranch, G.W.'s vision of a great western "plantation" was to be realized at long last.[1] Indeed, it was a time characterized by enormous contrast and change across the nation. The events of 1893 not only deeply influenced the Millers but also shaped the manner in which people would view the American West for generations to come.

In 1893, a cultural beacon gleamed brightly, far from Oklahoma Territory and the pastures along the Salt Fork. That year, on the southern tip of Lake Michigan, the city of Chicago put on an extraordinary show which captured the national imagination and offered glimpses of the future.[2] Formally dedicated in 1892 to celebrate the quadricentennial of Christopher Columbus' arrival in the Americas in 1492, the World's Columbian Exposition in Chicago was not ready to open to the public until May 1, 1893, but that did not discourage the flow of spectators.[3] Before the exposition closed six months later, more than twenty-seven million people—almost half the nation's population—had showed up to have a look.[4] They were eager to experience a spectacle that Richard Harding Davis, a prominent correspondent of the day, called "the greatest event in the history of the country since the Civil War."[5]

They came to Chicago to be lifted 264 feet into the air—two thousand passengers at a time—for fifty cents each on the world's first Ferris wheel.[6] They came to listen to the rousing military marches of John Philip Sousa and to see the first demonstration of the zipper. They came to munch on a new candied popcorn called Cracker Jack, to swig Pabst beer, and to dine on fresh cuts of beef from the fifty cattle slaughtered each morning to feed the crowds.[7] They came to view a duplicate of the Liberty Bell, to gawk at imposing Sioux chieftains "more civilized than many of their race," and to inspect an iron anchor from one of Columbus' ships.[8] They came to ogle the shapely gams of "Little Egypt, the Darling of the Nile," an audacious beauty whose belly-dancing skills on the mile-long Midway Plaisance made the word *hootchy-kootchy* part of the American vocabulary.[9]

Nearly every visitor—some arriving by boat and others riding the newly unveiled electrified "El" train—headed to Jackson Park, on the lakefront a few miles south of the downtown Loop.[10] There they roamed the 633-acre fairground site, which had been transformed from swampland into the magnificent "White City," or as some called it, "Great White City."[11]

Beyond the generous use of white paint on the architecture, White City was an appropriate name because it indicated the blatant racism that permeated the exposition and the nation it mirrored.[12] Citizens from a myriad of foreign nations were put on display. Condescending exposition officials and the general public treated most of them poorly—especially Asians and Africans. But the racism was not limited to those from overseas.

African-Americans likewise had a difficult time in Chicago. The majority of them could not land even menial jobs on the fairgrounds, and the only dining and restroom facilities for blacks were in the Haiti Building.[13] Ironically, "Aunt Jemima," the costumed black-mammy stereotype and commercial icon, made her debut at the exposition.[14] Frederick Douglass, the powerful abolitionist, and Ida Bell Wells, a former slave who had become a civil-rights activist and militant antilynching crusader, were troubled by what they found in Chicago.[15] They were among those who denounced the exclusion of blacks and produced a pamphlet titled "The Reason Why the Colored American is Not in the World's Columbian Exposition." On seeing White City in all its splendor, Douglass called it "a whited sepulchre."[16]

Nonetheless, architecture critic Montgomery Schuyler considered the gleaming phalanx of classically styled palaces and pavilions grouped around a lagoon that opened to Lake Michigan "the most admired group of buildings ever erected in this country."[17]

G.W. and Joseph Miller, toiling in the Cherokee Outlet, had no spare time for traveling to Chicago to attend the exposition. Tempting tales of exotic dancing girls on the midway were not enough to entice the Millers from the Land of the Fair God. They decided their time was better spent raising some of the beef cattle—"Texas Steers," as they advertised on their letterhead—that ended up as feasts for crowds flocking to the Great White City.[18]

Although Colonel Miller and his drovers chose not to appear in Chicago, two significant voices of the American West did make their presence known at the Columbian Exposition. One of those was thirty-two-year-old Frederick Jackson Turner, a history professor from the University of Wisconsin. The other was William F. "Buffalo Bill" Cody, the flamboyant showman and quintessential westerner.[19]

The buckskinned Cody and his Indians and daredevil entertainers, advertised as "Buffalo Bill's Wild West and Congress of Rough Riders of the World," were not official exposition participants.[20] That did not bother the old buffalo hunter, whose troupe performed twice daily—"every day, rain or shine"—just outside the walls of the exposition, in front of a covered grandstand that could hold eighteen thousand spectators.[21] Turner, however, was an invited participant. On the muggy evening of July 12, 1893, he read his academic essay "The Significance of the Frontier in American History" to an audience of bored historians at the annual meeting of the American Historical Association.[22]

Neither man knew the other. Turner declined an invitation to see Buffalo Bill's arena antics. Cody did not attend the presentation of Turner's lengthy frontier manifesto at the Art Institute building near the lakefront. Nonetheless, both men—each in his own way—left a lasting impression on how future generations would view and interpret the American West.[23]

In his thesis, Turner—who noted that according to the 1890 census, there was no longer a real frontier—marked the passing of an era.[24] After all, the infamous Dalton gang had been captured during a bank-robbery attempt in Coffeyville, Kansas, in 1892; the last of the Indian tribes had been vanquished; and the Cherokee Outlet was about to be opened to white settlers.

In concluding that the frontier was closed, Turner offered a eulogy for the single most important factor in molding American character and history. According to him, the westward advance of settlement had shaped the nation's development far more than any European influences. Turner's monumental argument inspired the shift of the focus of the study of American history, from New England and the Atlantic seaboard to the West.[25] Turner's landmark speech revolutionized the teaching of American history and influenced the profession for more than half a century.[26]

Although Colonel Miller certainly was no scholar, he most likely would have accepted Turner's view of the importance of westward expansion, and especially of the influences of such intrepid white men as Daniel Boone and Kit Carson. Certainly one of those "western heroes" who helped advance the frontier and its myth more than anyone else was Buffalo Bill Cody.[27]

In Chicago in that summer of 1893, as Turner sanctified the American West of myth, Cody—a master of commercial exploitation—did everything he could to keep the frontier alive. Not ready to hear a eulogy for the dying frontier, Cody realized that by marketing the romantic visions of the Old West in the performance arena, he could perpetuate himself and his illustrious career.[28]

In January 1894, soon after the exposition closed, fires of unknown origin destroyed many of the buildings of the White City.[29] Only still images, elaborate drawings, and gaudy posters survived that grand time in Chicago. But future world's fairs would soon be preserved by a new medium. In 1893, while crowds flocked to Chicago, Thomas Alva Edison, the "Wizard of Menlo Park," and his assistant, W. K. L. Dickson, created the first movie studio, at West Orange, New Jersey.[30] There they produced films for the world's first true motion-picture camera, known as the Kinetoscope, which they had invented in 1889.[31] Edison's coworkers dubbed the big, ugly tarpaper-covered structure the "Black Maria," slang for a police wagon, which it resembled.[32]

By 1894, Cody and his company, including sharpshooter Annie Oakley, journeyed to New Jersey and were filmed at the Black Maria, Edison's Kinematograph Studio.[33] Buffalo Bill and the movies proved to be a natural combination. Even though Cody never used film to his best advantage, it was not long before the screening of moving-picture images attracted large audiences across the country and advanced the mythology of the frontier.[34]

Out in Oklahoma Territory, the Millers, too, were destined to become part of the new medium that had such a lasting impact on popular culture. In less than sixteen years, the three Miller brothers would find themselves in the midst of the fledgling motion-picture business.[35]

Some folks might have agreed with Professor Turner that the frontier had died, but the Millers were determined that more than remembrances would remain of their lives and the empire they were building. They could not permit their lives and work to end up in ashes like the Great White City. Early on, they recognized the commercial potential of the Old West and its enormous public appeal.[36] Like Buffalo Bill, they knew the frontier had become merely entertainment. But they vowed that the real Wild West would always be found on the Salt Fork and in the camps and pastures of the 101 Ranch.

PART FOUR

The Real Thing

We come straight from the Land of Cattle, Corrals, Cabins, Cowboys, Cow-trails and Coyotes. . . . Our brand stands for Stern Honesty wherever it is stamped. It ensures fulfillment with every promise. We will make you feel the life-giving atmosphere of the Prairie, for we are "THE REAL THING."[1]

—101 Ranch show poster, 1907

OVERLEAF: Three future cowboys catch up on news of their heroes beneath a 101 Ranch Wild West show poster on Alma Miller England's barn in Ponca City, Oklahoma, 1930. Bethel Freeman *(center)* became one of Zack Miller Jr.'s closest friends and an advocate of later efforts to preserve the ranch empire. *(Frank Phillips Foundation, Inc.)*

Chapter 19

SHADES OF GRAY

In the fight over land usage the farmer was the victor. From the first opening of land for settlement by Anglos in 1889, it required merely eighteen years for Oklahoma to become a state. Few of the state's institutions, however, made the transition from cattle trailing to modern ranching and farming. One notable exception was the 101 Ranch.[1]

—James H. Thomas
"The 101 Ranch: A Matter of Style"

GEORGE Washington Miller spent most of the last ten years of his life looking over his shoulder. Throughout the 1890s and during the first few years of the new century, G.W. either sought vengeance on someone who had done him wrong or found himself on the dodge from the long arm of the law.

For a decade, beginning in 1893, the year of the founding of the 101 Ranch, Colonel Miller and his family faced legal disputes, weathered drastic changes in the way they did business, and were accused of several serious crimes. At the time of his sudden death in 1903, G.W. had just been indicted for rustling eighteen head of cattle and remained a prime suspect, free under bond, in the cold-blooded bushwhacker slaying of a Kansas man.[2] Several of the criminal accusations against Miller and his sons turned out to be untrue—malicious gossip or smears concocted by business rivals. But some of the complaints proved to be warranted. No matter the circumstances or the outcome, the Millers usually discovered a way to justify their actions.

There were also times when the Millers themselves needed justice. Their solution was usually to find those who had transgressed against them and dispense what they believed to be the appropriate punishment. One method of finding the suspects was to place an advertisement in the local paper. G. W. Miller ran the following notice in the *Winfield Courier* in 1893:

> Stolen out of my feed lot at West 9th Avenue Bridge, sometime during January, 8 head of fat hogs, most all black except one white stag, weighing about 175 pounds. No marks. I will pay $100 for thief and $50 for hogs or $25 for private information to their recovery.[3]

No record was left to reveal whether Miller ever retrieved his hogs, or if he obtained the "private information" needed to get his hands on the scoundrel. The thief would have been lucky to be apprehended by local authorities and marched off to jail to subsist for a spell on a diet of bread and water. If the Millers had gotten to him first, the outcome might have been less pleasant.

At the very least, the hapless thief would have received a good country whipping.[4] He also could have been shot or lynched from a cottonwood.[5] As the cowboys of that time put it, thieves answering to vigilante justice frequently were "treated like treasure," which meant they ended up buried with great care and affection in unmarked prairie graves.[6]

A pesty hog thief did little to endear Winfield to Colonel Miller, who had long been fed up with life in Kansas. On the other hand, Winfield offered attractive cultural amenities and creature comforts for Molly and diversions for the younger children that did not exist in the Twin Territories. For instance, Winfield boasted the Grand Opera House, a bowling alley, a cigar factory, a fire department, a dog catcher, gas streetlamps, a steam laundry, and a championship baseball team called the Winfield Reds, "composed of gentlemen and not of toughs."[7]

On summer afternoons, the Miller children devoured picnic lunches just outside town on the twin mounds called Cup and Saucer Hill, or they stalked imaginary outlaws in the famous Kickapoo Corral, a natural enclosure formed by the Walnut River and a high bluff where, long before, Indians had held cattle and horses stolen from settlers.[8] Zack, Alma, and little George rode with their mother in mule-drawn streetcars to attend the Winfield Chautauqua Assembly at Island Park.[9] Afterward, they usually ate a scoop or two of ice cream from the elegant soda fountain at the Columbian Parlors, with a second-floor veranda offering a magnificent view of Main Street, north and south.[10]

Although Winfield continued to serve as the family's home for several more years, G.W., Joe, and Zack had no time for dipping into the Columbian Parlor's handsome cigar case or for dancing on waxed floors during the busy winter social season.[11] Instead, they remained with their hired hands and cattle herds down in Oklahoma Territory, on the leased Indian lands of the new 101 Ranch.

They erected a sturdy corral and maintained their center of operations in a half-dugout sod-and-brush shanty, braced with lumber and set in the side of a bluff on the south bank of the Salt Fork River.[12] This simple dwelling would remain the 101 Ranch headquarters for ten years, until the Millers finally obtained clear title to several tracts of Ponca land and built a substantial ranch residence on the north side of the Salt Fork.[13]

No sooner had the Millers settled into their dugout ranch headquarters on the Salt Fork than disaster struck. It was not a natural disaster, but rather a catastrophe prompted by the business panic of 1893 and one of the worst depressions in the nation's history.[14] Economic activity declined by at least 25 percent; by late 1893, about five hundred banks and sixteen thousand business firms had gone under, and unemployment increased to between 15 and 20 percent nationally.[15]

As bread lines and vagrancy spread throughout the country, there were even reports of deaths from starvation.[16] More and more banks failed, the money supply dwindled, and the number of farm foreclosures soared across the Great Plains states. Conditions led worried farmers and Boomers to look to the Cherokee Outlet for salvation.[17] While the Millers continued with their cattle operation, thousands of new homesteaders began the transformation of the Twin Territories from a ranching to a farming economy.

For some time, to maintain viable operation of his sizable ranch holdings, Colonel Miller had disregarded his longtime commitment to dealing only in cash, and had borrowed large sums of money on credit.[18] It was a risky ploy that he soon came to regret. The strategy ultimately backfired when the J. J. Campbell Commission Company of Kansas City—the firm the Millers had used for years as an agent in all their cattle transactions—ran into serious difficulties brought on by the depression.[19] The directors fought to keep their overextended firm solvent, but it was too late. With little or no warning, the commission house went into receivership and closed.[20]

The day the Kansas City firm failed, the Millers had more than three hundred thousand dollars' worth of credit on the company's books, every dime of it due to the 101 Ranch for cattle sold.[21] To compound the problem, the commission house also had neglected to pay off notes amounting to one hundred thousand dollars against Miller livestock that it had sold to a Boston banking firm.[22]

Despite being deeply in debt without prospects for any immediate income, the Millers could not ignore the eastern bankers' demands for immediate payment of their outstanding loans. Colonel Miller despised the terms offered, but conceded that he had little choice except to comply. He agreed to surrender his remaining seventeen thousand head of cattle as payment for the defaulted loan.[23]

Before long, the bankers sent an emissary to Oklahoma Territory to take delivery of the Millers' cattle. He arrived at the ranch accompanied by a United States marshal. Because Colonel Miller was otherwise disposed, Jimmy Moore, the hard-drinking Irishman, and the temperate Uncle Doc Miller met with the bank representative and the lawman.[24]

After futile negotiations, Moore and Uncle Doc reluctantly acquiesced to the marshal's orders and supplied some cowboys to gather the livestock to be shipped to market. But by evening, when the first of the Miller herds had been assembled, G.W. had arrived in a violent mood. Everyone present, including sixteen-year-old Zack, saw at once that G.W. was in a burning rage—mad enough to kick his own cow dog.[25]

Using profanity that almost caused even Jimmy Moore to blush, Colonel Miller made it perfectly clear to the marshal and the bank agent that their timing was dead wrong. They had come too soon. G.W. growled that the cattle were so thin they would not bring enough money to pay off the hefty debt the Millers owed. As much as he hated to part with his steers, Miller argued that he would give up all his cattle within a few months, but only after they had had time to fatten on the Ponca tribe's bluestem grass so they would bring more money at market.[26]

The bank representative and the marshal wisely agreed. Miller's proposal made good business sense. No doubt the two men also took into consideration the well-worn saddle carbine Colonel Miller held at the ready and the presence of Jimmy Moore, Uncle Doc, and young Zack Miller, all cradling Winchesters in plain sight.[27]

By late 1893, almost every one of the Millers' remaining seventeen thousand head of cattle was rounded up and shipped as promised.[28] Because the Millers had had the opportunity to fatten the cattle, the sale price was considerably higher. Their revenues enabled them to pay off the loan. That was good news for the Millers. The bad news was that they were left practically penniless.[29]

"The eastern bankers sent in men who took all of our cattle," Zack told a journalist years later. "They took everything but the cripples and the runts. When they got through all we had left was eighty-eight old horses and a handful of cows. We were as flat as the prairie."[30]

But Colonel Miller did not intend to give up. Instead of sneaking off to his dugout on the Salt Fork and drowning his sorrows in a jug of hard liquor, he took stock of his life. He still had a devoted wife, a bright daughter, and three strong sons. They owned the fine residence at Winfield and leased thousands of acres from the Poncas and Otoes. Things could have been much worse.

Colonel Miller knew the main task was to rebuild the ranch, nearly from scratch. But first he had to carry the family through the winter and pay the thousand-dollar annual fee the government required to keep a lease on the Indian lands. For a grubstake, all the Millers had were a few cull steers, some broken-down horses, and three hundred dollars in cash.[31]

To generate quick income, Colonel Miller and Joe devised a scheme with Joe Sherburn, who had been awarded the government contract to furnish beef for the Ponca tribe.[32] Miller proposed selling to Sherburn, at a greatly reduced rate, all of the 101 Ranch's remaining cattle—nothing but culls, or inferior steers—which could then be passed off on the unsuspecting Poncas as better-grade beef.[33]

Sherburn liked the ruse but worried because the Poncas preferred to have their issue of beef delivered on hoof so they could do their own butchering and collect blood and entrails, a culinary delicacy the Indians favored almost as much as unborn calf.[34] Colonel Miller had a solution. The steers would be slaughtered on the Millers' ranch with the Poncas in attendance so they could take whatever they wanted after each steer was killed. G.W. put Zack in charge of the butchering, and told him to shoot each steer in the lungs so they would fill with blood before he died.[35]

The plan worked without a hitch. When the butchering was finished, the Poncas gathered up the gall and blood and returned to their camp.[36] Afterward, some of the Miller cowboys took the dressed beef to the Ponca agency where on at least one occasion, an inspector failed to detect the maggots in substandard cuts of meat, and G.W. and Joe received payment.[37]

Their schemes were not always successful. As one old cowboy, W. H. Day, recalled in 1937, Joe Miller "would get cattle from the stockyards in Kansas City and place them on his ranch to fatten. Later, he got a commission to provide cattle for the Indians. When they were grazing cattle on consignment from Kansas City, sometimes the commission men, or government men there, who sent out the cattle, would send men to count them. When the cattle were counted this way cattlemen would sometimes drive a herd from one place to another and thus the cattle were counted twice."[38]

Despite failing in an attempt to peddle putrid meat to the Ponca and Otoe Indians and getting caught red-handed in other shenanigans involving government beef contracts, the Millers kept the 101 Ranch from collapsing. Colonel Miller made enough money off the Poncas to keep his cattle outfit solvent through tough times. All his life, G.W. had taken advantage of people of color, and he was not about to change. He was determined that the 101 Ranch would endure at any cost.

During long winter evenings, G.W. and his two eldest sons sat huddled inside the snug dugout on the Salt Fork. They stoked fires with squaw wood, sipped cowboy coffee, and talked about ways to recover what they had lost. Occasionally Colonel Miller and his boys rode to Winfield to join the rest of the family at the big house on West Ninth. After dinner, all of them often gathered in the parlor and planned their future in Oklahoma Territory.[39]

During those winter parleys, Colonel Miller perfected what he believed to be an answer to their financial problems. His solution called for the Millers to diversify.[40] Instead of relying only on beef cattle for their livelihood, they would augment their operations with other types of livestock and, even more surprisingly, would also turn to agriculture. The Millers had already shown their talent as ranchers; now they would prove they could be good farmers also. To G.W.'s delight, the rest of the family agreed with his strategy.[41]

Because they had no time to prepare for a variety of crops, the Millers decided to gamble initially on wheat.[42] But first they needed cash for seed grain and plows. That meant they had to borrow another large sum of money, a somewhat monumental task given the poor health of the banking industry and the Millers' lending record. Undaunted, Colonel Miller put on his finest clothes and met with William E. Otis, president of Winfield National Bank.[43]

When G.W. presented his plan for farming Ponca lands, Otis did not hesitate. He knew the fertile prairie soil was ideal for yielding bumper crops of wheat. He quickly drew up the papers and loaned the Millers enough money not only to plant five thousand acres in wheat but also to purchase five hundred yearling calves.[44] With cash in hand, G.W. and his sons returned to his ranchlands on the Salt Fork. They paid nesters seventy-five cents or so per acre to break up the sod for planting, and they had their hired hands use cow ponies to plant thousands of acres in wheat.[45] But George W. Miller himself insisted on being the first to stick a steel plow into the earth.[46]

By the following spring, despite drought and chinch bugs, it was clear that the Millers were going to make excellent farmers. They and their crews harvested more than seventy thousand bushels of wheat, which sold at a record $1.20 per bushel in Chicago.[47] The grand gamble had paid off. The 101 Ranch was alive and well, and the Millers could once again run with the big dogs.

"56"

NOBODY EVER DOUBTED that the ranch and farm empire Colonel Miller had created in Oklahoma Territory would one day be run by his sons—Joseph, Zachary, and George. As the eldest, Joe had been given major responsibilities while still a boy, and on reaching his early twenties, he became a full partner with his father in the cattle trade.

Shortly after the 101 Ranch made the transition from a cattle operation to a functioning farm, Zack Miller, still only a teenager, took a more active management role in the family business. Like his big brother, the often pugnacious Zack was being groomed for ranch life when most boys his age still played childish games.[1] It was said that Zachary Taylor Miller was a cowboy all the way down to his liver.[2]

Much of Zack's range wisdom came from his father. Not only did he soak up knowledge by following G.W. everywhere he went, but the youngster also inherited Miller's instincts as a horse and mule trader and his ability to judge livestock. When Zack was an old man, he recalled his father's directions about buying livestock: "Son, when you ride through a herd of cattle one time, buy them—or turn them down. You go back for a second look, and nine times out of ten you'll beat yourself."[3]

In addition to learning all he could from Joe and Colonel Miller, Zack took instruction from many other capable teachers. After spending hundreds of nights under the stars, Zack memorized campfire tales told by old-time cowhands such as Milton Van Hook, J. D. Rainwater, and Charles Orr. The boy's teacher in stalking game and riding fast ponies was Comes From War, or "Comesy," as the cowboys called him, an old Ponca warrior who proudly displayed his collection of Sioux, Cheyenne, and Arapaho scalps, as well as his most prized trophy—the long blonde hair of a white woman.[4]

But of all the persons who crossed Zack's path when he was a boy on the ranges of Kansas and the Indian Nations, Jimmy Moore, the Irish cowhand who had joined the outfit in 1880, was his favorite. Jimmy showed Zack how to use a lariat and bull whip, and he looked out for the boy as though he were his own son.

Zack put to use many of the cowboying skills Jimmy had taught him when the newly christened 101 Ranch was fighting for survival after the collapse of the Millers' commission company in Kansas City. In yet another effort to generate some badly needed cash, Colonel Miller placed young Zack in charge of a horse-trading expedition to Louisiana which yielded a tidy profit of one thousand dollars.[5] Zack and Jimmy remained saddle pals through high and low times. When Jimmy died suddenly after a whiskey binge in a Ponca City hotel and was laid to rest with other 101 Ranch cowboys in a burial ground at Winfield, he bequeathed all his worldly effects to Zack. They included a 160-acre homestead, seventeen hundred dollars in cash, and a pair of matched mules.[6]

Memories of his Irish pal gave Zack comfort when in 1894, at sixteen years old, G.W. shipped him off to the newly opened Marmaduke Military Academy, in Sweet Springs, Missouri, halfway between Kansas City and Columbia.[7] Nothing about the academy was to Zack's liking, and he especially detested the lordly upperclassmen, endless parade-ground drills, and marching to classes in a scratchy woolen uniform. Fond recollections of calf brandings and varmint hunts on the prairie with Jimmy and the other Miller cowboys kept Zack sane during the brief time he spent at Marmaduke. When he finally returned to the 101 Ranch, it was unclear whether he had retained much book learning; it was, however, quite evident that he had "learned to drink and swear and hold authority in contempt."[8]

Zack had to endure only one more stab at formal schooling, when he turned eighteen and G.W. sent him to Spaulding Business College at Kansas City, which Joe Miller had attended.[9] Zack did not last very long at Spaulding. Instead of sitting through classes, he spent most of his time making deals at local stockyards and mule barns.

Back in the saddle at the ranch after his brief stint at Spaulding, Zack finally convinced his father that everything worth learning could be found on bluestem pasturelands, in line camps, and at spirited livestock auctions. That was the life for Zack Miller—the life he loved best.

Zack still had much to learn as he grew older and the 101 Ranch evolved into such a sizable operation that employees were assigned numbers for record-keeping purposes. Eventually, they even wore nickel-plated badges stamped with their numbers.[10]

One of those numbered workers—a seasoned line rider for the 101—taught Zack Miller the lesson of a lifetime. Like so many others, the cowboy's name was eventually forgotten, but his employee number—"56"—was burned permanently into Zack's mind.[11]

Just twenty-one years old at the time, Zack had grown so cocky he could "strut sitting down." Acting on orders from his father, Zack and a gang of armed 101 Ranch cowboys rode across the countryside and swooped down on homesteads near the Millers' big spread. Such "visits" were said to be a last resort after other attempts had failed to persuade local farmers to sell out and move on so the Millers could expand their holdings.[12]

When Zack and his band appeared at the farm of Eli Circle near the Noble County settlement of Red Rock, they did not know that someone else was in the farmhouse besides the farmer, his wife, and their five children. It was "56," one of the Millers' own line riders. He visited the farm regularly on his assignment of riding fences for the Millers, which took him to a far corner of the 101 Ranch near the Circle family's place. "56" often boarded and dined with the family, and they considered him their friend.[13]

Zack Miller was far from friendly when he and his men pulled up their horses at the Circle home and called out the farmer. One more time, Zack pointed out to Circle that the Millers had offered him a fair price for his land and that they even employed his own brother as a hired hand. Zack said they were willing to give Circle a job if he would sell out. Once again, Circle refused. He wanted to keep his farm.[14]

Unarmed and helpless, Circle stood alone and listened as Zack bellowed that the Millers had no alternative but to move the family forcibly off the land. At that moment, "56" stepped from the house. The lone cowboy, with a six-gun in his side holster, walked past Eli Circle and faced Zack and the mounted riders.

"I told you not to bother these people, Zack," said "56." "That still goes even if I take your pay. There's the gate, Zack. Get yourself through it. Just get on your way out of here. Take the boys with you."[15]

Zack sat on his horse and stared into the eyes of the man before him. Neither of them moved a muscle for what seemed like a very long time. Then without another word to Circle or to "56," Zack ordered his followers to leave.[16]

Although the big bunch of riders could easily have shot to pieces the farmer and his defender, Zack concluded that the Millers could get along just fine without taking the Circle place. He also reasoned that there was no sense in losing a perfectly good hand like "56."

From that time forward, the Circles' farm was never bothered. And until the day when he finally decided to go elsewhere, "56" continued to work for the Millers. Jimmy Moore might have been Zack's favorite, but the line rider with no name turned out to be one of the best teachers Zack Miller ever had.

Chapter 20

LORDS OF THE PRAIRIE

I remember when the Miller boys were roaming that country. They were big cattle men and had plenty of money and did just what they wanted to do. They would steal cattle, they would kill men. It seemed that the law could not handle them. . . . I was well acquainted with the Miller boys.[1]

—Recollection of W. A. Vines, 1937

THE bumper crop of winter wheat which the Millers harvested and sold in 1894 served as the catalyst that transformed the 101 Ranch into a diversified farm. For the next decade, the family-controlled empire grew and prospered as never before. The Millers, however, had to pay a price for their success.

As the ranch grew, Colonel Miller continued to teach his sons the fine points of entrepreneurship and risk taking. They proved to be able students. All three adhered to their father's basic business philosophy that anyone willing to take a chance might as well risk everything he had or not even bother.

"When we began here," Zack later explained in a magazine interview, "we figured it wasn't much harder to do things in a big way than it was to worry along in a small way. We figured it was no worse to fail big than to fail little; but ever so much better to *win* big."[2] Those were the words the Miller brothers lived and died by in the next forty years.

They also lived according to the work ethic instilled by their stubborn father's example. Like clockwork, the first one awake in the Millers' sod-covered dugout on the banks of the Salt Fork always was Colonel Miller. Once his eyes popped open, no one else within earshot stayed asleep for very long. Like a persistent rooster, G.W. peered outside into the inky heavens before every sunrise, and when he spied Venus radiant in the eastern sky, he bellowed, "Roll out of it! I can see the morning star!"[3]

Eager to turn the leased Indian lands into fields of cash crops, Colonel

Miller found the transition to farming relatively easy, especially because he had been raised on a flourishing Kentucky plantation. Long before he saddled his first cow pony, G.W. had amassed years of experience in farm management and animal husbandry. This time around, he no longer had a large slave force to do his bidding; he relied instead on hired hands and seasonal farm laborers to till the soil and tend the growing fields and grazing pastures.

Besides vast fields of profitable wheat, the Millers expanded their farming operations to include hundreds of acres of corn, alfalfa, and other crops, such as kafir and cane for fodder.[4] Zack Miller traded a beef to an Indian for a plow and another beef for a harness, and hitched up a pair of old cow horses.[5] After planting "nearly half a carload of watermelon seed," he ended up with a huge patch that yielded melons weighing as much as sixty and seventy pounds. The Millers sold off untold wagonloads of watermelons, mostly to a big wholesale seed outfit in Texas.[6]

While neighboring farmers tacked up warning signs to scare off would-be melon thieves, the Millers had so many surplus watermelons they could afford to give them away. The abundance finally reached the point that Colonel Miller had the boys post a big placard that boldly declared:

HELP YOURSELF TO A MELON
$10 FINE IF YOU DON'T GET ONE![7]

Ponca and Otoe Indians, cowboys, and farmhands from all around showed up to feast on the sweet pink flesh of the Millers' melons. Uncle Doc Miller, no doubt pleased to see folks quenching their thirst on something nonalcoholic, slapped together a brush arbor roofed with prairie sod and set out benches and tables. Using a slender-bladed knife with the skill of a surgeon, Uncle Doc served slices of ripe melon free of charge to those willing to dispose of the rinds and wash off the tables after they got their fill.[8]

The Millers purchased more livestock, including some dairy animals, draft and saddle horses, mules, hogs, and a few bison. They also added flocks of ducks, geese, and poultry. They shipped in calves by rail to replenish the herds which grazed in fenced pastures at the Bar L camp, just a few miles from the 101 headquarters.[9] They built crude bunkhouses for cowboys and line riders and constructed corrals and cattle chutes for branding, dehorning, and dipping.[10]

After twenty-two years of dealing exclusively in Texas longhorns,

Colonel Miller and his sons upgraded their expanding herds to include shorthorns and other purebred, registered cattle. They purchased breeding stock from several states in a continuing effort to improve the quality of the beef.[11]

The Millers scrambled to make these changes to keep up with the shifting trends of the ranch business. As historian Edward Everett Dale wrote in 1936,

> The lean, brown, hard bitten men who had laid out the foundations of the vast cattle empire in northern Oklahoma still remained, but except for the common cow hands who still retained many of the traits of the early cattlemen, they were comparatively few in number. They were giving place to a new group composed of individuals perhaps not quite as hardy and vigorous as were the early cattlemen, but who were men of education, broad vision, and intimate contacts with the world outside. Big business was coming to the plains and the new figures in the industry were business farmers in the highest sense of the term. . . . It was inevitable that men of this type should see at once the advantages to be derived by improving the breed of their herds and marketing animals at an earlier age. Wild, long-horned Texas steers five or six years old might be sold to the Federal government under beef contracts to feed the Indians, but they did not furnish a quality of beef desired by the markets of the nineties. Much of the American public, particularly in the east, insisted upon better beef than the coarse, stringy product derived from the longhorns. As a result the ranchmen of northern Oklahoma soon began to bring in large numbers of registered or high grade bulls from the corn belt states and even to import a great many breeding animals from Europe.[12]

Beyond the expansion of the 101 Ranch, the Miller family also increased in size in late 1894 when Joe took a wife.[13] At the age of twenty-five, Joe Miller ended his days as a bachelor with a reputation for girling and gambling in bit houses and whiskey mills from Smoky Row to San Antonio—at least for a little while.[14]

His choice for a bride was Miss Elizabeth Trosper, a pretty southern belle much like Joe's mother. Lizzie, as most people called her, hailed from Bethany, Louisiana, a small town just southwest of Shreveport on the Texas line.[15]

Raised in luxury, Lizzie grew up with her big brother, Jim, and their little sister, Alice, in a rambling house with high ceilings and a spacious yard of boxwood borders and immaculate flower beds, all surrounded by a white picket fence and tended by a flock of servants.[16] Her father, who every spring donned his handsome captain's uniform, complete with dress sword, for a reunion of Confederate veterans, owned and operated a large store in Bethany that sold everything from salt meat and bolts of calico to harnesses and coffins. The family also maintained a large farm and an active cotton gin, controlled lucrative timberland, and ran prize-winning Jersey cows and a herd of beef cattle just across the border in Texas.[17]

In the late 1880s, Jim, eldest of the three Trosper children, had left his academic studies to join his father, riding herd on some of their Texas longhorns bound for Hunnewell, Kansas. As they rode the Chisholm Trail, they became acquainted with the Millers.[18]

A few years later, while down south on a cattle-buying trip, Joe encountered the Trospers on their turf, and they enticed him to slip across the border for hospitality at their home, in Bethany. Joe, known to have an eye for the ladies, was impressed when he met Miss Lizzie. A natural beauty who had studied music, art, and elocution at a Nashville boarding school, Lizzie also developed her talent for piano with a year of study at the Conservatory of Music in Cincinnati.[19]

"She was considered by her contemporaries, one and all, to be an accomplished, charming, and beautiful southern lady," Lizzie's daughter, Alice Miller Harth, wrote many years later. "Papa [Joe Miller] was impressed by Mama's big blue eyes and tiny stature, not to mention her southern accent and winning ways. Manners were important. The courtship was carried on by correspondence. The bunch of letters in the attic trunk, which Mama kept tied with a blue ribbon, were very formal. They were written in a beautiful hand with many flourishes, but the spelling [Joe's] left something to be desired. One more visit was followed by a proposal and subsequent marriage."[20]

The wedding took place in December 1894 at the Trosper home. Joe, with his droopy mustache trimmed and his hair slicked down, looked the part of a prosperous cattleman in a handsome suit, cravat, and stiff white collar. Thanks to a fashionable Memphis dressmaker, the bride dazzled the groom and their guests in her stunning gown of lavender silk brocade, crinoline lined, with leg-of-mutton sleeves and mother-of-pearl buckles.[21]

Immediately after the ceremony and reception, the newlyweds boarded a northbound train for Kansas. Back in Winfield, Joe's family was surprised when he returned home with "a dainty little lady with a pretty trousseau and a southern accent," as Lizzie's daughter later described her.[22]

Soon after moving to Winfield, Lizzie began to wonder if she had made a mistake in settling in at the Miller residence on West Ninth Street. The clannish Miller family proved difficult to fit into. "Who thought to, or could have, prepared Mama for the critical reception she received?" wrote Alice Miller Harth. "It was culture shock on both sides. Each side had its standards and staunchly supported them. . . . Grandmother Miller tried to understand, was usually patient, and many times over the years stood by and for Mama. Alma didn't try. Mama tried, too, but found so many things hard and puzzling. Papa showed off this pretty novelty with the strange accent and lovely clothes. He was always a showman at heart."[23]

Although her husband soon left for his duties on the ranch in Oklahoma Territory, Lizzie discovered that she could keep quite busy at the main Miller residence in Winfield by engaging in social and cultural activities. Molly welcomed another female presence, especially because Alma was usually away at school.[24]

Satisfied that he had by now endured enough formal education, Zack had joined Colonel Miller and Joe at the ranch, but Lizzie saw plenty of her youngest brother-in-law, George Lee Miller, who lived at home with his mother and spent his vacations working on the ranch. By 1896, George—fifteen years old—had enrolled at Saint John's Lutheran College, housed in an impressive stone structure with Roman-arched portals, on East Seventh Avenue in Winfield.[25]

Many of the students were preparing for careers as theologians or ministers, but George stuck to bookkeeping and business courses.[26] After finishing at Saint John's, George took another business course, at Eastman Business College in Poughkeepsie, New York.[27] Blessed with a sharp mind for figures and finance even as a schoolboy, George showed a flair for business that would one day earn him a place as the financial genius of the 101 Ranch.

Unfortunately, young George was not yet prepared to aid his family with his financial talent. By the last half of the 1890s, even as they built up their ranch and farm operations, the Millers became embroiled in an array of legal problems caused mostly by questionable business practices and outright criminal acts.

All manner of outlaws found hiding places in the Osage Hills and throughout the Indian Nations, including the Daltons, the Doolins, Henry Starr, Ben Cravens, and many others. Sometimes the Millers had no choice but to cooperate with these notorious characters if they came to the ranch looking for help—"a man didn't dare to refuse an outlaw food or lodging," an old lawman who knew the Millers recalled in 1938.[28]

By 1897, the Millers' own illegal activities threatened to destroy their flourishing ranch. The first one to run afoul of the law was Joe. Part of the problem stemmed from his brief tenure as president of a "wildcat" banking institution in the Kay County town of Blackwell, Oklahoma Territory, where the officers' main goal was to make a quick personal profit.[29] When the Bank of Blackwell finally was forced to close, most depositors were left flat broke and very unhappy. Accusations flew fast and furious, and most fingers pointed at Joe Miller, the man at the helm.

Already under indictment for his part in the bank failure, Joe faced worse trouble when federal authorities charged him with passing counterfeit money while on a trip to New Orleans.[30] Joe claimed he was totally innocent and did not know he had been given bogus currency. His plea was futile, and none of Colonel Miller's business or political connections in Texas and Louisiana could help. While the family comforted a much distressed Lizzie, anticipating the birth of her second child, Joe Miller went to trial in federal court in New Orleans.

He was found guilty in March 1897, just as the nation observed the inauguration of William McKinley, a wealthy Republican, as twenty-fifth president of the United States. The presiding judge handed Joseph Carson Miller a sentence of five to fifteen years in the penitentiary.[31]

In Oklahoma Territory and in Winfield, the news about Joe's verdict greatly unsettled the entire Miller clan. "Word came last week that Joe Miller has been sentenced to 15 years in the penitentiary at New Orleans for being in possession of counterfeit money," reported the *Ponca City Courier* in Oklahoma Territory. "Miller is well known in this city, having a large lease in the Ponca reservation, and trading here. He was president of the Bank of Blackwell when it failed and is under indictment in this county as a wrecker of that bank."[32]

Instead of cooling his heels in an Orleans Parish prison, Joe was shipped off in irons to the Ohio State Penitentiary, at Columbus, in the new president's home state.[33] At home in Winfield, Lizzie grieved over their first daughter, who had died on March 27.[34] The Millers and many friends doubled their efforts to win Joe's release.

On October 14, 1897, J. W. Lynch, a wealthy rancher and Ponca City pioneer, left for Saint Louis, announcing that he intended to continue to Washington, D.C., to obtain a pardon for Joe Miller from President McKinley.[35] Less than a month later, two of Joe's supposed accomplices offered affidavits attesting to his innocence.[36] In one of the sworn statements, George Dice, also convicted of counterfeiting and serving time in Ohio, stated that Joe Miller "was in no way connected with me or to my knowledge knew anything concerning any counterfeit money."[37] B. A. Davidson, the other Ohio convict who wished to exonerate Joe, stated that he knew "positively that Mr. Miller had nothing to do with the passing or the attempting to pass or have in his possession any counterfeit money at New Orleans, for which he was tried and convicted."[38]

While Joe and his allies battled for his early release from prison, Colonel Miller faced his own serious legal problems in Oklahoma Territory. In late 1897, after having successfully harvested "a bonanza" of seventy-five thousand bushels of wheat off the Ponca reservation, Miller and two of his cowboys were tried and convicted of cattle rustling before a magistrate in the District Court of Noble County.[39]

Sentenced to six months in prison and a fine of three hundred dollars, G.W. furiously denied the allegations while he remained free on appeal bond.[40] He also protested that Frank Witherspoon, the rancher who had accused him of cattle theft, was a bitter rival in competition with the Millers for grazing rights on Otoe lands.[41]

Accusations flew while the two factions vied for the coveted pastures. At one point, young George L. Miller squared off with a Witherspoon cowhand and delivered a fist-whipping that only increased the tension.[42] When threats of open range war appeared to be real, G.W. had crates of new Winchester rifles shipped in from Kansas City and passed them out to his cowboys.[43] Fortunately, widespread violence never occurred.

Scandalous allegations that bidders from both sides paid bribes to the appointed agent of the Ponca agency, which supervised the Otoes and their rangeland, ultimately resulted in President McKinley's involvement.[44] He ordered the Indian agent to be removed from his post and prosecuted on criminal charges. Questions about the Indian land and terms of leases dragged on for years, and the Millers eventually wound up as one of the principal lessees of the Otoes' unallotted land.[45]

In the meantime, Joe Miller won his release from prison while his father avoided serving a day of jail time for rustling, thanks to legal technicalities. In 1899, the Supreme Court of Oklahoma Territory finally got around to the appeal of Colonel Miller's conviction for cattle theft. After careful review, the court found that Miller's arrest warrant had not been issued properly and his trial had been far too speedy.[46]

That year, on the brink of a new century, Joe Miller returned as general superintendent of the 101 Ranch, by then the largest wheat farm in the Twin Territories.[47] In late June 1899, it took four hours for Joe to make the six-mile trip around the great field with one of the ranch's self-binders. The twenty-four binders pulled by teams of horses cut a swath 150 feet wide across the golden stalks. More than two hundred men and three hundred horses worked in shifts around the clock, by moonlight and lantern, to gather wheat for the Millers.[48]

Just after that successful wheat harvest, Joe Miller moved his wife, Lizzie, and their second child, Alice—named for Lizzie's sister—from Winfield to the ranch.[49] Joe located a suitable homesite on land studded with cottonwoods, elms, and thickets of sand plums on the north bank of the Salt Fork, across the river from the dugout headquarters. Colonel Miller brought in a herd of goats to clear out the underbrush, and he supervised the construction of the five-room white frame house with a front porch.[50] It was ready for occupancy by October 1899, as Lizzie later recalled.[51]

Colonel Miller doted on his granddaughter. He kept Lizzie in a constant panic when he stomped into the small house, picked up little Alice, and tossed her around or slopped a mound of mashed potatoes from his plate into the baby's dish.[52] When Alice turned two years old, G.W. reduced her to tears by exploding an arsenal of fireworks. When she could barely walk, she had her own saddle and pony.[53]

Even when Joe and Lizzie had another child, a boy named George, for his uncle, little Alice remained the apple of Colonel Miller's eye. Likewise, she loved her grandfather, even though "he had skin like leather and wore clothes with ground-in dust and dirt" and "had absolute disdain for anything but the most casual grooming and was often an embarrassment to his family," as she later wrote.[54] One of G.W.'s favorite jokes was to board a train without buying a ticket, looking like a tramp in his rough-and-tumble cowboy duds. Just as the conductor was ready to evict him, Miller would produce a huge roll of folding money and peel off some bills. He repeated this routine in restaurants or any public place where he would be sure of attracting attention.[55]

Alice recalled,

> We children were fascinated by his personality and found him eminently satisfactory as a grandparent. Each week he hitched up the spring wagon and drove to town ten miles north across the prairie. . . . In the late afternoon of the day Grandfather went to town we placed ourselves on the steps of the front porch with our eyes glued to the horizon. When we saw a great cloud of dust we knew that Grandfather was approaching. The cloud of dust was occasioned by everything that could walk on four feet

> and be led by a rope tied to the wagon. Sometimes there would be a pony or donkey for us, but always there would be a huge brown sack of marshmallow bananas, candy corn, and gum drops.[56]

One of Alice's earliest memories of the house on the Salt Fork was of a reading table and kerosene lamp surrounded by stacks of seed catalogues and livestock journals. Every evening, the girl watched her father as he pored through publications in an effort to expand his knowledge of farming.[57] Alice explained,

> No one knew just what would grow best in this newly-turned soil so father had to experiment. He planted tobacco and found that the wind whipped the leaves to pieces. But wheat and corn, alfalfa, kaffir [sic], Sudan grass and sweet clover all sent hungry roots into the ground and tall stems above it. Eventually great fields were planted. The wind tore at them until they looked like disturbed lakes of yellow and green, but they held and gave to the wind nothing but their perfume. Along the sandy bank of the river watermelons grew like big balloons so eager to burst that, at the touch of a knife point, they split themselves.[58]

It appeared that the lean days had come to an end for the 101 Ranch. Time helped to heal many old wounds, and the Millers' domain was growing into a self-sufficient community that employed hundreds of people and was known across the nation. An admirer even suggested that Colonel Miller and his sons "were like medieval barons in the splendor of their court, in the gorgeousness of the retinues, in their prodigal spending."[59] They were resolved that nothing and no one would stop them, as long as that morning star appeared in the eastern sky. Indeed, at the dawn of the twentieth century, the Millers seemed invincible, poised to become one of the leading ranch dynasties of all time.

BUFFALO MAN

ONE OF THE most mysterious episodes in the saga of the 101 Ranch began at about the turn of the century, in the ranching and railroad town called Bliss. Established in 1898, in the rolling grasslands south of the Salt Fork of the Arkansas, the Noble County community was named for Cornelius N. Bliss, secretary of the interior.[1]

Bliss prospered alongside the 101 Ranch, and became the main shipping point for the Millers and a favorite gathering spot for local cowboys. Bliss also served as a temporary home for a great many railroad men who did not always get along with the Millers' crew.

From the beginning, the Millers ran into difficulties in business dealings with the Atchison, Topeka and Santa Fe Railway over bogus charges, neglect of rails and equipment, and sidetracking of livestock.[2] The squabbles frequently ended up in court. Even though the 101 Ranch was fast becoming a major enterprise, the Santa Fe was even larger and more powerful. The Millers often felt as though they were at the mercy of the railroad.[3]

Bad feelings between the railway and the Millers escalated in early 1900 when a Santa Fe news agent on a train passing through Bliss supposedly had trouble with Zack Miller and Frank Potts, a rider for the 101. Potts was said to be "a good, dependable cowhand, but there was a look in his eyes that made a man sorry for the horse he rode, the woman he wanted, or the man he hated."[4] The railroad worker claimed that Miller and Potts brazenly stole some of the cigars he was to peddle to passengers.[5] They denied the charge and maintained that to "get evidence of a criminal nature against the Millers," the railroaders had thrown several boxes of cigars out the car window into a 101 Ranch pasture, where outriders checking fences picked them up.[6]

The arresting officer in the Bliss cigar caper was George C. Montgomery, a detective for the Santa Fe Railway who had lived in Winfield, Kansas, since 1898.[7] Montgomery's friends recalled that on the street and on trains, he always kept a pair of six-shooters within easy reach and could shoot with both hands. He was described as "a daredevil on the road" but "a boy at home, full of fun and always sympathetic."[8]

Evidently Montgomery was not at all sympathetic to the Millers, however. Lawyers for the Millers claimed that not only were the charges against Zack Miller and Frank Potts trumped up, but when the two went to court in Oklahoma Territory at Perry, the railroad company intentionally delayed the train bearing them for five or six hours. As a result, the presiding judge—who the Millers believed worked in collusion with the Santa Fe—refused to continue the case, and the Millers were forced to pay a hefty fine plus court costs.[9]

After the court proceedings, Joe Miller and Montgomery reportedly exchanged heated words—and threw some punches—when Montgomery said the railroad company intended to break up the Millers' empire. As time passed, tensions mounted between the railroad and the Millers, and they exchanged more threats.[10]

By 1901, the situation intensified. One afternoon, Montgomery got off a train at Bliss just as Colonel Miller was about to board. Standing on the platform, the detective supposedly told Miller that he was nothing but an old man and that Montgomery could whip him.[11] Outraged by the impudence, Colonel Miller pulled a knife and lunged at Montgomery's neck. The railroader dodged the angry rancher, pulled one of his six-guns, and clubbed Miller over the head, leaving a nasty scalp wound. When Miller came to, he went to the ranch to get his shotgun, but by the time he returned to Bliss, the train and Montgomery were long gone.[12]

After that incident, the 101 Ranch cowboys regularly greeted every Santa Fe train, looking, in the words of one observer, like "a lynching party."[13] Throughout the territory, word spread that the Millers were out to get Montgomery and intended to "hang his hide on a fence at Bliss."[14] Montgomery never lingered when he came within range of the Millers, except when he was at his own home. He apparently felt safe in Winfield, even though the Millers' main residence was there.

Yet it was precisely at the Montgomery home on South Loomis, and not at some lonely railroad siding, where the Millers' nemesis was rubbed out—in a cold-blooded murder that took place on October 5, 1901.[15]

It was a Saturday night; Montgomery had spent the day in Winfield after a week of working in Wichita. Just after supper, he went to a table in the sitting room, slipped on a green eyeshade, and began to prepare weekly reports for the Santa Fe home office. Montgomery's wife had just gone to the bedroom to arrange some clothing; his mother-in-law was at the well drawing water; his youngest son, Guy, was in his bedroom; and the oldest son, Phil, was playing with a lantern in the yard.[16]

Suddenly a loud blast shattered the quiet night. Montgomery rose from his chair with his hands to his face and collapsed on the floor. His wife believed the oil lamp had exploded and ran into the yard screaming, "Help, the house is on fire!" When a neighbor raced to the home and reached Montgomery in the sitting room, his wife heard his final words, "My God, I am shot." He lived only a few minutes after having been struck in the face, neck, and breast by buckshot from a twelve-gauge shotgun blast fired through a window. Two of the pellets went into his left eye and entered the brain, one pellet penetrated his heart, and others perforated his lungs.[17]

The sheriff and railroad detectives began a massive investigation. Bloodhounds were brought in from Manhattan, Kansas, and boot tracks believed to have been left by the killer were found. From the moment that news of Montgomery's slaying got out, many people believed there was little doubt who was behind the ambush. "Suspicion Against Millers" read one bold headline, although other stories were not quite so explicit.[18]

On October 12, one week after the murder, Will C. Johnson, an Irishman hired to break horses for the Millers, was taken into custody at Bliss and brought to Winfield. After a "thorough sweating process," Johnson was arrested for the crime.[19]

Many observers at Johnson's preliminary trial in Winfield thought the prosecution's case was weak. Others pointed to testimony from a hardware-store clerk who said Johnson had purchased buckshot from him a few days before the murder, and to testimony that the defendant's feet fit the tracks left in the mud outside the victim's home. The authorities also recovered a train ticket Johnson had bought in Winfield to take him to Bliss the day after the murder. A judge ordered the cowboy back to jail to await trial.[20]

The case was far from being closed. On January 2, 1902, Noble County Sheriff George A. Foster tracked down and arrested Omar W. Coffelt, another 101 Ranch cowboy, at Del Rio, Texas, on the Mexico border.[21] Coffelt was taken by train to Kansas to be charged with Montgomery's killing. Born in 1868, Coffelt had come to the territory before the opening of the Cherokee Outlet and hired on as a line rider with the Millers.[22] After Coffelt's capture, more news stories appeared about the Millers, spurring Colonel Miller to write a long letter of protest to the *Wichita Eagle* that was reprinted in several newspapers.

"We are as anxious as any person for the truth regarding the killing to be known, but we do not care to be injured by unwarranted statements," wrote Miller. "The story from a Winfield man that Coffelt was once hangman at Fort Smith, Arkansas, is untrue. Coffelt never saw a man hanged in his life and was never at Fort Smith."[23] Colonel Miller went on to recount several of his family's encounters with Montgomery and to argue that none of the Millers had had a role in the murder.

"We are known to many of your readers and have done business with them, and do not wish these imputations to pass unnoticed by us," Miller's letter continued. "The fact of our having had trouble with the Santa Fe people and with Montgomery accounts for these indirect charges. There has not been a shadow of evidence to justify any of them. The truth is that we are too busy attending strictly to our own affairs and if we ever had personal difficulties with people we never have and never will resort to cowardly methods to settle them."[24]

Despite Colonel Miller's protests, rumors continued to circulate that the Millers and their cowboys were behind the murder. The gossip only increased after Johnson's case was continued and prosecutors proceeded with Coffelt's first trial. It ended in April 1902 in a hung jury when seven jurors voted for conviction and five for acquittal.[25]

Finally, on May 19, 1902, Colonel Miller found himself arrested by a constable for Montgomery's murder when his widow signed a complaint against G.W. and Zack.[26] Formal charges were never lodged against Zack, but Colonel Miller, represented by J. T. Lafferty, was brought before Judge L. H. Webb, who set a bond of five thousand dollars. The prosecution was convinced that a murder conspiracy had taken place and that G. W. Miller had hatched the plan and engaged his hired hands to carry it out.[27]

Exactly one month after Miller's arrest, Coffelt's trial began, and less than a week after that, another 101 Ranch cowboy—Bert Colby—was arrested and charged with complicity in Montgomery's murder. Colby, who had begun to work for the Millers when he was just a boy tending Zack's goat herd, was already under arrest at Enid, charged with the theft of three mules. Prosecutors promised to drop the three theft indictments hanging over Colby's head for his testimony against Coffelt, and said the murder charge was simply intended to hold Colby until he testified.[28]

While all this was going on, the Millers continued to flex their muscles and thumb their noses at the law. On June 12, 1902, three boys from Perry, including the marshal's son, went to the 101 Ranch to look for work. What transpired there was recorded the following day beneath the headline "101 Ranch Deviltry" in the Perry newspaper:

> The men at the ranch promised them something to do, but first started out to have some fun with the lads. One of the Wofford boys was roped after the manner of a wild steer. He was pretty thoroughly scared but not injured. Bert Wofford was told he could have a job with the cook but first he would first put himself in the hands of a barber. By threats and cajolery he was forced to sit while Zack Miller cut his hair with a pair of horse clippers. With a razor Miller shaved a streak entirely around and into the boy's hair, and then shaved upon the top of his head the figures of the ranch brand, "101." After this the boys escaped and made for home, arriving here about daylight Friday morning. Our citizens are very indignant at the disfigurement of the Wofford boy and the general treatment to which the boys were subjected. A warrant has been issued for the arrest of Miller.[29]

Coffelt's second murder trial, which included 110 prosecution and defense witnesses, soon overshadowed Zack's mischief. The defense featured testimony from almost every member of the Miller family, including G.W., all three sons, Molly, Alma, and Joe's wife, Lizzie. The trial ended in another hung jury, with nine votes for conviction and three for acquittal.[30]

Before Coffelt's next trial began, prosecutors made a formal murder charge against Colonel Miller and dropped the charge against Will Johnson. The third Coffelt trial ended on April 14, 1903, after testimony from 131 witnesses. Once again, the jury could not arrive at a verdict, this time giving a split vote of six for conviction and six for acquittal.[31]

On April 25, 1903, nine days after the conclusion of the third Coffelt trial, Colonel Miller suddenly died on the 101 Ranch, and the murder charge against him was dismissed.[32]

Determined that someone would pay for the killing of the railroad detective, the prosecution once again brought Coffelt before the bar of justice in November 1903. Bert Colby, who had been in jail since June 1902, was called as a state witness. In grueling cross-examination, however, lawyers for the defense showed that Colby had been coerced to swear against Coffelt to avoid a lengthy penitentiary term. For a fourth time, jurors were deadlocked—eight found Coffelt innocent and four guilty. It would be the last of the trials. The prosecution finally had had enough. On March 1, 1904, all cases concerning the murder of George C. Montgomery were dismissed.[33]

Bert Colby left the 101 Ranch, married an Osage woman, and established a fine ranch in Osage County. He remained one of Zack Miller's closest friends.[34]

In the years following the trials, Coffelt continued to work for the Millers. He and his wife, Lillie, raised four children. After Lillie died, in 1917, Coffelt stayed on and became a performer with the 101 Ranch Wild West show.[35] Distinguished by his long hair and beard, Coffelt developed a trained-buffalo act that became popular with audiences. The old cowboy came to love his buffalo so much that he preferred them to humans. He grew especially fond of a buffalo calf that Zack gave him. Even when the critter had grown to weigh eleven hundred pounds, Coffelt still went out in the pasture, gave a big holler, and the huge beast lay down and put its head in Coffelt's lap.[36]

The cowboys always speculated among themselves that Coffelt had been more than a line rider for the 101 Ranch. Some claimed that he had been an enforcer for the Millers, disposing of persons who got in the family's way. Stories of Coffelt as hired gun and as buffalo trainer were still being told long after the old man had died, in 1949. No matter who was telling the yarn about the eccentric old-timer, they never failed to use the word *lucky* when describing him. *Loyal* was another word usually heard. Coffelt—the crazy old buffalo man—had beat the hangman four times, and to his dying day, he remained true to the Hundred and One.

Chapter 21

FULL CIRCLE

The wheel is come full circle.[1]
—William Shakespeare
King Lear

CONSTANTLY embroiled in conflicts, George Washington Miller did not age gracefully. The founder of the 101 Ranch empire spent most of his last years locked in combat with rivals and foes. Some of his more serious quarrels were never resolved.

One of these feuds was the ongoing squabble between Colonel Miller and his most hated competitor, Abel Head "Shanghai" Pierce. Even long before the Miller family ran afoul of the law and became implicated in the unsolved murder case of George C. Montgomery, G.W. clashed hot and heavy with the explosive Texas cattleman who had once been his friend and partner. Both Miller and Pierce were known to resort to questionable business practices in their cattle trade, so it was difficult to pinpoint the problem or cast all the blame on one side.

Much of the rancor between the two stemmed from the old days of the Cherokee Outlet, when Pierce and Miller had a falling-out over a cattle deal. That was when Shanghai reportedly told G.W., "I can't stand you. You have got so bad you take cows before my own eyes. You have got more gall than any man I ever saw. When a man gets this bold, I can't watch him. . . . Mister Miller, I can't keep up with you. I will have to quit you. You bother me too much."[2]

Then when Miller confronted Pierce in his Pullman car as his train passed through Indian Territory, Pierce fired a blast from his shotgun that caused Miller to make a hasty retreat.[3] When he heard that Pierce was coming back through on another train, Colonel Miller showed up at the depot, carrying two Winchesters. The plan was for Pierce to use one rifle and Miller the other, so the two stubborn cattlemen could have an old-fashioned duel. But Pierce was not aboard the train, and the fight never took place.[4]

In late 1898, Colonel Miller appeared in a Galveston, Texas, courtroom as a witness on behalf of another party who accused Pierce of fraud in a cattle deal. Pierce's lawyer objected that Miller was not a fit witness because he had been convicted of cattle theft in Oklahoma Territory in 1897, but Miller protested loudly, pointing out that the sentence had been reversed. When Pierce took the stand, he shouted, "Miller is known to be the biggest liar on the American continent, and, not only the biggest liar, but the biggest thief; there is no dispute about that. He is not only the biggest liar, but the biggest thief and son of a bitch. He is under indictment now—he is under sentence."[5]

After the trial, Pierce and Miller continued to bellow threats and curses at each other. The strife persisted until December 26, 1900, when Shanghai Pierce died in his sleep after a holiday meal of turkey and raw oysters.[6] Although the two old rascals never had their duel, Colonel Miller probably felt some satisfaction about having outlived Pierce.

In spite of the violence and encounters with the law which came to be thought of as just part of business, the Millers worked hard to make the ranch profitable. If success required sending Zack Miller and Bert Colby to California in 1901 to buy mules needed by the British for the Boer War, the two would set off without hesitation.[7] If it required transforming more raw prairie land into cultivated fields, that was what they did. If it required taking risks by experimenting with livestock breeds, that was the way the Millers went. And if it meant coaxing some nester or homesteader to pack up and leave so the 101 Ranch outfit could have more land, there was no alternative. All the while, Colonel Miller and his family kept up their relationship with the Poncas and other Indian tribes in the area.

Indeed, the Millers understood that if the ranch was to prosper, they needed access to the land owned by these tribes. Joe's daughter, Alice Miller Harth, recalled the transactions of her childhood. "Our living room was always filled with Indians. In their blankets they huddled about the little round stove that was so hot when the corncobs had just been put in and which so soon became cold and needed refilling. In the summer the Indians sat on our porch, still in their blankets, no matter how warm the weather. They came so often and sat so long to get ponies, beeves, calico and all the things that father and grandfather seemed to know how to get for them better than they knew how to secure for themselves. On the other hand, the Indians had something that father and grandfather wanted—land."[8]

By 1902, the Millers had almost fifty thousand acres in pasture and under cultivation. Busy both as farmers and as stock raisers, they operated as the 101 Live Stock Company, with the main office in Winfield and the ranch address at Bliss, Oklahoma Territory.[9] It was a family affair. Colonel Miller served as president, his brother Walter T. "Uncle Doc" as vice president, and Alma as secretary and treasurer. All three sons also had specific roles. Joe was superintendent, Zack manager of livestock, and George manager of farming operations.[10]

In addition to land rental, the Millers shelled out about seventy-five thousand dollars a year in operating expenses. That still left plenty of profit. The livestock herds and thousands of acres sowed with wheat, corn, and forage crops generated close to five hundred thousand dollars in annual income. That required a work force of two hundred men and two hundred stout cow ponies.[11]

After a decade of successful farming and ranching on the Ponca pastures, the Millers were prepared to purchase the land they had been leasing from the Ponca and Otoe tribes for $32,500 annually.[12] This occurred in 1903, as the federal government continued to break up various Indian lands and dole out allotments to individual tribal members, enabling tribes to sell property with federal approval. When White Eagle received permission to sell some of the Ponca land, the Millers were finally able to buy some of the thousands of acres they had been leasing from the tribe.[13]

The combined purchased property and lands held under preferential leases from the Indians made the 101 Ranch a huge operation. The Millers' holdings extended through the lands of the Ponca, Otoe, Pawnee, and Osage tribes in four counties—Kay, Noble, Osage, and Pawnee.[14] No longer burdened with uncertainties, restrictions, and government red tape, the Millers at last felt comfortable about making permanent improvements on the land. They were especially anxious to draw up plans for a large headquarters residence to replace the sod dugout on the bank of the Salt Fork. Much of the prodding for a new home came from the women of the Miller family, especially Joe's wife, Lizzie, who became increasingly weary of putting up with all sorts of unexpected guests at her cottage beneath the elms and cottonwoods.[15]

Colonel Miller wanted the new 101 headquarters house to be the finest prairie palace in all of cow country. He told his family and friends that no cost would be spared. Influenced by the love of fine plantation homes in

Kentucky, the family planned a three-story frame residence with a basement and complete waterworks, to be built on the north side of the Salt Fork. The furnishings would come from the Millers' residence in Winfield.[16] J. W. Hiatt and his wife, Mary, soon purchased the Millers' Winfield home.[17]

While planning the new family residence, Colonel Miller stayed at his cow camp on the Bar L spread, just east of Bliss. In the winter of 1902–1903, he built a sod-and-brush shanty on the Bar L, along with a cook shack and sturdy canvas tent. A nearby spring gurgled up clear water.[18]

In addition to building a new ranch house and managing what had become one of the largest farms under fence in the country, Colonel Miller confronted plenty of problems and uncertainties. Although he had been freed on bond in the murder of George C. Montgomery, Miller seemed unable to steer clear of trouble.

On March 16, 1903, a Noble County grand jury meeting at Perry indicted G. W. Miller for the theft of eighteen head of cattle off Ponca lands, valued at thirty dollars each. Their owner, Thomas Stribling, had reported them stolen on January 19.[19] Colonel Miller's prospects appeared bleak, with the start of his murder trial in June and an accusation of cattle rustling.

But Miller never got his day in court to respond to any of the charges against him. He also never set foot in the ranch headquarters he had carefully planned. On a drizzly April afternoon, Colonel Miller got off a train at Bliss after a brief business trip only to find none of his cowboys at the station waiting with a pony or a rig to take him home. He thought nothing of it and struck out on foot, but during his five-mile hike to the Salt Fork, the rains kicked up again. By the time he reached the dugout, the old man was soaking wet and chilled to the bone. Instead of resting the next day, he helped Joe plant an orchard. The old man worked up a sweat and then became chilled. A pile of blankets and a few long tugs of whiskey were not enough help. Within a few days, Miller had pneumonia in both lungs.[20]

Molly came down from Winfield to be with her husband. A doctor arrived from Ponca City. G.W.'s three sons and daughter never left his side. Medicine and prayers brought comfort, but there was nothing more anyone could do for the old cattleman.

"Grandfather said he didn't want to live past sixty years of age," Alice Miller Harth later wrote. "His demands on life required enormous physical strength and he feared old age without it."[21]

Almost as soon as his illness was diagnosed, Colonel Miller realized that he would not recover. His sense of southern hospitality remained constant to the end. Three hours before his death, he made sure some friends who had ridden out to bid him farewell were fed a proper meal. He apologized that he could not join them at the table.[22] It was time for G.W. "to sing Indian"—to act fearlessly in the face of death just as Indians often did when they defied their fate by singing or chanting.

Colonel George Washington Miller, founder of the 101 Ranch empire, died quietly inside the old dugout headquarters on the Salt Fork. He was sixty-one years old. It was 2:30 in the afternoon on Saturday, April 25, 1903. G. W. Miller had gone west one final time. A newspaper headline said it all—"Spirit of 101 Ranch Gone."[23]

On Sunday, April 26, at 9:30 A.M, the Reverend Sims, the Methodist missionary at the Ponca agency, conducted a brief funeral service for Colonel Miller.[24] His family washed and dressed the old man and laid him in a coffin packed with ice so the body would keep while being shipped by rail back to Crab Orchard, the family home in Kentucky. Colonel Miller had wished to be laid to rest at the Fish place, in the burying ground alongside his baby sons and other kinfolk. An escort of G.W.'s favorite cowboys turned out in their best hats and boots and rode on each side of the hearse as it rolled from the ranch headquarters toward the depot at Bliss. Many Indians also accompanied the black hearse moving across the Millers' domain, past wheat fields, past stock pens and corrals, past herds of grazing cattle.[25]

The Ponca chief, White Eagle, and other tribal leaders paid their last respects to *Tesca-nu-da-hunga,* the mighty cow chief. They viewed Colonel Miller's body at the dugout, but they did not go with the others to the railroad station. A newspaper reporter who was there that day heard White Eagle quietly explain, "I would not weep where men and women could see. I must retire alone." All night long, the wail of Ponca mourners came from their distant camp. The next day, the Indians butchered many beeves and held a big feast to honor their departed friend.[26]

Molly and Joe went back to Kentucky with their dead patriarch. They laid out his body at the old Crab Orchard Springs Hotel so his Kentucky friends and family could say good-bye. Then they took him out to the cemetery on the Fish farm and buried him below the bluegrass sod, deep in the Kentucky soil. Before they returned to Oklahoma Territory, they placed a granite tombstone over his grave. Nearby were the resting places of G.W.'s grandparents, mother, and two young sons, Wilkes Booth and John Fish.[27]

Back on the Salt Fork, everyone felt like eating sorrow by the spoonful. Instead, they did just what Colonel Miller would have expected them to do. Zack and George and all the cowboys saddled ponies and rode the range from dawn until dusk. They roped and wrangled, they doctored sick animals, and they mended fences. They worked until their muscles burned and their bones ached.

And after a hot meal and a few hours of rest, they rose again and went out into the darkness of the new day. The old man was gone, with his bellow and roar, but that morning star still blinked in the heavens and showed them the way. A new era dawned on the ranch as the next generation took the reins.

THE YALLER DOG

BY THE TIME George Washington Miller succumbed to pneumonia on his sprawling 101 Ranch, the West of myth and the West of history had permanently fused to create the American dream. Many figures had a part in its creation, ranging from Frederic Remington and Charles Russell, the two best-known painters of western subjects, to Wild West showman William F. "Buffalo Bill" Cody and President Theodore Roosevelt—the "damned cowboy," amateur rancher, and famed Rough Rider who gave the American West the political and intellectual renown it had previously lacked.[1]

A host of new writers helped idealize the West and perpetuated the romantic myths of the frontier. One of them was Jack London, a socialist who wrote of the survival of the fittest, high adventure, and heroic struggle in the wilderness. Another was Zane Grey, who gave up a New York dental practice in 1904 to churn out scores of the most popular adventure novels of the American West.[2]

There was also O. Henry—the pen name of William Sydney Porter—a masterful short-story writer and creator of "The Cisco Kid" and other memorable characters.[3] On April 25, 1898, the day the Spanish-American War began, Porter was found guilty of embezzling bank funds in Texas. He acquired his famous pseudonym and scribbled a dozen fictional stories while serving thirty-nine months of a five-year sentence at the federal penitentiary at Columbus, Ohio, at the same time Joe Miller was imprisoned there.[4]

Notwithstanding the literary efforts of O. Henry and others, just after the twentieth century began, a towering best-seller appeared that created the archetypal cowboy hero and became the most influential western novel ever written. Published in 1902, *The Virginian*, by Owen Wister, a native of Philadelphia who went west for his health before studying law at Harvard, achieved instant success. In the five decades after it appeared, the book sold more than 1.8 million copies.[5]

Dedicated to the author's old friend Theodore Roosevelt, the book not only glamorized the Wild West, but also gave it relevancy. *The Virginian* made the cowboy a stalwart heroic figure and put him center stage in the nation's consciousness. In so doing, Wister helped to shape an image of the American West that would endure throughout the century.[6]

In the late spring of 1903, only a year after the publication of *The Virginian* and just as the body of George Washington Miller was being laid to rest in Kentucky, still another major influence on the public's perception of the West made its debut before pleased audiences across the country. Unlike Wister's endeavor, this creative effort was not a literary work but a film narrative with a western setting. In truth, it was shot on location in the "wilds" near Dover, New Jersey, and in the Edison studios.[7]

The Great Train Robbery, Edwin S. Porter's most celebrated film, was not the first western film, as some historians have claimed. However, the twelve-minute, one-reel film served as an important milestone in the history of motion pictures and set the standard for the western film as a genre.[8]

Several film elements introduced in *The Great Train Robbery* became staples in western movies for generations. Besides the robbery itself, it showed a saloon scene, an episode of bullies terrorizing a dude and, of course, a posse in pursuit of robbers, providing the consummate chase that remained standard fare in almost every western.[9] At the close of the film, audiences invariably shrieked in horror when mustached villain George Barnes faced the camera and blasted away at them with his six-shooter, an event that had absolutely no part in the plot.[10]

A former vaudeville actor using the stage name Gilbert M. Anderson (his real name was Max Aronson) was given a minor role in the film after assuring Porter that he was an accomplished horseman. In reality, the beefy actor could not even mount a cow pony, much less stay in the saddle; he was soon relegated to the ranks of "extras."[11] But even though he failed to get top billing, Anderson was excited by the possibilities film offered. Within a short time, he moved to Chicago and then to California in 1908, where he became known as "Broncho Billy" Anderson, the first true western movie star.[12]

By the time Broncho Billy figured out how to ride a horse, the three Miller brothers were well on their way to becoming deeply involved in the entertainment business as purveyors of western myth. But in 1903, as folks lined up to see *The Great Train Robbery* or eagerly devoured every word of *The Virginian*, the Millers carried on with their everyday trials and tribulations out on the Oklahoma Territory range. Joe, Zack, and George had no use for novels or nicklelodeons—not yet.

In August 1903, Martha "Calamity Jane" Canary died and was buried next to "Wild Bill" Hickok in Deadwood, South Dakota, and the nation's first cross-country automobile drive was completed.[13] It also was a time for the Millers to finish grieving for G.W. while they worked their fields and grazing pastures along the Salt Fork of the Arkansas River. The West of myth and the West of history may have blended elsewhere, but on the 101 Ranch, the Millers were still immersed in reality.

That same month, J. W. "Buck" Eldridge founded a saloon at the Noble County settlement of Red Rock. Word of the only "whistle-wetting" oasis for cowpunchers riding those parts quickly reached the 101 Ranch. On the day of the grand opening, Zack Miller and seventy-five of the Millers' cowboys rode to Red Rock. It was an occasion not soon forgotten, especially by the owner.[14]

Zack and the cowboys carried on all night long. They drank the shanty saloon dry and shot off so many rounds from their six-guns that the entire roof had to be replaced. Buck Eldridge was just happy to be alive after all the gunplay. "It was a tough country," he told a reporter many years later. "The celebration got going pretty good, and the boys got out their firearms. I'll never forget what happened. They riddled the roof of my shack and I decided right then and there that there would be no more gunplay in my saloon, and there never was."[15]

Eldridge also remembered how he came up with a name for his new establishment. "I believe I'll name it after that old yaller dog that came in last night," Eldridge told Zack Miller the next morning. "I think that'll bring me luck." Zack agreed, and the name Yaller Dog stuck.[16] It was celebrated in song and story, and even a poem was penned about the place:

I'm only a yaller canine, at best an ugly brute . . .
Old Buck is the only friend I have,
as around the street I roam.
And I still can tell my master's voice,
while this joint is home sweet home.[17]

Years later, when Zack and his brothers dealt with big-shot film directors and rubbed shoulders with actors who smelled nice but could not tell a horse from a cow, they thought back to Buck Eldridge and Red Rock and the Yaller Dog Saloon. As their West, the West of reality, slowly merged with the West of myth, the memories of those high times kept the cowmen from going crazy.

Chapter 22

THE MILLER BROTHERS

There were two keys to the success of the 101 Ranch. The first was the talents of its operators. The oldest son, Joe Miller, was an outstanding farmer who introduced the most recent scientific agricultural methods to the ranch. The second son, Zack, was a cattleman who brought similar innovations to beef raising and dairy farming. The third son, George L., was a financier who attracted the eastern capital necessary to pay for the modernization of the ranch.[1]

—John Thompson
Closing the Frontier

AFTER the death of George W. Miller, in April 1903, his three sons—Joe, thirty-five years old; Zack, twenty-five years old; and George Lee, almost twenty-two years old—assumed active management of the dynasty he had created from swapping cured hog meat for that first herd of sinewy longhorns. Under the Miller brothers' joint supervision and expert guidance, the 101 Ranch would grow into one of the most profitable ranching and farming operations in the West. That meant the Millers employed more cowboys to work the beef cattle and breeding stock and acquired additional hired hands to tend the flourishing pastures and fields of cash crops.

Many years later, Mack Wafer, who hired on with the Millers in 1903, recalled his time at the ranch. "I was paid twenty-five dollars per month, with room and board. At that time they had a big wheat crop and I ran the binder. They also raised cotton, all kinds of feed and corn and I did anything that there was to do, except ride fence line. The Miller brothers also had a large herd of buffaloes on the ranch."[2]

Soon after Joe and his mother returned from burying G.W. in Kentucky, the family made sure that his plans were carried out for a new residence to serve as the 101 Ranch headquarters. Colonel Miller left no last will and testament, but he had earmarked thirty thousand dollars of a life-insurance policy for Molly. She put the windfall to good use by buying more land and finishing construction of the three-story frame home on the north side of the Salt Fork, opposite the old dugout headquarters that G.W. had built in 1893.[3]

Before the house was completed, the family gathered for the first social event to be held there—the marriage of Alma, the only Miller daughter.[4] Her betrothed was William Henry England, a budding attorney and Cowley County native raised on a farm near Dexter, Kansas, site of his father's department store, England & Son. The couple's romance blossomed in Winfield, where England, educated primarily at Southwestern College in Kansas, taught in the public schools to earn money for the study of law. Alma, a Vassar graduate, was taking a teachers' preparatory course. Both of them were twenty-eight.[5]

The wedding, which the couple had postponed because of Colonel Miller's death, took place on October 31, 1903, at the new ranch headquarters. All three Miller brothers attended the nuptials, even though England was admittedly Republican. They knew he had worked on a farm and as a laborer when the railroad was built through Dexter, so he was industrious and would provide for their sister. Moreover, the Millers believed it would not hurt to have a lawyer in the family.[6]

The couple moved to Topeka, Kansas, where England served as federal court clerk before opening a law practice in Kansas City. Although Alma purchased his law books and helped him establish his career, she believed her husband's declaration that he had not married her for her money. Shortly after their marriage, Alma received her share in the family estate, including some properties outside the ranch holdings, and severed all other financial connections to the 101 Ranch.[7]

After Alma's wedding, the work crews finished details on the big frame home. On Christmas Day 1903—just a week after Wilbur and Orville Wright had made history with their flying machine at Kitty Hawk, North Carolina—Molly, all four of her children, and their families gathered in the dining room of the new house. They consumed platters of wild turkey and, of course, roast beef, at the first meal served in the residence that came to be called the White House.[8] Joe's daughter, Alice Miller Harth, later recalled it was "a tall, white frame house characteristic of prosperous midwestern farmers of the day. . . . An office was included on the downstairs floor with a door that opened into the residence. It was usually kept open because Grandmother liked to know what was going on; she often gave advice that was heeded. . . . One day an employee referred to her house as the White House, a name that pleased Grandmother and one that she encouraged."[9]

Near her grand residence on the prairie, Molly maintained a huge flock of geese as a source for down pillows. When plucking time came, Molly had a hired hand pen up the birds so she and Alice could snatch feathers from the squawking victims.[10]

The Miller matriarch employed a Chinese cook trained in the culinary arts and constantly eager to show off his skill at preparing gourmet dishes for Molly and the stream of guests who visited her spacious ranch residence. When she learned that squab on toast was popular among swank folks back east, Molly had a big nesting house built and stocked with pigeons. Soon Zack, George, and the other meat-and-potatoes men of the 101 Ranch sat down to heaping platters of squab.[11]

The trouble was that the pigeons reproduced so quickly that squab on toast became standard fare at almost every meal, including breakfast. The two bachelor Miller brothers soon found every excuse possible to dine with Joe and Lizzie, whose cook had not discovered the nutritional possibilities of unfledged pigeon. Rebellion at the White House was imminent until a resourceful soul—most likely Zack—came up with a solution. One evening, the door to the pigeon house was "accidentally" left open. The following day, beefsteak, pork chops, and country ham were restored as staples on the ranch menu.[12]

By that time, Molly had moved on to a new project. The big orchards Joe had planted were beginning to produce, and the gardens yielded so much that Molly and her helpers canned and preserved enough bushels of fruit and vegetables to feed practically all of Oklahoma Territory.[13]

"The business was growing and absorbing all the time of Papa and his brothers," recalled Alma Miller Harth. "Around the White House quite a large group of buildings began to grow. Because so many men had to be sheltered and fed, there were bunk houses and a large mess hall. To supply this a dairy was required as was also a packing plant, which supplied a part of the community too. The hides required a tannery and the vegetables a cannery. There were also stables, blacksmith shops, granaries, hog sheds, poultry houses, and a store."[14]

The Miller brothers operated the ranch as a family alliance, and with the encouragement and inspiration of their mother, the enterprise continued to grow by leaps and bounds. The ranch soon became known as the

Miller Brothers' 101 Ranch, with each of the three sons focusing on a different aspect of the partnership.

Although the brothers always consulted with Molly before any major transactions and kept her posted on all business affairs at the ranch, Joe Miller, as the eldest, assumed the leadership of the family. He also purchased some of the finest breeding stock in the Southwest and specialized in the agricultural aspects of the business, including the care of the orchards and fields. Zack, all cowboy, enjoyed buying, selling, and caring for the cattle and horses. George possessed the hard-nosed business talent, running the busy offices, overseeing financial operations, and negotiating contracts.[15]

It was a formidable combination of skills, with still more growth and successes to come. The Millers were poised to take center stage under floods of public limelight. Their impressive dominion would soon come to be considered the last bastion of the "Real Wild West."[16]

To make certain their growing empire had a voice in the affairs of the territory, the Millers began periodically to publish their own newspaper before the close of 1903. They named the paper the *Bliss Breeze* and listed Joe Miller as publisher on the masthead.[17] Joe had no intention of allowing the newspaper to detract from his duties on the ranch. He recruited a couple of young men to gather local news from ranches and communities and put the paper together. The idea behind the *Breeze* was to call attention to the successes of the ranch, but the Millers also had another motive—membership in the National Editorial Association.[18]

This affiliation with a professional organization led to a genuine turning point for the 101 Ranch. It took place in May 1904 when Joe Miller accompanied Frank Hilton Greer, editor and publisher of the Guthrie newspaper *Oklahoma State Capital*, and other territorial editors to a meeting of the National Editorial Association in Saint Louis.[19]

Although Greer was a staunch Republican leader known for his scathing editorials, Joe Miller was delighted to be part of the entourage going to the big parley in Saint Louis. Partisan politics had to be put aside. Joe had a definite plan in mind for the 101 Ranch—to induce the nation's editors to visit his family's farm and cattle spread. By enlisting the support of an enterprising publisher such as Greer, Joe Miller believed he would gain a powerful and persuasive ally to help make his case.[20]

"They ought to hold next year's convention in Oklahoma," Joe reportedly told Greer. "It would get the Territory more publicity than it's had since the land rush of eighty-nine."[21] Greer agreed and was even more excited when Joe spoke of sponsoring a visit to the 101 Ranch, where the editors could see cowboy and Indian stunts that "would pop the eyes right out of their heads!"[22]

Joe and the others in his party arrived at Saint Louis' handsome Union Station, with its cavernous train shed and the terminus for twenty-seven railroads.[23] To Joe, it seemed that the entire population of the world had gathered in the river city, the fourth-largest city in the nation and the site of the Louisiana Purchase Exposition. The extraordinary event marking the centennial of the Louisiana Purchase was considered by some historians to be the most remarkable of all world's fairs, rivaling even the 1893 World's Columbian Exposition in Chicago.[24]

The formal opening of the exposition took place April 30, 1904, just prior to the National Editorial Association convention, to be held May 19–21.[25] During the convention, which attracted newspaper editors and publishers from throughout the nation, Greer gave a presentation about the possibilities of Guthrie as a convention city, and then Joe was given a chance to make his pitch for the 101 Ranch.

Undoubtedly, Joe found inspiration in artist Frederic Remington's group of spirited statuary cowboys shooting up a western town that was positioned at the entrance to the Pike, the exposition's mile-long avenue of amusements.[26] Perhaps his excitement came from the parade of costumed Sioux and Plains Indians riding as members of the Wild West Indian Congress and Rough Riders of the World.[27] Whatever his motivation, Joe won the hearts of every member of the selection committee when he promised a spectacle like no other if the editors would hold their next convention at Guthrie and then visit his family's ranch on the Salt Fork.[28]

"Let me get a hundred good cowhands together, and I'll put you on a show the like of which your editors never saw," Joe Miller supposedly told Greer and the others. "I'll give them something to write about."[29]

The editors gave Joe Miller a resounding affirmative vote. The National Editorial Association scheduled its next convention for June 1905 in Guthrie, Oklahoma Territory, followed by a side trip to the Miller Brothers' 101 Ranch.[30] After the handshakes and cigars, Joe raced to the nearest telegraph office to send word to his family.

For several days after the convention broke up, hundreds of visitors were seen roaming the exposition grounds carrying glass canes the Miller family had prepared for the convention.[31] Each of the green-tinted walking sticks bore a red leather patch stamped with the message:

Meet Me At The Buffalo Chase
Cowboy Reunion
June 11, 1905
At The 101 Ranch
Bliss, Oklahoma

After distributing the canes and winning the bid for the next year's convention, Joe returned to Oklahoma Territory as soon as possible. He and his brothers met in the office at the White House and began to plan for the major gathering. They summoned their mother, the top ranch foremen, and some of the premium cowboy riders to the strategy sessions.

That busy summer of 1904 found the Millers also engrossed in the daily operations of their ranching and agricultural domain. Just to help feed the more than three hundred ranch and farm workers, they slaughtered a beef cow each day and fetched eggs from a flock of one thousand chickens. All the meat, vegetables, fruit, and flour consumed in the dining halls and at the line camps were products of the ranch. An immense herd of dairy cattle furnished milk and butter, and the ranch had thousands of head of graded cattle and Herefords, buffalo, mules, hogs, brood mares, and cow ponies.[32]

The hay from five thousand acres was cured each year for winter feed. From the first of July to November, as many as fifteen mowers worked in the hayfields. They raked four thousand tons of hay into piles of a half ton each and salted them down for the winter.

Besides farmhands, numerous blacksmiths, carpenters, and teamsters kept busy at all times. One team of men devoted the entire year to keeping all the fences in repair. Most of the cowboys, stationed at the headquarters or at one of the four outlying camps, roped and branded cattle and broke horses. They seldom mingled with the farmhands and harvesters. But every man, woman, and child drawing wages on the ranch—regardless of whether they were top wranglers, common laborers, or just kids hauling water to hay crews—knew the Millers and thoroughly understood the family's wishes.[33]

After the crop harvest and cornhusking of 1904, the Miller brothers determined it was time to see if they could still sponsor a proper roundup. It had been a long time since 1882, when Colonel Miller conducted that first roundup at the county fair in Winfield.

In the autumn, while the world's fair was still drawing record crowds to Saint Louis, the Millers held a "buffalo chase" on the ranch.[34] The public event was considered a dress rehearsal for the editors' convention scheduled for the next summer. They cleared some pastureland and constructed seating. Folks from Ponca City, Perry, and smaller communities showed up to watch the riding and roping 101 Ranch cowboys and a band of Indians in pursuit of a galloping buffalo bull along the Salt Fork River. Not a person who came was disappointed—most people in the crowd cheered themselves hoarse. The practice roundup was a complete success.[35] Joe Miller, who had made his debut as a bronc rider and roper at Winfield in 1882, had not lost his touch. Neither had the salty cowhands.

All winter long and into spring, as warm winds returned with steady rains, the Millers and their cowboys grew more anxious for their roundup extravaganza in June. Not one of them knew that when it was all over, all their lives would be changed—and so would the way the nation would look at the West.

THE WORLD'S FIRST COWGIRL MEETS THE CHEROKEE KID

AS THEY PREPARED for the national convention of newspaper editors in 1905, the Miller brothers grew anxious. They understood all too well that they not only had their work cut out for them, but that the risk of failure was great.

Tens of thousands of visitors, including a small army of powerful editorial and political influences from across the nation, were expected to descend on the 101 Ranch. It was essential that everything be in place and the ranch be put in top-notch shape. This was no easy task for a family which at the same time was trying to produce bumper crops of wheat and moneymaking herds of cattle.

Throughout the final months of 1904, a period highlighted by the closing of the Saint Louis World's Fair and President Theodore Roosevelt's stunning second-term victory, the three Miller brothers fully developed their plans and began work on their big entertainment event, to be staged along the Salt Fork near the ranch headquarters.[1] Those efforts gained more momentum in 1905.

Nothing other than the ballyhooed "buffalo chase" mattered to the Millers, even though, across the seas, causalities mounted in the war between Japan and Russia and, on American soil, the Supreme Court ruled in favor of the government's attempted suppression of unfair practices by Swift & Company and other large meatpacking concerns.[2] Not even a fiery Ty Cobb—"the Georgia Peach"—launching his major league baseball career in Detroit that spring or reports that Congress had halted the coinage of gold dollars distracted the Millers from their objective.[3]

Except for the essential ranch and farm activities and any substantial business decisions, the Miller brothers put everything else on hold in deference to their preparations for the anticipated Wild West gala. That included all their family and personal relationships—even with children, wives, and girlfriends.

Lizzie Miller, tending her daughter, Alice, and son, George, while pregnant with a third child due at midsummer, hardly saw her husband during the first half of 1905.[4] She spent her time overseeing household servants, receiving a steady flow of impassive Ponca Indian wives who dropped by uninvited, and gossiping for hours at a time with Mother Molly Miller at the White House. In the cool of the morning, Lizzie faithfully struggled over her precious garden of zinnias, marigolds, snapdragons, and sweet peas, all surrounded by chicken wire to keep out grazing goats and poultry.[5]

Meanwhile, Lizzie's determined husband, Joe, and his two younger brothers were out on the prowl. They were not searching for new breeding stock or the latest in farm machinery, but for talent to supplement their cadre of capable cowboy riders. Besides bossing the work crews as they cleared pasture for additional performance grounds and directing carpenters as they constructed more seats to augment those from the 1904 rehearsal roundup, the Millers hunted high and low for top-quality entertainers.

The ranch already boasted many skilled bronco fighters and rope tossers, but most of the hired hands were rough saddle tramps and unpolished working cowboys. The Millers believed a few rousing specialty acts were needed as crowd pleasers. Some of the finest trick ropers, bronc riders, musicians, and animal trainers drawing pay were already booked for the convention. But in the spring of 1905, the Millers acquired the services of a bona fide world-champion rodeo performer—a spirited nineteen-year-old named Lucille Mulhall, acclaimed from the Twin Territories to New York City as the original cowgirl.[6]

Weighing less than a pair of fancy Mexican saddles, Lucille not only threw steers and busted broncs but also stalked prairie wolves, branded cattle, and roped as many as eight running range horses at once.[7] She was an absolute showstopper. Schooled by stern nuns at two convents, Lucille, as described in 1900 by a New York journalist, could "play Chopin, quote Browning, construe Vergil [sic], and make mayonnaise dressing." The reporter noted that Lucille was "a little ashamed of these latter accomplishments, which are a concession to the civilized prejudices of her mother."[8]

When it came to rodeoing, Lucille had no equal. Elegantly clad in boots, ankle-length divided skirt, neckerchief, hat, and gloves, she put to shame men twice her age and size.[9]

Lucille came from a rather motley family background. Her parents, Mary Agnes Locke and Zachariah P. Vandeveer, were orphans. Her father, born in 1847 and left parentless at age eight, had been taken in by his uncle and aunt, the Joseph Mulhalls, an Irish Catholic family in Saint Louis. In addition to their young nephew, the Mulhalls later brought into their home young Mary Agnes, also a relative, and raised her as their own.[10]

Adopting his surrogate family's surname, Zack Mulhall, as he became known, squeaked through a few difficult semesters at the University of Notre Dame. He also played a bit of baseball for the Saint Louis Empires and labored on the livestock ferries along the Mississippi before going to work for the railroad.[11] Mary Agnes, twelve years younger than Zack, completed her schooling at Saint Mary's College at Notre Dame, a liberal-arts school for women, near South Bend, Indiana. Despite having been raised as siblings, Zack and Mary Agnes were clearly attracted to each other. They married in 1875, when he was twenty-eight years old and she was sixteen.[12]

Remaining in Saint Louis for almost fifteen years, they eventually had four sons and four daughters, but most of the children, including twin girls, died in infancy. One son, Logan, died of diphtheria when he was fourteen. Only two of Zack and Mary Agnes' daughters survived to adulthood—Agnes, nicknamed Bossie, born in 1877, and the spunky Lucille, born in Saint Louis on October 21, 1885.[13]

Others in the family circle included Georgia Mulhall, later billed in the Mulhalls' Wild West show advertisements as Mary Agnes and Zack's daughter to quiet gossiping tongues. In fact, she was an orphaned teenager named Georgia Smith who worked in a boardinghouse where Zack sometimes stayed when he was working for the Santa Fe Railway.[14] Although he brought her to Saint Louis to live with his family as a so-called adopted daughter, she eventually became Zack Mulhall's mistress. In time, he moved her to Kansas City where, in 1888, she bore Zack a son named Charles Joseph.[15]

When Charley was ten years old, Zack brought him to live with the rest of the family in Saint Louis. Mary Agnes, a devout woman, treated the boy like her own son. Zack and Georgia also had a second child together, a daughter, born in 1895. Georgia turned her second baby over to Zack's wife, who named the infant Mildred Madeline after her dead twin daughters.[16]

By then, the Mulhalls had been gone from Saint Louis for several years. Zack, who knew the Indian lands from his work as a railroader and was grazing a herd of cattle on leased Cherokee pastures, took part in the run of 1889 when Congress opened the Unassigned Lands for settlement. He staked his claim along Beaver Creek near the railway stop called Alfred. Eighteen miles to the north was the tent town of Guthrie, soon to become the bustling territorial capital.[17]

Immediately after erecting a temporary shelter on his homestead, Zack built stockyards and gave the railroad some land for right of way and a train station. He built a big, rambling family residence just west of town on his ranchlands that extended north into the Cherokee Outlet. When Mary Agnes and the rest of the Mulhalls arrived the following year, local citizens had already successfully petitioned the railroad to rename the town Mulhall in honor of Zack, the mayor at the time.[18]

The entire Mulhall brood—Bossie and Lucille, as well as Zack's children by Georgia, Charley and Mildred—took to ranch life. Lucille was considered a top cowhand by the time she was ten years old.[19] Mary Agnes tried with little success to shape her daughters into proper ladies. After Lucille's horse threw her while she was roping steers, her mother—over Zack's voluble protests—shipped her off to boarding school at the Visitation Convent in Saint Louis.[20] It was not a happy time for Lucille. In one letter to the Mulhalls, the concerned sisters at the convent wrote that "although her school work is good and she relates well to the other girls, it is breaking her heart to be so far from the ranch."[21]

Lucille was delighted when Zack brought her home to attend school at Saint Joseph's Convent in Guthrie. It meant she could return to the ranch on weekends and ride her beloved horses. Indeed, even her brief stay with the nuns at Guthrie failed to keep Lucille away from cattle. When one of the cows in the self-sustaining convent's livestock herd had difficulty delivering a calf, the troubled sisters summoned Lucille to help.[22]

Back on the ranch, Zack Mulhall noticed that his children, particularly Lucille and Charley, attracted compliments from all the cowhands by riding bucking horses and roping any critter in sight. When the mayor of Guthrie started to summon the Mulhall kids to entertain special visitors, Zack—who had dreamed for years of producing a Wild West show—gathered up his accomplished brood and hit the road.[23]

In 1899, Colonel Mulhall, as he became known throughout Oklahoma Territory and beyond, began to stage riding and roping contests—the type of rousing cowboy entertainment that the Millers called "roundups."[24] Mulhall's shows featured his organization of performers, dubbed "The Congress of Rough Riders and Ropers," but the main headliners were his offspring, including thirteen-year-old Lucille, riding her trained horse, named Governor. Adoring fans nicknamed him the "Wonder Horse."[25]

At first, the Mulhalls and their gang of riders and ropers did not stray too far from home. Then in 1899, an invitation arrived for Zack and his troupe to play the county fair back in his hometown of Saint Louis. It was just the break Colonel Mulhall had prayed for; he signed the contract immediately.[26]

One of the cowboy performers the Mulhalls brought along for the Saint Louis show was a young mixed-blood Cherokee trick roper, not long out of military school and fresh off the cattle ranges.[27] Neither Zack Mulhall nor the young man with an engaging drawl—who possessed an amazing talent for twirling a lariat and spreading his homespun humor—realized that one day he would be a national icon and the best-known American in the world.

Born November 4, 1879, in a two-story ranch house on the Verdigris River near the Cherokee Nation town of Oologah to Clem and Mary Schrimsher Rogers, the boy was named William Penn Adair Rogers.[28] The family called him Willie, and some of his cowboy associates later nicknamed him "Injun."[29] The Mulhalls, including Lucille, who was most impressed with the young man's roping ability, called him Billie. Within a couple of years, he would go by the name "Cherokee Kid" when he rode as a "Fancy Lasso Artist and Rough Rider" with Texas Jack's Wild West Show in South Africa.[30] Long after those names were discarded or forgotten, everyone would always remember him as simply Will Rogers.

Rogers, who never drew a paycheck from the 101 Ranch but spent a good deal of time on the Salt Fork range and became a close pal of the three Miller brothers, always credited the Mulhalls for much of his success. Thirty-two years after he first hooked up with the family and their show, Rogers, in his distinctive and often colloquially ungrammatical style, wrote about how the Mulhalls helped to shape his career. The story appeared in one of his popular syndicated newspaper columns, published in 1931, less than a month after Colonel Mulhall's death, at age eighty-four.[31] Rogers wrote in his column:

> My show career kinder [sic] dates from the time I first run into the Colonel (Mulhall). It was in 1899 at the St. Louis fair (not the World's Fair), just the big St. Louis fair they held every year. They had decided as an attraction that they would put on a Roping and Riding Contest.
>
> They were not called Rodeos, or Stampedes, in those days they were just what they are, a "Roping and Riding Contest." Well, I was pretty much of a kid, but just happened to have won the first and about my only

> contest at home in Claremore, Okla., and then we read about them wanting entries for this big contest at St. Louis. . . . Well, some one [sic] sent in my name, and the first thing I knew I was getting transportation for myself and my pony to the affair. Well, I went, and Col. Mulhall had charge of it. . . . But that gave me a touch of "show business" in a way, so that meant I was ruined for life as far as actual employment was concerned.
>
> Lucille was just a little kid when we were in St. Louis that year, but she was riding and running her pony all over the place, and that was incidentally her start, too. It was not only her start, but it was the direct start of what has since come to be known as the Cowgirl.
>
> There was no such a thing or no such word up to then as Cowgirl. But as Col. Mulhall from that date drifted into the professional end of the contest and show business, why Lucille gradually come [sic] to the front, and you can go tell the world that his youngest daughter Lucille Mulhall was the first well known cowgirl.[32]

As her colorful career progressed, Lucille Mulhall not only made her mark as a cowgirl but also became a featured performer with the Miller brothers' shows. The combination proved to be a stunning success.

Chapter 23

A STATE OF MIND

The heritage of the West was a state of mind, and would last much longer than the material circumstances that gave it birth.[1]

—Gerald D. Nash
Creating the West

BY 1905, the 101 Ranch, building on the foundation created by patriarch George Washington Miller, was fast becoming a significant gathering place for historical figures, celebrities, and notables from all corners of the globe. The ranch was poised to evolve into a fertile spawning ground for motion-picture stars, rodeo champions, and notorious characters. It also became a haunt for mythmakers, including the Millers themselves, always firm believers that the West was not just a region but a state of mind.

The first real hint of what was to follow for the Millers occurred at the roundup held on June 11, 1905, for the National Editorial Association. Those who attended remembered it as an epic occasion that brought together several prominent icons of the American West—Geronimo, Tom Mix, Lucille Mulhall, and Bill Pickett. On that remarkable afternoon, each of those legendary figures who rode for the Millers and the Hundred and One unknowingly nurtured the illusions and yearnings of generations yet unborn.

The Miller brothers had become mighty visionaries by the spring of 1905 as they feverishly readied themselves and their ranch for the approaching roundup. On April 10, at the height of their preparations, the Millers realized one of their dreams. Fortified by the memory of their late father as well as by gallons of powerful cowboy coffee, they met in the ranch office at the White House and formed a private corporation—officially named "The 101 Ranch"—under the laws of the territory of Oklahoma.[2] The following day, the three brothers scrawled their signatures on the necessary documents before Kay County notary public J. H. Lewis, who then affixed his seal and carried the sheaf of papers off to the territorial capital, at Guthrie.[3]

Naturally, the brothers chose Joe, the firstborn son, as president of the corporation, and George Lee as corporation secretary. They decided that Zack would act as the third and only other board director. The Miller brothers generated capital stock of three hundred thousand dollars for the new corporation by simply purchasing their own holdings in the Ponca and Otoe lands.[4]

The primary purpose of the corporation, as stated in the articles of incorporation filed with the secretary of Oklahoma Territory, was "to raise, to buy, to sell, to trade in, and to exchange livestock, and also all agricultural products and machinery and to buy, to sell, to lease, to exchange, and to trade in all lands and real estate necessary to be used to carry on the enterprise."[5] There was not a single mention of Wild West roundups, cowboy and Indian exhibitions, or mythmaking.

At the same time the Miller brothers were fine-tuning their corporation papers and arranging to entertain thousands of the nation's publishers and editors, newly inaugurated President Theodore Roosevelt was making his way through the Twin Territories.

On April 5, 1905, while en route to San Antonio, Texas, and one of the Rough Riders' reunions, the president's train chugged into Indian Territory.[6] Throughout that day, the southbound train ground to a halt for Roosevelt to make brief appearances at Vinita, Wagoner, Muskogee, South McAlester, Atoka, Caddo, and Durant. He vigorously waved at the adoring crowds and told them of the many advantages of single statehood for the two territories, a dream still more than two years from fruition.[7]

In San Antonio, after toasting slain comrades and reliving engagements against Spanish forces in Cuba with his former Rough Riders—"Teddy's Terrors"—Roosevelt and his entourage promptly retreated northward, toward the Red River and Oklahoma Territory. On April 8, they reached the territorial town of Frederick, where the high-spirited Roosevelt was anxious to spend several days hunting wolves with Comanche Chief Quanah Parker and John R. Abernathy. He was known as "Catch 'em Alive" Abernathy because of his ability to capture wolves with his bare hands, a barbaric but popular frontier activity.[8]

It was not Roosevelt's first experience with wolf hunting.[9] His first visit to Oklahoma Territory had taken place almost five years before, in July 1900. At the time, he was a vice-presidential candidate on the Republican ballot with William McKinley and had come to Oklahoma City as the guest of honor at a Rough Riders' convention.[10] For Roosevelt, the most exciting event during his stay in 1900 was the Fourth of July "Cowboy Tournament" staged at the fairgrounds. More than twenty-five thousand people showed up to watch a cowboy-and-Indian spectacle that featured Zack Mulhall's riders and ropers.[11]

The Frisco Cowboy Band, subsidized by the railroad through Mulhall's connections, provided stirring music.[12] Among the musicians decked out in big cowboy hats, chaps, boots, and spurs, lariat artist Will Rogers pretended to play a trombone. The young cowboy could no more play the instrument than perform brain surgery. In truth, Rogers was one of the ringers planted in the band by Colonel Mulhall, who advertised a prize of one thousand dollars if anyone in the audience could ride an outlaw horse without getting pitched or rope and tie a steer faster than one of his bandsmen. Of course, crack rider and roper Rogers or another of the equally skilled cowboys posing as a musician was the one Mulhall invariably picked if some sucker dared to take up the offer.[13]

Of the whole troupe of performers—which included James Mirrel, a top cowhand from Round Rock, Texas, who roped and tied a steer in fifty-one-and-a-half seconds—it was a teenage cowgirl who caught the crowd's attention and held them spellbound.[14] "Roosevelt was most enchanted with the daring feats of Lucille Mulhall, Oklahoma's lovely and talented horsewoman," observed one of the newspaper reporters covering the Oklahoma City event. "She rode beautifully throughout the contest and lassoed the wildest steer in the field."[15] It became obvious that Lucille had also lassoed Roosevelt's heart.

After the show concluded, Roosevelt invited the Mulhall family, including Lucille, Bossie, and Charley, to join him and a few of his Rough Riders at a private dinner. Lucille presented her host with the silk neckerchief she had worn that afternoon. An obviously pleased T.R. announced: "I predict a great future for the golden-haired girl of the West."[16]

A few days later, Roosevelt accompanied the Mulhalls back to their ranch, where he watched the Mulhall youngsters in action on horseback. A popular story with several versions emerged from Roosevelt's visit to the Mulhall Ranch. This tale began when the political candidate went riding one morning across the Mulhalls' rangelands and spied a large gray wolf.[17] Later, he told the Mulhalls of seeing the wolf and casually expressed a desire for the animal's hide. Apparently someone was listening.

"Lucille, without saying a word to anyone, had within a few days run the desired wolf down, roped it, beaten it to death with a stirrup iron, and had the skin mounted and sent it to the future president of the United States," a reporter wrote thirty-one years later. "When T.R. went to the White House the loafer wolf went with him."[18]

When he left the ranch to resume his busy political life, Roosevelt provided Lucille's proud father with some sound advice. "Zack, before that girl dies or gets married, or cuts up some other caper," Roosevelt told Colonel Mulhall, "you ought to put her on the stage and let the world see what she can do. She's simply great."[19]

As a result of his friendship with Roosevelt, Zack Mulhall received an invitation to bring his talented offspring and his cowboy band to Washington, D.C., to be part of the 1901 inaugural parade for President McKinley and Vice President Roosevelt.[20] The family and the band of musicians proudly rode at the head of the parade as Roosevelt's escort.[21] Afterward, during the reception at the vice president's residence, Lucille was thrilled to see on display the pelt of the wolf she had roped and killed for Roosevelt.[22]

Later that year, on September 6, 1901, an anarchist shot President McKinley during a reception in Buffalo, New York. Eight days later, after mouthing the words of his favorite hymn, "Nearer, My God to Thee," McKinley slipped into a coma and died. Almost twelve hours later, forty-two-year-old Theodore Roosevelt took the oath of office as the twenty-sixth president of the United States.[23]

Only a few weeks after taking office, Roosevelt removed William Jenkins from his post as governor of Oklahoma Territory, citing charges of official misconduct stemming from Jenkins' ownership of stock in a sanitarium contracted to provide care for mentally ill people in the territory.[24] Politically naive observers predicted that because of the Mulhall family's close ties with Roosevelt, the new president would appoint Colonel Zack as the next territorial governor of Oklahoma.[25]

Roosevelt's Republican pals protested loudly when they caught wind of rumors that the staunch Democrat Mulhall, who was closely associated with Saint Louis Democratic political boss Ed Butler, was a potential gubernatorial candidate.[26] If Zack Mulhall was ever truly a candidate—and no real historic evidence exists to back up that claim—he had little, if any, chance of being chosen.

Roosevelt's eventual choice for the post was Thompson B. Ferguson, editor of the *Watonga Republican* and a prominent member of the Republican party. Ferguson served until 1906. Then Frank Frantz, a veteran of the Spanish-American War who had been a captain with Colonel Roosevelt's Rough Riders and later acted as postmaster at Enid and as Osage agent at Pawhuska, became the last territorial governor.[27]

Zack may have been disappointed in not becoming governor, but he maintained his respect for Roosevelt as the Mulhalls continued to draw huge crowds at arenas across the nation. Lucille and the rest of her talented family kept up a whirlwind schedule, appearing at steer-roping contests, cattlemen's conventions, and county and state fairs from El Paso to Saint Louis, and scores of places in between. Astride her horse, Governor, Lucille became the featured performer of every show. Joining her were her sister, Bossie, and Mildred and Charley, the illicit offspring of Colonel Mulhall and Georgia. The latter also joined the Mulhall Congress of Rough Riders and Ropers, billed as another of the Mulhall daughters.[28]

The "Original Cowgirl," as most fans knew Lucille, acquired new nicknames on almost a daily basis. Reporters branded her as "The Daring Beauty of the Plains" and the "Deadshot Girl." One journalist, obviously carried away with both Lucille's ability and the use of adjectives, declared her to be: "The most fearless and famous roper and rider in the world . . . the Champion Beskirted Broncho Buster, the greatest female Conqueror of Hoofs [sic], Hides, and Horns; the most famous Lassoer in Lingerie; the Rarest Rough Rider and Roper in Ribbons and Ruches."[29]

A reporter in Omaha, Nebraska, took exception to the monikers being attached to the young woman with blue-gray eyes and "teeth that are as white as a wolf's" when he wrote, "Miss Lucille doesn't have to wear a label to prove that she is the genuine article. She wears her buckskins and pistol as gracefully as a society belle wears a Parisian gown and she knows more about roping steers than the average woman knows about embroidery."[30]

After Lucille set world records in steer roping and rode off with a grand prize of ten thousand dollars at a 1904 contest at Denison, Texas, she also became known as the "Queen of the West." That same year, the Mulhalls appeared at the famous Louisiana Purchase Exposition in Saint Louis.[31]

Included among Colonel Mulhall's crack performers at the world's fair was young Willie Rogers, back in the United States after a long adventure in England and South America and appearances with Texas Jack's Wild West Show as "the Cherokee Kid" in South Africa, New Zealand, Madagascar, and Australia.[32] Wearing a tight-fitting red velvet suit with gold braid—and more adroit than ever with a lariat—Rogers was being billed as "the Mexican Rope Artist."[33]

The Mulhall show, not officially sanctioned by world's fair officials, opened on May 3, 1904, on the grounds of the Saint Louis Fair Association, where county fairs were ordinarily staged.[34] In no time, the resourceful Colonel Mulhall and his Congress of Rough Riders and Ropers, wishing to avoid competition for fairgoers' dollars, formed an association with Frederick Cummins, an impresario with a contract to produce an "Indian show" near the entrance of the busy mile-long midway, popularly called the Pike.[35]

On May 19, just a couple of weeks after the show commenced, Joe Miller, in Saint Louis to attend the three-day National Editorial Association convention, made it a point to catch a performance. Afterward, Joe had time for a visit with his old friends, Colonel Zack, Lucille, and the other Mulhalls, and to trade stories with Will Rogers and various cowboy friends working for Mulhall and Cummins.

While at the world's fair, Joe also had an opportunity to meet Geronimo, the once-feared Apache chief who had been a prisoner of war since 1886.[36] Brought to Saint Louis under armed guard from Fort Sill in Oklahoma Territory, Geronimo made appearances with the Cummins show, crafted and sold souvenir bows and arrows to curiosity hunters, and posed for photographs with nervous visitors.[37] By the time Joe Miller departed the big city, he already had in mind several of the star attractions he wanted to present at the roundup for the nation's editors on the 101 Ranch the following summer. Near the top of the list were the names of Lucille Mulhall and Geronimo.

Colonel Mulhall's scheduled run of six months at the world's fair lasted only six weeks. On June 18, 1904, an ongoing feud between Mulhall and Frank Reed, the boss hostler for the Wild West show, over the unauthorized use of horses erupted into violence on the crowded Pike.[38] Before it was over, Mulhall reportedly drew a pistol and blazed away, striking Reed, one of Mulhall's own cowboys, and an eighteen-year-old bystander who some onlookers thought was fatally wounded. All three victims survived, but the story was carried by newspapers across the country and was featured in a front-page story in the *New York Times*.[39]

Mulhall was hauled off to jail but, according to reports in a Saint Louis newspaper, managed to call out to Lucille "to be a good girl and say her prayers before she went to bed."[40] Ed Butler, the city's powerful political boss and a Mulhall pal, quickly posted the bond of twenty thousand dollars. The Mulhall outfit was barred from the Pike, forcing the show to move from the fairgrounds to nearby Delmar Race Track.[41]

The Mulhalls continued their exhibitions until the world's fair closed, in December 1904, but they added the seventy-four-year-old Geronimo, "dressed in full regalia," twirling a lasso and riding his horse at a full gallop in pursuit of a steer. "The rope settled around the steer's neck on the first attempt," a newspaper reported. "In an instant the roper was off his horse and with all the speed of his youth, proceeded to tie the animal fast and sound. The exhibition clearly demonstrates that in spite of his years, Geronimo still possesses the strength and agility of any cowboy."[42]

In January 1905, Zack Mulhall, on trial in Saint Louis for assault with intent to kill in the triple shooting, was convicted and sentenced to three years in the penitentiary.[43] His appeal succeeded and he did not go to prison. However, a court upheld a damage suit brought against Mulhall for twenty thousand dollars by the young man who had almost died in the shooting. This caused a financial drain on the Mulhall Ranch.[44]

Desperate for cash, Colonel Mulhall looked for more work for his Wild West performers and jumped for joy when he negotiated a series of important bookings. He was especially pleased about the engagement with the Miller brothers for the National Editorial Association roundup in June 1905 at the 101 Ranch. Like the Millers, he knew the throng of editors would be of great publicity value to participants.

Then in April 1905, just after the Miller brothers completed the paperwork forming their new 101 Ranch corporation, both the Mulhalls and the Millers got a much needed boost. Colonel Mulhall and his Wild West show took the limelight as an attraction at the second annual New York Horse Fair, the high-society event of the season, held at Madison Square Garden.[45]

For Zack Mulhall, plagued by gossip and a mountain of legal expenses, the timing could not have been better. For the Millers, a New York City show provided an excellent opportunity to publicize their own approaching roundup at the ranch. Perhaps even more important, it served as yet another dress rehearsal for the Millers; several of the Mulhall performers later would ride for the 101.

Every cowboy and cowgirl was eager to gain more exposure and professional experience in the public arena, and no better venue was available than Madison Square Garden's full house of cheering New Yorkers. Among the 101 Ranch riders and ropers who journeyed east to perform with Colonel Mulhall were Joe and Zack Miller. Both remained dedicated to keeping alive that state of mind they called the West.[46]

It didn't matter whether the state of mind was real or fabricated. As historian Robert G. Athearn later wrote, "The story of the westering experience has still drawn packed houses for a long time. Whether we think of it as the West of the mind or as something geographical, it has been an enormous stage, with its characters set in place, ready to create the illusion that the audience has expected. This audience has paid its admission fee expecting to be enchanted, and the fact that it understood that this was all an illusion does not mean it was not satisfied. Nor does it mean that the characters were not telling the truth in their own way. If believed ardently enough, long and strongly enough to shape the way in which we live our days, anything becomes true."[47]

The Miller brothers would soon profit enormously from the American public's need to believe in the myth of the West.

KING OF THE COWBOYS

ONE OF THE performers who rode behind the Mulhall family and the Miller brothers when they paraded into Madison Square Garden in April 1905 was a twenty-five-year-old cowhand recruited from Oklahoma Territory.[1] Although the long procession of flamboyant entertainers and costumed Indians making the grand entry at the New York City show obscured him from public view, the young man would not go unnoticed for long.

Blessed with natural good looks but saddled with a somewhat checkered background, the cowboy had the given name of Thomas, after a maternal great-grandfather who made his living as a clergyman.[2] The other riders and ropers working the New York show, like everyone else who ever met Thomas, called him Tom.

Everything about the cowboy seemed clouded by half-truths or full-blown lies, including his own identity. The official program for the New York show listed him as "Tom Mixco, cow runner, from Old Mexico."[3] Both the last name and the place of origin were invented. His real name was Thomas Hezikiah Mix, and he hailed from Pennsylvania. When he turned eighteen and joined the army, Mix dropped the Old Testament name of Hezikiah and began to use Edwin, his father's first name.[4]

At one time a physical-fitness trainer and boxing instructor in the basement of the Carnegie Library in the Oklahoma Territory capital of Guthrie, Mix also had tended bar at the nearby Blue Belle Saloon on West Harrison Avenue.[5] He enjoyed his stint as a barkeep because the Blue Belle attracted the most influential people of the territory, including politicians, cattlemen, and visiting celebrities.

Built in 1890, Guthrie's favorite watering hole instantly became famous for concocting stiff drinks to quench the thirsts of parched gents. In addition, the management allowed a lively second-floor brothel to operate as an extra source of income.[6] A convenient iron catwalk spanned the alley and connected the upstairs parlors with the neighboring Elks Hotel, an interim residence for many territorial legislators—the most faithful clientele of the soiled doves and painted cats plying their trade in the bordello next door.[7]

While slinging straight whiskey shots and schooners of beer "across the mahogany" at the Blue Belle, Mix formed a friendship with Joe and Zack Miller. Although later a question arose about exactly which of the brothers first connected with Mix, evidently the Millers had made his acquaintance at the Blue Belle as early as 1902, during a cattlemen's convention in Guthrie.[8] Mix eventually hired on as a cowhand with the 101 Ranch—a beneficial move for himself as well as for the Millers.

Good-natured and engaging, Tom Mix at first glance looked like just another handsome grub-line rider, probably on the run from the law, angry creditors, a scorned woman, or himself. At best, he sported dubious credentials. After quitting school in the fourth grade, he made a career of holding odd jobs, was officially listed as an army deserter, and was about to end the first of his five marriages.[9]

Life for Mix had started calmly enough, far from the world of rodeo arenas and Wild West shows. Delivered by a midwife on January 6, 1880, in a modest frame home near Mix Run, Pennsylvania, midway between the Pennsylvania Railroad line and Bennett's Branch of the Susquehanna River, Tom was one of four children born to Elizabeth and Edwin E. Mix, a lumberman and teamster who made a living from the nearby mountainous forests.[10] When Tom was four years old, the Mix family relocated to the town of Driftwood, where the boy started school. Four years later, they moved to Du Bois, Pennsylvania, after Ed Mix became the coachman and superintendent of stables for John E. Du Bois, a local lumber baron who owned many fine thoroughbred and harness-racing horses.[11]

Tom gained a lifelong love of horseflesh from his father. Instead of tending to school lessons, the youngster preferred daydreaming or, better yet, hanging around the stables at the estate where his father worked. By the time he reached his tenth birthday, Tom had quit school and worked at a succession of menial jobs.[12]

He always found time for fueling fantasies. He eavesdropped on Union veterans as they reminisced about the pivotal battle of the Civil War fought near the southern Pennsylvania town of Gettysburg. He flocked to the knots of old men still able to recall the great migration of pioneers in Conestoga wagons, the original "prairie schooners" or "ships of the desert," manufactured in nearby Lancaster.[13] Tom's fertile imagination was further fired by dime novels and by his memorable visit to the fairgrounds for a performance by Buffalo Bill Cody and his Wild West entertainers, including sharpshooter Annie Oakley and a company of whooping and hollering cowboys and Indians.[14]

Even as a youth, Tom Mix found that his thick hair, flashing dark eyes, pearly white teeth, and muscular build were his greatest assets. When the United States declared war against Spain in 1898, the strapping eighteen-year-old immediately enlisted in the army.[15] Although his first assignment was to an artillery unit guarding the Du Pont powder works at Montchanin, Delaware, Mix still regarded himself as a dashing cavalier who could singlehandedly beat the Spaniards if given a chance.[16] Much to Mix's disappointment, the "splendid little war," which lasted only a few months, ended before he experienced a single day of combat.

Years later, inventive movie publicists and press agents bragged that Mix had fought alongside Lieutenant Colonel Theodore Roosevelt at Kettle and San Juan Hills in Cuba, and had seen action in the Philippine Insurrection, Boxer Rebellion, and Boer War. Not one word of it was true. Mix never left the eastern United States. He spent most of his army enlistment training recruits or serving at battery posts in Delaware, Virginia, New York, and New Jersey.[17]

Despite not having fired a shot or brandished a saber in combat, Mix did well in the army and moved up through the enlisted ranks until he was promoted to first sergeant of his battery.[18] Discharged in April 1901, Mix quickly reenlisted when he thought he might have a chance to see action in the Boer War, but that never happened. Instead, Mix kindled a romance with Grace Allin, a pretty schoolteacher he met during a furlough in Virginia. The young lovers were married on July 18, 1902.[19]

Weary of army life and anxious to spend more time with his wife, First Sergeant Mix took another furlough on October 20, 1902. It would be his last. Mix never returned to his outfit. Within a few days, he was reported as absent without leave, and finally his regimental officers had no other choice but to list him officially as a deserter.[20]

No arrest warrants were ever issued for the wayward soldier and, according to army records, no real effort was made to resolve the matter. Still, Mix apparently decided it was in his best interest to relocate. Naturally, he looked to the West—the land of his boyhood dreams and a good place to make a fresh start. By late 1902, Tom and Grace Mix, their marriage precarious from the start, had settled in Guthrie, Oklahoma Territory.[21]

Homesick and unhappy in her new surroundings, Grace found gainful employment as an English teacher while Tom taught physical-fitness classes, gave lessons to budding pugilists, and picked up bar tips from patrons at the Blue Belle Saloon.[22] Besides meeting Colonel Zack Mulhall and the Miller brothers at the Blue Belle, Mix also struck up a friendship with Thompson B. Ferguson, the Republican newspaper editor whom Teddy Roosevelt had appointed governor of Oklahoma Territory instead of Zack Mulhall.[23]

Impressed by the bartender's enthusiasm and flamboyant personality, Thompson proved particularly considerate when Mix's home life went sour. In 1903, Grace, with prodding from her family back east, had the marriage annulled. To help the despondent young man get over his deep depression, Thompson made sure Mix won the job as drum major of the Oklahoma Cavalry Band, even though he was neither a member of the territorial militia nor a musician.[24]

When the band played for the cornerstone dedication of the Oklahoma Building at the Saint Louis World's Fair in 1904, Mix was right there—dashing and unforgettable in his tall fur hat and elegant uniform, trimmed with lace and gold braid. A front-page Saint Louis newspaper story pointed out, "The handsome drum major, marching in the foreground, was a gallant figure who attracted a great deal of attention, especially from the ladies."[25]

At the world's fair, Mix also performed with Will Rogers and the Mulhalls before he returned to Oklahoma City, where the band had a performance. When the Oklahoma Cavalry Band left town on a long road trip, Tom decided to remain in Oklahoma City for a while.[26]

"The only thing that I could find to do was to be a bartender and I was always trying to find something else to do," Mix explained years later.[27] While serving drinks at a saloon on Robinson Street, Mix worked at a few other jobs and extended his network of contacts among the power brokers he encountered in Oklahoma Territory.

In March 1905, Captain Seth Bullock of Deadwood, South Dakota, put together what he called a Cowboy Brigade, a collection of western-style horsemen, to appear at President Roosevelt's second inauguration. Mix wanted to join, so he caught up with the train carrying Bullock's riders and horses at Omaha, Nebraska, and rode with them to Washington, D.C., for the celebration. On March 4, after Roosevelt took the oath of office, a dapper Tom Mix, sporting a six-shooter on his hip, fine leather chaps, and a new hat and neckerchief, rode with the Cowboy Brigade before the White House reviewing stand.[28]

In just over a month after the inauguration, Roosevelt would travel to Oklahoma Territory en route to San Antonio. By that time, Mix was back in Oklahoma City preparing for his next adventure—a journey to New York with Colonel Zack Mulhall and his entertainers, including Lucille Mulhall, the Miller brothers, and Will Rogers.

The Mulhalls and the Millers could not foresee that young Tom Mix would eventually reside in a California mansion and earn more than seventeen thousand dollars a week as the highest-paid Hollywood star of his day.[29] The thought would never have never crossed Will Rogers' mind that he and his saddle pal, whom he had dubbed "Tom Mixco" for the Madison Square Garden show, would both rise to unprecedented stardom and fame. But that was exactly what happened.

Thanks to hard work, luck, some distortions of the truth, and a few solid connections made over the bar and beneath the stained-glass windows at the Blue Belle, generations of America's youngsters would come to idolize Tom Mix. He would be known around the world as the first "King of the Cowboys."

Chapter 24

OKLAHOMA'S GALA DAY

The show started as one of the many by-products of an Oklahoma ranch empire founded by George W. Miller. . . . It is improbable that [the] Miller brothers got into show business entirely by accident . . . for there was a suspiciously large lot of top talent waiting at the 101 for all this lightning to strike.[1]

—Don Russell
The Wild West

TOM Mix was just one of many cowboys who participated in the roundup at the 101 Ranch in 1905. As the target date drew near, the Miller brothers decided to participate with Colonel Zack Mulhall and his gang at the Madison Square Garden show in April 1905. They packed their grips and caught an eastbound train at the Bliss depot.

It was to be the first of countless visits Joe and Zack Miller would eventually make to New York City; it was also to be one of their most unforgettable. As a behind-the-scenes observer at Madison Square Garden, Joe Miller planned to gain new and useful perspectives, while Zack would pick up invaluable experience out on the arena floor. The event would also serve as a rehearsal for several of the performers, including the renowned Lucille Mulhall; George Elser, a champion trick rider; and the jaunty Tom Mix, who were to participate in the Millers' massive gathering on the Salt Fork River in less than two months.[2]

After some struggle, Will Rogers also had won a spot in the company of riders and ropers bound for New York, thanks to lobbying on the part of Mary Agnes Mulhall, Colonel Mulhall's long-suffering wife. "When the time came for us to go to Madison Square Garden in New York in 1905 to put on our show for the big horse fair, Will wanted to go along," Lucille Mulhall remembered twenty-six years later.[3]

"He begged father for weeks, but father told him he couldn't be bothered with taking him along. Finally he went to enlist mother's aid. 'Make them take me,' he pleaded, so mother, who liked Will (we all did for that matter; he was such a good-hearted kid) told father he'd simply have to take Will with him. 'I can't be pestered with him around here,' was the way she put it."[4]

Many years later, Fred Gipson described Rogers' association with the Mulhalls and the Millers: "Will Rogers was one of the 101 bunch that went to Madison Square Garden that year. Will wasn't a regular 101 hand; he never was on the payroll. But for the last four or five years, he'd been coming down to prowl the Salt Fork range. He'd put up with the 101 outfit awhile, doing more cow work in a week than some riders would in a month, and never take a cent of pay for it. Then he'd drift over to the Mulhall range or throw in with some other cow outfit for a while. Just prowling, for the sake of prowling. . . . By the time he went to Madison Square Garden, Will could make his spinning trick ropes do just about anything but talk."[5]

When the Oklahoma Territory cowboys and cowgirls arrived in New York, the managers of Madison Square Garden put them into a block of rooms at a "big swank Fifth Avenue hotel."[6] That arrangement did not last long because of the high-hat staff and restrictive dress codes. As Zack Miller reportedly told the horrified hotel manager, "Why me and the boys had rather eat in a stable than dress up like show monkeys for a chance to eat in that damned dining room of yours."[7]

All the performers were relocated promptly to more suitable digs. Zack Miller, Will Rogers, Tom Mix, and most of the cowboys landed in the comfortable Putnam House, at Fourth Avenue and Twenty-Sixth Street, next door to Madison Square Garden. Single rooms at the Putnam rented for just fifty cents a night, and obedient bellhops fetched room-service drinks worthy of the Blue Belle in Guthrie or even the Yaller Dog Saloon, the rambunctious whiskey oasis at Red Rock, Oklahoma Territory.[8]

Everything about Manhattan—crowds of people from a variety of cultural and ethnic backgrounds, rumbling subways, and concrete canyons—amazed and energized the Millers and their cohorts from the open prairies of the West. Many of the men and women traveling with the Mulhall show, including Joe and Zack Miller, had been to Saint Louis, Kansas City, or Fort Worth, but none of those places compared with New York. Even the toughest bronc fighter could be rendered speechless by the many architectural monuments such as the twenty-one-story Flatiron Building. Completed in 1902 on what was said to be the windiest corner of the city, it was the best vantage point for an illicit peek at ankles and gams beneath long gowns on breezy afternoons.[9]

Yet nothing else—not even comely big-city ladies—was quite as exciting as opening night at Madison Square Garden. Famous as the nation's principal indoor place of amusement and the setting for national political conventions, championship prizefights, and circus performances, the Garden had been built on the site of abandoned railroad sheds that P. T. Barnum leased from Commodore Cornelius Vanderbilt in 1873 and turned into the Great Roman Hippodrome. Later, it was known as Gilmore's Garden and finally, in 1879, it became Madison Square Garden.[10]

The National Horse Show Association, established in 1883, secured the property with the assistance of prominent financier J. Pierpont Morgan, and in 1890 erected a new Madison Square Garden complex, with theater, restaurant, concert hall, and roof garden, all designed by New York architect Stanford White.[11] Constructed of yellow brick and Pompeiian white terra-cotta, the Garden's imposing tower was topped by a nude statue of Diana—the virgin goddess of hunting in Roman mythology—created by Augustus Saint-Gaudens, famed sculptor and one of White's former teachers.[12]

On that balmy spring evening of April 22, 1905, when Mulhall's Wild West riders swooped into the arena, the report of blank ammunition mixed with the cheers of an adoring audience of six thousand of New York City's social elite. The flags of nations from around the world hung from the girders. Beneath the tanbark, a layer of dirt was spread over the arena floor to a depth of four feet at the turns and eighteen inches in the center to provide footing for the horses and to protect riders in case of a fall.[13]

For opening night, after the completion of the conventional equestrian events and trotting races, Colonel Mulhall led the grand entry into the Garden. Behind him came the extended Mulhall family—Charley, celebrating his seventeenth birthday that day; ten-year-old Mildred, making her performance debut; Bossie and Georgia; and, of course, Lucille, on her trick horse, Governor, and wearing a beaded vest that Geronimo had given to her at the Saint Louis world's fair. Following the Mulhalls rode Zack Miller, Will Rogers, Tom Mix, Jim Minnick, George Elser, Otis and Curtis Jackson, William Craven, Jack Joyce, Charley Seymour, and other rough riders, costumed Indian riders, and the Cowboy Band.[14]

At Colonel Mulhall's request, Mix and Rogers wrote the colorful copy for the program, which included nine acts such as bronc busting, a recreation of a Pony Express ride, an Indian war dance, and trick riding and roping exhibitions. To perk up his friend's background for the program, Rogers conceived the catchy label "Tom Mixco, cow runner, from Old Mexico." Mix described mixed-blood Rogers as a "full blood Cherokee" and sprinkled in a few other biographical lies.[15]

The *New York Times*, in its review of opening night, praised the "genuine old fashioned broncho busting and steer roping," and gave special recognition to Lucille Mulhall, "Queen of the Range," and Will Rogers, "the only man in the world who can lasso both the rider and the horse at the same time with two separate ropes."[16]

Everywhere the cowboys and cowgirls went, the New York press corps followed. Stories appeared in all the newspapers about the Mulhall performers riding down Fifth Avenue in the Easter Sunday parade, and coverage was ample of a polo game between Durland Academy and the Mulhall cowboys, led by Zack Miller and Will Rogers. The more experienced players, from the riding academy, won the match, but Rogers was left with a passion for the sport that lasted for the rest of his life.[17]

Unlike cowboy Will Craven, who broke his collarbone when he was pitched off a bucking horse, or young Charley Mulhall, who was knocked unconscious after a bronc called Texas Pete pitched him to the tanbark, Rogers escaped physical injury.[18] His pride, however, was badly bruised by some "keen-looking girls" in box seats whom he tried to impress with his fancy rope tricks. Years later, Tom Mix remembered the incident during an interview with one of Rogers' biographers. "I asked him if anything was wrong, and he replied, 'I heard those girls say that they was strong for me till they read on the program that I was an Indian, and one of 'em said she could stand being entertained by the darkest inhabitant in Africa, but an Indian went against her nature.' "[19]

But Rogers' injured sense of self was healed during a matinée performance on the sixth day of the show. Lucille Mulhall was about to lasso an eight-hundred-pound Mulhall Ranch steer with a spread of horns five feet across when the critter suddenly leaped over a gate and climbed into the stands. Terrified spectators and musicians fled. A courageous but reckless usher grabbed the horns of the steer, which threw him across several tiers of seats. Six cowboys swinging lariats followed in hot pursuit, but it was Will Rogers who roped the steer and saved the day.[20]

"TEXAS STEER AMUCK IN GARDEN," screamed one erroneous newspaper headline. "The Indian Will Rogers ran up the 27th Street side and headed off the steer," the accompanying story reported. "As it passed from the corridor again in view of the spectators, he roped the steer's horns. Alone and afoot, he was no match for the brute's strength, but he swerved it down the steps on the 27th Street side, where it jumped again into the ring."[21]

The flood of publicity after the steer-roping incident brought Will Rogers to the attention of vaudeville promoters, who quickly convinced him to stay on in New York after the Mulhall show closed. Rogers jumped at the opportunity. Instead of returning to Oklahoma Territory with Colonel Mulhall and taking part in the Miller brothers' roundup, Will kept his room at the Putnam House and began to perform rope tricks on stage at a starting salary of seventy-five dollars a week.[22]

On June 11, 1905—the date of the great roundup and buffalo chase at the 101 Ranch—Will Rogers, billed as "The World Champion Lasso Manipulator," prepared to open his roping act at Keith's Union Square Theatre.[23] Within a couple of days of his New York stage debut, Rogers signed a contract with German-born impresario Oscar Hammerstein to appear at the Roof Garden of the Victoria Theatre, managed by Hammerstein's son Willie.[24] From then on, there would be no looking back for the Cherokee Kid.

In the meantime, on the rangelands of the 101 Ranch, the Miller brothers and their cowboys and cowgirls had little time to gloat about the successes of their friend Will Rogers. As soon as the Mulhall show was over, Joe and Zack Miller hightailed it back to the ranch to help George with final details for their upcoming June extravaganza.

The event would prove to be larger than they could have expected. As a later 101 Ranch brochure exaggeratedly claimed, "The Millers prospered as ranchers and their Hundred and One Ranch has been visited by many tourist bodies. The three young owners of the ranch had scant appreciation of its fame when they announced a programme [sic] of western sports and pastimes, including the killing of a wild buffalo by mounted Indians. . . . Taken a little by surprise, but not a bit aback, the Millers received more than 100,000 persons and gave a frontier entertainment in a thirty acre arena, that for reckless and spectacular realism, eclipsed anything in the annuals [sic] of the 'Wild West.' Five hundred Cow Boys and Cow Girls and nearly a thousand Indians, led by Geronimo, participated. This celebration has gone down in trans-Mississippi history as one of the epochal of the West."[25]

Although the Millers tended to greatly inflate facts and figures in much of their printed materials, the importance of their role in the worlds of entertainment, the arts, and business and industry cannot be diminished. Their 1905 roundup had a profound impact on American history and culture, as well as on the way the nation would view itself for a long time to come.

As the date for what most folks were calling "The Buffalo Chase" drew near, the three Miller brothers found themselves not only taking care of last-minute practical details but also dealing with mounting criticism of the event. Most of the concerns were raised by the more timid Oklahoma Territory newspaper editors who apparently were fearful that the wild and woolly affair would cause editors from the East to form the wrong opinion of Oklahoma Territory. Besides their fear of projecting a hackneyed image, the editors were also clearly affronted that the Millers had selected a female—Lucille Mulhall—as one of the featured performers.[26]

The Miller brothers, as stubborn as their father had been, refused to yield to detractors. They were gratified, however, when the editors of the *Lawton State Democrat*, in southwestern Oklahoma Territory, took up their cause and wrote a scathing editorial under the headline "The First To Her Rescue," denouncing the attacks against the Millers and Miss Lucille. Joe Miller was so impressed with the *State Democrat* commentary that he posted a copy for all hands to read.[27]

"Some Oklahoma editors are having all kinds of spasms because Miss Mulhall, an Oklahoma girl, is going to astonish those sedate and painfully dignified people of the East with a demonstration of what she can do in the way of riding a bucking bronco and roping and tying a steer," wrote the Lawton editors. "Those editors are quaking with fear that the goggle-eyed, bean-eating, blue-bellied, codfish aristocracy of the East will be shocked into forming a mistaken idea of Oklahoma and her inhabitants.

"Well, who cares for the opinion of those people, anyhow? We, the people of Oklahoma, have made this territory what it is today, and we have done so without the help or consent of the effete East. The chances are that any of those editors that are ripping their shirts up the back, would be a greater freak in Boston than Miss Mulhall. The first time one of them said 'laf,' he would be punched in the ribs with an umbrella and told to say 'lawf,' and if he mentioned a dog he would be arrested for not pronouncing it 'daug!' "[28]

The *State Democrat*'s editors did not stop there. In very direct language, their editorial went on to lambaste further their eastern counterparts and to defend Lucille's participation in the 101 Ranch show.

"Well, here's one newspaper that is going to stand up for Miss Mulhall.

She is an Oklahoma girl, an Oklahoma product, and we don't give three whoops in Hades whether those knock-kneed dudes and spindle-shanked dudesses of the East like it or not. We are ready to risk a stack of reds upon the proposition that the East can't trot out a girl that can duplicate the riding and roping of the Oklahoma Girl. Go it, Miss Mulhall, and show them there are no flies on an Oklahoma girl."[29]

Bolstered by the support from the Lawton newspaper, the Miller brothers waged an active campaign to counter any negative publicity. Each brother wrote scores of personal letters of invitation to editors and dignitaries, on new ranch stationery with a fancy letterhead which bore the claim that the 101 was "The largest diversified Farm and Ranch in the United States" and home to "The Finest Herd of Buffalo in Existence."[30]

In May 1905, Joe Miller put out a special edition of the *Bliss Breeze* which shamelessly plugged the ranch and the National Editorial Association convention in Guthrie.[31] The newspaper also provided the itinerary for the editors during their visit to Oklahoma and Indian Territories, including their three-day convention in Guthrie. On the front page, Joe ran a photograph of Lucille Mulhall, described as a "Champion Roper of the World," tying the feet of a roped steer. Beneath a large illustration of a pair of bison appeared the caption, "Say, Bill, the National Editors Will Eat Us at 101 Ranch on June 11th."[32]

Back in 1904 at the Saint Louis world's fair, when Joe Miller had made his successful sales pitch to the editors and convinced them to come to Oklahoma Territory for their next convention, he had vowed to feed them buffalo meat. The opportunity to dine on steaming hot cuts of bison became one of the principal ploys the Millers used in their publicity to attract crowds to the ranch.[33]

Just weeks before the big roundup, the Millers shelled out sixteen thousand dollars, plus four thousand dollars in related expenses, for an additional thirty-two head to supplement their buffalo herd of more than thirty healthy specimens. Joe Miller journeyed to Ravalli County, in the rugged Bitterroot Range country of far western Montana, to make the selections and see to it that the animals were safely loaded and shipped by rail to Kansas City and then to Bliss.[34]

The Millers touted their buffalo as "superb, full-blooded specimens of the one distinctive American animal which once roamed the area of the 101 Ranch in thousands." In their often overstated promotional material, the Millers estimated that they owned one-eighth of the five hundred bison that survived in the United States, and that their effort to gather more of the shaggy beasts helped to perpetuate the vanishing breed.[35]

Many people disagreed with the Millers. The announcement that a buffalo hunt would be held at the 101 Ranch proved to be even more controversial than the scheduled participation of Lucille Mulhall in the Millers' roundup. Rumors and ill-founded news reports that as many as one hundred bison would be killed and served for dinner brought complaints from a variety of sources, including conservationists and animal lovers throughout the nation.[36] Joe Miller encouraged the babble about a wholesale bloodbath by listing a "Buffalo hunt of herd of genuine buffaloes" as a featured event in the schedule of activities.[37]

One of the Millers' most obstreperous critics was Daniel Carter Beard, best known as Dan Beard or "Uncle Dan," a leading naturalist and artist who, in 1910, helped organize the Boy Scouts of America. After having received no replies to the angry telegrams of protest he had fired off to Joe Miller, Beard wired President Theodore Roosevelt, asking him to dispatch armed troops to the 101 Ranch to halt the buffalo slaughter.[38]

Roosevelt, "already hounded by the humane societies," reportedly asked the governor of Oklahoma Territory to dispatch the territorial militia to the 101 Ranch. By ignoring Beard's telegrams, Joe's ploy had worked. The result was exactly what the Miller brothers had hoped for—plenty of free crowd control.[39]

"I had requested the Adjutant-General of Oklahoma to permit two companies of soldiers to come up at my expense, which would have been about a thousand dollars," Joe Miller later explained. "The soldiers would have been glad to come, but the Adjutant-General refused. I was wondering how I should handle that crowd of sixty-five thousand people without soldiers, when Mr. Beard's telegram came. I saw a way. I said nothing. The troops came at the expense of the territory."[40]

To spice up the buffalo debate even more, the Millers announced that the once-feared Apache chief Geronimo was coming to the 101 Ranch under soldier guard from Fort Sill to shoot "his last buffalo" before the crowd of editors.[41] Then to further fuel the controversy and increase free publicity, Joe Miller planted news stories and spread rumors that he was offering one thousand dollars in cash to anyone willing to be scalped by Geronimo.[42] The Millers bet among themselves on the likelihood of anyone being brave or stupid enough to answer the challenge. Apparently, at least one person did.

"At last a man has been found who will accept Joe Miller's offer of $1,000 to have his scalp lifted by old Geronimo at the 101 Ranch during the National Editorial Association," reported the *Lamont Valley News* several weeks prior to Geronimo's arrival at the ranch. "A man by the name of Jim Scott of Kansas City. He's welcome to it as far as we are concerned."[43]

The short news report contained no statement of exactly who Jim Scott was or any mention of his mental condition. Skeptics believed that the mysterious Scott was nothing more than a figment of Joe Miller's imagination.[44] Ultimately, not one person took up the challenge to be scalped.

Assorted stories about Geronimo, buffalo hunts, and Lucille Mulhall—mostly placed by the Millers—generated tremendous nationwide interest in Oklahoma Territory and in the 101 Ranch. The coverage also assured a huge turnout for the National Editorial Association convention.

By June 7, 1905, thousands of editors and publishers had converged on Guthrie for the convention. With the exception of a stirring address by William Allen White, crusading editor of the *Emporia* (Kansas) *Gazette*, most of the convention activities were routine and predictable. In three days and nights, the editors elected officers, attended receptions and recitals, and listened to endless committee reports and speeches about such mundane topics as "United States Postal Laws and Rules" and "How to Secure and Maintain Circulation."[45] After the official business concluded each day, conventioneers fled to the Blue Belle Saloon, where they reportedly lapped up gallons of whiskey and beer like fired cowhands.

On Friday, June 9, hundreds of the editors departed Guthrie on a special Pullman train for Enid, where they were "royally entertained until midnight." From there, the train rolled south to Lawton, arriving in time for breakfast and a chance to watch military maneuvers at nearby Fort Sill before moving on to Anadarko, Chickasha, El Reno, and finally, Oklahoma City for the night. On the morning of June 11, the train chugged north to Bliss and the 101 Ranch.[46]

The Pullman filled with the nation's editorial elite was only one of at least thirty-five trains that descended on the ranch that day.[47] Not only did the Millers snare the National Editorial Association folks, they also pulled in members of the National Association of Cattlemen from Texas and the National Association of Millers, which was holding its annual meeting in Kansas City. Sizable delegations of visitors also journeyed to the ranch from Dallas, Saint Louis, New York, Boston, San Francisco, Los Angeles, and Minneapolis. Forty railcars—each crammed with passengers—were needed to accommodate the Chicago guests alone.[48]

The trains were so crowded that many travelers had to ride on top of the coaches. The Santa Fe Railway had laid special tracks from Ponca City to the fenced exhibition grounds in the big pasture on the south side of the Salt Fork River, west of Bliss. The railroad brought in one hundred section workers to tend the cars sidetracked all the way to the Ponca City yards. Station masters from Newton, Kansas, and Oklahoma City helped local officials handle the long lines of trains and the crowds.[49] The crush of people and clouds of dust reminded some observers of the staging grounds before the celebrated land runs. Many people were injured just getting to the 101 Ranch, and at least one man was killed while he hung from the side of a train as it was switching tracks.[50]

Not everyone came by train. Thousands of visitors arrived in wagons or buggies or on horseback.[51] Pickpockets, purse cutters, and watch stealers known as super twisters stayed busy all day and into the night. They preyed on city folk and country bumpkins alike while the growing crowds gawked at Ponca and Otoe Indians, cowboys and cowgirls, musicians, and other performers.[52]

The Millers had issued warnings that no hotel accommodations were available at the ranch or at nearby Bliss. Overnight guests who did not sleep in the trains or find a Pullman berth pitched tents on the prairie or along the Salt Fork. For miles in either direction on the riverbanks, evening campfires flickered. A procession of ranch wagons hauled fresh drinking water from a nearby pond, and when it went dry in less than a day, the teamsters turned to a second pond.[53]

By best estimates, at least sixty-five thousand men, women, and children showed up at the 101 Ranch, making it the largest gathering of its kind in the history of the Twin Territories.[54]

The Miller brothers called it "Oklahoma's Gala Day."[55] They hawked souvenir programs for a dime each. On the front, the event was given several names—Indian Celebration, Cowboy Reunion, Buffalo Chase, and Historical Exhibition.[56] The entire back page was devoted to a large advertisement for the American Steel and Wire Company of Chicago, the firm that had sold the Millers fifty thousand feet of field fencing to enclose the pastures and exhibition grounds.[57]

They sold these programs to the multitude of invited guests and unexpected visitors who milled in the dust and heat as they downed countless bottles of red soda pop and a mountain of melting hokeypokey ice cream.

The grandstand, a mile and a quarter long, quickly overflowed with thousands of spectators, all jostling for coveted seats.

Many of the onlookers hoped to see the famous Geronimo. The Millers had finally obtained permission from the U.S. War Department to bring the nation's most infamous prisoner of war to the ranch, if adequate security was provided. Six days before the show, soldiers transported Geronimo by train from Fort Sill. They were reinforced by seven troopers from a regiment of the Kansas National Guard.[58]

Phil S. Stover, a seventeen-year-old soldier, was one of those assigned to watch over Geronimo. Stover, the last survivor of the guard detail, recollected in 1971, "We took turns each night sleeping in Geronimo's tent. I've always felt lucky to have been a member of the outfit since we had to guard Geronimo. I had a wonderful time. . . . It's something no one would ever forget."[59]

About two o'clock that afternoon, a half hour later than the scheduled starting time, the grand parade—nearly one mile in length—entered the east entrance of the exhibition grounds. At the head were the three Miller brothers, riding fine horses outfitted with saddles and tack crafted by R. T. Frazier of Pueblo, Colorado.[60]

Immediately following the Millers came a cavalry band and a squad of soldiers escorting Geronimo, who was supposed to shoot "his last buffalo" that afternoon. As he rode in review by the cheering crowds in the grandstand, the Apache medicine man nodded and smiled, appearing to enjoy all the attention.[61] Perhaps the old Chiricahua warrior—whose homeland was the arid Southwest where no bison herds roamed—was amused because he was the only one among the thousands of people there who knew that, in truth, he would not be shooting his last but his *first* buffalo that day. Apaches had last hunted bison centuries before Geronimo was born.[62]

More marching bands—a dozen in all—came next, followed by a long procession of cowboys and cowgirls on spirited horses and Indians on paint ponies. At least seven tribes were represented—Ponca, Otoe, Missouri, Tonkawa, Pawnee, Kaw, and Osage. Next was a wagon train of prairie schooners and carts pulled by oxen, and finally a convoy of the Millers' newest farm machinery and plows.[63]

The program that Sunday afternoon was etched forever in the memories of all those in attendance. They would never forget the mock buffalo hunt and the herd that thundered into the exhibition grounds, chased by two hundred mounted Indians, many wearing flowing eagle-feather warbonnets.

After a fifteen-minute chase, it was time to kill a token buffalo for the editors' supper. Geronimo again made an appearance. Instead of shooting the old bull with a bow and arrow from horseback like the Plains Indians of yesteryear, Geronimo opened fire with a Winchester rifle from the front seat of a motorcar—a shiny new Locomobile, owned by Harold E. Thomas, a Chicago physician.[64]

The old warrior's first shot missed its mark and the bison had to be driven within point-blank range before one of Geronimo's bullets finally struck the animal high in the neck. Some witnesses close to the action claimed a Miller cowhand named Stack Lee had to "finish the job." Others recalled that Geronimo leaped from the vehicle and cut the bison's throat with a hunting knife before helping to skin the huge beast. The crowd, believing the extra rifle shots were all part of the act, cheered and applauded. Later that afternoon, Geronimo donned a top hat to pose for photographs from behind the wheel of the Locomobile, accompanied by three other Indian performers in more traditional headdresses.[65]

After the buffalo chase, the spectators beheld war dances and Indian stickball games, target shooting and bucking-bronc contests, and cowboys and cowgirls in horseback quadrille. Highlights included Lucille Mulhall and her horse, and George Elser, the "Champion Trick Rider of the World." Another big crowd pleaser was a daring Texas cowboy named Bill Pickett, billed by the Millers as "The Wonderful Negro Pickett," known for "Throwing Wild Steer[s] by the Nose with His Teeth."[66]

The final act of the roundup on Oklahoma's Gala Day came at just about sundown. Emotionally drained by the spectacles of the long afternoon, the sunburned audience watched as a line of ten prairie schooners appeared on a hill near the exhibition grounds. Many of the spectators had the impression that the wagon train was filled with sightseers arriving late for the show. In the gathering twilight, the wagons pulled into a circle about a half-mile from the performance grounds, where the drivers unhooked their mule teams, built evening fires, and pitched camp.[67]

Suddenly, as many as three hundred Indian warriors rode over the rise and swept down on the encampment. Gunfire and bloodcurdling cries echoed across the prairie. Some of the Indians and settlers engaged in vicious hand-to-hand combat. When one and then another of the wagons caught fire, a woman in the grandstand stood and screamed. The stunned spectators did not know if they were witnessing part of the roundup or an actual massacre.[68]

Just as pandemonium was about to erupt, a gang of mounted cowboys appeared from out of nowhere and, with guns blazing, routed the Indians and rescued the settlers. Before the audience could fully react, the cowboys and Indians united in a single force and rode at breakneck speed into the arena.[69]

To thunderous applause and cheers, they were joined by Lucille Mulhall, Bill Pickett, other star performers and, of course, the three Miller brothers. The deafening ovation lasted for a long time. It would ring in the Millers' ears for years to come. The 101 Ranch had begun its reign in the limelight.

BILL PICKETT:
The Dusky Demon

THERE NEVER WAS another cowboy quite like Bill Pickett. The world of brave bull riders, bronc busters, and steer wrestlers never saw his match. Across all of old cow country and throughout the rodeo circuit, if anyone ever dared to wager otherwise, the bet was quickly snapped up and the ante raised. Gambling on Pickett was sure money in the bank.[1]

Never mind that this cowboy was a black man with tinges of Cherokee and white blood, subjected to extreme racial prejudice.[2] Never mind that he was one of thirteen children born to dirt-poor former slaves. Never mind that he didn't get much formal schooling. Never mind that his earnings were almost always far less than those of white men who were not half the ranch hand he was.[3] In the long run, as far as the measure of the man went, none of that meant a damn thing.

Although the odds were stacked against Pickett from the beginning, he still emerged a winner—even in a world of inequality, bigotry, and intolerance. Old-time cowboys and rodeo riders, including many venomous race baiters, admitted that Pickett was the consummate champion. Among his many admirers were the Miller brothers and the men and women who rode for the Hundred and One.

Pickett, who spent most of his professional career as a faithful performer for the 101 Ranch, invented the rodeo event of bulldogging.[4] That alone was enough to ensure that Pickett would dwell forever in the hearts and minds of anyone with the gumption to participate in a Wild West show or a rodeo. Rodeo hands known as "doggers" especially revered Pickett.[5] Combination daredevil acrobat and brawny grappler, a bulldogger always needed more nerves than sense just to stay alive—let alone make a decent living and walk away with a trophy.

Pickett's style of bulldogging evolved into one of seven standard events in the contemporary sport of rodeo.[6] Steer wrestling, as it became known, consists of a rider jumping from a horse onto a running steer, then grabbing and twisting the animal's horns until he brings it to the ground. The performance is judged according to the time between the contestant's leaving the starting box and the moment when a field judge drops his flag to signify that the steer is down, with all legs straight out.[7]

Pickett's style of bringing down a runaway steer included one major and unusual technique not found in the modern sporting event. He would leap from his pony onto the steer's back, grab a horn in each hand, and dig his boot heels into the ground. After twisting the critter's head to bring up its nose, he chomped his teeth on the steer's tender lip and lunged backward, causing the beast to fall down. With flair, Pickett threw his hands into the air to show the audience that he no longer needed to hold the steer's horns.[8]

According to popular report, Pickett was a ten-year-old boy in central Texas when he first took notice of the mixed-breed bulldogs used on ranches to capture and hold cattle by the upper lip until a cowboy could rope them. Young Willie, as folks called him back then, figured if a dog could subdue a cow in that manner, so could a spunky kid. Pickett began to practice his "bite-'em-on-the-lip" procedure on stray calves, and soon graduated to bulldogging the beef cows and longhorn steers that ranged the thick mesquite brush country of Texas.[9]

As a young man, Pickett worked as a hired hand for several Texas ranches, picked cotton, and hunted game to serve as free lunches at the Buck Wills Saloon. In 1890, he married Maggie Turner, daughter of a white plantation owner and one of his black slaves. Eventually, the Picketts had nine children—seven girls and two boys. Both sons died in infancy.[10]

The family settled near Taylor, Texas, where Bill and his brothers operated Pickett Brothers Broncho Busters and Rough Riders Association. Their handbills, illustrated with a cowboy on a bucking horse and a solitary longhorn steer, advertised, "We ride and break all wild horses with much care. Good treatment to all animals. Perfect satisfaction guaranteed. Catching and taming wild cattle a specialty."[11]

During the 1890s, Pickett continued to bulldog steers with his teeth at county fairs across Texas, mostly arranged by rancher Lee Moore. In 1900, the Pickett brothers appeared at a fair in Colorado where Pickett put on a public exhibition of bulldogging that left crowds speechless.[12] By 1903, he had teamed up with Dave McClure, a promoter known as "Mister Cowboy," who booked Pickett at rodeos and shows in Arizona, North Dakota, Wyoming, and other ranching states. McClure—aware that blacks were automatically barred from entering most rodeo contests—focused on Pickett's mixed-blood heritage and billed him as "the Dusky Demon."[13]

During the 1904 Cheyenne Frontier Days celebration, held in Wyoming on August 30–September 1, accounts of Pickett's bulldogging appeared in many of the nation's daily newspapers and feature magazines.[14] "The great event of the celebration this year was the remarkable feat of Will Pickett, a Negro hailing from Taylor, Texas, who gave his exhibition while 20,000 people watched with wonder and admiration a mere man, unarmed and without a device or appliance of any kind, attack a fiery, wild-eyed, and powerful steer and throw it by his teeth," wrote John Hicks Howe in a patronizing article published in *Harper's Weekly*. "So great was the applause that the darkey again attacked the steer, which had staggered to its feet, and again threw it after a desperate struggle."[15]

It was not long before "the Dusky Demon" came to the attention of the Miller brothers while they assembled specialty acts for the 1905 buffalo chase and roundup at the 101 Ranch. When Joe Miller heard yet another story about the cowboy who was said to be the only professional bulldogger in the world, he dispatched Zack to the Fort Worth Fat Stock Show, where Pickett was performing. After he watched Pickett bulldog two feisty steers in a corral on the bank of Marine Creek, Zack was convinced that he could not leave Fort Worth without recruiting Pickett.[16]

Zack arranged a parley with Pickett and his newest manager, Guy Weadick, a talented trick-rope artist and vaudeville performer from Alberta, Canada. It was the start of a long relationship between the Millers and Weadick, known by the show name "Cheyenne Bill," who in 1912 would establish the legendary Calgary Stampede, an annual contest often called "The Greatest Outdoor Show on Earth."[17] It also was the beginning of an even longer alliance between the Hundred and One and Bill Pickett.

Zack Miller struck a deal. Weadick vowed that Pickett would not only appear at the ranch for the June 11, 1905, spectacle, but that he also would show up several days early to rehearse and meet other performers.

The afternoon of the big show finally arrived. The sixty-five thousand spectators knew they were in for a treat before the parade was even halfway into the performance grounds. After the buffalo chase, Geronimo's appearance in a motorcar, and the fancy riding of Lucille Mulhall and George Elser, bronc busters and steer ropers kept the spectators on the edge of their seats. Then it was time for Pickett.

Weadick picked up a megaphone and announced, loud and clear: "Ladies and gentlemen, the next event will be Bill Pickett, the Dusky Demon from Texas, who will leap from the back of a running horse onto a running steer and throw the steer with his bare hands and teeth."[18]

The audience gasped as a thousand-pound steer charged into the arena, pursued by a mounted hazer whose task was to keep the critter on a straight path in front of the long grandstand. From out of nowhere, Bill Pickett appeared. His mustache was neatly trimmed and he was dressed in a fancy matador outfit. Astride his bay war horse named Spradley, the bulldogger was later described as being "hard and tough as whalebone."[19]

Pickett coaxed the horse forward. In an instant, they were at full gallop and he was sliding off Spradley onto the huge steer's back. He grabbed a flashing horn in each hand, dug his boots into the earth, and twisted the steer's neck until its head was turned upward. Pickett's teeth gnashed on the steer's lip. The cowboy lifted his hands in the air and gave his body a twist. The steer fell on its side and lay perfectly quiet as Pickett rendered him helpless. The crowd jumped to its feet, as if one body. The applause was said to be deafening.[20]

The three Miller brothers, watching from behind the scenes, knew they had witnessed something special. Decades later, after bossing hundreds of champion cowboys and cowgirls, rodeo riders, and doggers, Zack Miller would still look folks straight in the eye and tell them, "Bill Pickett was the greatest sweat-and-dirt cowhand that ever lived—bar none."[21] Not a soul disagreed.

Chapter 25

SHOW TIME

Boys ten years old and younger have never seen a genuine Wild West show and we are going to make it possible for them to see one.[1]

—Joe Miller, 1905

THE roundup and buffalo chase hosted by the Millers on June 11, 1905, in their ranch pastures was a complete success and a springboard for the entry of the 101 Ranch into the world of big-time show business. Before the last train loaded with guests rumbled out of sight, the Millers knew they could no longer remain solely prosperous ranchers and farmers. The call of the open road, the roar of the crowds, and the promise of even more wealth from entertainment revenue could not be ignored.

The throng of editors and publishers among the sixty-five thousand visitors who attended Oklahoma's Gala Day had plenty to write about when the dust settled and they returned home. Unlike the masses of people who showed up that afternoon, the editors dined on succulent buffalo steaks cut from the single bison that Geronimo had killed. They also had the best seats in the grandstand. The resulting editorial coverage, in virtually every newspaper and magazine in the nation, immediately catapulted the 101 Ranch into the American public's imagination.

Within a short time, an official souvenir booklet about the 101 Ranch and the Millers' big roundup rolled off the presses. Bearing the portraits of the three brothers on the front cover, the booklets sold for fifty cents each to a steady stream of visitors who had heard about the buffalo chase and had journeyed to Bliss to see the ranch for themselves. Inside the booklet was a brief summary of the life of George Washington Miller and the story of how he and his family had launched their ranching and farming empire.[2]

James Bennie Kent, whom the Millers hired to develop the booklet, was a native of England. Kent had moved to Oklahoma Territory at about the turn of the century, where he opened a jewelry store in the town of Chandler and began his lifelong interest in photography.[3] The souvenir booklet contained scores of Kent's photographs depicting every aspect of the roundup, including the Millers on horseback greeting their guests, excursion trains arriving at Bliss, Geronimo killing the bison, and the buffalo banquet for the editorial delegates.[4]

But the single image in the booklet destined to become the most famous was Kent's portrait of Geronimo and three other Indians riding in an automobile across one of the pastures. The old Apache leader is wearing a top hat and his hands are holding the steering wheel. Kent added a patronizing caption: "Geronimo and Party in Automobile—Geronimo in Paleface Attire." Like Kent's many other portraits of soldiers, cowboys, and various ranch scenes, this photograph helped establish a striking and romantic representation of the 101 Ranch.[5]

This idealized image of the ranch came to represent the West in general. As historian James H. Thomas wrote, "The 101 Ranch not only survived and prospered, but also preserved much of the working cowboy's heritage. The cowboy's image, promoted by the 101 Wild West Shows, did help preserve the nation's romantic attachment to the cowpuncher's craft, but at the same time it presented a false impression of life on the plains. Hard work was euphemised as roping games; dusty clothing was replaced with sequined garments; cow ponies were often discarded for prancing stallions; and mundane line riding fell victim to staged cowboy-Indian battles. The Miller family, owner of the 101 empire, gave the public its money's worth."[6]

Encouraged by the overwhelming publicity and positive response from a cross-section of society, the Miller brothers decided to put the show on the road. Going into the Wild West show business seemed a natural move for the Millers. After all, they firmly believed that it was their father, back in Winfield, Kansas, in 1882, who had invented the roundup, as the family called rodeos.[7]

In his later years, Zack Miller always told visitors to the ranch that he and his brothers organized the 101 Ranch Wild West show when their cowboys were barred from appearing in rodeos in Wichita, Kansas, and Cheyenne, Wyoming, because they were considered "too professional."[8]

Certainly, the events the Millers staged were intended as showcases for their many skilled riders, ropers, and bulldoggers. But the Millers also wanted to do more than host roundups. They were interested in presenting the public with what they termed "A Real 'Wild West.' "[9] After much planning in the ranch headquarters office at the White House, the three brothers figured they could best accomplish that by staging mock battles between Indian war parties and settlers and reenactments of historic events which featured some of the original participants. To make their show even more authentic, the Millers assembled the true denizens of the windswept prairies and ranchlands—daring cowboys and cowgirls, lariat spinners, sharpshooters, Indian horsemen, herds of buffalo and longhorns, and plenty of renegade bucking horses.[10]

There was no shortage of models for the Millers to use or borrow from when preparing their early shows. By the time the family assembled its first company of 101 Ranch entertainers to take on the road, the idea of the Wild West show had become a firmly established part of western legend. The concept dated to as early as 1843, when P. T. Barnum put on his "Grand Buffalo Hunt" at Hoboken, New Jersey.[11] Although the Millers stubbornly maintained that their family had originated the roundup as public entertainment, even they had to admit that William Frederick "Buffalo Bill" Cody, the most flamboyant showman of his time, deserved most of the credit for bringing the Wild West to the world.[12] The Millers had attended performances of Buffalo Bill's Wild West and Congress of Rough Riders of the World, and they later developed a working relationship with Colonel Cody when he was in his sunset years.

The Millers learned all they could about the many Wild West shows and circuses which had appeared in the late nineteenth century. They became especially well acquainted with shows that sprang up and flourished during the first decade of the twentieth century.[13] The long roster of new shows barnstorming the nation included Broncho John, Famous Western Horseman, and His Corps of Expert Horsemen; Buckskin Ben's Wild West and Dog and Pony Show and Wild West; Cherokee Ed's Wild West; Dickey's Circle D Ranch; Diamond Bar Ranch Wild West; Luella Forepaugh-Fish Wild West; Hulberg's Wild West and Congress of Nations of the World; Lone Star Mary's Wild West; Texas Bud's Wild West; Tiger Bill's Wild West; and Wild Bill's Wild West.[14]

The shows came in all sizes. The largest were Cody's huge operation and Cummins' Wild West, which featured aging Indian chiefs and cowboy performers, along with elephants, camels, and an assortment of other creatures. The owners of some of the shows, on the other hand, only managed to turn out a few broken-down cowboys and some spent range horses for appearances at remote county fairs and rural carnivals. Buckskin Ben's Wild West Show was so small that Ben's busy wife beat the drum to attract a crowd and peddled tickets at the same time.[15]

Even outlaws saw an opportunity to make money by forming their own shows. In 1903, Cole Younger, surviving brother of the notorious Younger gang, and Frank James, eldest of the infamous James brothers, with financial backing from Chicago showmen, purchased the Buckskin Wild West Show.[16] Although the two ex-bandits figured they would be the greatest drawing feature of the show, their strategy backfired. "The show is without exception the poorest ever seen in our city," declared a newspaper in Maryville, Missouri, on August 29, 1903. The public agreed. The old Missouri outlaws could not make a legitimate comeback—the Cole Younger–Frank James Wild West lasted only one season.[17]

The majority of the thirty or so Wild West shows that popped up during the early 1900s vanished from sight just as quickly. In fact, from 1883 to the mid-1930s, more than one hundred Wild West shows came and went, although some were simply repackaged shows with fresh names, new partners, or different owners.[18] Indeed, as a 1967 editorial in *Real West* lamented, "The wild west show is gone, mourned by only a few who remember the thrill of the grand entrance parade. It brought the West to the East. Easterners could, for the price of admission, partake in the vicarious thrill of watching an Indian raid on a settler's cabin, the holdup of the Deadwood stage and countless other incidents that had been headlined in their newspaper, family story papers and in dime novels. It brought the West to life. . . . To most easterners the wild west show was their only contact with the West, and it made converts of them."[19]

Without a doubt, the two people who made converts of the Millers and most directly influenced their decision to enter show business were Colonel Zack Mulhall and Gordon William Lillie, an old Boomer and scout best known as Pawnee Bill. Both of the veteran showmen would remain lifelong friends of the Miller brothers, even though at times their own shows directly competed with that of the 101 Ranch.[20]

In September 1905, less than two months after the big roundup at their ranch on the Salt Fork, the Miller brothers and a company of 101 Ranch cowboys joined with the Mulhalls' Congress of Rough Riders and Ropers for a three-day show at the Interstate and Territorial Exposition in Coffeyville, Kansas.[21] It was the third time that year that the two families had appeared together in a public performance.

Once a popular cowtown remembered for a bloody raid by the Dalton outlaw gang in 1892, Coffeyville was in the midst of an economic boom sparked by the development of natural-gas and oil fields in Kansas and Oklahoma. Because of the town's prosperity and an extensive advertising campaign throughout the region, the exposition officials anticipated large crowds for the shows. Wooden bleachers nine tiers high stretched for a half-mile around an arena surrounded by heavy woven wire, similar to the fencing the Millers had used at their big roundup.[22]

On opening day, the heavens erupted and poured rain, leaving the race track soaked and the arena floor a sea of ankle-deep mud. Crowds did not materialize on the special trains provided by four railroads that served Coffeyville. Even though the sun finally appeared, fewer than three thousand persons—half the crowd anticipated—attended the first performance. Yet the Millers and Mulhalls persevered. Even when the pelting rains returned just as a steer-roping contest started, the performers gave the stalwart folks who braved the storm a show to remember.[23]

After twenty cowboys failed to catch a steer, Lucille Mulhall and Governor galloped through the mud and pools of water. In one minute and two seconds, "America's Cowgirl" had roped and tied the bawling steer. Horse races came next, but the slippery track made the conditions dangerous and the horses labored just to keep their footing.[24]

The Miller brothers' trained-mule act followed. If the late Colonel G. W. Miller, always an admirer of mules, could have been there with his three sons, he would have been pleased. The Millers' mules performed so well that the drenched crowd came back to life. One of the newspaper reviews described the mules' performance as "wonderful feats of skill and intelligence."[25]

Word of the show quickly spread throughout Coffeyville and the surrounding area. The next day, under a blazing sun, the grand parade through the town streets attracted enthusiastic flocks of onlookers.[26] Every performance that afternoon was memorable. George Elser, the fine cowboy who had ridden at Madison Square Garden and at the Millers' buffalo chase, re-created an abbreviated Pony Express ride by toting a mail pouch and changing mounts every one-eighth mile. A comedic race featured mounted contestants with spears who skewered potatoes from a box and then raced fifty yards to deposit them in a basket. Later in the day, the Millers' trained mules once again captivated the audience. So did a half-mile horse race with pitted White Eagle, the Ponca chief representing the 101 Ranch outfit, against Lucille Mulhall and a cowboy rider.[27]

While the crowd still cheered and applauded, a stampede of cattle was turned loose, with a gang of ropers and riders in hot pursuit. Then a bronc-riding contest, featuring Charley Mulhall, was followed by a balloon ascension, more horse races, and an Indian ball game. That evening, the Mulhall Cowboy Band concert and a Creek Indian ceremony brought the program to a close.[28]

On the third and final day of the show, the Miller brothers' mule act was moved to the first spot on the program. The Millers and their crew were due to appear at the Kansas State Fair at Topeka the next day, so they loaded the ranch personnel and stock early and rode the northbound train to the capital city.[29] The 101 Ranch Wild West Show was off and running. There was no looking back for the Miller brothers and their troop of riders.

From the start, the Millers made sure the men and women who rode for them—at the ranch and with the show on the road—were top hands. Many of those first cowboys and cowgirls who signed on with the Millers' early Wild West shows had been raised on ranches and completely understood cattle, horses, and the way of life the Miller brothers wanted to preserve.

Although the Millers insisted on having skilled hired hands, they were not as selective about the backgrounds of the people they hired. They could not afford to be. A few of those who showed up at the ranch looking for jobs as working cowboys or show performers sported checkered pasts. That never stopped the Millers from hiring anyone, including cold-blooded killers and thieves. Neither Joe Miller, a convicted felon, nor his brothers ever forgot that they and their family, including their father, had occasionally crossed the line of legality. Sometimes, if good help was short, the Millers even put convicts to work on the ranch.[30]

Of the hundreds of men and women who at one time worked for the Millers—as common laborers, cooks, roustabouts, cowhands, animal trainers, or entertainers—many were veterans of frontier life. Some of them remained with the 101 for their entire careers, but others did not last until the first paycheck. The true stories about various ranch hands and performers were often veiled in myth, hearsay, and bunkhouse invention.

Among the fleeting legends at the 101 Ranch was Frank Eaton, a cowboy, scout, and trail rider.[31] Born in Hartford, Connecticut, in 1860, Eaton was seven years old when he moved with his family to Kansas. The next year, his father, a Yankee veteran who belonged to a vigilante organization comprised of northern sympathizers and hired gunmen, was shot and killed in the door of the family home by former Confederates known as Regulators. At age fifteen, Eaton earned his celebrated moniker, "Pistol Pete," when an Indian Territory cavalry soldier observed the youth's competence as a marksman with a Colt pistol.[32]

Eager to avenge his father's murder, Pistol Pete Eaton wound up riding on both sides of the law. While still a teenager, he became a United States deputy marshal in Indian Territory, and he later took a job as a "troubleshooter" for a cattlemen's association.[33] It may have been a position similar to the one held by Omar Coffelt, the eccentric "buffalo man" who acted as an "enforcer" for the 101 Ranch for many years and was implicated in the 1901 murder of railroad detective George Montgomery.

During Eaton's short stint as a hand at the 101 Ranch, his fellow cowboys could not help but notice the eleven notches on the butt of his pistol. Six of the marks stood for the men he had killed while serving as a sworn law officer for Judge Isaac Parker. The other five represented his father's murderers whom Pistol Pete had methodically tracked down and killed. A sixth died before Eaton got to him.[34]

In later years, when some of the old Cherokee Outlet cowpunchers got together to reminisce and trade stories, Pistol Pete—with his great drooping mustache and waist-length braids decorated with ribbons—sometimes showed up. He still toted his Colt .45 pistol and always kept it loaded. "I'd rather have a pocket full of rocks than an empty gun," Eaton told the veteran cowpunchers. That gun was still loaded and by his side when Pistol Pete finally died with his boots on at age ninety-eight.[35] An enduring image of the Old West, a caricature of Frank Eaton as Pistol Pete was selected as the model for the official mascots of Oklahoma State University, New Mexico State University, and the University of Wyoming.[36]

Another 101 Ranch cowboy who reportedly had plenty of notches on his gun was Henry Grammer, a controversial figure in the early days of Oklahoma's Kay and Osage Counties.[37] Grammer bootlegged whiskey, brawled in saloons, shot straight from the hip, and was entangled in a long list of felonies, ranging from cattle rustling and bank robbery to cold-blooded murder. Some folks said he had the morals of a coyote in heat. Grammer was just the kind of cowboy the Millers were looking for when they put together their Wild West show.[38]

But the Miller brothers did not hire him just because he was tough and mean. They wanted Grammer because he was a natural crowd pleaser who could swing a rope and lasso running steers better than just about anyone in the Twin Territories. Long before Grammer became a world-champion rodeo cowboy, the Millers recognized the agile horseman's ability with a lariat. He first performed for the 101 Ranch when he was a young range rider, during the 1905 buffalo chase.[39]

In 1907, Grammer became what was commonly called a "squaw man" when he married an Osage woman and bought a ranch on the western side of the Osage Nation.[40] While punching cows, he continued to ride in Wild West shows for the Millers. Eventually, Grammer roped before many of the crowned heads of Europe and won the world's roping championship, a distinction he held for many years.[41]

In the early 1920s, Grammer was implicated in what was known as the "Osage Reign of Terror"—a scheme to cheat Indians out of their oil money, resulting in the murders of several Osages to gain control of their tribal headrights.[42] It was never certain exactly how many such murders occurred in Osage County between 1915 and 1925; some folks said at least two dozen, but others believed as many as forty homicides were committed.

In 1926, Grammer came to a violent end. He had just helped pistol-whip three men in a brutal fight when the Cadillac he was riding in mysteriously catapulted off the road about twenty miles west of Pawhuska, in Osage County. The champion roper, forty-two years old, died of a broken neck.[43] His death was never fully resolved, but for decades to come, rodeo fans talked about Grammer's roping feats.

Several of the Millers' performers started with the 101 as youngsters. James P. Collier, born in a wagon bound for Oklahoma Territory on a rainy day in 1891, was a thirteen-year-old runaway when a 101 Ranch cowhand found him trudging along a road and took him to the ranch headquarters.[44] After a plate of hot grub and some gentle questioning, Jim revealed that when he was eleven years old, two bandits had ambushed his father. The wounded man died in his son's arms as he tried to push his father's brains back into his skull. Within a few years, several more members of Jim's family had been killed, including his brother and sister-in-law, murdered in their sleep by outlaws who chloroformed them, robbed their house, and set it on fire.[45]

At the 101 Ranch, Jim's first job was opening and closing gates for line riders and helping the blacksmith and cook. By the time Jim turned fourteen, Bill Pickett had taught him how to break horses in the ranch corrals. Jim worked the June 1905 roundup for the National Editorial Association and then went on the road with the Millers.[46]

He soon became a versatile performer, riding in various historic reenactments and entertaining the crowds with fancy rope tricks between major show acts. Within a few years, when Princess Wenona joined the Millers' show, it was Jim who allowed the champion female sharpshooter to place an apple on his head and shoot it off, in the style of William Tell.[47]

Jim Collier later teamed with Emmett Dalton, the surviving member of the Dalton gang, and the pair traveled to county fairs and other events, peddling autographed photographs of the old outlaw. After working a series of jobs, Collier returned to the Miller brothers for their 1916–1917 show season. Then he finally moved on.

For the rest of his life, Collier kept his ties with the many show people he met along the way, including Will Rogers, Tom Mix, Buck Jones, Stepin Fetchit, and Spade Cooley, a western musician. In 1978, when Collier died in southern California at age eighty-seven, he still bragged that he had been one of the original 101 Ranch Wild West show performers.[48]

That was a boast that any cowboy or cowgirl who ever rode into an arena would have envied.

PAWNEE BILL

A TALE TOLD around bunkhouses and show arenas had it that "Pawnee Bill" Lillie, Wild West impresario and longtime friend of the Miller family, was the consummate frontiersman because, as a boy in Kansas, he had developed a taste for cow's blood.[1] Storytellers reasoned that without cattle, there would have been no cowboys, no roundups and trail drives, no rustlers, no range wars, and no wicked Kansas trail towns. Surely, then, anyone who was nourished by the very lifeblood of one the foremost symbols of the Wild West had to be special.

Imbibing the blood of cattle was something that G. W. Miller, Shanghai Pierce, and Zack Mulhall never tried. Not even the imaginative William F. Cody ever claimed to have partaken of blood of any sort, including bison blood, although the old rascal probably would have if only he had thought of it.

With some embellishments, Zack Miller liked to tell the story of the rather peculiar beverage on occasion. It proved especially effective whenever Pawnee Bill visited the Millers at the 101 Ranch and eastern dudes and ladies were in attendance, sipping powerful toddies and hanging on every word.[2] But as with so many of the other legends surrounding the Miller brothers and their cohorts, a clear vein of truth ran through the yarn. Just like the Millers, much of Pawnee Bill's true life was more interesting than the stories told about him.

Gordon William Lillie, born on February 14, 1860, in Bloomington, Illinois, was the eldest of four children of Susan Ann and Newton Wesley Lillie.[3] His Bostonian mother was the daughter of a noted banker, and his father had been born in Québec of Scottish parents. Although Gordon always remained small in physique, he developed into a sturdy youngster known for exceptional strength and athletic ability. When still a schoolboy, he worked nights and Saturdays at the big flour mill his father owned and operated.[4]

At about this time, Gordon Lillie succumbed to something incurable. He called it an "attack of Western fever," and explained that the condition was brought on by his visits with cousins from Kansas and their tales of

Indians, buffalo hunts, and life on the Indian Territory frontier.[5] The fever spread throughout Lillie after he devoured the dime novels of Ned Buntline and the periodical stories of such famous plainsmen as William F. Cody and James Butler "Wild Bill" Hickok.[6]

The raging fever peaked when both Buffalo Bill and Wild Bill, along with "Texas Jack" Omohundro, showed up in Bloomington, with hair cascading down their backs and wearing huge sombreros and buffalo coats. After young Gordon saw their show—*The Scouts of the Plains*—at Schroeder's Opera House, he knew he would never be happy until he moved west.[7] As he later explained, "Everybody had the itch to go West in those days, and I was no exception."[8]

The youngster's wish came true just a short time later when his father's mill burned to the ground and the family settled near Wellington, Kansas.[9] It was in the cattle country of Kansas where the story first emerged about Gordon Lillie's taste for cow blood.

Many years later, when Lillie was an old man reflecting on his colorful life and career from the comfort of the smoking room at his ranch outside Pawnee, Oklahoma, he spoke of those times. He recalled a bitter Kansas winter when he was a teenager and became so seriously ill with chills and fever that his parents feared he might die.[10]

Gordon Lillie's best pal in Wellington was the son of the local butcher who helped puny Gordon improve his health and become more robust.[11] The butcher suggested to Gordon's parents that he could be built up and invigorated by drinking fresh cow's blood—a fluid in great bounty at the man's place of business. Somewhat shocked by the proposed cure but anxious to raise a healthy son, the Lillies reluctantly agreed that their boy could try the strange diet supplement.[12] On slaughtering days, young Gordon faithfully showed up at the butcher shop to slurp down his quota of warm beef blood. Surprisingly, the regimen worked. "I am confident this was all that saved my life," he said years afterward.[13]

Back on his feet after a lengthy recuperation, Gordon taught school for a while, but soon succumbed to his yearning to roam the surrounding Indian country. After visiting local bands of Pawnee Indians and befriending a Pawnee named Blue Hawk who taught him some of his tribe's language and ways, Gordon Lillie and another young friend went to Wichita to find jobs as drovers on the Chisholm Trail.[14]

In Wichita, the youngster dined on longhorn steak, met the storied lawman Wyatt Earp and the Boomer leader David Payne, and became friendly with other prominent citizens.[15] But Gordon, not yet sixteen years old, also ran into serious trouble. When he came to the defense of an Indian being bullied by a cowboy named "Trigger" Jim Braden, he was forced into a gunfight and ended up killing Braden with a borrowed revolver. Although a coroner's jury acquitted the teenager, he decided he had had enough of town life and hightailed it south to spend time with Blue Hawk and other friends at the Pawnee agency in Indian Territory.[16]

The Pawnees fully accepted young Lillie and, after a brief spell as a buffalo hunter and trapper, he lived with the tribe. He listened to the stories of the elders, became proficient in their language, and at age seventeen served as an interpreter and teacher at the agency school. By the early 1880s, he had picked up the name Pawnee Bill, a sobriquet he would keep to his dying day.[17]

Pawnee Bill later hunted buffalo, worked as a cowboy and a teamster in the Cherokee Outlet, and became deeply involved in Payne's Boomer movement. By 1883, Lillie had reached an important juncture when he encountered one of his boyhood idols, Buffalo Bill Cody, and went on the road with him, working as an interpreter in charge of the Pawnees hired to appear with the show.[18]

Cody's Wild West, which met with overwhelming success, featured Indians as entertainers, along with cowboys, trick riders, and performers. When the show played Philadelphia, Lillie was standing on the showgrounds in front of the main tent when a fifteen-year-old schoolgirl walked by with her books under her arm. The girl smiled and then laughed out loud when the stocky frontiersman with long hair, sombrero, and buckskin clothes tipped his hat. Pawnee Bill lost his heart. "It was love at first sight, and I knew that she was the girl for me," he later wrote.[19]

Pawnee Bill went on to learn that May Manning, daughter of a prominent Philadelphia physician, had been raised as a Quaker and was a student at Smith College.[20] To most of those who knew the couple, it appeared that they had nothing whatsoever in common. Nonetheless, Pawnee Bill was determined to win May Manning's hand.

He showered the young woman with love letters and, after more excitement out West, returned to May's Philadelphia home, only to find that her mother had burned some of the correspondence he had sent.[21] The intrepid Lillie told May's parents of his abiding love for their daughter and tried to convince them that he could provide for her needs with earnings from a cattle ranch he was developing in Kansas. The Mannings remained somewhat skeptical, but before her suitor left, May had promised to marry Pawnee Bill.[22]

On August 31, 1886—a date Pawnee Bill described as the turning point of his life—May Manning, socialite newly graduated from Smith, and Gordon W. Lillie, flamboyant showman "of the plains country," became husband and wife.[23] In less than an hour after the ceremony, the newlyweds were aboard a train headed west to Kansas.

A year later, while her husband was "gallivanting around the country with a bunch of wild Indians," May gave birth to a ten-and-a-half-pound son.[24] Pawnee Bill hurried home, but the baby developed complications and lived only six weeks. To make matters worse, May had to undergo an operation and was left unable to bear any more children. She turned to her husband's chosen line of work and began her own career in what she called "western affairs."[25]

May threw every ounce of her being into Wild West show business. She learned to ride and rope, and "cultivated a taste for the rifle" by hunting prairie chickens and turkeys. May Lillie became known throughout the country as a true sharpshooter.[26]

In the spring of 1888, Pawnee Bill's Wild West launched a new season featuring Pawnee Bill and May Lillie, accompanied by some of their kinfolk and old friends, a huge troop of cowboys, Mexican riders, scouts, and Indians from five tribes—Pawnees, Comanches, Kiowas, Wichitas, and Kaws.[27] The press notices for May were stunning. She was hailed as the "Princess of the Prairie," the "World's Champion Woman Rifle Shot," and the "New Rifle Queen."[28]

Meanwhile, pressure mounted to open the Oklahoma Unassigned Lands to white settlement. Gordon Lillie returned to Kansas and organized scattered groups of Boomers into a colony. On the day of the land run—April 22, 1889—he led thousands of them into the "Promised Land." Finding himself an overnight national figure, Pawnee Bill parlayed the public attention and press reports into publicity for his expanded Wild West shows.[29]

Pawnee Bill toured his show around the United States and Europe for several years. In 1893, after the Cherokee Outlet was opened to white settlers, the Lillies moved to what became Pawnee County, in the countryside they liked so well, near the Pawnee agency.[30]

Throughout the 1890s and the first several years of the new century, Pawnee Bill found some of the best natural talent available. That included George Elser, the champion rider who later appeared with Zack Mulhall and the Miller brothers, and José Barrera, a native of San Antonio better known as "Mexican Joe."[31] Famed for his skill with a rope and as a horseman, Barrera went on to travel with the Miller Brothers' 101 Ranch show but returned to Pawnee to become Lillie's right-hand man.

Eventually, Pawnee Bill purchased almost two thousand acres southwest of Pawnee from his old friend Blue Hawk.[32] It was to be the site of Lillie's buffalo ranch—a sanctuary for the "monarchs of the plains." An ardent conservationist and activist in the buffalo-preservation movement, Pawnee Bill bought up all the pure-blooded buffalo calves he could locate. By 1906, he grazed sixty head of healthy buffalo, making it the third-largest privately owned bison herd in the nation.[33]

That year, Lillie joined in partnership with Edward Arlington, a veteran showman and former adviser to James A. Bailey of Barnum & Bailey fame. With Buffalo Bill and his retinue abroad playing the cities of Europe in 1906, the Pawnee Bill show had become the largest in North America.[34]

Always shrewd in business although sometimes generous to a fault, Lillie had no fears about his good friends the Miller brothers entering his world of Wild West entertainment. He figured there was plenty of room for everyone. So did the Millers. Through the years, Lillie and the Millers remained friends and allies in the effort to keep the so-called Wild West alive.

Chapter 26

"GOING UP"

I commend to your attention and study the superb specimens of my race gathered under the Miller Brothers' standard. They are real children of nature, by whom the official bounty of the white conqueror has remained untouched. Theirs has been the contented life of tepee and forest, far removed from the hated crowds. . . . weep with me for the days when we lived and worked and thought in our own way.[1]

—Charles Cowskin
Interpreter for Indians in 101 Ranch show

IN September 1906, the year Teddy Roosevelt scrawled his name on legislation which ultimately combined Oklahoma and Indian Territories into a single state, the Miller brothers hosted what was considered to be one of the largest Wild West shows in history.[2] The Millers focused all their energy on this next extravaganza, and the payoff earned them a bonanza of goodwill, publicity, and revenue.

Buoyed and somewhat astonished by the public enthusiasm for the 1905 buffalo chase and by the enormous success of their Wild West excursions through the Twin Territories and Kansas, the brothers wanted the next big ranch affair to be just as monumental as those events. The Millers therefore chose a landmark theme for their huge ranch production—the thirteenth anniversary of the September 16, 1893, Cherokee Outlet run, the greatest of all the openings of Indian lands.[3]

The celebration turned out to be yet another critical achievement for the Millers. By year's end, it had earned them a coveted invitation from President Roosevelt to bring their show to Virginia for the 1907 Jamestown Exposition.[4]

The production at the ranch on September 15–16, 1906, required the efforts of two thousand to three thousand people, including as many as one thousand Indians and five hundred cowboys and cowgirls.[5] The Millers were anxious to see a spectator in each of the twenty-five thousand seats around the immense pasture arena, three-quarters of a mile long and one-half mile wide.[6]

The show's printed program was crammed with paid advertisements from scores of businesses, many of which were closely associated with the Millers. Almost all the firms were based in Kansas City, at that time the largest marketplace in the region. Advertisements were placed by banks, jewelers, a mule wholesaler, printers, camp outfitters, and even an interior decorator.[7]

For a mere three dollars, Allmens Distilling Company of Kansas City offered to ship four full quarts of ten-year-old rye whisky, recommended by doctors as a "stimulant, tonic and invigorator." As a bonus for the discreet buyer, the bottles would be packed in "plain boxes, and they contain no marks to indicate contents." A full-page ad extolled the virtues of Eagle Brand Stock Dip, endorsed by the Millers themselves, to remedy mange and scabies and to remove lice and ticks from cattle, hogs, and sheep.[8] The list went on.

Although the size of the crowd did not equal the sixty-five thousand that had showed up in 1905, at least fifty thousand people from across the country descended on the 101 Ranch for the anniversary celebration.[9] Most of them came to Bliss on one of the twenty special excursion trains provided by Santa Fe Railway, complete with sleeper cars, drawing-room Pullmans, and Fred Harvey meals.[10]

The event began with the usual grand parade of Indians, cowboys, cowgirls, musicians, and featured performers. This was followed by a range of activities including Indian war dances, a simulated stagecoach holdup, a buffalo chase and, of course, the reenactment of the fabled race for land in the Cherokee Outlet.[11]

Hundreds of local farmers, their families, and even pet hounds showed up at the ranch to take part in the "land run." Many of those who came in their covered wagons, buggies, and on horseback had been participants in the real opening of the Cherokee Outlet. At the starting signal, all of them struck out in a rush, just as they had done thirteen years before. As the wave of wagons and riders raced at breakneck speed twice around the large arena grounds, great clouds of dust billowed into the sky. From the packed grandstand came the stirring march music of the band and the cheers of encouragement from the tens of thousands of spectators.[12]

One of the highlights of the celebration was the appearance of Bill Pickett, billed in the program as "Pickett, the Wonderful Negro, in his sensational Steer Catching and Throwing Act."[13] Pickett raced into the arena on his big bay, Spradley, seized a running steer by the nose with his teeth, and wrestled the critter to the ground.

Ever since his first appearance with the Millers in 1905, Pickett had continued to give his unusual bulldogging exhibitions. On two occasions, he even subdued a large bull elk. He had been in San Francisco just after the catastrophic earthquake and fire of April 18, 1906, when the city's business district was destroyed and the bodies of victims were stacked up at the morgue like cords of wood. Images of death and mayhem from that bruised and battered city would stay with Pickett for the rest of his life.[14]

In addition to the bulldogging, bronco busting, roping, and a simulated land run, the crowd also enjoyed the large numbers of "genuine Indians," representing more than a dozen tribes, that the Millers had brought together at their ranch.[15] Indian camps—studded with tepees and veiled by the smoke from countless cooking fires—surrounded the arena and flanked the Salt Fork. Visitors walked among Poncas, Otoes, Osages, Kaws, Pawnees, Cheyennes, Winnebagos, Kiowas, Comanches, Arapahos, Tonkawas, Apaches, and Sioux.[16]

From those earliest years of the Millers' Wild West shows, Indians came to the ranch by the hundreds, including some of the hereditary enemies of the Poncas, such as members of the Sioux tribe. At the 101 Ranch, the various bands of Indians lived, according to the Millers' propaganda, "as their ancestors once did."[17]

The Millers outfitted the Indians with all the necessary creature comforts, including medical care, shelter, water and feed for the pony herds, and fat beeves to slaughter. When the show went on the road, the Indians brought along their canvas lodges and their own basic clothing, except for headdresses and moccasins, which the Millers provided. Each Indian man appearing with the show received five dollars cash per week in pay, and each woman four dollars, far less than any of the white men and women who performed with the show.[18]

Many historians, Native American–rights activists, and Indian-policy reformers have questioned the motives of such showmen as the Miller brothers, Pawnee Bill, and Buffalo Bill who paid Indians such minimal wages to entertain the public. These critics also believed the use of "Wild West Show Indians" reinforced negative stereotypes by portraying them in a sensationalist and derogatory manner that perpetuated the racial myths of Indians as "wild" or "heathen savages."[19]

Some politicians and federal officials agreed with the criticisms and condemned the practice of using Indians in Wild West shows. Still, they begrudgingly admitted that no legal way existed to prevent Indians from exercising their right to participate in such exhibitions. Some detractors criticized the shows because they thought such displays glorified the Indians' traditional culture.

"Their surroundings in these tours are generally of the worst, and they pick up the most degrading vices," Thomas J. Morgan, commissioner of Indian affairs, wrote as early as 1890 in a report to the secretary of interior. "Instead of being favorably impressed with the religion of the white man, it is more than likely that they come to distrust it through what they unavoidably see, hear, and experience. Traveling about the country on these expeditions fosters the roving spirit already so common among them, encourages idleness and a distaste for steady occupation, and during their absence their families often suffer for want of their care and assistance."[20]

As commissioner of Indian affairs until his retirement, in 1894, Morgan also had taken exception with the Millers' relationship with Indians in other matters, especially the manner of killing beef cattle supplied to the tribes as part of their government rations.[21] The Millers had always allowed the Indian men to shoot cattle and then have the women and children butcher the animals where they fell, just as had been done on traditional buffalo hunts.

Morgan considered this a "savage sport" and wanted the practice stopped because it allowed Indians to maintain a traditional practice rather than adhere to the white man's ways. According to a directive Morgan issued, all slaughtering was to be done in a pen with only men present. He further specified that the "consumption of the blood and intestines by the Indians is strictly prohibited" since it "serves to nourish brutal instincts."[22] The Millers ignored the federal government's instructions and, for the most part, allowed the Indians who rode with their shows to butcher cattle just as they pleased.

But unlike the Millers, many other whites agreed with Morgan and other bureaucrats. They believed the best way for Indians to get along in the world was through assimilation. Yet many Indians—particularly in Oklahoma—did not see the need to act like white people or halt their participation in Wild West shows. Reflecting on this situation seventy-five years after the Millers' first shows, Native American scholar Rennard Strickland noted, "Oklahoma Indians have historically loved to perform, to play and dance for themselves or crowds, to 'play Indian' or just play. Colonial Indians traveling to Europe, Geronimo at the St. Louis World's Fair, the professional Indian dance troupe, the Osage ballerinas, Indians in Pawnee

Bill's and the 101 Ranch shows are all part of the same tradition. . . . Nor can any group of actors be as proud or arrogant as a group of Oklahoma Indians dressed by a Hollywood director in make-believe Indian costumes. If what one sees of the dances and the dancers, of the Indians at play, is just the outward performance, then one misses the spirit of the real world of Oklahoma's Indian people."[23]

Although Strickland's observations came decades after the heyday of the 101 Ranch shows, his views fit with the attitude of the Miller family, and especially of Joe Miller, guiding force of the 101 Ranch shows. Joe had remained a keen observer of the Indian way of life ever since he was a small boy riding the open range with his father.

Known by many of the Ponca people as "Joe Coga," which meant "Friend Joe," the eldest Miller brother realized that the most colorful and valuable assets of the 101 Ranch were the Poncas, on whose tribal land the major part of the ranch stood.[24] Joe maintained his bond with the tribe all his life. Ultimately, he received the highest honor the Poncas could give him—they adopted him into the tribe and made him a chief.[25]

This unusual event took place when Little Standing Buffalo, a former war chief of the Poncas and second in rank to head chief White Eagle, summoned the other leaders to his deathbed. A brave man, still proud of the Sioux scalps he had taken as a young warrior, Little Standing Buffalo spoke to the council of chiefs gathered around him of Joe Miller's long and close association with their tribe.[26]

He recalled Joe's solo boyhood ride across Indian Territory to Baxter Springs to tell the chiefs of the merits of the new land that waited for them in the West, and the time young Joe Miller had accompanied White Eagle and Ponca followers to the state fair in Alabama. Little Standing Buffalo reminded the others about the bitter winters when government rations were scarce and Joe and his brothers had given the Poncas extra beeves to keep their children from starving. Then the dying Ponca leader said that his last wish was for Miller to be made a chief. The others agreed, and Little Standing Buffalo eventually died content that his place in the council circle would be filled by a worthy successor.[27]

A delegation of Poncas came to the ranch and requested that Joe Miller attend their annual sun dance, a solemn and sacred ritual. As they put it, Joe was to come "just like Indian." Honored by the rare invitation but unaware that the tribe was about to adopt him, Joe donned moccasins, buckskin leggings, and a shirt adorned with intricate beaded and dyed porcupine-quill designs. He painted his face with the same colors and design used by Little Standing Buffalo, a coincidence that the Poncas regarded as a favorable omen. Joe left word at the ranch for several beeves to be driven to the Indian camp, and he brought along spotted ponies which he presented to prominent Poncas.[28]

After the exchange of gifts at the sun-dance lodge, White Eagle invited Joe to become a member of the Ponca tribe. Surprised, he accepted without hesitation, and was immediately turned over to two medicine men who taught him more of their tribal history and some of their most revered songs. After fasting and partaking in various ceremonies, the Poncas made "Joe Coga" a blood brother. They announced that he had attained warrior rank and had been given the name of *Mutha-monta*, which translated as "going up," to indicate that Joe was progressing to a higher status.[29]

After Joe's ceremonial presentation to the tribe as a warrior, the Poncas immediately returned him to the sun-dance lodge and informed him that he was to become the successor of Little Standing Buffalo. That status required two more days of ceremonies and instruction. At last, Joe was presented to the assembled tribe as *Waka-huda nuga-ski*, or "Big White Chief." Humbled by the experience, Joe sent word back to the ranch for more beeves, and two days of feasting and dancing ended the weeklong sun dance, which passed into the history of the Poncas as "the Sun Dance of the Big White Chief."[30]

Although he took his tribal responsibilities quite seriously, Joe Miller also parlayed his newfound leadership status with the Poncas into an even greater position of power and influence. Indeed, Joe's paternalistic attitude toward the Ponca people and all other Indians associated with the ranch appears clearly in the racially pejorative stories contained in early publications churned out by the 101 Ranch for its first Wild West shows.

"As 'White Chief of the Poncas,' Mr. Miller is the counsellor [sic], guide and protector of the tribe," stated one of the first show publications, commonly referred to as couriers. "The Indians come to him in all their diverse joyful or sorrowful circumstances. They seek his advice in marriage, sickness, births, death and divorce. He adjusts family differences, and is consulted on all money and land transactions. A constant procession of redskinned braves and squaws comes and goes at the 101 Ranch general offices."[31]

The Millers' close ties with the Poncas and other tribes ensured that large numbers of Indians joined in a variety of public events at the ranch and on the road for years to come. Only a few Indians accompanied Zack Miller and a bunch of the 101 Ranch cowboys to a 1906 roping contest and bronc-busting exhibition at Enid, but luckily, Lewis Schauss, manager of the Convention Hall in Kansas City, was in attendance and liked what he saw.[32]

Afterward, Schauss went to the ranch to book the Millers for appearances at Convention Hall during the November horse show. When the date came around, the Millers loaded seventy-five riders and ropers, as well as several carloads of livestock, at Bliss and headed to Kansas City. Although their appearance had had no publicity or advertising, the 101 Ranch performers so impressed local reporters on opening night that the resulting front-page coverage ensured sold-out audiences for the rest of the run.[33]

The Millers had tasted arena fame and found that they liked it. By the start of 1907, a year that brought the ranch even more national acclaim and ended with Oklahoma statehood, Joe Miller and his brothers had contracted a raging case of show fever. Just like Pawnee Bill Lillie and Buffalo Bill Cody, they recognized that there was no cure.

JANE WOODEND:
Fence Rider

As early as 1905, the Miller brothers played hosts to flocks of visitors from big eastern cities, anxious to learn how to ride, rope, and live a wrangler's life.[1] Occasionally a few young ladies and sometimes married couples appeared at the ranch, but the majority of the guests were young men whose fathers bankrolled their summer excursions to the 101 Ranch. The idea was for the pampered offspring to soak up experiences that could not be found in an Ivy League lecture hall or a corporate boardroom.[2]

For several years, until 1909, literally hundreds of these "dudes" and "dudesses," or "dudines," as the females were known, spent as long as four months each year on the ranch.[3] Most found the experience to be profound. For some, it proved to be life altering.

One of the Millers' guests recalled:

> We who were going to take a stroll over the world's most famous ranch began to hear it discussed as soon as our train had made its cautious progress over the Mississippi River, and the conversation turned to things western. Our first impression of the 101 Ranch, and it remained the last and enduring one, was its vastness. Five miles from the railroad station to ranch house and every step on 101 ground! And this only an inkling of its area!
>
> With a dexterous turn, our reinswoman deposited us at the wide-open front door and we entered the home of the Millers. A heartier welcome, more boundless hospitality, a greater generosity than pervades the 101 Ranch exists nowhere. The mother of the "boys" is mistress of the house, and everywhere are the evidences of her touch and personality. . . . It was not until the evening meal that the three brothers made appearance, one clanking from a roundup eight miles eastward, another from an inspection of fences that required forty miles in the saddle, and the third from the corn fields that had yielded thousands of bushels the previous year. Stalwart figures they were in long riding boots. As the boy of our party felt his hand squeezed, he turned quite pale. You could see it was the most momentous meeting of his life.[4]

At first, these guests and other sightseers drawn to the Hundred and One stayed in any available bunkhouse or "roughed it" in tents. But by 1906, the Millers had built about a dozen three-room cottages not far from Joe Miller's residence, in an elm grove on the north bank of the Salt Fork. These comfortable guesthouses came complete with baths and electric lights. Nearby was a clubhouse and a dining hall where waiters served wild game and beef dinners and fetched drinks cooled with ice hauled from Ponca City. The Millers named the settlement Riverside Camp.[5]

This new enterprise was tremendously popular from the outset. The fame of the ranch was spreading, and guests came not only from the United States but also from England, France, Germany, and Russia.[6] Boarders paid a fixed rate of twenty-five dollars per week, which covered room and board, and usage fees for a horse, saddle, and other equipment "necessary for full measure of enjoyment of life on the ranch." Children under twelve were charged half rate, and special terms could be arranged for married couples or two members of the same family. As a bonus, Mother Miller, the devoted hostess of the ranch, made herself available as "confidant and counselor of the feminine contingent of visitors."[7]

For the Millers, this enterprise not only educated outsiders and helped keep alive the image of the Old West, but even more important, Riverside Camp became yet another profit center. Besides the basic rental fee, all guests purchased from the Millers the appropriate attire for a proper 101 Ranch wrangler, including hat, boots, chaps, and shirts. Once properly dressed, visitors were photographed for identification purposes, just in case they became lost in the back reaches of the big ranch.[8]

Guests did not spend all their time lolling in hammocks strung from shade trees at Riverside Camp. They took part in roundups, branded calves, dehorned cattle, broke horses, rode fence lines, visited nearby Ponca camps, and attended Indian ceremonies and dances. For relaxation, they held shooting contests and twilight polo games on grassy pastures, and hunted for coyotes, prairie dogs, and game birds. On the south side of the Salt Fork, they fished and frolicked at Red Lake, a forty-acre expanse stocked with bass and crappie and swarming with ducks and geese. Some nights, after a chuck-wagon supper, the fledgling cowpokes gathered around campfires and slept under the stars.[9]

"We will furnish them a good mount and saddle and put them in camp down along the Salt Fork River," explained Joe Miller. "We will let them sleep out of doors, eat from the tail end of a wagon and live the regular cowboy life, but of course without much of the work unless they really want to work; then they will be given all they want. We'll send some of the cowboys who are pretty good fellows—good story tellers and all that—over to take care of them, and have a cattle round-up once in a while for their benefit."[10]

One of the "good fellows" Joe Miller spoke of was Tom Mix, the handsome young man who had tended bar at the Blue Belle Saloon in Guthrie and signed on with the Millers in 1905, when he appeared at the National Editorial Association roundup that attracted sixty-five thousand visitors to the ranch.

Mix was working on his second divorce—from Kitty Perrine, the twenty-two-year-old daughter of the owner of the Perrine Hotel in Oklahoma City, where Mix had lived after his first marriage ended. Mix and Kitty had been married on December 20, 1905.[11] Unfortunately, the groom spent most of his time on the road with the Millers or at their ranch. As a result, Kitty became unhappy and the marriage lasted less than a year.[12]

In 1906, his first full season with the Hundred and One, Mix acted as a host for the dude cowboys and cowgirls from back east. He received fifteen dollars a month, including room and board.[13]

Reports varied with regard to Mix's abilities as a cowboy. One veteran wrangler recalled, "Tom's duties at the ranch consisted mostly of just hanging around and looking pretty. He was not much of a cowboy as such when he first came to work for the 101. People used to say that Tom could get lost in an eight-hundred acre pasture."[14]

Lew Stockdale, a longtime Cherokee Outlet cowpuncher who later had a lease on the 101 Ranch and operated a livery stable in Bliss, remembered Mix in a slightly different light. "My best memory of the time is that of a little shaver named Tom Mix, who came to work on the ranch and with the rodeo. I'll never forget the night that Tom came in with rain frozen all over him, and I had to take a hammer to break him loose from the stirrups. Boys were better and stronger in those days, I can tell you."[15]

When Zack Miller was in his final years, preparing his memoirs with author Fred Gipson, he related that although Mix had to be taught how to properly saddle a cow pony when he came to the ranch, he proved to be a quick study. "In a little while, he could handle a horse or rope well enough to fool any dude," was how Zack described Mix. "And that was Tom's main job, anyhow, peddling loads to the pilgrims, betting them windies about the ranch, its wild and bloody history, and that sort of thing. And at that, Tom was an artist. To hear Tom tell it, he had won the Boer War single-handed after serving for years as a Texas Ranger. . . . Tom could color a story redder than a Navajo blanket. He told his scary tales so often that he finally got to believing them himself."[16]

It was Tom Mix, during his tenure as host for the Millers, who recruited quite possibly the most interesting, if not the most enduring, guest ever to abide at Riverside Camp. Her name was Jane Woodend. On first appearance, she was a most unlikely candidate to join the ranks of the rough-and-ready saddle tramps who rode for the 101.[17]

Jennie Louise Howard, born in New York in 1875, and her brother, James Watson Howard, born in 1884, came into the world with silver spoons in their mouths. Their mother, who died when Jennie was nineteen, was the daughter of James Watson, an extremely wealthy real estate dealer in New York. Jennie's father was Dr. F. F. Howard, an affluent New York physician and president of the Fourteenth Street Bank.[18]

At her mother's death, Jennie inherited a tidy sum of money, a handsomely furnished residence in a fashionable neighborhood at 58 West Seventy-first Street, and an annual income of ten thousand dollars a year. A similar fortune was left in trust for her brother, a frail lad known by his middle name, Watson.[19]

At about this time, Jennie, who spent much of her time riding her prized horses at Durland's Riding Academy, met Dr. William E. Woodend, who had graduated from Princeton at age sixteen and was a popular practicing physician in Manhattan. The good-looking doctor shared Jennie's love for fine horseflesh. In 1898, after a whirlwind four-month courtship and despite her father's protests, the two married and embarked on a lavish life in New York's high society.[20]

Not satisfied with a high-profile life as a prosperous doctor and his reputation as "the best dressed man in New York," Woodend convinced his wife to use some of her fortune to buy him a seat on the stock exchange so he could try his hand at high finance.[21] His success at trading stocks was phenomenal. Money flowed to Woodend as if by magic, and in only a few months he was listed among Wall Street's millionaires.[22]

Jennie continued to dazzle crowds as the most beautiful and daring rider in the tanbark arena. The belle of horse shows from New York to London, she won scores of trophies and blue ribbons with her favorite saddle horse, a bay gelding named "the Master," and with a remarkable collection of high-stepping harness ponies accumulated by her free-spending husband.[23]

Then, just as quickly as the Woodends' fortunes had risen, the bottom fell out with the advent of the "rich man's depression" of 1904.[24] The disastrous panic clobbered Woodend and other big operators on Wall

Street, and in his battle to stay afloat, he used up almost every cent of his wife's money. He then depleted Watson Howard's inheritance.[25]

While her bankrupt husband battled to keep their world from crumbling completely, the faithful Jennie—hoping to retrieve some of her lost fortune—also tried to find additional sources of money.[26] Relying on the elocution lessons she had taken years before at Vassar and a bit of amateur theater experience, Jennie turned to the professional stage. For a mere twenty-five dollars a week, with the promise of a five-dollar raise later in the run, she took a small part in a light drama called *Checkers*, playing at the Academy of Music.[27]

But after about two months of appearing on stage every evening and at each matinée, Jennie became seriously ill and withdrew from the play. She had contracted ptomaine poisoning by eating tainted cheese from a chafing dish of Welsh rarebit served to fellow cast members during a dinner party at the Woodend home. By the time she recovered, Kirk LaShelle, the show's director, had died during a trip to Paris and the play had closed. Jennie Woodend's stage career was over.[28]

After a few more months, Jennie—still recovering from the poisoning and with her marriage strained—began to break under the pressure. Her appetite disappeared, she lost a great deal of weight, and her physician forecast a complete collapse unless stringent measures were taken immediately. He suggested a trip.[29]

The Woodends liquidated some personal holdings, including real estate in the Bronx, and a family offered to lease their fine residence for five thousand dollars a month. Jennie and her faithful maid, Ellen Donovan, prepared for an extended sea voyage. But before they could depart, Jennie met Tom Mix.[30]

Friends had encouraged Jennie to get fresh air and take in the fine array of polo ponies and horses at a Wild West show playing in nearby New Rochelle, New York. That was where she encountered the affable young cowboy. During their conversation, she asked Mix if he knew of any locations in the West that might be beneficial for someone trying to regain her health.[31]

"I know just the place," Mix reportedly replied. "The Miller brothers' ranch in Oklahoma." He went on to tell Jennie about the vast 101 Ranch. Mix spoke of the three Miller brothers and Riverside Camp and the cabins for easterners who wanted to rough it. Jennie apparently liked what she heard, especially the part about the opportunity to ride first-rate horses at the ranch.[32]

Jennie corresponded with the Millers, and the following summer, she departed for the 101 Ranch with her brother, Ellen Donovan, and a wagonload of trunks.[33] The journey was just what the doctor ordered. Jennie loved everything about the Hundred and One—the people, the home-cooked meals, the outdoor life, the bracing air, and especially the pure pleasure of unlimited riding over open prairies.

Every summer for years to come, Jennie, accompanied by her brother and maid and sometimes her husband, returned to the 101 Ranch. Eventually the Woodends regained a fraction of their former wealth and purchased one of the small cottages at Riverside Camp, and Jennie began to spend even more time at the ranch.[34]

When Woodend later turned to the promotion of various theatrical enterprises, his wife joined up as a performer with the Millers' Wild West show. Although the social elite of Manhattan knew nothing of her double life, Jennie was featured as a daring cowgirl with the Millers for several seasons. Traveling with her maid in a special railcar and billed only as Jane Howard, she frequently appeared as a trick rider in the opening and closing acts and even rode broncos in the quadrille.[35]

But on May 2, 1911, during a 101 Ranch Wild West show performance in a Brooklyn arena, Jane Howard's true identity became known to the world.[36] On that fateful evening, a tiny pebble lodged in the forefoot of Jane's mount—a coal-black Kentucky thoroughbred named Chester—and caused the big horse to slip to its knees. Caught off guard, Jane was thrown to the tanbark. With the crowd watching, she was carried away and attended to at her home in Manhattan by a doctor who declared that she had sustained a badly wrenched ankle.

Although Woodend, when pressed by reporters, vehemently denied that his wife had become a cowgirl rider, it was clear that Jane Howard's cover was blown. For days after the accident, New York newspapers sported such startling headlines as "Ranch Girl, Injured, Really Mrs. Woodend," "Equestrian's Fall Reveals Identity," and "Mrs. Woodend a Cowgirl, Accident Reveals Secret."[37]

Relieved that the truth about her life as a show rider was finally known, Jane ultimately curtailed her appearances with the Millers' shows but continued to spend as much time as possible at the 101 Ranch. In time, Jane's troubled marriage to Woodend disintegrated and the two grew farther apart.

In 1920, Jane Woodend, as she was then known, and her brother, an invalid in declining health, moved permanently to Oklahoma, hoping to exist on thirty dollars of weekly allowance from her estranged husband.[38] When Joe Miller learned of her plight, he offered advice. "Buy the little place you're living on near Bliss and you and Watson stay out west here with us."[39] When she did buy a small five-room frame house just outside Bliss and tried to make go of it, Woodend quickly cut off her meager allowance.

Jane turned to the Millers, but instead of asking for a loan, she applied for a job as a hired hand on the ranch she had come to love so much. "Let me ride fences and pay me the thirty dollars a month you pay fence riders," she told them. "I love to be on the back of a horse and you know I could do the work well."[40] Without one word of discussion, the Millers put her on the payroll.

Jane Woodend, former queen of high society who could turn every head in Madison Square Garden, became one of the best fence riders the 101 Ranch ever had. Every morning, she saddled Joe, her trusty spotted cow pony, and with pliers in hand, spent the entire day riding mile after mile along the Millers' fences.[41]

Sometimes she covered fifty miles in a day. When she discovered a break in a wire fence, she dismounted, fixed it, and rode on until she found another. When she came upon stock ponds frozen over in winter, she broke the ice with a pick so the cattle could drink. On the coldest winter days, Jane wore a leopard-skin coat, the only remnant of the fabulous wardrobe from her New York life. By 1922, she had sold her last diamond to buy groceries. Watson looked after a flock of three hundred leghorn chickens that helped supplement his sister's cowgirl wages.[42]

On the walls of their house, Jane hung pictures from ceiling to floor. Her favorites were the autographed photographs of William F. Cody, Tom Mix, Neal Hart, and other cowboy entertainers. There were framed portraits of herself from years before in Manhattan, and a picture of her husband, whom she said she never stopped loving. Jane also had kept a silver loving cup from a long-ago horse show and a cluster of fading blue ribbons.[43]

A reporter who visited her in 1922 noted that Jane was fit and trim, and did not look to be in her mid-forties. "Her face is sunburned from much riding in the wind, and wrinkles around the eyes betoken the fact that she knows how to smile, and does it often," the reporter wrote. "She has a firmer handshake than 50 percent of the men one meets, and her quick, lively movements show her to be a person who lives every minute of the day."[44]

She told all the reporters and anyone else who ever asked that the best decision she ever made was to move to the 101 Ranch. She told them she had no regrets. "I've got everything on earth I want but canned peaches, and Watson and I are going to splurge some day and buy all we want of them."[45]

Watson Howard, always sickly, just wore out. In 1934, some cowboys found his frozen body lying alongside the road. Alone except for her ranch pals, Jane hung on to her little home, filled with bittersweet memories. She remained a working cowgirl until the day she died in 1938. She was laid to rest next to her brother in the Miller family plot at Ponca City.

When he was almost ninety, Joe Miller Jr., just a boy when he first met Jane Woodend, was asked who he thought was the best of all the cowgirls who rode for the 101 Ranch. He did not hesitate. "Why, Jane Woodend," he said. "She was spectacular. She rode in the shows and she rode the fences. You should have seen her ride."[46]

Chapter 27

SPINNING WHEELS

The Miller Brothers' shows achieved realistic synthesis of western culture. Their 101 Ranch production was an impressive reminder of a past that would never live again. Billed a "Real Wild West," the show was just that in every particular. It was an authentic display of ranch and frontier life as it had existed for years on the prairies of the Southwest.[1]

—Barbara Roth
"The 101 Ranch Wild West Show"

FROM their entry into show business and indeed throughout most of the early 1900s, except for a few bumps and obstacles along the way, the Miller brothers proceeded like unchallenged lords of the prairie. Although they stayed content while on the flourishing show circuit with their company of performers, the Millers also learned that sometimes their relationships with loved ones could be as difficult as trying to put socks on a rooster.

To continue to expand and diversify their holdings, the Millers paid a steep price on the home front. Generally, the three brothers' families suffered most, all at the expense of the constantly evolving and always demanding 101 Ranch empire.

Joe Miller had been married for a decade and had three children before his younger brothers followed suit. Zack was the next to take the matrimonial step. In 1906, he married Mabel Pettijohn, a spunky local girl who could handle a cow pony and whose father ran a boardinghouse at Red Rock, a small railroad town not far from the ranch headquarters.[2]

In keeping with the wishes of his late father, Colonel G.W. Miller, Zack broke out the barrel of blackberry wine that had been put up when he was born in Newtonia, Missouri, in 1878. Just as G.W. had instructed, the barrel had been tapped in 1899 when Zack turned twenty-one, and on Zack's wedding day, it was time to partake of the wine again.[3]

Although his brothers accepted Zack's decision to wed Miss Pettijohn, it was apparent that the Miller women did not exactly welcome her with open arms. "She [Mabel] was a peroxide blonde at a time when such a practice was looked on with disfavor as a sign of being in the lower caste of society," wrote Joe's daughter, Alice Miller Harth, in her memoirs.[4]

George Miller, the youngest of the brothers, was content to stage periodic stag parties at the ranch for a bit longer. Busy with the ranch and expanding family enterprises, George would not tie the knot until 1908, when he wed May Porter in Ponca City and brought her to live at the ranch. They had one child, a daughter named Margaret, who was born in 1912.[5]

"The bride [May] was a local girl—rather striking in appearance with milk white skin, blue eyes, and black hair—an Irish beauty," observed Alice Miller Harth. "Her modest background probably fostered dreams whose fulfillment were doomed to failure."[6]

Alice's memory, as she wrote many years later about family events, was accurate. Not only would her own parents' marriage finally fail, but her uncles' marriages ultimately ended in divorce also.

Ironically, the institution of marriage and the value of strong family ties often figured more in the way the Millers approached their work force than it did in their private lives. In 1906, when they experienced a drastic labor shortage, the brothers seriously considered Joe's plan to hire only married men as farm workers and encourage them to live on the ranch with their wives and children.[7]

"It is my idea to build the houses for the families, mostly at the headquarters of the ranch, and there establish the married men with their families," Joe Miller explained. "Then we will pay the married men their wages and we will furnish them their provisions at a reasonable rate, thus giving them all their time to devote to the duties on the ranch. The women in some cases we expect also to give employment. I think that by doing this we shall get rid of all the trouble caused by single men dropping in for a few days, and then getting tired of the game, and leaving us, just when we need them most."[8]

It was fitting that Joe did not discuss the proposed hiring policy at the ranch. His statements were instead delivered at the Hotel Baltimore in Kansas City, during one of the frequent trips that kept him far from his family.[9]

George Miller, with the savviest business mind of the three, usually stayed at the ranch to oversee the complex farming and cattle operations while Joe and Zack were almost always off traveling with the Wild West show. Joe's long periods away from his home on the Salt Fork took a heavy toll on his family, especially on his wife, Lizzie.

Besides their daughter, Alice, and first son, George William, they had Joseph C. Miller Jr., born July 7, 1905, less than a month after the National Editorial Association roundup.[10] Because his father was an honorary chief of the tribe, the Poncas honored "Little Joe" at the time of his birth with a ceremonial powwow. The dancing and rituals lasted three days and nights and required the exchange of gifts—bolts of calico and many ponies—along with five choice beeves to feed the crowd. By the time it concluded and the Indians returned to their camp, they had given the baby boy the Ponca name *Wah-Kiyah-Tunga*, which meant "Morning Star."[11]

Joe Miller was pleased that the Poncas had honored his newest son with a special name. Joe adored all three of his children and showered them with attention whenever he was with them. They returned their father's love and only asked for more, but for him the lure of the tanbark arenas and roar of the crowds were more powerful. His daughter, Alice Miller Harth, summed it up the best with a simple statement—"Father had always wanted to be a showman."[12]

In her memoirs, Alice further acknowledged the enormous impact the fulfillment of Joe Miller's ambition had on the rest of the family. "Father and his brothers were so busy that they were very poor family men," Alice wrote. "Everyone knows what happens to particles that cling to a fast spinning wheel. The wives and children were finally thrown clear. We children were reared by our mothers, but our business affairs were channeled through the main office, an arrangement by which my brothers and I knew our Uncle George better than we did our own father and our uncle knew us better than he did his own child."[13]

Despite a valiant effort, Lizzie Trosper Miller never fully adjusted to the lifestyle of Oklahoma Territory. Always looking for diversions, she acquainted herself with some of the more interesting guests at Riverside Camp, tended her flower garden, and tried her best to keep a full-time cook in the kitchen. When the ranch became widely advertised, Lizzie found solace in the people who would drive out on Sundays to look around. There were also, of course, cowboys and cowgirls and Indians, and even a 101 Ranch baseball team that played out of Bliss and included Tom Mix and George Miller on its roster.[14]

Lizzie enjoyed visits with Bill and Viola Vanselous, whose Big V Ranch adjoined the Millers' land to the west.[15] Vanselous, a hardworking farmer and stockman, was said to be the best-known range-mule dealer in the country, and later his Big V and its immense corn harvests became a favorite subject for Bennie Kent, the Pathé News cameraman. Like the Millers, Viola Vanselous was a Kentucky native. She had left her family's prosperous farm when she was a small girl and grew up accustomed to the rugged life in cattle country.[16]

Lizzie found the most effective medicine for her blues in trips with her three children to the Trosper home in Bethany, Louisiana, to visit her parents and old friends. It was also a great comfort that Mother Miller never failed to lend Lizzie a helping hand or offer her a shoulder to cry on, especially during those long spells when Joe Miller was away with the show.[17]

Finally, Lizzie decided she had had all she could stand. In 1907, she packed up her children and their belongings, left the house on the Salt Fork River, and moved to town. Because her husband was gone at the time, Lizzie had to shoulder the entire burden of finding a suitable home.

"I did not have much social life until I moved to Ponca City to send the two oldest children, Alice and George, to school," Lizzie later wrote. "Joseph, the youngest child, was only two years old at the time we moved to Ponca City in 1907. It fell to my lot to find a house to rent in Ponca City which turned out to be a very trying ordeal. Several hot days I drove a slow horse hitched to a buggy to town in search of one."[18]

Although the move was difficult, it may have been for the best. Indeed, Alice Miller Harth recalled in her memoirs, "From that time on our contacts with Papa were infrequent. We took vacations in the summer with the show and during the winter we visited some weekends in Grandmother's home where Papa had taken up residence. For all intents and purposes he was an absent parent. That left Mama with the whole responsibility for molding our characters. Not counting the effect the move may have had on the marriage, it probably worked out to our advantage."[19]

During the summer and autumn of 1907, while Lizzie and her children settled into a rented house in Ponca City and Oklahomans adjusted to the approach of statehood, the Miller Brothers 101 Ranch Wild West Show electrified enormous crowds throughout the country.[20]

Earlier that year, during the Millers' successful run at Convention Hall in downtown Kansas City, favorable press notices caught the eye of several big-time show promoters and even gained the attention of President Theodore Roosevelt. Already acquainted with the exceptional reputation of the 101 Ranch and its owners from his previous trips to Oklahoma Territory,

Roosevelt summoned the Millers and their performers to Norfolk, Virginia, for the Jamestown Exposition, a celebration marking the three hundredth anniversary of the first permanent English settlement in the New World.[21]

Joe Miller quickly dispatched an affirmative reply to Roosevelt.[22] But before the show left for Virginia—for what turned out to be a staggering one-hundred-day run—C. W. Rex and O. J. Cathcart of the C. W. Rex Company, promoters of the show billing for the Jamestown Exhibition, convinced the Millers to appear first in Chicago en route to the East Coast.[23]

On May 2, 1907, the 101 Ranch show opened a two-week run at the Chicago Coliseum, one of the nation's favorite venues for major sporting events, political gatherings, and marathon social bashes.[24] Although they did not know it at the time, the Millers would soon become close friends with a young man who had played a critical role in the creation of the Coliseum.

The rambling Gothic building covered two acres on the site of the old Libby Prison building, an infamous Confederate prison in Richmond, Virginia, that had been dismantled brick by brick, shipped to Chicago, rebuilt, and opened in 1889 as a Civil War museum. By the end of the century, when people had lost interest in the war and museum attendance dropped, local businessmen looked for another way to keep the structure profitable. They formulated a plan in 1897, after fire destroyed the city's original Coliseum.[25]

A group of investors, including Iowa banker and mahogany importer John Gibson, formed the Chicago Coliseum Company to build a new coliseum that would incorporate some of the ornate walls of the old prison building. Gibson selected his new son-in-law, an enterprising barber from Creston, Iowa, named Frank Phillips, to scour the countryside in a buggy carrying a satchel crammed with prospectuses and a list of potential investors. Phillips returned triumphant, with a stack of promissory notes and signed investment contracts. On August 26, 1900, with bands blaring and cannons booming, President William McKinley dedicated the new Chicago Coliseum.[26]

By 1907, Frank Phillips was far removed from Chicago. He and his brothers L.E. and Waite were busy with their banking and oil interests in Indian Territory, where they would soon meet and form lasting friendships with the Millers. Based in the town of Bartlesville, Frank and L.E. were just a decade away from founding Phillips Petroleum Company, one of the world's largest independently owned oil companies.

Hobnobbing with the Phillips brothers and other members of the flamboyant fraternity of Oklahoma oil tycoons and wildcatters would come soon enough for the Millers. On that balmy May evening in 1907 at the Chicago Coliseum, when chief bugler A. M. Wasser brought audience members to their feet and the grand entry commenced, the Millers had only one desire—to leave the crowd begging for more.[27]

As usual, only Joe and Zack traveled with the show, although George's name also appeared at the top of the program. Despite exaggerated numbers of Miller personnel in many of the newspaper reviews, about seventy Indians and ninety cowboys and cowgirls, including the band, performed at the Chicago show.[28]

Many of the Indian performers were Poncas, but others were Sioux from the Rosebud agency, led by Chief Black Elk; some Cheyennes, accompanied by Chief Bull Bear; a party of Arapahos from near Kingfisher, Oklahoma Territory; and Hopi Indians from Arizona.[29] During the two-week stay in Chicago, all the Indians resided in a camp created in the Coliseum annex which all paying customers were encouraged to visit before and after the shows.

Each of the performances opened with the obligatory grand entry, followed by the standard show events—Indian war dances, stagecoach and wagon-train attacks, capture and punishment of a horse thief, and reenactments of Pony Express rides. The Millers also added two new specialty acts in Chicago. These were not necessarily linked to the Wild West, but nonetheless they went over quite well with audiences and reviewers.[30]

The first of these was fancy precision riding on a highly trained horse by talented equestrienne Amelia Sommerville.[31] All other performers and every person in attendance sat transfixed while Miss Amelia and her light-footed steed pranced around the broad arena floor, in a gentle diversion from bronc busting, bulldogging, and the buffalo chase.

The other new act was Professor Dan Boyington with his trained ponies and buffalo and twenty "educated" mules that could march as well as soldiers, count and spell, waltz and polka, teeter on a plank, sit up like dogs on their hindquarters, answer questions by shaking their heads, and chew gum. Boyington's mules also pretended to faint and would not "come to" until revived with tender caresses and lumps of sugar. Boyington, who used flattery and sweets but never a whip when working with his animals, contended that mules and women were very much alike—neither could be completely understood.[32]

During the 1907 season, Boyington was billed as "Professor," but for the 1908 touring show, he took the name of "Uncle Dan" Boyington. He used that name during the rest of the years he and his four-footed pupils regularly appeared as a featured act with the Miller brothers.[33]

Beyond the staged events involving large numbers of mounted entertainers and rolling stock and the smaller specialty performers, it became apparent in Chicago that the 101 Ranch show's true bread-and-butter acts were those delivered by the Millers' expert cowboys and cowgirls. For years to come, those unsurpassed ropers and riders of wild steers and outlaw horses dominated arenas around the nation and, eventually, the world.

Throughout the 1907 season, the Millers boasted not only a select line of prime stock but a galaxy of top cowboy and cowgirl stars as well. A few of the entertainers who rode for the Hundred and One that year sported questionable pedigrees. One of the shadier figures was outlaw Henry Starr, who reportedly put in a brief hitch as a Miller ranch hand and was with the show in Kansas City at the start of the season.[34]

Among the most convincing performers with the 1907 show who went from Kansas City to Chicago and then to Virginia for the Jamestown Exposition were Dan Dix, Lon Seeley, Buffalo Vernon, Vester Pegg, Howard Compton, and George Elser, masterful horse breaker and trick rider. Bertha Ross, a champion lady bronc buster, and Fred Burns, famed as a rope juggler, garnered their share of praise. So did Bill Pickett, "the Dusky Demon," who threw steer after steer with his teeth.[35]

After their last performance of the two-week run at the Chicago Coliseum, the Millers' show journeyed to Norfolk, Virginia, arriving in time for the May 20 opening of the Jamestown Exposition. For several months at Norfolk, the 101 Ranch Wild West Show was to be a featured attraction of the spectacular "War Path," the amusement section of the exposition.[36]

The "War Path" was essentially a series of major historical displays and reenactments, such as the spectacular 1862 Civil War nautical engagement between the ironclads *Monitor* and *Merrimac* at Hampton Roads, and the decisive battles waged at Gettysburg and Manassas. Also featured were "Old Jamestown," a production about the storied relationship between Captain John Smith and Pocahontas, and several other re-creations of historical and literary events, ranging from the burning of colonial Jamestown and Paul Revere's ride to Ben Hur's fictional chariot races and the San Francisco earthquake, which had occurred just the year before the exposition opened.[37]

Visitors less interested in history took in a Japanese tea garden staffed by eighty striking geishas and maidens, the simulated crowded streets of Cairo and Seville, a Swiss village, and colossal amusement rides. The pious crowded around the so-called miracle painting *In the Shadow of the Cross*, and those seeking adventure flocked to see "Captain Sorcho and his Deep Sea Divers," or Colonel Francis Ferrari's Trained Wild Animals.[38]

But almost everyone who came to see the exposition's "War Path"—literally tens of thousands of visitors—made it a point to attend at least one performance of the Miller Brothers' 101 Ranch Wild West Show. The program, featuring sixteen distinct western acts, lasted a full ninety minutes.[39] Many of the people came back to see the show several times before the long run ended, in mid-October.

Joe and Zack were so encouraged by the staggering response to their show in Virginia that they made a hurried trip back to the ranch, quickly assembled a second road show, and shipped it to Brighton Beach, New York, a heavily populated residential area named for the famous resort in England.[40] Located at the southern tip of Brooklyn just east of Coney Island, it was called the "world's largest playground." The 101 show at Brighton Beach once again shattered all attendance records during a six-week run by luring in huge crowds to cheer for authentic "cowboys, cowgirls, and Indians" and to see bulldoggers such as Lon Seeley and Frank Maish.[41]

That busy summer, with two Millers shows playing at the same time on the Atlantic coast, Mother Miller accompanied Lizzie and her three small children to visit both places. Lizzie later reported, "New York gave me the thrill of my life."[42] For most New Yorkers, the Miller performers were the ones producing all the thrills.

Meanwhile, back at the Jamestown Exposition, the Miller family found plenty of excitement. Zack had brought his wife, Mabel, to Norfolk, and although she was in the last stages of pregnancy, the capable horsewoman remained a trooper. She rode with the rest of the 101 Ranch entertainers right up to the time of delivery.[43]

"Zack and Mabel rode in the performance everyday except for the few Mabel missed giving birth to a premature baby girl," wrote Alice Miller Harth. "The baby was totally rejected by her mother. Baby incubators were a curiosity, having just been invented, and were being displayed in use in a booth on the midway. The baby was sent immediately to be put into one. When Mabel was asked to indicate what name should go on the birth certificate she said she didn't care what they put on it. Her nurse suggested that, since the baby had been born in Virginia, why not name her for the state. And so Virginia was named."[44]

Even though some exposition officials were somewhat disappointed in the overall attendance numbers, the 101 Ranch show continued to pull in the lion's share of visitors. When one of the public's favorites, Bill Pickett, injured himself badly while bulldogging and had to rest for a week, the show went on. While Pickett recuperated, Lon Seeley, who shuttled between Brighton Beach and Norfolk, filled in, even riding Pickett's horse, Spradley, much to the pleasure of the audience.[45]

Before the Jamestown Exhibition closed, on October 12, Pickett had returned to the saddle. He went on with the 101 show to Richmond, Virginia, for a two-day stand, followed by nine days at the Georgia State Fair in Atlanta and a weeklong engagement at Louisville, Kentucky, that closed the 1907 season. The entire troupe of performers and stock arrived back at Bliss the morning of November 7, in time to mark Oklahoma's statehood celebration nine days later.[46]

Many more personnel returned to Bliss and the 101 Ranch than had left. Adding to the crackerjack cast of men and women who rode with the Millers in Kansas City and Chicago, several recruits appeared at the Jamestown Exposition. The best known was Lillian Smith, an illustrious rifle-shot champion of the world who had exhibited her uncanny skills in sawdust rings for years and had gathered accolades while touring Europe with Buffalo Bill's show.[47] Often appearing as "The California Girl," the lady sharpshooter was using the name "Princess Wenona" when she joined the Millers at Jamestown. The Millers outfitted her in a buckskin costume with feathers and billed her as "The Champion Indian Girl Rifle Shot of 101 Ranch."[48]

Another fresh but lesser-known addition to the Millers' show was Edward J. Milhau, a courtly New Yorker who, after a spat with his wife, walked away from his family business and headed to Norfolk to become a cowboy with the 101 Ranch show.[49]

The wranglers provided Milhau with proper cowboy duds and allowed him to put a few rank bucking horses through their paces. Milhau rode so well that the Millers offered him a job on the spot.[50] During the twenty-six weeks Milhau rode with the show, his wife learned of his whereabouts and joined him. They ironed out their differences and, at the end of the season, they went to Oklahoma with the rest of the troupe.[51]

Both of them worked for the 101 Ranch for five years, until Milhau's wife was killed when she was thrown from a spirited pony while riding as an extra in one of the early motion pictures being filmed at the ranch.[52] Soon after her death, Milhau drew his last pay and left the ranch forever.

Milhau eventually died at age eighty-nine. He left little behind except for a few things he always said were his most prized possessions. In the old man's room were those treasures—a pistol and gun belt, cowboy hat, and boots. It was the outfit he had worn when he was young and rode like blazes for the Hundred and One on the prairie and in that crowded arena not far from the sea at the Jamestown Exposition.

THE BAND PLAYED ON

Music was a key element for success in all Wild West shows, and the Miller brothers saw to it that the Hundred and One had the best bands money could buy. Throughout the many years that the Millers put shows on the road and for all their annual roundups held at the ranch, they always had a band to provide stirring music.

Often, they even had two bands with each of the 101 Ranch shows. Besides the regular group of musicians—who led the parades, played in the grand entries into the arenas, and serenaded the crowds during performances—a sideshow band generally featured Dixieland music.[1]

Through the years, the Millers employed some of the most sought-after band directors in the nation, such as Park Prentiss, W. B. Fowler, and Jack Bell.[2] Among other noteworthy directors were William Sweeney, who also conducted Buffalo Bill's Cowboy Band for twenty-six years; William Atterberry, the Millers' bandleader at the Jamestown Exposition and at many of the early 101 Ranch shows; A. B. Eastman, appointed band director at the start of the 1909 season; and Merle Evans, who later became a fixture with the famed Ringling Brothers and Barnum & Bailey Circus band.[3]

Evans took over the bandmaster's duties for the 101 at the start of the 1916 season, just before the Millers suspended their shows for a ten-year hiatus.[4] He replaced a man whom the Miller brothers and most of the old-time cowboys and cowgirls believed was the best conductor ever to lift a baton—the legendary "Professor" Donato La Banca. A native of Sicily, he had joined the 101 Ranch band as a trumpeter after the Saint Louis world's fair.[5]

Bandsmen said it was not at all unusual for La Banca to tear his clothing or break into tears if he became displeased with the way they played a particular composition.[6] During concerts, with hundreds of people in the audience, he was even known to stop the band if he detected one sour note. He would then bend on one knee and implore the Almighty to give him the strength to continue.[7]

Famed around the show circuit for choosing a broad variety of music, La Banca liked stirring marches and standard waltzes, such as "The Blue Danube," as well as selections by Verdi, Wagner, and Paderewski, and even the whimsical "The Glow-worm." The professor also composed a great deal of music, including a march which he called the "101 Ranch," much to the delight of the three Miller brothers.[8]

In 1912, La Banca was named director of the Military Band in Saint Charles, Missouri, a historic town on the Missouri River, just northwest of Saint Louis. By the following year, he had found it difficult to serve the hometown crowd in Missouri and act as director of the Millers' lively band. In the spring of 1913, La Banca and two local musicians, Joseph Pomilio and William Brown, left for Hot Springs, Arkansas, where members of the 101 Ranch Wild West show were preparing for another season. The Saint Charles newspaper openly questioned whether their new municipal bandleader could evenly distribute his time and talent.[9]

Within a couple of years, La Banca decided to make his life less complicated. He handed over the baton of the cowboy band to a successor and concentrated on his civic duties with the Saint Charles band.[10]

La Banca served as band director in Saint Charles for thirty years, with his municipal band playing at hundreds of concerts. He continued to compose numerous marches, including "The Spirit of Saint Louis," in honor of aviator Charles Lindbergh's 1927 solo transatlantic flight.[11] The La Banca home became a haven for visiting musicians, grandchildren and their friends, and any youngster desiring free music lessons from the maestro.

On November 22, 1942, La Banca's heart gave out and he died at his home in the old river town of Saint Charles. Two enormous trunks he left behind were filled with his copyrighted and handwritten music, a diploma from the Academy of Music in Palermo, and bundles of photographs and yellowed newspaper clippings. To honor the professor's last wish, several of his compositions which he had previously selected were played at his funeral. So many musicians showed up that day that there were not enough copies of music to go around.[12] It was a fitting tribute to the dapper bandmaster who had helped the performers of the 101 Ranch keep in sync.

The final send-off for Professor La Banca was a far cry from the simple burial eighteen years later of Pete Hale, another musician who had played out his heart on a cornet for the Hundred and One. Yet in his own way, Hale was just as important to the 101 Ranch as Donato La Banca and all the other conductors who directed the Millers' bands. He represented the hundreds of forgotten youngsters who had left family farms or fled big-city tenements and showed up at the ranch to join the cowboy band.[13]

Hale got his start in Kansas cow country, born in the Cherokee Strip in 1886. Named Ralph Hale at birth, he preferred to go by Pete, and that was the name that stuck. His grandfather was Q.A. Hale, who had put up part of his own land to found the town of Hunnewell, Kansas, in the 1870s. Later, Q.A. managed the big hotel that the Santa Fe Railway built in 1880, and then he leased it from the railroad for a dollar a year. It came to be called Hale House, and it was a popular haunt for unbroken cowboys and trail riders, many of whom rode for George Washington Miller and his outfit.[14]

As Pete Hale grew up on Hunnewell's "Smoky Row," his family noticed that he could play just about any band instrument he got his hands on. But the cornet became Pete's favorite and, when he acquired one of his own, he was said to have coaxed melodies out of that horn sweeter than the sound of angels' trumpets.[15]

Pete Hale was still a kid when he headed south with his cornet and joined the 101 Ranch Cowboy Band. Walter Douglas, one of Pete's pals from Hunnewell, also joined the band on slide trombone.[16] Several of Hale's cousins and other kinfolk already worked on the 101 Ranch, and they made the Hunnewell boys feel welcome.

Pete never cowboyed for the Millers. He only wanted to play that cornet of his, and that was what he did, every chance he got. Pete Hale and Walt Douglas and the other musicians, dressed in boots and big hats and leather chaps, traveled all over the country with the Millers' Wild West show. They went to big cities they had only dreamed about. They slept beneath crisp hotel linen and ate rich meals off china plates, served by uniformed waiters in fancy dining rooms. They learned to drink whiskey, a habit that haunted Pete for the rest of his days.[17]

Years later, after he left the Millers and stopped playing his cornet for pay, Pete returned to Hunnewell to stay. He never married. Folks said that when he was young, he had a crush on a girl, but she jilted him and he never took up with another. Sometimes on summer nights when the windows were open, passersby could hear the sweet music of his cornet.[18] He worked as a hired hand on farms and ranches and kept mostly to himself. Even though he drank heavily, Pete never looked for fights or bothered anyone. Most people who knew him said Pete Hale was just about the kindest man they knew, even when he was drunk.

In the 1920s, a barber in Hunnewell who regarded himself as quite a pugilist picked a fight with Pete, thinking a drunk man would be easy pickings. The two pulled on boxing gloves at the carnival and squared off in the ring. The barber was a full head taller than Pete and had more reach. But even though Pete was small, he had muscles like an anvil. The fight lasted only a few minutes. Pete moved right in on the fellow, jabbed him, and knocked him out cold.[19]

During the dry years of Prohibition, Pete managed to quench his thirst thanks to bootleggers and jars of illicit moonshine. By then, most of his family members—the once prominent Hales of Hunnewell—were gone. In 1939, the old Hale Hotel, a survivor from the roaring cow-town years, was razed.[20]

Years later, Pete went to work as a hired hand for Fred Strickland, a farmer born just northeast of Hunnewell in 1924. Fred and his wife, Velma, were aware that Hale had a weakness for strong drink, but they liked him and knew he could work as hard as three men when he was sober. Pete worked the Stricklands' fields with a team of mules that loved him because he fed them chewing tobacco and treated them with kindness.[21]

"I asked Pete if he had fun when he was younger and played in the band for the 101 Ranch," recollected Strickland. "He looked at me and kind of smiled and said, 'Freddie, I had too much fun, way too much fun.' "[22]

Not all of Hale's memories of the Millers were pleasant. During work breaks, he sometimes told Strickland about the "bad old days" at the 101 Ranch. "Pete had plenty of stories, and one he told was about the practice of the Millers hiring drifters with no family ties," Strickland recalled. "He told me that after those drifters were hired, the Millers let their wages accumulate, and all of a sudden that drifter would be gone—nobody would ever see them again. Pete thought that some of those men got paid off with a bullet instead of cash. The word was that their payoff was having another hired man take them out, shoot them, and bury them somewhere in that backcountry."[23]

Strickland helped build a cabin for Pete near the railroad tracks, and he walked to their farm every morning. On Saturday nights, the Stricklands drove him to town to cash his paycheck. Pete Hale always found someone to sell him some liquor. The bigger the check, the longer he stayed drunk. Finally, he traded his cherished cornet for a half-gallon of whiskey.[24]

When he was seventy-seven years old, Pete Hale had a heart attack and died in his sleep. The Stricklands took his body to the Hale family plot at Rosehill Cemetery near South Haven. Strickland's parents were buried there, as was John Hiatt, the Miller cowboy who had built the first fire for the 101 brand. They laid Pete to rest with some money he had stashed away to pay for his burial.[25]

The stone that marked Pete's grave listed his name—Ralph "Pete" Hale—and his dates, June 4, 1886, and February 15, 1964. A larger stone at the plot bore just three words—"Until We Meet."

There were no funeral marches, no crowd of admirers, and no brass-band procession when they laid Pete Hale to rest—just a few folks who knew the old man and had listened to his stories of his years with the 101 Ranch band. The only sounds they heard were the mournful prairie wind and a meadowlark's song.

Chapter 28

HARD KNOCKS

I always have wanted to go on a ranch so I would be devilish glad if you could put me on. I heard you run a show also. My parents is dead and in heaven. I have only one sister and she is married and don't want the trouble of me. I am 21, five feet, four inches tall, can ride any horse you ever saw and can knock the bull's eye every time. I learned to ride and shoot, can also throw a knife, also a lasso. Am fair, blue-gray eyes, golden hair, very short and curly. I am reckless and wild but can give you references if necessary as to my character.[1]

—1912 letter, Queen Hovermale, Olympia, Kentucky

AFTER the triumphs of the 101 Ranch's tremendous public events at home and on the road, 1908 to 1916 were undoubtedly the most satisfying and lucrative years for the Millers and their assortment of colorful entertainers. Throughout that incredible time, it seemed that literally every red-blooded American boy and girl—not to mention legions of grown men and women—wanted to run away and join the 101. They pictured themselves as either Wild West performers or working ranch hands.

Sadly, most of those failed to achieve their dreams. But a surprisingly large number of applicants saw their ambitions realized. They not only became involved with the road shows but, in the off-season, they found gainful employment on the Millers' vast ranch. Some of those who sent inquiries sought only honest labor in the fields and ended up as corn-huskers working for twenty dollars a month in wages, plus room and board.[2] Others, particularly those who had witnessed a Miller road show in a hometown arena, were desperate to become the next Princess Wenona, Lucille Mulhall, Bill Pickett, or Zack Miller.

Every day, bundles of correspondence arrived at the ranch headquarters. Letters asking the Millers for jobs came from immigrant orphans, surgeons and teachers, old soldiers, deaf-mute youths and men missing limbs, young ladies from Indiana, New Jersey bookkeepers, wayward husbands and discontented wives, Missouri farm boys, and Indians hoping to escape dreary reservations. Some of the job seekers were seasoned cowboys and cowgirls. Even convicts—a few of them former employees of the ranch—wrote to the Millers, asking for another chance.[3]

Experienced Wild West performers, professional musicians, vaudevillians, and those with specialty acts also responded to advertisements the Millers placed in *Billboard* and other entertainment and amusement trade publications. In addition to their many circus and Wild West show credits, the "pros" often enclosed photographs of themselves in action. A few of them, apparently feeling the need to make a more urgent pitch for a job with the show, went so far as to cable a flurry of overnight telegrams.[4]

The great response from job applicants and growing numbers of the general public who clamored to see the Millers' show made quite a convincing impact on the three brothers. As 1907 ended and the new year began, their enormous popularity filled them with hope for the coming year.[5]

Indeed, by the end of the brand-new year, the Millers not only would have produced an even larger show, as their farm and ranch enterprise continued to grow and prosper, but their lives would be further enriched when oil—"black gold," as folks called it—was discovered on the ranch. It was probably just as well that the Millers could not see that far into the future. There was no spare time that winter and spring to think about wildcat oil wells sprouting in their pastures.

In February, they conducted marathon meetings with their foremen and show bosses and began to schedule engagements and secure new talent for the coming season's tour of the country. That month, excitement erupted at the ranch when John Cudahy Jr., son of a major Chicago meatpacker, took a cabin at Riverside Camp for some rest and relaxation.[6]

One bitterly cold morning when young Cudahy rode along the banks of the ice-covered Salt Folk, he happened upon the Ponca Indian named Horse Chief Eagle, one of Chief White Eagle's sons, struggling with his pony in the water after they had broken through the ice while attempting to cross the stream. Thankfully, the easterner had spent time as a yachtsman and crewing on iceboats and could keep his composure in such an emergency. Cudahy leaped from his mount, tore off his coat and hat and, with no thought of his own safety, plunged headlong into the icy river.[7]

With just a few strokes, he reached Horse Chief Eagle and found that he was tangled in the reins and stirrups of the frenzied pony. Cudahy quickly pulled a knife and cut through the leather restraints, which allowed the kicking and plunging pony to swim free. With blood streaming from a cut in his head, Cudahy took hold of the weary Ponca and swam with him to shore. The exhausted pony struggled to reach shallow water but finally sank and disappeared into the Salt Fork.[8]

When they got to the bank, Cudahy placed Horse Chief Eagle on the remaining horse and they dashed to the White House. The Millers immediately summoned a physician from the Ponca agency. After dressing Cudahy's lacerated scalp and face and taping his two broken ribs, the government doctor announced that Horse Chief Eagle would recover, with nourishment and bed rest. He prescribed the same remedy for Cudahy, who was put to bed in his Riverside Camp cottage.[9]

Several days later, Horse Chief Eagle, along with one hundred Poncas, appeared at the ranch. When it became clear that the Indian wished to present his own daughter to Cudahy in gratitude for having saved his life, the bedridden Cudahy politely but firmly declined. That evening, the large delegation of Indians staged a tribute dance for Cudahy at the ranch and sent their appeals for his recovery into the winter heavens. Within a few weeks, Cudahy's health was fully restored and he returned to Chicago with stories of his grand adventure on the Salt Fork.[10]

The saving of Horse Chief Eagle's life was important to the Ponca people, considering that he eventually would succeed his father as the last hereditary chief of the Ponca tribe.[11] Beyond its impact on the Poncas, the Miller brothers also regarded "the Jack Cudahy episode," as Tom Mix called it, as a good omen for the future of their ranch and their Wild West show.[12]

Another "good sign" that caused the Millers to mount a show in 1908 was the decision of Major Gordon W. "Pawnee Bill" Lillie to depart from the road and base his Wild West show for the entire season at Boston's Wonderland Park.[13] While his show played in Boston that summer, Pawnee Bill made an unexpected trip to New York and met with the administrator of the estate of James Bailey—of Barnum & Bailey fame—who had died in 1906.[14] Bailey's executors, anxious to sell the Bailey interest in the Buffalo Bill Wild West, offered the deal to Lillie. After an initial parley with Colonel Cody at Keene, New Hampshire, where his Wild West was playing, and several more negotiation conferences, Lillie purchased the Bailey interest. He and Cody finally agreed to call their combined shows Buffalo Bill's Wild West and Pawnee Bill's Great Far East, popularly known as the "Two Bills" show.[15]

Lillie's wife, May, vehemently opposed the merger. Keenly aware of Buffalo Bill's reputation as a womanizer, hard drinker, and poor business partner, May reminded her husband that they had finally made their own show profitable and had nothing to gain from combining with Cody. Calling the merger "the craziest idea you have ever had," May further vowed never to travel with the "Two Bills" show, but to retire instead to their ranch at Pawnee and oversee the building of their new home on Blue Hawk Peak. It was a promise that Miss May—"Champion Girl Shot of the West"—kept, to the lasting regret of her husband and her many fans.[16]

The combined show would not make its first major public appearance until the 1909 season opener at Madison Square Garden. With Pawnee Bill's show rooted in Boston for 1908, Buffalo Bill's would be the only other large Wild West outfit on the road that season. The Millers would face little competition in 1908. Another bonus for the 101 Ranch show came when Edward Arlington, an extremely talented circus executive, left Pawnee Bill's outfit and formed a partnership with the Miller brothers.[17]

Although several well-connected "show people" had approached them, the Millers had turned down all offers until Arlington, a Barnum & Bailey veteran, unveiled his ambitious plans. Skilled as a general manager and transportation agent, Arlington proposed that he and his advance crews take total responsibility for practically all business affairs of the Millers' Wild West show, thus freeing the brothers to take care of other details and stay involved with their flourishing ranch and farm concerns in Oklahoma.[18]

William H. England, the Millers' lawyer brother-in-law, reviewed Arlington's proposal and helped hammer out the paperwork. Arlington and the Millers deposited money into a joint banking account from which all expenses were paid related to the assembly and maintenance of a road show, but with a stipulation that neither party could make withdrawals until the profits exceeded ten thousand dollars.[19]

George Arlington, Edward's father, was appointed general manager, with Edward acting as general agent and railroad contractor. Joe Miller was named managing director of the show, with Zack and George as his assistants, and with the understanding that George Miller would remain in Oklahoma and manage the ranch. The original Arlington and Miller agreement of 1908 would be extended to the 1909–1910 season and, with some alterations, would remain in effect through 1916, when the Millers halted their show-business career for several years.[20]

Throughout the winter months, Arlington scrambled to acquire a proper show train and accumulate the massive tents for arena, kitchen, and dining, as well as seating, wagons, and other gear for a large touring company. He also purchased the Millers' first calliope, an old circus relic that some of the show mechanics overhauled. Twenty-two of the railcars had been rebuilt and overhauled by the Pennsylvania Railroad in its Jersey City shops. A half-mile rail spur was constructed at Bliss for holding train cars. At the ranch, more saddle horses and mules were acquired and additional show stock, including more longhorns and bison to replace the many animals that had been accidentally killed or crippled at the Jamestown Exposition and Brighton Beach shows.[21]

By March, the flatcars, sleepers, and Pullmans began to arrive, loaded with men and materials picked up along the way. Soon, all the boardinghouses and rented rooms in Ponca City and Bliss were filled with workers and show staff.[22] So were the bunkhouses and cottages at the ranch, where daily rehearsals for all performers were under way.

At last, everything appeared to be in order. With their new partner's name and photographic image added to programs and couriers next to their own, the Millers, as cocky as ever, unveiled their Wild West show—but under their name only. It would take another two years for the show to become known as the Miller Brothers' and Arlington's 101 Ranch Wild West Show.[23]

On April 14—the forty-third anniversary of the shooting of Abraham Lincoln by G. W. Miller's hero, John Wilkes Booth—the Millers opened the 1908 season just a few miles north of the 101 Ranch, at Ponca City.[24] The mayor declared a legal holiday so local folks could attend the street parade and then proceed to the inaugural matinée and evening performances at the showgrounds on Grand Avenue.[25]

From Ponca City, the show headed to Guthrie and Oklahoma City, and then to Winfield and Wichita, Kansas, before playing a matinée at Fort Madison, Iowa. On April 23, the show opened a two-week return engagement at the Chicago Coliseum, followed by a week of one-day stands in Illinois and a six-day engagement in Saint Louis.[26]

Many of the performers appearing in the 1908 show had been with the Millers the previous year at Jamestown, but some new feature acts were added to the mix. One of those, without even a vague connection to the American West, was a detachment of Russian Imperial Cossack troopers with handsome uniforms and drawn sabers, under the command of dashing Prince Lucca.[27] Instead of riding cow ponies, the cossacks brought their own graceful horses that had been raised on the steppes of the Siberian border. Billed as the "Only Equestrian Rivals Of The Cow-Boy," the prince and his lighthorse cavalrymen, who formerly had served the czar, joined the 101 Ranch show after having performed for a season with Pawnee Bill Lillie.[28] The exotic daredevils' acrobatic exploits on galloping steeds made them a favorite with the audiences.

Another added feature were the *Guardias Rurales*, a group of stalwart Mexican vaqueros clad in the traditional costume of tight-fitting suits trimmed with fancy gold braid, broad sombreros, and jingling, burnished silver spurs.[29] Known for their horsemanship, the Mexican cowboys outfitted their sleek black mounts with horsehair bridles and inlaid leather saddles gleaming with silver conchas and mountings. They twirled lariats made from the fiber of the maguey plant, a source for the potent beverage they imbibed after each performance.[30]

Influenced by the historic reenactments they had seen at the "War Path" during the Jamestown Exposition, the Millers added a dash of their own history to the 1908 show. Instead of continuing with the simulated Indian attack on an emigrant wagon, they presented a specific incident—the "absolutely accurate reproduction of the sacking and burning of Pat Hennessey's wagon train, on July 4, 1874, and the foul murder of its passengers by Cheyenne Indians."[31] In the show courier, the Millers claimed that their father, G. W. Miller, had reached the grisly scene of the Hennessey massacre just a few days after it happened, while driving a herd of two thousand longhorns from Texas to market in Kansas.

To give the spectacle even more authenticity, the Millers employed Bull Bear, the Cheyenne chieftain who supposedly perpetrated the Hennessey outrage. Every day during the summer of 1908, the old warrior led a band of "blood-thirsty redskins"—as the Millers bluntly put it—in a fabricated attack on actors portraying the Irish freighter and his companions during their ill-fated journey on the Chisholm Trail.[32]

And to add yet one more dash of reality to the reenactment, W. W. Malaley, a former United States marshal of Indian Territory and the most prominent figure to join in the pursuit of the culprits, was hired to chase after Chief Bull Bear in the arena.[33]

Besides new productions, some familiar cowboy and cowgirl performers renewed their contracts with Arlington and the Millers. Princess Wenona, the champion rifle shot, and Bertha Thompson, a daring bronc buster, were the headliners. Mabel Miller, Zack's cowgirl wife, also rode with the show. Miss Mabel, far better at entertaining than at parenting, had left her daughter, Virginia, in Oklahoma, where Mabel's mother at Red Rock primarily raised her, except for periodic visits with Mother Miller at the ranch.[34]

One of the newcomers was Guy "Cheyenne Bill" Weadick, an old pal of Bill Pickett. Weadick and his wife, Florence La Due, with their trained horse named Poncho, appeared as "Weadick & La Due Lariat Experts," and were known as "the fastest roping act in vaudeville." Weadick, who created the successful Calgary Stampede in 1912, left the Millers in July 1908, after they reached Canada, but he and his wife rejoined the show in September at West Baden Springs, Indiana.[35]

By early summer, it had become painfully apparent that the season was not turning out as expected. In fact, it was only a few weeks into the new season before the Miller brothers and Edward Arlington figured out that the 1908 show was going to be anything but a moneymaker.[36] The combination of too many rookie performers and inexperienced management could not produce a profitable show.

Other factors contributed; during the first fifty days of the tour, it rained incessantly. The rain not only kept audiences small but also caused dangerous conditions in the arena. Horses and stock slipped and fell, injuring themselves and their riders. Inclement weather and lack of publicity contributed to a loss of at least thirty-five thousand dollars in the first month of the tour.[37]

After the sun finally came out, costly delays resulted from high water, scheduling foul-ups, and a train wreck near Dickinson, North Dakota, that killed two Miller cowboys and left several badly injured.[38] Tom Mix, Vester Pegg, Oscar Rixson, Charles Tipton, Dan Dix, Julia Allen, George Hoker, and George Elser were some of the badly injured bronc busters and riders that season. Besides the usual injuries sustained in the arena—broken arms, dislocated shoulders and hips, concussions, fractures, sprains, and cracked ribs—typhoid fever also struck the show at Winnipeg, Manitoba.[39]

One of those stricken with typhoid was D. Vernon Tantlinger, a veteran performer and one of the Millers' all-time favorite cowboy bosses.[40] Vern and his wife, Edith Tantlinger, a former schoolteacher from Pipestone, Minnesota, had been on the show circuit since the late 1890s.[41]

Vern, who attended Iowa State University before becoming a trick bicyclist and professional baseball player, shot objects out of the air while riding or precariously standing on a bicycle. He was also an expert with the rope and one of the world's greatest boomerang throwers.[42] His wife, Edith, had attended Mankato State Normal School in Minnesota before she gained fame as a trapshooter and a crack rifle shot, right up there with May Lillie, Annie Oakley, and Lillian Smith, who performed with the Millers as Princess Wenona.[43]

Starting with the opening performance of the 1908 season and for nine consecutive seasons, the Millers' show featured the Tantlingers. Vern acted as arena director, the show's Indian agent, and eventually as "Chief of the Cowboys." He also performed his unusual bicycle shooting act, rope throwing, and boomerang act. A dexterous rider and roper, Edith splintered thousands of glass balls and clay pigeons with her repeater rifle and shotgun and eventually became the "Chief of the Cowgirls."[44]

Starting on April 6, 1908, when she and her husband arrived at the train station at Bliss and were greeted by Mabel Miller and a hailstorm with stones as large as hen eggs, Edith Tantlinger kept a daily record of the show season, offering insight into the men and women associated with the 101 and their litany of injuries and show difficulties.[45]

Problems continued to pester the show throughout the long season. The legal squabbles alone, such as lawsuits over the deaths of the two young men killed in the train accident in North Dakota, kept the Millers in court for several years.[46]

In October, as the show pushed through the Deep South and edged along the Gulf coast, Lon Seeley, one of the Millers' best bulldoggers, was shot and killed in Gulfport, Mississippi, by George Varando, a policeman who mistakenly took the cowboy for an outlaw. As the mortally wounded Seeley fell to the ground, he shot his revolver, killing Varando.[47] The ensuing bad publicity so angered the Miller brothers that they finally threatened to file a lawsuit against the *New York Sun* for publishing false and damaging stories.[48]

With its many obstacles and crises, the 1908 season turned out to be a learning experience for the Millers and their ranch personnel. After appearing in more than eighteen states and several Canadian cities, the Millers' company played out its two-and-a-half-month southern tour in Louisiana and crossed into the Lone Star State. The tour finally concluded on December 3 at Brownsville in the Río Grande valley, at the southern tip of Texas.[49]

The Miller brothers, their performers, work crews, and livestock were battered and bruised. Everyone was ready for a well-deserved break. But instead of going home for rest and recuperation, the Millers only paused to regroup quickly before heading off in search of more adventure. On December 5, two days after the regular season closed, the 101 Ranch Wild West show pulled out of Brownsville and slipped across the border into Mexico.[50] The Miller brothers had gained a second wind.

PRINCESS WENONA:
The California Girl

TO SAY THAT Princess Wenona—a star attraction with the 101 Ranch shows for many years—was simply a crack rifle shot would have been a gross understatement. It would have been about as foolish as describing Lucille Mulhall as a fair horseback rider or saying that Will Rogers was handy with a lariat or that Bill Pickett had a way with steers.

During the long and illustrious history of the 101 Ranch and its many Wild West shows and entertainment events, scores of first-rate male and female sharpshooters worked for the Millers. None could compare with Wenona. Beyond the Millers, she also rode with Buffalo Bill Cody, Pawnee Bill, and several other notable Wild West productions. Throughout the golden age of Wild West shows, when plenty of expert marksmen dazzled audiences, Princess Wenona, on a piebald horse named Rabbit—a gift from Pawnee Bill—was the reigning rifle-shot queen of the sawdust ring.[1]

May Lillie, Edith Tantlinger, and other renowned female crack shots were not in her league. Even the highly publicized Annie Oakley—"Little Miss Sure Shot"—might not have been quite as handy with a rifle as Wenona. Indeed, an open antagonism burned for many years between Miss Oakley and her younger and highly accomplished rival.[2]

Wenona's true name was Lillian Frances Smith. She was born on February 3, 1871, at Coleville, California, a farming and trading hamlet in Mono County, due east of Sacramento on the Nevada border.[3] Throughout her professional show career, which spanned more than forty years, Lillian was almost always billed as a Sioux Indian "princess." She might not have been a Sioux chieftain's daughter, but the questionable claim was hardly ever challenged. There is no doubt, however, that Lillian was in fact Indian; the 1880 California census records display an *I*, which stood for Indian, and not a *W* for white, in the personal-description column next to young Lillie Smith's name.[4]

As with Tom Mix and some of the other Hundred and One performers, Lillian's rather hazy pedigree, especially in the later years of her career, was clouded with biographical information that came straight from press agents instead of from family records.[5] One of the more questionable stories alleged that she was the daughter of a lighthouse keeper on the Delaware coast and that when he saw how proficient she had become with a rifle, he moved the family to California so she could get more exposure. That version of her life, of course, totally contradicted the later account that Lillian was the daughter of Crazy Snake, "a fighting chief of the Sioux."[6]

According to publicity accounts from the mid-1880s, Lillian was only seven years old when she told her parents she had grown "tired of playing with dolls" and wanted her own rifle.[7] Her father, Levi Smith, reportedly gave her a .22-caliber Ballard rifle. Soon the child was "shooting forty mallards and redheads a day on the wing and bobcats out of the towering redwoods" in nearby Yosemite.[8]

As a way to promote the talented girl, her father entered her in local turkey shoots, including one in San Benito County, California, during the holidays of 1883. There Lillian supposedly shot so many turkeys that the stunned event officials finally persuaded her to drop out to give some of the local boys a chance.[9] By the time she was ten, Lillian had appeared in San Francisco, where "her marvelous accuracy and extreme youth" drew a great deal of attention. People said that in her first try at shooting glass balls with her prized .22, she shattered 323 in succession without a single miss, and then went on to post an incredible score of 495 out of a possible 500.[10]

The stories vary about just when and where Lillian Smith signed on with Buffalo Bill Cody's Wild West. Some of Cody's biographers and other writers of history have claimed that the showman "discovered" Lillian in 1885 while he was visiting a shooting gallery in Los Angeles and was "amazed at this young girl of fifteen [sic], who made his own efforts seem like the attempts of a novice."[11] Other Cody devotees are convinced that the girl did not join up with Buffalo Bill until 1886, when his Wild West was booked for a six-month engagement at Erastina, a resort on Staten Island, New York.[12]

Thousands of people attended the two daily performances at Erastina, including such notables as Mark Twain, P. T. Barnum, Elizabeth Custer, William Tecumseh Sherman, and Thomas Edison. One report stated that during a week in July, nearly two hundred thousand cheering spectators were "brought screaming to their feet with her [Lillian's] amazing ability."[13]

Sometimes billed as "The California Huntress and Champion Girl Rifle Shot" but mostly featured as "The California Girl," Lillian proved to be sensational with a shotgun, revolver, or rifle. She was especially expert at picking off targets while on horseback.[14]

With her unerring eye and a pair of lever-action Winchester rifles, Lillian could hit a plate thirty times in fifteen seconds, break ten glass balls on strings swinging from a pole, and then shoot the strings from the pole without a miss. For a dramatic finale, she would fire three times and miss—intentionally—a glass ball thrown in the air, but always shatter it to smithereens on her fourth shot.[15]

Neither the favorable reviews for "The California Girl" nor Buffalo Bill's obvious fascination with Lillian sat very well with Annie Oakley. She already faced heated competition in the arena from Johnny Baker, a teenage marksman called the "Cowboy Kid" who used marbles for targets.[16] All the attention being paid to young Lillian made Annie even more anxious.

Annie Oakley was especially touchy about her new rival's age. Not everyone noticed, but right about the time fifteen-year-old Lillian Smith joined the Cody show, Annie began to misrepresent her own age. She suddenly "lost" six years by telling reporters and fans that she had been born in 1866 and not 1860.[17] Overnight, Annie became a girl of twenty once again.

Because Annie was petite and youthful, she succeeded at her deception. At the same time, she noticed Lillian's tendency to gain weight. Although Annie did a good job of hiding her growing resentment for her arch rival, on several occasions she was said to have ridiculed Lillian's "ample figure" and "poor grammar."[18]

The conflict between the highly competitive and equally proud female sharpshooters intensified in 1887, when Buffalo Bill's Wild West invaded England to perform for six months as part of Queen Victoria's Jubilee, celebrating the first fifty years of her reign.[19] Although both sharpshooters received their share of favorable notices, both also took a pounding from partisan critics who were openly loyal to either Miss Smith or Miss Oakley.

By then, young Lillie, still a teenager, had taken a husband—the first of several. He was a reckless cowboy and champion roper named Jim Kidd, whom she had met and married in New York.[20]

Oakley had her own champion—her husband, Frank Butler, a sharpshooter who had given up his career to act as her manager. Butler and Oakley suspected that it was Kidd who wrote a slanderous letter that found its way into print, assaulting Oakley's name and reputation. They became especially perturbed about Lillian Smith and her cowboy boosters after a select entourage of Cody's entertainers was presented to Queen Victoria at a command performance staged at the Earl's Court arena.[21]

The event was momentous, if for no other reason than that Queen Victoria rose from her seat and bowed toward the American flag when it was presented, the first time a British monarch had saluted the star-spangled banner.[22] In spite of the fact that both Annie Oakley and Lillian Smith—the "American girls," as Victoria called them—curtsied before the monarch and received her compliments, the London press gave the lion's share of coverage to "The California Girl." The *Illustrated London News* published a sketch of Smith being introduced to the queen, but completely ignored Oakley.[23]

Meanwhile, a rift had developed between Oakley and her boss, the flamboyant Cody. Oakley's supporters contended that Buffalo Bill had become somewhat jealous of his female star after some British reviewers suggested that she was outshooting Cody.[24] Those hard feelings no doubt grew when Cody became aware of the lucrative side deals—exhibitions and shooting lessons—which Oakley and Butler were putting together with several fancy English gun clubs.[25] By the closing of the London engagement, Oakley and Butler had left Cody's Wild West.[26] "The California Girl" became Buffalo Bill's newest star.

But by 1889, the quarrel had ended between Cody and Oakley, and she rejoined his company of performers.[27] By that time, however, "The California Girl" was gone. She had moved on, satisfied that, at least in her own mind, she had bested Oakley, the so-called "Peerless Lady Wing-Shot."[28] A whopping purse of ten thousand dollars, offered by Buffalo Bill in 1887 to anyone who could defeat Lillian Smith in public exhibition shooting, went unclaimed for many years. Not even Annie Oakley, Johnny Baker, or Doc Carver ever took up the challenge.[29]

Back in the United States, Lillian Smith thrilled audiences across the country with her sharpshooting throughout the 1890s and the early years of the new century. But even though her professional career blossomed, her private life was never anything to brag about. The fluctuating weight problem plagued Lillian all her life, and her penchant for strong drink took a heavy toll. So did the many men Lillian became involved with and, in several cases, married.

After divorcing Jim Kidd, she wed other colorful figures through the years, including Wayne Beasley, a 101 Ranch cowboy who assisted her in her shooting act; Eagle Shirt, a Sioux performer with the Millers' shows; and Frank C. Smith.[30]

One of Lillian's longest relationships was with Smith, an expert rifle and pistol shot as well as a former Buffalo Bill performer and veteran Wild

West showman known as C. F. "California Frank" Hafley. Frank and Lillian formed an act and toured the country together from coast to coast, passing out promotional cards that bore a black clover design with a bullet hole through it and a printed message which read:

Shot by
Lillian F. Smith
'The California Girl'
Champion Rifle Shot of the World,
While Held in the Hand of
Frank C. Smith[31]

Later, when Lillian started to use Wenona as her stage name, the couple changed the name of the act to "Wenona and Frank—The World's Champion Rifle Shots," and Lillian "made up her face so she looked like a most charming Indian woman."[32] Sometimes she used the line "The Protégé of Queen Victoria," and bragged in publicity and program notes of owning "the only rifle ever held in the hand of Queen Victoria." Enthusiastic crowds marveled at Lillian's ability to snuff out a candle flame with her rifle, shoot the ashes off the cigar in her partner's mouth, and break small balls suspended from the brim of Frank's hat. In some private exhibitions, she even shot a dime from Frank's fingers without leaving a scratch.[33] The couple played in New Orleans, Boston, Omaha, Denver, Los Angeles, Washington, D.C., Kansas City, Saint Louis, Philadelphia, Buffalo, New York, and scores of other cities.

The Frontier Guide of 1904 described her as "Winsome Wenona, The Wonder of the West," and told how the Smiths had come to the assistance of Czar Nicholas II and Empress Alexandra of Russia.[34] Bulletproof vests ordered for the czar and his family were shipped to Pittsburgh to be tested by Princess Wenona. In the presence of the chief of police and a committee of Russian delegates representing the czar, Frank Smith wore each of the vests while Wenona calmly fired pistol shots at him at point-blank range. "Smith had the fullest confidence in Wenona's shooting," reported *The Frontier Guide*, "and never moved an inch while the bullets were coming towards him."[35]

At the close of the 1905 season with the Pawnee Bill show, Wenona and Frank joined other performers to spend the winter in the small town of Malden, Missouri, not far from Newtonia, where the G. W. Millers had lived after their departure from Kentucky.[36] To pass the time and generate extra income, Wenona broke some green colts for area farmers, including a black three-year-old nicknamed Spider who gave her a wild ride through the streets before he was finally tamed.[37]

After 1907, Lillian Smith made Oklahoma her official residence. Although she continued to appear with other shows and occasionally went on the road with a show of her own, Lillian—as Princess Wenona—became a fixture with the Millers' 101 Ranch Wild West productions. Her work became the focus of her life, especially after she and Frank eventually divorced. By 1909, Frank had remarried. Lillian reportedly never got over her split-up with the dashing Frank Smith.[38]

"Princess Wenona, who this year is with the 101 Ranch Real Wild West show which is to be here September 23, can truthfully be said to be a woman with a history," reported the *Ponca City Democrat* in 1911.[39] The newspaper presented yet another version of Lillian's early life. "During the early struggles of the pioneers in their westward course Wenona's parents were members of an emigrant train which was attacked by the Sioux Indians and nearly all members of the train massacred. Wenona's mother was among the few who escaped alive but was later captured by the Indians who attacked the train and was made prisoner. The chief of the tribe took a fancy to her and she unwillingly was added to his list of squaws. Some years later a daughter was born and this was Wenona."

By the mid-1920s, Wenona finally retired from show life. Many of the 101 Ranch performers had gone on to become major motion-picture stars. Others, like Wenona, were left behind in the arena dust—forgotten by the adoring public and fans and with no place to go. Fortunately, the Millers took pity on many of their old hands and entertainers and provided them a modest haven. The Millers had maintained some of the cabins at Riverside Camp, the retreat for summer tourists and eastern dudes. The Millers moved the show's old-timers into the cabins in exchange for light work around the ranch. Among those who found refuge there was Princess Wenona.[40]

Poor and lonely but still fond of male companionship, she ultimately took up with German-born Emil William Lenders, a prominent artist best known as a painter of Indians and western animals, especially buffalo.[41] Lenders, a colorful character in his own right, proved to be one of the more interesting of Wenona's men friends. Encouraged and befriended by Buffalo Bill Cody and Pawnee Bill Lillie, Lenders also credited the Miller brothers—especially Joe Miller, whom he met in the early 1900s—with advancing his career.[42]

"I found sunlight in Oklahoma," Lenders was fond of saying.[43] He also found a home at the 101 Ranch. The Millers' prairie empire provided Lenders with everything he was looking for as an artist—cowboys and cowgirls, herds of bison, cattle, and horses, wild game, and several Indian tribes dwelling nearby.

Lenders, with his trademark long, flowing hair, put his heart and soul into his work. To know his subjects, he regularly worked cattle and busted broncs on the 101 Ranch, traveled around the nation with Wild West shows, and lived among various Indian tribes. Lenders learned some Indian dialects and was said to have been made an honorary member of at least five tribes. In his later years with the Hundred and One, he appeared in at least one of the feature films produced by the Millers.[44]

During the many years he was associated with the ranch, Lenders formed a friendship with Princess Wenona. They ultimately became romantically involved, even though Lenders remained married to Eva Day, whom he had wed in 1898 in Philadelphia. She and the couple's daughter refused to move to Oklahoma.[45]

In 1922, the 101 Ranch Trust granted a mortgage of twenty acres in Noble County, south of Bliss, to Emil Lenders and Lillian Smith. They called their unassuming spread the Thunderbird Ranch.[46] They kept an array of animals at the ranch, including as many as forty-eight mongrel dogs—almost all of them strays. They also raised chickens, planted an orchard of five hundred peach trees, and maintained five hundred blackberry plants. Their vineyard of five thousand grapevines provided plenty of homemade wine, mostly for quenching Lillian's thirst for alcohol.[47]

Gradually, the romance lost its luster, and in 1926, Lenders left Lillian Smith and moved his studio into Ponca City.[48] Lillian remained alone except for her ragtag gang of animals. She considered writing her memoirs, but nothing ever materialized. In 1928, her beloved pony, Rabbit, died at age twenty-five, and she moved into Bliss, by that time renamed Marland for prominent oil tycoon and politician E. W. Marland.[49]

In spite of her failing health and lack of money, Lillian continued to care for her dogs and chickens and became a familiar sight in Marland and Ponca City, shuffling along on foot or riding in an old buggy with some of her faithful hounds trailing behind. Lillian's circumstances forced her to live frugally. She had few friends except for Jane Woodend, the once great horsewoman who also lived out her last days remembering past glories. Sometimes Zack Miller stopped by to pass a bit of time with Lillian, and

Bill Pickett, always a gentleman, never failed to treat the lady sharpshooter with the respect she deserved.[50]

Lillian did not survive the bitter winter of 1930, one of the coldest in Oklahoma history. Worn out in body and spirit, she died in the hospital at Ponca City on February 3—her fifty-ninth birthday.[51] Just two days before her death, "Happy Days Are Here Again," destined to become a song of inspiration during the bittersweet years of the Great Depression, broke into the charts.[52]

Lillian had designated Arthur Rynearson, a druggist in Marland, as the administrator of her last will and testament. It was a simple document. Lillian left most of her personal effects to the Oklahoma Historical Society, including a life-size portrait of herself, a beaded surcingle, a beaded blanket, a pair of silver-plated spurs, an ermine-trimmed buckskin squaw dress, four Winchester rifles, two gold-plated Smith and Wesson pistols, and a bulletproof vest from the batch she and Frank Smith had tested for the czar of Russia and his family in 1904. Lillian's personal papers and photographs went to Rynearson, and she bequeathed a picture of Joe Miller on horseback to Jane Woodend.[53]

"Would you kindly notify the persons named below when Our Father calls me home," Lillian had asked Rynearson in a letter of instruction written several months before her death. Among the ten names of old friends was "California Frank" Hafley—Frank C. Smith—Lillian's favorite former husband. She also requested that she be buried under her maiden name, Lillian F. Smith.

Zack Miller was away from the ranch, so his cousin W. A. Brooks helped with Lillian's funeral arrangements. Brooks, four cowboys, and a local newspaper reporter acted as pallbearers. It was the worst possible time for a burial. After days of snow, sleet, and freezing rain, the ground was frozen as hard as stone and the gravediggers cussed and moaned. Few people showed up at the windswept cemetery, but just before the coffin was lowered into an unmarked grave in the brittle earth, the clouds parted and the sun broke into view like a big glass ball. It was the best tribute of all to Princess Wenona—"The California Girl."[54]

Chapter 29

SOUTH OF THE BORDER

Reared in the open and living in the saddle, the cowboy of the 101 Ranch possesses a stature equalled only by the Vikings of the sea. The avarice of modern times is unknown to him. Covetousness is foreign to his nature. His simplicity is innate, his instinct primal, and unconsciously he is living history, never dreaming that his occupation is out of the ordinary or of interest to others. He comes to the full flower of manhood untainted by modern environment. Strong in his strength and weak in his weakness, the 101 cowboy stands as the ideal American. And, while he is no stranger to that cup that cheers, the smile of beauty or the turn of a card, these are mere pastimes to which he rises superior.[1]

—Joseph C. Miller, 1908

ALL three of the Miller brothers—even levelheaded George—possessed the nerves of cat burglars, the hearts of wildcatters, and the stamina that pulled skilled poker players through a three-night game. Even the highest risk did not put a damper on the brothers' spirits or curb their enormous appetite for life. Just like their lusty father, the brothers never flinched, never turned away from a fight, and never gave an inch.

Throughout the first three decades of the twentieth century—during times of both misfortune and prosperity—the Millers rolled up their sleeves, spit in their hands, and tossed the dice. Whether the venture involved investing in the speculative oil industry, forging headlong into the emerging motion-picture business, or trading with Mexican revolutionaries, the Millers remained high-stakes gamblers. They were not heedless, however, and in all of their diversified enterprises they obtained the most expert advice available.

Yet in the long run, they often operated well outside the boundaries of standard ethical business procedures and the legal process. And although it was never decisively proved in a court of law—as in the case of the George Montgomery slaying—it was generally believed that the Millers were capable of committing murder to settle a dispute or to gain financially.

Many times, their bullying techniques and risk-taking style worked in their favor, but not infrequently, the Miller brothers pushed too far and became their own worst enemies.

This tendency got the Millers into serious trouble at the close of 1908 when, instead of going home to the ranch to regroup at the end of a grueling and disastrous season on the road, the Millers took their 101 Ranch Wild West show deep into Mexico. It proved to be not only a memorable but an ill-fated journey that was doomed from the start. On the other hand, as they would later rationalize back at their ranch, the Mexican escapade gave the Millers and their performers, especially illustrious cowboy Bill Pickett, enough fodder for a lifetime of campfire tales.

The adventure started after a brief rest at Brownsville, Texas, while the Millers opted to take their show northwest along the Río Grande to the old border city of Laredo. On December 5, they crossed the river and entered Nuevo Laredo, the lively Mexican port of entry.[2] As soon as they left the United States, Joe and Zack Miller realized they had entered a hornet's nest. Although they felt far from welcome, they did not consider turning around.

The extraordinary Revolution of 1910, led by Francisco Madero against the dictatorship of President Porfirio Díaz—the aging Don Porfirio—was still two years in the future, but already the entire Republic of Mexico buzzed with talk of political agitation and insurrection and calls for reform.[3] Overly suspicious Mexican custom officials, supported by armed government troops, swarmed over the Millers' train. They spent an entire day and night searching through the railcars and personal belongings of the gringo entertainers.[4] "They [customs officials and soldiers] prized up the floor boards of the show wagons and looked under them," wrote Fred Gipson. "They opened the ten-gallon lard cans on the cook's wagon and stabbed bayonets into the lard, just to make sure. They all but stripped the eight blonde-haired hootchy-kootchy dancers in their search for implements of war. It was a shakedown that didn't leave a tent fold unexplored."[5]

At last, the Mexican officials permitted the show to travel. The Miller troupe rolled into the industrial city of Monterrey, on the east side of the Sierra Madre range, for a one-night stand and then proceeded southward to San Luis Potosí for performances on December 9–10.[6] By late on the afternoon of December 11, the 101 Ranch show had arrived in Mexico City—the oldest capital city in North America and the nation's most heavily populated marketplace and manufacturing center.[7]

It was the night before Guadalupe Day, and the city was especially crowded. Streets and markets teemed with curiosity seekers and pilgrims, some of whom had trudged hundreds of miles on foot. Most of them were making their way to the plaza surrounding the famous Basílica de la Virgen de Guadalupe, the brick church completed in 1709 to house a remarkable portrait and relics honoring the Virgin of Guadalupe, Mexico's revered patron saint.[8]

That evening, the Millers and their large cast of cowboys, cowgirls, Indians, musicians, and other entertainers rode through the busy streets and boulevards and then staged a magnificent illuminated parade down Paseo de la Reforma, the most handsome avenue in the capital city.[9] All along the wide, tree-lined boulevard, the riders attracted throngs of curious Mexicans. Aromas from food stalls and clouds of smoke from small wood fires to ward off the chilly night scented the air. Following a path that had once been used by Aztec kings, the parade continued through several wide *glorietas*, or traffic circles, adorned with monuments and flowers. They went on toward Chapultepec Park, the largest in the city, with its tiled fountains, lagoons, and bridle paths, rows of giant trees planted by the Aztecs before the Spanish conquest, and the president's summer residence.[10]

The following afternoon, at the circus arena on the Paseo in Porfirio Díaz Park, the 101 Ranch show opened a two-week engagement of matinées and evening performances that lasted until the day after Christmas.[11] From the first performance, Joe Miller quickly saw that the Mexican citizens were more concerned with the struggle of their daily lives and the general unrest in the country than they were with paying hard-earned pesos to be entertained by strange foreigners. The show's losses came to more than a thousand dollars a day. In addition, Mexican authorities gouged the Millers by slapping them with excessive daily fines if each performance did not begin precisely on time, or if they used a performer who had not been billed to appear.[12]

One of the main problems resulted from the Millers' featuring Bill Pickett—"the Dusky Demon"—in all the show advertisements and publicity although he was no longer appearing with the show. He was back in Oklahoma, helping with chores on one of the Miller cousin's farms.[13] In Pickett's place, seasoned cowboy Vester Pegg handled most of the bulldogging for the Millers in Mexico. To put a stop to the costly daily fines, Joe Miller wired his brother George, back at the ranch, to send Pickett immediately to join the other performers in Mexico City.[14]

Years later, Pickett recalled that the night before the telegram arrived at Bliss, he dreamed that he would receive a wire asking him to come to Mexico City to perform. In the dream, Pickett said, he also saw a large black bull chasing him. When he told his wife, Maggie, about the strange dream and said he was afraid to take the trip, she told him she believed the bull represented Satan, but if Joe Miller needed him in Mexico, he had better go. Pickett finally agreed. He asked George Miller for a train ticket and some whiskey to help get him through the long trip.[15]

Pickett boarded a train at Bliss but got only as far as Guthrie before he ran out of his supply of liquid courage. He got off the train to buy more liquor and got so drunk he awoke the next morning to find all his trip money gone. He wired back to the ranch, and George quickly dispatched another one hundred dollars. George also wired Joe and asked him to send a cowboy—preferably a teetotaler—to meet Pickett at Laredo and escort him the rest of the way.[16]

A sober Pickett and his vigilant attendant arrived in Mexico City on December 16, and the bulldogger went straight to work.[17] With Pickett finally performing, the Millers eliminated one of the daily fines.

The only difficulty Pickett encountered occurred one evening when he and Floyd Randolph and some other Miller show cowboys moseyed into a cantina not far from the railroad station and siding where the 101 Ranch sleeping cars were staged. Mugs of beer, shots of tequila, and powerful whiskey drinks cost less than a couple of cents in gringo currency at the watering hole. That meant the 101 Ranch hands—usually as dry as the dust in a mummy's pocket and suffering from bottle fever—could get good and soused for about a half-dollar.[18]

In addition to the Miller outfit, two Texas cowboys—one of them white and the other black—were at the long wooden bar, lapping up cheap drinks like fired cowhands. When the black cowboy started to mouth off about what a sorry place Texas was, Pickett—a loyal native of the Lone Star State—became riled, and a fistfight quickly erupted. In no time, Pickett had laid the other fellow out cold on the floor. Aware that the outburst would attract the law, Pickett and the other 101 Ranch cowboys took off like turpentined cats. They scrambled over a tall steel picket fence, raced down the railroad tracks, and were safe in their sleeping-car bunks before police arrived.[19]

The incident was nothing compared with the impending problems for Pickett and the 101 crew. This time, the trouble started at Café Colón—a more genteel establishment than the lowly cabaret where Pickett had knocked out his fellow Texan.[20] A preferred haunt for newspaper reporters, Café Colón also served as a popular rendezvous for matadors. Plenty of both were present the evening Joe Miller and his press agent, W. C. Thompson, went there to eat a late supper and, they hoped, to generate publicity for their Wild West show.[21]

Once seated, Miller and Thompson heard the chortles and muffled snickers of some bullfighters sitting nearby. When Joe turned and asked about their guffaws, the bullfighters replied that they had attended a matinée of the Miller show that afternoon. They said they had been especially interested in seeing Pickett, the daredevil bulldogger who, some reporters in Mexico City were suggesting, had created a sport that came the closest of any to bullfighting. One newspaper had even gone so far as to claim that Pickett's bulldogging act was a more spectacular show than any Mexican bullfight. After watching Pickett in action, the insulted bullfighters said, they were not impressed. They laughed contemptuously and said even a novice bullfighter could accomplish Pickett's act, and in less time.[22]

Bristling with anger and humiliation, Joe immediately challenged the matadors to try their hand at bulldogging if they thought it was so easy. Bienvenida, celebrated as the leading matador in Spain and Mexico at the time, accepted the dare on behalf of his fellow bullfighters. The confident matador agreed to appear at the showgrounds at ten o'clock the next morning to bulldog a steer and "teach the boasting Americans a lesson in courage and grace," as one of the newspapers reported.[23]

To make sure his Wild West show received even more publicity from the battle with bullfighters, Joe Miller purchased advertising space in a newspaper, and challenged any pair of bullfighters to bulldog a single steer in the same time it would take Pickett to throw two steers.[24]

Not one bullfighter responded to Joe Miller's advertisement. Even the illustrious Bienvenida failed to appear in the showring at the appointed time. When he was finally tracked down at his hotel, he said the bull-ring authorities who held his contract had prohibited him from risking life and limb in any activity except fighting bulls in the national arena.[25]

Although he had plainly gained at least a moral triumph, Joe Miller was not satisfied. Back at the Café Colón before a large gathering of reporters and dumbfounded matadors, he announced that he would wager five thousand pesos that Pickett, barehanded and alone, could best the most bloodhungry, man-hating fighting bull in Mexico. This new challenge, along with a few pointed insults that questioned the bravery of matadors in general, appeared in all the local newspapers on December 20.[26] Joe's contemptuous statements created such an uproar that the public demanded that he and his "Dusky Demon" make good on the challenge. The bull was back in Joe's court.

Realizing that they could sell thousands of tickets for such a spectacle, the managers of El Toreo, one of the city's foremost bullrings, guaranteed to cover the impulsive wager and arranged for Pickett to appear in their arena. They also drafted ground rules for the contest pitting Pickett against a Mexican bull, including stipulations that he appear on horseback and wear his customary red shirt. They insisted that he stay in the ring for at least fifteen minutes and spend five of those minutes on the bull's head after he had thrown the animal to the ground.[27]

The unusual encounter at the Plaza El Toreo was set for December 23, at four o'clock in the afternoon. All the newspapers carried major stories with such bold headlines as "PICKETT WILL FACE SPANISH BULL ALONE" and "GREATEST SENSATION IN THE HISTORY OF THE NATIONAL SPORT OF MEXICO. NEVER BEFORE A MAN SO BRAVE." Handbills and posters were plastered on walls and trees throughout the Federal District, advertising the "Grand Human Taurine Struggle," which would feature "Pickett, The Fierce Phenomenal Black from Oklahoma."[28]

According to bullfight enthusiasts, the cowboy who was used to dogging steers did not stand a chance against a fierce half-ton toro bred with other fighting bulls on a ranch where they were isolated from human contact and constantly culled to eliminate weakness and keep the bloodline pure. Fans wagered that as soon as Pickett rode into the arena, his death was inevitable. Bookmakers gave Pickett only four minutes to live after he entered the ring.[29]

If Pickett could pull off his daring stunt, not only would the Millers win the five-thousand-peso bet, but they also would receive the daily gate receipts for the twenty-five thousand bullring seats which, that afternoon, turned out to be a cool forty-eight thousand pesos.[30]

But Pickett was not worried. He told Joe and Zack that there was not a bull on earth he feared. He asked his bosses only to promise him that if things went wrong and he ended up dead, they would carry his body back home to the 101. He told them to be sure to bury him deep in the earth so the prairie wolves could not scratch out his bones. Zack and Joe gave him their word, but despite the odds, they were confident that he would win.[31]

By early afternoon on December 23, every seat was sold. The elderly

President Díaz and several government officials sat among the spectators. The entire company of the 101 Ranch cowboys and cowgirls turned out to cheer on Pickett. High in the seats, a Pathé motion-picture cameraman set up his tripod to record the spectacle on film. Just before Pickett's appearance, a group of costumed matadors strutted into the ring bearing an elaborate black coffin on which was inscribed *El Pincharino*, "one who has been gored."[32] Pickett immediately flashed back to his dream about a big black bull chasing him. Recalling that Maggie had believed the bull symbolized the devil, he shuddered with dread.

Zack Miller thrust a bottle of rye whiskey toward Pickett, who drained about a half-pint before he handed it back. Then, with his good Stetson hat in place and resplendent in a red shirt, ducking overalls, and knee-length boots, the bulldogger swung into the saddle and rode his faithful bay horse, Spradley, into the ring. Pickett was ready to face the fighting bull named Frijoles Chiquitos, or "little beans," a ferocious animal with thick neck, sharp horns, and a speckled hide that gave him his name.[33]

Pickett's entrance received mingled hisses and cheers and loud booing as the Mexican bullfighters, in their fancy garb, led the catcalls. Then, just as a trumpet sounded, a battered wooden gate was thrown open wide and the snorting and fuming Frijoles Chiquitos dashed into the ring. The crowd roared with approval.[34]

Surprisingly, Picket felt relieved when he saw Frijoles Chiquitos, with purple flecks across his broad back and shoulders. He figured that because the bull in the dream had been solid black, perhaps this brute was not the devil but just another flesh-and-bone-creature, albeit an immense and nasty one.[35]

Once Frijoles Chiquitos noticed Pickett, mounted on Spradley, the bull made a charge like a runaway locomotive across the arena floor. Pickett was in for the fight of his life. So, too, was the raging bull.

Pickett immediately realized that the riders serving as his hazers—Zack and Joe Miller and Vester Pegg—could not get in position to drive the bull toward him so he could leap on its back. In the mêlée, the bull's horn hooked Pegg's horse, Silver, in its flank.[36] As the other hazers tried to keep from harm's way and fired blank pistol cartridges in the bull's face, Pickett maneuvered for the best bulldogging approach but failed at several attempts. The bloodthirsty crowd jeered and howled at Pickett as the bull kept up its relentless attack.

Suddenly the bull whirled and charged Pickett and Spradley from the rear. Spradley was unable to avoid the rush, and one of the bull's horns plunged into his rump, ripping it open. The tough cow pony screamed horribly and went down on his rear quarters. Pickett leaped from his wounded horse, dove between Frijoles Chiquitos's bloody horns and fastened his arms around his thick neck. Every man, woman, and child in the arena stood as one.[37]

Surprised by the man clinging tightly to his back, the bull tried everything possible to dislodge the human cargo. Pickett hung on for dear life while the bull bucked and tossed and battered him against the arena walls. Even when the bull stood still and violently whipped his massive head and shoulders from side to side to shake Pickett off, the tenacious cowboy stuck like a sandbur.

The crowd, sensing that the bull was weakening and that the gringo was on the verge of humiliating their beloved national sport and disgracing the haughty matadors in attendance, began to hurl a shower of missiles—seat cushions, bottles, stones, oranges, bricks, canes, even open knives—into the ring. A cushion struck Pickett full in the face, and a chorus of approval followed. The cheers grew louder when a stone hit Pickett on the cheek and drew a steady stream of blood. Next, a facial wound Pickett had received while bulldogging a few nights earlier reopened and began to bleed profusely. Pickett only tightened his grip.[38]

Finally, a beer bottle flung from the stands struck Pickett hard in his side, breaking several ribs. Blood gushed from the wound and flowed into his boots. A reporter for the *New York Herald* watched Pickett tumble to the ground and described the scene: "He groaned in sudden pain, gasped for breath, cast a last, imploring, agonized look at us, his long time friends, and loosed the iron clasp which had defied the fury of as fierce and strong a bull as ever pawed the earth of El Toreo."[39]

Pickett lay limp and writhing in excruciating pain just a few feet from the bull. Snorting and partially revived after at last getting the bothersome cowboy off his back, the bull lowered his head and horns. But before the bull could charge and finish off Pickett, a solitary figure—naked from the waist up—hurdled over the barricade.[40]

It was Vester Pegg, acting on specific orders from clear-thinking Joe Miller. Pegg had stripped off his red shirt, and he waved it frantically as he ran toward Pickett and the bull. The ploy worked. With the bull's attention temporarily diverted, Pickett struggled to his feet and staggered to the barricade where outstretched arms pulled him to safety. Meanwhile, Pegg beat his own hasty retreat and escaped the confused bull's wrath.[41]

By this time, the spectators had become a seething mob that howled with outrage. Furious because the bull had failed to kill the gringo bulldogger, they also realized that Pickett had stayed on the back of Frijoles Chiquitos much longer than necessary for the Millers to win their sizable wager. In an astonishing feat which would define his entire life, Bill Pickett had remained on the bull's head and horns for seven-and-a-half minutes and had spent thirty-eight-and-a-half minutes in the ring.[42]

The mob rained spittle and debris into the ring and on the cowboys scrambling to find cover. Joe and Zack ran a herd of steers into the ring to clear out the frightened horses and induce the bull to exit the arena floor. President Díaz and other government officials tried to restore order by dispatching two hundred mounted soldiers to the scene. It took nearly two hours before the 101 Ranch performers could safely leave the sanctuary they had found behind a large iron gate in a corner of El Toreo.[43]

Meanwhile, the gravely wounded Pickett was concerned only about his horse. When he managed to stagger out of the arena, Pickett went directly to Spradley, draped his arms around the quivering animal's neck, and bawled like a baby. He insisted that Spradley, in obvious agony and weak after losing a great deal of blood, be looked after before anyone treated Pickett's own injuries.[44]

An old Mexican man who witnessed the scene assured Pickett and the others that he knew a sure-fire remedy, and he sent a boy to fetch two red bananas from a street vendor. When the youngster returned, the old man thrust the ripe fruit deep into Spradley's wounds. Miraculously, the horse stopped quivering within minutes, regained its feet, and was led away. Within a short time, the swelling had subsided and Spradley was declared fully recovered, without even a slight limp and with only a scar to remind folks of the ugly encounter in the bullring.[45]

Despite protests from some bullring officials, upset because other horsemen had been in the ring while Pickett fought the bull, Pickett had more than fulfilled the requirements of the wager. Joe Miller collected his bet and all of the gate receipts. Pickett received his standard road wages of eight dollars a week plus room and board.[46]

The 101 Ranch Wild West Show concluded its Mexico City engagement on December 26. As soon as the last performance ended, the show headed north. The long show train paused at San Antonio. It encountered some excitement before the next stop, at Fort Worth, when two workers blew open the safe in the ticket wagon and attempted to abscond with the profits. Both culprits were captured and the loot was recovered.[47]

The weather soon turned bitterly cold, and although the show was billed to appear at Gainesville, Texas, Joe and Zack canceled the stop and gave the order to continue to Oklahoma.[48] All the hands breathed a sigh of relief. A new year was dawning. When Bliss came into view, the performers of the Hundred and One clapped and cheered and told one another that the little town had never looked so good. Although the Miller brothers were also glad to be home, the financial success of their Mexican escapade had taken some of the sting out of the grueling 1908 season. The future looked bright.

WILLIE-CRIES-FOR-WAR

AFTER THE 1908 show season, it took George L. Miller's keen mind to come up with yet another source of income so the 101 Ranch empire could expand beyond ranching, farming, and entertainment. George saw to it that fountains of "black gold" spouted and gushed on the 101 Ranch. The groundwork for that auspicious development—the Millers' entry into the lucrative oil business—came to pass in the waning days of 1908.[1]

It had been a tumultuous year. The Miller family's Wild West show had taken its share of hard lumps during the long and grueling road trip through the United States, Canada, and Mexico, which culminated with the near catastrophe involving Bill Pickett in the bullring at Mexico City. Through it all, George had kept the home fires burning and maintained a positive attitude.

Even in November, when beefy Republican presidential candidate William Howard Taft crushed William Jennings Bryan at the polls, George Miller kept his spirits high, figuring that politicians would come and go and there would be more chances down the road for the Democrats.[2] He soon had abundant reason to be so optimistic.

Thanks to Ernest Whitworth Marland, an ambitious wildcatter who had found his way to Oklahoma, George soon would learn that reservoirs of natural gas and crude oil percolated beneath the prairie sod. George quietly hosted Marland that December while Joe and Zack and their Wild West performers made headlines in Mexico City. George's ranch visitor would forever alter the Millers' lives and fortunes.[3]

Neither Miller nor Marland had any way of knowing it at the time, but the partnership they were on the verge of forming would eventually produce enormous sums of income for all parties. Their alliance would also enable Marland to become a major industrial force and a political leader of national consequence.

After Marland had become a big-time oil baron and politician in Oklahoma in the turbulent 1930s, he enjoyed recalling family history for friends and associates. He talked of his father, Alfred, an English gunner in the Crimean War who had been wounded at age fifteen at Balakavia, on the coast of the Black Sea.[4] Marland noted with pride that the famous English nurse Florence Nightingale had tended to his father while he recuperated.[5] In 1934, when Marland took the oath of office as governor of Oklahoma, he placed his right hand on the worn leather-bound Bible which Nightingale had given to his father in 1854.[6]

In 1860, Alfred Marland sailed to America to make his fortune. After brief service as a Confederate soldier, he soon became a wealthy mill owner in Pittsburgh and married Sara McLeod, an attractive widow with five children.[7] He and Sara had two daughters and a son, Ernest Whitworth Marland, born in 1874.[8]

E. W. Marland graduated from the University of Michigan law school in 1893 and returned to Pittsburgh. His father had gone broke in the crippling money panic and resulting depression which gripped the nation—the same economic downturn which had caused the Miller family to turn to diversified farming as a way to boost their cattle empire.[9] Marland wasted no time in finding gainful employment. He clerked in a law office for ten dollars a week, passed the bar exams, and was sent to the Pennsylvania oil fields to examine titles, prepare contracts, and acquire land for future development. He purchased real estate for himself. He also took night classes in civil engineering, which led to his lifelong interest in geology and his ability to locate oil-bearing formations beneath the earth's surface.[10]

In 1903, Marland wed the bright and witty Mary Virginia Collins at her family's home in Philadelphia. It was said that Virginia was attracted to Marland because of his gambler's instinct.[11] By the time he reached his thirty-third birthday, Marland's gambler's instinct had made him a millionaire.[12] He barely had time to adjust to his lofty status before the panic of 1907 struck the nation, causing an industry collapse as banks suspended cash payments. Within a year, E. W. Marland was flat broke but far from defeated.[13]

In December 1908, Marland's luck turned. During a visit to the new state of Oklahoma, he met George Miller, and together they stalked the broad dimensions of the 101 Ranch.

Marland became acquainted with the Miller family through the son of one of his half sisters, Colonel Franklin R. Kenney, a friend of George L. Miller.[14] When Marland suffered economic losses and expressed a desire to escape his home in smoke-clogged Pittsburgh, Kenney arranged for Marland to visit the 101 Ranch.[15]

"Not only was the time propitious for E.W.'s arrival at Ponca City, but the spirit of the people was in harmony with his own," Marland's biographer, John Joseph Mathews, would later write of Marland's first trip to Oklahoma. "... The people of the plains took pride in their generosity and were more interested in working out a rhythm for chance than in basing their hopes on the constancy of agriculture. One gambled on wheat and cattle in the early days of the Outlet. One soon learned to laugh at his own pitiful activities on the great red, wind-swept land."[16]

Arriving at the White House clad in stylish knickerbockers, Norfolk jacket, and spats, Marland wasted no time in persuading George Miller to give him a grand tour of the ranch properties. As they made their rounds, Marland kept his eagle eyes peeled for rock outcroppings and other telltale signs of natural gas and oil beneath the rolling prairie.[17]

Thoroughly convinced of the presence of rich deposits in the area, Marland asked George Miller to give him a lease on the Miller ranchlands and to help negotiate additional leases from the Ponca tribe. George agreed to help, and the 101 Ranch Oil Company was formed.[18] Others who joined the venture included W. H. McFadden, a retired steel executive from Pittsburgh; James J. McGraw, a Ponca City banker; and John J. McCaskey, a Pittsburgh produce broker.[19]

In February 1909, as his proud mother and wife watched alongside an anxious Marland, George Miller staked the first well near the ranch headquarters.[20]

The conditions soon proved to be horrible. Instead of using big draft horses, drillers had to rely on cow ponies and cumbersome oxen teams to haul rig timbers, tools, and casings from the depot at Bliss. Gas pipelines snaked through the Millers' alfalfa and wheat fields. The Poncas watched in amazement and with growing concern for their land.[21]

Ellsworth Collings, in his history of the 101 Ranch, quoted Running-After-Arrow, an elderly Ponca Indian who watched as the first gas well was brought in on the ranch. He indicated that the gas roaring from the earth was an evil omen. "Uh-h, no good, no good," Running-After-Arrow supposedly said. "Beautiful country all die now. Cattle die. Ponies die. No good, no good. Beautiful country soon all gone."[22]

The inaugural well, drilled with Manila cable and old-fashioned tools, proved to be a dry hole. The Marland interests abandoned it at a depth of twenty-seven hundred feet. They pushed forward. The next seven wells hit gas, providing just enough income to continue the search for oil.[23]

Financing became more difficult with a subsequent series of failures, yet Marland refused to give up his dream. He worked as hard as his roustabouts. Sometimes he even cooked for the drilling crews, or he drove teams of oxen through the mud to deliver pipe and supplies. When time allowed, Marland continued to ride around the ranch in search of more drilling sites. Now and then, George Miller rode with him.[24]

"George L. Miller was showing me around the Ranch one day and we rode up a hill to see the cemetery of the Ponca Indians," Marland recollected in a 1934 newspaper interview. "The Indians placed their dead on wicker platforms above the ground. I noticed by the outcropping of the rock on the hill that the hill was not only a topographical high but also a geological high. A little further investigation showed it to be a perfect geological dome."[25]

Marland itched to start drilling. Unfortunately, the site—"high on a swell of the plains" near Bois d'Arc Creek, a tributary of the Salt Fork—was where the Poncas buried their warriors. It was on the allotment of a Ponca tribesman named Willie-Cries-for-War. It was the Poncas' hallowed ground, forbidden to whites.[26]

Marland faced a delicate problem. He found a solution when George Miller intervened. Because the Millers remained close friends of the Poncas, George arranged for conferences with the Ponca chief, White Eagle. After much coaxing and compromise, Miller and Marland finally swayed White Eagle to their way of thinking. The old chief gave them permission to drill at the burial grounds, provided that they located the well on the slope rather than the crest of the hill.[27]

Completed in June 1911, the Willie-Cries-for-War No. 1 flowed at a rate of 120 barrels a day. Located right in the midst of the 101 Ranch, the well marked a major oil field and the first oil production west of the Osage lands. It also brought a flood of wildcatters to the state.[28]

When the well came in that June day, Marland was working on the Salt Fork, busily laying a gasoline pipeline. Some of the crew members heard the roar coming from the Willie-Cries site and summoned Marland, who arrived in time to see the gusher. Later, Marland remarked, "I am sorry for the man who has missed the big thrill that comes to the wildcatter when his well, on which he has worked night after night and day after day, comes in a gusher."[29]

As George Miller and Marland watched the Willie-Cries roar to life, Chief White Eagle remained guarded. He feared he had made a mistake by allowing the whites to drill for oil on sacred land. "It will mean great trouble for me, for my people, and for you," White Eagle told Marland.[30]

Despite White Eagle's dark prophecy—many folks called it a curse—Marland stepped up drilling operations. The profits grew to be substantial.

In a short time, he built a tremendous income as the 101 Ranch property continued to yield oil. Marland and his chief allies, the Millers, were on their way to new fortunes.

Nevertheless, legends die hard. Many years later—long after Marland had lost his money and the Miller family's kingdom had collapsed and blown away—some Poncas still told the story of White Eagle's fateful prediction. They said the old chief had spoken only the truth. They said his curse would haunt forever what had once been the Millers' land. Not a living soul could argue otherwise.

PART FIVE

Galloping Ghosts

The Old Wild West is gone. The sands of time drift thicker and thicker over the days of the open range, of great cattle herds, of reckless, free-riding men on horseback. The physical existence of the Old West is recalled only by a deserted trail town, a crumbling adobe wall, a stretch of trampled ground that was once a boulevard of cattle traffic. Only a scant few of the old cowboy breed remain, gnarled old-timers whose memories are filled with the lore of the past. To those remnants of the cowboy legion, the ghosts of yesterday beckon as they gallop with the sweeping prairie winds.[1]

—Stan Hoig
The Humor of the American Cowboy

OVERLEAF: Roger Glen Taylor *(left)*, sign painter for the Miller brothers' movie trucks, and Oscar Wallcott, champion rodeo rider, pose with the *Passing of the West* production truck, circa 1924. *(Jerry and Ruth Murphey Collection)*

One of a series of souvenir postcards made from individual frames of a movie filmed on the 101 Ranch in 1915. *(Michael Wallis Collection)*

Leather band from one of the glass walking canes distributed by Joe Miller at the Saint Louis World's Fair in 1904 to entice visitors to the ranch in 1905 for what became known as Oklahoma's Gala Day. *(Jerry and Ruth Murphey Collection, courtesy John Dunning)*

A 1906 postcard printed in Germany showing Zack Miller and his first wife, Mabel Pettijohn Miller. *(Jerry and Ruth Murphey Collection)*

Hundred and One Ranch cowboys and cowgirls cross the Salt Fork River south of the summer camp, 1908. *(Michael Wallis Collection)*

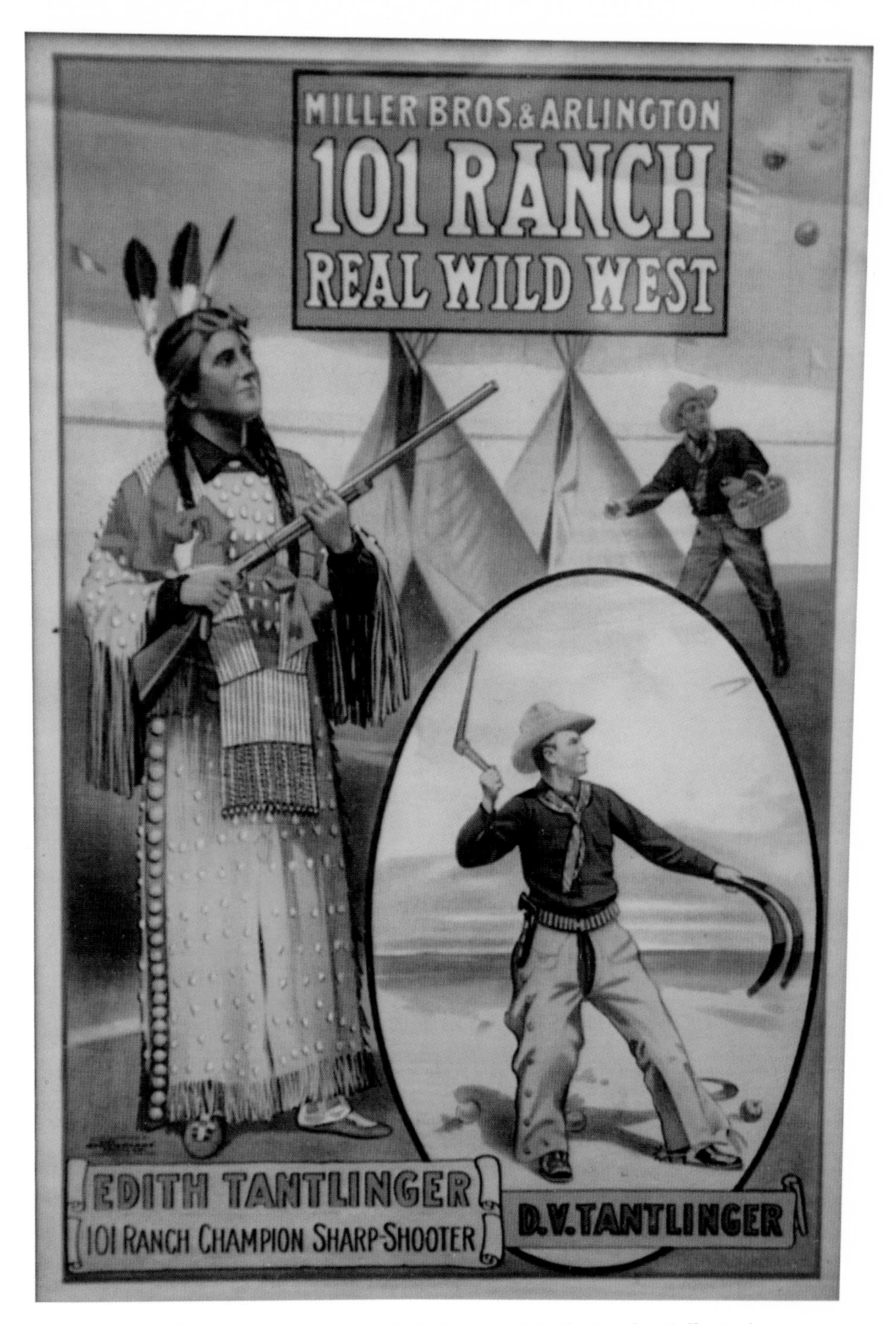

A 101 Ranch show poster, 1912. *(Jerry and Ruth Murphey Collection)*

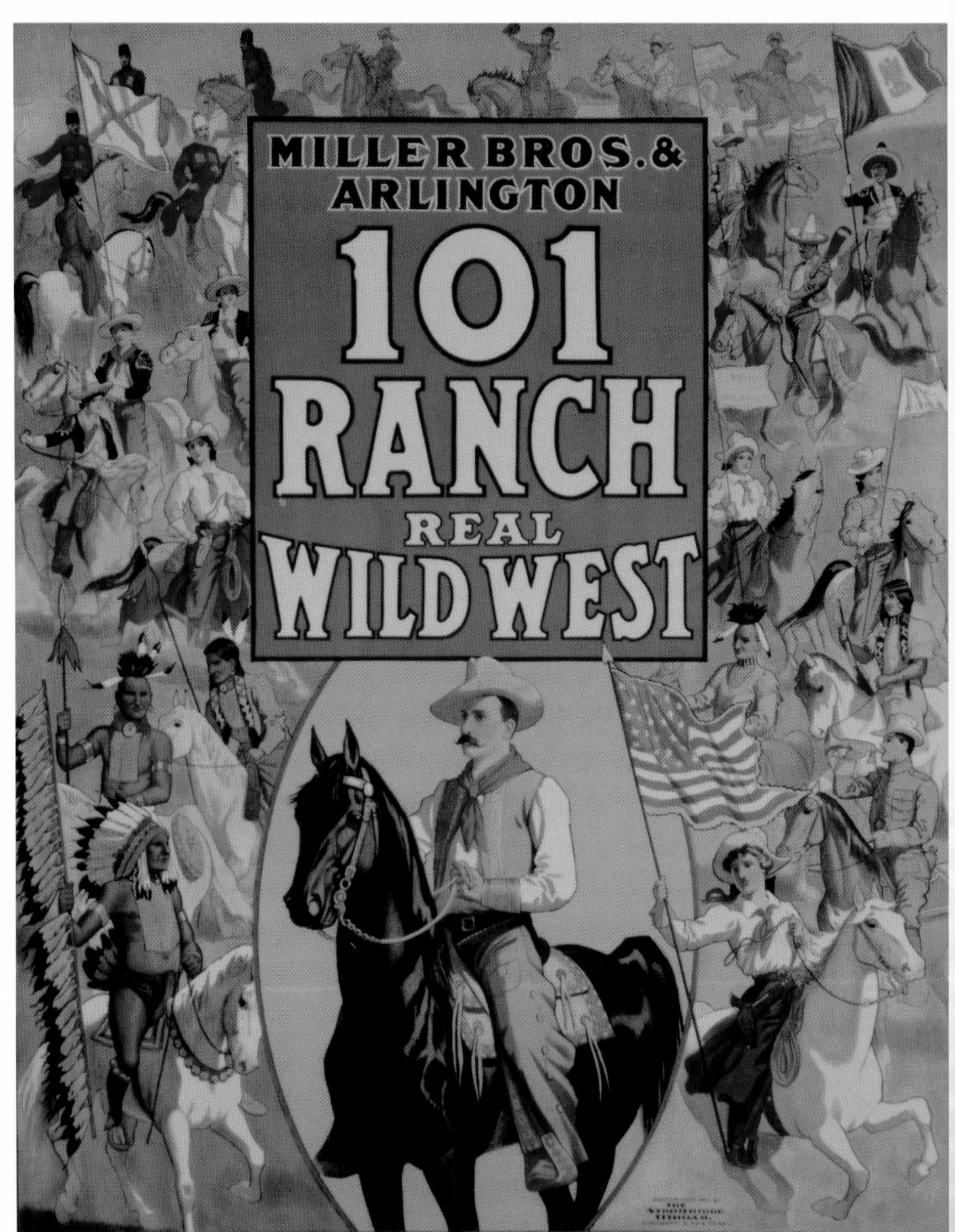

A 101 Ranch show poster, 1911. *(John Larbus Collection)*

Portrait of Joe C. Miller in his best cowboy duds, circa 1915. *(Frank Phillips Foundation, Inc.)*

Image of Bessie Herberg on one of the poster stamps distributed to show patrons. *(Jerry and Ruth Murphey Collection)*

The Miller family's first White House, just north of the Salt Fork River, was destroyed by fire in 1909. Note the mounted longhorn and buffalo heads above the porch. *(J. D. and Maxine Welch Collection)*

The Miller family's second White House, an imposing structure erected in 1909, became the nerve center for the Hundred and One empire. *(Michael Wallis Collection)*

Chief Good Boy was one of the Poncas who took part in the traditional Indian wedding ceremony of Joe Miller and Mary Verlin Miller in 1927. *(Michael Wallis Collection)*

ELECTRIC POWER HOUSE AND SEED CORN BINS ON MILLER BROS. 101 RANCH.

The 101 Ranch became a self-sufficient kingdom with its own electric plant, waterworks, and general power plant. Note the ranch cafe in the foreground. The small silo at far left served as the ranch jailhouse. *(Michael Wallis Collection)*

A LITTLE FUN FOR THE BOYS. MILLER BROS. 101 RANCH.

The Millers' cowboys and cowgirls never lost their passion for taming broncos. *(Michael Wallis Collection)*

THE NORMAN FILM MFG. CO.
PRESENTS
BILL PICKETT
WORLD'S COLORED CHAMPION....
"THE BULL-DOGGER"
Featuring The Colored Hero of the Mexican Bull Ring
in Death Defying Feats of Courage and Skill.
THRILLS! LAUGHS TOO!
Produced by NORMAN FILM MFG. CO.
JACKSONVILLE, FLA.

Opposite: One-sheet poster for *The Bull-dogger*, a film starring Bill Pickett, by Norman Film Manufacturing Company, 1923. *(Jerry and Ruth Murphey Collection)*

A "50 Bucks" bill used as currency by ranch hands and workers on the 101 Ranch. It has been said that the slang terminology *bucks* originated with the use of the word on 101 Ranch currency. *(Michael Wallis Collection)*

K. LEE WILLIAMS
PRESENTS
MILLER BROS. 101 RANCH
WESTERN FEATURE
"DAYS OF THE BUFFALO"

Opposite: Hundred and One Ranch movie poster depicting a bronc tamer reputed to be Yakima Canutt, circa 1921. *(Jerry and Ruth Murphey Collection, courtesy Charles Wade III)*

A 1925 show pass signed by George L. Miller and issued to Oklahoma oil baron Waite Phillips. *(Michael Wallis Collection)*

OFFICIAL REVIEW
AND HISTORY OF THE
GREAT WILD WEST

MILLER BROS.

101 RANCH

ZACK T. MILLER

JOSEPH C. MILLER

WILD WEST

GEORGE L. MILLER

I. M. SOUTHERN & CO., PUBLISHERS, N. Y. & CIN

Opposite: A 1910 show poster. *(Jerry and Ruth Murphey Collection)*

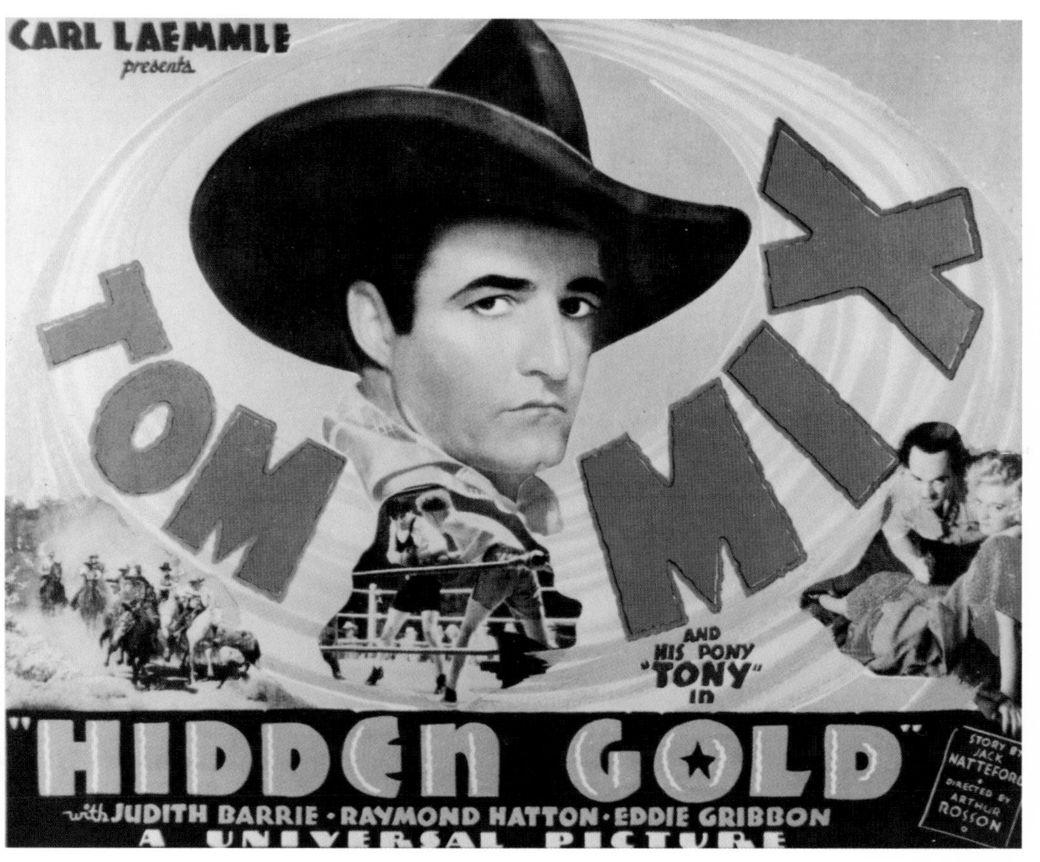

In 1932, Tom Mix made several sound westerns at Universal, including *Hidden Gold*. *(Michael Wallis Collection)*

Located south of the 101 Ranch headquarters, just across the Salt Fork River, Cowboy Hill is the final resting place of Zack T. Miller; Jack Webb, a trick roper and trick shot artist; and Sam Stigall, 101 Ranch foreman for thirty-five years. *(Suzanne Fitzgerald Wallis)*

Chapter 30

CREATING THE WEST

The Old West might pass from sight elsewhere in the land, but the Miller brothers ensured it would linger forever at the 101.[1]

—Kevin Brownlow
The War, the West, and the Wilderness

THE lucrative oil and gas business enabled the Millers to set their sights on new targets, including the fledgling motion-picture industry. From the first time the Miller brothers caught a glimpse of a moving picture—more than likely *The Great Train Robbery* at some vaudeville house or storefront nickelodeon during one of their Wild West show tours back east—they were hopelessly and forever hooked. Undoubtedly, the dancing images of Edwin S. Porter's ten-minute western milestone, filmed in the wilds of New Jersey, thoroughly entranced the Millers.[2]

Although many folks clucked their tongues and judged the nascent film business to be nothing but pure folly—even more risky than the oil game—the Millers were willing to take a chance. As early as 1908, they began a close relationship with the motion-picture business—a union that would last for years.[3]

Such an association, the Millers firmly contended, served as an important communication device and offered the 101 Ranch a means to participate actively in the social and cultural changes occurring across the nation. Filming western dramas also allowed the tenacious Miller family to maintain their abiding loyalty to the past and leave what they believed would be a fitting tribute to their rich heritage.

While they were at it, the three brothers hoped, they might even make some money. They figured that perhaps the movie business could be turned into yet another source of profit for them. But even as they started to work with some of the brightest of the early filmmakers, the Millers found that turning a profit was easier said than done.

The new year had only started when a succession of trials and tribulations arose in the Millers' daily operations. The show train packed with bone-weary cowboys and cowgirls had barely returned to the railroad town of Bliss when the first calamity struck. At about two o'clock in the morning of January 12, 1909, a fire erupted in the Millers' White House. Within an hour, the imposing ranch headquarters had burned to the frozen ground.[4]

The blaze, which originated in the heating system in the basement, was a veritable inferno by the time it was finally detected by Little Sol, George Miller's favorite pet dog, who smelled the rising clouds of smoke and awoke his sleeping master. Sadly, the faithful dog perished in the flames.[5]

Although none of the occupants was seriously injured, rumors flew about for many years afterward that not just the dog but also a human being had died in the fire. Some folks firmly believed that George Washington Miller, who had succumbed to pneumonia in 1903, had survived the illness and had secretly lived for six more years in the White House cellar.[6]

One popular story suggested that the old man had only feigned death as part of an elaborate ploy to evade the murder charge against him stemming from the 1901 shotgun slaying of railroad agent George Montgomery at Winfield, Kansas. Some people even claimed to have seen Miller on the porch of the White House years after his supposed death. They, of course, offered no explanation for the funeral service conducted for Miller in Kentucky in April 1903, where a crowd gathered at the Crab Orchard Springs Hotel and many people paraded past his open coffin.[7]

The Miller family scoffed at rumors that Colonel Miller had been hiding as a fugitive in the cellar, but they could not avoid the terrible truth of the fire.[8] They were especially shocked at how quickly the house had filled with thick smoke and how the flames had consumed the substantial frame structure as if it were only a child's paper dollhouse.

Mother Miller—snug in a feather bed with her young granddaughter, Alice, beside her—first caught a whiff of the fumes only fifteen minutes before the walls of the big house crashed to the ground.[9] The family and their eastern guests—thoroughly exhausted after spending the previous day sleighing across the prairie—fled the inferno in their bedclothes. They raced into the bitterly cold darkness and huddled, some of them barefoot, in the freshly fallen snow.[10]

"In spite of protests from the women folk," as the Bliss newspaper put it, "George L. Miller went into the house after all had deserted it" in a futile attempt to rescue his dog and salvage a few belongings. When he emerged, George lugged out some clothing and a trunk containing his mother's diamonds and other expensive jewelry.[11]

Nothing else was saved. The three-story White House, along with the Millers' heirloom furniture, personal possessions, and ranch documents, was completely destroyed. The loss was estimated at more than twenty-five thousand dollars, but the residence and contents were insured for only about one-fourth the actual cash value.[12]

The Millers were already exhausted by their Wild West road trip, which had concluded with the Bill Pickett episode in the Mexico City bullring. On top of that, they had also had to deal with the two wayward employees who had robbed the safe in the ticket wagon.

The situation had not improved when they reached Oklahoma. Joe and Zack had returned to the ranch to learn from George about the budding partnership with E. W. Marland and his interest in developing oil operations on their property. They had scarcely met the eager oil prospector and had only begun to explore ways of working with him. Now they faced the unsettling business of drilling for oil on their ranchlands without an office or even a proper place to call home.

As if the disastrous fire had not been enough, more bad news followed. Later that morning, word reached the Millers that one of their most dependable employees had died at a Bliss roominghouse. Henry Breslow, canvas foreman for the Wild West show, had succumbed to tonsillitis after a short illness. The attending physician reported that the cowboy had become quite weak and had no resistance to fight infection. Like so many of the Millers' hired hands, the twenty-eight-year-old bachelor was simply worn out after a grueling season on the road.[13]

Although they faced adversity, the Miller brothers refused to cry over their losses. Instead, they parleyed with their mother at Joe's home in Ponca City. Then—while cowhands smothered the dying embers of the White House fire—they rode back to the ranch to confer with several of their most trusted hands.[14]

Not a soul who knew the Millers harbored any doubts about what would happen next; the only question was exactly when rebuilding would commence. The answer came loud and clear just days after the fire. The Miller brothers publicly announced that they would construct an even more impressive home. Work would begin at once.[15]

By February 17—the day Chiricahua Apache leader Geronimo died of pneumonia at age eighty, still in captivity as a prisoner of war at Fort Sill,

Oklahoma—the Millers had started to create a new family home and office. They had cleared the piles of debris, removed burned timbers, and opened discussions with architects.[16]

Joe Miller, acting as general superintendent of construction, oversaw the project. He worked closely with a consulting architect, whom he ordered to design a building so fireproof that a bonfire could be set in every room without damaging the house.[17] Money was not an obstacle, and by the time the new house was completed, the Millers had shelled out thirty-five thousand dollars.[18] They felt it was worth every dime.

The result was a three-story fortress built primarily of steel and reinforced concrete and topped with an asbestos roof. Only the flooring, doors, and ornamental woodwork could burn in case of another fire. Individual energy plants furnished the seventeen-room residence with electricity, hot and cold running water, steam heat, and hot and cold ventilation. Designed and constructed in a colonial style with massive porticoes on two sides and a porte cochere to shelter arriving guests, the new home resembled antebellum mansions the Miller family had known in Kentucky.[19]

The first floor included a spacious living room, den, library, dining room, and kitchen. Nine bedrooms, each with its own bath, and another comfortable living room occupied the second floor. The third floor was a single huge room filled with enough four-poster beds to sleep as many as a hundred guests during rodeo season and other special occasions. Affectionately called the "attic," this top-floor dormitory was decorated with scores of pictures of cattle and bison. Throughout the house, colorful Indian rugs were scattered on the polished floors.[20]

Most evenings after dinner, the billiard parlor was the favorite retreat for the brothers and their friends, and the breezy screened porch off the third level afforded an impressive panorama of the ranch. Drinking toddies or sampling sumptuous fudge ordered by the case from a Kansas wholesale grocer, guests gazed out at the Miller domain. An ornate wrought-iron fence surrounded a grassy lawn landscaped with shrubbery, flower beds, and a variety of trees. Beyond the manicured grounds stretched the striking valley of the Salt Fork and the Millers' orchards, vineyards, fields planted in alfalfa, wheat, and corn and, farther away, tens of thousands of acres of pasturelands where herds of cattle and horses grazed.[21]

After work crews finished the interiors, they painted the exterior walls bone white. Mother Miller and her sons fittingly named the place the White House after the home they had lost in the fire.[22] The Millers loved their new mansion and predicted that it would stand forever. It had taken some doing, but the Miller brothers' empire had become a significant influence on the national scene. Nevertheless, while the Millers' entertainment, farming, and ranching enterprises continued to prosper and they finalized plans to enter the lucrative oil business, the new year would soon become a time to bid good-bye to a fabled era. For the Millers, that would mean a long, slow, and often agonizing farewell.

By 1909, some people realized that the passing of what came to be called the Old West was at hand. Perhaps some of them saw the writing on the wall when Frederic Remington, creator of more than twenty-seven hundred works of art that symbolized the American West of myth, died that year at age forty-eight in Connecticut.[23] Still others recognized that the end was in sight because of the advancement of modern technology. As more rail and telephone lines crisscrossed the land, Henry Ford mass-produced Model T automobiles, and pioneer aviators made further advances, the rural West quickly became far less isolated. The time had come for guardians of the range such as the Millers to acknowledge the inevitable changes in their way of life.

Yet they also knew that at least for the time being, their agricultural enterprise, oil exploration, and other profit centers would serve them well. The Millers paid heed when the federal government declared 1909 the most prosperous year in the history of American farming, with corn considered the most valuable product—worth even more than all the silver and gold bullion in the nation.[24]

Bumper crops of corn and wheat and the promise of even more riches from oil wells spouting across Indian lands convinced the Millers that they could retain the spirit of the Old West, at least for a little longer. One of the main methods for accomplishing this goal was to take the Miller Brothers 101 Ranch Real Wild West—as they started to call their extravaganza in 1909—to as many cities and towns as possible.[25]

From the beginning of the 1909 season until the advent of the Great War in Europe, the 101 Ranch show remained a steady income producer for the Millers. Profits ranged from a low forty-seven thousand dollars in 1909 to a high of two hundred thousand dollars in 1915, when their two road companies toured the nation. One troupe of entertainers became a featured attraction at the Panama-Pacific International Exposition in San Francisco, attended by about thirteen million visitors during its run, which marked the opening of the Panama Canal.[26]

In the early spring of 1909, amid meetings with E. W. Marland, the Miller brothers and their show-business partner, Edward Arlington, finalized plans for the coming season. Once again, Arlington, an equal owner of the Wild West show, acted as the advance man, in charge of all routing. Joe Miller served as show manager, and Zack directed each performance.[27]

Zack—in a big white Stetson, colorful neckerchief, and tooled boots—also had a role in the program so he could display his marksmanship while riding full tilt around the arena on a trained Arabian stallion named Ben Hur. George, as usual, remained in Oklahoma to direct ranch, farm, and oil activities.[28]

Vern Tantlinger and his wife, Edith, refreshed from the rigors of 1908, returned for the new season. Tantlinger was boss of the cowboys for many years, but the boomerang act was his specialty. His assistant was Zu-Rah, billed as an Australian aborigine, who always caught the flying weapon bare-handed as it whirled through the air.[29]

Most of the 101 Ranch regulars also came back, including the cowboy musical band and such headliners as Prince Lucca, chief of the cossacks; Sioux Chief Eagle Feather; Vester Pegg; George Hooker; Otto Kline; Johnny Frantz; Frank Maish; Neil Hart; Sammy Garrett; Bernie St. Clair; Otto Kreinbeck; Chester Byers; Esteven Clemento; Guy Weadick and his wife, Florence La Due; Pat Christman; John Mullens; and Dan Dix. Miss Amelia Sommerville and her horse, Columbus, were a featured act until midsummer in Connecticut, when they left to join California Frank's Wild West Show. Maude Burbank and her noble steed, Dynamo, replaced them.[30]

Uncle Dan Boyington and his trained mules appeared, as did such assorted circus stars and sideshow acts as Captain George Devere, the tattooed man; Casibanka, the Singalese conjurer; the Ramons, gifted jugglers and battle-ax throwers; a fifteen-man minstrel troupe; and trainers and handlers, with their snarling lions, leopards, tigers, and performing bears.[31]

Princess Wenona, the best female shot alive and perhaps the most accurate woman sharpshooter ever, never failed to leave audiences cheering and yelling for more as she shattered target after target from the back of a horse racing at full speed. Zack's wife, Mabel, rode with the gang of dauntless Miller cowgirls, which included such able horsewomen as Goldie St. Clair, Bertha Ross, Maude Jameson, Dolly Mullens, Mary Fitzpatrick, Marie Morrison, and Marie Killinger.[32]

Besides Poncas and members of other tribes from near the 101 Ranch, many of the Indian performers for the Millers' Wild West show were Sioux recruited by Vern Tantlinger from Pine Ridge Reservation in South Dakota. Sioux who signed contracts to ride with the 101 included Alex Iron Bear, White Butterfly, Two Dog and Mrs. Two Dog, Sam Cuts Grass, One Feather, Bessie One Feather, Yellow Wolf, Good Boy, Charles Red Bear, White Star, Shout At, Laura Bear, and Sam Running Horse.[33]

Weekly wages for the Sioux performers varied from one dollar for children to seven dollars for grown men. Contracts stipulated that the Millers pay for all travel, food, medical attention, and clothing, "except for one set of Indian clothes, head dress, moccasins, etc."[34]

Bill Pickett, still recuperating from his ordeal in the bullring in Mexico City, did not perform his standard bulldogging act for the Millers during most of the 1909 season.[35] Unable to rejoin the show until September, Pickett took his wife, Maggie, and their daughters to a ranch north of Chandler, Oklahoma, where he handled basic chores and mended his wounds. In Pickett's absence, Dell Blancett—another fearless rodeo rider who served a few years later with the Canadian armed forces and died on the western front—took over the bulldogging act, with help from three or four other top cowboys.[36]

Although Pickett did not appear at many of the major stops—including Kansas City, Indianapolis, Cincinnati, Pittsburgh, Cleveland, and Boston—vivid images of him in action flashed before thousands of people across the United States.[37] A French film crew from Pathé-Frères had recorded the dramatic confrontation between Pickett and the fighting bull in the crowded Mexico City arena in December 1908. Throughout 1909, moving pictures of Pickett riding Spradley flickered across theater screens throughout the nation. One of several films of Pickett and other 101 Ranch riders that were later lost, the early action documentary served its purpose by inspiring even larger audiences to turn out for the Millers' Wild West shows.[38] Many more such films followed.

The showman behind some of the first one- and two-reelers shot on the 101 Ranch was William N. Selig, a pioneer film producer and former magician who had operated a successful minstrel show.[39] After Colonel Selig, as most of his associates called him, visited the 101 Ranch, the lives of the Millers were never quite the same.

A Chicago native, Selig entered the infant film business in the mid-1890s after witnessing a demonstration of the Edison Kinetoscope in Dallas. With assistance from a machinist friend, Selig developed what became known as the Selig Standard Camera and the Selig Polyscope, a film projector. By 1896, Selig had rented a Chicago loft and started to produce such films as *The Tramp and the Dog* (1896), followed by *Trapped by*

Bloodhounds, or, A Lynching at Cripple Creek (1905), *The Count of Monte Cristo* (1908), and *Dr. Jekyll and Mr. Hyde* (1908), under the name of Selig Polyscope Company.[40]

When former president Theodore Roosevelt set out on his famous African hunting expedition in 1909, Selig lobbied unsuccessfully to accompany the safari with a camera and film T.R. bagging big game. Undaunted by rejection, the audacious and enterprising Selig purchased an aging lion at a bargain price and acquired the services of a vaudeville actor who bore a slight resemblance to Roosevelt. Selig also hired some Chicago citizens to portray African tribesmen.[41] With the aid of a few tropical plants, optical trickery, and clever editing, Selig's director created a jungle scene in an indoor studio in which "Roosevelt" shot and killed the king of beasts. Selig's timing was perfect. His creation was ready for release when news came out of Africa that Roosevelt had bagged a lion. Within days, the film, *Hunting Big Game in Africa*, appeared in theaters around the nation. Audiences who paid to see it honestly believed they were witnessing Teddy Roosevelt's slaying of an African lion.[42]

Encouraged by this success, Selig acquired an entire zoo and churned out a series of animal and jungle films. He also financed expeditions to exotic lands to obtain authentic footage for future creations. One of those locales was the faraway reaches of the Miller brothers' 101 Ranch in Oklahoma.[43]

Realizing the impact of motion pictures and the large audiences the newfangled medium reached, the Millers did not hesitate to allow film production on their Oklahoma cattle spread in the early spring of 1909.[44] Still, the advent of film work on the ranch could not have come at a worse time. The new White House was under construction, the Marland interests had hatched their drilling schemes on the prairies, and plans were well under way for the next Wild West show season.

To make things worse, just as trains bearing the film crews pulled in at Bliss, a shipment of more than fifteen thousand head of cattle arrived from various points for summer grazing at the Hundred and One.[45] Many of the cowboys and cowgirls hired to tend the cattle and handle daily chores also had to serve as primary actors and extras for the movies being filmed on the ranch. Eager to get the western moving pictures filmed on locale and in the can, the Millers and the filmmakers persevered.

The Selig Polyscope crews used the Miller cowhands at work on the 101 Ranch as the backdrop for three films that spring. Featured players in those screen dramas included Van E. Barrett, John Kenyon, George L.

Graves, Laura Roth, and Carroll McFarland.[46] But of even more importance to the motion-picture industry and especially to the developing genre of western films, Colonel Selig also "discovered" a personable 101 wrangler that spring. His name was Tom Mix.

After completing the grueling 1908 show season—his third with the 101 Ranch—Mix began to spend more and more of his time at Dewey, Oklahoma, to court Olive Stokes, a Scottish-Cherokee cowgirl barely twelve when Will Rogers had introduced her to Mix. By 1909, she had matured into a stunning young woman.[47]

On January 19, 1909—only a week after the Millers' White House burned to the ground—eighteen-year-old Olive became the third of Mix's five wives. It was said that Miss Olive was as good a rider and roper as most men.[48]

Following a Montana honeymoon with his bride, Mix rode the circuit for the Wilderman Wild West Show of Amarillo, Texas. Everything went well for a while, but Mix quit the outfit during a Denver engagement when he was denied a pay raise. He and Olive moved on to Seattle and formed their own show, made up of about sixty performers and actors and forty Blackfoot Indian riders. The show proved successful, although Mix was wounded in the hand during an attempted armed robbery of the show payroll, which he and Olive thwarted.[49]

When their Seattle show closed, Tom and Olive joined Will Dickey's Circle D Wild West Show for a hitch, and then Mix returned to the Millers and the 101 Ranch. Although some credible sources claimed Mix worked for the Millers at the time, it remained debatable exactly who paid Mix's cowboy wages in 1909 when he and Selig became acquainted on the Oklahoma plains. Only twenty-nine years old, Mix had invented various aspects of his life and spiced up his professional résumé with exaggerations and, in some instances, outright lies.[50]

Selig later said that despite the embellishments, the instant he met Mix he knew he had found a natural for the silent screen. He immediately put the handsome cowboy to work as an extra and a scout for film locations for a low-key movie entitled *Ranch Life in the Great Southwest*, directed by Francis Boggs and released in 1910.[51] Boggs, the Selig company's ace director, was murdered a few years later in Los Angeles when a Japanese gardener, irritated by the noise from a film crew on location, went berserk and began to shoot his gun wildly, killing Boggs and wounding Selig.[52]

An abundance of gunslingers still prowled Oklahoma when Selig and Boggs made their films on the 101 Ranch. The locale also offered plenty of good horsemen and rugged cowpokes. When Selig needed a horse to be ridden over a cliff in an action scene, Mix volunteered. Impressed by the stunt, Selig enlisted Mix for future films. This started Mix on a journey to become the top motion-picture attraction in the world and one of the highest-paid stars of his time.[53]

The Selig experience also guaranteed that the 101 Ranch name would remain center stage for a long time to come. Those first motion-picture adventures convinced the Millers that by memorializing their riders and ropers on film, they could keep alive the old traditions their father had instilled in them.

Indeed, by producing their own creative concoction—a blend of myth and reality—the Miller brothers ensured that the Hundred and One would endure as one of the last links with the Old West.

CONEY ISLAND

THROUGHOUT THE MANY years the Miller brothers produced Wild West shows, casualties commonly afflicted the crews and performers. Besides broken bones, sprains, concussions, dislocated shoulders, and fractured skulls sustained in arena spills, train derailments and other accidents took a toll, sometimes with deadly results.[1]

Most of the riders who toured with the Millers' Real Wild West also worked at the ranch and returned to Bliss at the end of the season, right along with the riding stock. As a rule, professional performers who did not work as cowhands spent the off-season mending wounds. But some of them looked for ways to earn additional money or sought further excitement from adoring fans.

At the close of the Millers' successful 1909 show season, several of their top 101 Ranch performers decided to spend the winter in warmer climes.[2] Vern and Edith Tantlinger, Vester Pegg, Frank Maish, George Hooker, Jim Garrett, Chester Byers, and Ethel (sometimes spelled Etheyle) and Juanita Parry were among the headliners who temporarily signed on with the IXL Ranch Wild West Show and headed to South America. They arrived at Buenos Aires for the opener on December 18 and spent the next four months making the rounds of stadiums and arenas throughout Latin America.[3]

By April 4, the entourage of 101 Ranch riders had finished the show circuit and returned to the United States. From New York, they quickly made their way westward to Saint Louis in time to rendezvous with the rest of the Miller-Arlington personnel and prepare for the 1910 season opener, on April 16.[4]

After a week's run in Saint Louis, the show moved into Ohio for stands at Dayton, Springfield, Columbus, and Cambridge. From Ohio, the Miller-Arlington outfit played several major cities, including Pittsburgh, Philadelphia, Washington, and Baltimore, before hitting New England and New York state.[5]

After a well-received run at Perth Amboy, New Jersey, the 101 Ranch Real Wild West departed the industrial city at the mouth of the Raritan

River, and on May 22, the show train pulled into Brooklyn for a weeklong stand.[6] Advertisements in area newspapers described the mighty rolling circus of entertainers, laborers, animals, and tons of equipment as "The Only True, Possible, Pretentious Western Frontier Exhibition" and "Without a Counterpart Anywhere on Earth."[7]

At the railroad siding that bright morning, hundreds of local people came out to watch teamsters and hostlers, with their teams of muscular horses, unload the show stock and equipment. The crowd swelled and then moved in a great wave to Fifth Avenue and Third Street, where crews erected a tent city on the old circus lot.[8]

Because it was the Sabbath, no performance or parade was scheduled until the following day. With a free afternoon and evening, Joe Miller decided his employees might benefit from a little diversion. At high noon, Joe gathered his show people around him and surprised them by saying, "Let's all go to Coney Island!" He did not have to repeat it.[9]

By two o'clock, more than one hundred of the Millers' cowboys, cowgirls, and Indian entertainers were ready to invade the famous seaside amusement park. As the large party of colorfully dressed western entertainers, led by Vern and Edith Tantlinger, walked to the railroad station, they attracted a great deal of attention. Acting on Joe Miller's orders, the show's publicity crew and press agents had tipped off the New York newspapers. A small army of reporters tagged along to record the events of that unusual day.[10]

At the Third Street station, the startled ticket agent for the elevated railroad was alarmed at the sight of the performers. At first, he believed he was about to be caught in an Indian uprising. His fear dissolved when Joe Miller appeared with a fistful of greenbacks to buy tickets for everyone.[11]

The 101 Ranch gang went directly to Coney Island—six miles of beachfront billed as the "world's largest playground," on a peninsula at the southern tip of Brooklyn. Named *Konijn Eiland*, or Rabbit Island, by early Dutch settlers, it was the place where Henry Hudson had landed in 1609. It was an island in name only; most of the old tidal Coney Island creek that separated it from the rest of Brooklyn had long been filled in.[12]

Coney Island had become a resort by 1829 when the first hotel, the Coney Island House, was built at Norton's Point in Sea Gate, a residential community. Other hotels soon sprang up, followed by bathhouses, dance halls, freak shows, fun houses, and sundry rides and attractions.[13]

After arriving at about four o'clock, the 101 Ranch visitors went to Luna

Park, largest of the Coney Island fun spots. Created in 1903 by Frederick Thompson and Elmer S. Dundy, the Luna Park complex included dozens of rides, a broad lagoon, and a popular ballroom.[14] Fred Thompson himself met the Millers' cowboys and Indians at the entrance, along with a complete musical band and a huge crowd of curious New Yorkers. The giant playland, the masses of people, and the vast expanse of ocean that lay before them combined to dazzle the visitors from the West.[15]

The next few hours went by in a flash, as Joe Miller and his Wild West bunch rode every ride and visited every attraction in the park. They thrilled at being whirled, jolted, battered, and tossed upside down. Among their favorites was the Ferris wheel, but many of the performers also enjoyed the Chute-the-Chutes—speedy incline coaster cars that careened into a body of water, resulting in giant splashes and whoops and screams even from veteran riders and ropers. Chief Plenty Horses stated unequivocally that one ride on the exciting Chute-the-Chutes was more than enough, but young Red Eagle was so thrilled that he refused to give up his seat and rode for hours.[16]

A throng of New Yorkers followed the cowboys, cowgirls, and Indians around the park. The locals said they would never forget the sight of champion cowpoke George Hooker trick riding on a bobbing merry-go-round mount or Indian women, with babies secure in cradleboards, whizzing down the steep Helter Skelter slide. Mexican vaqueros, with their fancy duds and wide sombreros, found a friend in a newspaper reporter who spoke fluent Spanish and served as their interpreter while they made their way through the amusement park.[17]

Somehow, amid all the hubbub, Vern Tantlinger noticed that Bill Pickett was missing. Tantlinger asked around, but none of the other cowboys had seen the bulldogger. Aware of Pickett's notorious thirst for alcohol, Vern worried that he had wandered off in search of strong drink. Tantlinger enlisted "Rocky Mountain" Hank Walker, the skilled driver of the show's overland Deadwood stagecoach, to find Pickett. By the time the sun disappeared and tens of thousands of glittering electric bulbs flashed awake around Luna Park, neither Walker nor Pickett had returned.[18]

Finally, when it appeared that everyone had had enough thrills, Joe Miller led his tired and hungry employees to a preferred Surf Avenue restaurant for an acclaimed Coney Island fish dinner. Meanwhile, Tantlinger looked over his shoulder for any sign of Pickett or Walker. He also alerted policemen assigned to herd crowds of onlookers away from the 101 Ranch diners to keep their eyes peeled for two wayward cowboys.[19]

Just as waiters delivered bowls brimming with chowder and platters heaped with sole, soft-shell crabs, and steamed clams to the performers, Pickett and Walker calmly strolled into the restaurant. Without a word of explanation, they pulled up chairs, tied napkins around their necks, and started to eat.[20]

"I should have expected this," Tantlinger was reported to have said. "Neither one of those two rascals was ever known to have missed a free meal."[21]

Between forkfuls of fish, Walker told the others he had finally tracked down Pickett on Surf Avenue. The famed bulldogger was standing on the corner, carefully counting the passing automobiles, and had lost track of the time.[22]

After dinner, all hands boarded a train and returned to the Fifth Avenue lot for a good night's sleep before they launched their Brooklyn run. Awaiting the 101 Ranch performers that summer and autumn were more performances in New England, followed by shows at crowded arenas in Saint Louis, the state fair in Minnesota, and scores of sites across the Midwest and Deep South.[23]

But for the remainder of 1910 and for many years after, the memory of the Sunday stayed with those who had followed Joe Miller to Coney Island. It was a special day for the men and women of the Hundred and One—a fragment of time they would warmly recall the rest of their lives.

Chapter 31

CALIFORNIA DREAMING

Against the great natural background of the Far West, in itself dramatic, the Western developed from melodrama toward epic. From 1911 till today, the majesty of plains, deserts, and mountains has given an importance beyond itself to the feeblest Western. Whatever plot is spinning, the background reminds us that these films are part of the national drama of the winning of the wilderness.[1]

—Richard Griffith and Arthur Mayer
The Movies

HORSE operas and the Hundred and One always seemed a natural fit. The Miller brothers and their salty, sassy bunch of rawboned cowboys and cowgirls, rough riders, and entertainers were tailor-made for the movie business.

Unfortunately, the people who truly played a role in the birth and evolution of western motion pictures were never properly asked to identify the most significant influences on their craft. If such a poll had been taken, anyone possessing a morsel of common sense would have been obliged to include the Miller brothers and the lively men and women who rode for the Hundred and One. A few might even have felt compelled to place the Millers near the top of the list.

Despite the Millers' great impact on American cinema in the formative years of the industry, many of those associated with the 101 Ranch—including some members of the family—thought the Millers never received sufficient credit for their efforts.[2]

"My father and uncles and the rest of our family and outfit did a damn sight more than their share to boost the cowboy picture business at a time when not many folks even had a clue what it was all about," recounted an indignant Zack Miller Jr. in his waning years. "One hell of a lot of fine men and women who became big shots in Hollywood and household names on movie screens around the world got their start with the Hundred and One. The Miller boys and their big gang should have been acknowledged more than they were for the important part they played in keeping the great American dream alive."[3]

According to Zack Miller Jr. and some other family members, this perceived lack of recognition may have occurred in part because the Millers were involved with several major endeavors on a variety of fronts. Simply put, the Millers were spread thin. The family's Wild West touring companies and other ventures upstaged their film work. At the same time the Miller brothers plunged headlong into the motion-picture business, they also busily pursued ranching and farming operations, produced Wild West shows, and became deeply involved with oil-drilling ventures on Oklahoma Indian lands.

Still, as Zack Jr. vehemently insisted to his dying day, no one could honestly deny that the Miller brothers played an instrumental role in the conception and evolution of western films, a genre founded more on myth than reality.[4]

Zack Jr. conjectured that his father and uncles believed that motion pictures would buy them time to preserve their rich heritage. Perhaps he was right. Perhaps the Millers recognized what film historian Kevin Brownlow would discuss in his book *The War, the West, and the Wilderness*.[5]

"Westerns offered employment to men who had known no life other than life on the range and for whom no security remained," wrote Brownlow. "It offered a rich prize to the rodeo rider. It gave outlaws a chance to vindicate themselves through re-enactments of their criminal past, to deter future crime. And it staged the last great drive of Texas longhorns. The motion picture not only reconstructed Western history—it became an extension of that history."[6]

Conceivably for those reasons, the Millers had hired photographer Bennie Kent, the Englishman from Chandler, Oklahoma, known for his trademark derby hat and cigar. Toting his huge boxy still camera across the prairies and pastures, Kent took photographs that forever captured the Millers' famed June 1905 roundup—Oklahoma's Gala Day—featuring Geronimo, Bill Pickett, and Lucille Mulhall performing before tens of thousands of spectators near the Salt Fork River. Just a few years later, Kent switched to a motion-picture camera to document other key events at the ranch. Beyond Kent, the ability of film to extend history and to reconstruct legends convinced the Millers to involve themselves with early film production companies such as Pathé-Frères, the French crew that recorded Pickett's ballyhooed bullring appearance in Mexico City, which *Billboard* magazine was still heralding in 1911.[7]

More important, preservation also motivated the Millers to work with some of the first feature filmmakers from back east. That included the Polyscope Company of Chicago, run by movie pioneer William N. Selig, the resourceful and prolific producer who shot a series of rudimentary western flickers at the Millers' ranch in 1909.[8]

Beyond the Polyscope films made at the ranch, Selig's association was advantageous to the Millers because he transformed their hired hand Tom Mix into a cinematic cowboy hero. Of all the many movie stars and film luminaries through the decades who were connected to the Millers and the 101, none shone brighter than Mix. Even though his lustrous star at times became a tad tarnished, mostly because of his predilection for shenanigans and the backlash from ill-timed scandals, the handsome Pennsylvanian proved his worth. His personal problems aside, anyone who hired Mix knew that he meant money in the bank whenever he came into the public eye and flashed his grin.

With the start of the 1910 season, Mix—as flamboyant as ever and accompanied by Olive Stokes, his attractive third wife—was once more appearing with the Miller brothers.[9] He also stood on the verge of becoming a major figure with Selig's film company. Before Mix could enjoy fame and glory by riding a blindfolded horse over a bluff into the flood-swollen Salt Fork for Selig's cameras, he accompanied the 101 Ranch show to Mexico City in September 1910 for the centennial celebration of Mexican independence from Spain.[10]

Mix's old friend Bill Pickett, fully recovered from the injuries he had sustained in the bullring during his earlier visit, also returned to Mexico City. By the beginning of 1910, Pickett had moved his family into a large house just east of Bliss on a leased section of the 101 Ranch, and he was raring to ride the show circuit.[11]

While appearing with the Millers in Mexico City, three top cowboys—Mix, Pickett, and Stack Lee—staged the same stunt Will Rogers had pulled a few years before in New York that had started him on the road to stardom. Lee and Mix turned a bull loose in the grandstands in Mexico City, sending spectators into a panic.[12]

Seemingly from out of nowhere, Pickett rode into the ring on his pony. Without hesitation, he expertly roped the bull and dragged it from the stands before anyone was hurt. The resulting applause and cheers were thunderous. It also was widely rumored that the Millers collected plenty of pesos from a wager they had made with Mexican officials that the gringo riders would take control of the situation in an allotted period of time.[13]

Whether it was deliberately staged or not, the 1910 event in Mexico City went much smoother for the 101 Ranch riders than had their previous appearance. The performers, especially Pickett and Mix, made favorable impressions on the curious crowds.

While the 101 Ranch performers captivated their fans, a local youngster with no place to call home found favor with Zack Miller. When the successful run in Mexico City concluded, Zack and his wife, Mabel, returned to the United States with the orphan in tow. Just ten years old when Zack smuggled him across the border into the United States, the boy had a shadowy past. He soon picked up the nickname Muchacho, a common Spanish word for "boy" or "lad."[14]

Little was known of the youth except that his mother and father had worked as lion tamers in a Mexican circus and had been killed by the big cats during a performance. When the frantic boy tried to pull his parents to safety, the lions badly mangled one of his arms. Circus performers rushed to the child's rescue as he watched his parents being ripped to shreds before his eyes.[15]

Some folks back in Oklahoma, including Zack's brothers, thought it most curious that Zack and Mabel would take on another youngster. It had become obvious to even a blind mule skinner that Zack and Mabel's marriage had soured under the strain of road travel. Both of them had developed a wandering eye, and the distance between husband and wife widened. Moreover, both of them seemed incapable of adequately caring for their daughter, Virginia, without help from Mabel's family or from Mother Miller. As it turned out, Zack treated the Mexican boy like a personal servant and never really considered him his son, even though whispered rumors circulated that Zack and Mabel had legally adopted the orphan.[16]

In Oklahoma, Muchacho promptly made friends with young Jack Baskin, a ten-year-old from Red Rock and Mabel Miller's first cousin. The two boys, known as mascots for the 101 Ranch show, went on the road with the performers. In her spare time, Mabel taught English to the Mexican boy. Zack saw to it that he earned his keep by waiting on tables at the White House and tending to Zack's horses.[17]

"For some curious reason, he'd [Muchacho would] have nothing to do with the other Mexicans with the outfit; he threw in with the Indians, taking on their dress and manners, learning their language," explained Fred Gipson in *Fabulous Empire*. The boy, anxious for his own identity, began to call himself Sky Eagle.[18]

"He was a shrewd one, this little Sky Eagle," wrote Gipson. "He watched everything that went on around the show, and by the time he was eleven or twelve years old, he'd learned more about human nature than many a man learns in a lifetime. At fifteen, he was using this knowledge to his own advantage."[19]

Sky Eagle later worked as a sideshow huckster and peddled bottles of snake oil and liniment—mostly mixtures of cheap whiskey, dried flowers, gasoline, oil of mustard, and rattlesnake oil. Besides convincing gullible visitors to the Millers' Wild West shows to purchase his potions and aphrodisiacs, Sky Eagle also showed that he had a way with the ladies.[20]

Of course, growing up on the 101 Ranch meant the boy had role models all around him. He was in the constant presence of natural-born yarn spinners, tale tellers, pathological liars, and outrageous saddle tramps whose lives remained forever embroiled in illusion and myth. Some of them, such as Tom Mix, had become obsessed with reinventing their biographies to suit their needs. In the case of Mix, it was constantly a chore just to separate fact and fantasy. It also was just as hard for him to avoid trouble.

Soon after the 101 Ranch gang returned to the United States from the Mexico adventure in 1910, Mix ran head-on into more problems—this time with the Miller brothers themselves. His legal squabble with the Millers erupted after Mix "borrowed" a steed from the 101 Ranch corrals to ride in an Oklahoma City rodeo he had entered.[21]

Disaster struck when Mix rode into the arena and took a tumble from the high-spirited mount. Everyone knew what happened as soon as they heard the sharp pop that sounded like a rifle shot and saw him writhing in pain on the floor of the arena. Mix had broken his leg. A few kindhearted pals lugged Mix to a hospital to have the leg set while other ranch hands arranged to have the Millers' horse stabled at the nearby Mulhall Ranch. While Mix was on the mend, the horse he had appropriated from the Millers mysteriously vanished from Colonel Mulhall's place. That prompted the Miller brothers—who angrily claimed that they had not given permission to Mix to borrow the animal in the first place—to seek immediate legal action. They filed an embezzlement charge against Mix in Kay County court.[22]

Observers who knew the parties on both sides of the dispute saw the obvious irony of the situation, considering the Millers' own brushes with the law, including criminal charges of livestock theft and murder. Folks also recalled that in his younger years, Joe Miller had served hard time in prison on a counterfeiting conviction. Old-timers agreed that by bringing criminal charges against Mix, the Millers would keep him in line and make sure he remained a 101 Ranch cowboy. If that was indeed their plan, the scheme misfired.

On October 31, 1910, J. E. Burns, the county attorney, arraigned Mix.[23] He maintained his innocence and waived a preliminary hearing. County Judge Claude Duvall held Mix over to answer the felony charge and fixed his appearance bond at a hefty one thousand dollars. Mix and his wife scraped up some money, but he never paid the bond and never served a day of jail time. Instead, Mix hired Sam K. Sullivan to defend him in the criminal case brought before District Judge William Boles.[24]

The legal action was due to be heard in court on January 16, 1911, but Mix failed to appear. Although the case was supposedly dismissed, no further entries appeared in the official court records, so the matter remained in legal limbo for years.[25]

The embezzlement charge seems to have been forgotten. Then in 1929—nineteen years after the supposed horse theft—Zack Miller and Mix locked horns again, over a breach-of-contract suit against Mix. The two aging cowboys ended up in a lengthy legal battle as Miller tried in vain to use the old horse-theft case for leverage against Mix.[26]

But a few years earlier, after Mix had become a big-time movie star, he had been able to put aside his differences with the Millers and admit that his greatest early days were with the 101. In 1926, when he was one of the most popular figures in Hollywood, Mix still expressed warm feelings for the Millers and the ranch. His reminiscences appeared in a *101 Ranch Magazine* story published that year:

> In the old days, with the blue sky above me, a good horse under me, the vast acreage of the old 101 Ranch rolling green about me and a bacon-filled atmosphere from the chuck wagon calling me, I was the richest of men. How rich, the recent years alone have told me.
>
> My fondest recollections are those of my early days on the 101 Ranch and I attribute my present standing in the great industry of which I am a part to the training I received and experiences when working under the 101 brand. I could name hundreds of incidents and scenes in my pictures

> that really had their origin and happened along the banks of the old Salt Fork River.
>
> To me there had always been an inspiration in the broad expanse of far-stretching prairie, the ranch houses and the low corrals of the 101. But above all of these, I remember with keenest interest and happy memory my association with the three wonderful Miller boys—each so different in character and temperament—and yet each reflecting so important an understanding and part in the development of that great country.
>
> When one remembers the various individuals that were employed in the conduct of the wide-stretching Miller ranches, it is a marvel that anything was ever accomplished. I can safely say that some of the toughest cowpunchers, and likewise some of the best, were graduated from the old school of the 101. . . . In the daily gatherings of this bunch, altho [sic] now engaged in a different line of work, there still remains the same twang and breeze of the sage, as in the good old days when we squatted around the 101 chuck wagon, for we who have polished saddle leather and dragged our muddy loops for the Miller boys, are banded together with strong and everlasting ties of an enduring friendship.[27]

Unquestionably, his experience on the 101 Ranch not only shaped Mix and his movie career but also influenced many others. The 101 Ranch served as a proving ground for numerous western motion-picture stars.[28] Nevertheless, as important as their big Oklahoma ranch became to the film industry, the Millers would not have had nearly the same impact on the movie business without a second locale they secured more than a thousand miles to the west—in the foothills and on the raw studio lots of sunny southern California.[29]

More than forty years after G. W. Miller had headed his family west, the Millers finally reached the golden land of California. With help from their cowboys, cowgirls, and Indian performers, the Miller brothers established a foothold there. From the moment they arrived on the West Coast, in 1911, the Millers recognized that at long last they had fulfilled their father's dream.

This land on the western edge of the nation was where the ambitious George W. Miller had planned to establish a cattle ranch during those turbulent years after the Civil War. Although the Millers' westward journey had been decades in the making, they always believed the timing was ideal for their arrival on the roaring Pacific shore.[30] But unlike their crusty father, the Miller brothers were not interested in punching cattle or breaking horses in southern California. They had other plans.

Resolved to become active participants in the film business taking shape in the Los Angeles area, the brothers wanted to sustain the traditions they had grown up with on the cattle trails and open prairies. The Millers understood the West of old, when anarchy threatened law and order. They had ridden on both sides. The Millers knew the "real Wild West" had lasted only a couple of decades, but cinema could preserve their favorite myths.

Eager to take their rightful place as genuine trailblazers of the motion-picture industry, the Millers quickly committed themselves to becoming a major force in the development of that peculiarly American film genre known as the western. By the time they started the 1911 Wild West show season, plans for the Hundred and One's operations in California were well under way.[31]

That spring, the Miller cowhands loaded fresh livestock in railcars as scores of well-rested performers boarded an eastbound train. Meanwhile, the rest of the Miller-Arlington show emerged from its eastern winter quarters at Passaic, New Jersey, in preparation for the new season opener on April 8, 1911—a one-week run at the Boston Arena.[32]

As the new season begun, Zack Miller, whose tumultuous marriage to Mabel was about to unravel, journeyed to New York City. There he took charge of the Millers' sale of "50 Classy, Well-bred Saddle and Polo Ponies" at a public auction.[33]

"In the consignment one will find the choice pick of over 1,000 head of horses sired by the best stallions and foaled by western and Indian mares," stated the Millers' advertising flyer for the April 19 auction. "Several of them are half-bred Arabians from our well-known show stallion, Ben Hur. . . . In the entire bunch we offer but three horses that pace, two of them being pintos from the late Comanche Chief Quanah Parker. . . . This being our first sale, we are offering our very best stock, knowing that one good horse sold to the right party will do more to advertise our horses than all the literature we could distribute. . . . We are proud of this bunch of horses and you will be, too, if you get any of them."[34]

While Zack oversaw the successful sale of the horses, the Miller-Arlington show departed from Boston and played to packed houses beneath an enormous canvas tent at Philadelphia.[35] Then the show traveled to Baltimore before heading to Trenton, New Brunswick, Newark, Brooklyn, and several points in New York and New England.[36]

After appearances at sixteen stands across Pennsylvania in June, the 101 Ranch troupe spent the rest of the summer performing in Michigan, Wisconsin, and Illinois. Everywhere the show traveled, it faced fierce competition from traveling circuses such as Ringling Brothers, Forepaugh-Sells, Barnum & Bailey, and the Al G. Barnes Wild Animal Show. In many towns, two or more of the outfits played within a week of each other.[37]

Finally, the show train headed west. The long string of horse cars, flats, and sleepers was painted yellow, except for the last car, which was bone white. It carried Madame Marantette's trained horses, named Chief Geronimo, Sun Flower, and Saint Patrick, a jumper capable of clearing an obstacle six feet four inches in height.[38]

After playing engagements across Oklahoma and Texas, including major stops at Tulsa and Dallas in late September, the troupe anticipated the season finale, planned for October 21 at El Reno, Oklahoma, the old cattle-trail town west of Oklahoma City. However, instead of calling it quits for the year, the Millers decided to extend the season. After El Reno, they continued with stops throughout Texas, New Mexico, and Arizona until they reached California.[39]

On November 8, the long show train ground to a halt at Barstow, a Santa Fe Railway town that once had served as a desert junction for overland wagon trains and later as an outfitting point for Death Valley expeditions.[40] Within a few years, movie producers would use the rolling Mojave landscape and nearby mining towns such as Victorville as backdrops for western motion pictures, including many which starred 101 Ranch veterans, including Tom Mix and Hoot Gibson. In late autumn 1911, however, the Millers' cowboys and cowgirls were content to make local citizens' hearts flutter with trick riding and roping antics during a dozen stands in towns south and east of Los Angeles, including Long Beach.[41]

The last performance of the season was staged on November 22 at Pomona, an orchard center appropriately named for the Roman goddess of fruit and trees, just east of Los Angeles at the foot of the San Gabriel Mountains. After spending seven-and-one-half months on the road and traveling by train 14,097 miles though twenty-five states from the Atlantic to the Pacific, the Miller-Arlington 1911 season had come to a close.[42]

Instead of returning to Oklahoma, Joe Miller decided to winter the show in Los Angeles. Founded in 1781 just as the American Revolution was drawing to a close, Los Angeles was no longer a sleepy little town. By 1911, Los Angeles was in a period of tremendous growth. In the first decade of the twentieth century, the population had soared from slightly more than 100,000 to nearly 320,000.[43]

After their months on the road, Los Angeles looked like heaven on earth to the exhausted bronc riders, trick ropers, Indian entertainers, and sharpshooters. Joe Miller's performers were delighted for the chance to bask in the sunshine, feel the caress of warm salt breezes beneath stately palms and eucalyptus trees, and feast on luscious grapes, citrus, and abalone, fresh from the sea.

The show stock and equipment were quartered on the spacious grounds of the Los Angeles Gun Club. A large number of the performers and show workers secured rooms at the St. Marks Hotel in Venice, a pleasure town known as the "Coney Island of the West," just south of Santa Monica on the roaring Pacific.[44]

Other 101 Ranch performers leased oceanfront cottages on the Venice beach at reduced winter rates. The boarders at Venice that winter of 1911–1912 included the Tantlingers; Wayne Beasley and bronc buster Jim Kidd, both former husbands of Princess Wenona; Lillian Smith—Princess Wenona herself—back in her native California; the high-riding Parry sisters; clown Dan Dix; and lady bronc rider Lulu Parr. A cowgirl fashion plate, Parr had closed the regular season riding with the Buffalo Bill and Pawnee Bill Wild West Show but had quit to join the 101 troupe for the extended trek to the Pacific coast.[45]

Joe Miller was so pleased to have finally arrived in California that he immediately rented a sprawling house at Venice with a view of the ocean. He soon went back to the ranch headquarters in Oklahoma for the holiday season but returned with his family to Venice in January 1912.[46]

The 101 Ranch show people made their presence known in Venice from the beginning. When the railcars bearing the show equipment, stock, and performers rumbled down the spur track at the rear of the Sunset Avenue barns in November, an overloaded flatcar tipped over and destroyed two wagons.[47]

Despite the mishap, the Millers' grand parade through Venice started on time. Hundreds of Venetians turned out to listen to the boisterous calliope and watch the cowgirls, rough riders, costumed Indians, cossacks, bison, horses, and three marching bands.[48] It marked the beginning of a love affair between the Hundred and One and the residents of the resort city by the sea.

Founded in 1905, Venice was the dream of Abbot Kinney, a wealthy and eccentric tobacco magnate and real estate developer who envisioned what he called a "Venice-of-America"—a seaside renaissance town of Italianate buildings, single-lane bridges, and gondolas floating down a sixteen-mile network of concrete canals.[49]

After helping to create the new coastal town of Santa Monica, Kinney formed a land syndicate and began to develop an expanse of nearby marshland and sand dunes that had once served as cattle pasture but had become so flood prone it was no longer suitable. The seaside marshes were destined to become the town of Venice, but in the early years, most southern Californians called the development "Kinney's folly."[50]

Despite his many detractors and the violent Pacific storms that wreaked havoc on new construction along the coast, Kinney persevered. On July 4, 1905, when Venice-of-America opened, more than forty thousand enthusiastic visitors enjoyed choral serenades, gondola excursions, and patriotic speeches. Cascades of fireworks erupted above the bathhouse, swimming lagoon, and wooden pier.[51]

Kinney tried his best to market his new coastal community as a cultural showcase, but the lectures, poetry readings, musicals, and Chautauqua meetings he sponsored failed to attract large numbers of tourists. Even an appearance at the Venice Auditorium by the celebrated and controversial French actress Sarah Bernhardt in 1906 was not enough to boost the lofty goals Kinney had set for his renaissance city. He finally admitted that what the public most clamored for at Venice were profitable sideshow freaks, amusement rides, and honky-tonk attractions.[52]

The Midway-Plaisance, or Midway, along the swimming lagoon featured rows of amusements and exhibits such as head-hunting Igorots from the Philippines, dancing girls, snake charmers, a bearded lady, camel rides, and a moving-picture theater. Some of the most popular attractions included Chiquita, a thirty-two-pound woman who stood twenty-eight inches tall, and "Bosco Eats Them Alive," a man who dined on wiggling reptiles. Barkers wielding huge megaphones enticed tourists into tent shows, and pickpockets and scam artists wandered through the crowds.[53]

Venice proved to be the perfect lair for the Millers and their entertainers. Within a few weeks after their arrival, the Millers' performers and workers blended in with the locals and renewed friendships with members of the Al G. Barnes Wild Animal Circus, also wintering in the resort town.[54]

Members of the 101 Ranch company turned out for Venice's Christmas festivities. Decorations and pepper boughs festooned buildings, and palm trees sported ribbons and streamers of holly. Santa Claus arrived in a sleigh pulled by four Shetland ponies and distributed gifts to eleven hundred children. Guests enjoyed turkey dinners and a masquerade ball, but the most popular event took place on the pier, where more than one hundred Indians from the 101 Ranch show set up camp. It took four cooks and a team of assistants almost twenty-four hours to prepare a feast of barbecued ox. The crowd needed less than one hour to consume the entire meal.[55]

As the year came to a close, watch parties were formed around town to welcome 1912. On January 1, a large group from Venice, including the 101 Wild West Band and several Miller performers, departed for Pasadena, overlooking the San Gabriel Valley, to take part in the annual Tournament of Roses and to march in the Rose Parade.[56]

Until 1916, when the famed collegiate football game was instituted, the pinnacle event of the Pasadena celebration after the parade was a thundering chariot race. At the 1912 event, some 101 Ranch riders—Oscar Rixson, a tough bronc buster, and Melvin Saunders, a fine Roman rider—upstaged the chariot race. They were seeking the hand of Lillie Francis, a cowgirl who could not make up her mind which suitor to choose as a husband. A pony race was held to help with the decision.[57]

Betting was fast and furious. Saunders had the upper hand because the race was Roman style, with riders standing astride the backs of unsaddled ponies. The race began with the two men and their mounts side by side, but at the close of the two-lap dash around the tournament field, Rixon pulled ahead of Saunders and held on to win. Rixon galloped to the grandstand and shouted to Miss Francis, "I've got you, kid!" Then he gathered the blushing young woman in his arms and placed her on a spare pony while he remounted his steed. The two disappeared in a cloud of dust.[58]

When they reappeared at Venice the next day, a minister performed their wedding ceremony. Afterwards, Rixon's fellow cowboys sponsored a rousing party. When the celebration finally broke up—amid a fusillade of yells and noisy six-shooters—the Rixons caught a train bound for a honeymoon at the 101 Ranch.[59]

Soon after the holidays, Joe Miller concluded his visit to Oklahoma and returned to Venice and his beach home. He immediately plunged into the good life of southern California. Joe delighted in sightseeing and deep-sea fishing, and he enjoyed splashing in the ocean surf with his children. One afternoon, acting on gut instinct as usual, Joe purchased a sizable orange grove and sprawling walnut orchard.[60]

He told his friends that his first love would always be his adopted homeland of Oklahoma, where he had roamed since he was a boy riding the prairies of old Indian Territory. But that winter, Joe also plainly nurtured a love for California. He knew it was a big and bold land filled with promise and hope—a place of wild freedom and incredible risk.

In California, people could escape their pasts and invent new lives. For the Miller brothers and the renegades and misfits who followed them, California was where their dreams could all come true.

BISON 101

SOON AFTER ESTABLISHING a winter headquarters for their Wild West show at the resort city of Venice, California, the Miller brothers became even more involved with the motion-picture business than they had been in Oklahoma. By the end of 1911, the Millers sought to use moving pictures as yet another profit center like their ranching, farming, oil exploration, and road-show ventures.

On the surface, it appeared to be a shrewd and lucrative maneuver; indeed, cinema proved quite successful at first. Yet in a cruel twist of irony, the Millers, by fully embracing the film industry, signed the death warrant for the Hundred and One. Although it would take many years, the advance of competitive western movies—which continued to gain in popularity—steadily chipped away at the audience base for the Millers' Wild West extravaganzas. In the 1930s, after the advent of the Great Depression and talking films, the public's tastes changed—the era of the Wild West show came to an end.[1]

However, as the western film genre developed in California and other locales—borrowing showmanship from Wild West spectaculars and from authentic characters who had helped to shape the American West—the Millers had no reason to fear the future. By late 1911, they had become comfortable with the advances in modern technology. That autumn, with a significant corn crop ready to harvest at their ranch on the Salt Fork, the brothers still advertised for huskers at the pay rate of three cents per bushel and board, or four cents per bushel without board.[2] At the same time, they sought improved agricultural equipment to make the hard work easier and, more important, to cut expenses and help reduce their large labor force.

"This machine [tractor] will plow an acre an hour on 15 gallons of gasoline per day and will use about the same amount in hauling on the road," Joe Miller wrote in 1911 to an associate in Guthrie, Oklahoma. "It will easily do the work of eight horses. While we do not think that it will entirely displace the horse on the farm, it certainly is a great convenience and is much cheaper and better than to feed horses, as well as the saving of men."[3]

Throughout the first two decades of the twentieth century, the Millers negotiated lucrative deals with several manufacturers for tractors and other farm implements, automobiles, and large sums of cash—all in exchange for product endorsements and the use of the 101 Ranch for the production of commercial films and print advertisements.[4]

Although the Millers did not seem to notice it at the time, all the boosts in technology took a toll on the way of life the three brothers had always claimed to respect and wished to preserve. Their rural locale became less isolated. The 101 Ranch that Colonel George Washington Miller knew so well, in becoming more accessible, was a far different place than the cattle spread he had founded.

"Advances in agricultural machinery enabled farmers to earn a living on land that had defied profitable cultivation," observed Paul O'Neil in *The End and the Myth*. "And as early as 1911, when a flight pioneer showed that coyotes could be hunted from an airplane, ranchers foresaw that stock on remote sections of their land could be inspected from the skies. Even the cowboy on horseback—the very symbol of the American West—would finally be outmoded as the guardian of the range."[5]

In the final days of 1911, the Miller brothers were aware that within the coming year, New Mexico and Arizona would be admitted as states. They cheered for Jim Thorpe, an Oklahoma favorite son and possibly the world's greatest athlete, poised to win the pentathlon and decathlon at the 1912 Olympic games in Stockholm, Sweden. The brothers watched with interest as the palatial White Star ocean liner *Titanic* prepared for its maiden transatlantic voyage in April from Southhampton, England, to New York.[6]

All was right with the world and all was right with the Millers and their Wild West riders. They considered themselves as infallible as the mighty *Titanic*.

Like many other people of means, the Millers had become thoroughly comfortable with the new technological advancements of the time, including a telephone system that connected even the most remote ranch locations to the headquarters on the Salt Fork. They were fascinated with fancy motorcars, efficient farm machines, and airplanes. The brothers were especially impressed with the motion-picture cameras that recorded every aspect of their ranch life.

The Millers soon discovered that the people who owned those cameras were just as impressed with the large company of cowboys, cowgirls, and Indians in the employ of the Hundred and One. After touring several California beach resorts and cities and settling at Venice for the winter, the Millers and their entertainers attracted numerous independent filmmakers struggling to gain a foothold in the new industry taking root on the Pacific shore.

Choosing from the bunch, the Miller brothers made a deal with New York Motion Picture Company (NYMP), which had been founded by Charles O. Bauman, a former streetcar conductor; Adam Kessel, once a bookmaker; and Fred J. Balshofer, a stereoscopic-slide photographer who had turned to making motion pictures in 1905.[7] Within a few years, Balshofer recognized that his career transition had been a smart move—nickelodeons quickly replaced vaudeville theaters as the primary exhibitors for motion pictures. By 1908, more than five hundred nickelodeons in New York City alone attracted as many as two hundred thousand people a day.[8]

With headquarters in Brooklyn, NYMP became officially incorporated in 1909, with Kessel as president, Bauman as vice president, and Balshofer as secretary-treasurer and general manager.[9] NYMP filmed some of the earliest western movies at locations across the Hudson River in New Jersey, near the town of Coytesville and at Fort Lee—known as the first American movie capital, long before Hollywood acquired that designation.[10]

Using the image of a bison as the trademark and name for one of their ancillary film ventures, by late November 1909 the filmmakers had moved this operation—the Bison Moving Picture Company—and some of their best stock players to sunny California, where they could make pictures year-round.[11]

The film locations and facilities in New Jersey and New York would no longer serve as the center of the motion-picture business. Since the turn of the century, the infant technologies of motion photography and the electric light made it essential to shoot all films in open sunlight. Even interior scenes were usually shot outdoors.[12]

The summer season back east was not nearly as long as in California, which seemed to have eternal sunshine. That reason alone would have been sufficient for production companies to forsake the East Coast and make California the major film center. But there was another persuasive motive for the move.[13]

By 1908, Thomas Edison—eager to ward off competition—had organized several other film producers, including Vitagraph, Biograph, Kalem,

Lubin, Selig, Essanay, the French Pathé-Frères and Méliès. The companies acknowledged Edison as the inventor of the motion picture and agreed to produce films only with his permission. Participants not only turned over all their patent claims but also paid Edison a royalty fee for the right to produce and distribute films in the United States.[14]

Together, they formed the Motion Picture Patents Company (MPPC), known as the Patents Trust—a blatant attempt to monopolize and control the film industry. The MPPC arrogantly asserted that only its members could produce, distribute, and exhibit motion pictures. In effect, those who tried to make films without MPCC permission risked harsh penalties, including criminal prosecution and even imprisonment.[15]

Although the strong-arm tactics of the powerful Patents Company monopoly forced several filmmakers out of business, some dauntless independent producers—including NYMP's Bison company—looked for ways to continue to make their own films. Many of those independents simply packed up and left New York. They moved to Cuba, Florida, Louisiana, Texas, New Mexico, and California to avoid prosecution by the trust.[16] California—not as hot and humid as some of the other places—was close to the Mexican border if MPPC lawyers and detectives came snooping around. It proved to be the ideal locale.

More than a half-century later, in a book he coauthored about the formative years of the film industry, Fred Balshofer recalled those turbulent early days of the Bison company in southern California: "We were among the first of the moving picture companies to begin building a moving picture center in California. . . . As early as January, 1910, . . . we photographed scenes around Hollywood, riding out horses from the studio in Edendale to the picturesque hills over the winding roads. There were some adobe buildings on a fair-sized ranch just west of LaBrea Avenue and Hollywood Boulevard where we photographed many horse chases, gun battles, stagecoach holdups and other similar scenes for our Bison pictures before we discovered Griffith Park. Griffith Park was a beautiful place with tree-covered hills, ideal for western pictures. It was only a few miles from our studio, and many times we set up an Indian village and left it there for days at a time in the section now known as Griffith Park golf course."[17]

In 1911, the Bison company—featuring Hoot Gibson, Art Acord, Tex Cooper, George Gebhardt, Charles Inslee, Princess Mona Darkfeather, Jack Conway, Frank Montgomery, and several others—made films in Big Bear Valley, a remote summer resort in the San Bernardino Mountains, east of Los Angeles.[18] The location was isolated and somewhat perilous because of its steep terrain, so it kept the Bison players out of easy reach of the Patents Company detectives. That autumn, a surge of cold weather and the threat of snow in the mountains forced the company to return to Los Angeles. It was just about that time that the NYMP made its first contact with the Miller brothers.[19]

Fred Balshofer later wrote:

> Bauman learned that the Miller Brothers 101 Ranch Wild West show was in winter quarters at Venice, California, just a few miles down the coast from our location. Together we went to look over the show and the possibility of using it in our Bison pictures during the time they were wintering there. We talked out a deal with Joe Miller who was in charge of the show. I made out a personal check for a thousand dollars, payable to the Miller Brothers 101 Ranch to bind the deal.
>
> Our arrangement gave us the use of about seventy-five cowboys, twenty-five cowgirls, and about thirty-five Indians and their squaws, who spoke no English. One of the tribe, a rather fat squaw who called herself Minnie, was their teacher and interpreter. We hired Jim Brooks, manager of the show, who was a powerful ex-cowpuncher well able to rustle everybody up at sunrise and parade them up the coast to our sanctuary in the Santa Ynez Canyon, to be in charge of them. We also had the use of twenty-four oxen, some bison, and many horses complete with trappings, as well as prairie schooners and stage coaches.[20]

Rejuvenated by the association with the Millers, Bauman and Balshofer immediately went back into film production. They also came up with a new name for their company. In deference to the Miller brothers, it would be known as the Bison 101.[21] Although the company was short-lived, it would have a lasting impact on the film industry.

Chapter 32

INCEVILLE

Those were the days.[1]
—Hoot Gibson

THE deal forged in California between Fred Balshofer and Charles Bauman of the New York Motion Picture Company and the Miller brothers—which almost overnight created Bison 101 films—turned out to be a smart move for the movie company. With a huge gang of genuine 101 Ranch cowboys and Indians on the payroll, the frustrated founders of NYMP regained some of their swagger.

They had grown weary of looking over their shoulders for Al McCoy, the most tenacious of the Motion Picture Patents Company investigators. The Edison interests had employed McCoy and his cohorts to harass and track down any of the independent film producers who refused to kowtow to the imperious film monopoly and pay tribute in the form of substantial royalties.[2]

The NYMP executives and their Bison crews knew from firsthand experience that the Patents Company's so-called detectives liked to play rough. Many of them were little more than thugs, quite capable of using strong-arm tactics to terrorize the independent filmmakers they stubbornly pursued. Often, the companies being tormented by Patents Company operatives adopted similar techniques of intimidation just to stay in business.[3]

Allan Dwan was one of the early independent filmmakers in California who finally resorted to using guards armed with Winchesters to protect his film crews and actors. "The Patents Company hired goons for gunmen," recalled Dwan many years later. "If they saw a bunch of people working and it wasn't one of their companies, they'd shoot a hole through the camera. Without the camera you couldn't work, and cameras were impossible to get. The reason we came to places like California was to get away from these goons. Around Chicago and New York your life was in your hands if you went out with a camera. You'd find a bullet whizzing by your ear—bang, a hole in your camera. And so we sneaked out to California and hid away in little places. We worked in areas where you could see everything around you, and we stationed sentinels. I got my cowboys, the three Morrison brothers, together with one or two they hired in the neighborhood, and told them, 'If these fellows bother you, pop at them. Hit them in the foot, or something, but don't kill. Just let them know you're there.' "[4]

Like Dwan, Balshofer and Bauman hired cowboy muscle to protect their business interests. They appreciated it that the Millers and their rough riders were not about to allow gumshoes from back east to push around the Bison 101 film crews. The Miller brothers had not achieved their success as cattle barons and entertainers by pussyfooting around with folks who dared to get in their way or threaten their livelihood.[5]

Besides providing a substantial security force, the 101 Ranch served as the major outfitter and purveyor of livestock and personnel for the film company. For twenty-five hundred dollars a week, the Millers supplied a cadre of Indians, cowboys, cowgirls, and some of the most gifted performers on the show circuit.[6]

Soon after signing their agreement with the Bison company, the Miller brothers dispatched their trusted cousin W. A. Brooks and a group of the toughest 101 Ranch riders to protect the crew and actors and the film company's newest property lease—a spread of almost twenty thousand acres near Santa Monica. Brooks ordered fences and warning posters to be erected and placed armed cowboys on regular patrol around the huge tract of land. He also posted armed guards at the one ranch entrance, near Santa Ynez Canyon.[7]

Although most film historians credit Balshofer and Bauman with securing the services of the Millers and their personnel, other people claimed responsibility for bringing together the Bison Company and the Hundred and One.[8] One of the most vocal was Thomas Harper Ince. Not only a resourceful entrepreneur and spirited visionary, Ince was a gifted producer, director, actor, and screenwriter. Many film pioneers recognized Ince as the originator of the studio system.[9]

Born into an acting family in 1882 at Newport, Rhode Island, Ince made his stage debut at age six, appearing in vaudeville shows. He went on to appear on Broadway and in various road productions before moving to films, first as an actor and later as a director of several Biograph pictures.

Ince soon joined German-born Carl Laemmle's Independent Motion Picture Company, known as IMP.[10]

A production company founded in 1909 in defiance of Edison and the Motion Picture Patents Company, IMP prospered because of the diminutive and eccentric Laemmle's ability to recruit talented directors and actors such as Ince, Harry Salter, Florence Lawrence, King Baggott, and Mary Pickford, known as "Little Mary." When Laemmle became fearful of Patents Company detectives, he dispatched Ince and Pickford to Cuba to make IMP's films out of harm's way.[11]

In September 1911, Ince left IMP. Later that autumn, Ince—accompanied by his wife, cameraman Ray Smallwood, and a couple of other actors—arrived in Los Angeles to join New York Motion Pictures as a Bison director at the princely salary of $125 a week.[12]

"One day I hit upon the idea of putting on some Indian and Cowboy [sic] pictures in the mountain passes down Santa Monica way," Ince later explained in his version of how the Millers became partners with Bison. "So I leased the land and contracted with the Miller Brothers for the use of their entire stock, the '101 Ranch show' having just arrived at one of the nearby beach resorts for the summer months."[13]

But Ince's explanation did not fit with the commonly accepted timetable. In truth, the Millers had arrived in California in November 1911 to spend the winter and not the busy summer season, when their Wild West show was still on the road. Ince came to the West Coast at about the same time as the Millers. The deal between Bison and the Hundred and One was announced in the December 2, 1911, issue of *Moving Picture World*, days after the negotiations were completed.[14]

Regardless of which party initiated the relationship with the Millers and their outfit, Ince took control of film production at Bison 101 in California. Meanwhile, Balshofer pondered moving the entire company to the Millers' spread on the Salt Fork. During a business trip back east to inspect the latest Bell & Howell camera, Balshofer visited the 101 Ranch.[15]

Balshofer later wrote:

> Taking the railroad out of Chicago, I continued my trip to Ponca City, Oklahoma. Joe Miller met me at the train and we drove over some rough roads for almost an hour before finally reaching the ranch. The purpose of my visit was to ascertain if it would be possible to make our 101 Bison pictures in Oklahoma, as all of the Indians, cowboys, livestock, and other

paraphernalia we were using on the coast would be leaving in April [1912] to join the Miller road show. The Miller Brothers ranch was a vast spread of perhaps ten miles wide by fifteen miles long. Everything we needed for making western pictures was on that ranch, including a herd of bison, and close by was an Indian reservation [sic] where we could hire real Indians in their colorful native costumes. On a rise overlooking the layout was the Miller home. It was a mansion, painted white, and a real showplace. It was illuminated and heated by the natural gas readily available on the ranch. The oil actually oozed out of the ground in numerous places. This accessible oil eventually brought a fortune to the Miller family."[16]

Balshofer felt comfortable on the 101 Ranch and was impressed with the many resources he found there, but he ultimately decided against the move to Oklahoma. He found that as a potential movie site, the ranch lacked the spectacular scenery of the Santa Ynez Canyon near Santa Monica, where his crews shot most of the Bison 101 pictures. Balshofer recalled about his visit to the 101 Ranch:

> This new country was as flat as a pancake and had the further disadvantage of the stormy winter months which made it impossible even to consider making such a change. Joe and his brother Zack talked it over and felt they could get additional Indians, cowboys, and livestock, plus a couple of stagecoaches and other equipment around the ranch to make up their road show. This meant that they would have to take only their star performers from the group wintering at the coast. So we made a deal. Joe agreed to go along with me to California to straighten things out there, while Zack was to stay at the ranch to rustle things at that end. After Joe had selected what he needed from their winter quarters in Venice, California, we moved the rest of their outfit to our Santa Monica Canyon location. I persuaded Joe to let Brooks stay with us, and he was put in charge of looking after the Millers' interests as well as ours. It wasn't an easy task to arrange housing and a mess hall for the people and shelter and corrals for the livestock in such haste. Brooks helped to ease the situation by having the Indians set up their own tepee village almost at the crest of the south ridge of the canyon, and there they lived all by themselves.[17]

Will Brooks, who had worked with his cousins the Millers since the late 1880s, emerged as a key figure in the movie venture. Brooks proved remarkably masterful at solving the endless logistical nightmares which plagued the movie company, including the difficult problem of feeding hundreds of cast and crew members on location. Every day at high noon, Brooks and his helpers set up tables covered with identical sack lunches of premade sandwiches, cakes, and fresh fruit for the long line of hungry actors, extras, and workers. They simply picked up sacks and drew beverages of their choice from large urns of ice water, cold milk, and hot coffee.[18]

When the actors at Inceville discovered that large numbers of rattlesnakes and insects also resided on the movie ranch and slithered and crawled into the canvas tents used as dressing rooms, log cabins were quickly built. Later, more spacious barrack-style buildings replaced them and also served as a commissary and costume shop.[19]

Meanwhile, the enterprising Ince—pleased to have a rollicking company of real cowboys and Indians at his disposal—began production of another western film. The two-reel spectacle, *War on the Plains*, won instant praise from even the most demanding critics. "The true history of early life in the Wildest West is being written on film," gushed *Moving Picture World.* "The impression that it all leaves is that here we have a presentation of Western life that is real and that is true to life, and that we would like to see it again and again so as to absorb more of the details."[20]

Always a showman, Ince even suggested that with *War on the Plains*, featuring a throng of 101 Ranch riders and performers, he might have created the definitive western movie. "Forthwith the western sprang into instant favor," said Ince. "Producing companies everywhere set about the manufacture of cowboy and Indian films. Wild West shows were besieged with offers of employment to their members."[21]

By the time Ince filmed *War on the Plains*, almost all of the Bison 101 pictures were being produced on location at the company's twenty thousand acres in the rugged Santa Monica Mountains. The property had been part of a Spanish rancho named Topanga Malibu Sequit, for the three old Indian villages in the area. Dubbed the Miller 101 Bison Ranch, the big spread—rolling land covered with oak, chaparral, sage, and poppies—became known as Inceville.[22]

"Soon a Western town set, as well as living quarters, were [sic] built, together with a complete village of tepees for the Indians, somewhat removed," renowned historian William H. Goetzmann and his son, William N. Goetzmann, wrote of Inceville in *The West of the Imagination.* "As an organizer and producer, Ince was a genius who foreshadowed the studio moguls of the 1920s and '30s."[23]

Ince's ability to get the job done and improve working conditions impressed the Millers and their cowboys and cowgirls. To make life on location more bearable, the director installed a water system at Inceville for actors and crews.[24] But the Miller brothers and the cast of characters from the 101 Ranch most admired Ince for his work ethic—he toiled as hard and long as the lowliest laborer on the movie set. The Millers believed the ranch deserved to be named for the tireless director.

Inceville became a make-believe place where dreams came true. Part of the magic came from its location between the mountains and the ocean, not an easy site to reach. Visitors had to put up with "a road leading from Santa Monica, choked with dust in summer, and impassable with mud in winter. On rainy days everybody used to ride horseback from the Japanese fishing village where the car line ended."[25]

By February 1912, three months after Tom Ince and the Miller brothers arrived in California, their film company had produced four epic two-reeler movies—*War on the Plains, The Indian Massacre, The Battle of the Red Men*, and *The Deserter*.[26] The trade magazine *Film Fancies*, in its February 24 issue, declared, "The world has gone wild over the 101 Bison pictures. Critics who have seen Mr. Ince's work proclaim him the [David] Belasco of the moving picture business, and none can with fairness dispute his right to the appellation."[27]

Ince's early successes were made possible in large part by the quality cast and livestock from the 101 Ranch. The ranch horses were always top grade, and horseback riders didn't come any better than the men and women who rode for the Millers. The top-notch riding forced the film company's actors and actresses to improve their own equestrian skills; they often found themselves being pursued by gangs of extras who were some of the finest riders in the world.[28]

In some instances, such as with young film star Mabel Normand, this meant climbing on a horse for the first time. Normand was a Boston native who had spent much of her youth in New York as an artists' model before becoming an actress and moving to California. Will Brooks taught her to ride on a 101 Ranch mount, just like several other city-bred thespians at Inceville. Within a short time, Normand was able to do many of her own horseback stunts.[29]

Besides the Millers' talented cowboys and cowgirls riding for the film company, a sizable force of Indian entertainers added their considerable horseback skills to movies under production at Inceville. Many had appeared with the Millers' touring companies and some had also performed with Buffalo Bill Cody, Pawnee Bill Lillie, or in one of the other major Wild West shows. Several of the Indian performers, especially the Oglala Sioux from Pine Ridge Reservation in South Dakota, had direct ties to legendary warriors from the past. Some of them had fought as young men in fierce engagements against the United States Army, including the Battle of the Little Bighorn.

One of the elders with the Millers' Indian troupe was Lone Bear, former high chief of the Sioux, a medicine man in Sitting Bull's camp, and a veteran of the 1876 battle with George Armstrong Custer.[30] Instead of riding ponies at Inceville, Lone Bear spent most of his time in Venice, where many of the Millers' show people resided.

Late in 1912, Lone Bear was reunited with a figure from the distant past—Henry Stanley, a Civil War veteran and old Indian fighter, visiting California from his home in Kansas City. While sightseeing on the Venice Pier with tourists, Stanley spied a bent figure wrapped in a blanket. As he came closer, the old soldier recognized Lone Bear. After the Black Hills campaign, when Lone Bear was taken prisoner and jailed at Fort Sill near Lawton in what was then Indian Territory, Stanley was a soldier guard. The two men had become acquainted and developed a friendship.[31] After having been out of touch for decades, the two elderly men met several times during Stanley's vacation. They talked of their youth and remembered the old times. Before Stanley returned home, Lone Bear presented his former guard with a special gift—a piece of soft elk skin covered with beads.[32]

Luther Standing Bear, who had joined the Millers in 1911, was another popular 101 Ranch Sioux who enjoyed mixing with the swarms of visitors at the Venice Pier. He operated an archery concession on the pier that helped supplement the wages he earned as a movie extra and actor.[33] A capable actor and showman, Standing Bear was even more competent with his bow and arrow. At the pier, several Japanese archers, clad in elegant kimonos and bearing their homeland's traditional bows and arrows, frequently challenged Standing Bear to shooting contests. None ever bested the Sioux marksman, with his unerring eye.[34]

Employing Indians in films was not a new concept for the folks at Bison 101. Even before it combined forces with the Miller brothers, the Bison company had used Indian actors—particularly Young Deer and his wife, Red Wing—in some of its early movies shot around Fort Lee and Coytesville, New Jersey.[35] However, when it came to character leads, filmmakers always cast white actors and actresses such as Evelyn Graham or Charles Inslee. In the 1909 Bison film *The True Heart of an Indian*, Inslee donned a black wig with braids and wore a breechcloth.

After Tom Ince became a principal director for the film company in California, he saw to it that William Eagleshirt, an Oglala, was one of the first Indian actors to land a major role in the westerns produced at Inceville.[36] By using real Indians such as Eagleshirt—an imposing figure in flowing warbonnet and authentic Sioux costume—Ince won much critical acclaim.

Although other movie companies tried to match these celebrated Bison 101 films, none could ever duplicate the pictures made at Inceville. Both Ince and the Millers knew much of the popularity of their movies came from the large numbers of Indians in the casts. "The Indians were of the Sioux tribe," Ince wrote, "from one of the government reservations, who had been loaned to the wild west show [the Millers']. When I took them over, I had to sign an agreement with the Indian commissioner in Washington according to which the Indians were to have certain hours of schooling. I furthermore had to assume full responsibility for their well being and care."[37]

Ince's condescending attitude toward Indians carried over to other aspects of the movie business, including publicity and marketing. To boost cinema ticket sales, press agents put out the word that the Indians of Inceville were so dangerous that guards had to keep them from scalping other members of the cast and crew. It also was rumored that a hapless white actor was severely wounded by a crazed Indian wielding a tomahawk and that the film directors and their assistants constantly had to prevent Indian extras from loading their weapons with live ammunition during filming.[38]

The exaggerations and outright lies told about the Inceville Indians became so outrageous that even Ince had to come to their defense. "Arousing their anger sufficiently to attack the enemy with any semblance of reality was one of the hardest things I ever had to tackle in my whole career in motion pictures," Ince admitted when pressed about his Indian actors.[39]

The blatant racism of the time was a key factor in the decision not to award starring roles to Indians. Beyond bigotry, the quandary of giving Indians better billing was further exacerbated because—except for traditional dances and ceremonials—play-acting was not part of the culture of most Indian tribes. Their main contribution to early westerns came from the air of authenticity their very presence brought to the screen.[40]

That was why Ince and other directors relegated Indians to small parts or roles as crowd-scene extras but invariably preferred non-Indians for lead roles. Some of those recruits chosen to "play Indian" in early western moving pictures included Anna Little, an aspiring California actress who went on to play in other westerns with such stars as Art Acord; Francis Ford, older brother and mentor of film director John Ford; and Sessue Hayakawa, a Japanese actor who toured the American West in 1913, where Ince saw him and offered him a movie contract.[41]

Throughout this period, the more vocal Indian actors attempted to expand their influence on the films under production at Inceville. Led by Luther Standing Bear, these activists pointed out to Ince that his films would be even more authentic if he used more Indians in major roles. A frustrated Standing Bear offered to provide script ideas and even volunteered to serve as a language coach for the other Sioux actors. To the Indians' disappointment, Ince never agreed to any of their suggestions.[42]

As Ince and his associates continued to crank out more films in California throughout 1912, the Bison 101 parent company, New York Motion Picture Company, led by Charles Bauman and Adam Kessel, founded another production studio in New York City. They dubbed the new operation Keystone Film Company and hired away from Biograph a seasoned director named Mack Sennett.[43] Sennett—a true comedic genius—attracted to Keystone such leading players as Fred Mace, Ford Sterling, Henry "Pathé" Lehrman, and brunette beauty Mabel Normand. By March 1912, after shooting several comedy pictures in and around New York, the entire Keystone operation, including its lineup of film stars, migrated to California.[44]

"All our [Bison 101's] western pictures were being made out at our rapidly growing studio within the fenced-in area in Santa Ynez Canyon [Inceville], where trespassing became too dangerous for the detectives of the Patents Company," recalled Balshofer. "This meant our Edendale [Los Angeles] studio was idle, so we made it the permanent studio for producing our Keystone comedies. It was there that Sennett began making them, all split-reelers, about the middle of April, 1912."[45]

Within a short time, Keystone would add several more up-and-coming stars to its entourage, including Roscoe "Fatty" Arbuckle, Charles Chaplin, Marie Dressler, Gloria Swanson, Ben Turpin, Chester Conklin, Phyllis Haver, and many others.[46] For those bright young directors, there was no looking back. Their optimism proved contagious—at least for a while.

As the power struggle between the Patents Company and the independent filmmakers continued, the feisty casts and crews at Edendale and Inceville thumbed their noses at the world. After all, they reasoned, they had the protection of the Miller brothers and their gang of riders toting shotguns, Winchesters, and bows and arrows—they had the Real Wild West as guardians. It would be a short but sweet ride that none of them—especially the Millers—would ever forget.

HOLLYWOOD-ON-THE-ARKANSAS

ALTHOUGH CALIFORNIA ENDED up as the primary locale for the film industry, many of the motion pictures produced in the early years had an Oklahoma setting or featured an abundance of native-born or adopted Oklahomans. The fervent love affair between Oklahoma and the movie industry resulted in large part from the influence of the Millers and the 101 Ranch.

During the first three decades of the twentieth century, nearly every film, especially the western movies with an Oklahoma connection, could have been traced to the Miller family or to one of their associates. Even as the Millers and their outfit basked in the sunshine of southern California, their 101 Ranch on the Salt Fork of the Arkansas acted as a springboard for scores of well-known performing artists and others who left their marks on Hollywood.[1]

The extensive Hundred and One empire contained many of the ingredients necessary for a western movie—cowboys, cowgirls, Indians, herds of horses, cattle, and bison, and wide-open spaces. In spite of the fact that film directors such as William Selig, Fred Balshofer, and Thomas Ince ultimately chose California as a base for their studios and film locations, the 101 Ranch distinctly influenced the industry, if only because of the actors and actresses it produced.[2]

Throughout the early 1900s, many Oklahoma cowboys and cowgirls made the natural transition from riding the range to performing with Wild West shows and then effortlessly shifted to western films for a bit of easy money. Not only did numerous moving-picture cowboys and cowgirls come from the 101 Ranch, but several of the earliest motion pictures shot in Oklahoma either were produced on the Millers' spread or involved their close friends.[3]

One example was *The Wolf Hunt*, filmed in 1908 by Bennie Kent, the pioneer cameraman who worked on and off for the 101 Ranch for many years. It featured some of the Millers' cohorts, including former lawman and rancher John B. Abernathy and William M. Tilghman, an old buffalo hunter and famous federal marshal from the days when George Washington

Miller drove Texas cattle up the good grass trails. The movie's genesis had occurred several years earlier when President Theodore Roosevelt, en route from a Rough Riders reunion in Texas, paused in Oklahoma Territory for a wolf hunt. Roosevelt had been captivated by Oklahoman Jack "Catch 'em Alive" Abernathy, who chased down wolves and subdued them with his bare hands.[4]

With encouragement from T.R. to document his daring deed on film, Abernathy founded Oklahoma Natural Mutoscene Company. *The Wolf Hunt* was shot in one week in the Wichita Mountains with Kent behind his Curtis motion-picture camera and Tilghman acting as director. As promised, an enthusiastic Roosevelt proudly showed the movie to cabinet members and guests in the East Room of the White House in February 1909.[5]

Along with Abernathy and a gang of horsemen, Al Jennings—a familiar Oklahoma character and reformed outlaw well acquainted with the Miller brothers—appeared in the chase scenes of *The Wolf Hunt*. Jennings also had received star billing for his role in a film produced in 1908 by Oklahoma Natural Mutoscene Company—a one-reeler, *The Bank Robbery*.[6]

In the late 1890s—about the time Joe Miller ended up in prison on a counterfeiting conviction—Jennings' criminal calling was interrupted by a penitentiary term after a bungled train robbery. "The word 'notorious' was often applied to outlaw Al Jennings, but it referred more to his failures than to his skill," explained film historian Kevin Brownlow. "He had the unhappy experience of blowing up the safe of a baggage car, only to find the car wrecked and the safe unharmed. In an attempt to save the day, Jennings robbed the passengers, grabbed a bunch of bananas and a jug of whisky from the wreckage, and rode away."[7]

Jennings did not get very far. Eventually the long arm of the law snatched him up. After Jennings had languished in prison for five years, President William McKinley commuted his sentence. In 1907, President Roosevelt granted the inept desperado a full pardon. A contrite Jennings immediately returned to Oklahoma, where he opened a law practice in Lawton and started his profession as a movie actor.[8]

In *The Bank Robbery*, shot in Cache, Oklahoma, just west of Lawton, Jennings basically played himself and provided technical expertise while Tilghman directed the production and Kent captured the action on film.[9] The movie company hired citizens of Cache to play Jennings' outlaw gang and posse members, as well as townsfolk in crowd scenes filmed on dusty streets and after working hours at the local bank. Some of the gunfight and robbery scenes proved so realistic that a bystander vaulted out of a bank window and raced to find law officers.[10]

Kent also filmed *A Round-Up in Oklahoma*, a one-reeler which Tilghman directed for Oklahoma Natural Mutoscene Company. Produced during the summer of 1908 on the 101 Ranch, the movie related the story of some hardworking drovers herding cattle up the trail from Texas to Kansas and warding off the attacks of renegade Indians. The script was custom-made for the Millers and the cowboys and Indians in their employ.[11]

Within a few years, some of the Millers' top riders found more juicy acting roles when Geronimo Film Company, an independent outfit based in Lawton with a studio location in the Wichita Mountains, began to produce movies billed as "True To Nature Western Films." Fred Phillips, youngest brother of Oklahoma oil tycoons Frank and Waite Phillips and a friend of the Miller brothers, acted as the film company's treasurer.[12]

Vern and Edith Tantlinger, who helped direct the Millers' Wild West cowboys and cowgirls, landed starring roles in *The Sign of the Smoke*, Geronimo Film Company's big western of 1915. The five-reeler also featured White Parker, son of Quanah Parker, with support from "Miss Fay Kent and Full Cast of Competents," a reference to the one hundred Comanches who appeared in the movie.[13]

In the early 1900s, more fledgling film companies sprouted on the Oklahoma prairies along the banks of the Arkansas River. Appropriately, the most successful producers of these horse operas were peace officers, outlaws or, in several instances, both.

One of the best examples was the ubiquitous Al Jennings, who had learned the art of storytelling while doing time in an Ohio penitentiary where he befriended William Sydney Porter, better known as celebrated author O. Henry. Based on the success of one-reelers shot in 1908 by Oklahoma Natural Mutoscene Company, Jennings continued his sporadic film career. He also began to dabble in politics. By 1914, the retired outlaw became a candidate for governor of Oklahoma, the state that had once placed a hefty bounty on his head. "If elected I promise to be honest for a year—if I can hold out that long," Jennings boasted during a campaign stop. He also told voters that they could trust a train robber far more than they could trust dishonest politicians. During the Democratic primary election, Jennings managed a strong third-place finish, garnering more than 24 percent of the vote.[14]

That same year, Jennings again played himself as a train robber and acted as technical adviser in *Beating Back*, an action-packed film set in

Oklahoma but shot in New Jersey. The film portrayed peace officers as incompetent, callous, and self-serving and depicted Jennings as a victim of circumstances, driven into a life of crime.[15]

The film so incensed veteran lawman Bill Tilghman that he decided to set the record straight by making a film of his own. Tilghman—along with his old running mate, Chris Madsen, and former United States Marshal E. D. Nix—formed Eagle Film Company in Oklahoma City.[16] Captain Lute P. Stover, whose army unit had provided the guards for Geronimo when the Apache captive made his celebrated appearance at the Millers' 101 Ranch in June 1905, was hired to write a script with assistance from Tilghman. Bennie Kent, resplendent in his ever-present derby hat and with his coat pockets crammed with cigars, acted as chief photographer.[17]

Together, they produced *The Passing of the Oklahoma Outlaws*, a six-part film re-creating the high crimes and subsequent demise of several of Oklahoma's most notorious desperadoes—Al Jennings, Henry Starr, Bill Doolin, and Cattle Annie and Little Britches. Filming continued throughout the winter and spring of 1915.[18]

Many of the leading roles were filled by former law officers such as Nix, Madsen, and J. F. "Uncle Bud" Ledbetter. The cast also featured several members of the Millers' 101 Ranch Wild West show. After a special preview showing in Chandler, Oklahoma, in July 1915, *The Passing of the Oklahoma Outlaws* premiered in Oklahoma City that summer and was shown across the state and nation. For the next eight years, Tilghman busily traveled with his morality flicker and lectured on the folly of a life of crime.[19]

In 1924, Tilghman came out of semiretirement when a delegation of citizens from Cromwell, Oklahoma, asked him to clean up the oil boomtown, reputed to be the wickedest community in the state.[20]

"If I don't get killed in a gun fight," said seventy-year-old Tilghman, "I'll have to go to bed some day and die like a woman, and I don't want to do that."[21] Tilghman got his wish. One November evening, a drunken prohibition officer shot him down and killed him in Cromwell. His body was taken to the state capitol in Oklahoma City, where it lay in state with a guard of honor for three days.[22] Many of the mourners who doffed their big hats and paid final respects at Tilghman's coffin hailed from 101 Ranch.

"Tilghman was the most colorful lawman to involve himself in pictures, but several lesser-known personalities added color of their own to early pictures," Brownlow wrote. "Pat Fields, a nephew of Henry Starr, who became a lawman instead of an outlaw, was a friend of Tom Mix and spent several years playing supporting roles in Mix Westerns."[23]

Oklahoma bank robber Henry Starr—like Joe Miller, Al Jennings, and O. Henry—served time in the penitentiary at Columbus, Ohio. Starr later worked briefly at the 101 Ranch, and involved himself in the movie business while he continued his outlaw life. Just as Tilghman and his company were filming *The Passing of the Oklahoma Outlaws*, Starr and his bandit band attempted to pull off a feat never before accomplished—robbing two banks at the same time.[24]

Starr selected Stroud, Oklahoma, as his target. As Starr later explained to Tilghman, "When I came to Stroud to look it over, I saw it was just as easy to rob two banks as one, so I decided to kill two birds with one stone."[25]

Starr's plan to loot a pair of banks—a deed the Dalton gang had failed to do years before at Coffeyville, Kansas—went off without a hitch. In broad daylight on March 27, 1915, Starr and his gang made their move. Shortly after riding into town, the seven unmasked outlaws struck like lightning at the Stroud National Bank and the First National Bank of Stroud.

However, as Starr and the other brazen bandits mounted their horses and prepared to ride out of town with six thousand dollars, Paul Curry, a seventeen-year-old butcher's apprentice, took potshots at the gang with a sawed-off .30-30 Winchester rifle used for killing hogs. Curry's aim was true. One of the slugs tore through Starr's hips, and he fell from his horse.[26]

"I'll be damned," Starr told the authorities who arrested him. "I don't mind getting shot, knew it would happen sooner or later. But a kid with a hog gun—that hurts my pride."[27]

News of the audacious attempt to loot two banks at one time spread quickly. Tilghman, seventeen miles away in Chandler, where his company was filming *The Passing of the Oklahoma Outlaws*, strapped on his guns and rushed to the scene to help local authorities pursue the other gang members. After making additional arrests, Tilghman returned to Chandler and film production. Bennie Kent also came along and filmed Starr lying wounded at the hospital. Kent even recorded on film Zack Mulhall, the old showman and rancher and pal of the Millers, visiting the injured bank robber.[28]

At his trial a few months later, Starr pleaded guilty to bank robbery and was sentenced to twenty-five years in the state prison at McAlester.

Before guards ushered him from the crowded courtroom, he went over to Curry, shook his hand, and congratulated him for his courage and marksmanship.[29]

Predictably, Starr was an model inmate at McAlester. He taught spelling and composition to fellow prisoners, served as the prison librarian, and won sympathy because of his damaged leg. Paroled for good behavior in 1919, Starr followed the example of former outlaws Emmett Dalton and Al Jennings and went into the movie business, purchasing a quarter interest in Pan-American Motion Picture Company in Tulsa.[30]

Historically, Tulsa had been a rough-and-tumble town where outlaw gangs found refuge in territorial days. Fugitives usually lurked on Standpipe Hill, a lofty perch just north of the Frisco tracks which allowed them to use spyglasses to see if lawmen's horses were tied to hitching posts along city streets.[31]

"If they [outlaws] spotted no lawmen's mounts from their lookout . . . they boldly walked Tulsa's streets, ate at its cafes, and traded at its stores," wrote Oklahoma historian Danney Goble. "Typical purchases included suspicious amounts of gunpowder and ammunition. Otherwise, they hardly bothered local businesses, since both parties assumed a live-and-let-live attitude, the outlaws receiving shelter, the businesses security."[32]

With the discovery of rich deposits of oil and gas in the region, Tulsa shook off its frontier image and transformed itself into a center of trade and commerce. Some of the same outlaws who had once used Tulsa for a hideout went on to serve on the police force or joined one of the many motion-picture companies with headquarters in the city. A few, such as Emmett Dalton—sole survivor of the Dalton gang's 1892 Coffeyville, Kansas, raid—did both.[33]

After serving time in a Kansas prison for the Coffeyville raid, Dalton believed police work and moviemaking would be his best pursuits. Although he eventually moved to California, Dalton started his movie career in Tulsa, where he took notice of the successes of local film producer William Smith's motion-picture company. In 1912, Dalton produced *The Last Stand of the Dalton Boys,* which a critic described as "a mediocre three-reel account of his lawless career." Dalton's *Beyond the Law*, an expanded film version of the same story, came out in 1918. In this film, Dalton not only played himself but also appeared as his slain brothers Bob and Frank.[34]

During this period, several studios in the Tulsa area turned out nothing but action-packed western movies. It was a golden opportunity for some of the old Oklahoma desperadoes, including Dalton and Starr, to "go on the scout" and ride the outlaw trail once again.[35]

In 1919, Starr and his partners in Pan-American Motion Picture Company produced *Debtor to the Law,* the film story of Starr's ill-fated attempt to rob two banks in one raid. Film production started in Stroud, where actual locations, including the banks, were used. Starr played himself, as did Paul Curry, the young marksman who had shot Starr out of the saddle as he tried to make his getaway. Other supporting roles went to bank employees and local residents.[36]

Problems besieged the film from the start. Interior shots in the banks were poorly filmed and had to be scrapped. George Rhems, the director, became thoroughly disgruntled with the script as well as with Starr, who proved to be totally unsatisfactory as an actor, even when playing himself. Patrick S. McGeeney, a popular western novelist of the time, was recruited to breathe new life into the story, and Shamrock Motion Picture Studio stepped in to help with production at its studios in San Antonio. Starr stayed on as a technical consultant but William Karl Hackett, a noted screen actor, replaced him in the lead role.[37]

Although the finished movie did not attract many favorable reviews, *Debtor to the Law* became enough of a success to earn Starr at least fifteen thousand dollars under the film company's profit-sharing agreement. Starr never received a dime, however. Ironically, the man whom many people considered the most notorious bank robber of all time was cheated out of his share of profits by his partners.[38]

Unable to afford legal help to recover his money and afraid of going to California to pursue film opportunities because of an outstanding warrant against him from an 1893 Arkansas robbery, Starr decided to stay in Oklahoma and make more movies. All he needed was another grubstake. He turned to old friends, including the Millers, for financial assistance. Most of the folks he approached were obliging and offered Starr modest loans.[39]

"Every now and then, Henry would show up at some 101 cow camp," Fred Gipson wrote years later in his book about the 101 Ranch. "Zack [Miller] learned to like the man and got after Henry to quit the outlaw game. And once Henry did quit for a spell. . . . But the next thing anybody knew, Henry was making long rides again, following the dim trails and watching back over his shoulder like a coyote."[40] Finally, to come up with the money he needed to pay his growing pile of bills and to stay in the film game, Starr determined that the time had come to do what he did best—rob a bank.[41]

The last time Zack Miller saw Henry Starr was on February 2, 1921, when Starr showed up in a motorcar at the 101 Ranch. He tried to convince Milt Hinkle, one of the Millers' veteran rodeo riders, to take a few days off and accompany him on a trip to Texas and Arkansas.[42] Zack still had a fondness for the rascally Starr because he had once worked on the ranch and had briefly appeared with the Millers' Wild West show, but Zack smelled a polecat. He told Hinkle not to leave the 101 Ranch.

Many years later, Hinkle recalled Zack's exact words of advice. "Zack said, 'Milt, I have a job for you to do, so don't you go any place with that fellow. You are headed for trouble. You know you just missed getting into trouble a few years ago, so take my advice, don't go.' " Hinkle did just as Zack told him, and Starr drove off without another word.[43]

On February 18, Starr and three companions drove into Harrison, Arkansas, in an automobile.[44] They parked and strolled into People's National Bank with their .45-caliber pistols drawn. Starr wore a stylish dark pinstripe suit and silk cravat. The armed men held frightened customers and employees at gunpoint and began to scoop up cash. Former bank president W. J. Meyers happened to be there and remembered that twelve years before, he had hidden a rifle in the vault. While the robbers were busy collecting their loot, Meyers grabbed the weapon—a .38-40 Winchester Model 1873 rifle—and opened fire. The slug slammed into Starr, severing his spine. He crashed to the floor and his accomplices fled empty-handed. All of them were soon captured.[45]

On February 22, Starr died on a jail cot. His mother and new wife were at his side. The couple had been married one year to the day. Also present was a son from an earlier marriage, Theodore Roosevelt Starr, named for the cowboy president who had granted Starr a pardon years before.[46]

"I have robbed more banks than any man in the United States," Starr had told his doctor the day before he died. "It doesn't pay. I was in debt two thousand dollars and had to have money, so I turned bank robber again. I am sorry but the deed is done."[47]

Although he died in debt, Starr received a decent burial. Years earlier, he had paid a Tulsa undertaker for a proper coffin and funeral. Just as Starr requested, he was laid to rest just north of the little town of Dewey, Oklahoma.[48] The procession of cars and horseback riders extended from the graveyard clear back to town. It was the largest funeral in Dewey's history. A contingent of mourners from the 101 Ranch had ridden across the Osage prairies that winter day to say farewell to one of their own.[49]

"Outlawing had got into his blood and he couldn't quit it," Zack Miller explained in *Fabulous Empire*. "Just like hooch will sometimes get the upper hold on a man."[50]

Zack's summation of Henry Starr validated another explanation of his life that the bandit himself had once offered years before his death: "Life in the open, the rides at night, the spice of danger, the mastery over men, the pride of being able to hold a mob at bay—it tingles in my veins. I love it. It is wild adventure."[51]

Like so many others, Starr's life and death instantly became entwined in myth and legend. He had made the transition from the days when outlaws rode quarter horses and wore boots and jeans to a time when they arrived at banks in swift motorcars and wore tailored business suits and neckties.

Henry Starr's story was pure Hollywood. It was pure Oklahoma. And like the lives of so many other cowboys, it was the stuff of movies.

Chapter 33

A VANISHING BREED

The West vanished for the Indian and the drover; it vanished for the cowboy. Simultaneously it reappeared in all the same places, and in movies and rodeos. It's like fire. Hollywood, calf tables, and depreciation schedules can't kill it.[1]

—Thomas McGuane
Foreword, *Vanishing Breed*

THE Miller brothers and their diverse empire flourished even as darkening clouds overshadowed Europe and the rest of the world—an omen of what would be called the Great War. Yet while the century reached its adolescence and approached its turbulent teen years—a span marked by great violence and radical change—the Millers had enough time only for the moment at hand.

Like most of the nation, they entertained no thoughts of global warfare. The Millers believed that Democratic presidential candidate Woodrow Wilson—who would eventually win the 1912 and 1916 elections—would keep the United States out of squabbles between foreign nations far across the sea.[2]

Antics on the mountainous movie lots of Inceville, distractions along the beachfront at Venice, and the constant flow of activity at the sprawling 101 Ranch in Oklahoma guaranteed that the Millers and their outfit stayed very much grounded in the present. Political assassinations, U-boat attacks, and poison gas could not even be imagined as the Millers and their partner, Edward Arlington, prepared for several more seasons with their popular and profitable Wild West extravaganzas. Early in 1912, the Millers and Arlington ran advertisements in *Billboard* and other trade publications seeking new cowboy and cowgirl talent for their show.[3] As usual, the ads brought a flood of responses from across the nation to the New York offices of Miller Brothers & Arlington, on West Fifty-second Street, in the heart of Manhattan. It seemed that everyone wanted to ride for the Hundred and One.

From the White House office at the ranch in Oklahoma, George Miller kept the business running as smoothly as the new Cadillac automobile he purchased in 1912.[4] The Millers' brother-in-law, William England, a successful lawyer in Kansas City, remained a trusted legal confidant to George and his brothers. England regularly communicated with George on such family business matters as paying medical bills and providing a stipend for Walter T. "Uncle Doc" Miller, elder brother of G. W. Miller. Uncle Doc's declining health kept him hospitalized in Winfield, Kansas.[5]

Unfortunately, not all the Miller family affairs could be handled as smoothly as shelling out a few dollars to care for an ailing uncle, buying expensive jewelry for the womenfolk, or quietly slipping a financial contribution to a politician in exchange for favors. The stormy marriages of the Miller brothers proved much more difficult.

Although he tried to be a good father, Joe Miller's marriage suffered greatly from his penchant for the ladies and the great demands the diverse ranch business placed on his time, thereby keeping him apart from his wife and children. However, of the marriages of the three brothers, Zack's union with Mabel Pettijohn was particularly tempestuous.

By 1912, Zack and Mabel's stormy six-year marriage had finally played out. On shaky ground almost from the start, the relationship only eroded further during the long road trips and separations which led each to accuse the other of infidelity. The fact that they had a daughter, Virginia, did little to cement the couple, and neither was especially proficient or attentive when it came to parenting.

In 1911, at the insistence of his brothers, Zack, resolved to terminate the marriage, had hired a crack private investigator named Harry Edward Stege to track Mabel's movements.[6] Stege, former superintendent of the Bureau of Identification at Kansas City and Oklahoma City, had established a detective agency in Oklahoma City with Shirley Dyer, a veteran law officer and former chief of detectives in Oklahoma City.[7] By 1913, Stege—known for using innovative criminal investigative and identification procedures—would join the Tulsa Police Department, becoming the first of four generations of Harry Steges to serve on the city's force.[8]

"We are in receipt of information as to the present whereabouts of your wife from a friend of ours," Dyer wrote to Zack on December 28, 1911. "And having heard that your [sic] seeking to get legal service on her without result we take this means of informing you, thinking that perhaps you may be still interested in locating her for the same or other purposes."[9]

On January 2, 1912, Stege sent a detailed follow-up dispatch to the ranch in care of George Miller. "I have succeeded in getting hold of our informant in the matter concerning (HER) and he insists that he saw her here on the streets on two different occasions and after the suit had been filed and that he knows her well having seen her with the show many times."[10]

Stege further reported that Mabel had been spotted purchasing a train ticket in the company of a man who had formerly worked with the Millers' show. "We shall keep our eyes and ears open for anything in the line and inform you of the same," wrote Stege.[11] Ultimately, proper divorce papers were served and processed and the marriage ended.

Supported by his brothers and the rest of the extended 101 family, Zack used the flurry of activity at the ranch in Oklahoma and on the movie lots in California to help him forget the bad times and look forward to a bright future. He was not disappointed in the new show season, and neither were his brothers.

The 1912 season was unusual for the Miller and Arlington Wild West show because every show date was played west of Ohio, with no appearances in any of the larger metropolitan areas.[12] As always, it was an action-packed year.

Early that spring, just prior to launching the show's long tour, the Millers produced a no-holds-barred rodeo on the Lucky Baldwin Ranch near Arcadia, just east of Los Angeles, at the foot of the San Gabriel Mountains.[13] Purchased in 1875 by a flamboyant silver-mining magnate named E. J. "Lucky" Baldwin—the man who founded Arcadia and helped introduce horse racing to southern California—the ranch, part of a Spanish land grant, had become a showplace.[14]

Years later, the Los Angeles State and County Arboretum—a 127-acre garden of exotic flora and fauna—would be created on part of Baldwin's estate. The old ranch was also eventually discovered by the movie studios in nearby Hollywood. Some folks claimed it became the most photographed spot in the world. Through the years, many film projects such as Tarzan flicks, Bing Crosby's *Road to Singapore*, the classic movie rendition of *The African Queen*, the television series *Fantasy Island*, and the miniseries *Roots* were filmed or partly filmed there.[15]

But in 1912, there were no signs of any of the scores of stars who would come to the place for film projects. Instead, the big crowds of Californians who flocked to the ranch watched Joe Miller and his handsome riders swoop into the arena, sending clouds of powdery dust into the air.

The Millers' show formally opened the new season at Santa Monica on Saturday, March 23. For two hectic weeks, the outfit played bookings in more than a dozen southern California cities—Long Beach, Pomona, San Bernardino, Pasadena, Anaheim, San Diego, Los Angeles, Escondido, Santa Ana, Corona, and Redlands. The three-day stand at Praeger Park in Los Angeles included a contest of Olympic track and field stars designed to raise funds to send the athletes to the forthcoming Olympic Games at Stockholm, Sweden. Joe Miller and Edward Arlington saw to it that the Olympic Games Committee received an ample percentage of the advance ticket sales and posted a ticket wagon on the showgrounds.[16]

Jack Hoxie, a native of Kingfish Creek, Oklahoma, and a square-jawed cowboy destined to become a star in numerous Hollywood silents and talkies, appeared with the Millers for the first time during the early spring shows in California.[17]

Weeks of strenuous rehearsals paid off. The ranch show concluded its swing through southern California at Venice with a pair of performances, described as "a swan song," before leaving for the road. The *Venice Vanguard* commended the 101 Ranch performers for their fine deportment and pointed out that the show folks had spent a great deal of their earnings at restaurants and hotels while wintering in the beach city.[18] The newspaper neglected to mention all the additional money the Millers' performers had left at the city's numerous brothels, saloons, and gambling dens, where they played roll-down games, razzle-dazzle, and chuck-a-luck.

At the close of the second Venice production, the Miller crews packed up all the winter gear at the athletic field and headed for the railroad station. Reinforcements of fresh horses and riders arrived from the headquarters ranch in Oklahoma. With a large complement of cowboys, cowgirls, and Indian performers left behind for film work at Inceville under the direction of the Millers' cousin Will Brooks, the rest of the outfit boarded the waiting Santa Fe trains and headed north over the Tehachapi Mountains into the San Joaquin Valley.[19]

The Miller-Arlington show performed every single day without a break from April 8, when the run opened at Bakersfield, California, through May 11, at Idaho Falls, Idaho. Along the way came a five-day stand at San Francisco, a two-day stand at Oakland, and a string of one-day appearances throughout northern California, including Fresno, San Jose, Lodi, Oroville, Stockton, and Auburn. The show then crossed the Sierras into Nevada for stops at Reno and Winnemucca.[20] Even the catastrophic news of the sinking of the ocean liner *Titanic* that April failed to keep fans away from the Millers' shows.

After appearances across Idaho and Utah and stops at fourteen towns in Montana and Washington, the show journeyed into British Columbia for performances at New Westminster and Vancouver. From there, the outfit crossed Puget Sound aboard the steamer *Princess Mary* and a pair of Southern Pacific barges to play at Victoria, the picturesque city on the tip of Vancouver Island, considered by Joe Miller as the banner site of the show season.[21]

The show returned to the United States for appearances throughout the Northwest before returning to Canada. During the rest of the summer and the fall, the show stopped in the Dakotas, Minnesota, Iowa, and Nebraska, and barnstormed Wisconsin, Illinois, Indiana, Ohio, Kentucky, Missouri, Kansas, Oklahoma, Louisiana, Texas, and Arkansas.[22]

"The 101 Ranch Wild West has more railroad cars, more wagons, more seats, more horses, more buffaloes and long-horned steers, more cowboys, more cowgirls, more Indians, more Mexicans, and more and greater variety and multiplicity of novel and original, individual and collective features than any other solely western exhibition in existence to-day," the Miller and Arlington 1912 show program boldly proclaimed.[23] The program discussed in vivid terms the "equine outlaws" and "bucking bronchos [sic] who hate mankind" and were "demons incarnate, a menace to life and limb."

The Millers reserved the most colorful descriptions for the white performers. They were depicted as "masters and mistresses of the lariat, who can make a coil of slender rope act as if enchanted," and as "keen-eyed and clean-hearted cowboys and cowgirls, grown brown and strong on the tremendous stretches of Oklahoma range-land owned by the Miller Brothers."[24]

On the other hand, the Millers portrayed their Indian entertainers as "pure blooded people of the wild old days" and in other equally patronizing terms. The show program proclaimed:

> Many famous chieftains are enrolled among the hundred Indians Miller Bros. & Arlington have gathered from many reservations. With them come wrinkled squaws, young belles of the wigwam, gay braves, and papooses, swinging uncomplaining on their mothers' back.
>
> In spite of government and in spite of education, the Indian clings to

> old customs and old traditions. The men remain strangers to work and refuse to be introduced. They insist upon the wife performing all labor, whether there be one or three. The squaws of the 101 Ranch Wild West carry the baggage, build the fires, erect the tepees and saddle the horses. Their reward from their stronger mates is generally a cigarette, which the squaws relish immensely.[25]

Such descriptions apparently worked. Every performance drew great numbers of patrons, all of them anxious to see cowboys and Indians, Mexican vaqueros, the Imperial Russian Cossacks, and such novel events as auto polo, in which the daring contestants competed in speedy motorcars instead of on the backs of swift ponies.[26]

The 1912 season was not without misfortunes. In Wisconsin one August night while the show train made the sixty-five-mile run from Beaver Dam to Milwaukee, a fire erupted in a railcar loaded with canvas horse tents. The train screeched to a halt near a creek and a cowboy bucket brigade led by Wayne Beasley, one of Princess Wenona's former husbands, quickly extinguished the blaze and averted tragedy.[27]

Just five nights later, while en route to Lancaster, Wisconsin, one entire section of the train struck a spread rail, demolishing five cars. Fortunately, no human lives were lost, but five valuable arena horses, including a roan bucking bronco, and five team horses were killed and thirty horses were injured. In a pouring rain with lightning streaking the night sky, the show veterinarian, assisted by a local animal doctor and some others, put the most severely injured animals out of their misery and treated the rest of the wounded stock.[28]

Joe Miller appeared shocked by the disaster. Not only was the balance of the season's schedule at peril, but he felt genuine affection for every animal connected with the show, even the draft horses and mules.[29]

"Now, in the manner of a general on a battlefield, he locked up his grief, saw to the welfare of the injured animals, and then took stock of the situation," wrote Jerry Armstrong for *The Western Horseman* in describing Miller's behavior. "In short order, hurried wires were sent the management of the Chicago Union Stockyards. The Chicago firm cooperated fully in the emergency; in a matter of hours horses from the stockyards were on their way to Miller as replacements for the casualties."[30]

The later part of the tour included some of the performers' favorite dates because they were back among familiar sights and with old friends.

The show paused at Winfield, the former Miller hometown in Kansas, and held many appearances in Oklahoma, including stops at Tulsa, Shawnee, Okmulgee, Bartlesville, and Nowata.[31]

Just west of Tulsa, at the Creek County seat of Sapulpa that September, 157 of the Millers' cowboys turned out when Teddy Roosevelt delivered an impassioned ten-minute campaign speech while running for president as the Progressive Party candidate. When Roosevelt told the crowd of more than fifty-eight hundred people that "the Republican Party is dead and that in November we propose to bury the Democratic Party," the loudest cheers reportedly came from the members of the Miller-Arlington show.[32]

Nevertheless, everyone present—most likely even Roosevelt—knew that the Millers would maintain their Democratic connections, as did the vast majority of ranch personnel. During the 1912 campaign, George Miller—busy with running the business office, buying new roadsters for family members, and negotiating oil leases—corresponded with top Democratic Party officials on strategy for candidates to use in the race against Republicans and Progressives.[33]

The closing date of the Millers' 1912 season came only eleven days after the election—a show given on November 16, at Hot Springs, Arkansas, scene of the final four performances, held in connection with the state fair. During the long season, the Millers' Wild West show had staged 421 performances, traveling 17,280 miles through twenty-two states and three Canadian provinces.[34]

After spending two days at the ranch headquarters on the Salt Fork, Joe Miller departed on a special train for California to check on his landholdings and film projects. Accompanying him were two carloads of fresh stock, fifty cowhands, and a large delegation of Ponca Indians.

Joe relished his respite in the California sunshine, even though Los Angeles and the beach communities were clearly growing increasingly crowded. A new car park built on the Venice Pier was filled to capacity by noon every day of the week. That November, a frustrated California secretary of state declared that "there already were 80,000 machines [automobiles] in California and an average of 71 being purchased daily, the greater number of autos being owned by residents of Los Angeles County."[35]

Despite the crowds of people and the motor traffic, Joe Miller still found plenty of benefits to living on the Pacific shore. Joe kept close tabs on the family enterprise there. Throughout the year, even when the show season was at its peak, Joe stayed in close contact with Will Brooks at Venice through letters and overnight cables. Joe made sure that a steady flow of livestock, feed, and supplies from the headquarters ranch in Oklahoma was routed to the Millers' California operation.[36]

In September, Joe had taken temporary leave from the road show and hurried to Venice to negotiate another contract with the Bison 101 film company. Despite the contract, the relationship between the 101 Ranch and the movie company was far from ideal.[37] Problems had surfaced earlier in the year, while the Miller-Arlington outfit traveled its show circuit. Several independent film companies had organized in an attempt to overcome the powerful Patents Company's stranglehold on the industry. Two of the main independents to join the amalgamation were film pioneer Carl Laemmle's IMP company and New York Motion Picture Company, the parent of Keystone and Bison 101.[38]

By June 1912, the new company was unveiled to the public. The participating independents chose the name Universal Film Manufacturing Company, or simply Universal, as most Hollywood people came to call the studio.[39] The honeymoon period lasted only a brief while before the various entities began to vie for domination of the new company.

"When NYMP joined the sheltering umbrella of Universal, a power struggle led to a resurgence of the kind of warfare the company had been formed to avoid," explained film historian Kevin Brownlow. "The NYMP laboratory in New York was attacked twice by gangsters, and Irwin Willat, who was there for the second raid, recalls several shots being fired. Universal's strong-arm men were all set to storm the Santa Ynez canyon [Inceville] in a similar manner. Had they done so, history might have recorded the first battle of a new Civil War, for the 101 [Ranch] people were spoiling for a fight."[40]

Balshofer stated that such descriptions were overly dramatized and "out of all proportion." Still, he also admitted that as one of the combine's first moves, some of Universal's "strong-arm men" attempted to take possession of NYMP's New York property. "What fighting there was lasted for about ten minutes," wrote Balshofer. "George Dobbs, who worked in the chemical room, had the misfortune to lose one eye, but no else suffered any injury. The police arrived and put an end to the fray."[41]

Although Balshofer acknowledged that the "Santa Ynez Canyon studio would have been a real prize for Universal," he played down the toughs' attempt to take control of Inceville.[42] "Brooks, who was in charge of our Indians, had them dress in full regalia and cover their faces with war paint," wrote Balshofer. "He then asked them to parade on a ridge well in view of anyone approaching the canyon along the beach road, the only way to get in. One of our several prop cannons we used in our Indian and soldier pictures Brooks placed pointing in the direction the enemy expected to come and had his Indians carrying army muskets and jumping and hopping in an Indian war dance. The whole thing was staged by Brooks. Some of the cowboys joined in the fun and fired their guns in the air, using blank cartridges."[43]

The Millers' cowboys and Indians did not care if they protected Inceville from the Patents Company goons or the operatives from the Universal combine trying to take control of the property. As far as the outfit was concerned, any brawl was worth fighting, regardless of the opponent.

The fierce struggle among the various Universal partners continued that summer and throughout the autumn. In the end, the umbrella company of Universal, with Laemmle at the helm, won out and fully absorbed NYMP. The net result brought rapid and drastic changes in various studio operations, especially for Keystone and Bison.[44]

As Laemmle and other studio heads emerged as the indisputable power players at Universal, they made further attempts to control the NYMP properties in California. These properties included not only Inceville but also the company's Edendale location, where many of Mack Sennett's slapstick comedies, featuring Mabel Normand and other leading comedy stars, were produced. Universal finally brought suit against NYMP, which resulted in hotly contested legal battles involving an array of expensive lawyers.[45] "In the end, we did not have to turn the company over to Universal for stock," wrote Balshofer, "but they did win from us the right to use the name Bison films."[46]

This stunning development not only changed the makeup of the film industry but also had a major impact on the Miller brothers and the relationship between the 101 and the California motion-picture studios. "Universal offered an armistice in return for a certain sum; they also demanded the name of Bison for their own product," wrote Brownlow. "The NYMP, caught out over a contract, submitted, and the unromantic Kay-Bee (for Kessel and Bauman) was substituted for the Ince product. Universal (which later won Francis Ford and other Ince personnel) shipped in their own Indians, cowboys, and longhorn cattle, producing elaborate Indian-and-military Westerns along the Ince lines, under the trademark of 101 Bison. Miller Brothers promptly sued to prevent this unauthorized use of 101, but Universal clung to the charismatic brand. Their 101-Bison

[sic] pictures were often impressive, for former Ince directors like Ford and Frank Montgomery made them, but the magic—the Ince touch and the Inceville dust—were [sic] missing."[47]

In no time, Laemmle—with his own production units in place at Inceville—began to make western films under the old Bison 101 name, while Thomas Ince and some of his followers departed to build a new studio in Culver City. "When we lost the right to use the brand name Bison films to the Universal company, we rechristened the same unit Broncho films," wrote Balshofer, "but they never were quite as popular as the original 101 Bisons, and we lost quite a bit of business."[48]

With the arrival of 1913, as the new Broncho and Kay-Bee studios began to make silent films in and around Venice, Joe Miller had returned to his beloved 101 Ranch in Oklahoma. Content to let Will Brooks sort out the confusion caused by the movie folks, Joe joined his brothers to plan the next season of their Wild West show.[49] The ranch operations were running quite smoothly, thanks to the efforts of all the Miller brothers, especially businesslike George. The brothers worked hard all winter to prepare the Wild West show for the upcoming season and put their ranch affairs in order.

During the winter, George devoted much of his time to hiring and firing and other personnel matters. Although no shortage of applicants existed for the variety of tasks at the ranch or with the road shows, not all candidates proved acceptable. Even though the Millers routinely hired outlaws or ex-convicts, including hardened killers and bank robbers, the one thing they could never tolerate was someone who stole from the ranch itself. That was an unforgivable sin. A clear illustration of this policy came in January 1913 when a woman identified as Mrs. Anson Yeager wrote an innocent letter to the Millers inquiring about her younger brother, Edward Engstrom, who had taken a job with the Wild West show.[50]

"I thought I would write a few lines and find out how my brother Edward Engstrom is getting along in the circus world of yours," wrote Yeager from her home in Moline, Illinois. "I hope he is satisfactory and does his work well. Now if you can will you please give him a chance at riding. . . . For I truly would like to see him gain a high reputation as long as he intends to lead that life. You see Edward is twenty and will be twenty-one the 15th of Feb., 1913. And surely he ought to be able to better himself immensely. Hoping you will try to help me make my wish come true."[51]

The rapid reply to the letter was brief and to the point.

Dear Madam—

Your letter of January 27th is just received, and I regret very much to have to write this letter.

I enclose you, herewith, a reward card, offering $100.00 reward for the arrest and conviction of a horse thief.

I beg to further advise that your brother, Edward Engstrom, is the man mentioned in this card, and he was captured at Arkansas City, Kan., on the morning of Jan. 30th, where he was attempting to sell the horse and saddle for $30.00, and he is now in jail at Newkirk, Oklahoma, and will, no doubt, plead guilty to horse stealing.

He was probably very fortunate in falling into the hands of the sheriff instead of falling into other hands when being caught with the goods.

Very truly yours,
George L. Miller[52]

Fortunately, most of the Millers' workers remained dedicated to the ranch and the family which employed them. One of the most dependable hands was Bill Pickett. The Millers' star bulldogger and chief attraction, Pickett spent the winter of 1912–1913 breaking horses and steers for the next show tour, which followed the same basic route as the 1911 tour.[53]

The troupe traveled the circuit in a twenty-eight-car show train made up of a half-dozen sleepers, eight stock cars, and fourteen flats. Four brave rodeo clowns—Dan Dix, Bill Caress, Billy Lorette, and Joe Lewis—worked the arena floors, starting with the 1913 season opener, on April 5 at Hot Springs, Arkansas.[54]

One of the Millers' featured newcomers for the 1913 season was Iron Tail, an Oglala Sioux war chief, born in South Dakota in 1850. He said his mother chose his name after witnessing a herd of stampeding buffalo with their tails straight up in the air "as if made of shafts of iron." As a young warrior, Iron Tail fought in the War of the Black Hills of 1876–1877 and served as an aide to Sitting Bull at Little Bighorn. In the late 1880s, he joined Buffalo Bill's show and accompanied Cody on a European tour in 1889.[55]

Iron Tail remained with Buffalo Bill even after the old showman merged his outfit with Pawnee Bill Lillie's show, in 1908. But the combined Buffalo Bill's Wild West and Pawnee Bill's Great Far East lasted less than five years. By 1913, Cody's poor management skills and his proclivity for reckless investment had taken a toll, and the show was on the verge of disaster.[56] Some of the entertainers from the "Two Bills" show jumped ship long before the show closed that summer. Iron Tail was one of those who left the heavily indebted Cody and Lillie and took a job with the Millers' outfit.

The Sioux warrior's timing was ideal. On February 21, 1913, the United States Treasury issued its new five-cent piece—a nickel depicting a buffalo on one side of the coin and an Indian's head in profile, said to be of a likeness of Iron Tail, on the other side.[57] In production until 1938, the "Indian head–buffalo" nickel became one of the most famous coins in American history. More than one billion were minted. Although James Earle Fraser, the noted sculptor who designed the coin, later said he had used at least two other Indians as a composite model for the new nickel, the Millers made no mention of anyone but Iron Tail in their show publicity, starting with that first show of the 1913 season, at Hot Springs.[58]

Joe Miller, riding at the head of the opening-day parade on the stallion called Ben Hur, looked especially regal mounted on his new saddle, custom-made by S. D. Myres, the celebrated leather craftsman from Sweetwater, Texas.[59] Valued at an astonishing ten thousand dollars, it became known as the finest fancy saddle ever made. The elegant hand-carved leather saddle, with a silver-and-gold horn and stirrups bound with silver and overlaid with gold, was covered with fifteen pounds of silver and gold and encrusted with 166 diamonds, four garnets, 120 sapphires, and seventeen rubies.[60]

Following Joe came Professor Donato La Banca and the stirring cowboy band. The bandsmen marched smartly in a parade that featured a new calliope, scores of floats, and an endless procession of cowboys and cowgirls, cossacks, and more than one hundred Indian riders.[61] All three Miller brothers attended the opening show. Their mother, Molly Miller, and Joe's wife, Lizzie, also were on hand with some of their lady friends from Ponca City. They rode in an automobile through the streets of Hot Springs, waving at the crowds massed along the curbs.[62]

The *Ponca City Courier* sent a team of reporters to cover the spectacle. "Immediately after the opening," the newspaper reported, "Zack Miller left for the South with a bunch of cowboys, to corral a great bunch of 10,000 cattle which he has purchased and which he will ship to the 101 ranch as rapidly as possible. This is one of the greatest cattle purchases ever made, and will require 350 cars to ship. Shipments will begin April 20, and will continue until the entire bunch has been domiciled on the ranch and turned loose to feed on the great range. Mr. Miller will then go to Europe, to consumate [sic] a big show deal, inaugurated by Joe C. Miller, and which is expected to create a sensation when announced."[63]

Joe had spent several weeks during the winter in London and on the Continent, especially in Germany, arranging for the so-called big show deal. After his return to the United States that spring—just as the road show of 1913 started its national tour—the Millers unveiled their plans. At long last, the 101 was going global. In the tradition of Buffalo Bill Cody, the Miller brothers and Edward Arlington shipped a sizable part of their show to Europe.

Negotiations that winter between Joe and German circus impresario Hans Stosch-Sarrasani led to the appearance of a large troupe of Indians from the 101 Ranch with the Sarrasani Circus, billed as "the grandest show ever seen in Europe."[64] Based at a six-thousand-seat arena in Dresden, Germany, the circus featured a broad range of attractions such as wild-animal acts, tumblers, jugglers, and a complete Wild West show.

Stosch-Sarrasani requested the services of some "real Sioux Indians" in hopes of making his European tour more authentic. The Millers complied by dispatching fifty Oglala Sioux under the direction of Wayne Beasley, the intrepid Hundred and One cowboy who had led the bucket brigade which doused the train fire during the 1912 season. Beasley and his Sioux charges made the transatlantic crossing in the spring of 1913 and reported directly to the circus, at Dresden.[65]

Everything went according to plan until early July, when seventeen of the Indians announced that they had grown weary of touring Germany, Austria, and Belgium. They further stated that because of their homesickness and the poor treatment they received at the hands of German border police, they wished to return to the United States. Joe tried to placate them by sending souvenir watch fobs made from the new Iron Tail nickels for Beasley to distribute.[66]

When some of the Indians left the European tour and returned to the United States, Joe sent urgent letters of appeal to the authorities at Pine Ridge agency in South Dakota, the home of most of the Sioux working for Beasley. "Several of our Indians have got tired of the show business and have gone home," Joe wrote to agency Superintendent John R. Brennan while on tour with the show that July. "I have been able to pickup [sic] a few Indians up here in Michigan, and these, with some coming from the Rose Bud [sic] Agency, will give me all I need. . . . Should any of the Indians who come in complain of mistreatment or things not going right with the show, I would be very glad to have you write to Iron Tail or any of the Indians on the show [on the U. S. tour], and they will tell you that there is no show on the road that takes as good care of the Indians and treat [sic] them as well as we do."[67]

The situation worsened when a circus tiger mauled the young daughter of Dick White Calf as she passed the cage. "I sent her to the hospital," Beasley wrote Joe, "and don't think it is anything only flesh wounds."[68]

When Joe Miller refused to release the disgruntled Indian performers from their contracts, the Oglalas came up with a plan.[69] Contrary to the morals clause of their contracts, the Sioux began to imbibe large quantities of alcohol—a relatively easy feat because liquor was readily available and many circus fans insisted on buying the Indians all the beer and schnapps they could consume. Yet even when some of the Sioux became so drunk they could no longer stand, Beasley remained firm about their contracts.[70]

Besides keeping tabs on the European tour and overseeing the ranch show as it traveled across the United States, the Miller brothers also struggled with film projects and a variety of critical ranch transactions. One of the most profitable deals the Millers made that summer came in June, when they contracted to supply three thousand cavalry and artillery horses to the Greek army, in the midst of a bloody war in the Balkans.[71] Working with their business contacts in London, the Millers gathered several hundred horses before meeting with Greek army inspectors and shipping the stock from the port of Galveston, Texas.[72]

During the hectic summer months, the Millers also watched with great interest as the Buffalo Bill and Pawnee Bill show finally closed and the two old showmen declared bankruptcy. "While they [the "Two Bills"] were going broke," Joe Miller wrote an American associate in Berlin that July, "our business has steadily increased and this has been the best season we ever had. I can only attribute it to the fact that we deliver the goods and they did not."[73]

In August, all three Miller brothers attended the Buffalo Bill sale in Denver, where they purchased seventy-eight of the best show horses for an average of sixty-one dollars a head.[74] "I bought the big end of their Arena stock, all of the wardrobe and costumes, the lighting plant, and considerable other stuff," Joe Miller wrote on August 25. "Was very sorry indeed to see such a grand and big outfit like that finish as it did."[75]

Later that summer, after Zack and his cowboys finished rounding up ten thousand head of cattle in Florida, he left New York aboard the *Emparator*, bound for Europe. By the time Zack arrived in Germany, the situation with the unhappy Indian entertainers had improved because of Wayne Beasley's diligent efforts. Ultimately, most of the Oglala performers who had gone to Europe with Beasley finished the season. The majority even showed up for another European tour the next year.[76]

Back in the United States, the Millers' 1913 season developed into a fast-paced journey. The outfit visited several states, highlighted by a two-week stand at Brooklyn, a long New England excursion, and major stops at Cleveland, Pittsburgh, Washington, Baltimore, Boston, New York, Buffalo, and Detroit. Finally the show headed south to Oklahoma and Texas, playing to big stands at Dallas and Fort Worth before closing on October 28, at Houston.[77]

Most of the 101 Ranch livestock and entertainers returned to the ranch for the winter. The Millers shipped much of the show equipment to Lakeview, New Jersey, for repairs and storage until the opening of the 1914 season.[78]

Instead of resting for several months at Bliss, some of the better 101 Ranch riders opted to remain in the saddle that winter. After the final performance at Houston, the Millers sent three baggage cars loaded with horses, tack, and supplies to New York City, where Edward Arlington planned a tour of several South American cities throughout the winter, including major shows at Buenos Aires, Montevideo, and Rio de Janeiro.[79]

Crack performers whom Arlington recruited from the 101 Ranch and the defunct "Two Bills" shows departed Brooklyn from Pier 9 on November 1, 1913, aboard the *S.S. Varsara*, bound for the first port of call, in Argentina.[80] Vern Tantlinger, with his trusty boomerang packed in a grip, acted as the arena director. Among the headliner performers were such champions as Bill Pickett, Chester Byers, Lulu Parr, Jane Fuller, Mabel Kline, Ed Bowman, and Iona and Milt Hinkle.

The voyage south soon became a trying experience for humans and animals alike. The Atlantic grew rough and stormy, and everyone aboard ship was seasick. Pickett became so ill that he thought he might die. He later said that only constant thoughts of his wife, Maggie, and his children back in Oklahoma kept him going.[81]

Trick roper Hank Durnell, stricken with smallpox, stopped eating and refused to leave his bunk. Finally some pals dragged him to the top deck for fresh air. Durnell begged his friends to throw him overboard to end his suffering, but he eventually recovered.[82]

Four of the Indians aboard, also victims of smallpox, did not regain their health. Chills and high fever took hold of them and they died. Sailors sewed the pockmarked bodies in canvas and buried them at sea, far from their home in the grasslands of America.[83]

Following the wild voyage of twenty-eight days, the outfit at last reached land. Arlington sneaked his ailing performers off the ship and bribed the health officials at Buenos Aires, but when a livestock inspector found that one of the show horses had contracted glanders, a contagious and often fatal equine disease, he ordered all the horses to be shot and burned.[84] Pickett uttered a prayer of thanks that he had shipped his trusted steed, Spradley, back to Oklahoma for the winter. Replacement horses and livestock were purchased, including a mule for rodeo clown Billy Lorette, and the Wild West show went on as promised.

An avalanche of favorable newspaper coverage, placed by Arlington and his lackeys, helped publicize the show. Everywhere the outfit went that winter, tremendous crowds turned out to see it perform. On some days, Arlington staged three performances to accommodate the swarms of fans who came to cheer for Pickett and the others.[85]

But even though the South Americans received the shows well and the tropical drinks laced with rum went down smoothly, the Wild West riders sensed the change that rode the warm winter winds washing over the land. Indians with the outfit—still silently mourning the loss of their friends at sea—said they smelled death all around them.

With the arrival of 1914, as revolution raged in Mexico and the world prepared for war in Europe, that distinctive aroma of death would become more familiar for everyone. The vanishing breed of men and women who rode for the Millers and the Hundred and One would be no exception.

HOLLYWOOD BUCKAROOS AND THE GOWER GULCH GANG

THROUGHOUT THE SILENT-MOVIE era and long after the arrival of talkies, a drove of motion-picture notables—ranging from flashy matinée idols and glamorous starlets to big-shot directors and fearless stunt doubles—bragged about their ties to the Hundred and One. All of them called the Millers their friends.

Most of those luminaries—including Tom Mix, Mabel Normand, Neal Hart, Jack Hoxie, Buck Jones, Hoot and Helen Gibson, Ken Maynard, and other big-screen headliners of the teens and twenties—enjoyed friendships with the Millers.[1] Some who worked in the various Miller film projects, such as Normand; Helen Ferguson, star of many action genre silents; and Jack Mulhall, a prolific leading man from New York state (who was not related to Colonel Zack Mulhall), came to the world of film with impressive show-business backgrounds.[2]

Several of these trained actors with excellent theatrical credentials started their screen careers with the Millers at Venice or Inceville, just as film producers moved westward to escape the long reach of the Motion Picture Patents Company. Yet even in California, the big eastern trust tried to force the smaller independent companies out of business. The harassment continued until "Uncle Carl" Laemmle merged several "patent pirates" into Universal Film Manufacturing Company. Laemmle and the independents fought back, and at last federal government antitrust action disbanded the film monopoly.[3] By that time, an endless stream of young men and women had appeared in southern California, ready to find their niche in motion pictures.

As a rule, those cast in early western movies, especially extras and bit players, arrived in California by way of Wild West shows and rodeos, theatrical stock companies, and vaudeville. Many of them had worked as cowboys or cowgirls on the 101 Ranch or had ridden with the Millers' Wild West show. Often, they just showed up with hat in hand at the Millers' White House in Oklahoma, or they haunted one of the movie sets in California, hoping to nab a part in a western flicker.

Sometimes, aspiring movie recruits—including a few who went on to become legendary film stars—were literally plucked off the streets of Hollywood. Originally part of an old land grant, the district of Los Angeles that became known as Hollywood consisted of rich farmland planted in bell peppers, melons, and citrus when Horace W. Wilcox, a Kansas prohibitionist and real estate developer, and his wife, Daeida, moved to the Cahuenga Valley in the late 1800s.[4]

Staunch political and social conservatives, the Wilcoxes hoped to start a temperance colony on their land just north of the La Brea tar pits. In 1891, they began to subdivide the huge farm and sell parcels for $150 an acre. By 1903, they had incorporated their growing community and Daeida Wilcox decided to name the new city Hollywood.[5]

In 1910, Hollywood—all four square miles, with a population of about four thousand sober souls—agreed to be annexed to Los Angeles to avail itself of the city's sewage system and to obtain potable water from Sierra snowmelt in Owens Valley. That decision would fundamentally reshape the "obscure and dusty suburb" with a reputation as a haven for piety and virtue.[6]

At once, filmmakers and their camp followers began to move into Hollywood. Al Christie and David Horsley, of Nestor's Film Company, established the first Hollywood studio in 1911, in a rented tavern and barn at the corner of Sunset and Gower, where they ground out a series of short westerns.[7] Cecil B. DeMille, son of an Episcopalian clergyman, moved to Hollywood the next year after deciding that Flagstaff, Arizona, did not "look western enough." He went into partnership with vaudeville musician Jesse L. Lasky and his brother-in-law, Samuel Goldfish, a glove salesman who later changed his name to Samuel Goldwyn. By 1914, their film company had produced *Squaw Man*, starring Dustin Farnum. DeMille shot the six-reeler—generally considered the first full-length motion picture produced entirely in Hollywood—in a barn on the corner of Selma Avenue and Vine Street.[8]

In the next few years, several more fledgling movie moguls established studios in Hollywood. Like Laemmle, Goldwyn, and Lasky, most of them were immigrant Jews with eastern European roots, such as Adolph Zukor, William Fox (born William Fried), Louis B. Mayer, the Selznicks, and the four Warner brothers, sons of Polish Jews.[9] Although Jewish movie magnates might not have had much in common with the Millers on the surface, like the three brothers, they were highly motivated risk takers, unafraid of a high-stakes gamble.

As these and other movie people and their associates arrived, Hollywood's population swelled, especially during winter when cowboys and cowgirls came for seasonal employment. Because the studios had not yet formed the Central Casting Bureau, hopefuls looking for work in western flickers for five dollars a day and a box lunch congregated near the Hollywood barns where most of the films were produced. Assistant directors from various studios regularly patrolled the neighborhoods and streets, lined with cafes and stores, especially Joe Posada's boot shop, a favorite place to purchase handmade western footwear.[10]

The studio boys also checked out the corner of Hollywood Boulevard and Cahuenga Avenue—the most popular hangout for out-of-work cowhands and rodeo riders, refugees from Wild West shows, and other movie aspirants. This location came to be referred to as the Waterhole, after a nearby saloon where patrons waiting to be discovered by filmmakers played marathon hands of poker and gin as they sipped high-octane tequila, mescal, and whiskey.[11]

Within a few years, as Hollywood continued to grow, the immediate area became known as "Poverty Row" because of all the struggling independent film studios located there. The proper Christian citizens of early Hollywood resented the studio "gypsy camps" and posted signs in rooming-house windows declaring, "No Dogs or Actors Allowed."[12] The blunt admonition had no effect on the migration of Hollywood newcomers, who continued to arrive in droves.

Eventually, after the old Waterhole saloon had dried up, the movie extras made the nearby Columbia Drugstore, at Sunset and Gower, their meeting place. Site of that first Hollywood studio, the busy intersection became the new cowboy hangout. They lovingly dubbed the corner Gower Gulch.[13]

Numerous veterans of the 101 Ranch and Inceville joined those from the Waterhole—and later from Gower Gulch—who found gainful employment with the studios. Neal Hart—a former cowpuncher and sheriff in Wyoming who became known as "America's Pal"—was just one of the former Hundred and One riders who ended up in Hollywood after touring the Wild West circuit.[14]

Not all members of the Gower gang were macho cowboys. Some came from the Millers' storied cowgirl ranks, such as Jane Bernoudy, a world-champion horsewoman while with the Millers, and once the fiancée of the cowboy film star William S. Hart.[15] The Millers always cherished the letter

Jane sent to them from El Paso in 1912 when she replied to their advertisement in *Billboard* and told of her ability as a rider and spinner of ropes. The handsome Miss Bernoudy performed with the 101 Ranch shows and then rode onto the silver screen through productions at Inceville and later at Universal City.[16]

Although in later years several of Hollywood's biggest western stars of all time—including the big four, Tom Mix, Hoot Gibson, Buck Jones, and Ken Maynard—still spoke fondly of the 101, other Hollywood notables linked to the Millers had no clear and immediate connections to either the ranch or Oklahoma. Yet long after the 101 Ranch had been relegated to history books, some of those more unlikely associations proved valid. Indeed, the influence of the Millers clearly extended well beyond the lifetime of their ranch and reached a broad spectrum of the world of entertainment.

Even Elizabeth Taylor and John Wayne, legendary Hollywood icons who did not emerge as movie stars until years after the collapse of the Miller dynasty, can be linked to the Hundred and One and Oklahoma through their families and friends. Die-hard boosters of the Miller legacy have argued that there never would have been a Liz Taylor or a Duke Wayne, at least as the public came to know them, without the Hundred and One.[17]

The impact of the Miller brothers on John Wayne's life and career is not difficult to understand. Born Marion Michael Morrison in Winterset, Iowa, in 1907, the actor who became known as John Wayne forged his career in Hollywood in the 1920s under the tutelage of some of the Millers' most illustrious Hollywood associates.[18]

One of the primary influences on Wayne was John Ford, the younger brother of Francis Ford, who worked as a director and actor with Thomas Ince during the busy Bison 101 times at Inceville. Born Sean Aloysius O'Feeney in Maine in 1895, John Ford had changed his surname, just as did his elder brother, whom he followed to Hollywood in 1913.[19] After starting his movie career as an assistant prop man and set laborer, young Ford became a stunt double for his brother. In 1915, he appeared as a hooded Ku Klux Klan rider in D. W. Griffith's controversial epic film of the Civil War, *The Birth of a Nation*.[20]

John Ford soon found his real niche in Hollywood when he became a director. For the rest of his long life, Ford captured the poetry of the western landscape better than anyone, earning six Academy Awards while making 136 pictures. Fifty-four of those pictures were westerns, including forty-one silents films which featured such 101 Ranch alumni as box-office sensations Tom Mix and Hoot Gibson.[21]

Ford gave John Wayne his big break in 1930 when he recommended the former college football player to director Raoul Walsh for the lead role in *The Big Trail*, which also featured Marguerite Churchill, the attractive brunette who eventually married cowboy movie star George O'Brien.[22] The film's success marked a turning point for Wayne and the start of his long association with Ford, which produced such classic western films as *Stagecoach, Red River, She Wore a Yellow Ribbon*, and *The Searchers*.[23]

Other significant cowboy stars with 101 Ranch affiliations appeared with Wayne in many of Ford's western films. One of the best known was Yakima Canutt, recipient of a special Oscar "for creating the profession of stuntman as it exists today and for the development of the many safety devices used by stuntmen everywhere."[24]

Born in 1895 on a farm in the Snake River hills of Washington, Enos Edward Canutt started to break horses as a boy and began his tour of the professional rodeo circuit in 1912, before he turned seventeen.[25] He picked up his colorful nickname in 1914 at the Pendleton Round-Up in Oregon during a bucking-horse event when he was mistakenly identified as a cowboy from the Yakima River region. A photographer caught Canutt in midflight after having been pitched from his mount and captioned the picture, "Yakima Canutt leaving the deck of a Pendleton bronc." His fellow cowboys began to use the exotic name, which many of them soon shortened to "Yak."[26]

In a decade of rodeo competition, Yak Canutt built a national reputation as a fearless bronc rider, bulldogger, and all-around cowboy. By the time he joined the 101 Ranch outfit for a brief fling during the 1914 Wild West show season, Canutt—already a rodeo champion—had become a well-known figure to most of the 101 Ranch cowboys.[27]

A photograph of Canutt on a bucking horse named South Dakota, taken on May 15, 1912, by famed rodeo photographer R. R. Doubleday, caught the Millers' attention.[28] The same picture later served as a model for the image on token coins minted by the Millers for their employees to use at the ranch store and with selected merchants in Ponca City and other towns near the ranch. Cowhands and workers could draw against payday by accepting the trade tokens and signing their names. The brass "broncs," as folks called them, came in denominations of five, ten, fifteen, and twenty-five cents, with the coin's value on one side and on the other side an engraved image of Canutt astride the bucking horse. Old-timers later vividly recalled attending the fall roundup shows at the 101 Ranch when cowboys and cowgirls rode past the grandstands and tossed handfuls of Canutt "broncs" to the crowds.[29]

Canutt's appearances at rodeos and Wild West shows led to his being cast for stunt work and bit parts in westerns and action pictures in the early 1920s. Although his voice, which he said sounded "like a hillbilly in a well," caused him problems in the late 1920s when the silent era gave way to talkies, his athletic ability and ease at executing difficult stunts on the first take guaranteed him a place in Hollywood history.[30]

For decades, Canutt thrilled motion-picture audiences with his daredevil performances, as he stunt-doubled for some of the biggest Hollywood stars—Roy Rogers, Gene Autry, Clark Gable, Kirk Douglas, Errol Flynn and, of course, John Wayne.[31] Canutt's lengthy friendship and professional association with Wayne started in the 1930s and continued for four decades.

"Marion Morrison [John Wayne] wanted to be an actor too, and he especially wanted to play cowboys in the movies," wrote W. David Baird and Danney Goble in their history of Oklahoma. "Unlike Yakima Canutt, however, Marion Morrison had no sense at all of how to ride a horse or even how to walk like a real westerner. It was the 101's Yakima Canutt who showed him how to ride and how to walk with a cowboy's rolling gait, the skills that Canutt had displayed for the Miller brothers. . . . When Marion Morrison changed his name—to John Wayne—he remembered the lessons. Everyone who has seen the Duke play a cowboy, thereby has been touched by a small piece of the legacy of Oklahoma's 101 Ranch Wild West Show."[32]

The legacy of the 101 Ranch was also preserved through John Wayne's close friendship with another Academy Award winner—Ben Johnson, the Oklahoma wrangler and world-champion cowboy whose father, Ben Johnson Sr., rode briefly with the Millers' outfit.

Born in Arkansas in 1896, Ben Sr. was four years old when his family moved to Tulsa so his father could work as a livestock auctioneer. Ben left home while still in fifth grade after seeing some of the early cowboy moving pictures, including crude one-reelers featuring wranglers from the 101 Ranch. He wanted to become a cowboy.[33] By the time he was fourteen, Ben Johnson had fulfilled his desire. He hired on with the Miller brothers and took up residence at the 101 Ranch. The youngster tended cattle, repaired fences, and acted as a bunkhouse barber. He skillfully wielded his four straight razors, with wooden handles and tempered German steel, which he kept in a soft leather carrying case branded with the inscription "Ben Johnson, 101 Ranch, Bliss, Oklahoma, March 1912."[34]

When not busy punching cattle or trimming whiskers, Johnson broke horses for the British government prior to the entry of the United States into World War I. He also began to compete in rodeos. A great bronc rider and roper, Johnson took home many prizes and top honors. He established a world record for calf roping in 1923 and held it for three years. In 1927, he set a steer-roping record with an average time of eighteen seconds for three steers. By that time, Johnson had married and he and his wife, Ollie, were raising three children—two girls and a boy named Ben Jr., who became known simply as "Son."[35]

Long before he even started to shave, Son Johnson picked up occasional paychecks by chasing steers across the bluestem pastures for his father, foreman of the Chapman-Barnard Ranch, a big Oklahoma cattle spread in Osage County. Son probably would have remained in Oklahoma, riding, roping, and winning his share of championships at rodeo arenas, if it had not been for the lure of Hollywood.[36]

Not satisfied to be just a range cowboy, Ben Jr. arrived in Hollywood in the early 1940s, working as a horse wrangler in *The Outlaw*, the sensual western made by Howard Hughes, which also launched the career of Jane Russell.[37] After maneuvering his way through the ranks as a stuntman, Ben Johnson got his big break when he crossed paths with John Ford and ended up being cast in *Fort Apache*, starring Henry Fonda, Maureen O'Hara, and John Wayne.[38]

More western film roles followed for Johnson, including parts in *Three Godfathers, She Wore a Yellow Ribbon, Shane*, and other classics.[39] In 1953, Johnson took time off from making movies to return to the rodeo arena, where he won a world title in team roping. Many more movie roles followed, and in 1971 Johnson won an Oscar for his work in *The Last Picture Show*.[40]

A frequent visitor to his old stomping grounds in the Osage country before his death in 1996, Johnson eventually appeared in three hundred films. Four hundred mourners attended his funeral at the small Oklahoma town of Pawhuska. They gathered in front of his casket with cowboy hats clutched to their chests and listened to a single fiddler play "Just a Closer Walk with Thee."[41]

Ben Johnson died less than two years after the passing of an elderly woman who had appeared before primitive movie cameras at the 101

Ranch at the same time Ben Johnson Sr. worked for the Millers. A girl from Kansas filled with burning ambition, she became famous as the mother of Elizabeth Taylor, the ultimate Hollywood celebrity.

Born in London, Taylor—an Academy Award–winning screen actress who many fans believed hailed from British lineage—actually came from purely American stock. Her mother, Sara Viola Warmbrodt, was born in 1896, three miles north of the Oklahoma border at Arkansas City, Kansas—a small town about halfway between Winfield and Ponca City, in the heart of Miller country. Elizabeth's father, Francis Taylor, was born in Springfield, Illinois, in 1897 and reportedly lived in Arkansas City as a young man before moving to New York.[42] As a schoolgirl, Sara took part in theatrical productions in Arkansas City and neighboring towns.[43]

Her big break came in 1914 after she won a contest which landed her a role in *One from the Flames*, a film shot entirely on the 101 Ranch.[44] Stunningly beautiful and confident, the young lady from Kansas turned many a cowboy's head during the long days of production. Although not a major player in the film, Sara found that the Millers' movie provided her with the incentive to stretch her acting talent. Adopting the stage name Sara Sothern, she left Kansas and followed the stock-company circuit. By the early 1920s, the budding actress had appeared in productions on Broadway and had even journeyed to England, where she landed a few lead roles on stages in London's illustrious West End.[45]

Back in New York City in 1925, Sara made screen tests, but she was too old for ingenue roles in the movies.[46] While looking for work in Manhattan, she became reacquainted with Francis Taylor, by then a promising fine-art dealer, and they soon married. Eventually they settled in England, where their son, Howard, was born in 1929, and their daughter, Elizabeth, in 1932.[47]

In the winter of 1937–1938, the Taylors paid an extended visit to Arkansas City because of illness in Francis' family. For two months, Elizabeth and Howard attended a local school. Elizabeth—already a striking beauty—impressed the other children and charmed the adults with her decided English accent.[48]

In 1939, with World War II approaching, the Taylors left their home in England and moved to California to join Sara's widowed father, running a chicken farm near Pasadena. The family lived at Pacific Palisades, and Francis Taylor opened an art gallery at the Beverly Hills Hotel.[49] In California, little Elizabeth caught the attention of movie scouts. Her strong-willed mother cajoled the girl to become an actress; as gossip columnist

Hedda Hopper bluntly put it, quoting a woman who had known the Taylors in Arkansas City, "she had driven Liz to be the actress she [herself] could not have been."[50]

Sara Taylor's wishes came true. When the Kansan who launched her career at the 101 Ranch died in 1994, her illustrious daughter was known as the last great Hollywood-made star.

By that time, Gower Gulch was just a distant memory. The drugstore cowboys and cowgirls had long disappeared, along with their old hangouts. Yet the famed Hollywood sign still loomed on the nearby slopes of Mount Lee, with letters fifty feet high and thirty feet wide, erected in 1923 to advertise a housing development called Hollywoodland. In 1949, city officials chopped off the *land*.[51] The word *Hollywood* remained as a reminder of the glorious past, when sinewy wranglers and beautiful trick riders from the 101 Ranch had walked the streets below, looking for their moment in the sun.

Chapter 34

WHERE THE WEST COMMENCES

The Old West is not a certain place in a certain time, it's a state of mind. It's whatever you want it to be.[1]

—Tom Mix

THE Hundred and One empire continued to gain in reputation and stature, even as Hollywood claimed its rightful place as the world's dominant film center and war and revolution broke out across the Atlantic. In due time, however, these developments exacted a heavy toll on the 101 Ranch, as did a series of business calamities, natural disasters, and the deaths of several figures critical to the success and well-being of the Millers' domain.

Indeed, the period from 1914 to 1924 proved especially challenging for the Millers, setting the stage for the eventual collapse of their ranch, which occurred a few years later. Through it all, the brothers held to the archaic traditions of a family operation dependent on a plantation economy. For the Miller brothers and their faithful followers, the 101 Ranch allowed them to assume their place in history. In the words of a future popular song, the ranch had become the place "where the West commences," the epitome of the western experience.[2]

As the Miller brothers moved into their middle-aged years, they ballyhooed their great holdings while prospering as ranchers, farmers, oil prospectors, and showmen. At heart, however, they remained, first and foremost, horse traders. They never lost their love of haggling over a choice stallion or cutting a deal in a stock pen, with their fancy tooled boots ankle-deep in ripe manure. George Washington Miller would have applauded his three sons' unwavering aptitude for raising and swapping choice horses and mules.

Although Joe and George were quite competent at breeding and marketing horses and other livestock, Zack was the most skilled of the three. He had the most flair, particularly in the bartering end of the business. No one could wrangle a deal quite like Zack.

Back in 1901, the rest of the Millers first witnessed his natural skill at trading when Zack, with help from his pal Bert Colby, went to California and bought and sold mules for the British army to use in the Boer War.[3] In a short time, Zack had parlayed seventeen hundred dollars into an impressive seventy-five thousand dollars in investment earnings.[4] Zack helped the 101 Ranch turn another quick profit, in 1913, by supplying thousands of steeds to the Greek army fighting in the Balkan War.

Then, in January 1914, Zack entered into his most famous trading deal of all, which ended up involving much more than horses. It may not have been the most lucrative transaction he ever made, but it was pure adventure—just the kind of shenanigan that earned the Millers a notable place in the lore of the Wild West of myth and imagination.

The incident occurred during one of Zack's stock-buying expeditions along the war-torn Texas-Mexico border, the scene of ferocious combat between Mexican government troops and revolutionary rebel forces led by Doroteo Arango, an unschooled cowboy-bandit known as Francisco "Pancho" Villa.[5] Soon after reaching the border, Zack became one of the few persons in history to purchase an entire army. The sale included herds of livestock, weapons, ammunition, saddles and tack, and a vast array of equipment and supplies—everything but the soldiers themselves.[6]

Zack's escapade began on January 8, 1914, when he departed Marfa, a west Texas trading point, and made his way to Presidio, an isolated ranching town on the Río Grande.[7] Just across the border in Ojinaga, Mexico, waited a sizable herd of mules valued at four thousand dollars which Zack had purchased and wished to ship by rail back to the 101 Ranch.

Zack found that hotel lodging was difficult to secure in Presidio because of crowds of newspaper reporters, photographers, and curious *turistas* milling about the streets. All of them had flocked to Presidio to watch the pitched battle, under way since January 1, on the other side of the river between the Mexican soldiers and Villa's troops. While waiting for the fighting to stop and the border to reopen so he could claim his herd of mules, Zack and an associate acquired spyglasses and a jug of mescal and found a high point above the Río Grande where they could watch the show.[8]

Meanwhile, Pancho Villa busied himself upriver at El Paso, negotiating a Hollywood movie contract with Mutual Film Corporation. According to popular legend, Villa—eager to bolster his image and make money off gringos—sold the film rights to the Battle of Ojinaga for twenty-five thousand dollars, with stipulations that all fighting must be carried out during daylight hours for optimum filming conditions and the cameraman had to be consulted about all battle plans.[9] Just like the Millers, Villa realized the value of motion pictures as a means of influencing history and the interpretation of events.

In his published memoirs, Villa prudently included no mention of the filmmaking venture. Instead, he wrote of journeying southward from Juárez to join his troops on the border, pausing only to raid ranches and enjoy suppers of roast beef.[10] Finally, on January 10, Villa reached Ojinaga. In just one hour and five minutes—according to Villa's account—he led his brigades to victory over forces commanded by Generals Salvador Mercado and Pascual Orozco.[11] The defeated government troops sustained heavy losses, including at least four hundred deaths. Smoke and the sickening aroma of death hung heavy over the border while the survivors fled across the Río Grande to take refuge in Texas.

"The next day I gave orders to clear camp, after giving the inhabitants of the town assurances of safety," wrote Villa. "Colonel John J. Pershing, in command on the other side of the river, asked permission to visit me in our territory. We greeted each other courteously. He congratulated me on my successes and I praised him for sheltering the defeated troops, since this spared me from being responsible for further casualties."[12]

From his vantage point at Presidio, Zack watched the entire "tangled, bloody slaughter" unfold before him.[13] He never forgot the carnage he witnessed. "The Villistas poured shot and shell into the retreating *federales*, knocking wagons clear out of the water, killing men, killing horses, dogs, women, jackasses," wrote Fred Gipson, drawing on Zack's graphic recollections. "The screams of the wounded and dying were sharp and shrill against the rattle and thunder of the Villista gun-fire. There were long bloody streaks in the muddy waters of the Río Grande that day; the catfish and turtles would feed well for a week."[14]

Among the hordes of refugees who survived the river crossing and surrendered to American authorities at Presidio were several thousand federal soldiers and their camp followers, including grieving women and lost and frightened children. The refugees also included at least thirty-six hundred horses, mules, and burros, large numbers of cattle, pigs, chickens, and fighting cocks, and a forlorn menagerie of terrorized and homeless pet dogs, cats, parrots, and monkeys.[15]

The situation had no precedent in American history. Because the United States was not at war with Mexico, the American authorities could not officially accept the Mexicans' surrender offer, and the troops and equipment could not be considered spoils of war. While the Americans searched for a solution, the defeated Mexicans were disarmed and placed under guard at refugee camps strung out along the road to Marfa.[16]

As soon as he learned that the Mexican government had authorized the sale of the army livestock and equipment, Zack quickly submitted a bid to the Mexican consular office in San Antonio, offering to purchase the entire lot for forty-five thousand dollars.[17] While the Mexican officials considered the proposal, Zack wired his brother Joe at Bliss:

COME AT ONCE HAVE BANK GIVE ME FORTY-FIVE
THOUSAND DOLLARS CREDIT OR BRING THAT MUCH IN GOLD
GOT A HELL OF A BIG DEAL ON[18]

With Zack's telegram in hand, Joe Miller sped off to Ponca City. He secured a bank draft for forty-five thousand dollars and caught the next train for south Texas. At Presidio, Zack and Joe did everything possible to close the deal with the Mexican government.[19]

Neither of the Millers complained when a blue norther suddenly struck, causing the shivering refugees—whose meager supply of sotol stalks, yucca, and greasewood ran out—to throw four hundred fancy cavalry saddles and bridles into the campfires.[20] The slow-burning leather prevented the Mexicans from freezing to death. Comfortable at their hotel, the Millers were concerned mainly with securing additional horses and livestock.

Once the transaction was completed, the defeated Mexican soldiers were transported by train to Fort Bliss, at El Paso, and many of the civilian refugees were sent to Brownsville, where they could be safely returned to Mexico through the border town of Matamoros.[21] All the while, Zack and Joe worked through the snarls of red tape and, when necessary, bribed government officials. They also called on their friend William Jennings Bryan, secretary of state under President Wilson, to intervene on their behalf. Bryan dispatched a wire to United States Customs officers ordering them to waive their usual $3.50 per head duty on the horses and other livestock the Millers purchased.[22]

Finally, after much arguing and negotiating with corrupt bureaucrats and nitpicking brand inspectors, the Millers took possession of the horses and cattle. Pleased with the livestock deal, the brothers eventually sold back to the Mexican government a dozen wagonloads of munitions and weapons, ranging from machine guns and pistols to daggers and machetes.[23]

Some of the herds ended up going to Texas pastures controlled by the Millers. Several railcars loaded with horses, mules, and calves were shipped northward to Bliss. At the 101 Ranch, the wiry Mexican army horses, accustomed to scant rations and hard riding, quickly grew fat in the lush pastures. "Most of the horses sold to a New York buyer at sixty dollars a head," wrote Gipson. "Two hundred and thirty went into the Miller Brothers 101 Wild West Show. Of these, some ninety head finally wound up as courier ponies in the battlefields of Flanders. Back in the thick of another war."[24]

By the time the bookkeepers had completed their tallying, the 101 had taken in more than sixty-five thousand dollars on an investment of forty-five thousand dollars.[25] Once again, Zack Miller had proved his worth as a trader.

At the 101 Ranch that winter of 1914, the Millers were still celebrating the Mexican transaction when they received the sad news that their longtime friend and ally White Eagle had died at age seventy-eight.[26] After more than fifty years as Ponca chief, White Eagle had resigned shortly before his death. His son Horse Chief Eagle became the last hereditary chief of the Poncas.[27]

Christian missionaries at the Ponca agency fussed over White Eagle's body and insisted that the shrouded corpse be placed in a coffin and given a "Christian burial." The chiefs' followers disagreed. Although they allowed the use of a casket, a delegation of Poncas dressed White Eagle in his chieftain's regalia, consisting of a warbonnet, scalp necklace, beaded and fringed doeskin clothes, and moccasins. They painted the old man's face with clay pigment. Before they lowered the coffin into a grave on a limestone ridge, at the tribal burying grounds at the settlement named for White Eagle, some of the Ponca attendants bored a small hole in the lid to give White Eagle a bit of fresh air.[28]

The Poncas also observed an old burial custom reserved for their most respected warriors. They led White Eagle's favorite pony to the gravesite and tied a slipknot around the animal's throat. Then they strangled the pony to death, thus assuring that the dead chief would have a proper mount to ride into the hereafter.[29] Followers blanketed the grave with an abundance of food to sustain the warrior on his journey. In the Ponca tradition, a large American flag was placed on a nearby pole and left to flutter and flap in the wind and rain until it was faded and shredded.

In 1927, thirteen years after White Eagle's death, the Miller brothers created a monument to the revered Ponca chief on a tract of ranchland not far from Bliss, which by then had been renamed Marland.[30] On a hill overlooking the broad pastures of the 101 Ranch, the Millers' building foreman, Sam Stigall, erected a cairn. It was just like the signal mounds used by Indians to guide them on their treks across the land in the days before the coming of white settlers and ranchers.[31]

In tribute to the chief, Stigall and his crew placed a white eagle, carved in stone, atop the fourteen-foot-tall rock shaft. Crazy Snake, a faithful companion of White Eagle who had participated with him in the tribe's sun dances, helped dedicate the marker.[32] Horse Chief Eagle, White Eagle's son and successor as chief, and many other descendants, in their full tribal regalia, also joined in the ceremonies, which included dancing, prayers, speeches, and a great feast.[33]

In 1914, Joe Miller felt particularly saddened on that bitterly cold February day when word came to the White House of White Eagle's passing. When he learned that the old chief had died of pneumonia caused from exposure after walking from the agency to his home and was found along the road nearly frozen, Joe recalled that his own father had died under similar circumstances.[34] Joe—the so-called white chief of the Poncas—also fondly remembered his own experiences as boy and man with White Eagle and the Poncas.

Nonetheless, Joe Miller and his brothers had little time for grieving. They had only two months to complete preparations for the show's 1914 season opener at New York's Madison Square Garden. The show opened on April 20, two days after Barnum & Bailey closed, with daily performances extended for three weeks, until May 9.[35]

Included in the Millers' entourage of riders and ropers was Charles Frederick Gebhart (sometimes spelled Gebhard or Gebhardt), a fearless bronco buster destined to become known to movie audiences of the twenties and thirties as Buck Jones.[36] Mustered out of the army, with his chest covered with sharpshooting medals, on October 23, 1913, at Texas City, Texas, Jones spotted a newspaper advertisement for riders with the Millers' show at nearby Galveston. He made a beeline for the showgrounds and hired on after a successful tryout.[37]

Johnny Baker, a world-famous crack shot and such a familiar figure with Buffalo Bill Cody's Wild West that he virtually was known as Cody's adopted son, became a featured performer with the Hundred and One in 1914.[38] Known far and wide as "The Cowboy Kid," Baker joined up with the Millers after the breakup of Cody and Pawnee Bill Lillie's show the year before.[39]

Several of the world's foremost cowgirl performers made their debuts with the 101 Ranch show during the 1914 season. One of the finest was Ruth Scantlin, whose earliest experience with busting rank broncos occurred while she grew up as a pigtailed girl on ranches and farms in Missouri with her kid brothers Clarence and William.[40]

Ruth, who could ride as well standing on her head as she could sitting in the saddle, became more and more restless and left home while in her early teens. She soon became a dedicated rodeo rider, inspired by Lucille Mulhall and "Prairie Rose" Henderson, a flashy cowgirl who rode professionally as early as 1906 and became one of the all-time great champion bronc riders.[41]

At the 101 Ranch, prior to the start of the show season, the spunky Miss Scantlin changed her name to Ruth Roach after she met and married Bryan Roach, a superb bronc rider with the outfit. The newlywed couple made a great team in the Millers' Wild West show repertoire.[42] Ruth Roach—a blonde beauty decked out in fringed outfit, silk blouse, high Stetson, and stitched boots—cut a stunning figure on the hurricane deck of a bucking cayuse.

During the spring of 1914, Jackie McFarlin, another nimble teenage cowgirl, made her first arena appearance as a trick rider and roper with the Miller brothers.[43] Born in 1896 in Oklahoma Territory, she was the daughter of Jess McFarlin, a Confederate veteran from Crab Orchard, Kentucky, just like G. W. Miller. McFarlin named his daughter Mary Elizabeth Lease McFarlin, for Mary Elizabeth Lease, a fiery orator known as the "Kansas Pythoness" who came into political prominence as a Populist party agitator when she exhorted Kansas farmers "to raise less corn and more hell."[44]

Nicknamed "Leasey" by her family, the McFarlin girl was only a two-year-old when her father landed the job as manager of the dairy department at the 101 Ranch and her mother began to cook for the Millers' sizable workforce. Jess McFarlin and his crew milked seventy-five head of cows twice a day until 1904, when the Millers purchased the first automated milking machine in Oklahoma Territory. When she was ten years old, Leasey began to earn money by gathering eggs from the flock of two thousand prolific leghorn hens.[45] At about the same time, the little girl discovered horses, and her life changed forever.

Along the Salt Fork and across the broad meadows, Leasey McFarlin learned to ride and rope. All those who saw her ride knew she was a natural. Early on, she became fast friends with Will Rogers, Tom Mix, Hoot Gibson, Buck Jones, and many other future stars, long before some of them were even known by those household names. At the start of her career with the Millers, the young woman took the stage name Jackie McFarlin. The handle stuck, even after her marriages to Johnny Roubideaux, a Missouria Indian cowboy, in 1919, and to cattleman DeWitt Laird, in 1944.[46]

As a show cowgirl for the Millers, Jackie eventually became the lead rider for the "Oklahoma Cowgirls," the show's top female performers, who were ordered always to appear "wholesome" and were never allowed to wear rouge or lipstick in public. Wearing a fringed buckskin skirt, shirtwaist silk blouse, wide-brimmed hat, cuffed leather riding gloves, and gleaming boots, Jackie McFarlin flashed an enormous smile as she rode for her first appearance with the Millers at Madison Square Garden.[47]

After the successful run of shows in New York to launch the 1914 season, the Miller and Arlington outfit crammed onto a train comprised of scores of flats, horsecars, sleepers, and wagons. On May 11, the show opened in Philadelphia, nine days after the Ringling-owned organization, known as "the Greatest Show on Earth." Next came a series of performances throughout Pennsylvania and New York state and a weeklong stand in Boston, which put the Millers ahead of the competing circus on the show circuit.[48]

Altogether, the Miller show spent thirty-one weeks on the road during the 1914 season. Traveling more than nine thousand miles by rail, the troupe visited 155 cities in twenty states while putting on 373 performances. The performers spent almost the entire season east of the Mississippi River, except for the final week, when they played to sellout audiences in several Arkansas cities, closing on November 21 at Hot Springs, site of the show's winter quarters.[49]

The real excitement in 1914 came in May, near the end of the New York engagement. That was when the Millers and Arlington split up their Wild West show and dispatched a large section of riders and stock across the Atlantic to perform in England.[50] Although this second unit was not nearly as large as the main show touring the United States, some of the Millers' best hands made the journey to Great Britain. They included many of the performers who had spent the fall and winter on tour in South America and had returned to the United States just in time for the season opener at Madison Square Garden.[51]

Led by Zack Miller, who borrowed Joe's ten-thousand-dollar diamond-studded saddle to impress British crowds, and with Johnny Baker, Buffalo Bill Cody's "adopted" son, acting as arena director, the Millers carefully chose their prime headliners and star attractions to go to England. The company included Bill Pickett, Guy Weadick and Florence La Due, Milt Hinkle, George Hooker, Ruth Roach, Mabel Clive, Lottie Shaw, Chester Byers, Fred and Ed Burns, Lottie Aldridge, Stack Lee, Jane Fuller, Hank Durnell, Lucille Mann, Alice Lee, Babe Willets, and Dot Vernon.[52] Zack also brought along a cowboy band, a mule caravan, bucking horses, longhorn steers, buffalo, prairie schooners, Mexican vaqueros, Russian cossacks, and sixty-five Indians, mostly Oglalas.

During the transatlantic journey, the Miller performers often gathered around a grand piano and belted out a brand-new song entitled "On Ranch 101 (The Wonderful One Is You)," with words by Ballard MacDonald and music by Harry Puck.[53] Although the song never caught on like "St. Louis Blues" or "By the Beautiful Sea," two of the big musical hits of 1914, for some of the show hands, the tune became almost sacred. Composed for the Millers, the catchy melody could be heard every evening drifting from the salon of the ocean liner.

Side by side across the prairie wide,
They were riding, he and she,
A Western gal and eastern pal,
"I'm going back East, Sal," said he;
Tears sprang to her eyes as she answered in surprise:
"If you mean that, and you ain't just making fun,
Guess you like it back East best?"
"No!' said he, "My heart's out West,
Though I'm leaving Ranch One Hundred and One."
(Chorus)
In the mountains of blue, In the rippling streams,
There are fortunes in silver and gold,
O'er the plains roam the herds beyond fondest dreams,
In this land filled with wealth untold,
Like a fairy tale, unfolding wonders on Ranch One Hundred and One,
But the wonderful one is you.[54]

Before long, even members of the ship's crew and passengers, including some enthusiastic travelers from first class, sang along with the Miller outfit.

By the time the liner reached port in England, everybody aboard knew all the verses of the song by heart.

Billed as the "World's Greatest Wild West Show," the Miller and Arlington production opened in London in late May at the Anglo-American Exposition, a celebration marking a century of peace between the American and British peoples.[55] The exposition—staged in the remodeled Shepherd's Bush Stadium and the surrounding exhibition grounds, known as White City—made the Miller performers instant celebrities throughout the British Isles.

The cowboys and cowgirls, Indians in warbonnets, and wild beasts of the prairies outdrew all the other exhibitions and attractions. The 101 Ranch show became even more popular with Londoners than the model of the Panama Canal, a panoramic reproduction of the New York City skyline, or the American daredevil known only as "Crazy" Curran, who looped the loop in a motorcar at breakneck speeds inside the Motordome, a rough wooden structure which resembled a huge teacup.[56]

During the stay in London, Zack leased a spacious abode owned by the widow of a noted physician. Located on Holland Road, the richly furnished residence came with a complete domestic staff, including a cook, butler, maids, gardeners, and a governess for Zack's young daughter, Virginia.[57] Members of the Wild West show found lodging at various London hotels, and the show workers and Indian performers set up a comfortable camp on the stadium grounds.

After hours, Zack and his top performers became the toast of London, picked up in chauffeured motorcars and honored at lavish receptions hosted by such notables as the Earl of Lonsdale and Sir Thomas J. Lipton, a merchant, philanthropist, and yachtsman remembered for his many futile attempts to win the America's Cup. Wishing to repay the Millers' hospitality when he had visited California and toured Inceville in 1911, the famed tea mogul also entertained Zack aboard a private yacht, where liquor flowed generously.[58]

At first, Bill Pickett did not enjoy such favor among the English. As had been the case in several cities in the United States, humane societies and animal-rights activists vehemently protested Pickett's using his illustrious teeth to bulldog steers.[59] London Humane Society officials also complained about the methods used by the Miller wranglers during public demonstrations of horsebreaking.

Ultimately, the humane society persuaded local authorities to arrest Pickett and charge him with cruelty to animals. Zack promptly paid the fine, which amounted to about twenty-five dollars in American money, but instead of curtailing his star cowboy, Zack encouraged Pickett to continue the rodeo act. Aware of all the publicity the show received as a result of the widespread newspaper coverage of the bulldogger, Zack cut a deal with the authorities.[60] Each week, he cheerfully covered the prescribed fine while Pickett continued with what some London journalists called nothing but "horrible steer torture." Despite the unfavorable press, Pickett's popularity steadily rose with the general public.

Soon the controversial bulldogger received invitations to dine with some of the most illustrious citizens of London, such as the Earl of Lonsdale, who threw a huge dinner party at his castle in Pickett's honor. Pickett proved even more popular at the stadium. A highlight of the tour came when he successfully bulldogged a wild Scottish Highland steer at two performances.[61]

All summer, the Miller and Arlington outfit turned out each day for two ninety-minute shows—matinée and evening—which drew record crowds to Shepherd's Bush.[62] Frequently, the cheering audiences included not only prominent Londoners such as Robert Baden-Powell, the British soldier who founded the Boy Scout movement, and an assortment of high-society types but also British nobles and several European monarchs. King George V and Queen Mary sat spellbound in the royal boxes, thoroughly captivated by the saucy cowgirls, Indians in war paint, and wizards of the lasso.[63]

Just before the bronc competition at one of the matinées, Zack's daughter, Virginia, dressed in her best cowgirl outfit, curtsied before the king and queen and presented them with a bouquet of fresh flowers. Recalling the incident in *Fabulous Empire*, Fred Gipson wrote, "King George got so excited watching old 'Chain Foot' [a notorious bucking horse] try to unload a bronc peeler that he forgot and started clapping his royal hands like a commoner. And the Queen caught him at it and slapped his hands to stop him. And little Virginia came away from the royal tribune with her mouth open and her eyes round as saucers."[64]

After the final act of the show, a jubilant King George, surrounded by his entourage, received the performers at the stadium gate, where he repeated over and over: "Most wonderful exhibition! Most wonderful exhibition!" As the entertainers bowed to the sovereigns, one of the attending nobles whispered to Zack that this was the first time in memory that the royal party had not made an early exit but had remained for an entire event.[65]

King George's mother, Queen Alexandra, attended another matinée performance. She was accompanied by her sister—Dowager Empress Marie of Russia—other members of the British royal family, and four motorcars filled with knights, generals, and European royalty.[66] Empress Marie and her fellow Russians paid special attention to the high-riding cossacks racing around the stadium in their elegant uniforms. Others preferred the cowboys and cowgirls, the whooping Indians, and the pioneer scouts reenacting scenes from the 101 Ranch that they had only imagined or had seen on movie screens.[67]

"Queen Alexandra took so many snapshots during the entertainment," reported the *Daily Chronicle*, "that her camera had to be replenished with a fresh spool of films; and before she left the Stadium she specially requested that the entire series of photos bearing on the performance should be forwarded in order to supplement her own collection. As the Royal party drove off, the members of the company—Indians, cowboys, and all—lined the route and heartily cheered the departing guests."[68]

Unfortunately, the cheers drifted away and the good news reported in the newspapers quickly evaporated. On June 28, just two days after Queen Alexandra's visit to Shepherd's Bush to see the Miller and Arlington show, shockwaves rippled across Europe. On that day, a Serbian nationalist fanatic gunned down Archduke Franz Ferdinand, heir to the throne of Austria-Hungary, and his wife, the duchess of Hohenberg. The slayings occurred as their motorcar passed through the streets of Sarajevo, in Bosnia.[69]

"The assassination comes like a clap of thunder to Europe," wrote the *Daily Chronicle*. Indeed, the threat of war had hung over Europe for years. With the scene set for conflagration, the murders of the Austrian archduke and his wife in an obscure provincial capital provided just the spark needed to trigger the Great War, eventually known as World War I. The worst armed conflict the world had yet seen, it commenced within a month and lasted four years.[70]

Based on the tremendous success in London and resultant invitations to bring the Miller and Arlington show to Paris, Barcelona, Berlin, and Saint Petersburg, Zack had been busily planning a comprehensive tour of the Continent.[71] But by mid-July, as troops mobilized and the European powers declared war on one another, many of the royal leaders who, months earlier, had sat together watching the Millers' Wild West show had become avowed enemies. Zack wisely scrapped all plans for an extended European tour.

By the first week of August, armed conflict had erupted on two European fronts as Germany invaded Russia, France, Belgium, Luxembourg, and Switzerland. Within days, more European nations, including England, joined the fray. On August 4, the British, vowing to protect Belgium and the French coast, declared war on Germany. The following day, the United States government formally announced its neutrality and ordered the cruiser *Tennessee* to set sail for Europe with five million dollars in gold to aid stranded American citizens.[72]

On August 7, the war literally arrived at the doorstep of the 101 Ranch show when two London policemen and five British soldiers called on Zack at his Holland Road residence. When the butler summoned him, Zack—fully expecting to be presented with yet another summons for Pickett's arrest—told the servant to send the visitors away and make a proper appointment. Instead, they charged up the stairs and burst into Zack's bedroom, where the leader of the grim-faced delegation announced that they had come as official representatives of King George V.[73] The officer then handed Zack a royal warrant which read:

National Emergency *Impressment Order under Section 115 of the Army Act*

To Zack T. Miller, 68 Holland Rd. W.

His Majesty, having declared that a national emergency has arisen, the horses and vehicles of the 101 Ranch Show are to be impressed for public service if found fit (in accordance with Section 115 of the Army Act), and will be paid for on the spot at the market value to be settled by the purchasing officer. Should you not accept the price paid as fair value, you have the right to appeal to the County Court (in Scotland the Sheriff's Court), but you must not hinder the delivery of the horses and vehicles, etc. The purchasing officer may claim to purchase such harness and stable gear as he may require with the horse or vehicle.

Charles Carpenter, Sergt.
Place *Shepherd's Bush Exhibition*
Date *7th August, 1914*[74]

"I didn't know whether I was going to get a dime for my animals or whether I was contributing them to the cause of King George," Zack later recalled. "When I went down to the show Monday morning I hardly knew my horses. They were all sporting King George's brand."[75]

Immediately, Zack made his case with several high-ranking British contacts, hoping they could halt the wholesale requisition of the animals and equipment. All such attempts proved fruitless, as did Zack's efforts to bribe the authorities. Within a few days, the British government had completed its confiscation of nearly all of the Millers' show livestock and property, leaving only a few trained horses and miscellaneous personal equipment.[76] Most of the horses seized by the British had originated from the herd which Zack had purchased from the Mexican government on the Texas border.

"My father [Joe Miller] often wondered how the British cavalry performed on those Mexican mustangs and Wild West broncos," Joe Miller Jr. later related. "Knowing how much he cared about animals, I'm sure he fretted for a long time over their fate on the battlegrounds of France and Belgium."[77]

The British government also seized the Millers' stagecoach, show wagons, and souped-up automobiles used in the motor-polo exhibitions. In exchange for one hundred head of horses and equipment, Zack received British banknotes which came to the equivalent of approximately eighty thousand dollars in American money.[78] As he cleverly augmented this payment through a monetary rate-of-exchange scheme, Zack faced other difficulties, such as helping his distressed and displaced performers to find a way home.

Prince Lucca and his Imperial Russian Cossacks felt they must return to Mother Russia to help defend their homeland. They boarded a cross-channel packet to France and then made the long journey to Russia. "When this is over," Zack told a weeping Lucca, shortly before the cossacks departed, "I'll still have a place for you boys." But Lucca knew better. "For us, sir, it is over now," he told Zack. "We shall never see the 101 again."[79] The courtly Lucca's prediction proved correct, and Zack never learned the cossacks' fate on the Russian front.

In addition to worrying about getting the rest of the show personnel safely home to the United States, Zack fretted over the fate of the Oglala Sioux Indians who, under contract to the 101 Ranch, were touring Europe for a second consecutive season with a German circus.[80] All standard methods of communications between England and Germany had ceased. Zack dispatched a series of frenzied cables to Joe in the United States, who wired Miller associates in Germany.

After taking a circuitous route to England by way of Norway, Denmark, and Holland, all the Sioux performers eventually found their way to London. They told anyone willing to listen their stories of escaping from

German authorities, who had arrested another band of Oglalas, from Colonel Cummin's Wild West, and accused them of being Serbian spies. Only the intervention of the American consul general in Hamburg had secured the other band's release from a German prison.[81] While Zack hunted for space on any ships bound for the Americas, the Sioux riders and dancers and some of the other Miller entertainers continued a modified schedule of performances, despite being greatly hampered by the absence of proper horses and show stock.

Booking passage to the United States proved no easy feat. With German U-boats stealthily patrolling the seas, any ship flying the Union Jack made an attractive target for deadly torpedoes.[82] To add to Zack's difficulty, most of the British steamship companies refused to sell tickets to Indian passengers. The United States War Department attempted to assist the stranded Americans, but it estimated that naval ships would not be prepared to depart from Newport News, Virginia, for at least a month.[83]

By early September, after the Battle of the Marne in France, Zack managed to get at least some of his employees, along with salvaged remnants of livestock and equipment, on a few of the American freighters and tankers still floating in English ports. Later that month, Zack and the rest of the show personnel finally secured passage aboard the *St. Paul*, a U.S. mail packet bound for New York.[84]

The 101 troupe, along with more than seven hundred other refugees, crammed into the cabins, makeshift berths, and staterooms of the *St. Paul*, a ship designed to carry no more than 250 first-class passengers. Unlike the voyage to England, the return crossing featured no regular gatherings around a piano to belt out tunes about the 101 Ranch. The transatlantic journey—which cost the Millers an additional twenty-five thousand dollars—proved most uncomfortable, but the overcrowded ship finally reached the United States unscathed on September 21.[85]

Within a few days of the *St. Paul*'s arrival, some of the Indians, disgruntled over Joe Miller's refusal to pay them for their extra performances in England, returned straightway to Pine Ridge Reservation in South Dakota. As far as Joe was concerned, the Indian refugees from the Sarrasani Circus performed in London "as a matter of pass-time while they were waiting for an opportunity to return home." In an explanatory letter to John Brennan, the Indian agent at Pine Ridge, Joe suggested "that if you would issue each Indian on the Reservation a big fat cow, there would be several who would kick because they had no calf."[86]

Despite the pay conflict and Joe's contemptuous attitude, several of the

Oglalas joined the Millers' main road show, which performed for American audiences until late November. Meanwhile, Zack beat a hasty retreat to the 101 Ranch for an emergency meeting with his brothers, their brother-in-law, William England, Mother Miller, and other trusted family advisers.

"Zack had taken the best part of the Miller Brothers 101 Wild West Show to England with him," Fred Gipson noted years later. "Now the prize horses and mules were gone. Every trick car and vehicle that could be of any possible use to the British war machine had been taken over. The Cossacks were fighting in Russia. The whole outfit was badly disrupted and disorganized."[87]

In spite of the huge setback, the Millers persisted. Losses from the 1914 London show and European tour were substantial but not catastrophic. The three brothers decided that although many of the physical assets of their show had gone to the war effort, their ranch could still provide personnel, stock, and everything else needed to maintain the show. Along with their partner, Edward Arlington, the Millers cut their losses and pushed forward with plans for the next season.[88]

In 1915, the Millers and Arlington again threw caution to the winds and put out two 101 Ranch Wild West shows. Their primary road show's first public performance came on February 20 at the opening of the Panama-Pacific International Exposition, held in San Francisco to commemorate the opening in 1914 of the Panama Canal, which had brought the city closer commercially to the Atlantic ports of North and South America.[89] More importantly for the resilient citizens, the exposition confirmed the remarkable rise of San Francisco from the ashes of nine years before, when an earthquake and the fires that followed reduced much of the city to shapeless mounds of rubble and a sea of molten ash.

Officials told the Millers that they expected the exposition to draw more than thirteen million visitors during its yearlong run. Performances took place in an arena at "Rainbow City," built beside the famed Presidio, once a garrison for Spanish soldiers originally known as Castillo de San Joaquin, which had evolved into a sprawling U.S. military reservation. Bill Pickett and other Miller hands who had seen the havoc caused by the deadly quake of 1906 marveled at the reconstructed city.[90]

Cowboy star Tom Millerick, who eventually joined with his brother Jack to become the top rodeo stock contractors and producers on the West Coast, had recruited many of the riders and ropers at the exposition show. More show hands hailed directly from the rangelands of the 101, and still others came from the film studios and movie lots of southern California.[91]

Joe Miller headed up the lavish production, backed by some of his most reliable veterans and such specialists as Pickett, sharpshooting star Princess Wenona, bandleader Park Prentiss, and rodeo clown Dan Dix. The celebrated cowboy character Duke R. Lee, who had been breaking horses for the English army, acted as the exposition show announcer. Lee, a talented bronc buster, had been with the Miller brothers during their early years on the road but had taken a leave of absence because of his chronic sleepwalking. When the show traveled by train at night, sound-asleep Lee would leave his berth and wander like a zombie through the sleeper car. On several occasions, he came dangerously close to stepping off the speeding train. During the show's run in San Francisco, with no trains to worry about, Joe figured Duke Lee could sleepwalk in relative safety if his hotel room was on the ground floor.[92]

Cuba Crutchfield, considered one of the best trick ropers in the business, made his debut with the Millers at San Francisco. To stir interest, Crutchfield put up a cash pot of one thousand dollars and had Joe Miller place an advertisement in *Billboard*, daring all competitors to a roping contest, with winner take all. Crutchfield never lost a cent because no one dared take up the challenge.[93]

Pedro Leon, yet another expert roper with a flair for drama, performed daily with a maguey lariat and ready loop in each hand. Leon thrilled the crowds by first lassoing four galloping horses and riders with his left hand, and then—almost simultaneously—roping four horses and riders headed in the opposite direction using his right hand.[94]

"Booger Red" Privett, a famed bronc peeler and Irish teetotaler who constantly chewed a cigar, served as arena director for the San Francisco show. Born Samuel Thomas Privett Jr. in 1858 on a Texas cattle spread, the diminutive redhead picked up his picturesque moniker as a thirteen-year-old when he and a chum packed a hollow tree with gunpowder for a big Christmas bang. The ensuing blast killed the other boy and nearly blinded young Privett, causing another friend who accompanied him to the country doctor to declare, "Gee, but Red is sure a booger now, ain't he?" From that day, Privett became known as "Booger Red."[95]

A longtime pal of Bill Pickett and a highly respected champion cowboy, Privett merged his Booger Red Wild West Show with the Miller and Arlington outfit just prior to the 1915 season opener. His teenage daughter, Ella, accompanied Booger Red to California and quickly became one of the favorite performers at the San Francisco Exposition.[96]

Ella Privett's star shone particularly bright on the afternoon the 101 show sponsored a ten-mile relay race, a grueling event which called for each of the four riders to use five horses and change mounts every half-mile. The lone female entrant, Miss Ella—despite crashing through a fence at breakneck speed near the seventh mile marker—came in second, just behind Tom Millerick on a fast string of his fine horses.[97] Thousands of spectators shot to their feet and cheered the plucky Texas girl.

"A strong wind swept across the course, filling the air with dust, and at times the riders were lost from view," reported the *San Francisco Chronicle*. "All the riders pounding around the track in the dust storm, with the twenty changes of mounts, found the race a hard ordeal, but they yielded the honors for gameness to the little cowgirl, as she was carried away exhausted in the arms of her father, 'Booger Red' from Texas."[98]

Besides captivating everyone who saw her ride in San Francisco that day, Ella won the heart of Hank Linton. A Kansas cowboy and trick roper with the Millers, Linton competed in the relay race and came in third, just a breath after Ella. Linton, who always vowed he would marry a gal smart enough to beat him, courted the teenager all season, oblivious to the objections of her protective father.[99] On November 27, 1915, while still performing with the Millers' road show, the lovers wed on horseback outside a Baptist church in Port Arthur, Texas. Ella was eighteen and Hank was twenty-seven.[100]

Booger Red, who died in 1925, need not have worried about his daughter's welfare. She and her cowboy husband rode together for many years and stayed happily married until 1967, when Hank died at their home in Sapulpa, Oklahoma. Ella took his body back to Cherryville, Kansas, and buried the old roper in a family plot, just as he had wanted.[101]

The relationship between Ella Privett and Hank Linton was not the only romance in the air during the Panama-Pacific International Exposition. Miss Bessie Herberg, with cascading blonde curls and fair skin, not only appealed to the spectators who watched her take the "educated horse" named Happy through his paces, but she also bewitched Joe Miller.[102]

Joe, approaching his forty-seventh birthday, fell hard for Bessie, who was young enough to be his daughter. Just watching the youthful horsewoman was not nearly enough. In no time, they became blanket companions, as old-time cowboy called lovers. Joe and Miss Bessie turned up as familiar figures at such public places as the Saint Francis, Fairmont, and Palace Hotels; the dining room of the Mark Hopkins; and the rustic seafood houses and sidewalk stands along Fisherman's Wharf.[103]

When the 101 Ranch motion-picture department later shipped equipment and crew to San Francisco to churn out a series of western movies on location, Joe made sure that both he and Bessie had roles in the productions. The movie company's favorite location was due south of the Presidio in Golden Gate Park, a half-mile-wide and four-mile-long expanse created from barren sand dunes in the 1870s. Much of the filming of *Neola of the Sioux,* a 101 Ranch movie featuring an Indian maiden called Neola, Pedro Leon, Mae Fierst, and Duke Lee, took place in the picturesque park, dotted with rhododendrons and ferns and a string of artificial lakes.[104]

The movie outfit's crowning achievement included the filming of a complete exposition show performance. Called *The Exposition's First Romance,* the five-reel western starred Joe Miller, Clara Freeman from the popular "High Jinks" Company, and Duke Lee.[105] The ruggedly handsome Lee won a lead part in several of the 101 Ranch pictures, usually in the villain's role, while continuing as the exposition show announcer. Eventually the pace became overwhelming, and Lee had to decide between announcing or continuing in films. He chose the movies, and Chief Eagle Eye took on the job of announcing the shows.

Bessie Herberg also got plenty of exposure in the feature film. A portrait of the cowgirl graced advertisements which urged theater operators to book the Millers' newest film, based on "an Actual Romance Woven Around the Panama-Pacific Exposition." In the photograph, a smiling Bessie, clad in a smart riding outfit and mounted on her trusty stallion, looked the part, perched on a fancy tooled-leather saddle—a gift from Joe Miller.

Back in Oklahoma, reports of Joe's amorous indiscretions reached his long-suffering wife, Lizzie. A faithful spouse ever since Joe had brought her from Louisiana as a bride, in 1894, she had heard plenty of gossip through the years about her husband's philandering. Often, Lizzie and her children, along with Mother Miller, had joined the road show to stay close to Joe. It came as no surprise to anyone that as the rumors about Joe's dalliance with Bessie continued, Lizzie reacted by packing up her two sons, Joe Jr. and George, and teenage daughter, Alice. They boarded a train for San Francisco.[106]

"I think Papa would have adored having Mama dress as a cowgirl and be a constant travelling [sic] companion," Alice Miller Harth observed many years later. "Heaven forbid! as far as Mama was concerned. . . . Mother had never dreamed she was marrying a circus man. . . . It posed a problem outside her experience and training for rearing a family. She finally decided that travel was educational if not taken in too large doses. Mother never rode, but we children had made for us riding outfits of fringed leather, our own little high-heeled cowboy boots and real Stetson hats."[107]

On arrival in San Francisco with her brood, Lizzie quickly discovered that her husband had changed his plans. Instead of remaining at the exposition for the rest of the year, Joe had decided to take the show on the road. Although it may have appeared that such a maneuver was only an attempt to escape from his family, Joe had been mulling the situation ever since spring, when exposition attendance figures began to decline rapidly. Disbanding the production in San Francisco and linking up with Miller and Arlington road show offered Joe an attractive option.[108]

The Millers' number-two show for the 1915 season—a traveling production with a great number of top-notch performers and Professor Donato La Banca as bandleader—had opened on April 10 at Hot Springs, Arkansas, and then had gone on the road. "It is bigger, better and grander than ever, and that is putting it mildly, for some of the greatest acts ever dreamed of in a Wild West show have been added to the program of last year," boasted George Miller to a reporter.[109]

The show was to have traveled directly to Texas, with an April 14 performance set at Dallas, followed by appearances at Fort Worth and six other Texas cities. Those plans changed because of a quarantine necessitated by an outbreak of hoof-and-mouth disease which temporarily prohibited the shipment of any livestock into the Lone Star State.[110] The quarantine, however, did not keep the Millers from making money.

For weeks before the road show opened in Arkansas, Zack and George Miller wrangled with Texas livestock officials and prepared for the coming season. They also devoted long hours to further enriching the 101 Ranch empire's coffers by selling horses and mules for the war effort. For several days in March, the brothers huddled in Fort Worth's Westbrook Hotel with a commission of horse dealers representing the Italian government on a mission to purchase cavalry mounts. "These men know a horse when they see one," quipped Zack. "Give them good horses to inspect and they will pass upon a horse a minute. They know what they want when they see it and it doesn't take them any longer to reject a horse than it does to accept one. It is a pleasure to work with these men, as no time at all is lost."[111]

Although the Millers made tens of thousands of dollars by buying and selling livestock bound for Europe, transportation obstacles appeared insurmountable. To get around the shipping problem, the Millers, with characteristic flamboyance, bought their own ship.

"Joe C. Miller of the 101 Ranch now in Frisco has stated that at the present time it is almost impossible to secure means of transportation to Europe from Galveston of the stock he is purchasing for the belligerents and it was decided that the Miller brothers should purchase their own steamship," reported the *Ponca City Courier*. "Zack Miller made a flying trip to New York and closed the deal with a German maritime concern for the purchase of a vessel at a price of $450,000. While this figure seems exorbitant, Mr. Miller stated that the vessel will have paid for itself when it has made four trips with stock."[112]

The purchase of the German vessel won approval from the British and French governments, with the understanding that during the war the steamship would be used only to transport livestock to Allied nations battling the kaiser. At the close of hostilities, the Miller brothers would refit the interior to comfortably house and transport their show performers on a five-year tour of the world. "In this way," newspapers reported, "the show will play maiden territory, week stands, at an expense of about 25 percent of the present transportation outlay."[113]

Unfortunately, Germany's escalated attacks on neutral shipping, especially around the British Isles, curtailed the Millers' maritime ambitions. Throughout the spring of 1915, more merchant ships and steamers fell prey to German torpedoes and mines. On May 1, a U-boat, without warning, torpedoed the American tanker *Gulflight*. Just six days later, a German submarine sank the Cunard Line steamer *Lusitania*, bound from New York to England, killing 1,198 people, including 124 Americans.[114] The Millers continued to ship as many horses and mules as possible to Allied forces, but they postponed all plans for future European tours.

During April and May, Joe Miller busily placated both Bessie Herberg and his anxious wife. With a wary eye on plummeting attendance figures, Joe also divided his time between the exposition in San Francisco and the road show making its way around the country.

Just days after the *Lusitania* sank, Joe and his brothers added a new wrinkle to their Wild West venture. After a bit of haggling, they signed a deal with prizefighter Jess Willard, who on April 5, under the scorching sun in Havana, Cuba, had won the world's heavyweight championship in the twenty-sixth round by knocking out Jack Johnson, the first black man to hold the title.[115]

A native of Kansas, Willard stood well over six feet six inches tall and weighed 250 pounds. Known as the "Great White Hope," the behemoth instantly became a national hero and the idol of all those who believed the prestigious boxing title needed to be restored to the white race.[116] The Millers were confident that Willard had all the drawing power necessary to attract crowds of patrons to their show. They congratulated Edward Arlington for having signed Willard to a contract for a summer tour with their outfit.

According to the terms of the deal, Willard received one hundred thousand dollars for five months of personal performances, staged boxing demonstrations, and appearances in all the grand-entry processions but none of the street parades. In addition, the Millers and Arlington supplied the champion and his entourage (wife, son, manager, trainer, sparring partner, and assorted guests) with a brand-new private railcar, a chauffeur and automobile, a chef, and a porter.[117]

Willard and his sparring partner, Walter Monahan, joined the Miller show at Minneapolis on May 10, at the start of a two-day stand.[118] Wearing cowboy attire and billed as "a cowboy from Kansas, crack rifle and revolver shot, expert swimmer, [who] never drinks or smokes," Willard became an instant hit with the public at stops in Chicago, Detroit, and Buffalo. For an extra twenty-five-cent fee, fans of the "one and only Jess" watched the cowboy pugilist spar with an opponent. Soon, extra performances were booked to accommodate throngs of fans.[119]

One of the Miller bronc riders claimed he saw Butch Cassidy, the notorious "Wild Bunch" leader supposedly killed years before in Bolivia, in attendance at a performance. Otherwise, there was little excitement left in San Francisco. Inspired by the glowing reports from the road show, Joe Miller closed at the exposition on June 14. He packed up everything on railcars and took the whole outfit back to Bliss for fresh stock.[120]

On June 25, at Erie, Pennsylvania, the two shows combined and finished the season as a single unit known as "The 101 Ranch Wild West Show With Jess Willard."[121] Besides the performers Joe had brought from the exposition, others who took part in the joint show that season included the Tantlingers, Clarence Schultz, José "Mexican Joe" Barrera, Bryan and Ruth Roach, Beatrice Brosseau, and the picturesque Tex Cooper, as show announcer and parade marshal. After stops throughout the nation, Jess Willard and his crew left the show at New Orleans in late October, as his contract dictated. The 1915 season closed for the Millers on November 20, in their home territory at Ponca City. During thirty-four weeks and more than twelve thousand miles on the road, the show had played 188 dates in twenty-three states. It ended a record-breaking season with net profits reported at more than two hundred thousand dollars.[122]

That winter, as the war continued to rage in the trenches of France, the Miller brothers must have felt like old bronc busters itching to climb back on and win the gold. While the prairie winds wailed outside, the Millers rested in the comfort of the White House. They also counted their blessings and breathed a collective sigh of relief at having triumphed over two difficult years.

SATURDAY'S HEROES AND HEROINES

MOTION PICTURES—AS well as the legion of screen idols the film industry created—brought great change to the nation's cultural scene and permanently impacted the public's leisure and entertainment habits. Movies also affected how Americans viewed their own history. This was especially true of westerns, a thoroughly American cinema genre.

Early western movies, such as those made on the 101 Ranch or films shot in California which featured the Millers' star entertainers, were "characterized by sincerity of sentiment and a poetic spirit," according to some motion-picture authorities.[1] These observers pointed out that film patrons believed they were actually witnessing "not merely casual entertainment but, rather, a serious and dignified visual discussion of an era which had already passed into the nation's heritage."[2]

In reality, a powerful group of filmmakers and influential sources, including the Millers and their associates, deliberately manipulated the past and reconstructed historical events to suit scripts crafted to lure large crowds. During the creative process, some shifting occurred in the public's leisure interests. As westerns grew in popularity, the appeal of other established entertainment institutions not only diminished, but in some instances faded completely from the scene.

The demise of the great Wild West live extravaganzas, such as the ill-fated Buffalo Bill Cody and Pawnee Bill Lillie joint creation called the "Two Bills" Show, occurred between 1900 and the start of World War I. Some of the Millers' elder performers from the show circuit insisted that the passing of this type of public entertainment resulted primarily from the steady advance of motion pictures.

"It was the movies that killed the wild west show, movies and the war," Edith Tantlinger, the rifle sharpshooter dubbed "queen of the cowgirls" during the years she rode for the Millers, declared in a 1920s interview.[3] "But the movies sounded the doom even before the war. Movies had no real cowboys. Supers hired by the day, in chaps and sombrero that a real cowpuncher would not be caught dead in, spoiled the dare-devil spirit of the west. . . . For they have cranked the wild west out of America. With the coming of the movie, the old wild west show was doomed, and with the passing of the show passes the interest in the real days of the plains. It's about time for us to quit, too."

Vern Tantlinger, longtime cowboy boss for the Miller brothers, agreed with his wife's assessment of the movie business and its impact on their way of life. "The wider the hat, the less cowboy, I always say," observed Vern. "We were in the movies ourselves, and we know. The action and spirit and color of a wild west show is [sic] lost in the pictures. Western pictures are going. Even Bill Hart and our friend Tom Mix will soon find their day, like ours, is waning."[4]

Certainly not everyone, including Mix, Hoot Gibson, Buck Jones, Ken Maynard, and the 101 Ranch veterans who earned fortunes from film work, concurred with the Tantlingers' negative appraisal of movies. Instead, Mix and the others turned their backs on rodeo riding and traveling the long and arduous show circuit. They remained in Hollywood and championed cowboy motion pictures as they watched the population of southern California mushroom, in large part because of the flourishing cinema business.

"From 1914 into the 1920s, Hollywood grew from a handful of wooden bungalows in an orchard realm into a village where elaborate mansions reared themselves above streets of box-shaped stucco dwellings," wrote Jesse L. Lasky Jr., a noted screenwriter. "Hilltops sported bogus Spanish haciendas where the stars, directors, and producers were grandly housed above the hovels of the technicians and extras who fed the growing factories."[5]

After 1915, Hollywood and Los Angeles not only underwent a tremendous growth in population but also experienced a conspicuous change of attitude toward the motion-picture industry. This positive perception extended to movie people, who had formerly been ostracized and branded as undesirables. With big money came respectability and acceptance; it seemed that money could buy both.

For example, by 1915 Charlie Chaplin, who went to work at Keystone for $150 a week in 1913, pulled down a stunning ten thousand dollars each week. Appearing with such established stars as Fatty Arbuckle and Mabel Normand, the brilliant comedienne who learned in Inceville how to ride a horse, Chaplin became the toast of the town. By that time, the industry's annual payroll had reached twenty million dollars. Even the skeptics had to admit that movies and those associated with the film industry had clearly arrived.[6]

Many of the motion-picture newcomers riding at the vanguard came straight from the bunkhouses and show arenas of the 101 Ranch. As the twenties began to roar, a significant number of leading ladies and men, stunt performers, screen villains, directors and producers, screenwriters, and matinée heroes and heroines who staked their claims in Hollywood proudly listed on their résumés time spent with the Hundred and One.

The Miller brothers remained in the movie business for years after they stopped wintering their show performers at Venice and after Inceville vanished from the scene. Indeed, the 101 Ranch film crews ground out action flicks well into the 1920s. Besides the Millers' feature films and Pathé serials, such documentary filmmakers as Bennie Kent and A. D. Kean—an unsung Canadian hired by Zack Miller and known as the "Cowboy Cameraman"—produced numerous quasi documentaries of the 101 Ranch road shows as well as of the ranch roundups staged at the popular performance grounds along the Salt Fork.[7] Always aware of their show's familiar catch phrase—"The Real Wild West"—the Millers made sure the 101 Ranch remained the foremost training ground for western film stars and performance artists.

Unfortunately, not all the heroes and heroines who graduated from the ranks of the 101 troupe enjoyed lives with storybook endings like the romanticized characters they portrayed on the big screen. Naughty behavior and moral transgressions among stars and starlets in the carnival atmosphere of Hollywood attracted as much public attention as the blazing klieg lights on a movie set. Frequently, vicious and reckless gossip toppled theatrical careers destined for greatness.

The Millers never quite adapted to the strange behavior of Hollywood, which included well-publicized scandals and misfortunes involving various associates and friends. For instance, in 1921 the Miller brothers were startled to learn that a despondent and unstable John Cudahy, a family friend and the son of a prominent meatpacker, had shot the top of his head off at a palatial mansion on Hollywood Boulevard.[8]

Long before he went to southern California, Cudahy first experienced the West at the 101 Ranch. The Millers distinctly recalled Cudahy's visit to their old Riverside Camp in 1908 and how he had rescued Horse Chief Eagle from the Salt Fork River after the Indian's pony broke through the ice. Six years later Horse Chief Eagle succeeded his father, White Eagle, as the last hereditary chief of the Ponca tribe.[9] When news of the Hollywood suicide reached the Millers' White House, they toasted Cudahy's memory on behalf of the Ponca people.

All three Miller brothers—the progeny of a frequently brutal frontier—had long been acquainted with violence in all forms. They had been known to mete out their brand of justice and to seek retribution which sometimes included vicious and lethal physical acts. Throughout the many years the Millers devoted to ranch life, the oil business, and the entertainment industry, they also witnessed their share of suicides, shoot-outs, and brawls involving their personnel.[10] Nevertheless, some misadventures—especially those involving women in their employ—stirred the hearts of even the hardened Miller men.

One of the most tragic examples was Mabel Normand, perhaps the most talented comic actress of the silent screen era. She held the dubious distinction of becoming one of the first movie stars associated with the Millers to wind up a victim of violence—a cruel verbal ambush which left her image permanently tarnished by rumor and innuendo.

Once described by her longtime lover Mack Sennett as being "as beautiful as a spring morning," the amusing Mabel always kept her ties with the Millers, their cousins Will and Jim Brooks, and other friends she had made on the dusty movie sets at Inceville.[11] However, while Mabel won starring roles in numerous hit films for Goldwyn, she also became caught up in the wilder side of the Hollywood social scene. Mabel's rather careless lifestyle raised eyebrows and inspired unsubstantiated tales of cocaine addiction.[12]

Other stories of Mabel abounded. On the evening of February 2, 1922, William Desmond Taylor, a suave Irish-born film director whose early movie projects had involved 101 Ranch personnel, was found shot to death on the floor of his Hollywood bungalow on South Alvarado.[13] Taylor had been linked romantically with several popular stars, including Mabel Normand and Mary Miles Minter. A murder inquest revealed that Mabel was one of the last people to have seen him alive. Although the police never considered her a suspect in the unsolved crime, lurid newspaper reports suggesting otherwise further sullied Mabel's reputation.[14]

A short time later, authorities named her chauffeur—discovered with Mabel's pistol in his hand—in the shooting death of Hollywood millionaire Cortland S. Dines. Once again, the press had a field day. Even adoring fans turned against the actress and her films. She made her last movie in 1926. Ill with tuberculosis and pneumonia, Mabel Normand died at age thirty-five on February 2, 1930—eight years to the day after Taylor's mysterious murder.[15]

The next day, just as the news of Mabel Normand's death broke, another of the Millers' former heroines died. Lillian Smith—the great rifle shot better known as Princess Wenona—passed away at age fifty-nine in a Ponca City hospital after having suffered through a bitterly cold prairie winter.[16] Ironically, two of the most talented women ever associated with the 101 Ranch had died within less than twenty-four hours of each other in Oklahoma and Hollywood—locales which had made the Millers and their empire the focus of public attention.

"Every person who ever drew a pay check from the Miller brothers and even those folks who visited the ranch had value and when they got into some kind of trouble, or when they died, well, that really meant something to the family," recalled Zack Miller Jr. many years later. "No one, and I mean that, no one was ever forgotten—not a single soul."[17]

The Millers lost other Hollywood friends as well. Thomas Ince, pioneer film director and an intimate of the Miller brothers and the Bison 101 film crews, became another of the early celebrity casualties.

Ince's great period of turning out epic western films, which began with the Millers in 1911, had ended by 1914. In November of that year, the Millers, embroiled in more contract disputes with the Hollywood crowd, decided to sever their ties with Ince. Joe Miller sold off all his landholdings in California. The Miller brothers gathered up five thousand head of horses, including many from the corrals and stables at Santa Ynez Canyon, and shipped them to the Allied forces in Europe. Only about two dozen Indian riders, a small herd of cattle, and 150 saddle horses were left at Inceville.[18]

Ince stayed busy shooting westerns starring William Surrey Hart, a popular Shakespearean actor who had been Ince's roommate during lean days together on Broadway. Despite the fact that Inceville was only a shadow of what it had been before the Millers lost their contract and withdrew from California, the place captivated Bill Hart after only one visit. "Tom [Ince] called and took me out to the old camp," Hart later said. "The very primitiveness of the whole life out there, the cowboys and the Indians, staggered me. I loved it. They had everything to make Western pictures. The West was right there!"[19]

Hart became a top box-office attraction known for making starkly realistic westerns. He eventually directed many of his films and also worked closely with the famed Clifford Smith, a 101 Ranch veteran and a leading director during the silent era. Another key member of the creative team was noted cinematographer Joseph H. August, who began his career at

Inceville and later created images for some of John Ford's most distinguished films.[20]

Inceville, known for a time as Hartville, eventually fell prey to the elements. Frequent brush fires, costly production delays because of the thick Pacific fog, and punishing storms along the coastal road took a heavy toll on the once spectacular movie location. Inceville served as a back lot until 1922, but within two more years directors largely abandoned it after another fire destroyed the few remaining sets.[21]

John Gilbert, a dashing leading man remembered for his starring roles as a celluloid lover opposite Greta Garbo, broke into films as a bit player at Inceville. Not long after the Santa Ynez location fell into disuse, Gilbert spoke with great sadness of the old days when Pedro Leon, the 101 Ranch rider and actor, bossed the gang of Inceville cowboys, resplendent in their sombreros and chaps.[22]

"Occasionally, I take a long afternoon drive up the beach beyond Santa Monica," Gilbert recalled. "Where buildings and stages and western streets of Inceville used to be, are now the red flags and orange placards of a new subdivision called Castellammare. My stomach sickens as I turn my eyes seaward and pass this hideous destruction of what was once my glorious playground."[23]

Tom Ince, to all appearances not nearly as sentimental about the demise of Inceville as Gilbert and others who had worked there, walked away from the site that once bore his name and never looked back. In 1915, Ince, with assistance from property developer Harry Culver, created a new, gleaming white studio on farmland at Culver City.[24] Along with his film credentials, the visionary director's reputation for being ruthless and difficult also grew. By 1918, after quarrels with his associates, Ince built yet another studio, one mile east of the old one, where he made features as an independent producer.

Then on November 19, 1924, Thomas Ince, the pioneer filmmaker who had captured images of the Millers' best riders in the California hills, died mysteriously and without warning. He had just celebrated his forty-second birthday. Ince's death was officially attributed to angina pectoris, or heart failure, resulting from an ulcer and acute indigestion.[25] According to the authorized account, Ince died at his recently completed Benedict Canyon residence, Días Dorados (Golden Days), surrounded by his loving wife, three sons, and two brothers.

Gossip about Ince's sudden passing persisted in Hollywood and beyond. Lurid tales of the director's death circulated through the Miller family conferences at the White House. According to the rumor mill, Ince was a murder victim who had died of "lead poisoning" after having been shot while aboard the *Oneida*, a luxury yacht owned by newspaper magnate William Randolph Hearst.[26]

One version of the story claimed that Hearst suspected Ince of having an affair with his young lover, chorus girl turned actress Marion Davies. When Hearst supposedly discovered the pair romancing aboard his own yacht, he produced a revolver and shot the hapless film director to death. Another rendition of the rumor, again lacking confirmation, suggested that the fatal bullet had been intended for Charlie Chaplin, whom Hearst actually had found with his protégé, Davies. When Hearst began to shoot wildly, he missed Chaplin and accidentally killed Ince.[27]

No matter what had transpired, Ince's puzzling death rocked Hollywood, and the Millers felt the shock waves at the 101 Ranch. However, not all members of the Hollywood crowd associated with the Miller brothers ended up victims of bad luck. Plenty of glamorous entertainers and film notables went on to lead happy and productive lives and reveled in their experiences with the Hundred and One, in Oklahoma and in California.

A few of these more illustrious notables were William Desmond (not to be confused with the director William Desmond Taylor), a muscular Irishman cast in many of the action pictures at Universal, mostly serials and westerns; Helen Ferguson, star of *Wild West*, a Pathé serial costarring Jack Mulhall, produced in three months in 1925 on the 101 Ranch and directed by Robert F. Hill, director of the first Tarzan movie; Helen Holmes, a true serial queen and heroine of many Hollywood action pictures; and Sid Jordan, noted cowboy movie scoundrel, especially in Tom Mix productions.[28]

Several others from the Millers' outfit put in time as working cowboys and saddle tramps before they became film stars. Miles "Bud" Osborne, a proud Texan and one of the better known genuine movie cowpokes, ranched for a spell before performing with Buffalo Bill and with the 101 Ranch show. Beginning in 1915 as a player in some of Ince's productions, Osborne appeared in literally hundreds of silent and sound westerns, most often as a low-life heavy. Osborne, who never forgot the lessons he learned as a rider for the Millers, became known as one of Hollywood's finest horseman and "stage coach manipulators."[29]

Art Acord, an Oklahoma native and honest-to-goodness cowpuncher, starred with Wild West shows before becoming a screen cowboy and stunt performer in one-reelers shot in New Jersey by Bison Film Company. Sometimes using Buck Parvin as a screen name in early two-reelers, Acord later served with valor in France during the Great War and was awarded the Croix de Guerre for bravery under fire at Verdun. Acord went on to fame as one of the leading cowboy actors of the 1920s, when western serials became firmly established staples of independent and major studios.[30]

The roguish Acord turned to bootlegging and ran into trouble with the law after he failed to make the transition to sound westerns. After serving a hitch in prison, Acord drifted to Mexico with a rodeo outfit and ended up flat broke from incessant gambling. In 1931, he was found dead from cyanide poison in a Mexican hotel.[31] The death was ruled suicide, but some of the old riders claimed Acord really had died in a knife fight when he was found in bed with another man's wife.

Jack Hoxie—like Acord, an Oklahoma-born movie star with ranching and rodeo credentials—rode in the grand entry with the 101 Ranch show in Los Angeles in 1911 and appeared with the outfit in 1912. By 1916, he had launched his film career as an extra and bit player. Although critics pegged Hoxie as a burly and athletic cowboy but a mediocre actor, his screen presence appealed to youngsters who enjoyed fast-paced pictures with plenty of action and stunts. Hoxie played western leads for several independents until the advent of talking pictures. Between 1923 and 1927, Hoxie's popularity at the Universal lot was second only to that of another former Miller rider, Hoot Gibson.[32]

During the early 1930s, when only Zack survived of the three Miller brothers, Hoxie once again joined the 101 Ranch show. He made many appearances, along with his trained dog, Bunkie, and his wonder horse, Scout. Hoxie later performed with a variety of Wild West enterprises before retiring to a small ranch in the Oklahoma Panhandle. The old matinée cowboy died in 1965 at age eighty, proud to the very end of his glory days with the Millers.[33]

Inspired by actual characters as well as historic events, all of these silent-picture western stars with 101 Ranch connections paved the way for future big-screen cowboys and cowgirls and their faithful sidekicks. As a result, in the years between the world wars and throughout the heyday of the western motion picture, most American youngsters and countless adults flocked to neighborhood movie houses or big-city picture palaces every Saturday afternoon to see their favorite sagebrush heroes and heroines of the silver screen.

Elmer Kelton, an award-winning writer of western fiction who grew up in Texas feasting on Saturday matinées, recalled[34]:

> We realized that many movie cowboys were not real cowboys at all. We could tell that by the way they mounted a horse, the way they sat in the saddle, or just the way they wore their hats. But there was the redeeming nameless but dependable Gower Gulch gang, outlaws in one picture, possemen in the next, who got on a horse like a real cowboy and rode as if they had been born to it.
>
> The *reel* West was often a lot more fun than the *real* one. The heroes dressed better, and heroines never got their hair mussed up. Problems always got solved in the final reel. In life, many problems never got solved, and those that did seemed to be replaced by new ones just as troublesome. . . . when myth collided with reality, Hollywood almost always chose the myth.[35]

And whenever Hollywood chose myth over reality, so did the public. Watching someone ride into the sunset provided the very best escape from the problems of the world. The favorite mythmakers dashing across Hollywood's Wild West range in the 1920s and into the bittersweet 1930s were Ken Maynard, Buck Jones, Hoot Gibson, and Tom Mix. This charismatic quartet became known as the "Big Four" of cowboy actors. Every one of them was a memorable box-office buckaroo. Every one of them left his own distinctive brand on the motion-picture screen. Every one of them had the Millers and the 101 Ranch to thank—at least in part—for his success.

Born in Indiana in 1895, Ken Maynard was the youngest of the famous foursome.[36] Taught to ride and handle horses while a toddler, Ken Maynard began his show business career in 1914 as a circus and rodeo trick rider with several outfits on the circuit, including the 101 Ranch Wild West show.[37] After serving with the army during the Great War, Maynard joined the Ringling Brothers circus and became head rider in the show's Wild West event. Maynard's skill at freestyle riding—perfected while appearing with the Millers and several other outfits—brought him to the attention of Hollywood moviemakers. A big break for Maynard came in 1924 when he played the role of Paul Revere opposite Marion Davies in *Janice Meredith*, a production of William Randolph Hearst's Cosmopolitan Pictures.[38]

With his movie earnings, Maynard bought a palomino for six hundred dollars. He named the handsome steed Tarzan at the suggestion of his friend Edgar Rice Burroughs, author of the popular adventure novels. Before long, Maynard started to appear in a series of quickie independent western movies which featured him as a bashful hero astride his loyal wonder horse.[39]

Maynard vaulted from silents to talkies by becoming the screen's first singing cowboy—a straight shooter who never smoked or drank in a picture. Ironically, an off-screen addiction to alcohol took a heavy toll on Maynard's demeanor and his relationships with fellow actors and directors.[40] Eventually, Maynard's argumentative behavior and thin musical talent inspired movie executives to hire another warbler—Gene Autry, a budding cowboy star. Will Rogers had discovered him in 1928, when Autry was on duty as a telegraph operator at the railroad station in Chelsea, a small Oklahoma town on Route 66.[41]

Maynard left films for a while and went back to the rodeo circuit. He returned to the screen briefly and then retired, except for rare appearances at state fairs and bit parts in movies. Maynard refused to watch any of his old films, and he shunned most television westerns. His wife, Bertha, a former aerialist with Ringling Brothers, died or, as Maynard put it, "went away," in 1969. Until the end of his life, the man who had prided himself on his clean screen image was known to keep a plentiful supply of cigars and bourbon in the refrigerator.[42]

"I'm no legend," the aging cowboy actor told a reporter in a 1969 interview. "I hate the word."[43] Ken Maynard died in 1973 at age seventy-seven, after having spent several years alone with his memories in a musty trailer in the San Fernando Valley.

Maynard certainly was not forgotten. "It was a real treat when I could plunk down my dime to see Buck Jones or Ken Maynard do their rough riding and take on the bad guys," recalled author Elmer Kelton, twenty-three years after Maynard's passing. "Somehow they made real life more pleasurable. They caused our childhood imaginations to run free and made us see adventure where we might otherwise have found drudgery."[44]

As much as the public adored them both, Ken Maynard and Buck Jones never really liked each other. Professional jealousy strained their relationship almost from the start. On a few occasions, Maynard's obnoxious behavior, especially when he had a snoot full of whiskey, nearly brought the two to blows.[45]

Jones first encountered Maynard in 1914, just before the two young rodeo riders started their film careers. Only the year before, Jones, fresh out of the army, had signed on with the Miller brothers. During two three-year hitches in the army, Jones had patrolled the turbulent Mexican border and had been shot in the leg during a jungle skirmish with fierce Moro bandits in the Philippines.[46]

With his badly wounded leg fully mended and his discharge papers in hand, Jones joined the 101 Ranch show on the road in Texas in late 1913.[47] Jones already knew about the Millers. Born Charles Frederick Gebhart in 1891 at Vincennes, Indiana, the youngster—who developed a lifelong love of horses while hanging around livery stables and livestock auctions—grew up hearing tales about the 101 Ranch and the Millers' "Real Wild West."[48]

Going by "Buck," a nickname he most likely picked up as a soldier, the young man took a menial job currying horses for the Millers. "I put resin on my chaps to help me hold the saddle, and drove horseshoe nails into the heels of my boots to keep my spurs on," Jones fondly recalled in 1938. "Then I went over and asked for a tryout."[49] At first dubious about the youngster's expertise with bucking stock, Joe Miller nonetheless appreciated his courage and gave him a shot. Joe and the other hands were impressed. Soon, Charles "Buck" Gebhart had earned his spurs, and he became known as the outfit's top bronc tamer.

During that initial winter spent with the Millers, Jones appeared in his first motion picture, filmed in its entirety on the 101 Ranch. The untitled production, made to promote the ranch, featured many of the Millers' cowboys and cowgirls and starred Duke R. Lee, the well-known character actor, and an Indian damsel called Princess Sunshine. Based on Jones' experience as a combat soldier, he was cast as a cavalry sergeant.[50]

In 1914, during the opening stand of the 101 Wild West show at Madison Square Garden, Jones became captivated by Odille Dorothy Osborne, better known as Dell, a teenage trick rider and roper who had run away from home in Philadelphia to become a star performer for the Millers. Dell fell just as hard for the rugged bronc rider. When he learned that his sweetheart had signed with the Julia Allen Show for the next season, he resigned from the Millers' outfit—bound for its ill-fated appearance in England at the start of World War I. Jones took a job with the Allen show and, in 1915, he and Dell Osborne married on horseback in a circus arena before a cheering audience in Lima, Ohio.[51]

During the early part of the war, the couple settled in Chicago where, for $7.50 a day, Jones broke and trained horses for the British and French armies at a remount depot in the stockyards. Then in 1917, after performing with other shows and circuses, he and his wife moved to Bliss, Oklahoma. They enjoyed another brief stint with the 101 Ranch Wild West before joining the Ringling Brothers circus—a move that brought them to California, where in 1918, their only child, Maxine, was born.[52] Soon after, Dell began to work as a movie double and rodeo rider. Jones became a film extra and stunt double for Bill Hart; Tom Mix; William Farnum, brother of Dustin Farnum, star of *Squaw Man*; and Marshall Farnum, at one time chief director for the 101 Ranch motion-picture department.[53]

Before long, Jones had moved from the stunt ranks to starring roles. Starting in the early 1920s, he appeared in numerous films for Fox studios, first as Charles Jones and then as Buck Jones—the name that became known in households across the nation.[54] For many years, Jones—the ultimate cowboy good guy—and his gray gelding, named Silver, averaged at least eight movies a year for theatergoers mesmerized by the myth and reality of Hollywood westerns.

For a time, Jones, with his wife and daughter, appeared with his own family Wild West show, but the big screen beckoned him back. By 1935, Jones had become the top cowboy draw at the box office for Universal and Columbia. The following year, Universal founded the "Buck Jones Rangers," a youth fan club with more than five million faithful members.[55]

As happened with so many other cowboy stars, Jones found that fame was fleeting. With the advent of World War II and the decline of his popularity, Jones went on tour with other movie stars, selling millions of dollars' worth of war bonds. On November 28, 1942, he was among those gathered in the Back Bay district of Boston at the famous Coconut Grove when a fire turned the nightclub into a blazing inferno.[56] Panicked crowds of servicemen and others celebrating a football victory were trampled in the rush for exits. Many more victims perished in the smoke and flames.

A popular account claimed that Jones initially escaped the fire unharmed but returned at least three times to help save others trapped in the burning building. That night, 492 people lost their lives. Jones was one of the 181 survivors. Badly burned and barely breathing, he clung to life for two days and died a hero on November 30, 1942.[57] Buck Jones' remains were returned to California. His loving wife scattered his ashes over the Pacific, just as he had wished.

Hoot Gibson—yet another member of the "Big Four" with strong links to the Millers—mourned the tragic loss of Buck Jones. Gibson lived another twenty years and remained active in western movies until near the end of

World War II. In 1959, Gibson made a comeback of sorts when he took a role in *The Horse Soldiers*, a John Ford film which starred John Wayne. Gibson had first encountered Ford forty years earlier when the cowboy played supporting roles for the director's early westerns shot at Universal.[58]

Long before meeting Ford or even setting foot in Hollywood, Gibson had earned a solid reputation as a daredevil rodeo cowboy. Born Edmund Richard Gibson at Tekamah, Nebraska, in 1892, he picked up the picturesque nickname "Hoot" while working as a bicycle messenger for Owl Drug Company.[59]

At age thirteen, Gibson left home to join a traveling circus. After being stranded in the wilds of Colorado, the resourceful youngster decided to become a cowpuncher, and by his fifteenth birthday, he could break outlaw horses and tame wild cattle as well as any grown man. A salty wrangler before he could shave, Hoot Gibson, by some credible accounts, began to perform with the Miller Brothers 101 Ranch Show as early as 1907.[60]

Gibson quickly developed into an accomplished rodeo performer while appearing with the Millers. Prior to winning the title of "World's All-Around Champion Cowboy" at the historic Pendleton Roundup in 1912, Gibson toured the nation as a bronc buster and bull rider along with his pal Art Acord, a champion bull rider in his own right and a stunt rider for the Bison company.[61]

The moody and mercurial Acord became Gibson's favorite sparring partner during impromptu fistfights on various movie locations. "They'd just stand up and beat the hell out of each other," recalled Tim McCoy, another early western star. "And then they'd come to the bar and have a drink. They loved it."[62]

In 1913 at Salt Lake City, Gibson hooked up with Rose Helen Wenger, a fine trick rider from Ohio who performed for the Miller brothers. Better known by her middle name, the perky cowgirl began to make films in 1911 for the Bison 101 Company under the direction of Tom Ince.[63]

Helen Wenger soon became Helen Gibson. Although her film career soon took off and she became the star of many serials and westerns, the rough-riding Gibson had to settle at first for bit parts. After his service with the Army Tank Corps in World War I, Gibson's prospects brightened. He landed several supporting roles with John Ford and, by 1919, was starring in his own series of two-reelers, usually playing a likable, carefree cowpoke.[64]

Hoot and Helen split up in 1920, but Gibson's career never faltered.

His daring on the screen was famous, and the public approved. Once asked by a director, with tongue firmly in cheek, if he would consider risking a dangerous fall from a racing horse for five dollars, Gibson replied, "Make it ten dollars and I'll let him kick me to death!"[65]

Gibson galloped through hundreds of films, received four vans filled with fan mail every week, and at his peak earned $14,500 a week for Universal Pictures. A lavish spender, Gibson survived several marriages and many career swings while collecting a fleet of expensive race cars and a stable of thoroughbred horses. He also survived the crash of one his four airplanes while competing against Ken Maynard before forty thousand spectators at a 1933 air race in Los Angeles.[66]

Pulled from the twisted wreckage of the biplane, the unconscious Gibson appeared badly bruised and lacerated. As the ambulance stretcher passed worried bystanders, the cowboy regained his senses. He grinned at the fans and said, "You can't kill me."[67]

Throughout a long entertainment career, Gibson retained his sense of humor. After retiring from movie work, he tried to break into television and then attempted to start a dude ranch near Las Vegas. Both undertakings ended in failure. In his last years, Gibson relied on a movie pension and Social Security and worked as a friendly celebrity greeter at a posh Las Vegas casino hotel, appropriately named the Last Frontier. Hoot Gibson died of cancer in 1962 and was buried in Hollywood, wearing his full cowboy regalia.[68]

Like his old friend Hoot Gibson and the rest of the "Big Four," the celebrated Tom Mix—best known of all the 101 Ranch movie stars and considered by many western devotees to be the greatest cowboy luminary of all time—also lived life to the fullest. Yet Mix came to a tragic end much like Buck Jones and some of the other stars who had died too soon.

For Mix, the end came on October 12, 1940.[69] It was a Saturday—the day of the week reserved for the movie matinées that Mix and the others had made so popular and which had made him so famous. Tom Mix met his end far from the ranges of the old 101 Ranch. He was in Arizona—home of the Apache, the gunfighter, the cavalry dragoon. He was in the land that he and other western film stars had helped to make indelible in the minds of moviegoers around the world.

Wearing an immaculate cream-colored western dress suit, a trademark ten-gallon hat, and the fanciest tooled boots money could buy, Mix told some friends that he felt fit as a young bronc rider. Fans who saw him that day when he paused for lunch never guessed that he was sixty years old.[70] Mix was tanned and trim and his hair was still as black as the coal mined from the Pennsylvania countryside where he was born.

Mix drove a custom-built Cord roadster with his initials raised on the tread of the tires so he could leave the distinctive letters in the dust wherever he went. Millions of movie fans had adored his trick horse, Tony, but Mix also took pride in knowing that he was one of the first cowboy stars to use the automobile in his films.

On that Saturday afternoon in 1940, the wild days and nights spent with the Miller brothers on the 101 Ranch must have seemed like lifetimes past. Mix had been through five marriages, had ridden the Wild West show circuit for the Millers and had cowboyed on their legendary ranch, and had even put in a brief stint as night marshal at Dewey, Oklahoma.[71] That record alone would have been enough to satisfy most folks. Beyond those accomplishments, Mix had become the top box-office attraction in the nation. By 1922, he earned a staggering $17,500 a week, making him the highest-paid Hollywood star of his day.[72] He went on to make—and subsequently lose—millions of dollars while cranking out countless movies.

Mix tried his damnedest not to let the glories of the past slip away. Through the years, he rendezvoused with other old-timers to reminisce about the Hundred and One and bygone times in early Hollywood. "There wasn't much real West left when I knew you back on the 101 Ranch," Mix told a journalist he had first met in the early 1900s in Oklahoma. "There ain't none at all now. And besides, you don't know how sick I am of things here. I've ridden every inch of this country on location for pictures. I've seen the same mugs and done the same things day in and day out for years. I can't work the way they work nowadays."[73]

After movies broke their silence, Mix realized his trail was about played out. He earned and lost plenty of money in an attempt to revive his career with yet another Wild West show tour. The film roles dried up. His speaking voice was never very good. The last movie he made was a serial in 1935.[74] Gene Autry, Roy Rogers, and other "singing cowboys" had taken over the big screen.

Still, Mix did not give up. In 1940, before he took his final ride across the desert, Mix visited his old studio, by then called Twentieth Century–Fox. He sought out John Ford, one of the most respected directors in Hollywood. Although Ford was busy shooting *The Grapes of Wrath*, he made time to take Mix out to lunch. The old friends recalled their days together in the teens and twenties when Ford was starting as a director and Mix was fast becoming one of the first film superstars. Over coffee, Ford looked Mix in the eye and told him the hard truth, knowing his old pal would want it straight. "This picture business has passed you by a long time ago," Ford said.[75]

After Ford returned to his movie set, Mix visited with Sol Wurtzel, the studio manager, and he heard the same thing—it was time to quit. Then Mix looked up R. Lee "Lefty" Hough, the studio production manager. They shook hands and hugged, and Mix sat in his office and they talked. "He was a little seedy, with the boots, the hat, the white suit and everything," Hough remembered years later. "He had lost a million dollars in the circus, and there was no money left."[76] Like Ford and Wurtzel, Hough pulled no punches.

"We sat there and talked a while and I could see he was quite depressed. 'Lefty,' he said, 'I don't know what I'm going to do.' I couldn't answer. I walked with him to the gate. He stood there in the vestibule, and there were pictures of the big stars, Tyrone Power and everyone else on the wall. Here was the guy that had made our goddamn studio what it was, looking for a spot."[77]

Despite his friends' advice, Mix still believed he had at least one more comeback in him. Refreshed after a series of personal appearances around the country, Mix felt he could endure the tough times and reclaim at least some of the grandeur he had known. He decided to go back to California one more time. The day before his trip across the Arizona desert, a visit with old friends—western writer Walt Coburn and Sheriff Ed Echols, a pal from long ago at the 101 Ranch—had boosted his morale.[78]

Over strong drinks and hand-rolled cigarettes at Coburn's ranch residence in the Santa Catalina foothills near Tucson, the threesome chewed over their past. "Ed and Tom got to telling about traveling with the Zack Miller 101 Wild West Show, and about all the cowhands who rode broncs and roped steers and bulldogged—men such as Bill Pickett, Neal Hart and Henry Grammar," Coburn later wrote. They spoke of first meeting Will Rogers at the Millers' ranch on the Salt Fork and how they had remained friends through the years, right up until Will's tragic death with Wiley Post in an airplane crash in Alaska, in 1935.[79]

"Tom said that during those same years he had been involved in expensive lawsuits," recalled Coburn. "Zack Miller of 101 fame was suing him for breach of contract. He was also involved in lawsuits over alimony. And as Tom talked a note of bitterness crept into his rambling. Once a man was beset by troubles, some men he had once called friends were trying to tromp his guts out. But Tom Mix was never a man to call quits. The image Tom Mix had built up throughout the years as a cowboy hero was still intact."[80]

Coburn and Echols encouraged Mix to imitate the old bronc riders who, whenever a pitching stallion bucked them off, climbed right back on, grabbed a handful of mane, and held tight. Energized and confident, Mix had plenty to mull over during his journey back to Hollywood.

On the morning of October 12, he took off in his Cord, bound for Florence, Arizona, to see Harry Knight, a former rodeo champion who had been married to one of Mix's daughters. Mix then planned to motor west to California.

At a filling station, an attendant told Mix to be on the lookout because a bridge was out up ahead and there were detours near Florence. Mix doffed his big white hat, flashed a smile, and pushed on. "I've got to be close to Hollywood come sundown," Mix told the attendant as the Cord roared away, leaving a trail of "TMs" imprinted in the dust.[81]

Eighteen miles south of Florence on Highway 98, a work crew repairing a bridge over a dry wash had just put up detour signs and wooden barriers at about two o'clock that afternoon when they spied a cloud of dust and saw the Cord speeding along. The flashy roadster never slowed. It crashed through the barrier and flipped over in the wash. Workmen rushed to the scene and dragged Mix clear of the wreckage.[82]

They found Mix impeccably dressed and his body unmarked by wounds. He had died instantly, with his boots on and seventy-five hundred dollars in cash and traveler's checks in his pockets. His neck was broken, apparently by a metal suitcase stashed in the car. A rumor circulated through Hollywood that the suitcase had been filled to bursting with twenty-dollar gold pieces. As film historians would later note, this became the ultimate Mix myth—that his life had been ended by the very stuff that, as far as he was concerned, had given it meaning.[83]

In Hollywood, Mix's family, friends, and fans gathered to say their farewells. William S. Hart showed up at the mortuary, as did Mary Pickford and other movie stars, including some who had once ridden for the 101 Ranch. Gene Autry paid tribute to the man who had paved the way for so many big-screen cowboys. Lawyers for the Mix estate tried to secure an American flag from the Veterans Administration to drape over the casket during the funeral, but the old question came up about Mix having been an army deserter. When officials refused the request, John Ford pulled some strings and got a flag. Mix was laid to rest with full military and Masonic honors.[84]

Before the silver-plated coffin, which bore his famous initials in large block letters, was removed from the funeral parlor, Ford rushed forward with tears streaming down his cheeks and placed a bone-white Stetson on Mix's coffin. Monte Blue, a part-Cherokee cowboy actor with two hundred film credits, said some final words and orchestra leader Rudy Vallee crooned Mix's favorite song, "Empty Saddles."[85]

They laid him in a grave in the Whispering Pines section of Forest Lawn Memorial Park, not far from the resting places of Douglas Fairbanks, Jean Harlow, and Marie Dressler. Mix was buried in his best outfit, complete with glossy black boots and a belt buckle which spelled out his name in diamonds.[86]

Out in the Arizona desert at the place where the Cord had tumbled off the highway, a statue of a riderless pony on top of a rock monument was erected to honor Mix. The plaque bears this inscription:

IN MEMORY OF TOM MIX
WHOSE SPIRIT LEFT HIS BODY ON THIS SPOT
AND WHOSE CHARACTERIZATIONS AND PORTRAYALS
IN LIFE SERVED BETTER TO FIX MEMORIES OF
THE OLD WEST IN THE MINDS OF LIVING MEN

Hollywood also remembered Mix. On one of the big soundstages at Twentieth Century–Fox, they placed a bronze plaque dedicated to the memory of Tom Mix and Tony, his famed movie horse, who died two years to the day after Mix.[87]

Years later, youngsters with hope in their hearts and stardust in their eyes would hurry by the stage on their way to an audition. A few of them noticed the plaque. Only a few asked about Mix. Those who did got the same answer. Grizzled stagehands or a director who happened to be nearby set the record straight.

"Who was Tom Mix, you ask. Don't you know, kid? Why, he was hot stuff around here. He was the 'King of the Cowboys.' "

Chapter 35

TRAIL'S END

Everything has an end.
—Masai saying

THE Miller brothers failed to see the approaching collapse of their empire. In spite of telltale omens, they truly believed the 101 Ranch would last forever. Charging ahead through the 1920s, the Millers took no notice that, as old cowhands might have put it, they had become hopelessly caught in their own loops.[1]

It was not as if they did not have enough time to halt the downfall of their kingdom. Although it seemed rapid when compared to the length of time it had taken to build up the empire, the end of the 101 Ranch did not occur overnight, but rather during an agonizing sequence of strategically placed jabs, slaps, and blindside punches.

The total effect of the Millers' actions and misconduct through the years played a role in determining their fate. What helped bring them down was not so much crimes as sins of omission. The Millers' fortunes were bound to the shackled human beings their father and other kinsmen had bought and sold like horses and mules back in antebellum Kentucky. Their destiny was sealed when they rode roughshod like feudal lords over anyone who dared get in their way, or when they paid slim wages to a champion cowboy like Bill Pickett just because he was black, or when they brought Geronimo to their ranch as a prisoner in irons with soldier guards and put him on public display like a captive mustang.

If they had paid more attention, perhaps the Millers would have seen the avenging ghosts of history in the eyes of the Poncas, Otoes, Pawnees, Sioux, and other native people they had taken for granted for such a long time. Instead, the Indians who rode for the Millers and those such as the Poncas and Otoes who surrendered their land and their lives to the 101 Ranch simply took the place of African slaves whose blood and sweat had helped to establish the initial grubstake which financed the Millers' empire.

And if they would have looked deep into the eyes of the Indians they patronized and defrauded, the Millers might have seen even more. They might have glimpsed their own future and made amends before it was too late. Hard lessons could have been learned by listening more closely to the Poncas who spoke of the old ways and how their lives had been changed by presumptuous white men such as the Millers.

For the Poncas, tribal memory was essential. They believed it was important to recall the past, before the whites gave them smallpox and whiskey and false treaties. Tribal elders wanted young people to understand how things had been before the intrusion of Baptist and Methodist missionaries—all of them eager to rescue "pagan" souls through fiery sermons and by submerging Indian brethren in the shallows of the Salt Fork River.

Elderly Ponca women stirring kettles of thick soup over campfires and men who still wore otterskin caps and broadcloth blankets clung to the old religion and ceremonials. They recalled the clan taboos and the rites of the sun dance and the Ghost Dance. They knew by memory the love songs and lullabies piped on cedar flutes and eagle-bone whistles. They recited the tribal legends and customs and practiced herbal remedies. They remembered the death whoops of battle, horse-stealing raids on Sioux camps, and the ghostly thunder of endless bison herds rumbling across the plains.

The Poncas knew stories from the days when their tribe had thrived in what became South Dakota and Nebraska, long before their people were brought first to the Quapaw agency near Baxter Springs, Kansas, and then to the lands along the Salt Fork—the "hot country," as it became known.[2] They carried with them memories of peyote chiefs, keepers of magic and myth, and wise shamans who could predict their own deaths.

The Ponca people often thought of the dead. In the old days, when a member of the tribe died, relatives would cut off their own hair and slash their arms and legs with a knife. They would mourn for a long time and sometimes they would stop eating for several days. They held lengthy farewells.[3] It was said that occasionally the spirits of the dead hovered about as ghosts, and the Poncas told many tales about encounters with them. Sometimes ghosts cried or whistled, and when the living heard such sounds late at night, they would set out a bit of food or water to appease the restless spirits. Occasionally the spirit of a dead person would be reincarnated, while others stayed on earth and pestered the living.[4]

There were those who believed that perhaps some of the Ponca spirits mixed with the ghosts of the forgotten cowboys who had perished on the ranch. Both Indians and whites spoke of the dark side of the Millers and how certain cowhands suddenly had vanished without a trace. It was rumored that they had crossed their bosses once too often or that they possessed something of value. Mostly young, unattached men who led nomadic lives, they supposedly wound up shot dead and buried beneath the well-trodden earth of the mule yard or the buffalo pasture, with only their handsome saddles and tack left behind for the Millers to claim.[5] These unproved stories of bushwhacked wranglers lying in unmarked graves circulated beer joints and domino parlors long after the passing of the 101 Ranch.

Some of the Poncas believed the stories, true or not. They also believed that all of those ghosts—cowboy and Indian alike—lingered on the ranch. They could be heard in the evening songs of the coyotes and the whistle of prairie wind through stands of cedar and elm.

When some of the Ponca people heard the cries and trilling of those footloose spirits, they thought of White Eagle and all the other old chiefs of the tribe who had come before him. They also remembered White Eagle's grim prophecy after he realized he had made a terrible mistake by allowing the Millers and E. W. Marland to drill for oil and gas on the Poncas' sacred land. "It will mean great trouble for me, for my people, and for you," White Eagle had told Marland.[6] An old Ponca man called Running-After-Arrow agreed with White Eagle. When he stood with George Miller and watched an early gas well roar to life, he muttered, "No good, no good. Beautiful country all die now. Cattle die. Ponies die. No good, no good. Beautiful country soon all gone."[7]

Even years after White Eagle's death, many Poncas avoided the stone memorial that the Millers had built on a hilltop to honor him. The Poncas said the whispers of ghosts were especially resonant at that place, and they gave the monument wide berth. They had come to believe that the predictions of Running-After-Arrow and White Eagle turned out to be a curse—a curse laden with the ring of truth, the inevitable truth of history.[8]

Along with the curse on the white men and the land they had ravaged, the Poncas also recalled an old custom of warriors in battle—a practice that earned the tribe the name "Head-cutters" among some of the southern Plains people.[9]

When Ponca warriors killed an enemy in combat, they scalped him and cut off and discarded his head. Next, they severed his hands at the wrist and cast them off. Finally, they slashed his back in a checkerboard style, described as "making a drum of the enemy's back."[10] These rituals of death were considered acts of bravery, worthy of boasting about around campfires.

Without wielding a scalping knife or war club, the Poncas would gain their revenge on the white hunters of oil who took advantage of them. Throughout the 1920s and into the 1930s, the Ponca people beheld the last great surges of success experienced by Marland and the Millers, as well as their ultimate collapse.

The Poncas witnessed oil baron E. W. Marland's sudden rise and his decline. They saw him flounder and fall and finally lose his riches as his personal and political life disintegrated. They watched silently as the mighty 101 Ranch was slowly and symbolically scalped, beheaded, and taken apart limb by limb, parcel by parcel, piece by piece. They saw everything in their world come full circle and return to the way things used to be, until only the land, the Salt Fork, and the ghosts remained.

An omen of the gradual erosion of the Millers' empire came at the close of the 1915 season, which featured the "Jess Willard Side Show." Although it was one of their most prosperous seasons, with a net profit of more than two hundred thousand dollars, the Miller brothers knew it was a fluke.[11] They credited the season's substantial financial success to the increase in foreign money entering the United States in exchange for war supplies; more disposable cash became available to the public, which used it on shows and other leisure activities.[12]

Suspicious of unstable conditions around the globe, Joe Miller recognized the importance of finding another major celebrity name for the 1916 show season to replace cowboy pugilist Willard—"The Great White Hope"—who had since joined up with the Sells-Floto Circus. In casting about for such a notable, Joe and impresario Edward Arlington connected with none other than William F. "Buffalo Bill" Cody—previously a fierce competitor of the Millers and a living metaphor for the way generations of Americans imagined the Wild West.[13]

Since the breakup of his partnership with Pawnee Bill Lillie, which resulted in a constant stream of legal squabbles, Cody had experienced little success at making a comeback. He remained in heavy debt to Harry H. Tammen, the notoriously shrewd Denver newspaper publisher and an owner, along with Frederick G. Bonfils, of the Sells-Floto Circus.[14]

Back in 1913, after loaning money to the bankrupt Cody, Tammen swallowed up the "Two Bills" show and then held Cody as financial hostage. Referring to Tammen as "the man who had my show sold at sheriff sale, which broke my heart," Cody refused to surrender.[15] Despite staggering debts and poor health, the old scout tried all sorts of schemes—including filmmaking, lecture tours, and circus appearances—to remain afloat financially and to regain some of his past glory.

Cody finally managed to take care of his debt and break away from Tammen's clutches. In early 1916, Cody cut a deal with the Miller brothers—the only ones at the time with a major Wild West show still in operation.[16] It would be Buffalo Bill Cody's last stand, as well as the final show season on the road for the Millers until 1925.

Failing to gain any share of ownership in the Millers' show, Cody settled for a performance fee of one hundred dollars a day and one-third of all the daily profits of more than $2,750. At first, this arrangement turned out to be fairly lucrative for all parties. During one week alone early in the season, Cody pocketed $4,161.35 in income.[17]

"Preparedness" had become a popular catchword by 1916, as more and more Americans found it difficult to follow President Wilson's neutrality stance in the face of global warfare. Cody seized on this patriotic cause and made it the show's theme. The show, presented by the Miller and Arlington Wild West Show Company, was billed as "Buffalo Bill (Himself) and 101 Ranch Wild West Combined, with the Military Pageant [of] Preparedness."[18]

Probably only a few patrons who turned out to see Buffalo Bill and the 101 Ranch riders noticed the omission of the word "Brothers" from the show bills and programs.[19] Because of a disagreement brewing among the three Miller brothers over whether to take out a road show in 1916, Zack and George remained at the ranch to concentrate on the family's ranching, farming, and oil-exploration ventures. Zack and George felt that supplying raw materials and livestock for the war effort was more than enough to keep them busy.[20] Consequently, in 1916, as had been the case for much of the year before with Jess Willard, only Joe joined with George and Edward Arlington in producing the road show.

To make their novel production a reality, Cody and Joe Miller convinced the United States War Department that regular army troops were needed for the military spectacle. Top army brass immediately saw the propaganda value of exposing large audiences of Americans to a show made up of 101 Ranch riders, Buffalo Bill Cody, and—as the show courier put it—"an army of Uncle Sam's gallant defenders of Old Glory."[21] It promised to be a recruiting officer's dream.

In early March, Cody and Joe Miller received word from Major General Hugh L. Scott, chief of staff of the U.S. Army, that he had ordered several regimental commanders to furnish soldiers and artillery pieces for the "Military Pageant of Preparedness."[22] The timing of the letter from Scott, a Kentucky native and advocate of the selective service, was especially noteworthy. The day before, Mexican revolutionary leader Francisco "Pancho" Villa had raided Columbus, New Mexico, and killed seventeen American citizens. On the day Scott sent his approval letter for the "loan" of soldiers to the Cody-Miller show, the army dispatched five thousand troops to Mexico. Within two more weeks, Brigadier General John J. Pershing and thousands of soldiers under his command pursued Villa as part of a punitive expedition.[23]

By late April, soldiers on special furlough to participate in the show began to arrive at Ponca City. Although every branch of service was represented, most of the troopers came from cavalry units stationed at the Presidio, Fort Bliss, Fort Sam Houston, and several other locations. Included were veterans of the Thirteenth Cavalry from Columbus, New Mexico, and the fabled Seventh Cavalry, commanded many years earlier by George Armstrong Custer.[24]

The program included a thrilling depiction of the Columbus raid, batteries of artillery field guns in action, displays of military horsemanship and maneuvers, and spectacular street parades, all punctuated by flying guidons and blaring bugle calls. "It is a rousing, exhilarating display of military power in embryo," wrote a New York reporter. "It is our army in the making. It is a promise of America's great defensive host when the people have been thoroughly aroused to the necessity for military preparedness."[25]

In truth, even with the addition of Cody and his military pageant, the show itself had changed very little from past Miller productions. Merle Evans—later a band boss with the Ringling Brothers and Barnum & Bailey Circus—took up the bandleader's baton, succeeding perennial favorite Donato La Banca. A new group of Imperial Russian Cossacks, led by Prince Tepho, joined the show, as did troupes of Arabian and Japanese acrobats and gymnasts. The Tantlingers came out for their final tour with the 101 show. Johnny Baker, happy to be associated again with Cody, acted as arena director.[26]

A troupe of cowgirls—described in the show program as the "sauciest, happiest, loveliest assemblage of femininity that ever galloped"—included Joe Miller's supposedly secret lover, Bessie Herberg, who sometimes went by the name Bess Carter. Other familiar female bronc busters, trick riders, and ropers were Fox Hastings, Florence La Due, Martha Allen, Beatrice Brosseau, twin sisters Ethel (Etheyle) and Juanita Parry and, at certain key dates, Lucille Mulhall—longtime Miller family friend and an enduring crowd pleaser. Among the prominent cowboy performers were Hoot Gibson, Bill Pickett, Mexican Joe Barrera, Chester Byers, Hank Durnell, Tom Kirnan, Henry Grammer, Fred Beeson, Montana Jack Ray, and other top hands from the 101 Ranch headquarters and the Millers' remote Bar L division.[27]

Cody felt comfortable appearing with the show and he trusted Joe Miller. He also welcomed the chance to be reunited with sharpshooter Johnny Baker and with Iron Tail, the famous Sioux warrior whom the Millers used to great advantage because his likeness appeared on the popular buffalo nickels. Iron Tail led a hundred painted warriors in daily attacks on the Deadwood stagecoach during show appearances across the nation.

After a successful start, the 1916 season began to sour. Iron Tail developed pneumonia during the tour and had to be hospitalized in Philadelphia. The old warrior knew his time was running out, and he longed for his beloved South Dakota hills. He slipped out of the hospital, bought a one-way ticket with part of his show wages, and boarded a westbound train. On May 28, as the train reached Fort Wayne, Indiana—a state name meaning "Land of the Indians"—Iron Tail died.[28] His passing saddened Cody and Joe Miller and left a melancholy shadow over the entire outfit.

Nonetheless, the show continued, and in early August it enjoyed a run of twelve days at the New York Stampede at Sheepshead Bay Speedway in Brooklyn. Tens of thousands of fans turned out for performances, including Theodore Roosevelt and Will Rogers, who invited his old 101 Ranch friends to see him twirl a lariat and crack jokes as headliner of the Ziegfeld Follies on the roof of the New Amsterdam Theatre.[29]

After the New York Stampede, the show encountered problems in Chicago. A concerned Mayor William Hale "Big Bill" Thompson, head of the local Republican political machine, thought the display of military might would anger the large number of German-American citizens—all potential voters—in his city. To avoid canceling the eight days and nights of performances, some clever publicity agents temporarily dropped the "Military Pageant of Preparedness" portion of the production. The show was renamed the Chicago Shan-Kive and Round-Up for the duration of the run, with an explanation in the program that *Shan-Kive* was an Indian expression which meant "a good time."[30]

The ploy worked. Mayor Thompson, apparently placated by the simple name change, gave his consent to be named "Honorary Director General" of the Shan-Kive, and Cody acted as "Judge Supreme" of all the rodeo contests. The panel of honorary judges included Joe Miller; his old friend J. W. Lynch, from Ponca City; William A. Pinkerton, of the noted Chicago detective agency; and several prominent business and political leaders. Not everyone enjoyed the Chicago run. Champion bulldogger Bill Pickett, going head-to-head in competition with Ed Lindsey, had all he could take of Chicago when he saw that the posted rules bluntly stated, "Positively no biting allowed," an obvious reference to Pickett's unusual style of bringing down steers.[31]

As the season continued, the novelty of the show appeared to lose its appeal, and audience interest waned. After weeks of inclement weather and an epidemic of infantile paralysis, or poliomyelitis, among the nation's children, the overflow crowds of spectators that had turned out at earlier appearances dwindled. Naturally, so did the profits. To make matters worse, Joe Miller and Edward and George Arlington fell ill with influenza during the tour and all three had to be hospitalized.[32] Even in their absence, Cody persisted, never failing to make a single parade or performance.

Cody's own health was failing fast. Uremic poisoning prompted a deterioration of his kidneys and heart, and an ailing prostate made it difficult for the old man to ride his white stallion without considerable pain. Johnny Baker faithfully hoisted Cody into the saddle behind the scenes at every appearance until finally the old showman had to ride into the arenas in a buggy pulled by a pair of matched steeds.[33] To the end of the run, he delighted loyal fans with his marksmanship—a young man tossed glass balls into the air for Buffalo Bill to shatter with his rifle.

Cody hung on until the final performance of the season. It came at Portsmouth, Virginia, on November 11, 1916, just after President Woodrow Wilson, in his bid for reelection, had eked out a narrow victory over Republican Charles Evans Hughes.[34] As soon as the show closed, Cody bade farewell to Johnny Baker, the Arlingtons, and Joe Miller. Thoroughly exhausted, Cody headed due west to Colorado to regain his health, write more autobiographical pieces for William Randolph Hearst, and prepare for his next adventure.

None of those grand plans was meant to be. Cody's health continued to deteriorate, and by the end of the first week of the new year, a death watch began for the old scout. Joe Miller and others who had been so close to Cody during his last year on the road heard the news with disbelief. Johnny Baker rushed from New York to reach his foster father and oldest friend, but he arrived too late.[35]

At precisely five minutes past high noon on January 10, 1917, William Frederick "Buffalo Bill" Cody—one of the prime creators and packagers of the mythical American West—died, six weeks before his seventy-first birthday. For a day, the old showman managed to take center stage once more, even stealing the limelight from a world war. Telegrams and messages of condolence poured in from President Wilson, Teddy Roosevelt, King George V and Queen Mary of England, and other heads of state, old soldiers, army generals, children, and dignitaries from around the world.[36]

Pawnee Bill Lillie reflected on the sad news from his fourteen-room sandstone bungalow atop Blue Hawk Peak, the sprawling buffalo ranch he and his wife, May, maintained near Pawnee, Oklahoma. "Time smoothes everything," wrote Lillie. "Buffalo Bill died my friend. He was just an irresponsible boy."[37]

Not far from Pawnee, Joe Miller sat dazed and utterly exhausted in the White House. On a table before him, the front page of the *Tulsa World* bore the headline: " 'Buffalo Bill,' Hero of Young America, Dies at Denver After Nervy Last Fight."[38] Without daring to admit it, Joe must have recognized that the death of Buffalo Bill Cody signified the passing of the West of myth. In the coming years, Cody would be joined by many others with 101 Ranch ties—Henry Starr in a failed bank robbery, Buck Jones in a tragic fire, Will Rogers in a plane crash, Tom Mix racing back to Hollywood, May Lillie and Lucille Mulhall in car accidents, and so many others.

All of that lay far ahead, even as the decline of the 101 Ranch began to show in various ways after the deaths of Iron Tail and Buffalo Bill. As the Indian curse on the white men and the land they had corrupted took hold, the Millers went into a tailspin and plunged to the earth. Time, once on their side, had turned against them.

After the death of Buffalo Bill Cody in January, the year 1917 did not improve for the Millers, especially for Joe. His sexual escapades on the road, particularly his blatant liaison with the attractive Bessie Herberg, not only angered Mother Miller but finally got the best of Joe's wife.

Raised a Louisiana belle, Lizzie never had adjusted to life on the ranch and marriage to a showman. Throughout her turbulent twenty-three years with Joe, she always had felt her husband was more wed to his family business than to her. By 1917, as Joe spent even less time with his family because of pressures of the ranch, squabbles with his brothers, and frequent trysts with his cowgirl lover, Elizabeth Trosper Miller decided enough was enough.

"One afternoon, when I was in my late teens, I had been horseback riding out at the ranch," recalled Alice Miller Harth, Lizzie and Joe's eldest child. "The house was quiet. No one was downstairs so I went upstairs where I heard voices and, through an open door, I saw Mama and Grandmother [Miller] talking in Grandmother's room. I went in and threw myself across the bed. The conversation had stopped for a few minutes after I came in, then continued.[39]

"What had I walked into? Surely this was a dream. No, it wouldn't be a dream. I was hearing Grandmother's voice. She was telling Mama about Papa's infidelities on the road. I was shocked—stunned would be a better word but, if Mama felt any surprise or shock, she took the news very calmly. After a period of quiet contemplation she observed that, such being the case, she would have to get a divorce. She would call her brother, Jim, and have him come up to take care of the details."

After the divorce in 1917, Lizzie remained in Ponca City for many years. She ultimately moved to Tulsa, where she died in 1962, at age ninety-one, in the home of her daughter, Alice. Lizzie Miller never remarried, but kept alive the memories of her life as part of the Hundred and One kingdom.

With Lizzie's departure in the spring of 1917, just as the United States Congress voted to go to war, all three of Mother Miller's sons were once again bachelors. Zack had been single for several years, and George's four-year marriage to May Porter had ended shortly after their only child, Margaret, was born, in 1912.

"George was preoccupied with business every day and all day," recalled Alice Miller Harth of her uncle. "Social activities of the kind May would have enjoyed were out the window. Only occasionally did Grandmother ask her to ride into town. Then along came an uncomfortable pregnancy and the baby cried all night. Now three people were enclosed by the same four walls and all must have been miserable. It is easy to imagine the loneliness and frustration that prompted May to pack up the baby girl called Margaret and leave for home and a divorce."[40]

Unlike George, who preferred to stay close to the White House so he could oversee the various family ventures, including lucrative holdings in the oil patch, Joe Miller had little interest in sitting in an office or boardroom. Although Joe always paid special attention to the ranching and farming enterprises, he could never shake his abiding passion for show business. Joe never lost his love for the big parades and the applause of fans crowded into an arena.

Between 1916 and 1918, Joe stayed away from the ranch for long periods while he tried to keep the Millers' Wild West show alive. Joe continued his efforts despite overwhelming odds as well as his brothers' desire for the family to get out of the entertainment business. George and Zack wished to abandon show business because of the financial boost they enjoyed by selling large quantities of beef, supplying the military with horses and mules, and—thanks to the new oil and gas fields being explored—furnishing some of the fuel for the war.

Even after the close of the 1916 season and Buffalo Bill Cody's death in early 1917, Joe remained far from the Salt Fork for long spells, returning only for brief visits. During this turbulent period, while his divorce from Lizzie was finalized, the gulf grew even wider among the brothers.

By the time the United States entered the Great War in Europe, Joe had sold off the equipment and his interest in the show to Edward Arlington. That year, the former 101 Ranch outfit went out as the "Jess Willard (Himself in the Flesh) and the Buffalo Bill Wild West Show and Circus."[41]

A hodgepodge of sideshow freaks, derelict clowns, trained elephants, and acrobats, the show featured Johnny Baker as both an arena director and a replacement sharpshooting star for the deceased Cody. Various Miller personnel stayed on with the show, including Merle Evans and his band, Tex Cooper as announcer, and several cowboy and cowgirl performers, although many male entertainers hung up their spurs and enlisted in the military. Dogged by problems ranging from bad weather and transportation snags to a scarcity of workers because of the war, the show floundered even after Willard took control of the operation. By November, the show mercifully had folded. Although Willard wanted to go on the road at least one more year, he concluded his career in outdoor show business to focus on his calling as a professional boxer. As 1918 dawned, not a single Wild West show survived on the circuit.[42]

Throughout the first part of the year, while hostilities continued in Europe, the Miller brothers persisted in waging war among themselves on the Salt Fork. Joe mostly kept his distance from Zack and George. He relied on notes from his sister, Alma, and telegrams from friendly associates in Oklahoma to keep him abreast of family and business activities at the 101 Ranch.[43]

Buffalo Bill Cody (*far right*) looks on as Joe Miller (*left center*) confers with retired army general Hugh Scott, 1916. The soldiers—including Charles "Buck" Jones (*second from left*), who went on to fame as a movie cowboy hero—appeared with Miller and Cody in their combined Wild West show. *(Jerry and Ruth Murphey Collection)*

Known as "The Great White Hope" while he was heavyweight boxing champion of the world, Jess Willard became a featured attraction with the Millers' Wild West show in 1915. The pugilist remained a close ally of the Millers and was a guest at the 101 Ranch during the great flood of the Salt Fork River in 1923. *(Jerry and Ruth Murphey Collection)*

Mabel Normand in the 1923 Mack Sennett production *Suzanna.* Perhaps the most talented comic star of the silent screen, Normand learned to ride a horse at Inceville with instruction from Will Brooks, the Millers' cousin. *(Michael Wallis Collection)*

A popular hero of big-screen westerns for more than three decades, Hoot Gibson (shown at right in an early silent feature) earned his spurs and launched his career as a daredevil rodeo cowboy on the Hundred and One. *(Michael Wallis Collection)*

One of Hollywood's most popular cowboy stars in the 1920s and '30s, Buck Jones joined the 101 Ranch show on the road in Texas in late 1913. He soon became one of the outfit's top bronc tamers and forged friendships with many other future celluloid heroes and heroines. *(Michael Wallis Collection)*

Following a stint as a trick rider with the 101 Ranch Wild West Show prior to his service in the army during the Great War, Ken Maynard (shown at right in *Drum Taps*) soon came to the attention of Hollywood moviemakers. Maynard later vaulted from silents to talkies by becoming the screen's first singing cowboy. *(Michael Wallis Collection)*

Yakima Canutt, who almost single-handedly created the profession of movie stuntman, was already a rodeo champion when he joined the Millers for the 1914 Wild West show season. The image of this daredevil astride a bucking horse appeared on brass coins called "broncs," used by the Millers' cowhands and workers as trading tokens at the ranch store. *(Michael Wallis Collection)*

Kentucky native Jesse Briscoe appeared with the early 101 Ranch Wild West shows and was still riding for the Millers in London in 1914. A skilled stuntman and movie extra, Briscoe was killed in a horse fall in 1922 on the Paramount studio lot. *(Ken Theobald Collection)*

Film star Jack Hoxie, an Oklahoma native with plenty of cowboy credentials, appeared with the Millers' show as early as 1911. After starring in many independent films, Hoxie briefly rejoined the 101 Ranch show in the early 1930s. *(Frank Phillips Foundation, Inc.)*

Fred Burns (*left*), bronc buster turned actor, and Jack Mulhall, prolific leading man of Hollywood silents and early talkies, in a scene from *On with the Show*, shot on the 101 Ranch in the mid-1920s. *(Frank Phillips Foundation, Inc.)*

Advertised as "the country store with the city ways," the second 101 Ranch store was built in 1918 by Austrian prisoners of war. *(Frank Phillips Foundation, Inc.)*

Tony, a captive black bear chained in front of the 101 Ranch store, was addicted to soda pop and served as a popular attraction for visitors during the Roaring Twenties. *(Jerry and Ruth Murphey Collection)*

The 101 Ranch, frequently called "the greatest diversified farm on earth," included a vast complex of commercial buildings such as the cider works, which processed hundreds of barrels of sweet apple cider each autumn. *(Bethel Freeman Collection, courtesy The Glass Negative, Ponca City, Oklahoma)*

Many old-timers believed the Ponca curse was at work in June 1923 when rampaging waters from the Salt Fork River inundated the 101 Ranch and surrounding area. *(Courtesy The Glass Negative, Ponca City, Oklahoma)*

Equestrian football contests between 101 Ranch cowboys and Indians became a crowd pleaser at roundups on the ranch and, after 1924, when the road shows were revived. *(Courtesy Circus World Museum, Baraboo, Wisconsin)*

Throughout the 1920s, thousands of fans flocked to the Millers' roundups and special events. At left, Lucille Mulhall takes a bow during one of her many appearances at the 101 Ranch. *(Jerry and Ruth Murphey Collection)*

Famed rodeo photographer Ralph R. Doubleday captures 101 Ranch cowgirl Fox Hastings in action during the bulldogging event at the 1930 Houston Rodeo. *(Jerry and Ruth Murphey Collection)*

In this Doubleday photograph, 101 Ranch cowgirl Ruth Roach, wearing boots she had won during the 1930 Houston Rodeo, feeds her pet spotted pig. *(Jerry and Ruth Murphey Collection)*

During a Miller Brothers Wild West show at a roundup in Newkirk, Oklahoma, cowboy Guy Schultz leaps from a speeding automobile to bulldog a steer. *(Jerry and Ruth Murphey Collection)*

A painted Ponca rider poses with his horse during a 101 Ranch roundup. *(Frank Phillips Foundation, Inc.)*

Joe Miller watches one of his show elephants help sow wheat 101 Ranch style, circa 1925. *(Frank Phillips Foundation, Inc.)*

In 1924, the Millers unveiled the annual National Terrapin Derby at the ranch roundup grounds, which often earned winners thousands of dollars in prize money. Above, attendants prepare some of the entries for the 1926 race. *(Courtesy The Glass Negative, Ponca City, Oklahoma)*

Known far and wide as "the elephant girl," Selma Zimmerman bossed the Millers' trained pachyderms during the 1920s. *(Bob Kerr Collection)*

The bannerline of the Millers' sideshow and Indian village attracted crowds of curiosity seekers throughout the late 1920s. *(Bob Kerr Collection)*

Workers drive in a big-top stake for a performance of the Miller Brothers 101 Ranch Wild West Show. *(Frank Phillips Foundation, Inc.)*

Counting the day's receipts in front of newly painted wagons at Marland, Oklahoma, just prior to the opening of the 1925 season. *(Bethel Freeman Collection, courtesy The Glass Negative, Ponca City, Oklahoma)*

Born in 1882 in one of Buffalo Bill's show wagons, Glenn "Ammunition Shorty" Kischko was the son of a cossack performer. Kischko served as a gunsmith for the Millers until 1926. The baskets shown above contain glass and resin balls used as targets by sharpshooters in the 101 Ranch Wild West show. *(Jerry and Ruth Murphey Collection, courtesy George Virgines)*

A cossack trick-riding troupe performed with the 101 Ranch Wild West show in the 1920s. *(Jerry and Ruth Murphey Collection)*

José Barrera, known as "Mexican Joe," appeared as a fancy roper and horseman with several Wild West shows, including the Millers'. In later years he served as foreman of Pawnee Bill Lillie's buffalo ranch near Pawnee, Oklahoma. *(Jerry and Ruth Murphey Collection)*

Oil tycoon E. W. Marland reputedly had a "nose for oil and the luck of the devil." The ambitious wildcatter, with help from the Millers, leased Indian land for oil and gas exploration as early as 1909. *(Jerry and Ruth Murphey Collection)*

A Marland Oil Company service station on the main street of Marland (formerly Bliss), Oklahoma, 1924. Building in background was built by the Miller brothers as offices for their show's winter quarters. *(Courtesy The Glass Negative, Ponca City, Oklahoma)*

In 1925, at age ninety-five, Ezra Meeker—celebrated pioneer of the historic Oregon Trail—began to make appearances with the revived 101 Ranch road show. Meeker (shown at right with Joe Miller) remained with the show until his death, in 1928. *(Frank Phillips Foundation, Inc.)*

Aerial view of the 101 Ranch headquarters on the Salt Fork River, circa 1925. Note the White House, circled on right, and the new roundup arena in the lower left corner. *(Courtesy* Daily Oklahoman*)*

Joe Miller (*fourth from right*) inspects a herd of 101 Ranch cattle, circa 1926. Veteran cowboy Bill Pickett is second from right. *(Frank Phillips Foundation, Inc.)*

Ponca tribal elders conducted a traditional Ponca wedding ceremony for Colonel Joe Miller and his bride, Mary Verlin Miller, in 1927. *(Frank Phillips Foundation, Inc.)*

The Miller brothers—(*left to right*) Joe, Zack, and George—in front of the big top, circa 1927. *(Frank Phillips Foundation, Inc.)*

The funeral of Colonel Joe C. Miller—considered to be the most impressive in Oklahoma history—at the White House, 101 Ranch, October 24, 1927. *(Frank Phillips Foundation, Inc.)*

Jack Quait, trick rider, appeared with the Millers' show from 1929 until it closed, in 1931. *(Michael Wallis Collection)*

The final parade of the Miller Brothers' 101 Ranch Wild West, August 3, 1931, Washington, D.C. The show closed forever the following day. *(Jerry and Ruth Murphey Collection)*

Zack Miller (*left*) and his old friend Bert Colby in front of Colby's home in Osage County, Oklahoma, circa 1948. *(Joe Colby Collection)*

For weeks at a time, Joe traveled far and wide, mostly by automobile. He purchased a boatload of range cattle from Honduran ranchers at the stockyards in Jacksonville, Florida; dabbled in a few high-dollar deals with stockbrokers; and set up prizefights for his friend Jess Willard, who was still the world's heavyweight champion. In a steady stream of correspondence scribbled on hotel stationery, Joe remained in constant contact with Bessie Herberg (going by Bess Carter), at her home in Bliss.[44]

Sprinkled with such endearments as "Dear Cutie," "Dad would sure like to see Cutie now," "Dady [sic] sure lonesome today," and "am sorry to hear Cutie has a cold," Joe's letters to Bess came from New Orleans, Montgomery, Selma, Jacksonville, Memphis, Saint Louis, Pittsburgh, Kansas City, Chicago, and other cities. Joe often gently chastised his lover for not writing him more often, and he spoke of being homesick for the ranchlands along the Salt Fork. "I sure would like to see the place," Joe wrote to Bess in May 1918 from the Morrison Hotel in Chicago, "but the way I feel I don't think I will show up there for some time. Think it best for me to stay away."[45]

In the same letter, Joe also complained about Jess Willard's constant indecision and his reluctance to committing to a fight date in Cumberland, Maryland. "I had a hunch he [Willard] might get cold feet. Well, I have just had a talk with him and his feet are frozen up to his knees. Now he wants to back out and call it off."[46]

Soon after writing the letter, Joe ended his working relationship with Willard, although the prizefighter would remain a close friend. Within fourteen months of Joe's letter to Bess, Willard would be dethroned as world heavyweight champ by a savage puncher who fought under the name Kid Blackey, or the Manassa Mauler—a nickname taken from the Colorado town where he was born. His actual name was William Harrison Dempsey, but by the time he pummeled Willard into submission before forty-five thousand spectators at the Toledo Arena on July 4, 1919, he was better known as Jack Dempsey.[47]

By then, Joe Miller had patched up his differences with Zack and George and had returned to the fold at the 101, prompted by the failing health of Mother Miller. As early as May 1918, about the time Joe was trying to arrange prizefights for Willard, he learned of his mother's poor physical condition. "Have had the blues all day," Joe wrote Bess from Chicago. "Don't feel much like writing now. Had a letter from my sister. Said Mother was quite sick and hinted that I come in but the way I feel don't think I could do it. Not now anyway."[48]

Doctors who examined Mother Miller found that she had cancer and there was little that could be done. As his mother's condition worsened and the attending physicians came to the White House and predicted that the end was near, Joe dropped everything he was doing and returned at once to the 101 Ranch.

In her book coauthored with Ellsworth Collings about the 101 Ranch, Alma Miller England presented a sanitized but accurate account of the conflict among her three brothers and an explanation of Joe's return to the ranch during the summer of 1918.

"It seems that since the Miller family was operating the Ranch as a unit, very little consideration was given to just which name under which title to the land was recorded," wrote Alma and her coauthor. "Apparently most of the land purchased by Mrs. Miller with the life insurance money of her husband was actually taken in patents from the government to two of her sons, Zack and George. Joe was busy with his farming interests and had little mind for the office affairs. In 1917 a disagreement arose between [sic] the brothers and Joe's interest was bought by the other two, so that at the time of Mrs. Miller's death, there was none of the land in his name. He was gone from the ranch for two years and returned when Mrs. Miller was dying."[49]

Although he found his mother in rapid decline, Joe was elated to be back at the ranch. The three Miller brothers hammered out their differences and, drawn together by their mother's illness, restored their close alliance. Joined by Alma and other relatives and friends, the brothers spent as much time as possible with their ailing mother.

She had always been a vital and robust woman, and her loved ones were not accustomed to seeing her bedridden. They recalled the many years she had devoted to her family and the ranch, continually doling out advice to children and grandchildren or lending a sympathetic ear to hundreds of cowboys, cowgirls, and oil-field hands who worked for the Millers.

As early as 1912, Mother Miller and her sons had begun to enjoy big royalty disbursements from the wildcat oil and gas wells. The 101 Ranch Oil Company found a ready market for its vast supply of gas, and—at a cost of a half-million dollars—they laid a pipeline to the town of Tonkawa.[50] The sale of gas from the plant enabled the Millers and E. W. Marland to continue the search for additional pools of oil. New discoveries opened up even greater opportunities, and daily production figures soared. Many of the drilling sites, each yielding hundreds of barrels every day, were on

Indian allotments, including two hundred acres known as the Iron Thunder land, at the very heart of the oil field.[51]

"One of the lucky landowners is Mrs. George W. Miller of the 101 Ranch," reported the *Ponca City Democrat* as early as 1912. "Mrs. Miller has lived most of her life in the West, and has been acquainted with large business transactions, having dealt in herds of cattle and horses, but she never before enjoyed an income so easily obtained as that which is flowing hour by hour from the three wells on her 200-acre farm in the heart of the Ponca field. Her income from royalties is now $100 a day, to be greatly increased as new wells are brought in."[52]

Molly, born and bred a Kentucky lady, appreciated her great influx of wealth and especially enjoyed how the affluence enhanced her role as the official hostess of the 101 Ranch. "She was a grand dame—a gregarious matriarch kind of figure who loved to be in the thick of things," Joe Miller Jr. recalled of his grandmother many years later. "She enjoyed watching the motion pictures being produced on the ranch and she visited the Wild West shows out on the road. When those oil wells came in out in the South Ponca Field and she started receiving those big royalties, well, then, by golly, she got herself a chauffeur-driven twelve-cylinder Packard and she'd go to town and call on her friends. She really loved life."[53]

During the last days of her life, Molly presented pieces of her jewelry, mostly diamond rings, brooches, and necklaces, to every member of her family. One morning, close to the end, she had the attending nurse summon the three Miller brothers. "Now listen here," she told them, "I'm up here in this bedroom and it's too lonesome. I want to go downstairs to the living room where I can see people and enjoy the comings and goings."[54] Her sons carried their mother downstairs and placed her in her bed, set up in the sunlight-drenched living room. Folks in fancy dress came to the ranch to pay their respects, and grizzled cowhands doffed their dusty hats and tiptoed into the room to say so long to the snowy-haired lady.

There in the White House, encircled by those who cherished her the most, Mary Anne Carson Miller completed her journey. She died just a month before her seventy-second birthday, on Sunday morning, July 28, 1918, and was laid to rest in the I.O.O.F. Cemetery in Ponca City. Mother Miller died at peace, knowing her three boys were friends once again.[55] Some of the old-time hands who survived from the early years of the ranch declared that after the passing of Mother Miller, the Hundred and One was never quite the same.

Her last will and testament, drafted while the brothers were still quarreling when Joe was away from the ranch, transferred all the ranch holdings to Zack and George and named them as the sole executors of her estate.[56] Infuriated with Joe because of his romance with Bess Herberg, Mother Miller disinherited her eldest son and terminated the original 101 Ranch private corporation agreement, drawn up by the brothers in 1905. According to provisions of her final will, additional portions of property from outside the boundaries of the ranch proper were set aside for Alma and for grandchildren and some close friends.[57]

On her deathbed, however, Mother Miller had a change of heart. This came about after she reportedly extracted a promise from Joe that he would give up Bessie, his pretty cowgirl from Minnesota. Satisfied with her son's pledge, Mother Miller made a codicil to the will, giving Joe 160 acres in the bend of the Salt Fork where he had developed a large prize-winning apple orchard.[58]

Joe tried his best to keep his word to his mother, even though he continued to look after Bess for several more years. The two of them ran some livestock and entered into oil and gas leases with Gypsy Oil Company on acreage Joe provided to Bessie near Bliss. They named the modest spread the 50–50 Ranch.[59]

Bess managed the small ranch after she and Joe went separate ways. In the early 1930s, Bess, often referred to as Buckskin Bessie, married Marshall Blackwell. Eventually they operated a general-merchandise store near the White Eagle settlement south of Ponca City, and later Blackwell moved to Ardmore, Oklahoma, where he managed a second store.[60]

Eventually gaining a reputation as a crusty lady fond of giving candy to Indian children, Bessie owned numerous animals, including a Great Dane, a warthog, peacocks, and a sorrel saddle horse. In her store, she displayed an autographed photograph of Buffalo Bill, a 101 Ranch branding iron, and the fancy saddle Joe Miller had given her many years before.[61]

Early on the morning of September 6, 1943, a fire of mysterious origin flashed through the living quarters of the store at White Eagle. Buckskin Bessie's badly charred body was found in the smoldering ashes.[62] At the funeral, some Ponca Indians honored their friend by presenting her family with a ceremonial peace pipe. Then Bess was laid to rest at Ponca City in the cemetery where many of her old comrades were buried, including the love of her life—Joe Miller.

Although Joe showed reluctance when it came to severing the relationship with Bessie in the early 1920s, Zack and George had no concerns about their older brother's love affairs. Their differences with Joe stemmed solely from business matters. Once Joe made it clear that he was willing to cease the Wild West road shows, the two younger Miller brothers were satisfied. To placate Joe, George and Zack even agreed to continue to produce public shows at the spacious roundup grounds near the Salt Fork.

Once the brothers reconciled in 1918, there even had been talk just before Mother Miller died of her changing her will to include Joe and formally reinstating him as an equal partner. Instead, Zack and George verbally agreed to restore the partnership. They gave Joe a one-third interest in the entire ranch property, so no further written changes or amendments were made in the will other than the addition of the rider giving Joe the apple orchard.[63]

Alma's husband, William England, attorney and legal adviser for the ranch, was not satisfied with such an arrangement, however. England convinced his brothers-in-law that more than a verbal contract and handshakes were necessary to protect the integrity of the family partnership. England foresaw complications which might arise on the death of any of the partners. In the next few years, England drafted a detailed written agreement designed to prevent the dissolution of the partnership in case of the death of one of the brothers.[64]

Will Brooks and J. E. Carson—the Millers' Kentucky cousins who had been with the ranch for many years—were elected trustees and charged with administering the agreement. Called the Miller Brothers 101 Ranch Trust, the arrangement did not become effective until September 12, 1921, when Joe, Zack, and George signed the final document. As equal partners and shareholders in the trust, each of the brothers received one-third of the one hundred thousand shares issued.[65]

With the signing of the trust agreement, everything appeared to be in order once again for the Millers and their ranch. By then, the nation had to rely on bathtub gin, Choctaw beer, and other creative concoctions prevalent during Prohibition, which took effect in 1919. The Miller brothers, however, toasted the 1920s and their own accomplishments with the best bootleg Scotch purchased by the profits from cattle, crops, and reservoirs of rich Oklahoma crude oil and natural gas sucked from beneath the prairie sod.

Ironically, the most popular stories about the Hundred and One—tales of celebrity visitors, exploits of daring performers, and the business achievements of the ranch—came from those final years of the Millers' operation. In a way, the ranch could have been compared to a terminally ill person who seemed stronger and appeared to rally, suggesting a glimmer of hope just before death. Between World War I and the onset of the Great Depression, the wheeling and dealing Millers entered a state of deceptive euphoria. They continued to make bold headlines around the world, even as time began to run out for them and the 101 Ranch.

Much of the lore that endured long after the last Miller departed the scene in the mid-1930s emanated from the ranch itself—a veritable livestock and agricultural kingdom, frequently called "the greatest diversified farm on earth."[66] The operation not only included crop fields and grazing pastures but also a vast complex of commercial buildings encompassing the White House, including an oil refinery, filling station, restaurant, electric plant, meatpacking plant, tannery, dairy, laundry, harness shop, ice plant, and cannery. This was in addition to a seemingly endless network of barns, silos, corrals, livery stables, and blacksmith, machine, woodworking, and repair shops.

The 101 Ranch store was for many years the principal mercantile center for hundreds of Miller employees as well as farmers and ranchers from across northern Oklahoma and part of southern Kansas. A combination general-merchandise outlet and department store, the Millers' emporium offered a wide selection of goods, including many products produced on the ranch itself.

By 1918, business was so good that the brothers decided to build a larger store on the site of the original frame structure just south of the White House. At the time, the ranch suffered from a severe labor shortage because many of the Millers' cowboys and field workers had left to serve in the military during World War I. To solve the problem, George Miller called in some markers with the family's political allies and arranged for the federal government to transport by rail thirty Austrian prisoners of war from an East Coast internment camp. Sam Stigall, who years before had acted as carpentry foreman for the construction of the White House, took charge of the prisoners and saw to it that they drew the same pay as everybody else on the ranch.[67]

Housed in old cottages left standing along the Salt Fork, the prisoners worked in the agricultural fields but devoted most of their time to building the two-story stucco store building, with spacious living quarters upstairs. Often, they ate their meals across the road in the 101 Ranch cafe, where chefs and cooks turned out memorable dishes and boasted that everything served came straight from the ranch with the exceptions of coffee, sugar, and olives. It soon became evident that the POWs enjoyed working on the fabled ranch so much that there was no need to post guards. At war's end, some of the Austrians decided to settle in the area instead of returning to their homeland.[68]

Advertised as "the country store with the city ways," the ranch store sold freshly butchered meats and poultry; bushels of peaches, apples, melons, grapes, and other produce; and jugs from the two hundred barrels of sweet cider the 101 Ranch processed each autumn. While attendants in white dusters gassed up automobiles out front with fuel refined on the premises, soda jerks inside the store stayed busy whipping up ice-cream treats from the nearby ranch diary, where herds of purebred Jersey and Holstein cows produced an enormous surplus of milk, butter, and high-test cream.[69]

Shoppers had a broad range of choices—everything from ostrich feathers for stylish fans and boas to jars of apple butter and jelly produced on the ranch and "guaranteed to keep all winter, if you can keep the children away from it."[70] Miller employees used the 101 Ranch scrip, printed in denominations ranging from five dollars to one hundred dollars, and ranch-minted coins known as "broncs" to buy such things as saddles, overalls, or lard.

Although the store proved popular with the Austrian prisoners and with many ranch employees and visitors, not everyone harbored good feelings about what transpired there. For some of the Indian people laboring in the Millers' novelty factory, the ranch store became a symbol of exploitation and abuse. Despite long hours spent producing goods for the store and for a thriving wholesale trade, the Ponca and Otoe employees received far less than fair wages.[71]

Day in and day out, these Indians performed what amounted to drudge work, turning out large quantities of beaded belts, rugs, clothing, drums, rattles, bows and arrows, jewelry, and trinkets. The Millers marked up the Indian piecework and sold it at the store along with postcards depicting life on the ranch, Mexican curios, and an ample assortment of children's chaps, vests, hats, gun belts, and other inexpensive cowboy souvenirs.[72]

Customers and patrons who clogged the store after performances at the big ranch roundups left with keepsakes from the ranch, which the Millers proclaimed "the connecting link between the old and new west, the one place in all America where life as it was lived on the great plains in the early days shakes hands with the present."[73] No one, including the silent Indian workers who needed the hard-earned wages, seemed to question the pittance they received for hours of tedious menial toil.

Yet mistreatment of Indians at the ranch store went far beyond exploitative wages, and there would be much more serious repercussions. Bitter memories lingered for years, stemming from numerous accounts of Indians who traded at the ranch store and were cheated out of money or, in some cases, finagled out of their land allotments.[74]

These victims included several Ponca and Otoe men who came to the Millers' store before going off to fight for the United States during World War I. Store clerks and cashiers reportedly told the young men that chances were slim to none that they would survive the fierce combat in the trenches of France. They supposedly encouraged the Indians to sell their 160-acre allotments to the ranch and enjoy the proceeds before being shipped overseas.[75]

"I remember well when I was there [the 101 Ranch] that the man who ran the store used to handle the signing of land leases for the Millers," recalled 101 Ranch alumnus Jack McCracken before his death, in 1972. "He would get the Indians to sign the lease with the usual X, then give them a sack of flour or a sack of spuds as payment. He also told them to go down to the slaughter house and help themselves. Well, at the slaughter house they would find, *maybe*, a head and a lot of tripe which was all the off fall [offal] left there. So the Millers had another 160 acres leased for another year. I've seen those deals made many times."[76]

The Millers invariably denied such misdeeds. Instead, they pointed to the long-standing, albeit paternalistic, relationship between the Miller family and various Indian tribes, especially the Poncas and Otoes, who leased thousands of acres of land to the 101 Ranch. In two books about the ranch—both coauthored or heavily influenced by the Millers—the family was portrayed as being generous to a fault when it came to their "red-skinned friends" and their inability to handle fiscal matters.[77]

Fred Gipson wrote in *Fabulous Empire*:

> The rent money which the 101 paid for farming and grazing leases was turned over to the Indians through the Office for [of] Indian Affairs. By white man's law and custom, this was as far as the Millers' dealings with the Indians had to go. But Indian ways are not the ways of a white man. The Indians were friends of the Millers, and, to an Indian, friendship works both ways and is on a lot higher level than mere dollars and cents. And to whom but a friend should a man go when he is broke and hungry?
>
> So when a Ponca was hungry, he went to the 101 for food. When he

> was broke, he went to the 101 for money. When he needed advice on the strange laws shoved upon him by the white man, the 101 was the first place he headed. . . . But saving for a rainy day isn't an Indian's way of doing and plenty of times the lease money the Poncas received from the Millers failed to cover the debts they made. When this happened, none of them hesitated to hit up the 101 for a loan, promising to pay when the lease money came again.[78]

Likewise, in her tribute book about the 101 Ranch and her family, Alma Miller England made sure the Millers were cast in the best possible light concerning their business affairs with Indians. She depicted the Ponca men as "strangers to work" who would "sit for hours carving some weird design without looking up or saying a word."[79] She also emphasized the generosity of Joe Miller, a trait which she admitted enhanced his popularity and influence with the tribe.

"The heaviest of Colonel Joe's duties was in looking after the thousand Indians who owned much of the land of the 101 Ranch and who looked upon him as a father," wrote Alma and her coauthor. "They called him at all hours on the telephone, camped in his door yard, brought all their troubles to him, borrowed money from him, made presents to him. . . . The Indians were honest, but their lease money was not always enough to pay their debts, so the debts continued. They owed the Millers as much as $22,000 at one time."[80]

Twenty-two thousand dollars might have been an astronomical sum to the Poncas, but it meant nothing to the white men who fueled the Oklahoma oil boom. It represented a pot at a Saturday-night poker game or a roll of the dice for wildcat tycoons such as E. W. Marland and Louis Haines "Lew" Wentz, another Ponca City oil millionaire who liked splashing his money around town.[81] It was spare change for the big independent developers like the Millers who held some of the region's most productive oil and natural-gas producing leases.

Marland, always working in concert with the Millers, organized Marland Refining Company in 1915, and two years later absorbed the 101 Ranch Oil Company, with offices in a nondescript one-story frame building on First Street in Ponca City.[82] He then erected a refinery on the south edge of town, expanding his operations into refining and marketing petroleum products. The Kay County Gas Company, which he also controlled, assumed natural-gas distribution.[83]

In 1920, Marland incorporated his refinery into Marland Oil Company.

Before long, the firm's red triangle insignia became familiar at gas stations throughout the state and region.[84] In the next several years, Marland continued to enjoy spectacular success as a wildcatter and was involved in a series of important discoveries, including the Blackwell, Garber, Billings, Burbank, and Three Sands fields.[85]

Already a multimillionaire, Marland—with a "nose for oil and the luck of the devil"—watched as enormous sums of money poured into his coffers, thanks to the seemingly endless gas and oil production on Indian lands controlled by the Millers.[86] In 1920, Marland's holdings alone were valued at eighty-five million dollars. In the next decade, Ponca City—described by one eastern writer as "the Athens of the West"—doubled in size.[87]

To honor E. W. Marland, the town of Bliss was renamed Marland in 1922. It seemed a fitting tribute for the risk taker who had done so much to boost the Millers' income by developing field after field.

Oil derricks and drilling sites, dotting the 101 Ranch as far as the eye could see, brought in thousands of barrels of oil daily. By 1921, several important oil fields were developing on the Millers' ranchlands—two on the ranch proper, about five miles northeast of the White House headquarters; one on the Bar L lands in the Ponca country; and another on ranch holdings in the Otoe country, which became known as the Watchorn field, after Robert T. Watchorn, president of Watchorn Oil and Gas Company.[88] Between 1923 and 1930, the oil earnings of the Hundred and One totaled more than $1.3 million, not including profits from the ranch filling station and refinery. During the same period, income from oil wells on the Millers' ranchlands accounted for an average of $190,000 annually.[89]

Much like their cronies—E. W. Marland, the Phillips brothers of Bartlesville and Tulsa, and Lew Wentz, whose independent oil company was raking in a million dollars a month by 1927—the Millers luxuriated in the oceans of money washing over Oklahoma in the teens and 1920s.[90] According to some critics, when it came to oil and gas royalties and lease income, the Millers literally made out like bandits.

"It always bothered me to see the Miller Brothers played up as heroes when they defrauded Indians of land greater in value than train and bank robberies committed by the Daltons, Doolins, James and other bandits combined," wrote Ferdie J. Deering, veteran journalist and editor, in a confidential memorandum in 1982.[91] A longtime columnist for the *Daily Oklahoman* and editor for forty years of *Farmer-Stockman Magazine*, Deering devoted years to tracking the U.S. Justice Department's legal action against the Miller brothers and the probe of their questionable business dealings with Indians.

A lengthy investigation of the Millers began in the early 1920s, and a federal grand jury returned forty-nine criminal indictments charging the brothers with defrauding the Poncas of large tracts of allotted lands between 1917 and 1920. The ensuing litigation dragged on for years in lower federal courts and eventually ended up before the United States Supreme Court.[92]

"Out in Oklahoma the Miller Brothers, of the famous Ranch 101, were indicted for swindling the Indians, wards of the Government, out of valuable oil lands," wrote Samuel Hopkins Adams in 1939 in *Incredible Era*, a biography of President Warren G. Harding and his corrupt presidency. "They had powerful connections in both the Republican and the Democratic camps. . . . The Millers were notorious in Oklahoma for this sort of chicanery. One of them [Joe Miller] was a convicted counterfeiter. At the lowest valuation, the land out of which they had jockeyed the Indians was worth $380,000; any fines assessed would have left them with a handsome profit."[93]

Herbert M. Peck, U.S. district attorney in Oklahoma City in the early 1920s, represented the Department of Justice in the case against the Millers. In the late 1960s, Peck, a respected attorney who came to Oklahoma in 1908 and remained active in state affairs until his death in 1972, provided Deering with a taped summary which recounted the investigation, the Millers' trials, and subsequent events.[94]

"The Miller brothers' case was one of the most notorious cases that I handled while I was United States district attorney," Peck stated in his taped account. "It seems the Department of Justice for many years had endeavored to secure competent evidence against the Miller brothers to present to a grand jury, and each time, the investigators sent here from Washington were wined and dined by the Miller brothers and returned with no concrete evidence against them for their actions in defrauding the Indians."[95]

That changed, however, when A. Mitchell Palmer, known as the "Fighting Quaker," became U.S. attorney general in 1919, during the final term of Woodrow Wilson. Palmer, harboring ambitions to become president, was an overly zealous patriotic reformer who orchestrated the infamous "Red Scare Raids" against Communists and alien "radicals."[96] Palmer was also determined to prove that the Miller brothers had deceived the federal government while they hoodwinked large numbers of Indians.

After recruiting a pair of "competent and thoroughly honest investigators," Palmer dispatched them to Oklahoma, where they devoted two years to scrutinizing every facet of the case against the Millers. Much of the evidence came from one of the 101 Ranch's bookkeepers, who had become suspicious when he found glaring discrepancies in many of the leases and warranty deeds between Ponca and Otoe Indians and the Miller brothers.[97]

"Under the federal law, incompetent Indians were not permitted to deed their property without the consent of the Indian Department in Washington," Peck explained years later in his tape-recorded account. "But they were permitted, without the consent of the Indian Department, to lease their lands for agricultural purposes for a period of five years. The scheme adopted by the Miller brothers to secure possession of these Indian lands was rather unique. They knew that the Indians had this land to rent for agricultural purposes and the Miller brothers had many times secured many of these leases, so the Indians were very familiar with this practice."[98]

The Millers, according to Peck, secured leases on many tracts of oil-rich land in this manner. Then when they wished to obtain ownership, they simply had the unsuspecting "Indian and his squaw" sign what was described as an agricultural lease, which in fact turned out to be a warranty deed for the property. This allowed the Millers to do whatever they wanted with the land, including exploring for oil and gas. After John C. Newton, the Millers' chief clerk, notarized the deeds, they ended up in the ranch vault until the time came for the Office of Indian Affairs to pass on the competency of various Ponca and Otoe people.[99]

In Oklahoma—where the Millers lavishly entertained them at the White House—the visiting commissioners usually followed their hosts' recommendations on the competency of the Indians at question. The end result was that the secretary of the interior would recommend that the Indians be given deeds, or patents, to their allotments so they could transact business without interference from the federal government.[100]

Peck related,

> The Miller brothers for years had been using this same practice in securing land from the incompetent Indians, and had in their employ in the city of Washington, D.C., a lawyer who was thoroughly familiar with the practice and kept in very close touch with these recommendations made by the commissions that were sent out to determine the competency of the Ponca and Otoe Indians.
>
> Just as soon as the patent, or deed, to the Indian allotment was signed

> by the General Land Office, this particular attorney of the Miller brothers would wire the Miller brothers that on a certain date a certain patent, or deed, was signed, giving the allotment absolutely to the Indian who had been declared competent. The Miller brothers would then have the notary public date the deed which he held in his safe, which the Indian thought was an agricultural lease, and file the deed for record.
>
> Several weeks later, the Indian would receive from the government his patent, or deed, to his allotment, and then he would go out and endeavor to sell this particular tract of land to some people who lived in the area. And, if a sale were made, then an investigation would be had of the abstract and it would be discovered that the land had theretofore been sold to the Miller brothers and the Indian no longer held any title to it.[101]

Satisfied with the findings of his crack investigators, which led to multiple criminal indictments, Peck held out for lengthy prison sentences for the three Miller brothers. Aware that serious trouble loomed for them, the Millers assembled an impressive legal corps for their upcoming federal trial, in 1923. They also reserved two full floors in the posh Skirvin Hotel in Oklahoma City, near the federal courthouse, to house their attorneys, family members, and a parade of anticipated defense witnesses.[102]

Meanwhile, the national political scene had dramatically changed with the election, in 1920, of Republican President Warren G. Harding and Vice President Calvin Coolidge. After taking office in 1921, Harding—a seasoned Ohio politician—rewarded several of his cronies by appointing them to important offices, including various cabinet posts.

A key member of this inner circle, which came to be known as the "Ohio Gang," was Harry M. Daugherty—lawyer, lobbyist, and Harding's campaign manager. Daugherty, who replaced A. Mitchell Palmer as U.S. attorney general, became associated almost immediately with much of the corruption spawned during the Harding administration. By 1923, when Harding suddenly died in office, it became clear that Daugherty took more than a passing interest in the federal government's case against the Miller brothers. John E. Todd, Daugherty's well-connected law partner, was named legal adviser on the Millers' defense team.[103]

"Daugherty professed surprise at learning that his former partner was connected with the case," Samuel Adams explained in *Incredible Era*. "The Attorney General's capacity for amazement was unlimited. On his advice, Mr. Todd withdrew from the [Miller] case. He did not, however, return any part of his two-thousand-dollar fee [to the Millers.]"[104]

The stage was set for a lengthy trial before federal Judge John H. Cotteral, with testimony from scores of witnesses, including many Poncas and Otoes. However, the proceedings came to an abrupt halt when the Millers suddenly entered guilty pleas. Stunned by the unexpected move, U.S. attorney Herbert Peck had no choice but to go along with the decision. "On the morning that the Miller brothers decided to plead guilty," Peck later explained, "I received a telegram from Attorney General Daugherty in which he directed me to say nothing at all to the judge in open court with reference to the punishment to be meted out to the defendants. The attorney general knew that I was insisting upon a penitentiary sentence and he . . . was willing to accept a fine."[105]

Judge Cotteral assessed the Millers a modest fine of ten thousand dollars for having illegally acquired Indian land valued at more than $380,000, and the three brothers walked out of the courtroom without having to serve a single day in jail. The judge explained that the fine, which Peck considered a slap on the wrist, was sufficient punishment because of the several civil lawsuits which could be brought against the Millers, thus breaking up the 101 Ranch and returning the land to the rightful owners.[106] Cotteral, however, underestimated the power of the Millers and their contacts in high places in the federal government.

After the criminal trial, Peck prepared to file on the Millers and proceed with the civil cases to restore the land to the Indians. Before Peck could carry through with his plans, the attorney general ordered him to cease all work concerning the Millers and to allow Daugherty's office to assume full control of the matter.[107]

Even though civil suits were filed to reclaim the disputed land for the Indian owners, Peck saw the writing on the wall. He realized that Daugherty had allied himself with various big oil interests and that the action would undoubtedly bog down in the courts and end up in favor of the Millers. Peck's worst fears came true when he found that the two investigators "who were overactive in securing evidence" against the Millers had been discharged from their jobs.[108]

In 1924, while serving as vice president and trust officer at First National Bank in Oklahoma City, Peck received a subpoena to report to Washington, D.C., to testify before a United States Senate committee investigating Attorney General Daugherty.[109] Members of Harding's administration were suspected of shady dealings, including Daugherty, Secretary of the Navy Edwin Denby, and Interior Secretary Albert Fall. Indeed, Fall eventually went to prison for his role in the infamous "Teapot Dome" scandal, involving the leasing of federal oil reserves to private interests.

During lengthy testimony before the panel of senators, Peck discussed Daugherty's preoccupation with the Millers' criminal case. Peck held his ground, although some pertinent correspondence and telegrams had mysteriously vanished from the files and he faced intense grilling from Republican members determined to uphold Daugherty's actions.

"This Miller brothers' case is the only one I handled while I was a district attorney in which the attorney general himself handled matters directly from his own office," Peck told Senator Burton K. Wheeler of Montana, committee chairman. "I suggest you have records of his office brought into court."[110]

Wheeler issued a subpoena for the records, but Daugherty refused to comply with the order. The matter was referred to President Coolidge, who had succeeded Harding. Finally, Daugherty produced some of the files, although he further angered senators by refusing to appear before the committee. The missing documents were eventually located and Peck's testimony was substantiated.

In March 1924, Daugherty—who managed to escape conviction on charges of conspiracy to defraud the government—was forced to resign as attorney general. His ouster came at the request of Coolidge, who stated that Daugherty had become a source of "increasing embarrassment."[111]

In Oklahoma, the Miller brothers and their lawyers battled civil suits and managed to win dismissals on some of the counts against them. "Politics is at the bottom of all these charges," George Miller told the *Oklahoma City Times* in a 1924 interview. George, who conducted all Indian land matters for the 101 Ranch, vehemently denied any intentional fraud or wrongdoing and insisted that the charges were based on erroneous information. He also said that Peck's testimony before the Senate committee "sounded foolish" and that it was "absurd" to charge that Daugherty "ever exerted himself in my behalf."[112]

The government's charges against the Millers dragged on through the court system. In 1926, Judge A. G. C. Bierer of Guthrie was appointed special master to take further testimony and make recommendations. After six weeks of hearing witnesses and arguments, the judge ruled generally in favor of the government, although the Millers also emerged victorious on several points. Both sides filed exceptions, and the litigation continued for several more years, with hearings and motions in various federal courts.

Ultimately, the scores of original counts against the Millers dwindled through government dismissals or judicial rulings.[113]

Finally, in 1931, the remaining counts came before the Tenth Circuit Court of Appeals, in Denver. The judges unanimously ruled in favor of the Miller brothers and declared that they had not unfairly induced the Indians to sell their lands. Besides finding that the Millers "did not actually entice, advise or assist the Indians to apply for their fee patents," the court declared "that the Indians were charged no more for the goods and merchandise that they purchased at the ranch store than elsewhere; that any plan or purpose of the Miller brothers to buy these Indian lands, when they became salable, was a lawful intention to do a lawful act."[114]

The federal lawyers appealed the decision to the United States Supreme Court. On October 17, 1932, after hearing arguments, the justices refused to review the case, thereby upholding the circuit court's ruling.[115]

"Thus the long and technical litigation left the Miller brothers in rightful possession of all the 17,492.31 acres of deeded land purchased from the Indians," pointed out Alma Miller England and Ellsworth Collings in their book about the ranch, published five years after the final court action. "The land returned to the Indians, as a result of the litigation, was not part of the 101 Ranch proper but included scattered holdings, ranging in small tracts from twenty to one hundred and sixty acres. The Federal court found that the brothers had not in any instance acted fraudulently and that in only two of the forty-one counts had technical errors occurred in the purchases. The court, however, found that twenty of the Indians, from whom purchases had been made, were incompetent despite government ruling to the contrary at the time the purchases were made. The court, furthermore, ordered that these lands be returned to the Indians with the government paying back in full to the Miller brothers the purchase price of $30,649.90."[116]

It proved to be a hollow victory. By the time the long legal war between the government and the Millers had concluded, two of the brothers were dead and their 101 Ranch empire had collapsed. The sad prophecy—the curse on the white men uttered so long before—echoed across the pastures, masked only by whispers of wind brushing against the heart-shaped leaves of cottonwoods, gnarled specters guarding the contrary Salt Fork.

NOTHING BUT COWBOYS, COWGIRLS, AND INDIANS

Life is just a moving picture;
And we see it in a glass—
The sorrowful and tragic;
As the figures rise and pass;
So what's the use of weeping,
For before our tears are dry
There comes another picture
With a rainbow in the sky.[1]
—Joe Miller

WHEN all was said and done, the Miller brothers—Joe, Zack, and George—were in fact nothing but cowboys. In spite of their extensive agricultural enterprises, oil and gas deals, Wild West shows and roundups, motion-picture projects, and other activities, the Millers never did shake their powerful desire to work with cattle on the range.[2] True to the revered cowboy saying, all three of the Miller brothers died with their boots on.

Until the bitter end of the 101 Ranch empire in the 1930s, the core of the ranch remained cowboys and cowgirls—men and women who broke broncos, doctored sick cows, branded calves, and mended fences. That was what the Hundred and One had been all about from the start, when Colonel George Washington Miller and his gang of loyal "cowhunters" and drovers swapped hog meat for Texas longhorns and herded them north up the good grass trails.

Diversification had saved the ranch empire as early as the 1890s, when the Millers, hoping to bolster lost revenue from a sagging cattle market, expanded their horizons with the establishment of a major farming operation. Thirty years later, long after the patriarch was dead and buried beneath Kentucky bluegrass, his three sons continued to ranch and farm on a major scale, but they found themselves spread too thin, with family problems and other interests. Although they tried their level best to keep alive the ranch, as well as the mythical West, by reprising their Wild West shows for several years starting in the mid-1920s, the Millers and their entire outfit were destined for a head-on collision with the stark truth of the times.

Yet many years after the collapse of the 101 Ranch in the early 1930s, the cowboy endured as the archetypal hero. For better or for worse, much of the credit for creating the image of the quixotic cowboy and his female counterpart belonged to the Millers and their accomplices—the cowboys and cowgirls and, to some extent, the Indians employed at the 101 Ranch.

"There is, in America, no more pliable figure than the cowboy," observed the *New York Times* in 1998. "He is whatever we want him to be whenever we need to imagine him. He rides in from somewhere else, driving cattle, chasing badmen, fleeing the past or simply mulling over the landscape as it looks from the back of a horse. He is as artificial as the worst of movies can make him, and he is more authentic than even the truest of stories that are told about him. How richly we have elaborated the myth of cowboys—surrendering the reality nearly completely in the process. . . ."[3]

For a long period of time, the romantic West of the "cowboy and Indian"—the West of the imagination—blended with the West of reality on the Millers' ranch along the Salt Fork. The resulting concoction proved to be an intoxicating brew. Yet in the twilight of the Millers' astonishing empire, that same mixture fed the decay which chewed away at the heart and soul of the 101.

Matters were not helped by the Indian curse. Some of the toughest cowboys believed in the spell that the Poncas were said to be have cast over the Millers and others who violated the Indians' land. Even when those cowboys were old men, gnarled and scarred after too many seasons in the saddle, they swore on their dead mothers' eyes that the inescapable Ponca curse had taken a greater toll on the 101 Ranch than all the problems the Millers caused for themselves.[4]

They believed the curse definitely was at work in 1923. It proved to be another year of highs, when ranch income soared because of the Watchorn oil field as well as staggering agricultural production. However, the year also brought many lows, as legal disputes over the validity of titles to Indian lands piled up for the Millers. Then in June, while elsewhere in the nation flappers danced the Charleston and moviegoers applauded a German shepherd named Rin Tin Tin, the rains came to the 101 Ranch.

Hard rain had started to fall two months earlier and continued as the Millers hosted their old show-business friend Jess Willard and his manager, Ray Archer, at the White House. They planned a June 10 cowboy and cowgirl reunion and ranch roundup in Willard's honor, including an appearance of the former heavyweight champion in an exhibition boxing match.[5]

A crowd gathered at the ranch early that Sunday, just as huge storm clouds erupted in a deluge. Thunder boomed across the prairies, daggers of lightning flashed through the summer sky, and sheets of torrential rain fell without respite. The Arkansas, Chikaskia, and Salt Fork Rivers—already swollen from a succession of recent storms—raged out of control, as did Bois d'Arc, Cow Skin, and Bird's Nest Creeks.[6]

Within a few hours, chocolate-colored floodwater inundated the ranch and many of the headquarters buildings. Rampaging waters quickly covered the saturated pastures, engulfed the two-lane highway connecting the town of Marland to Ponca City, and washed away the nearby bridge over the Salt Fork, leaving the span twisted like a crumpled newspaper. The Millers lost more than four thousand acres of ripening corn. Entire poultry flocks and thousands of head of livestock, including a herd of three thousand hogs, drowned. Eventually, the river grew to two miles in width, and water rose to the second-story porch of the ranch store.[7]

"The porch of the White House was out of the water with about two inches to spare," recalled Clair Nickles, a Ponca City machine-shop operator who made his way to the ranch through pelting rain in a motorboat to help with rescue operations. "We cut fences to keep the fat hogs from cutting their throats. And we had a time avoiding one of the buffaloes that got inside the fence around the White House and charged the boat."[8]

Joe Miller, who had only recently suffered a broken leg in a ranch accident, hobbled about on crutches like a landlocked sea captain, shouting commands at frantic cowhands as water gushed into the White House basement and seeped beneath the front door.[9] Along with his brothers and ranch foremen, Joe directed Nickles and other able-bodied boys and men who braved floodwater to rescue stranded employees, visitors, and livestock. Ranch cooks worked around the clock, serving coffee, fried chicken, ham, and mounds of biscuits to flood victims, including two hundred area refugees huddled at the White House.

"We moved people from the store porch to the White House and people were sleeping everywhere," explained Nickles, who spent several days in his boat bringing food and fresh water to workers and their families. "One lady had perched on top of a piano and didn't want to leave, but we dragged her out."[10]

Evacuees, wrapped in blankets, stood in numbed silence on the second-floor gallery of the White House and watched as dead horses and cows, automobiles, fences, and the remains of buildings floated downstream in the churning water. Jess Willard, while waiting for the flood to subside, broke away from a marathon poker game at the White House and played a heroic role by rescuing marooned families and helping to save endangered livestock.

Meanwhile, Nickles and his friends dealt with a gang of frenzied monkeys which some ranch workers had unchained from their poles when the floodwater continued to rise. "They were perched on hayracks and fences, everywhere," said Nickles. "The water kept climbing and the Millers wanted us to rescue those monkeys. But they can be pretty vicious, and, of course, they were pretty mad about the state of things, so after a couple of battles we gave up and let them sit out the flood."[11]

Joe's celebrated eleven-hundred-pound boar, known as "The Great I Am"—a grand-champion hog pampered in lavish quarters which included a tile bath, electric fans, and a staff of specialists to exercise and feed him and provide a harem of alluring sows—was hustled to safety on the second floor of the White House.[12] For several days, the front gallery of the Millers' residence was crowded with displaced people and a strange menagerie of domestic and wild beasts—everything from prize poultry, calves, and hound dogs to snakes, skunks, and prairie chickens. "By God, old Noah didn't have much on us," Joe said, laughing. "We've damned near got a pair of everything on earth."[13]

There was little else to amuse Joe and his brothers. The widespread devastation to the ranch and surrounding countryside became more apparent as the water finally began to recede, exposing crop damage in the fertile bottomland. To help stem future floods, the Millers constructed a levee several miles in length along the Salt Fork, not far from the ranch headquarters. But the havoc had resulted in more than a quarter-million dollars in damage to the 101 Ranch.[14]

Always enterprising, Joe recouped some of the losses by immediately starting a public ferry service at the Salt Fork crossing. The Millers maintained the ferry at their own expense, charging a dollar for every car or horseman except drivers of Fords—the most common automobile in the area at the time—who had to pay fifty cents more. Doctors, regardless of mode of transportation, rode free.[15]

The ferryboat earned the Millers about twenty-five thousand dollars. It remained in operation until August 1924, when state dignitaries dedicated a replacement bridge, built at a cost of fifty-eight thousand dollars. They christened the new steel bridge with a bottle of crude oil from a well in the Tonkawa field owned by Wentz Oil Corporation, leaving a large oily stain on the bridge roadway which remained for years. After the ceremony, the Millers threw a party for five hundred guests at the White House, complete with sweet cider, cake, and iced watermelons.[16]

Ten times that many people showed up at the ranch later that year for a soirée arranged by George Miller and his cousin Will Brooks. The crowd of five thousand came to celebrate the paving of the highway from Ponca City to the ranch and beyond to Marland, the Millers' headquarters town, where Brooks served for several years as mayor. When the moon rose, an outside wall of the ranch office building served as a screen for showing western motion pictures, which featured some of the notable 101 Ranch alumni. Afterward, partygoers sipped bootleg liquor and danced the night away on the freshly laid concrete highway.[17]

Regardless of paved roads, stronger bridges, and stout barriers to hold back floodwaters, people who knew the fickleness of Oklahoma weather and believed in the Ponca curse recognized that nature would always have the upper hand over all those who tried to tame the land and the elements.[18] The Salt Fork—which flooded the ranch again in 1926 and drowned cowboy Ralph Rhoades when his horse became entangled in a submerged fence—remained a contrary stream, inclined to go exactly where it pleased.[19]

Not long after the flood of 1923, the ranch was struck by a combination of blows. By August of that year, while the Millers still reeled from flood damage, the rains stopped altogether. The severe drought and hot winds which followed exhausted the soil and left the few intact growing fields parched. Fully 90 percent of the surviving corn was a failure, and the Millers' entire wheat crop was ruined.[20] The following month, still more misfortune visited the 101.

William H. England, Alma's husband and the Miller brothers' trusted legal adviser, died suddenly on September 22, 1923, at age forty-eight, in Ponca City. His untimely passing struck a hard blow to the community, as well as to Alma and the couple's three sons and three daughters.[21] An adept lawyer who briefly considered a run for United States Congress in 1921, England had maintained his own legal practice for many years while also handling legal affairs for the Hundred and One.[22] With their big cowboy hats in hand at the burial service, the Millers knew they would miss their brother-in-law's wise counsel in business and personal matters.

By the time of England's death, all three of the Miller brothers had at last acquired the honorary title of "Colonel"—the coveted epithet of respect among southern gentlemen that their father, George Washington Miller, had been given as a young man on the family plantation in Kentucky. In 1915, Oklahoma Governor Robert Lee Williams made Joe an honorary colonel. George became an honorary colonel in 1919, thanks to Governor J. B. A. Robertson. Finally, in 1923, Governor John C. "Jack" Walton designated Zack an honorary colonel on his staff.[23]

It seemed only appropriate that Zack—often considered the "bad boy" of the Miller family—was the last of the brothers to gain the ceremonial rank, and even more fitting that the honor came from Jack Walton, a former mayor of Oklahoma City and one of Oklahoma's most controversial governors. A champion of patronage but a foe of the powerful and influential Ku Klux Klan, Walton began his term as governor with a square dance and gigantic barbecue—with meat ranging from beef and pork to possum and bear—for three hundred thousand revelers at the state fairgrounds. Within less than ten months of his inaugural feast, Walton had been impeached and convicted on eleven charges of high crimes and misdemeanors, including campaign fund illegalities, padding of state payrolls, excessive use of pardoning power, suspension of the writ of habeas corpus, misuse of the National Guard, and general incompetence in office.[24]

Like Walton, Zack Miller frequently found himself the brunt of wrath and criticism. Often his harshest detractors were Zack's own family members, some of whom accused him of being lazy, crude, and generally offensive.[25] Zack often served as the scapegoat for the rest of the family. Indeed, much of the blame for the failure of the 101 Ranch ended up on Zack's shoulders, partly because Joe and especially George, both of whom died in the late 1920s, had managed to escape their share of criticism.

"Zack's presence at home was distracting because he had a habit of playing cards, drinking, and sometimes fighting with his cowhands," recalled his niece, Alice Miller Harth. "I can think of just one way he contributed to the business and that was his skill at cattle buying. He was encouraged to pursue this activity because it kept him away from home.

"Then on one of Zack's buying trips to Louisiana, he found a country place that he wanted to buy. This arrangement was readily agreed to by his brothers. It offered a more or less permanent solution to a problem—one that would keep Zack occupied at a distance."[26]

Zack named his combination ranch-farm the 101 Ranch Louisiana Plantation. Located near Sicily Island, Louisiana, in the rugged upland pine and hardwood forests of Catahoula Parish, just across the Mississippi River from Natchez, Mississippi—the oldest city on the great river—the plantation occupied much of Zack's time in the late teens and the 1920s. Zack and his resident manager, A. L. Curry, oversaw all farming and livestock operations, which included large herds of cattle, hogs, mules, and horses. The plantation boasted a sizable pecan grove, supported hundreds of acres of commercial timberland, and produced harnesses, saddles, and other leather goods.[27]

Unknown to Joe and George, their wandering brother used the Louisiana plantation for much more than running livestock and growing bumper crops of pecans and pulpwood trees. For several years, the Sicily Island estate served as a love nest for Zack and his longtime private secretary and companion, Marguerite Blevins.

Zack's niece Alice Miller Harth described Marguerite as "a perfect example of a Tennessee Williams character—a fading southern belle." Zack, who met Marguerite in the autumn of 1915, seemed to be drawn to the young woman's "finely chiseled features and refined manner [which] seemed to give credence to her charm." Alice also noted that Marguerite's "demeanor was more that of a nervous attendant, more ready and able to bring a drink than to take dictation."[28]

Although the two became lovers almost immediately after Marguerite went to work for Zack, he kept her far removed from family, friends, and the principal 101 Ranch spread in Oklahoma. The rest of the Millers knew nothing of the close relationship between Zack and Marguerite, even after the pair journeyed to the Mexican border, ostensibly on yet another cattle-buying trek. They were secretly wed in a Mexican civil marriage ceremony on August 8, 1919, at Piedras Negras, a port of entry on the Río Grande, opposite Eagle Pass, Texas.[29]

Finally, after years of carrying on the clandestine relationship, Zack again married Marguerite in a ceremony attended by a few of their Louisiana friends at Natchez, Mississippi, on February 6, 1921. Later that year, Marguerite bore Zack a son, whom they named Zack Jr.[30]

Perhaps out of shame or fear of adverse reaction to his choice of a second wife, Zack continued to keep his marriage secret from his immediate family in Oklahoma. It was not until the turbulent year of 1923 that the rest of the Millers learned that Zack had wed and was the father of a two-year-old son.[31] George Miller became quite upset when he learned of Zack's marriage. George reminded Zack that in 1921 he had listed himself as a single man with his signature on the Miller Brothers 101 Ranch Trust partnership papers. At George's insistence, the deed of trust was reexecuted in 1924, amending Zack's marital status and adding Marguerite's signature. That year, Marguerite gave birth to a second child—a daughter named Tassie Blevins Miller, whom the family called Blevins.[32] The tumultuous marriage proved toxic to both Zack and Marguerite and would eventually end in a bitter divorce and custody battle just as the 101 Ranch folded.

"Zack, I'm sure, had no desire to marry again," Alice Miller Harth disclosed in her 1983 memoir. "However, ensuing events proved that Marguerite, the so-called secretary, had definite plans for marriage. Later, I learned that she followed him from his place in Louisiana where they lived until events brought them back to Oklahoma."[33]

Although he had remarried and produced two more lively Miller offspring, Zack showed no signs of settling down. He continued to frustrate his brothers, particularly in his failure to keep them posted on his various business activities and exact whereabouts. "When you left here I particularly impressed you with the importance of letting us know where you were all the time, but we have not heard from you," scolded George in a letter sent to Zack at the Sicily Island plantation in 1924. "On two occasions [Lew] Wentz's office has called us asking where we could reach you by wire, and we could not give any definite information. I wish you would be more thoughtful along these lines."[34]

George's reprimand appeared on an official Miller Brothers 101 Ranch letterhead which, in bold type, unabashedly proclaimed the family operation to be "The Largest Diversified Farm And Ranch In The United States."[35] The Millers' old boast may have been wearing thin in some circles, but until just before the ranch finally went under and was scattered to the winds, few persons dared challenge the bold assertion. In fact, right up to the end, the Millers and their supporters did everything possible to publicize the image of the 101 Ranch.

Corb Sarchet, pioneer Oklahoma journalist and close friend of the Millers, wrote in 1927,

> The 101 Ranch is the one remaining big ranch of the old cattle country to be held intact. Others have been cut up into smaller parts or parcels to fit the purse. With the advent of the new order of things, the Miller brothers established schools, churches and built roads and bridges for the

> benefit of their own workers and for the general welfare of the community at large.
>
> While the 101 Ranch is the only place left in the southwest where the genuine old wild west may be depicted, yet the importance of the ranch lies in the fact that it is one of the most extensive live stock and agricultural experimental farms in the world. . . . It is a domain within itself, larger than some of the European principalities.[36]

In those final chaotic years of the ranch, when revenue from oil production continued until the Great Depression dried everything up, the Millers made history and brought international fame to their ranch. Always willing to gamble, the brothers accelerated research into improved agricultural methods and expanded into new and better markets for their ranching and farming operations.

After recovering from the devastating Salt Fork flood of 1923 and the subsequent drought, the Millers quickly developed new varieties of seed corn, including such hybrids as White Wonder and the speckled Improved Indian Squaw, which could withstand Oklahoma's severe weather conditions. Even in the disastrous year of 1923, the Millers grew seventy-five thousand bushels of White Wonder seed corn on one thousand acres, and shipped more than fifty thousand bushels to growers throughout the nation.[37]

By 1925, the Millers cultivated immense commercial orchards of apple, peach, and black walnut trees, maintained bountiful vineyards, and produced record crops of wheat, milo, and alfalfa. Often referred to as the "foremost farmers of the world," the Millers planted five thousand acres in corn and four thousand in wheat. The 101 also yielded every conceivable vegetable and fruit—from figs, Bermuda onions, melons, and Irish potatoes to okra, peanuts, persimmons, and frost-proof cabbage. The Millers transported two hundred experienced pickers from the Louisiana plantation to Oklahoma to tend twenty-five hundred acres of cotton, which was then ginned on the ranch. This tremendous quantity of crops helped bring the ranch's gross income for 1925 to a stunning $1,070,512.[38]

Besides the vast farming and horticultural activity, the Millers maintained the largest herd of registered Duroc-Jersey hogs in the world and the largest herds of registered Holstein and shorthorn cattle in the United States.[39] Tens of thousands of head of cattle, horses, mules, sheep, and hogs grazed and grew fat in pens, corrals, and pasturelands.

With all the abundance on the ranch, the Millers and their cowhands had to be on the constant lookout for predators; in the spring of 1925, a single wildcat killed great numbers of sheep and lambs, including twenty newborn lambs, in just one night. A posse of 101 Ranch hunters, led by crack shot Stack Lee, relentlessly searched the Salt Fork and Arkansas River bottoms until they cornered the wily cat and riddled it with bullets.[40]

The Millers also had to be on the lookout for looters of the human variety. If such culprits were caught, justice was swift, whether the Millers decided to involve the civil authorities or handle the matter themselves. Yet sometimes even the hard-nosed Millers showed mercy. Such was the case in the mid-1920s when Joe Miller and John Newton, a teamster from Marland who boarded midget performers from the Millers' shows, tracked down some reckless hog thieves.

"My dad went down to feed a dozen or so hogs he owned jointly with Joe Miller and he found that a couple of the shoats had been stolen from the pen," related Arthur "Capper" Newton years later. "He called Mister Joe and they summoned the sheriff, and the three of them set out on the trail. It had snowed, and they found fresh hog blood and some tracks and signs out in a pasture, and they went straight to this little shack along the river."[41]

Inside the shanty, Joe and the other men discovered two frightened couples and a bunch of small barefoot children preparing to cook the stolen swine, which they had already dressed out. Capper Newton said:

> My dad told me that it was real quiet for a long time. No one was quite sure what Joe Miller would do, even if the sheriff was there. They could plainly see that those folks were dirt poor and the kids were plenty hungry. Then Joe spoke up and said to my dad, "Newton, half these hogs are yours, what do you want to do about this?" My dad said it appeared the people needed the hog meat, and as far as he was concerned they could have his share. Old Joe Miller agreed and said they could have his part, too. The sheriff gave the people a good talking-to and told them that when it warmed up they needed to leave Noble County.
>
> On the way back to the ranch, Joe told my dad that he didn't like to see anybody in jail. He said he had been there himself years before for counterfeiting money and didn't wish it on anyone. Besides, there was more than enough to go around and the Hundred and One sure wouldn't be missing a couple little ol' pigs.[42]

Indeed, throughout the 1920s—when the ranch used honeysuckle as cattle forage, planted acres of lettuce for baby chicks to dine on, and treated champion breeding stock better than they did most people—the Miller brothers thought only in terms of thousands whenever it came to their limitless herds, flocks, acreage, or other holdings.

So vast was their empire that by 1927, the Millers, hopeful of improving internal communications, organized their enterprises into the Wheel Club, which consisted of the eighteen ranch department heads. The group's wagon-wheel hub symbolized the ranch, and the eighteen spokes represented each of the departments—agriculture, oil and gas, hogs, horses, cattle, dairy, packing plant, light and power, Indians, poultry, accounting, horticulture, construction, sales and store, land, legal, show, and moving pictures.[43]

A close working relationship among the spokes of the wheel was vital to the ranch's success. All the departments were connected to one another and to the headquarters by the ranch's private telephone system. Every Monday evening, after a three-course dinner and cigars at the ranch cafe, Wheel Club members shared problems, voiced complaints, and planned for the future of the extended domain.[44]

The Millers' abundant assets, as well as their skill at making deals, became apparent during the spring of 1927, far from home. That spring, the Florida legislature attempted to regulate the cattle industry by passing laws which closed the state's open range and stipulated that all cattle be subjected to a treatment against disease and ticks known as dipping. Florida ranchers opposed these drastic measures. They believed the combination of expensive fencing and the cost of gathering and dipping great numbers of beeves would be prohibitive. Many cattlemen left the business and sold off their herds.[45]

Consequently, the market became flooded with thousands of cattle and the Millers pounced on the opportunity and traveled immediately to Florida. In what Colonel Zack Mulhall and some of the other old-time cattlemen described as the "greatest single movement of cattle in forty years," Zack and George Miller gathered thirty-six thousand bulls, steers, heifers, and calves, including, in one bold stroke, a single herd of nine thousand beef cows.[46]

After summoning Bill Pickett and a gang of Oklahoma cowboys and ponies to Florida and leasing several grazing pastures throughout the Deep South, Southwest, and Mexico, the brothers transported the great herds on thirty trains comprised of eight hundred cattle cars. Ten thousand head of the Florida stock were shipped to the ranch on the Salt Fork for conversion into beefsteak at the Miller's busy slaughterhouse. The rest were fattened on leased pastures and shipped to markets across the nation.[47]

Each day, just for local consumption, the ranch packing plant processed a minimum of one hundred head of hogs and fifty head of cattle, dispensing hamburger, hams, and slabs of bacon throughout the area from a fleet of refrigerated trucks. In addition to their range and purebred herds, the Millers successfully crossbred buffalo with Brahma cattle, producing a new disease-resistant breed which they dubbed "Bramola."[48] When the Millers crossed a common range cow with a buffalo bull, the resulting "cattalo" gained worldwide recognition. One of the beasts—a strapping seventeen-hundred-pound critter—was butchered and served up piping hot at the "other" White House, in Washington, D.C., to President Calvin Coolidge and his guests.[49]

Beyond the intensive crossbreeding programs with commercial livestock and horses, the Millers also received a great deal of national attention for their numerous horticultural experiments, most of them the brainchildren of Joe Miller. Although he remained a rancher by trade and a showman by choice, Joe enjoyed growing fruit trees and field crops. Through the years, he kept meticulous records of his research involving various plants and crops, including such details as soil analyses, growing conditions, and profit-and-loss statements.

Joe successfully raised Kentucky tobacco in the Oklahoma soil and produced hybrid corn, wheat, and superior grain crosses for winter pasturage. He also grafted a great variety of fruit- and nut-bearing trees such as the imported Japanese persimmon with the Oklahoma native; various types of black walnuts; hickory trees with pecan scions; and the local variety of pecan with the soft-shelled variety grown on the Millers' Louisiana plantation.[50]

Joe Miller's scientific farming and achievements with assorted grains, fruits, berries, and trees—especially his techniques of crossbreeding, hybridization, and grafting—eventually came to the attention of Luther Burbank, the internationally famous horticulturist. Burbank pored over Joe's field notes and records, and the two men developed enormous respect for each other's abilities and broad knowledge of cultivated plants. A steady exchange of correspondence passed between them until Burbank died, in 1926 at Santa Rosa, California.[51]

The 101 Ranch, and especially Joe's livestock, agricultural, and horticultural research and experimentation, became well known even in academic circles. Oklahoma Agricultural and Mechanical College at Stillwater, which later became Oklahoma State University, required that its agricultural students spend at least two full weeks in residence at the 101 Ranch, observing the assorted livestock and farming operations as part of their official course work.[52]

Meanwhile, the public flocked to the spread to see the roundups and the exotic menagerie which roamed the pastures alongside herds of cattle, horses, and working stock or was confined to pens and cages at the headquarters. Ranch visitors could see not only Arabian stallions, oxen, and bison, but also caribou, zebras, elephants, camels, ostriches, wild boars, lions, tigers, anteaters, chimpanzees, elk, and other species.[53] The Millers had purchased many of the animals from a circus and had used them as exhibits in the revived ranch shows from 1925 to 1931, but some were kept for the Millers' research and rather unorthodox crossbreeding experiments.

The Millers never missed a trick. In the summer of 1924, an eleven-foot-long alligator that Zack shipped to the ranch from the Louisiana plantation became a big attraction. Less than a year later, the Millers played a joke on their old friend and political ally William Jennings Bryan, noted lawyer, orator, and three-time Democratic nominee for president. The opportunity came during the famous "monkey trial," which pitted Bryan against Chicago lawyer Clarence Darrow, defender of John T. Scopes, who had been charged with teaching Darwin's theory of evolution to high school science students.[54]

While the two prominent barristers argued in July 1925 whether man was descended from apes, Zack Miller arrived at the highly publicized trial, in the mountain town of Dayton, Tennessee. Zack brought with him Bozo, also called Big Joe, the 101 Ranch's friendly show ape. "You are the finest specimen I have ever seen," Bryan was heard to say as he nervously shook hands with the gorilla at Zack's request.[55] Photographers snapped away. Out of deference to the obviously flustered Bryan, Zack promised that none of the photos would ever be used for publicity purposes. Five days after the trial concluded, with Scopes being found guilty and fined one hundred dollars, Bryan fell over dead. Physicians attributed his death to cerebral hemorrhage, leaving the Millers to wonder if their ape stunt had played a part in Bryan's sudden passing.[56]

"Those Miller brothers were a crazy, wild bunch," as John Gibson Phillips Jr., oil tycoon Frank Phillips' oldest grandson, recalled years later. "I was always told about when they convinced one of their cowboys to make love with a big ol' female gorilla they had on the ranch. I think that maybe the Miller boys actually thought they could end up with some sort of incredible crossbreed creature. Of course, nothing ever came of it and I never learned if that cowboy was able to consummate the act or just how drunk he had to get before he approached that animal. Just thinking about it kept me awake at night for a long, long time."[57]

Other people were also surprised by the Millers' menagerie. It was said that during the late 1920s, many travelers swore off all bootleg hooch after crossing the Salt Fork bridge near the 101 Ranch, where they suddenly encountered grazing camels or elephants pulling farm machinery across the rolling pastures. Still others contended that the experience had the opposite effect, causing many ranch visitors to turn to strong drink.

"During the palmy days that existed for the 101 Ranch, while the trio of brothers was in charge, guests had to expect most anything happening," reported the *Daily Oklahoman.* Such was the case one summer evening when George Miller hosted a poker party for several oil executives in the White House dining room. "No attention was paid to Zack Miller when he entered the dining room, nor to the fact that he carried a gunnysack in one hand. Zack stood around awhile, watching for an opportunity. Then when all were busy studying their hands, he lifted the sack and emptied a half dozen sprawling bull snakes in the center of the table." George Miller later said, "Zack sure broke up that party. My guests never waited to go through the doors, they went out the windows and whatever else was possible. They never did come back that night."[58]

Still, it took much more than bull snakes and friendly apes to keep people away from the 101 Ranch. Page after page in the guest register, kept on a library table, contained names of the famous and the infamous—presidents, foreign royalty, society matrons, political and business leaders, writers, adventurers, and movie stars. If all three of the Miller brothers happened to be absent from the ranch, Will Brooks, their cousin and the affable mayor of Marland, played host at the White House and introduced everyone to the striking bust of Geronimo, which the Millers claimed contained the spirit of the great Apache leader and possessed supernatural powers.[59]

A few of the more notable guests during the years included Theodore Roosevelt, William Howard Taft, Warren Harding, Sarah Bernhardt, William F. "Buffalo Bill" Cody, General John J. Pershing, Mary Roberts Rinehart, Ty Cobb, John D. Rockefeller Jr., William Jennings Bryan, William Randolph Hearst, John Ringling, Edna Ferber, Jack Dempsey, Wiley Post, Mae West, and William Allen White.[60] Famed Antarctic explorer Richard

E. Byrd climbed aboard one of the Millers' elephants and raced across the ranch pastures. During a 1928 tour, bandleader John Philip Sousa enjoyed riding and roping events, as well as Indian dances, and he was made an honorary member of the Ponca tribe by Horse Chief Eagle, who gave "the march king" a fancy warbonnet and an Indian name meaning "the Chasing Hawk."[61]

Another guest who enjoyed each of his visits at the ranch was Ezra Meeker, one of the pioneers who blazed the Oregon Trail. Born in an Ohio log cabin in 1830, Meeker wrote of his adventures in the far West and made several more trips over the trail in an oxcart, the last when he was ninety-three years old. Asked to make personal appearances with the revived 101 Ranch road show in 1925, Meeker, then a spry ninety-five, refused even to consider the job unless given a ten-year contract. Meeker explained he wanted "a permanent job—not one that would play out in two or three years." The Millers gave him the contract, and the famed trailblazer with long snowy white hair and beard fulfilled it until his death, in 1928.[62]

During those last years, many of the visitors—no matter if they were celebrities or just plain folks—would not think of leaving the 101 Ranch without visiting Tony, the Millers' captive black bear, who held court in front of the ranch store. Although the Millers had kept other bears—including Teddy, a trained black cub which Zack raised on condensed milk and used as a drawing card during the early years of the Wild West shows—Tony was by far the most famous animal on the ranch.[63]

William H. "Bill" McFadden, an adventurous pioneer in the oil business and one of E. W. Marland's early backers, brought the cub to the 101 Ranch and presented it to the Millers after a hunting trip in Mississippi.[64] Tony usually resided at the end of a stout chain. But when he took to crawling inside vehicles parked near the store, the gregarious bear was relegated to an old gorilla cage which at other times served as a jail for drunken cowboys when the silo ordinarily used as a holding tank was full. During winter and on sweltering summer afternoons, Tony found refuge in a den he had dug beneath the sidewalk. Yet even on the coldest or hottest days, Tony could be coaxed out by the offer of a bottle of soda or sweetened water, which he would grab between his paws and slurp down in an instant.[65]

Tony was addicted to soda pop and consumed it by the case, much to the delight of the store manager, who charged eager visitors a nickel a bottle for Tony to drink. The poor creature drooled at the mere sight of a bottle and threw a tantrum if he was teased, which unfortunately happened far too often. Jackie McFarlin, a former Miller cowgirl, was left with a large scar on her hand after Tony took a swipe at her when she was too slow in presenting him with a bottle of his precious soda.[66]

On another occasion, Bill Pickett and Wes Rogers, the Millers' top ranch foreman, had to resort to their best roping techniques to get Tony into a truck so he could appear briefly in a movie being filmed on the ranch pastures. Both men survived the ordeal unscathed, and by day's end, Tony was back at the store, guzzling his favorite beverages and snapping up candies.[67]

Finally, the sugary treats took a toll. Tony swelled to an unhealthy three hundred pounds and became sick and listless from a kidney aliment. In 1931, during the waning days of the ranch, Tony the bear curled up and died.

Melvon Lewis, a solid cowboy who, like his father and brothers, worked for the Millers for several years, was given the chore of disposing of Tony's great carcass. "When that poor bear died he looked like a big, ol' fat hog," recalled Lewis. "I got a team and hooked him up to a chain and dragged his body by my house so my wife, Gracie, could see him and then I took him to the packing plant. They skinned him out and gave his hide to Zack and I fed that bear—just a big bunch of lard and fat—to the hogs. That was how it all ended for Tony."[68]

By the time Tony was rendered into hog slop, the end also was drawing near for the 101 Ranch. During that sad summer of 1931, creditors stopped the latest version of the Millers' Wild West show dead in its tracks. The final loss of the ranch itself was soon to follow. The Hundred and One—much like the Millers' obese black bear—had grown out of control. Yet those final years, marked by the resurrection of the Millers' famed road shows in 1925, allowed the 101 a last bit of grandeur.

Colonel Joe had always hoped to recapture the glory days of the Millers' original road shows which, at the urging of George and Zack, the brothers had disbanded during World War I. In 1920, Joe had helped to organize the Cherokee Strip Cow-Punchers Association (CSCPA), a fraternity of veteran cowboys and cattlemen of the famed Cherokee Outlet.[69] The Millers wrote to all the old hands and wranglers they could locate, inviting them to a roundup and buffalo barbecue at the ranch. Hundreds of cowboys—some of them well over eighty years old—responded. On September 5, 1920, the Millers staged a great show in the buffalo pasture south of the ranch headquarters.[70] Even a heavy rain could not dampen spirits. The old-timers huddled together, bellowing out trail songs, swigging hard cider, and recounting experiences from their early days on the open range.

The next afternoon, after the completion of the riding and roping events, every man present cheered when Joe Miller suggested making the reunion an annual Labor Day affair. Joe was elected the first president and served until his death, when Zack took the reins. "Boys, the 101 Ranch is yours, anywhere you say, make camp," Zack told the crowd. "If you want the White House location, we can move it. We give you a lifetime lease on as much land as is needed for your accommodation."[71] The members unanimously selected a site on a grassy bluff on the south side of the Salt Fork, not far from the road and the river bridge. It soon became known as Cowboy Hill.[72]

Throughout the 1920s, the Millers not only hosted the annual reunions each Labor Day, but they also continued to hold Sunday-afternoon contests at the ranch roundup grounds, featuring champion performers from across the West. Large numbers of city and farm folks from Oklahoma and neighboring states showed up for the roundups and stayed until all the broncs were bucked and the last bull was ridden.

Then in May 1924, the 101 Ranch once again hosted a convention of the National Editorial Association. Although the second time around was not as spectacular as the first gathering of editors and reporters, in 1905, the fifty thousand visitors produced an avalanche of fresh publicity about the Millers' shows.[73] In addition to writing about the numerous riders and ropers, many of the newspaper and magazine editors focused on yet another new and improbable event unveiled at the 1924 convention—a turtle race.

Joe came up with the novel event, dubbed the National Terrapin Derby—which soon became a nationwide fad—after watching small box turtles crawling around to escape the strong summer sun. For weeks, youngsters scoured the pastures and river bottoms for turtles, worth a dime each to the bounty hunters. They brought bushel baskets filled with turtles to the ranch roundup grounds, where each contestant paid a two-dollar entry fee, with one dollar going into the pot for the first-place winner and the rest to be split between second and third places. Everyone who entered was assigned a terrapin identified by a bright yellow number painted on its shell. Many entrants brought their own turtles for the race, but some borrowed from the ranch "herd," kept in a shady pen and fed slices of fresh watermelon.[74]

Just like bettors at horse races, the Terrapin Derby participants had racing forms listing the colorful names of the entrants, their numbers, and the names of the owners. Preliminary elimination races narrowed the field to forty or fifty. The finalists were placed in a circular pen in the middle of the roundup grounds. As Fred Olmstead, the official derby starter, gave the signal, the top of the pen was raised off the ground, allowing the turtles to leave the enclosure and crawl seventy-five feet toward a circular finish line.[75]

With only 214 entrants in the 1924 race, the winner, Shingles, owned by Ponca City Mayor Harry Cragin, received $214.[76] But as word spread and the derby grew larger each year, the prize money soon became significant. In 1925, the derby had more than eleven hundred entries. By 1930, the first-place winner—Goober Dust—crawled away with seventy-one hundred dollars and a silver loving cup for owner Clara Day, who used her winnings to pay off a farm mortgage and buy a new automobile.[77] Usually, most of the prize money ended up going to a charity or some worthwhile cause, but no one knew for sure just how much loot was collected from all the heavy side betting going on in the stands.

The positive response from the National Editorial Association gathering at the ranch, as well as the other events staged at the roundup grounds, prompted a rebirth of the 101 Ranch Wild West road shows. After overcoming George's arguments against returning to the sawdust trail, an inspired Joe Miller, with Zack as an ally, began to plan the return of the touring shows for the 1925 season. Because of Joe's arm-twisting, the brothers, including hesitant George, put up one hundred thousand dollars each to get the wheels turning and put the show back on the road.[78]

By late August 1924, the Millers' workers were busily processing lumber, cut from the timberlands at Sicily Island, for new show wagons and thousands of bleacher seats. Cotton grown in the Millers' Oklahoma fields was woven into canvas for the enormous tents and arena walls, and hides from the family's cattle were transformed into harnesses and tack for show horses and stock.[79] Plans also called for thirty thousand pounds of meat, fruit, and vegetables produced on the ranch to be shipped every ten days in refrigerated cars to the show lots. Once the provisions arrived, cooks would turn out hot meals for five hundred workers and entertainers at the mess tent within forty minutes.[80]

On September 6, 1924, *Billboard* carried the news of the Millers' plans with the headline "101 Ranch Wild West Will Again Take To The Road."

To back up the announcement, the Millers purchased the entire Walter L. Main Circus on October 1. They took possession not only of railcars, wagons, costumes, and the assorted equipment of a three-ring circus, but also of elephants, lions, tigers, camels, monkeys, and other trained animals.[81] With the exception of elephants and camels, which traveled with the show, the animals were sold or remained at the ranch on the Salt Fork.

The Millers' new touring show—called the 101 Ranch Real Wild West and Great Far East—left Marland in thirty new steel railcars, including a magnificent private car for the family, and opened on April 22, 1925, at Oklahoma City. Clint Finney, a nationally known showman, served as general agent and advance man. "California Frank" Hafley and Colonel Zack Mulhall signed on as arena directors, Ed Bowman was chief of cowboys, and the flamboyant Tex Cooper, married to Nona, one of the show's midgets, did the announcing.[82]

Many of the Millers' proven cowboy and cowgirl performers returned to the show circuit, including Bill Pickett, Mexican Joe Barrera, Reine Hafley Shelton, Tad Lucas, Stack Lee, and Milt and Mildred Hinkle. Jack Webb, who would stick with the Millers until the ranch folded, joined the show in 1925 as a roper and sharpshooter billed as "America's most sensational trick and fancy rifle and pistol shot." The show also featured Indian riders, Russian cossacks, Richard Swift's Zouave Drill Team, Ezra Meeker with his ox team, and other Old West historical dramatizations, such as the robbery of the Deadwood stagecoach and a mock buffalo hunt.[83]

However, because the Millers now had to compete with major circus outfits, they relied less on authentic western experience. Instead, they turned to the spectacular by adding several sideshow, animal, and freak acts. These included the versatile Selma Zimmerman, a crack pachyderm trainer known as "the elephant girl"; Montana Hank, an eight-foot tall, 360-pound cowboy; Madame Leatrice, "Queen of Reptiles"; Chief Ino, fire-eater and sword swallower; and Dr. Frank La Marr, who lectured on the curse of opium use. Jack Bost, a female impersonator, led the ballet of Oriental dance girls; Prince Nemo walked on swords; and Darlie Wonder appeared as frog boy, alongside a curious display of three-legged humans, tattooed persons, costumed midgets, snake handlers, mind readers, and magicians.[84]

Press releases ginned up by show flacks described the 101 Ranch Real

Wild West and Great Far East as "the most magnificent tented attraction ever put on wheels."[85] The public disagreed. Attendance figures started out high, with turnaways at some performances, but crowds dwindled as the season wore on.

Although the Millers' outfit toured twenty-nine states and one Canadian province during the 1925 season, the show lost money.[86] The Miller brothers had to deal with intense rivalry from other large circus interests; new governmental regulations; and rising costs from expensive advertising, train accidents, and lawsuits. They also continually battled adverse weather, ranging from frigid temperatures at the start of the season to heat waves later in the year. Heavy rains fell all summer and into the fall, keeping spectators away. At Evansville, Indiana, a cyclone tore through the showgrounds, and in Pennsylvania, a violent windstorm ripped the arena tent to shreds. In Boston, the temperature soared so high that people stayed away from most of the performances.[87]

As usual, the Millers and their show bosses had to address personnel problems which frequently arose from excessive drinking and gambling. After the show pulled out of Saint Louis, some of the cowboys decided to "steal" Colonel Joe's famous jeweled saddle to create badly needed publicity. The stunt backfired, and they ended up getting shot at by police and thrown in jail before embarrassed show officials bailed them out. Some of the predicaments with show workers were easily solved. For instance, in mid-July, Julia Little Snake, a 450-pound Ponca woman, temporarily quit her job as the show's fat lady because the seat she had to occupy during appearances was "too hard even with a pillow."[88] Sadly, most of the problems the Millers faced on the road proved more difficult.

After two sleeping cars on the show train caught fire and burned on the tracks near Gainesville, Georgia, the Millers braced themselves for an onslaught of competition across the south from the Ringling Brothers and Barnum & Bailey Circus. In early November, the Millers' outfit limped into Birmingham, Alabama, where the brothers cut their losses by suddenly closing the show and canceling the final two weeks of booked appearances.[89]

"When the Millers entered the entertainment business again in 1925, they faced a rival more potent than the movie," Winifred Johnston wrote in 1935 for *Southwest Review*. "Frontier Days entertainment had become an annual event in many western communities and had almost fulfilled the place once held by the traveling Wild West Shows. The prototype of the modern rodeo emerged in the Pendleton Roundup and the Madison

Square Garden Rodeo. The Wild West Show could not compete with this and other relatively inexpensive entertainment media. This competition, coupled with the increasing expense of producing big top entertainment, marked the end of the 'fabulous wild west.' "[90]

The 1926 season was not any better for the Millers' combined touring show. Once again, competing circuses and foul weather played key roles in the show's failure. Powerful winds and torrents of rain ripped canopies, snapped tent poles, and kept paying customers at home. When an especially severe storm struck the show at Erie, Pennsylvania, a falling pole killed one of the fans scrambling for cover.[91] Performances throughout the tour were shortened, postponed, or scrubbed.

After a grueling tour of several western states, the show returned to Oklahoma that autumn only to be greeted by the worst rainstorms of the year. Floodwaters covered much of the state and region. At the 101 Ranch, the treacherous Salt Fork once again flowed over fields and pasturelands. The flood drowned hundreds of head of livestock and two thousand turtles—racers from the annual National Terrapin Derby, kept in a two-acre fenced pasture.[92] On top of everything, an epidemic of hoof-and-mouth disease broke out in several neighboring states where performances were booked, forcing the Millers once again to cancel the season early. At the close of 1926, the Millers' road show had lost $119,970.[93]

One of the few bright spots of that season had come in Chicago on August 2, when Joe Miller remarried at the age of fifty-eight. His bride—Miss Mary Verlin—hailed from Grand Rapids, in the center of western Michigan's fruit-growing belt. She had gone to Ponca City to visit her aunt and uncle, Mr. and Mrs. C. R. Rhodes, owners of the Arcade Hotel, formerly known as Rhodes House. At the Arcade, with its Spanish-style stucco exterior and red tile roof, Mary became acquainted with Colonel Joe.[94]

Sparks of passion immediately flew, and the old cattleman pursued the shapely, dark-eyed beauty with all the intensity he could muster. Although he had grown a bit paunchy, Joe, with his drooping mustache and powerful presence, proved irresistible to the young woman. Clearly half her husband's age, Mary was often mistaken for Joe's daughter when the couple appeared together while on the road with the Wild West show.

Following their brief wedding ceremony, Joe and his bride departed Chicago in the Millers' private train car, bound for Racine, Wisconsin, site of the show's next performance. Performers and workers threw a huge party in the newlyweds' honor on the showgrounds, inside a mess tent banked with baskets of flowers. More than seven hundred guests toasted the occasion and shouted their approval as the happy couple sliced a three-foot-tall wedding cake.[95]

Back in Oklahoma the next spring, just before the start of another difficult and costly show season, some of the Millers' close friends and Ponca tribal leaders staged a celebration to recognize Joe and Mary's marriage. This event grew so large that it required the entire ranch arena and grandstands to contain the well-wishers. Dressed from head to toe in Indian wedding costumes, the couple had agreed to be remarried according to tribal custom. Mary, in the style of a proper Ponca bride, wore her hair in braids. Horse Chief Eagle and the Ponca elders appeared, along with many of their people. Yellow Bull and his wife, the oldest living married Poncas, acted as official escorts for the Millers throughout the ritual and the wedding feast which followed.[96]

The Millers' Indian nuptials remained a popular topic of discussion around Ponca City that spring of 1927 as the couple settled into the new house Joe had built just north of the ranch. Then in May—exactly nine months after their Chicago wedding—Mary gave birth to a healthy son. The baby was born at the hospital in Ponca City on the eve of Charles Lindbergh's historic solo flight across the Atlantic. A few of Mary's friends and her mother, from Grand Rapids, were on hand for the birth of the little boy, whom Mary named Jack Rhodes Miller.[97]

Joe was not there to welcome his new son. He was hundreds of miles away, on the road at Clarksburg, West Virginia, riding herd over his failing Wild West show. When he received the wire with the good tidings, Joe wept with joy. To mark the event, he had his company of western and circus entertainers put on a free matinée for the public.[98]

At the time of his son's birth in 1927, Joe was already a grandfather. His daughter, Alice—a mother with two young daughters—had taught school in Ponca City before marrying Dr. Charles Pittman Harth, a Kentucky native and osteopathic physician.[99] Both of Joe's older sons—Joe Miller Jr. and George W. Miller Jr.—had completed much of their university training and were being groomed for management of the 101 Ranch empire. Like her brothers, Alice remained close to her father but recognized that they were all witnessing the end of a way of life that would never be repeated.

Alice later wrote of that time,

> The three brothers realized they had created a personality. It had a name. It also partook of other human characteristics.It became ill with mortgages, crop failures, low prices for stock and bad seasons for the show. At such times it had to be watched and attended with anxiety for each breath might be the last. When it grew lusty with bountiful harvests, good prices, successful seasons on the road and then oil—its demands could not be denied. Because they loved it so they wanted to protect its future. Insurance seemed to be the answer. Each brother took out a large policy made payable, at his death, to the surviving brothers, or in the event two died, to the surviving brother. They were all very tall and very strong at the time this happened and I am sure expected to live a long time. Life is uncertain. Father was the first to go, and soon after this agreement was made.[100]

Joe Miller had looked forward to his return to Oklahoma at the close of the 1927 season. It had become painfully clear that the revived ranch shows—marked by misfortune and poor management—would never turn a profit, let alone gross the eight hundred thousand dollars earned between 1908 and 1916 by the Miller-Arlington productions. Throughout the 1927 tour, the Millers' show encountered the same woes that continually besieged it from 1925 until 1931—foul weather, fierce competition, rising expenses, and injuries to personnel and spectators, which often ended in costly litigation.

Back at the ranch that October, Joe worked his way through mounds of correspondence and assorted paperwork that had accumulated in his absence. In the mornings, he met with his brothers, ranch department managers, or lawyers overseeing a variety of legal issues which troubled the Millers. By evening, after a horseback ride along the Salt Fork, Joe returned to his new home, about five miles north of the White House. He was preparing for the homecoming of Mary and their baby, whose name Joe had changed from Jack Rhodes Miller to Will Brooks Miller, in honor of the Millers' favorite cousin. After spending nearly all summer accompanying Joe on the road with the show, Mary had gone to Grand Rapids for a brief visit and to retrieve their five-month-old son, who had been staying with her mother.[101]

Early on the morning of October 21, Joe drove from his home to the ranch. After breakfast, a foreman asked him to settle a dispute involving money between two of the show roustabouts. Each had accused the other of cheating, and the quarrel had led to a fistfight. One of the workers had had to be restrained in the seed house. Joe summoned the men and carefully listened to both stories. When they finished, he asked them to give him all the money they had between them, which amounted to nine dollars. Joe divided the cash equally between the pair and then walked them out to the highway in front of the White House. Joe told one of the men to start walking south and the other one to head north, and he advised both of them to never again set foot on the ranch.[102]

Satisfied that the matter had been resolved, Joe went to the ranch store to pick up a few groceries. He chatted with other shoppers, loaded the boxes into his automobile, and left for his residence. Before driving off, he told Zack that his car had been acting up and, although he was not much of a mechanic, he intended to fix it that afternoon. Then Joe waved at some cowboys visiting in front of the store and touched the brim of his hat. It was ten o'clock in the morning and the last time anyone saw him alive.[103]

Will Brooks, the cousin from Kentucky who had joined the Millers as a youngster and helped them build their empire, was the one who found Joe. Some of Joe's old-time pals had stopped by the White House, and at about three o'clock that Friday afternoon, Brooks went to Joe's home to bring him back to the ranch for a visit.

On arriving at Joe's place, Brooks heard a car engine idling, and he headed to the garage. The doors were partly open, and he went inside. The car hood was up, and Brooks spied a pocketknife and several screws on the running board. On the ground next to the car was Joe Miller, stone-dead.

Attending physicians and others called to the scene had no doubt about what had happened. They surmised that Joe had been tinkering with the car engine and had been overcome by carbon-monoxide fumes. Some family members guessed that Joe might have first suffered a fatal heart attack, because his arms were crumpled beneath his body, indicating that he had had no time to break his fall when stricken.[104]

Joseph Carson Miller had courted danger throughout his fifty-nine years. He had been the guiding hand of the Hundred and One. His passing stunned the Miller family and all those who worked for them. While they waited for Joe's young widow and baby son to hurry home from Michigan, Zack and George remained secluded at the White House, mulling over their brother's life and times. For them, Joe's death was like losing their father all over again. "Joe has gone," Zack wrote to a friend just days after

Joe died. "His death is a great loss to us and we hardly know how we are going to adjust ourselves to his absence."[105]

Many of those who attended Colonel Joe's funeral, on October 24, considered it the most impressive in Oklahoma history. The day before, he had lain in state in the living room of the White House, and about ten thousand mourners representing all walks of life passed by the open coffin for a last glimpse of Colonel Joe. His funeral service was moved to the veranda, and almost as many people returned for the ceremony. Hundreds of messages and telegrams offering sympathy poured into the ranch from around the world. Tier after tier of floral offerings covered the veranda, reaching all the way to the roof. Appropriately, the family chose Clint Finney, the capable general agent for the Wild West productions, to oversee the services and lay out Joe's final route.[106] The old showman would have been proud.

It turned out to be an ideal autumn day—balmy weather and clear skies, with just a hint of breeze off the broad ranchlands. Flags flew at half-staff, and Russian cossacks in their handsome regimental uniforms served as ushers. E. W. Marland, Lew Wentz, the Phillips brothers, and several other oil barons and corporate captains came to pay their respects on the lawn of the White House, beneath trees planted by Joe.[107] They sat among statesmen, families of show freaks, movie stars, cowboys and cowgirls, and everyday folks who had known and loved Joe.

Schools in Ponca City and neighboring communities were dismissed so children could attend the service. Like so many others, Oklahoma Governor Henry S. Johnston, an old family friend and legal adviser, openly wept when a minister from the Christian Church in Ponca City delivered a stirring eulogy and a young woman sang Joe's favorite hymn, "The End of a Perfect Day."[108]

A large group of Indians appeared, consisting mostly of Poncas. Led by Horse Chief Eagle and Crazy Bear, they stood in mourning blankets beside the coffin and then, one at a time, each quietly spoke to Joe in the Ponca dialect, which he had learned as a boy riding the frontier ranges. After they finished, each of them dropped an eagle feather, symbolic of the soul's flight, into the coffin.[109] Then the Poncas chanted a death song to the beat of ancient drums, and Horse Chief Eagle spoke, recalling only the good times and not the bad.

"Our brother Joe, he is one of us," Horse Chief Eagle told the hushed crowd. "He is gone. When he went away, it meant more than anything to the Indian. The Indian weeps because our brother Joe will not be good to us any more. He has reared us from boys, some of us. He gave us encouragement. God is a right God, so the Indian says. He gives each man a time. We all have a time. You see paint on our faces. We paint our faces because our brother Joe who has lived with us all these years is dead. That is all. We are sad."[110]

When he finished speaking, Horse Chief Eagle gently laid a pouch of tobacco, a pipe, and a chief's feather on Joe's chest. The casket lid was closed, and the pallbearers—Pawnee Bill Lillie, Zack Mulhall, and some of the old cowpunchers—carried Joe's body to the waiting hearse. His prize Arabian show stallion, Pedro, stood nearby, with Joe's cowboy boots reversed in the stirrups and his worn chaps draped over the horn of the famous jewel-studded saddle.[111]

They buried Joe beside Mother Miller in a grave shaded by a stand of elms. Afterward, many of the mourners returned to the White House for food and drink and to swap stories about Joe. The Poncas further honored their adopted white chief in their own manner. True to the Ponca custom, Joe had set aside one thousand dollars to be used for tribal burial rites and the giveaway feasts always held at the death of a member of the tribe. The money purchased twenty-five hundred yards of calico, a stack of thick blankets, and twenty ponies, given as gifts at the feasts.[112]

"As the funeral procession wended its way to the family plot near Ponca City, those of us who were sensitive to the thing that was happening realized we were seeing the beginning of an end to an era," wrote Joe's daughter, Alice Miller Harth. "The things that we had known so well and taken for granted could not survive in a changed world. They were fast becoming an anachronism."[113]

Soon after Joe's death and burial, his grief-stricken widow, Mary Verlin Miller, decided that without the man she adored, life on the 101 Ranch offered no pleasant prospects for her or her young son. Mary liquidated her holdings, packed up her belongings and, with little Will Brooks Miller in tow, moved far away. "The new wife," as Alice Miller Harth referred to Mary, "collected her insurance money and took the baby to Michigan, where she had lived before marrying Papa. They vanished from our lives and we wonder what happened to a half-brother we never knew."[114]

At a family meeting in the White House living room after Joe's passing, Alice, her eyes swollen from crying, clutched her father's special watch, which had, instead of numerals, letters that spelled out "Joseph Miller."[115] She and her two brothers listened as their uncles laid out future plans for the Hundred and One.

"The show will go out as usual—that is what Joe wanted," George told them. Everyone nodded in agreement, but down deep, they knew better. George immediately began in earnest to train his two nephews, George W. Miller and Joe C. Miller Jr., to become active participants in the management of the family empire. Both young men had grown up around the ranch, had traveled on the road with their father, and were familiar with the show routine.[116]

In April 1928, the reorganized 101 Ranch Real Wild West and Great Far East, with Zack and his nephews in control, launched yet another six-month tour of the United States. It featured a variety of circus acts and talented cowboy and cowgirl performers such as Tex Cooper, Pete and Hilda Workman, Jack Webb, Joe Barrera, Buddy Kemp, Turk Greenough, Selma Zimmerman, and Jack Brown.[117] On the home front, George Miller tried to manage the ranch and pay off the mounting debts which resulted from crop losses, a severe decline in oil and gas royalties and, ironically, the heavy financial drain of the road show.

Mail pouches stuffed with billing invoices and legal filings arrived at the Millers' office daily. George's worries grew, and before long, he changed management strategy. Although he continued to supervise farming and livestock operations through his managers in the Wheel Club, George also stayed absent from the ranch for long periods while he went on the road to manage the show, allowing Zack to take care of cattle business in Florida and check on the Sicily Island plantation.[118] Zack and George continued with business as usual, but nothing seemed to go their way. Although they put their best face forward, the brothers knew that Joe's death had taken the heart out of the Hundred and One. Everyone from laborers to top hands missed Colonel Joe's personal touch and passion for the ranch and its myriad activities.

Zack became more distressed with each performance of the 1928 season, which proved to be another failure for the Millers. George responded by plunging even deeper into the oil business, heavily mortgaging the Millers' holdings in Louisiana and elsewhere, hoping to make a big killing to pay off the show's deficits. It proved to be a foolish and costly maneuver. But George Miller was not the only risk taker who found oil to be a fickle mistress that year. Extravagant wildcatter E. W. Marland, longtime associate of the Millers in the oil patch, was also about to be permanently changed, apparently by that old Ponca curse.

Marland's wife, Virginia, had died in 1926, just as he began to erect a palatial fifty-five-room mansion in Ponca City.[119] Soon after her death, Marland publicly demonstrated an amorous interest in Lydie Roberts—his wife's niece, whom the Marlands had legally adopted, along with her brother, when the girl was ten years old. Marland later had the adoption annulled. In July 1928, he shocked everyone when he wed the painfully shy beauty and moved her into his new $5.5 million "Palace on the Prairie," with its leather-lined elevator, dozen bathrooms, and indoor handball court. The groom was fifty-four and the bride was twenty-eight.[120]

In 1928, however, while high-riding Marland spent money like a drunken cowhand and chased foxes across his elegant estate, the price of crude oil dropped and overproduction reached a critical stage. To maintain his lifestyle and to expand operations of Marland Oil, he quickly overextended himself by borrowing enormous sums of money from powerful Wall Street bankers, who soon took charge of Marland's board of directors. Within a short time, Marland had lost control of his company, which the new management merged with Continental Oil Company, soon known as Conoco.[121]

Marland and his young wife closed the mansion where they had lived for only a brief time and moved into a small guesthouse on the estate grounds, where he plotted his comeback. The stock market crash of 1929 snuffed out those dreams. Marland found himself flat broke, but instead of trying to reestablish himself in the oil business, he went into politics. He became a "New Deal" Democratic congressman for two years and then, in 1934, was elected Oklahoma's tenth governor.[122]

Bitter and melancholy after his term as governor, Marland eventually withdrew from public life and returned to Ponca City, where he died a broken man in 1941. At the end, he was left with only the fading memories of the time when he came to the 101 Ranch to hunt for oil. Perhaps he recalled the grim prophecy of those old Poncas and the last words of his father—"Oh, if Ernest had not gone after strange gods."[123]

Much as Marland had done in 1928, just before the oil bubble burst, George Miller pursued those same strange gods as he scrambled to keep his family empire afloat. However, as the year continued with little or no relief in sight, he and Zack became more uneasy. Finally, out of sheer desperation, the Millers tried quietly to unload the Wild West show and sell the entire road outfit to a rival circus combination.[124]

Zack had been unobtrusively courting potential buyers throughout most of the 1928 season. By early September, after considerable haggling, he cut a deal with American Circus Corporation (ACC)—an entertainment conglomerate headed by Jerry Mugivan and Bert Bowers, two rough-and-tumble grifters from Peru, Indiana.[125] Negotiations continued at a meeting between both parties in Chicago in November and concluded the next month at the 101 Ranch when the ACC signed an option to buy the show. A bill of sale, dated December 17, was drawn up, and the Miller brothers publicly confirmed the deal and announced their retirement from show business in the trade magazines.[126]

Just three days later, however, the transaction fell apart. Zack had already signed the bill of sale and had called in his younger brother for his endorsement. George, with pen in hand, glanced over the contract one last time and discovered an objectionable clause which would give the circus syndicate use of the Miller name and the right to sell stock to the public to finance the corporation. George refused to sign.

"We are retiring entirely from the show business in order to concentrate all our efforts on our other lines of business," George announced in a statement to the press, "but we refuse to allow the name Miller brothers on stock exploitations to bolster up the holdings of the American Circus Corporation."[127]

Zack attempted to patch together the scuttled transaction, but even more hidden loopholes in the contract surfaced and he too gave up. During the holidays at the White House, the Millers once more regrouped and examined their options. As the last year of the turbulent 1920s arrived, the Millers formed new plans and resolved to return to the road in the spring of 1929 with their Wild West show.

In late January 1929, George, anxious to generate operating capital, spent a week in Texas looking over new oil properties and inspecting a wildcat well being drilled southeast of Big Spring. He returned to Oklahoma with renewed confidence, and on February 1 he met a few cronies at Ponca City's Arcade Hotel for an evening of cards and conversation. In the wee hours of February 2, after numerous games of pitch and several rounds of drinks, George took his leave.[128]

During the night, a combination of sleet and snow had begun to fall, and city streets were slick with ice and appeared to be treacherous. Lew Wentz did his best to convince George to get a room at the Arcade and wait out the storm. George, always a gambler, bet his pals that even with foul weather and bad roads, he could be at the ranch in record time. It proved to be a fatal wager.[129]

Fifteen minutes after his big Lincoln roadster roared off into the darkness, George Lee Miller—forty-seven years old—was killed. He died instantly at about two o'clock that morning on Highway 77, southwest of Ponca City. His car apparently had skidded and overturned on an icy curve. When Oscar Clemmer and another local man came upon the wreck two hours later, they found George's body pinned beneath a front wheel with his head crushed.[130]

"To me the death of George Miller means that I have lost a dear old friend," said an anguished Gordon "Pawnee Bill" Lillie in a newspaper interview. "The years have taken a heavy toll of these friends of mine and I grieve for every one of them."[131]

For the second time in less than sixteen months, thousands of mourners gathered to bury one of the Miller brothers. Once again, flags were lowered, flowery editorials appeared in newspapers across the land, and streams of telegrams and tributes arrived at the White House, where George's body lay in state. A troupe of the Millers' Arab performers, wintering back east, commended George's spirit to Allah during a special memorial ceremony held in New York.[132]

All the businesses in Ponca City were closed for the funeral service, which was conducted at the municipal auditorium instead of at the ranch because of inclement weather. The Miller family—including George's seventeen-year-old daughter, Margaret—laid Colonel George to rest beside his mother and brother Joe. The Ponca tribe then held its traditional rituals in remembrance of George.[133]

Of G. W. Miller's sons, only Zack survived, with his back against the wall, leaving him little or no time for sorrow over his losses. Zack, with help for a short time from his two nephews, tried to keep the family operation buoyant in very treacherous waters. It proved to be a futile task, guaranteed for failure. The 101 Ranch not only suffered from the death of George L. Miller early in 1929, but in October of that year, at the close of another losing season for the show on the road, the bottom fell out of the stock market, heralding the arrival of the world's greatest economic depression.

Cynical pundits could almost smell blood and the stench of doom washing over the ranch like deadly floodwaters from the Salt Fork. Longtime Miller critics joined with pessimistic family members to put the kiss of death on the ranch. They continually whined and lamented the tragic passing of George, the family's so-called financial wizard, and predicted the breakup of the ranch because of Zack's supposedly inferior business competence. Even Zack's sister, Alma Miller England, harbored misgivings and eventually let them be known.

"There were, no doubt, many business managers as highly trained in finance as Colonel George L. Miller but it was seemingly impossible to secure one with all the requisite qualities possessed by George L. Miller," Alma and her coauthor, Ellsworth Collings, wrote in 1937. "This fact was demonstrated, again and again, in Colonel Zack Miller's attempt to fill the place of his dead brother. Any such arrangements always ended disastrously to the ranch, largely because co-operation in thought and agreement in action was [sic] conspicuously absent. As a result, a chaotic condition finally developed in the ranch affairs and, in the end, brought ruin to the whole thing. If Colonel Zack Miller could have had the support of his dead brothers, there is no question but the 101 Ranch would have weathered the world's economic upheaval as it did the panic of 1893."[134]

Faced with insurmountable problems, Zack, fifty years old at the time of George's death, fought on, despite suffering the consequences of errors in judgment which all three Miller brothers had made throughout the 1920s. Amazingly, he produced the Wild West road show for three more grueling and costly seasons. Believing, as many others did, that the economic depression would be short-lived, Zack and his nephews secured a mortgage of more than a half-million dollars to finance the ranch operations and cover mounting debts.[135] There was no improvement or relief, however, and the situation only worsened in 1930.

Although the ranch continued to produce livestock, grain, hay, and oil, the markets—and thus incoming cash—had dried up. Prices of farm products, oil, and livestock dropped to new lows, while taxes and overhead soared. With each new loan to cover rising costs, legal bills, and show losses, the Millers were forced to terminate employees and shut down entire departments. By the end of 1930, as creditors closed in on Zack, the 101 Ranch suffered a net loss of more than three hundred thousand dollars.[136]

Besieged on all fronts, Zack stubbornly took the show on the road again in 1931, in hopes of luring a buyer, as he had done a few years earlier. By that time, Zack's nephews, each of whom had married and had ambitions of his own, had severed their ties with the show. George W. moved to Ponca City and established a law practice, and Joe Jr. launched a fifty-year career in the consumer-finance business.[137]

Unable to attract potential buyers for the show, Zack plugged along, but the events of 1931 were overwhelming. The spring and summer brought a litany of woes—notes due on ranch property, fallout from lawsuits and countersuits with Tom Mix over breach of contracts and slander, inflexible creditors unwilling to extend loans, and family members dissatisfied with Zack's management style. In March, eighteen months after Zack sued Marguerite for divorce on charges of infidelity, he won custody of his son and daughter. The cost of the ongoing legal battle, which would last two more years, only added to the towering stack of past-due bills.[138]

Out on tour that summer—while President Herbert Hoover tried to convince growing numbers of jobless Americans that they had nothing to worry about—the Miller Brothers 101 Ranch Wild West Show played to shrinking audiences. Finally, in early August, Zack and his discouraged company pulled into Washington, D.C. Even though he had not been able to cover salaries for some workers for two months and many of his employees had become openly rebellious, Zack still had high hopes. Those prospects were soon dashed. Instead of the anticipated twenty-four thousand dollars in ticket revenues for four performances during the two-day stand, the box office reported a take of only six thousand dollars.[139] It was the end of the line—the show folded.

"The saddest day of my life was the day the 101 Ranch show closed in Washington, D.C.," remembered Jack Quait, a top trick rider with the Miller outfit at the time, who died in 1996, at age eighty-eight.[140] Quait's simple words echoed the sentiments of a legion of cowboys, cowgirls, and fans.

Zack returned to the ranch in Oklahoma that month, only to face creditors and learn that his nephew, George W. Miller, and the Exchange National Bank of Tulsa, representing the heirs of the late George L. Miller, had filed a petition in district court asking that the 101 Ranch be placed in the hands of a receiver.[141] The action was deemed necessary because of Zack's inability to pay the delinquent taxes and outstanding debts. After some debate, the court appointed as receiver Fred C. Clarke, a rancher from Winfield, Kansas, and former major-league baseball player and manager. On September 16, 1931, the court confirmed Clarke's appointment as receiver. For the first time since its founding, the 101 Ranch passed from the control of the Millers.[142]

Clarke, handicapped by lack of funds and inexperienced in managing operations the size of the Hundred and One, suspended his plans for revitalizing the ranch. Instead, he announced that the vast pastures and crop fields would be broken up and leased to individual farmers and that all personal properties—saddles, cattle, hogs, chickens, combines—would be liquidated.

A story published in the *Daily Oklahoman* poignantly described the scene on March 24, 1932, when everything on the ranch but the White House and its contents went on the auction block:

> There were sad doings here Thursday, marking the passing of a great Oklahoma institution, the 101 Ranch, internationally famous symbol of a young state that rides 'em cowboy. A picturesque crowd of more than 3000 persons turned out for the receiver's sale of all property of the Miller Brothers' 101 Ranch Trust, a few coming to buy, but a vast majority simply to walk stolidly along the dusty lanes and watch with calm solicitude the disintegration of the greatest showplace in the West. Over in the historic White House of the ranch, Colonel Zack Miller, sole survivor of the trio of brothers which made the place famous, roared defiance to the world, threatening to blow up the mansion, and even fired a shotgun in the direction of attorneys seeking a conference with him. . . . The lonely man there in the famous White House, living among his dead hopes, bellowing defiance from his sickbed, simply typified the already half-forgotten, glorious yesterdays of Oklahoma.[143]

Zack, who called the public auction "legal robbery," was arrested and briefly detained for chasing lawyers with his shotgun. After posting bond, he returned to his bed, suffering from what doctors diagnosed as a nervous breakdown. But Zack was forced to summon his courage on April 2 when he received more bad news. Bill Pickett, the famed "Dusky Demon" and faithful bulldogger, had died in a Ponca City hospital, two weeks after having been kicked in the head while taming an unbroken chestnut gelding at the 101 Ranch.[144]

Pickett, the originator of steer wrestling and as true a cowboy as ever rode for the Miller brand, never regained consciousness. Will Rogers spoke of Pickett's passing on national radio, and Zack Miller rallied enough to scribble a rambling, sentimental poem about Pickett and arrange for the funeral to be held on the front gallery of the White House. More than one thousand people—mostly cowboys, cowgirls, and Indians—gathered to say good-bye to Pickett, about sixty years old, who had been loyal to Zack and the ranch to the very end. After a preacher spoke and read Scripture, they buried the old cowboy near the stone monument for White Eagle, south of the ranch headquarters. As his fancy coffin was lowered into the earth, a choir sang "Swing Low, Sweet Chariot."[145]

Others buried on the windswept hill in the 1930s kept Pickett company—James E. "Curbstone Curby" Smedley, an ox-team trainer for the Millers' show; Henry Clay, a black cowboy who had taught Will Rogers some rope tricks; Gladys Hamilton, the nine-year-old daughter of a Miller hired hand; and Jim Gates, a farm laborer who had been shot to death at a dance. Pickett's favorite bulldogging horse, Spradley, was said to have been buried nearby.[146]

Undoubtedly, the death of the fearless Bill Pickett, occurring on the heels of the ranch auction, contributed to Zack's strange behavior and his belief that he had become the victim of a vast conspiracy. For days at a time during that grim spring of 1932, Zack remained bed-bound, refusing to eat. Much of the time, he appeared delirious. Selma Zimmerman, the cowgirl elephant trainer, acted as a nurse for Zack and faithfully tended to him. Several examining physicians suggested that he might not be able to recover from the breakdown, which prompted Corb Sarchet, a devoted friend, to begin to compose Zack's obituary.[147]

Suddenly, Zack appeared to be his old self once more. He later revealed that he snapped out of his condition by chewing mescal buttons from a peyote cactus and imbibing a peyote brew prepared for him by a delegation of Ponca Indians who performed a healing ritual at the White House. Zack swore that the religious ceremony and the vivid hallucinations he experienced by ingesting the peyote helped him more than all the white man's medicines.[148]

In the sizzling summer of 1932, Zack came back out swinging. July brought shocking news stories that to keep at least part of the 101 Ranch spread going, Zack was negotiating a big land-purchase deal with Chicago gangster Al "Scarface" Capone.[149]

The plan called for the notorious gangland leader and his brothers, John and Ralph Capone, to purchase jointly several thousand acres of the ranch for $125,000.[150] A Ponca City real estate broker suggested that the Capones would manage the ranch after Al gained release from the federal prison at Atlanta, Georgia, where he was serving time for tax evasion. The Capones would then divide the land into forty-acre and eighty-acre farms to be worked as a colony and truck-farming cooperative by hundreds of Italian immigrant families. News reports claimed that the Capones had approached Zack after their offer to buy Woolaroc, the Oklahoma ranch retreat of oil magnate Frank Phillips, was turned down.[151]

Many people, including the Capones' attorneys, scoffed at the notion of the infamous criminal family moving to Oklahoma. Although some folks branded the scheme as nothing but another Zack Miller publicity stunt, others feared that the Capones would use the ranch as a front for illicit criminal activities. A gleeful Zack did not provide any comfort for those who worried about the proposed transaction.

"We have a wonderful spring here on the property and if the booze business comes back a brewery and distillery could be put here and the by-products all fed into the livestock," Zack wrote to one of the Capones' agents in July 1932.[152]

That month, after Ponca City Mayor Dan Kygar received queries about the Capones from a Chicago newspaper, he responded with a dose of humor. Kygar wrote:

> I have no information in regard to purchase of the famous 101 Ranch by Capone brothers. But we have outlived the Daltons, Al Jennings, Ben Cravens, Henry and Belle Starr, Al Spencer and [two] gubernatorial impeachments. If the Capones can give us new thrills, send them along, but advise them to bring their bodyguards with them. All Oklahomans excel in steer juggling, bronc busting and bulldogging. They take theirs straight. Advise them to spike their weak beer with some of our hill corn and make their advance. The old ranch has already been tamed by the encroachments of civilization. A little Chicago culture will do no harm. Inform the Capone brothers they should see me first. I'll extend them an Oklahoma welcome, where children cut their teeth on forty-fives and thirty-eights, and the keys to the city, and assure their protections until they become acclimated. After that, they must look out for themselves.[153]

The Capone scheme, much to Zack's disappointment, fell completely apart by autumn. Still, Zack fought on with renewed energy. Represented in his legal battles by Henry S. Johnston, another hapless Oklahoma governor, who had been impeached and removed from office in 1929, Zack sought a new operating receiver and filed for the dismissal of Fred C. Clarke on grounds that he was incompetent.[154] More defiant than ever, Zack also remained painfully aware of all that his father and brothers had sacrificed to make the 101 Ranch a truly remarkable empire.

At about that time, Marguerite Blevins Miller filed suit against her estranged husband in Oklahoma, seeking overdue separate-maintenance payments and lawyer fees. By late November, after the landslide election of Democrat Franklin D. Roosevelt as president, Zack still had not complied with a court order to pay temporary alimony. The high sheriff and some deputies paid a call to the White House, arrested Zack, and threw him into the Kay County jail, at Newkirk, for contempt of court.[155]

The moment he learned of Zack's predicament, eccentric William H. "Alfalfa Bill" Murray, governor of Oklahoma and a Miller ally, intervened. He issued an executive military order demanding that Zack be released from "false imprisonment" in the county jail, and pardoned him of all offenses of which he had been convicted. Murray's clemency decree charged collusion by the ranch creditors and Marguerite to deprive Zack of his personal property.[156]

To emphasize the seriousness of the matter, Murray directed Adjutant General Charles F. Barrett to execute the order, "using such force as may be necessary." Barrett quickly dispatched two National Guard officers, Lieutenant Colonel Elmo D. Flynt and Captain Ted Heywood, to Newkirk, where authorities protestingly released Zack from jail.[157]

For a time, Zack believed his luck had changed for the better once more. All the assault charges from Zack's terrorizing lawyers during the auction at the White House were dismissed. In early 1933, Zack finally was granted a divorce decree, and on March 25, the court approved the dismissal Zack had filed against Clarke.[158] Clarke was found guilty of gross neglect and was replaced as receiver by Zack and two trustees. The court awarded Zack management of the remaining ranch lands, which lay in ruin, until January 1, 1935. He had less than two years to come up with seven hundred thousand dollars to redeem the loans on the 101 Ranch.[159]

For the next two years, Zack fought on as the courts approved the sale of various parcels of land. Believing in Roosevelt's slogan for the troubled nation that "the only thing we have to fear is fear itself," Zack pulled together enough cowboy and cowgirl troopers to put on a modest show at the 1933 "Century of Progress" exhibition in Chicago. More schemes followed. Zack tried to persuade New York Yankee slugger Babe Ruth to become his partner and launch another national tour.[160] After each performance, Zack visualized the great "Bambino" putting on a hitting display and passing out thumbprints and autographed baseballs to all the fans, but Zack's dream never got to first base.

At the end, after he tried to borrow money from everyone he knew and sold off many of his possessions, Zack was reduced to peddling Indian tom-toms and cheap trinkets from the ranch store. All that remained for him was the White House and a few furnishings.[161] Then came the foreclosure and final injunction, demanding that Zack vacate his family home.

On July 25, 1936, the entire contents of the twenty-two-room White House were auctioned off, including furniture, Indian rugs, antique guns, buffalo overcoats, and a prized Lenders portrait of White Eagle. A reporter from the *Daily Oklahoman* described the scene at the ranch that blistering July afternoon:

> Grim, gray-haired Zack T. Miller stood in the shadows of the old White House Saturday and watched the last of his vast empire crumble under the hammer of the auctioneer. He stood without visible emotion, although his face set in hard lines as one by one his personal belongings went on the block, ending another epic of the Old West.
>
> The sale ended, and bargain hunters scattered. The last of the three famous sons of a famous father stood on the steps of the big white mansion, and gazed over what once was a 110,00-acre ranch. Perhaps he saw another time, when 50,000 [sic] persons gathered in 1905 to cheer the first annual roundup that later grew into the Wild West circus. Miller looked at deserted, fallen farm buildings that once housed the state's finest blooded cattle and hogs. He looked over weeds and disorder where once were showplace orchids [orchards], wheat fields, packing houses and power plants. Miller walked slowly down the steps to the car of his sister, Mrs. Alma England, and drove toward Ponca City.[162]

With money raised from the auction, Zack won a reprieve on the foreclosure and returned to the White House for a brief time. When that last appeal was denied, he knew there was no use fighting anymore, and he packed his few remaining possessions. Just before sundown on March 29, 1937, Zack Miller left the White House for the last time, without locking the door and without looking back.[163]

In the years leading up to World War II, concerned local citizens made a concerted push to reclaim and preserve the White House and the headquarters property and create a state park, but nothing ever came of the effort.[164] By 1941, the land had been sold to the Federal Farm Security Administration and divided into small farms as part of a government resettlement program. Within two years, many of the buildings were torn down for scrap, and by 1943, the once magnificent White House—the architectural hub of the old Miller empire—was leveled to its foundation.[165]

As he watched those sad developments, Zack pondered different options. For a time, he considered moving to British West Africa, where some of his old hands had put together a successful cattle operation, but ultimately he decided he was too old to start over as a rancher. He never believed he was too old for the Wild West show circuit, though. Zack hit the comeback trail numerous times. As late as 1949, while touring the south with one of his shows, he was briefly jailed in Georgia for refusing to pay a fine for speeding.[166]

Ultimately, Zack ended up in a wheelchair. He hired a young man to push him around, and they made the rounds of sale barns so the old cattleman could see livestock. Sometimes he stopped to visit his older daughter, Virginia Miller Flood, at her home in Midland, Texas, and he kept up with his two other children and many of the old-timers who had ridden for the Hundred and One.

Finally, near the end of 1951, Zack moved into the home of his younger daughter, Blevins Miller Gibbs, at Valley Mills, Texas, just west of Waco. After Zack's six weeks in a hospital, cancer had chewed up his liver. Everyone but Zack figured it was time for him to die. Just before he breathed his last, a bedridden Zack told Blevins, "Give me a couple of days and I'll be out of here."[167]

On January 3, 1952, with Blevins and Zack Jr. at his side, Zachary Taylor Miller, seventy-three years old, closed his eyes and died.[168] He died in Texas, where so many years before, his father had swapped hog meat for steers to start the Miller kingdom.

They brought Zack home to Oklahoma, back to the land he loved. Funeral services were held in the old ranch store. About six hundred friends and family members came, bundled up in overcoats to ward off the cold. After the preacher's brief eulogy and Scripture reading, some of Zack's best pals—Bert Colby, Jack Webb, Robert Little Dance, and other genuine cowboys and Indians—took the metal casket to a special place.[169] They did not reduce the old man's body to ashes and shoot the remains toward the west from a cannon, as Zack had directed in his last will and testament. Instead, they honored Zack by burying him close to the banks of the Salt Fork, deep in the earth of Cowboy Hill.

Years later, two more 101 Ranch veterans—Jack Webb, the trick roper and sharpshooter, and Sam Stigall, a Miller cowboy and foreman—were laid to rest nearby. In 1986, the kinfolk of Odis James Farmer scattered his ashes on the grassy hill, fulfilling the wishes of an old man who had left his home in Missouri at fourteen to join up with the Miller gang and work for the Hundred and One.[170]

As the years passed, hardly any physical trace of the 101 Ranch remained standing. The land was divided up, and eventually almost all traces of the buildings were lost or decomposed. In 1987, a mysterious fire destroyed the historic 101 Ranch store, which for many years had served as the home of Zack Jr. and his mother, Marguerite, who took her own life there with a revolver in 1963.[171] The Salt Fork continued its assault, cutting deeper and deeper into the land.

But sometimes if the morning light is just right, or late at night, when the moon makes puzzling shadows, those who know what was once there pause along the two-lane road running across the pastures and over the Salt Fork. They let their minds play tricks. In the thistle and clumps of sumac and out in the tall grass, the wind sounds like strong cow ponies on the move. Hundreds of ghosts are difficult to silence. The beating drums, the solemn chants, the crack of pistols, the waves of applause cannot be stilled.

None of what happened there can ever be forgotten.

EPILOGUE

Putting together the story of the Miller family and their remarkable empire and of all those who rode for the 101 Ranch has proved to be the realization of a dream for an author whose heroes have always been cowboys. Writing about the lively bunch of wranglers, Indians, entertainers, and others of the Hundred and One, and weaving an explanation of the West of which they were so much a part—a place where reality and imagination collided and became one—have been obligations that I will always cherish.

I was lucky from the start to find men and women who pulled no punches, but laid their souls bare as they guided me through time and space to reveal the true and often unbelievable story of the 101 Ranch. I am honored to have become friends with Ruth and Jerry Murphey, who tirelessly do everything in their power to keep alive the legacy of the 101 Ranch. I will never forget my time with members of the Miller family, especially Joe Jr. and Zack Jr. I will forever treasure my days and nights spent stalking history with Sam Hill, Kenneth Goodeagle, Jack Quait, Rex Spangler, Arthur "Capper" Newton, Bethel Freeman, John Cooper, and so many others who kept me on the right path.

By sharing their own treasure trove of stories and knowledge, they gave me a human bond to the 101 Ranch. For me, this was a truly significant experience which helped me forget my disappointment with the woman keeping bar in Ponca City who had never even heard of the ranch and had no inkling what had transpired there.

My sole regret is that I was born too late to be a part of it all. Just spending a day on the 101 Ranch in its time of glory would have made many of my boyhood dreams come true.

I did have a taste once, an inkling, and then I let it slip away. When I was seventeen years old, I worked a summer job on a black Angus cattle ranch not far from Eureka, Missouri. The rancher peddled insurance policies by day and oversaw his cows and hayfields in the evenings and on weekends. My days were spent cutting brush, helping to mend fences, and putting up bales of hay which stretched across the fields as far as the eye could see. From time to time, I escorted amorous bulls to pastures where cows waited. In Celtic mythology, Angus was the god of love; it soon became clear to me how this particular breed of cattle got its name.

A few years later, I put in a hitch as a hired hand at a fancy guest ranch outside Santa Fe. There I dug corral postholes and fed and watered palominos and paint ponies after they had lugged city dudes and turquoise-jeweled Dallas dowagers over mountain trails.

I have lived in Taos, Tulsa, and Austin, and have roamed throughout the West—from Calgary to Guadalajara. I found solace on the banks of the Mississippi River in the upper reaches of the Last Chance Saloon for a dollar-a-day rent and the promise that if I did not retrieve my mail from the barkeep by four o'clock every afternoon, I might end up fighting drunks who would use my letters for drink coasters.

I have witnessed a lifetime of rodeos, powwows, cockfights, whorehouse brawls, and goat ropings. I have been shot at, knifed, kicked, fallen down drunk, stepped on by cows, chewed on by dogs, and sucker punched.

I have written countless stories and several books dealing with damn near every aspect of western life, from tumbleweeds and rodeo clowns to tequila and coyotes.

I have met Belle Starr's great-great-granddaughter, Pat Garrett's son, Pancho Villa's widow, and Tim McCoy, one of the finest old-time cowboy movie stars. I have spent serious time with Charlie Dunn, Sam Lucchese, Enid Justin, Tony Lama, Buck Steiner, and many of the other great cowboy boot makers.

I have known wild-bronc riders, rodeo clowns, barrel racers, and Freckles Brown—the champion bull rider who bested the old fighting toro dubbed Tornado.

I was best man at an Oklahoma Panhandle wedding staged beneath the new moon and Venus and presided over by a preacher who had been blinded years before by the kicking hooves of a mustang. Coyotes serenaded the bride and groom, and the nuptial flowers were black-eyed Susans I had picked from along a graveyard fence. We feasted on banana cream pie baked by a Mexican cook at the stockyard cafe, and we washed it down with bootleg wine supplied by a local cowpoke.

I drove across the grazing pastures of the LBJ Ranch in the Texas hill country in a Cadillac with Lady Bird Johnson at the wheel. Afterwards, we sipped tall glasses of iced tea spiked with sprigs of peppermint she had picked from the garden.

I spent hours atop a pine tree watching young eagles learn to fly, and I chased wild boar through mesquite thickets with a fifth-generation Texas rancher.

I have trooped over tallgrass prairie, mountain peaks, glaciers, and deserts, and have witnessed southwestern sunsets so spectacular they could make a hardened criminal weep.

I have stalked the dimensions of the south Texas ranch where storied cattleman Shanghai Pierce introduced Brahma cattle to the United States in 1878.

I have shaved with snowmelt from the Rockies; rafted the Arkansas, Chama, Colorado, and Río Grande gorge rapids; climbed Hopi mesas; eaten buffalo suppers; and tended bar in a hotel where locals claim Billy the Kid once washed dishes.

I rode with posses led by Texas Rangers and deputy sheriffs on the trail of cold-blooded murderers and cutthroat thieves.

I have done all these things and am a native of Saint Louis—the storied "Gateway to the West"—but I have never considered myself a cowboy, not even during that long-ago summer when I worked those few head of cattle or when I drew wages on that fancy dude ranch. The real cowboys and cowgirls who rode the range for the 101 Ranch probably would have laughed at me.

But in my eyes, my mother's father, Bert Dorsey, was a pure-blood Texas cowboy, the genuine article, brought back to life in my boyhood dreams that through the years became gospel truth.

My grandfather was born deep in the proverbial heart of Texas, in the first week of 1876. That year, George Armstrong Custer and his troopers met their demise on the Little Bighorn River; James Butler "Wild Bill" Hickok was killed during a poker game in Deadwood, Dakota Territory; and the notorious James gang was shot to pieces during a bank-robbery attempt at Northfield, Minnesota.

Down in Texas that year, Reconstruction was coming to a close with the adoption of a new state constitution. The fabled Texas Rangers were at the peak of their power, doing battle with renegade Kiowas and Comanches, cattle thieves, and bandits on the long border with Mexico.

My grandfather was born in cow country, not far from the Chisholm Trail. It was said—and I always chose to believe—that young Bert could take up his sack of Bull Durham and his rolling papers, known as "cowboy bibles," and make a tightly rolled smoke with one hand while on horseback. Bert was mostly Irish; he was all Texan.

A year before Bert came into the world, my grandmother Mary Bohnert was born in Germany, in 1875, just about the time Crazy Horse and Sitting Bull and hundreds of other Sioux people were deemed "hostiles" by the United States government. After coming to America with her family when she was a little girl, my grandmother eventually settled in Kansas City. She recalled that folks were still talking about Jesse James, who had recently met his end at the hands of the Ford brothers, up the road in Saint Joseph, Missouri.

At about the turn of the century, Mary moved to New Orleans to keep house for one of her brothers, an artist who maintained a studio not far from the French Quarter. My grandmother formed friendships with several other young ladies, and they met regularly to visit and make fancy silk neckties. Soon a man began to sell the neckties. One day, my grandmother and her friends decided to have some fun; they wrote their names and addresses on small slips of paper and stuffed them inside the ties before they were boxed up. That particular batch of neckties ended up in stores across Texas.

Soon after, my grandfather Bert Dorsey—recently returned from having served with the Second Texas Regiment in the Spanish-American War—rode into Ballinger, Texas.

He was in town that day to prepare for a relative's wedding, for which he needed a new necktie. Bert sauntered into the general store and picked out a tie. As he handed it to the clerk, a slip of paper fell out and fluttered to the floor. Bert picked it up and saw the name and address of a young lady from New Orleans. He sent her a letter and she wrote back. They became penpals. Soon Bert hopped a train and went to New Orleans to meet the young woman. They got along from the very beginning.

Bert Dorsey and Mary Bohnert married and raised a son and a daughter, my mother. In due time, the family moved to Saint Louis. Bert died there in the veterans' hospital in 1939 and was buried at Jefferson Barracks, an old army post overlooking the Missouri River. His grave—with a bone-white soldier's marker—on a grassy hill is where I visited him as a boy. In 1964, my grandmother passed away, and was buried in the same grave.

Although I never met my grandfather, I remember my grandmother very well. When I was a boy, she lived in an apartment attached to our house, and almost every afternoon I visited her. On entering her world, I would become mesmerized.

As I sat in her rocking chair, she folded hats for me from the pages of the *St. Louis Post-Dispatch.* We devoured shortbread cookies and sipped strong tea as we sang old cowboy tunes and barracks ballads. These were songs from long ago—songs of war and patriots, songs about men who earned slim wages driving herds to market and spent their time roping, branding, and doctoring livestock. There were poems set to music about men like my grandfather when he was a young Texan, who found enjoyment with a quiet smoke in front of a campfire before stretching out beneath the evening sky. There were lyrical tributes to soldiers who had left ranches and farms to fight for an America that had long since vanished.

My grandmother also told me stories. She talked for hours about coming to this country as an immigrant girl and about being alive when Jesse James and Geronimo were on the scout. She told vivid tales about Bert Dorsey and his life in Texas. In my mind's eye, I pictured my grandfather's face, complete with its crow's-feet and creases, and my nostrils quivered at the imagined trace of sour mash on his breath. I would sit in that old rocker until it was pitch dark and then creep home to the supper table. Later, those stories and songs came back to me in my dreams—visions of horsemen and cattle drives, of soldier boys clad in khaki, and of a young Texan finding a girl's name inside a fancy necktie.

I was given my first pair of cowboy boots when I could barely walk. I had chaps and a cowboy hat and wore a gunfighter's belt with a toy six-shooter. I grew up chasing imaginary desperadoes through the fields and forests near my home. On weekends, my father took me to a dirt track where I rode ponies until he had spent all his money. I was weaned on Saturday matinées, television shoot-outs, and sweet tales of that grandpa I never knew. Whenever I heard the strains of Rossini's *William Tell Overture*, known to me then as the theme song for *The Lone Ranger*, I sprang into action and jumped on my faithful rocking horse. Another tune that sent me into action was "Pony Boy," considered one of the peppiest of the synthetic "cowboy" songs:

Pony Boy, Pony Boy,
Won't you be my Tony Boy?
Don't say "no," Here we go
Off across the plains.

Marry me, Carry me
Right away with you.
Giddy up, Giddy up, giddy up
Whoa! My Pony Boy.[1]

I am lucky to have so many memories. Indelible images of cowboys and cowgirls have filled my life from childhood on and have nourished my imagination. I drank from a plastic mug shaped like Roy Rogers' head and pretended the milk was red-eye whiskey. I discovered arrowheads in the soft mud of creek banks and in freshly plowed soil. I held off Apache war parties and legions of outlaws from the safety of Christmas-tree forts. I met two of my cowboy heroes—Hopalong Cassidy and the Cisco Kid—on different occasions in the parking lot of Famous & Barr, a Saint Louis department store. I stood there on the asphalt, looked them in the eye, gulped hard, and shook their hands. I did not wash mine for at least a week after those meetings.

Military school, baseball, college, the marine corps, marriage, jobs, a writing career, replaced my cowboy dreams as I became an adult. I have not been to visit Bert and Mary at Jefferson Barracks in many years. I am not sure I could even find the grave anymore.

But sometimes I pull out old photographs I keep stashed away in a drawer. They are family remembrances—sepia portraits of young Bert Dorsey and his bearded father working with a horse. There are photographs of Bert in Texas, standing next to a porch covered with morning glories. He looks bashful but happy. In another picture, Bert is sitting in a horse-drawn carriage, dressed to the nines, and next to him is my grandmother, who wore gloves and a stylish hat. These images were an inspiration to me during the writing of this book about the 101 Ranch.

The Roy Rogers mug has a place of honor in my study, along with more treasures—photographs of bull riders and bronc busters, memorabilia from the men and women of the West who have filled my adult life, piles of books filled with Old West yarns, pieces of barbed wire, buffalo and cattle skulls, eagle feathers, a hangman's noose, an ancient spur, a lucky coyote's fang.

There is one small box which I consider special. Inside are rusted trigger housings, buckles, hobnails, floor tiles, and bits of shattered china and glass. All of it was dug from the dirt and dust of what was once the 101 Ranch. During the development of this book, these totems often kept me from despair while I sat at the word processor, straining to tell the story of G. W. Miller and his family. They were a link to my past.

It is my sincere hope that this book will forever serve as a tribute to all the old cowhands I was privileged to encounter—and even to those like my grandpa who may have been cowboys only in the minds of their grandchildren. But most of all, preparing this story has also given me another opportunity to be a cowboy. I think Bert Dorsey would have been proud.

ENDNOTES

EPIGRAPH

1. Quoted in Richard W. Slatta, *Cowboys of the Americas* (New Haven, Connecticut: Yale University Press, 1990), p. 123. Note: According to Slatta, this song is of unknown authorship.

INTRODUCTION: THE HUNDRED AND ONE

1. *Official Review and History of the Great Wild West, Miller Bros. 101 Ranch Wild West* (New York: M. Southern & Co. Publishers, 1910), p. 27.
2. Glenn Shirley, foreword to *The 101 Ranch*, by Ellsworth Collings and Alma Miller England (Norman: University of Oklahoma Press, 1937, 1971), p. vii.
3. *Time*, 11 February 1929.

PART ONE: THE DARK AND BLOODY GROUND

1. Mary Bolté, *Dark and Bloodied Ground* (Riverside, Connecticut: The Chatham Press, Inc., 1973), p. 7.

CHAPTER 1: KENTUCKY HOME

1. Quoted in John Fetterman, "The People of Cumberland Gap," *National Geographic*, November 1971, p. 594.
2. Darcy O'Brien, *A Dark and Bloody Ground* (New York: HarperCollins Publishers, Inc., 1993), p. 1.
3. Mrs. M. H. Dunn, comp. and ed., *Early Lincoln County History* (Stanford, Kentucky: Lincoln County Historical Society, n.d.), p. 1; Lewis Collins, *History of Kentucky*, vol. 2 (1877 edition republished by Kentucky Historical Society, 1966), p. 468.
4. William O. Steele, *The Old Wilderness Road: An American Journey* (New York: Harcourt, Brace & World, Inc., 1968), p. 3.
5. Dunn.
6. Collins, pp. 477–478.

Daniel Boone: America's First "Cowboy"

1. John Mack Faragher, "But a Common Man," p. 31 of an *American History Illustrated* article based on Faragher's research for *Daniel Boone: The Life and Legend of an American Pioneer* (New York: Henry Holt and Company, 1992).
2. Ibid., p. 35.

3. Elizabeth A. Moize, "Daniel Boone: First Hero of the Frontier," *National Geographic*, December 1985, p. 841.
4. Ibid.

CHAPTER 2: REBEL CHILD

1. Words and music by Stephen Collins Foster. It is said that Foster's inspiration for this song came during a visit to Kentucky in 1852. Another claim is that Foster's earlier version of the song resulted from the success of Harriet Beecher Stowe's book *Uncle Tom's Cabin*, which began with the lines, "Oh goodnight, goodnight poor Uncle Tom, grieve not for your old Kentucky home." Foster's song eventually was made the official state song of Kentucky.
2. Steven A. Channing, *Kentucky: A Bicentennial History* (New York: W. W. Norton & Company, Inc., 1977), p. 95.
3. Marc McCutcheon, *The Writer's Guide to Everyday Life in the 1800s* (Cincinnati: Writer's Digest Books, 1993), pp. 211–223.
4. Allan R. Leach, "A Glimpse From the Past," *The Lincoln Ledger*, Stanford, Kentucky, 22 April 1987, p. 10.
5. Zack Miller Jr., interview by author, 9 September 1988.
6. Ibid.
7. Ibid. References to the Kit Carson relationship also appear in some undated Carson family records and correspondence.
8. Carson family records provided by Rockcastle County Historical Society, Inc., Mount Vernon, Kentucky.
9. Ibid.
10. Ibid.
11. Mrs. M. H. Dunn, comp. and ed., *Early Lincoln County History* (Stanford, Kentucky: Lincoln County Historical Society, n.d.), p. 80.

P. T. Barnum Invents the Wild West

1. M. R. Werner, *Barnum* (New York: Harcourt, Brace and Company, Inc., 1923), p. 39.
2. Ibid., p. 299.
3. Ibid., p. 68.
4. Ibid., p. 69.
5. Ibid., p. 70.
6. Ibid., pp. 238–239.
7. Ibid., p. 241.

CHAPTER 3: HEAR THE WIND BLOW

1. Burke Davis, *The Civil War: Strange and Fascinating Facts* (New York: The Fairfax Press, 1982), p. 24.
2. Ibid., p. 25.
3. Ibid., pp. 79–80.
4. The lone notation "Civil War Co. D" appears on one of the John Evans Carson family charts provided to the author by Rockcastle County [Kentucky] Historiçal Society. Given his age, station in life, and ability with horses, Judge Carson likely would have served as a cavalry officer.
5. Information and data provided to the author in October 1994 by Ron D. Bryant, curator of rare books and director of library reading rooms, Kentucky Historical Society, Frankfort, Kentucky. Bryant's search of the *Report of the Adjutant General of the State of Kentucky, Confederate Kentucky Volunteers, War 1861–65*, vol. 2 (printed by authority of the legislature of Kentucky) revealed a listing for seven men named George, G.W., or George W. Miller. Six of them had enlisted in Trimble, Letcher, Harrison, Magoffin, and Breathitt Counties, and one—a George W. Miller—had enlisted in Madison County, not

far from George Washington Miller's home county of Lincoln. Bryant also located one listing for a George Washington Miller in the *Index of Confederate Pension Applications, Commonwealth of Kentucky*, compiled by Alicia Simpson. But this listing was for a resident of Floyd County, and the application was received June 20, 1912, nine years after G. W. Miller's death on his ranchlands in Oklahoma Territory.

6. Kentucky Historical Society, "The Battle of Perryville," *The Bulletin of the Kentucky Historical Society* 5:5, October 1979, p. 55.
7. *Report of the Adjutant General of the State of Kentucky, Confederate Kentucky Volunteers, War 1861–65*, vol. 2 (Utica, Kentucky: Cook and McDowell Publications, 1980), pp. 86–87.
8. Dr. Albert E. Castel, *The Guerrilla War, 1861–1865*, special issue of *Civil War Times Illustrated*, Historical Times, Inc., 1974, p. 30.
9. General William T. Sherman to Leslie Combs, 11 August 1864, quoted in *The War of the Rebellion: A Compilation of the Official Records of the Union and Confederate Armies*, 129 vols. (Washington: Government Printing Office, 1880–1901), series 1, 39, pt. 2:241.

Under the Black Flag

1. Zack Miller Jr., interview by author, 9 September 1988.
2. Accounts of alleged crimes by of G. W. Miller and other Miller family members are based in large part on research compiled by historian Richard Kay Wortman, Arkansas City, Kansas, and on reports in contemporary newspapers, particularly the Ponca City (Oklahoma Territory) *Daily Courier*. The Millers' criminal activities will be discussed at greater length in later chapters.
3. The 1995 Grolier Multimedia Encyclopedia, Ver. 7.0.2, Grolier Electronic Publishing, Inc., 1995.
4. Paul Kooistra, *Criminals as Heroes: Structure, Power & Identity* (Bowling Green, Ohio: Bowling Green State University Popular Press, 1989), p. 28.
5. Michael Wallis, *Pretty Boy: The Life and Times of Charles Arthur Floyd* (New York: St. Martin's Press, Inc., 1992), p. 52.
6. Quoted in Paul W. Meredith, *Violent Kin!*, October 1993, p. 1. Note: *Violent Kin!*, quarterly newsletter published in Miami, Florida.
7. Jay Robert Nash, *Bloodletters and Badmen: A Narrative Encyclopedia of American Criminals from the Pilgrims to the Present* (New York: M. Evans and Company, Inc., 1973), pp. 457–458.
8. Paul I. Wellman, *A Dynasty of Western Outlaws* (New York: Bonanza Books, 1961), pp. 59–62.

CHAPTER 4: KENTUCKY FAREWELL

1. Words and music by Stephen Collins Foster. See endnote 1 in chapter 3 for further explanation and background.
2. Miller family records and recollections, passed down from several family sources.
3. Ellsworth Collings and Alma Miller England, *The 101 Ranch* (Norman: University of Oklahoma Press, 1937, 1971), p. 4.
4. Ibid.
5. From a memoir, "What Goes Up," by Alice Miller Harth, daughter of Joseph C. Miller, son of G. W. and Mary Anne Carson Miller. This family remembrance was written some years prior to Harth's death in Tulsa, Oklahoma, in 1987. Note: Harth's statement that her grandparents were not related is incorrect. They were second cousins.
6. Ibid.
7. Collings and England, p. 4.
8. Steven A. Channing, *Kentucky* (New York: W. W. Norton & Company, Inc., 1977), p. 141.
9. Correspondence of Allan R. Leach, Stanford, Kentucky, to Zack Miller Jr., February 7,

1988. "Tradition has it that G.W. was so happy someone had shot Abraham Lincoln that he named his son Wilkes Booth," Miller said.

10. Ibid.
11. "Thus always to tyrants," state motto of Virginia.

The South's Avenging Angel

1. Paul I. Wellman, *A Dynasty of Western Outlaws* (New York: Bonanza Books, 1961), p. 59.
2. Burke Davis, *The Civil War: Strange and Fascinating Facts* (New York: The Fairfax Press, 1982), pp. 236–237.
3. Ibid.
4. Alex Adwan, "The Tale of Oklahoma's Own John Wilkes Booth," *Tulsa World*, 11 June 1995.
5. Ibid.
6. Ibid.
7. Ibid.
8. Ibid.

PART TWO: GO WEST, YOUNG MAN

1. From James Parton, *Life of Horace Greeley*, 1855. John Babsone Lane Soule (1815–1891) first used the term "Go West, Young Man" in an 1851 article published in the *Terre Haute* (Indiana) *Express*. Greeley (1811–1872) often is credited as the author. Greeley did use the phrase in dozens of *New York Tribune* editorials, often adding the afterthought "and grow up in the country." Thousands of people, including George Washington Miller, heeded that advice. Even though Greeley helped found the Republican Party, backed Abraham Lincoln, and fought for such causes as abolitionism and black suffrage, the crusading journalist's admonition to "Go West" probably appealed to Miller. Certainly Miller must have approved of Greeley's seeking amnesty for former Confederates, signing Jefferson Davis' bail bond in 1867, and becoming a major critic of Ulysses S. Grant during the former Union general's graft-ridden presidential administration.

CHAPTER 5: CALIFORNIA BOUND

1. Carey McWilliams, *Southern California Country* (New York: Duell, Sloan & Pearce, 1946), pg. 126. ". . . the caption of a broadside dated March 25, 1870, announcing that a 'party of fifty' residents of Marshall, Michigan, had been formed to visit Southern California to select a colony site."
2. Alice Miller Harth, "What Goes Up," a family memoir.
3. Material from Newton County Historical Society, Neosho, Missouri, including 1870 Newton County census documents.
4. McWilliams, p. 126.
5. Ibid., p. 127. Historical novelist Stewart Edward White (1873–1946) was noted for authentic tales of adventurous life in the American West.
6. Ibid.
7. David B. Gould, *Gould's St. Louis Directory for 1874* (Saint Louis: David B. Gould Publishers, 1874), p. 23. According to Gould, by 1874, Saint Louis had a population of 473,560, making it the eleventh-largest city in the world, surpassed in the United States only by New York and Philadelphia. "No city in the Union, perhaps none in the world, is increasing with the rapidity of St. Louis and the causes which have induced this remarkable increase in the last decade have just begun to operate. The same causes will produce the same results in the next decade—results that will astonish the most sanguine," Gould wrote.
8. Gerelyn Hollingsworth, "Legitimate Theater in St. Louis, 1870–1879," *Missouri Historical Review* 69:3, April 1975, p. 267.

9. Ibid., p. 263.
10. Francis Hurd Sadler, *St. Louis Day by Day* (Saint Louis: The Patrice Press, 1989), pp. 122–123.
11. Ellsworth Collings and Alma Miller England, *The 101 Ranch* (Norman: University of Oklahoma Press, 1937, 1971), p. 5.

Ned Buntline

1. Paul O'Neil, *The End and the Myth* (Alexandria, Virginia: Time-Life Books, 1979), p. 54.
2. Ibid.
3. Eric Foner and John A. Garraty, *The Reader's Companion to American History* (Boston: Houghton Mifflin Company, 1991), p. 622.
4. Thomas W. Knowles and Joe R. Lansdale, eds., *Wild West Show!* (New York: Wings Books, 1994), p. 30.
5. Edward Buscombe, ed., *The BFI Companion to the Western* (New York: Da Capo Press, Inc., 1988), p. 75.
6. Ibid.
7. Ibid.
8. William H. Goetzmann and William N. Goetzmann, *The West of the Imagination* (New York: W. W. Norton & Company, Inc., 1986), pp. 290–291. The Goetzmanns also point out, "Without even knowing it, Buntline also invented the cowboy as media star. Texas Jack, with his deadly lasso, was the first known performer to use the lariat on stage. He was the archetypal cowboy, though referred to, like Cody, as a scout," p. 291.
9. The relationship of Cody and the Miller brothers is discussed in greater detail in subsequent chapters of this book.
10. Quoted in Knowles and Lansdale, p. 49.

CHAPTER 6: HOME ON THE RANGE

1. This traditional cowboy tune generally is attributed to Brewster Higley, who was born in Rutland, Vermont, in 1823 and reportedly died at Shawnee, Oklahoma, in 1911. Higley was a country doctor in Kansas when he published the words to the song in the December 1873 issue of *The Smith County Pioneer*. Daniel E. Kelley, a guitarist from Gaylord, Kansas, added the music. Lyrics and music first appeared together in 1904 under the title "An Arizona Home," with credit given to composer William Goodwin, a claim that was dismissed in 1934. Folklorist Alan Lomax described the song as "the cowboy's national anthem." It is the official state song of Kansas.
2. Randolph B. Marcy, *The Prairie Traveler* (by authority of the U.S. War Department, 1859; reprint, Bedford, Massachusetts: Applewood Books, 1993). Note: In 1849, Captain Randolph Barnes Marcy charted a wagon road from Fort Smith to Santa Fe along the Canadian River. His guidebook, first published by authority of the United States War Department in 1859, served as a standard for travelers for many years.
3. Ellsworth Collings and Alma Miller England, *The 101 Ranch* (Norman: University of Oklahoma Press, 1937, 1971), p. 5.
4. *The WPA Guide to 1930s Missouri* (Lawrence: University Press of Kansas, 1986), p. 405. Originally published by Duell, Sloan and Pearce under the title *Missouri: A Guide to the 'Show Me' State*, copyright 1941, by the Missouri State Highway Department.
5. Eventually the telegraph poles disappeared, but the road became part of U.S. Route 66, a paved highway linking Chicago and Santa Monica, California, which opened in 1926.
6. Zack Miller Jr., interview by author, 12 October 1988.
7. Ibid.
8. Michael Wallis, *Pretty Boy: The Life and Times of Charles Arthur Floyd* (New York: St. Martin's Press, 1992), p. 54.
9. Ibid. Many reporters of the day and critics of the Missouri outlaw's admiration society guffawed at the letter purportedly written by Jesse James or a member of his gang. They believed none other than John Newman Edwards, the zealous champion of the James

family, had penned the epistle. Whoever wrote the letter must have been disappointed, because in the presidential election of 1872, U.S. Grant defeated Horace Greeley by a wide margin. True to the words of this letter, Jesse James continued his bandit life.

10. Howard L. Conrad, ed., *Encyclopedia of the History of Missouri*, vol. 4 (New York: The Southern History Company, 1901), p. 577.

"Wild Bill"

1. John S. Bowman, gen. ed., *The World Almanac of the American West* (New York: World Almanac, 1986), p. 203. Note: "James Butler 'Wild Bill' Hickok, 1837–1876. In an era when fiction and reality overlapped to a degree rarely seen, 'Wild Bill' Hickok worked both as an effective lawman and as a caricature of himself on the stage."
2. During several visits to Springfield, Missouri, in the preparation of this book, the author encountered a variety of local citizens, including chamber of commerce officials, who made it a point to show him the "exact spot" where the Hickok-Tutt duel took place.
3. Clyde A. Milner II, Carol A. O'Connor, and Martha A. Sandweiss, eds., *The Oxford History of the American West* (New York: Oxford University Press, 1994), p. 401.
4. Thomas W. Knowles and Joe R. Lansdale, eds., *The West That Was* (New York: Wings Books, 1993), p. 221.
5. William C. Davis and Joseph G. Rosa, eds., *The West* (New York: Smithmark Publishers, Inc., 1994), p. 104. Note: In 1874, a character known as "Cemetery Sam" described himself as a "gunfighter." By about 1900, the term *gunfighter* had replaced *man-killer* or *shootist* in a generic sense.
6. Paul Trachtman, *The Gunfighters* (New York: Time-Life Books, 1974), p. 38. Note: In 1867, Hickok reportedly swore to Henry M. Stanley that he had "killed over a hundred" when asked how many "white men" he had dispatched. Several credible sources, however, believe that Hickok probably killed fewer than ten men in his tumultuous life on the frontier.
7. George Constable, ed., *The Old West* (New York: Time-Life Books, 1990), p. 376.
8. Edward Buscombe, ed., *The BFI Companion to the Western* (New York: Da Capo Press, Inc., 1988), p. 238.
9. Ibid., pp. 26–27, 45.
10. Ibid., p. 114. Note: The *BFI Companion* states, "Robert Dykstra in *The Cattle Towns* calculated that in the heyday of Dodge City, Abilene and other Kansas towns there was an average of only 1.5 homicides a year, and in these only a third of those victims who were killed by gunfire managed to shoot back."

CHAPTER 7: PRAIRIE CITY

1. Floyd C. Shoemaker, *Missouri—Heir of Southern Tradition and Individuality* (Columbia: State Historical Society of Missouri, 1942), p. 444.
2. Ellsworth Collings and Alma Miller England, *The 101 Ranch* (Norman: University of Oklahoma Press, 1937, 1971), pp. 5–6.
3. Ibid., p. 5.
4. Zack Miller Jr., interview by author, 9 September 1988.
5. 1870 Newton County census and records of Newton County Historical Society, Neosho, Missouri, provided to the author in February 1994.
6. *History of Newton, Lawrence, Barry and McDonald Counties, Missouri* (Chicago: The Goodspeed Publishing Company, 1888), p. 197.
7. Ibid., p. 181.
8. Ibid., pp. 316–319.
9. Anne Cope, "Newtonia: Village with a Vivid Civil War History," *Neosho* (Missouri) *Daily News*, July 11, 1984), p. 7; Nathan H. Parker, *Missouri as It Is in 1867* (Philadelphia: J. B. Lippincott & Co., 1867), p. 341.
10. *History of Newton, Lawrence, Barry and McDonald Counties, Missouri,* pp. 316–319.
11. Douglas Hale, "Rehearsal for Civil War: The Texas Cavalry in the Indian Territory,

1861," *The Chronicles of Oklahoma*, fall 1990, p. 225. Note: The D-guard knife took its name from the distinctive shape of the guard on the handle. These knives were of local, not military, manufacture.

12. Edwin C. Bearss, "The Army of the Frontier's First Campaign: The Confederates Win at Newtonia," *Missouri Historical Review*, April 1966, p. 311. Note: This article by the renowned historian and Civil War authority is the most comprehensive and detailed account of the first Battle of Newtonia.
13. *History of Newton, Lawrence, Barry and McDonald Counties, Missouri*, p. 322.
14. Ibid., p. 387.
15. Ibid., p. 388.
16. Ibid., p. 387.
17. Collings and England, p. 6.

The Bandit Queen

1. James A. Browning, *Violence Was No Stranger* (Stillwater, Oklahoma: Barbed Wire Press, 1993), p. 240. Note: Some writers give February 5, 1846, as the date of birth.
2. Glenda Carlile, *Buckskin, Calico, and Lace* (Oklahoma City: Southern Hills Publishing Company, 1990), p. 98.
3. Ibid., pp. 98–99. Note: Many writers have stated that Bud and Myra Shirley were twins. He was six years older than his sister.
4. Jerry J. Gaddy, *Obituaries of the Gunfighters: Dust to Dust* (Fort Collins: The Old Army Press, 1977), p. 68. Note: This reference to Belle's shooting ability first appeared in the 15 February 1889, edition of the *Weekly Elevator*, Fort Smith, Arkansas.
5. Zack Miller Jr., interview by author, 9 September 1988.
6. Anne Cope, "Newtonia: Village with a Vivid Civil War History," *Neosho* (Missouri) *Daily News*, 11 July 1984, p. 7. Note: In 1996, the Mansion House still was occupied, and stories of the "black room," Quantrill, and Belle Starr still were circulated widely.
7. Ibid.
8. Ibid.
9. "Frontier Justice," *The Joplin* (Missouri) *Globe*, 12 September 1991, p. 8D.
10. Ibid.

CHAPTER 8: GONE TO TEXAS

1. Quoted in Robert West Howard, *This Is the West* (New York: Rand McNally & Company, 1957), p. 159.
2. Correspondence from Lincoln County historian Allan R. Leach, of Stanford, Kentucky, to Zack Miller Jr., Grass Range, Montana, 7 February 1988.
3. Ibid.
4. Ibid.
5. John Marquart, *Six Hundred Receipts Worth their Weight in Gold* (Philadelphia: John E. Potter and Company, 1867), p. 238.
6. C. H. Miller, "George Miller as I Knew Him," *The 101 Magazine*, January 1926, pp. 7–8. Note: The entire account of the fight between the Printer's Pride and the Irish Wonder is based on C. H. Miller's eyewitness account, published in the January 1926 issue of *The 101 Magazine*.
7. C. H. Miller, "Newtonia's Most Beautiful Woman," *The 101 Magazine*, March 1926, p. 11.
8. Ibid. Note: The entire account of the Newtonia beauty contest is based on C. H. Miller's eyewitness account, published in the March 1926 issue of *The 101 Magazine*.
9. Early Miller family ranch records, provided by Zack Miller Jr., October 1988.
10. Ibid.
11. Ibid.
12. Winfred Blevins, *Dictionary of the American West* (New York: Facts on File, Inc., 1993), p. 148.

Jesse Chisholm's Trail

1. Zack Miller Jr., interview by author, 9 September 1988.
2. Ibid. Note: According to Zack Miller Jr., his grandfather's respect for Native Americans was evident early on, when the Millers encountered various tribes in Missouri, Kansas, and Indian Territory.
3. Don Worcester, *The Chisholm Trail: High Road of the Cattle Kingdom* (New York: Indian Head Books, a division of Barnes & Noble, Inc., by arrangement with the University of Nebraska Press, 1980), p. xi.
4. Kent Ruth and Jim Argo, *Windows on the Past: Historic Places in Oklahoma* (Oklahoma City: Oklahoma Historical Society, 1984), p. 11.
5. David Dary, *Cowboy Culture: a Saga of Five Centuries* (Lawrence: University of Kansas Press, 1981), p. 188.
6. Frank S. Wyatt and George Rainey, *Brief History of Oklahoma* (Oklahoma City: Webb Publishing Company, 1919), p. 72.
7. Ibid.
8. Ibid., p. 73.
9. *The WPA Guide to 1930s Oklahoma* (Lawrence: University Press of Kansas, 1986, originally published by the University of Oklahoma Press in 1941 under the title *Oklahoma: A Guide to the Sooner State*), pp. 368–369.
10. Stan Hoig, *Jesse Chisholm: Ambassador of the Plains* (Niwot: University Press of Colorado, 1991), p. 159. Note: Professor Hoig's biography of Chisholm separates fact from fiction and paints a portrait of this frontier figure that surpasses the many myths created about him.
11. Ibid., pp. 171–172.
12. G. W. Miller's rifle, in the 101 Ranch Collection of Jerry and Ruth Murphey, Corpus Christi, Texas, is a model 1873 Winchester carbine shipped from the manufacturer in 1874. Stamped on the left side of the receiver is an inscription added later: "Col. G. W. Miller, 101 Ranch."
13. Note: Folklorist and author Dr. Guy W. Logsdon states in his book about cowboy music, *"The Whorehouse Bells Were Ringing" and Other Songs Cowboys Sing* (Urbana: University of Illinois Press). p. 60, that "The Old Chisholm Trail" originated in the early cattle-driving days and is one of the oldest songs, if not the oldest, with a cowboy theme.

CHAPTER 9: TRAILS SOUTH

1. Quoted in Howard La Fay, "Texas!", *National Geographic*, April 1980, p. 444.
2. Ellsworth Collings and Alma Miller England, *The 101 Ranch* (Norman: University of Oklahoma Press, 1937, 1971), p. 8.
3. Ibid., p. 10.
4. John Rolfe Burroughs, *Where the Old West Stayed Young* (New York: Bonanza Books, 1962), p. 3.
5. A description of Colonel Miller's first trip to Texas was gleaned from contemporary records, files, and correspondence, including diary entries of James D. Rainwater, supplied to the author by Zack Miller Jr. in 1988. Note: James Rainwater appears on the 1870 Newton County census as a fourteen-year-old male from Arkansas. Colonel Miller hired him at about that time, and he remained with Miller and, later, at the 101 Ranch for years. Rainwater finally left the Millers and moved to California, where he worked in the circulation department of the *Los Angeles Times*. He died in Saint Louis, Missouri, in 1933.
6. Ibid.
7. Albert Castel, "A New View of the Battle of Pea Ridge," *Missouri Historical Review*, January 1968, pp. 136–151.
8. Ibid., p. 150. "Some historians have termed Pea Ridge one of the decisive battles of the Civil War because, they assert, it so discouraged the Confederates that they abandoned their effort in the West. . . ."

9. Neal R. Peirce and Jerry Hagstrom, *The Book of America: Inside 50 States Today* (New York: W. W. Norton & Company, Inc., 1983), p. 481.
10. Rainwater diary notes, provided by Zack Miller Jr.
11. Ibid.
12. Ibid.
13. Ibid.
14. William J. Butler, *Fort Smith, Past and Present: A Historical Summary* (Fort Smith, Arkansas: The First National Bank of Fort Smith, 1972), p. 97.
15. Ibid.
16. Ibid., pp. 98–99.
17. Ibid., p. 99. Note: In March 1871, Congress moved the Western Arkansas Federal District Court from Van Buren to Fort Smith and gave the court jurisdiction over Indian Territory.
18. David Fitzgerald, *Portrait of the Ozarks* (Portland, Oregon: Graphic Arts Center Publishing Company, 1995), p. 26.
19. Rainwater diary notes.
20. Ibid.
21. Arrell Morgan Gibson, *Oklahoma: A History of Five Centuries* (Norman: University of Oklahoma Press, 1981), p. 161. Note: The date of McAlester's origin is usually given as 1872, when the Missouri-Kansas-Texas Railroad tracks reached J. J. McAlester's store. He later became embroiled in a controversy over mineral royalties with the Choctaw tribe until a compromise was reached. He eventually became lieutenant governor of Oklahoma.
22. Francis L. Fugate and Roberta B. Fugate, *Roadside History of Oklahoma* (Missoula, Montana: Mountain Press Publishing Company, 1991), p. 1.
23. Ibid., pp. 54–57. The town called Stringtown originally was to have been named Springtown, because of nearby springs, but a Missouri-Kansas-Texas Railroad official misspelled the name with a *t* and the mistake never was corrected.
24. Ibid., p. 62; Rainwater diary notes.
25. Fugate and Fugate, p. 62.
26. Rainwater diary notes.
27. Ibid.
28. Ibid.
29. Ibid.

The Hanging Judge, Frontier Vigilantes, and Stone-cold Killers

1. Arrell Morgan Gibson, *Oklahoma: A History of Five Centuries* (Norman: University of Oklahoma Press, 1981), p. 132.
2. Ibid.
3. Ibid., p. 133.
4. Quoted by Bob Lancaster, "Bare Feet and Slow Trains," *Arkansas Times*, Little Rock, June 1987, p. 88.
5. William J. Butler, *Fort Smith, Past and Present: A Historical Summary* (Fort Smith, Arkansas: The First National Bank of Fort Smith, 1972), p. 104.
6. Ibid., p. 112.
7. Ibid., p. 107.
8. Ibid., pp. 111–112. Note: George Maledon became almost as well known as Judge Parker. The hangman kept his oiled rope coiled inside a basket which he ceremoniously carried to the gallows for each execution. It was said that Maledon took great pride in his work and never bungled a hanging.
9. David D. March, "Sobriquets of Missouri and Missourians," *Missouri Historical Review*, April 1978, p. 252.
10. Mary Hartman and Elmo Ingenthron, *Bald Knobbers: Vigilantes on the Ozark Frontier* (Gretna: Pelican Publishing Company, 1988), p. 6.
11. Ibid., p. 7.
12. Ibid.

13. *History of Newton, Lawrence, Barry and McDonald Counties, Missouri* (Chicago: The Goodspeed Publishing Company, 1888), p. 298.
14. Ibid., p. 322.

CHAPTER 10: SAN SABA COUNTRY

1. Don Edwards, *Classic Cowboy Songs* (Layton: A Peregrine Smith Book published by Gibbs Smith Publisher, 1994), pp. 66–67. Note: This traditional cowboy song is about a retired cowpuncher expressing his nostalgia for the good old days in Texas. Some sources credit the music to Kenneth Chapman. According to Don Edwards, the song first was recorded by Vernon Dalhart in 1926. "The song was most likely written by some old-time cowboy and not by Carl Copeland and Jack Williams, who were credited as writers and assigned a copyright in 1935," Edwards writes.
2. In a 1989 conversation in Tulsa with the author, Waldo Emerson "Dode" McIntosh, former principal chief of the Muscogee Creek Nation, explained that he believed the South's famed Rebel yell had been taken from the Creeks and that the Texans had adopted their yell from that. According to McIntosh, the yell was a combination of a turkey gobbler's cry and a series of yelps. McIntosh, the fourth member of his family to serve as Creek chief, often started various tribal and civic festivities with this distinctive Creek war whoop. McIntosh died in 1991 at age ninety-eight.
3. Early drovers on cattle trails wore heavy, knee-high leather boots pulled on by canvas loops or leather "mule-ears." The traditional western-style boot, or classic cowboy boot, was developed in 1879 by Herman Joseph "Daddy Joe" Justin, a cobbler in Spanish Fort, Texas, who made boots for cowboys and drovers of longhorn cattle going on the Chisholm Trail. By 1890, Justin had moved his boot-making operation to Nocona, seventeen miles south of Spanish Fort. Most credible boot makers credit Justin with having made the first genuine pair of cowboy boots.
4. Seth Moore family, quoted in *San Saba County History, 1856–1983* (San Saba: San Saba County Historical Commission, 1983), p. 427. Note: David M. Williams, county attorney of San Saba County, provided this book and other important research information and historical documentation in March 1994.
5. Ibid., pp. 38–39. Note: From an account of pioneer life in San Saba County from the Andrew Jackson "Jack" Brown family. "One time Jack Brown and the men of the settlement were after some Indians who had stolen a number of their horses. While his wife and small children were at home, the Indians stole Mrs. Brown's favorite pony that she kept in a log barn behind the house. They took him upon a hill, built a fire and roasted him. They danced around the fire and ate the meat. When the moon went down they left."
6. James Rainwater diary notes, provided by Zack Miller Jr., 1988.
7. Ibid.
8. Ibid.
9. Alma Ward Hamrick, *The Call of the San Saba: A History of San Saba County* (Austin, Texas: Jenkins Publishing Company, 1969), p. 261.
10. Jym A. Sloan, *Old Timers of Wallace Creek* (San Saba: The *San Saba News*, 1958), pp. 42–47, 49–50. Note: "In the 1890's Riley Harkey retired from active business. Barbed wire had come into general use as a practical material for fencing large areas of land. Mr. Harkey enclosed all of his land with barbed wire fencing and reduced the numbers of his cattle herd. Years after he reached the 80 years milestone Uncle Riley, late of an afternoon, would mount his little dun pony and ride out into the pasture to drive up the milk cows," p. 49. On January 5, 1920, Harkey died peacefully in a rocking chair before a fireplace at the home of his daughter, Mary Ella Taylor, a few miles west of San Saba.
11. Rainwater diary notes.
12. Ibid.
13. Ibid.
14. Sloan, pp. 27–29. Note: John P. Robbins was born in San Saba County in 1853 or 1854.

He died there in 1929 and was buried in Wallace Creek Cemetery, remembered by some as the "Oldest Cowboy in San Saba County."

15. Rainwater diary notes.
16. Ibid.
17. Ibid.
18. Ibid.
19. Ibid.
20. Kent Ruth, *Oklahoma Travel Handbook* (Norman: University of Oklahoma Press, 1977), p. 173.
21. Ibid.
22. Okmulgee Historical Society and the Heritage Society of America, *History of Okmulgee County* (Tulsa, Oklahoma: Historical Enterprises, Inc., 1985), p. 76.
23. Ibid.
24. Ibid., p. 78. Note: When the "Unassigned Lands" of Indian Territory were opened to white settlers, Minda accompanied older kinfolk to witness the fabled land run of April 22, 1889. She climbed the scaffold and remained there while John Prettyman made his famous photograph of the run. In later years, Minda and her first husband, John Ross, lived at Perry, Oklahoma Territory, where she became a good friend of the Miller family at the 101 Ranch. She also rode cow ponies in the Osage country with Lucille Mulhall, the popular performer billed as "America's First Cowgirl."
25. Rainwater diary notes; records supplied by Baxter Springs (Kansas) Historical Society, June 1994.
26. Rainwater diary notes. Note: At the close of his diary entries for the first trail ride, Rainwater wrote that he primarily had served as the helper who rode at the tail end of the herd. He observed that for future trips, "I have thought there should be two men at the tail."

Cowboys

1. Winfred Blevins, *Dictionary of the American West* (New York: Facts on File, Inc., 1993), p. 93.
2. Ibid.
3. Peter Watts, *A Dictionary of the Old West* (New York: Promontory Press, 1977), p. 102.
4. Quoted in C. L. Sonnichsen, *I'll Die Before I'll Run* (New York: Harper & Brothers, 1951), pp. 20–21.
5. Quoted in Richard W. Slatta, *Cowboys of the Americas* (New Haven: Yale University Press, 1990), p. 45.
6. Walter Prescott Webb, *The Great Plains* (New York: Grosset & Dunlap, 1931), p. 254. Note: When Webb's book was published, statutes governing firearms were more restrictive in Texas, Oklahoma, and many parts of the United States. Ironically, those laws were changed in the 1990s, permitting more people to carry concealed weapons, thus giving new meaning to the term *Wild West*.
7. Ramon F. Adams, *The Old-Time Cowhand* (New York: Collier Books Edition, 1971), p. 5.
8. Dianne Stine Thomas, ed., *The Old West* (New York: Prentice Hall Press, Time-Life Books, Inc., 1990), p. 302.
9. Slatta, p. 166.
10. Ibid., p. 18.
11. Ibid., p. 168.
12. Note: Bill Pickett, a significant part of the 101 Ranch story, will be discussed in greater detail later in this book.
13. Note: In 1971, some forty years after his death, Pickett became the first black to be elected to the National Rodeo Cowboy Hall of Fame, which is part of the National Cowboy Hall of Fame and Western Heritage Center, in Oklahoma City.
14. Bailey C. Hanes, *Bill Pickett, Bulldogger* (Norman: University of Oklahoma Press, 1977), p. 20.

CHAPTER 11: THE COWBOY'S DREAM

1. N. Howard (Jack) Thorp, *Songs of the Cowboys* (Lincoln: University of Nebraska Press, 1984), p. 40. Note: Some sources, including Thorp, suggest that this anonymous cowboy song may be ascribed to the father of a Texas Ranger captain. The lyrics have been sung to various tunes, but its original was more than likely the melody of "My Bonnie."
2. Zack Miller Jr., interview by author, 9 September 1988.
3. *Third Annual Report of the Denver Board of Trade*, 1872, p. 61, quoted in Ernest Staples Osgood, *The Day of the Cattleman* (Chicago: University of Chicago Press, 1929), p. 46.
4. Ellsworth Collings and Alma Miller England, *The 101 Ranch* (Norman: University of Oklahoma Press, 1937, 1971), p. 6.
5. Ibid., p. 11.
6. Lincoln County, Kentucky, records provided by Ray W. Settle and others, 1993.
7. Ibid.
8. James Rainwater diary notes, provided by Zack Miller Jr., 1988.
9. Ibid.
10. Ibid.
11. Ibid.
12. Note: Rainwater failed to mention whether Colonel Miller retrieved the two thousand dollars in gold before the culprit took his leave.
13. Ibid; also see Opal Hartsell Brown, "Penal Institutions and Punishment in Indian Territory," *Frontier Times*, April 1985, pp. 44–48. Brown writes: "Each of the Five Nations had its own police force: sheriffs and lighthorsemen. These men took the accused before the court or council, which pronounced the sentence: a fine, scourging, or both, or death by hanging or firing squad. Punishment varied little from tribe to tribe: 25 to 100 lashes on the bare back, depending on the crime. Both men and women were scourged, then released. If a prisoner had the same charges brought against him three times, he usually drew death. Murder, rape, and sometimes theft drew death sentences. If an Indian killed a Negro, however, he could pay the owner and escape death. Those condemned to die were released until their scheduled execution. One man went home to finish his crop and cut enough wood for his family to use during the winter. Silan Lewis, once a Choctaw sheriff, returned two years after his trial to face execution. Honor was considered the Choctaw's top priority."
14. Lincoln County, Kentucky, records provided by Ray W. Settle and others, 1993.
15. Ibid.
16. Zack Miller Jr., interview by author, 9 September 1988.
17. Account based on Corb Sarchet feature story, "Vivid Pageantry of the 101 Ranch—Symbol of Our Changing Times," from the 23 April 1939 edition of the *Daily Oklahoman*, Oklahoma City, p. 46, provided by the Pioneer Woman Museum, Ponca City, Oklahoma, 1995.
18. Ibid.

Standing Bear: Chief of the Poncas

1. Note: Chief Standing Bear of the Ponca tribe should not be confused with Lakota tribesmen also named Standing Bear, such as Luther Standing Bear and his kinsmen. The Standing Bear name (sometimes spelled StandingBear) also is found in Osage County, Oklahoma, home of other Native American people who claim family ties to both the Sioux and Osage tribes.
2. Irene Sturm Lefebvre, *Cherokee Strip in Transition* (Enid, Oklahoma: Cherokee Strip Centennial Foundation, Inc., 1989), p. 101.
3. Ibid.
4. H. Glenn Jordan and Thomas M. Holm, eds., *Indian Leaders: Oklahoma's First Statesmen* (Oklahoma City: Oklahoma Historical Society, 1979), p. 101.
5. Ibid.

6. Ibid., pp. 101–102.
7. Ibid., p. 102.
8. Thomas Henry Tibbles, *Standing Bear and the Ponca Chiefs* (Lincoln: University of Nebraska Press, 1972), p. 7.
9. Ibid., pp. 8–9. Note: During their journey, the Ponca chiefs lived mostly on a few pieces of bread and some corn they pounded with stones. They slept on the open prairie or sometimes found shelter in haystacks.
10. Ibid., p. 9. Note: According to Standing Bear's account, the telegram cost $6.25 to send from Sioux City, Iowa, to Washington, D.C.
11. Ibid., p. 10.
12. Ibid., p. 13.
13. Jordan and Holm, pp. 102–103.
14. Ibid., p. 103.
15. Ibid., p. 104.
16. Ibid. Note: Standing Bear's married daughter also died during the trip to Indian Territory. After the Poncas' arrival, the chief also lost a sister, and a brother almost died. Reportedly, the chief said that as his son was dying, he had a final request: "I would like you to take my bones back and bury them where I was born." Standing Bear stated that he could not refuse his son's request.
17. James H. Howard, *The Ponca Tribe* (Lincoln: University of Nebraska Press, 1995), p. 36.
18. Ibid.
19. Angie Debo, *A History of the Indians of the United States* (Norman: University of Oklahoma Press, 1970), p. 211. Note: At that time, Henry Tibbles (1840–1928) was acting as the newspaper's editor-in-chief.
20. Ibid.
21. Ibid.
22. In his book, Tibbles quoted Standing Bear as saying he had held his religious beliefs "since the missionary came up from Omaha Agency . . . and told me the right way."
23. Quoted in the *Ponca City* (Oklahoma) *News*, 14 September 1952, p. 16.
24. Ibid.
25 From the epilogue of Henry Tibbles' book, originally published in 1880 as *The Ponca Chief*, by Lockwood, Brooks of Boston.
26. "Ponca Indians' 'Trail of Tears' Led from Nebraska to Oklahoma," the *Ponca City* (Oklahoma) *News*, 14 September 1952, p. 10.
27. Ellsworth Collings and Alma Miller England, *The 101 Ranch* (Norman: University of Oklahoma Press, 1937, 1971), p. 131.
28. Note: According to anthropologist Alanson Skinner in 1915, as quoted in Howard, *The Ponca Tribe*, p. 6, "Apparently the Ponca, together with the Omaha and Osage, retained the old Middle Mississippian custom of removing the entire head from a slaughtered enemy."

PART THREE: THE CATTLEMAN'S LAST FRONTIER

1. William W. Savage Jr., *The Cherokee Strip Live Stock Association: Federal Regulation and the Cattleman's Last Frontier* (Columbia: University of Missouri Press, 1973), p. 7.

CHAPTER 12: THE FIRST COW TOWN IN KANSAS

1. Jim Hoy, *Cowboys and Kansas: Stories from the Tallgrass Prairie* (Norman: University of Oklahoma Press, 1995), p. 4.
2. Records supplied by Rockcastle County Historical Society, Mount Vernon, Kentucky, April 1994.
3. Ibid. Note: According to Rockcastle Historical Society records, Minnie Carson Bennett, a family relative, was eight years old at the time of the shooting death of Judge Carson. "Uncle Judge was killed by a man named Smith, over war talk," Bennett was quoted as

saying when she was eighty-seven years old. "I remember the tape on the holes where he was shot." No further information has surfaced concerning the shooting, the alleged killer, or the disposition of the case.

4. Alfred J. Kolatch, *Dictionary of First Names* (New York: Perigee Books, the Putnam Publishing Group, 1990), p. 302.
5. Ellsworth Collings and Alma Miller England, *The 101 Ranch* (Norman: University of Oklahoma Press, 1937, 1971), p. 29.
6. Ibid., p. 6.
7. Family records provided by Zack Miller Jr., 1988.
8. Fred Gipson, *Fabulous Empire: Colonel Zack Miller's Story* (Boston: Houghton Mifflin Company, 1946), p. 1.
9. Assessment List of Personal Property, Newton County, Missouri, 1878. Note: The record used for assessment purposes indicates that George W. Miller owned three horses valued at $105, eight head of cattle valued at $60, twenty hogs valued at $40, and other personal property valued at $230.
10. *History of Newton, Lawrence, Barry and McDonald Counties, Missouri* (Chicago: The Goodspeed Publishing Company, 1888), p. 301.
11. Miller Brothers 101 Ranch Collection, Western History Collections, University of Oklahoma Library, Manuscripts Division, Norman, Oklahoma, hereafter referred to as the 101 Ranch Collection, OU. Note: Several collections in the Western History Collections pertain to the Miller family and the 101 Ranch. These include several thousand photographs and posters, scrapbooks, outsize materials, correspondence, financial and business records, legal papers, contracts, leases, adjudications, and several miscellaneous collections of documents. The Miller Brothers 101 Ranch Collection alone is quite extensive. It consists of almost forty linear feet, or about one hundred document boxes, each a treasure trove of invaluable data.
12. Ibid.
13. Ibid.
14. Harold C. Evans, chief ed., *Kansas: A Guide to the Sunflower State* (New York: Viking Press, 1939), pp. 441–442.
15. *Scenes Near Baxter Springs* (Chicago: The J. M. W. Jones Stationery & Printing Co., 1888), p. 7. Note: This was a promotional booklet sponsored by the Baxter Springs Investment Company to counter the town's image as a wild and unruly cow town. "Baxter Springs is not one of those new crude towns where law and order and refining influences are conspicuous for their absence," p. 6.
16. Records and documents provided by Baxter Springs (Kansas) Historical Society, 1994.
17. Ibid.
18. Ibid. Note: Remembered as having a keen business mind, six-foot-seven-inch Baxter was described variously as a "mild-mannered preacher," a "gun-toting preacher," and even a "spiritualist medium." He was killed by gunfire on January 26, 1859. His widow moved to Bonham, Texas. During the Civil War, one of his sons enlisted with Federal troops and served throughout the war with an Illinois regiment, while two other sons joined the Confederate Army.
19. *The Baxter Springs Story, 1858–1958* (Baxter Springs, Kansas: Centennial Historical Committee, 1958), p. 6.
20. *Quantrill's Raid at Baxter Springs*, Official Reenactment Program, 6 October 1985. Note: Major General James G. Blunt had distinguished himself at several engagements, including the battle at Newtonia, Missouri. The disastrous clash with the overwhelmingly superior force which Quantrill led at Baxter Springs was one of the few reverses of Blunt's military career. A physician in civilian life, Blunt never resumed his medical practice after the war. He was committed to an insane asylum in Washington, D.C., in 1878 and died there in 1881.
21. Note: Some sources claim eighty Union soldiers died, but the most credible authorities maintain that ninety-three perished.
22. Ibid., p. 7. Note: Quantrill's losses were relatively light, with two killed and two wounded in the raid on the fort and one killed and one wounded in the massacre on the prairie north of Baxter Springs. In 1870 and 1871, the remains of the Federal soldiers who had

died in the massacre were removed from temporary graves and reinterred in the National Cemetery block at the burial ground just west of Baxter Springs. It was the second such plot to be designated in the nation; the first was at Gettysburg.

23. Records and documents provided by Baxter Springs (Kansas) Historical Society, 1994.
24. Note: The building at 1101 Military Avenue which formerly housed the Baxter Springs Bank, where the robbery occurred, eventually became the site of Murphey's Restaurant. Until the restaurant moved to a nearby location, the proprietors proudly handed out to legions of Route 66 travelers postcards telling the story of the Jesse James robbery.
25. *The Baxter Springs Story,* p. 11.
26. Ibid., p. 10.
27. Ibid.
28. Records and documents provided by Baxter Springs (Kansas) Historical Society, 1994.
29. The 101 Ranch Collection, OU.
30. Marc McCutcheon, *The Writer's Guide to Everyday Life in the 1800s* (Cincinnati: Writer's Digest Books, 1993), p. 244.
31. Ibid.
32. Ibid., p. 250.
33. Michele Morris, *The Cowboy Life* (New York: A Fireside Book, Simon & Schuster, 1993), p. 44.
34. Cathy Luchetti, *Home on the Range: A Culinary History of the American West* (New York: Villard Books, 1993), p. 92.
35. Rod Gragg, *The Old West Quiz & Fact Book* (New York: Promontory Press, 1986), p. 117.
36. Ibid.
37. Ibid., p. 119.
38. A standard trail herding song, probably written in the 1880s.

Miss Molly: The Kentucky Connection

1. Zack Miller Jr., interview by author, 9 September 1988.
2. Joseph Miller Jr., interview by author, 3 October 1994.
3. Alice Miller Harth memoirs, 1983.
4. Alice Miller Harth, "What Goes Up," a family memoir.
5. Zack Miller Jr., interview.
6. Dee Brown, *The Gentle Tamers: Women of the Old Wild West* (Lincoln: University of Nebraska Press, 1968), pp. 11–12. ". . . the western woman was more by far than a face hidden in a ragged sunbonnet. Often her bonnet was gay with color and ornamented with flowers, sometimes she wore French millinery, the latest styles from Paris. . . . Whatever her dress, she had endurance, she had courage, sometimes she was wilder than the land she tamed."
7. Emerson Hough, *The Passing of the Frontier* (New Haven: Yale University Press, 1921), pp. 93–94.
8. Sandra L. Myres, *Westering Women and the Frontier Experience 1800–1915* (Albuquerque: University of New Mexico Press, 1982), p. 261. Note: Most of the women who went along on cattle-herding trips were the wives or daughters of the herd owner or owned the cattle themselves and thus had a monetary stake in the operation.
9. Records supplied by Ken Theobald, Danville, Kentucky, February and March 1994.
10. Ibid.
11. Ibid. Note: Ken Theobald, a distant relative of the Briscoes through marriage, has assembled a collection of 101 Ranch material, including many records, photographs, and personal items owned by the Briscoes.
12. Ibid.
13. Correspondence from Mike Sokoll, veteran 101 Ranch cowboy, to Ken Theobald, 26 March 1986.
14. Ibid. Note: John Ford remade the film in 1949, starring John Wayne, Harry Carey Sr., and Harry Carey Jr.
15. Theobald records.

CHAPTER 13: THE SALT FORK OF THE ARKANSAS

1. "Oklahoma Hills," words and music by Woody Guthrie and Jack Guthrie, copyright 1945 by Michael H. Goldsen, Inc., copyright renewed 1973 by Michael H. Goldsen, Inc. Note: Famed balladeer Woody Guthrie, wrote this song in the 1930s, and his cousin Jack Guthrie, a popular cowboy singer, popularized it in the 1940s. The author of this book used Guthrie's song title for the name of a book of essays, published in 1992 by St. Martin's Press, New York.
2. Phillips Collection of the Miller Brothers 101 Ranch Collection, Western History Collections, University of Oklahoma, Manuscripts Division, Norman, Oklahoma, hereafter referred to as the 101 Ranch Collection, OU.
3. D. Earl Newsom, *The Cherokee Strip: Its History & Grand Opening* (Stillwater, Oklahoma: New Forums Press, Inc., the Oklahoma Legacies Series, 1992), p. 1.
4. Ibid.
5. Ibid.
6. Note: The confusion over the usage of *Cherokee Outlet* and *Cherokee Strip* continues. Most people still use the term *Cherokee Strip* when referring to lands contained in the Cherokee Outlet. The *Ponca City* (Oklahoma) *News* of 9 September 1973 published a story (p. 17-F) in a special supplemental edition in an attempt to clarify the terms. "Every time Cherokee Strip (Outlet) anniversaries approach, someone voices his objection to the term Cherokee Strip used instead of the correct name, Cherokee Outlet. But no community that we know of has even held a Cherokee Outlet celebration and no newspaper has published a Cherokee Outlet edition. A great percentage of those who live in the Outlet know they don't live in the Strip, but no one seems to get worked up to the point of doing anything about it. Most annoyed by the adulteration, probably, are old timers who actually live in the Cherokee Strip area."
7. Victor E. Harlow, *Oklahoma* (Oklahoma City: Harlow Publishing Co., 1949), p. 245.
8. 101 Ranch Collection, OU.
9. Ibid.
10. Ellsworth Collings and Alma Miller England, *The 101 Ranch* (Norman: University of Oklahoma Press, 1937, 1971), p. 23.
11. Lu Celia Wise, *Indian Cultures of Oklahoma* (Oklahoma City: Oklahoma State Department of Education, 1978), p. 98.
12. Note: The story of Ponca Chief Standing Bear and his role in the tribe's history is discussed in depth in a previous chapter.
13. Frank Eagle, "Ponca Indian Chieftain," in *The Last Run: Kay County, Oklahoma, 1893*, stories assembled by the The Ponca City Chapter of the Daughters of the American Revolution (Ponca City, Oklahoma: The Courier Printing Company, 1939), pp. 335–338.
14. *Buffalo Bill and 101 Ranch Wild West Combined* (Philadelphia: The Harrison Press, 1916), unnumbered pages. Note: This publication, issued by the Millers, served as their official magazine and daily review during the time the 101 Ranch show featured Buffalo Bill Cody.
15. Ibid. Note: A thorough account of the Millers' first visit to what became Ponca lands and the site of a Miller ranch is presented in the article "How the 101 Ranch Found a Home in the Ponca Country," in the 1916 101 Ranch show publication.
16. Ibid.
17. Note: White Eagle met on at least one occasion with President Rutherford B. Hayes and conferred with numerous federal officials in attempts to win back Ponca lands in Dakota Territory. In 1879, White Eagle composed an eloquent letter addressed to the people of the United States in which he made yet another impassioned plea for assistance. A portion of that letter reads: "When people lose what they hold dear to them the heart cries all the time. I speak now to you lawyers who have helped Standing Bear, and to those of you who profess to be God's people. We had thought that there were none to take pity on us and none to help us. We thought all the white men hated us, but now we have seen you take pity on Standing Bear when you heard his story. It may be that you knew

nothing of our wrongs, and, therefore, did not help us. I thank you in the name of our people for what you have done for us through your kindness to Standing Bear, and I ask you to go still further in your kindness and help us to regain our land and our rights. You cannot bring our dead back to life, but you can save the living."

18. Ibid.
19. Ibid.
20. Ibid.
21. Note: Most of these passages from the 1916 Miller brothers' publication were used verbatim, but not credited, by Ellsworth Collings and Alma Miller England in their book, *The 101 Ranch.*
22. Ibid.
23. Ibid.
24. The 101 Ranch Collection, OU.
25. Fred Gipson, *Fabulous Empire* (Boston: Houghton Mifflin Company, 1946), p. 6.
26. Ibid.
27. Ibid.
28. Ibid; 101 Ranch Collection, OU.
29. 101 Ranch Collection, OU.
30. Note: In Glenn Shirley's foreword to *The 101 Ranch*, by Collings and England, the name is spelled *Tesca-nu-da-hunga.* That spelling also appears in several periodical and journal references and in some material in the 101 Ranch Collection at the University of Oklahoma. In his book *Fabulous Empire*, Fred Gipson spells Colonel Miller's Ponca name without hyphens as *Tescanudahunga*, and translates it as "the biggest cow boss," p. 182.

Boomer Sooner

1. William W. Savage Jr., "Of Cattle and Corporations: The Rise, Progress, and Termination of the Cherokee Strip Live Stock Association" *The Chronicles of Oklahoma*, summer 1993, p. 139.
2. Ibid.
3. Irene Sturm Lefebvre, *Cherokee Strip in Transition* (Enid, Oklahoma: Cherokee Strip Centennial Foundation, Inc., 1993), p. 50. Note: "The Cherokees grew very resentful at this infringement of cattlemen upon their Outlet lands and objected. After an effort to interest the federal government in buying the Outlet, wherein Congress was reluctant to do so, the Cherokees in 1867 levied a tax, which amount was increased in 1869."
4. The 101 Ranch Collection, Western History Collections, University of Oklahoma Manuscripts Division, Norman, Oklahoma, hereafter referred to as the 101 Ranch Collection, OU. Note: William Savage also points out in his summer 1993 story in *The Chronicles of Oklahoma* (cited above) that most cattlemen operating on the Cherokee Outlet thought of the tribal taxes as routine expenses and were "more than willing to cooperate with the Cherokees," p. 139.
5. Note: According to Savage in *The Chronicles of Oklahoma*, some cattlemen who did not want to pay the levies posted mounted guards to warn of approaching tax collectors. "Were one to be sighted, a brief stampede to the north would ensue and the herd would be on Kansas soil by the time the Cherokee official arrived," p. 140.
6. Lefebvre, p. 50; documents from Oklahoma Historical Society, Oklahoma City, 1994.
7. H. Wayne Morgan and Anne Hodges Morgan, *Oklahoma: A History* (New York: W. W. Norton & Company, 1984), pp. 46–47.
8. Ibid. Note: Some of the Boomers were "veterans of the earlier Black Hills invasion," p. 47.
9. A. P. Jackson and E. C. Cole, *Oklahoma! Politically and Topographically Described, History and Guide to Indian Territory* (Kansas City: Ramsey, Millett and Hudson, 1885), pp. 150, 71. Note: The name *Oklahoma*, a Choctaw phrase meaning "red people," can be traced to an 1830 Mississippi treaty. In 1866, Choctaw Chief Allen Wright suggested Oklahoma as a name for Indian Territory.

10. John Thompson, *Closing the Frontier: Radical Response in Oklahoma, 1889–1923* (Norman: University of Oklahoma Press, 1986), p. 48. Note: "The Boomers. . . . consisted mostly of modest farm families. These settlers, however, almost certainly were unknowing agents of the railroads. The connections between the railroads and the Boomers has not been conclusively demonstrated, but the consensus is that historian Arrell M. Gibson was correct in labeling the homeseeker a 'stalking horse' of the railroad interests."
11. Ibid., p. 49.
12. Arrell M. Gibson, *Oklahoma: A History of Five Centuries* (Norman, Oklahoma: University of Oklahoma Press, 1981), p. 158.
13. Bonnie Speer, *Moments in Oklahoma History* (Norman: Reliance Press, 1988), p. 15. Note: Elias Cornelius Boudinot's father, who was prominent in tribal affairs, was named Buck Watie but changed his name to Elias Boudinot.
14. Edwin C. McReynolds, *Oklahoma: A History of the Sooner State* (Norman: University of Oklahoma Press, 1954), p. 283.
15. Ibid., pp. 283–286. Note: "David L. Payne's biographers have sometimes tried to picture him as a rugged, dynamic, courageous fellow. . . . But he was not a great pioneer of the Western Plains. . . . His physical stamina was lacking. . . . Exposure and the hardship of long marches gave him rheumatism. . . . Payne died suddenly on November 28, 1884, at the age of forty-eight," p. 286.
16. Ibid.
17. Ibid., p. 288. Note: President Harrison issued the proclamation on March 23, 1889, during his third week in office.
18. Ibid.
19. Lu Celia Wise, *Indian Cultures of Oklahoma* (Oklahoma City: Oklahoma State Department of Education, 1978), p. 115.
20. Ibid.
21. "Yale Boola," by A. M. Hirsh, copyright 1901. Note: The lyrics of "Yale Boola" include "Boo-la, Boo-la, Boo-la, Boo-la, Boo-la, Bool-la, Boo-la, Boo-la, When I meet sweet Adelina, Then she sings her Boo-la song." At the University of Oklahoma, the melody is the same, but instead of "Boo-la, Boo-la," the Sooners sing, "Boomer Sooner."

CHAPTER 14: "101"

1. Fred Gipson, *Fabulous Empire* (Boston: Houghton Mifflin Company, 1946), p. 2.
2. Corb Sarchet, "Necrology: Col. George L. Miller," *Chronicles of Oklahoma*, June 1929, p. 194.
3. Note: Sheriff Pat Garrett killed William Bonney, known as Billy the Kid, in Fort Sumner, New Mexico Territory, on July 14, 1881. The sensationalized gunfight involving the Earp brothers and others took place in the vicinity of the OK Corral in Tombstone, Arizona Territory, on October 26, 1881. On September 19, 1881, ten days after George L. Miller was born, President James Garfield died of gunshot wounds he had received in Washington, D.C., on July 2. Vice President Chester A. Arthur was inaugurated as the twenty-first president of the United States on September 20.
4. Sarchet, p. 194.
5. Ibid.
6. Various Miller family records provided to the author; the Miller Brothers 101 Ranch Collection, Western History Collections, University of Oklahoma, Manuscripts Division, Norman, Oklahoma, hereafter referred to as 101 Ranch Collection, OU.
7. 101 Ranch Collection, OU.
8. Claude H. Nichols, "Hard Times in Baxter Springs," *History of Baxter Springs* (Baxter Springs: Centennial History Committee, 1958), pp. 9–10, and other records and material supplied by Baxter Springs (Kansas) Historical Society. Note: "The old frontier town of Baxter Springs continued to exist in its largely forsaken and shrunken condition, after the longhorn drive shifted westward. . . . Had it not been for quick and successful action by some of the heavily invested men in Baxter Springs in changing the sentiment of the public, Baxter Springs would certainly have perished from the earth. . . . It was

rediscovered in the 1880's that the spring from which the town took part of its name possessed health giving properties. The springs were extensively advertised and the move resulted in reviving confidence in the future prospect of the whole community. A bath house and a sanitorium were built, and hundreds of people came to receive benefits from the health-giving water. Thus Baxter Springs was able to survive these difficult years. . . ."

9. Records supplied by Cowley County Historical Society, Winfield, Kansas, and by Richard Kay Wortman, regional historian, Arkansas City, Kansas, 1994.
10. Records supplied by Richard Kay Wortman.
11. Ibid.
12. 101 Ranch Collection, OU; 101 Ranch records and material provided to the author by Jerry and Ruth Murphey, of Corpus Christi, Texas, the premier 101 Ranch collectors. Note: Included in the Murpheys' vast collection of documents, correspondence, ranch records, and publications, hereafter referred to as the Murphey Collection, are many references to the origin of the 101 brand in the official 101 Ranch programs prepared and published for the Millers' Wild West shows.
13. Murphey Collection.
14. Joseph B. Thoburn and Muriel H. Wright, *Oklahoma: A History of the State and Its People*, vol. 2 (New York: Lewis Historical Publishing Company, Inc., 1929), pp. 500–501.
15. Murphey Collection.
16. Glenn Shirley, foreword to *The 101 Ranch*, by Ellsworth Collings and Alma Miller England (Norman: University of Oklahoma Press, 1937, 1971), p. ix; also see p. 16.
17. Ibid., p. ix.
18. Ibid.
19. Ibid., pp. 16–17; various documents from the Murphey Collection and the Miller Brothers 101 Ranch Collection, OU. Note: In their book about the ranch, Collings and England gathered information about the other 101 Ranch, near Kenton, Oklahoma, from Fred Hollister, a Colorado cowboy who had worked for that outfit.
20. 101 Ranch Collection, OU; also discussed by Collings and England in *The 101 Ranch*. Note: "In 1893, the company began to dispose of its cattle and it is claimed Colonel Miller purchased the remnant of the herd and the 101 brand and adopted the name for his ranch. This explanation seems unlikely since it is definitely established that Colonel Miller selected his 101 brand in 1881 and used it that year in branding cattle on the Deer Creek and Salt Fork Ranches. Even though he purchased the cattle and brand of the 101 Company near Kenton, the fact remains he had been using the 101 brand a number of years previous to that transaction," p. 17.
21. Zack Miller Jr., interview by author, 9 September 1988.
22. Ibid.
23. Sam and Bess Woolford, *The San Antonio Story* (Austin: The Steck Co., 1950), p. 91. Note: This book, which includes a selection of rare photographs, was published by Joske's of Texas as a public service.
24. Ibid., pp. 91–93.
25. Ibid., pp. 93, 94, 107.
26. Ibid. Note: Roy Bean (c. 1825–1903) settled in San Antonio after the Civil War. He married and fathered children and resided for several years on South Flores Street. Bean moved to west Texas in the early 1880s. He ended up dispensing rough justice and rotgut liquor and keeping a pet bear named Bruno on the banks of the Río Grande at Langtry, Texas.
27. Ibid.
28. Ibid., p. 96.
29. James A. Browning, *Violence Was No Stranger* (Stillwater, Oklahoma: Barbed Wire Press, 1993), pp. 104–105. Note: John Wesley Hardin moved to El Paso to practice law. John Selman shot and killed him on April 19, 1895, and he was buried in Concordia Cemetery in El Paso. Hardin's ground-level grave marker was placed there in 1965 after a lengthy feud between a local citizen committee and cemetery officials who did not want the grave

identified. On April 5, 1896, almost one year after Hardin's death, a fellow law officer shot and killed John Selman just outside Wigwam Saloon, on San Antonio Street. Selmon's grave, near Hardin's, remained unmarked in 1996.

30. Zack Miller Jr., interview by author, 12 October 1988.
31. Ibid.
32. Documents and records supplied by the Menger Hotel, San Antonio, Texas, and the National Trust for Historic Preservation, Washington, D.C.
33. Ibid; Materials provided by Tom Shelton, Library Department, the University of Texas Institute of Texan Cultures at San Antonio, and in Cecilia Steinfeldt, *San Antonio Was: Seen Through a Magic Lantern* (San Antonio: San Antonio Museum Association), p. 124.
34. Steinfeldt, p. 112.
35. Anne M. Butler, *Daughters of Joy, Sisters of Misery: Prostitutes in the American West, 1865–1890* (Urbana: University of Illinois Press, 1985), p. 117. Note: Reform movements were aimed at stopping prostitution in San Antonio, and in 1868, one effort drove prostitutes beyond the city limits. But when local authorities saw that the women were living without proper food or shelter, they relented, and soon the "sisters of misery" were back, plying their trade.
36. Steinfeldt, pp. 112–113. Note: "Just as the chili queens and their colorful stands were a local and unique institution, so also was the food they served unique to San Antonio. Historians agree that the Mexican food served in the city did not originate in Mexico but was indigenous to Texas, and they hypothesize that chili, in all likelihood, was invented in San Antonio. . . . By the 1880s the chili stands had become one of San Antonio's major attractions," p. 113.
37. Ibid.
38. Ibid.
39. Ibid., p. 114.
40. Zack Miller Jr., interview by author, 12 October 1988.
41. Ibid.
42. O. A. Cargill, *My First 80 Years* (Oklahoma City: Banner Book Co., 1965), p. 125.
43. Ibid.
44. Ibid.
45. Zack Miller Jr., interview, 12 October 1988. Note: "My father loved to tell the story of those cowboys tearing up that saloon in Texas," related Zack Miller Jr.
46. Gipson, pp. 1–2.
47. Ibid., p. 2.
48. Shirley, foreword to Collings and England, p. ix; Zack Miller Jr., interview, 12 October 1988.

Devil's Rope

1. Ellsworth Collings and Alma Miller England, *The 101 Ranch* (Norman: University of Oklahoma Press, 1937, 1971), p. 15.
2. Ibid.
3. David Dary, *Cowboy Culture: A Saga of Five Centuries* (New York: Alfred A. Knopf, Inc., 1981), p. 308.
4. Ibid.; records furnished to the author in 1995 by the Devil's Rope Museum, McLean, Texas. Note: This fascinating museum, in a brick-and-masonry building that used to house a brassière factory in the heart of a key Route 66 and Texas Panhandle town, is an unequaled monument to barbed wire.
5. Dary, p. 308; Devil's Rope Museum records.
6. Ibid., both references above.
7. Walter Prescott Webb, *The Great Plains* (Boston: Ginn and Co., 1931), p. 295, quoting Edwin Ford Piper's *Barbed Wire and Wayfarers*, Macmillan Company. Note: Webb, one of America's most distinguished historians, told the story of the rise and effect of barbed wire in his provocative book. "There is something primitive about the name 'barbed wire'—something suggestive of savagery and lack of refinement, something harmonious

with the relentless hardness of the Plains. . . . It fended well against wild cattle and served excellently for the inclosing [sic] of vast areas of land which could not be inclosed [sic] under the old time-consuming and expensive methods of rock, rail, and hedge. Barbed wire was a child of the prairies and Plains," pp. 295–296.

8. Henry D. and Frances T. McCallum, *The Wire That Fenced the West* (Norman: University of Oklahoma Press, 1965), p. 21. Note: As Dean Edward Everett Davis wrote and was quoted in Webb's *The Great Plains*, "Barbed wire and windmills made the settlement of the West possible," p. 270.
9. Ibid., p. 21.
10. Ibid., p. 22.
11. Ibid., p. 20. Note: The McCallums cite information recounted by W. H. Hudson Jr., a railroad vice president, who reported that near Sherman, Texas, railroad ties of bois d'arc made in 1888 were used for more than sixty-five years.
12. Roscoe Logue, *Under Texas and Border Skies* (Amarillo, Texas: Russell Stationery Co., 1935), p. 21. Note: "Col. Charles A. Goodnight, who drove the first trail herds, proper, across the Texas Plains, claimed the distinction of using the first practical chuck wagon ever devised." In 1996, the author of this book verified with Goodnight descendants in Texas the story that Goodnight used bois d'arc wood for the first chuck wagon.
13. James D. Horan, *The Great American West* (New York: Crown Publishers, 1959), p. 184. Note: "He [Glidden] was granted a patent on November 24, 1874. The patent, number 157,124, is one of the most important in western history. . . . Barbed wire is as completely American as pumpkin pie or wild turkey. The strands which stretched across the plains of the early West helped to change its history. It bred lawsuits, feuds, violence and murder, but it played a major role in bringing the West to agricultural prominence," p. 184.
14. Ibid., pp. 184, 194.
15. Michael Wallis and Suzanne Fitzgerald Wallis, *Songdog Diary: 66 Stories from the Road* (Tulsa: Council Oak Publishing, 1996), p. 56. Note: A popular story related to the authors from a variety of sources during the preparation of their book, the "Bet-a-Million" Gates story is also related by David Dary, in *Cowboy Culture: A Saga of Five Centuries*, p. 313.
16. Thomas W. Knowles and Joe R. Lansdale, eds., *The West That Was* (New York: Wings Books, 1993), p. 305.
17. Ibid.
18. McCallum and McCallum, p. 70. Note: According to the authors' text notes, some of their sources contended that Gates used the Main Plaza, but most reliable authorities always have maintained that the nearby Military Plaza was the scene of Gates' demonstration.
19. Ibid.
20. Note: Most sources put the number of steers used in the demonstration at twenty-five, but other estimates vary from sixty longhorns to as many as 135.
21. Ibid., pp. 71–72.
22. Note: By 1880, eighty million pounds of barbed wire had been sold in Texas alone.
23. William W. Savage Jr., *The Cherokee Strip Live Stock Association* (Norman: University of Oklahoma Press, 1990), p. 35.

CHAPTER 15: WHERE THE COYOTES HOWL

1. There are several versions of this old cowboy song, which is often called "Bury Me Not on the Lone Prairie." The verse used to open this chapter is contained in a version quoted in N. Howard (Jack) Thorp (1867–1940), *Songs of the Cowboys* (Lincoln: University of Nebraska Press, 1984), pp. 62–63, a book that reproduces the 1921 edition published by Houghton Mifflin Company, Boston. Thorp first published the collection of cowboy songs in 1908. A New Yorker who came to the West "to be a real cowboy," Thorp collected the original songs of cowboys from 1889 to 1908. He credited authorship of "The Dying Cowboy" to H. Clemons, Deadwood, Dakota Territory, in 1872, but Thorp further stated that he first heard it sung in 1886 by Kearn Carico at Norfolk,

Nebraska. Most sources list the author as anonymous or unknown. In *The Cowboy Sings*, edited by Kenneth S. Clark and published in 1932 by the Paull-Pioneer Music Corp., New York, it is noted that the song was "A sort of 'Cry of the Valkyries' among cowboy songs, with a bit of the 'coyotes' howl' in it," p. 53.

2. Based on definitive and conclusive records provided by Jerry and Ruth Murphey, of Corpus Christi, Texas, primary collectors of 101 Ranch material; a variety of Miller family records; and the Miller Brothers 101 Ranch Collection, Western History Collections, University of Oklahoma, Manuscripts Division, Norman, Oklahoma, hereafter referred to as 101 Ranch Collection, OU. Note: The first Miller ranching operation was the L K Ranch, 1871, the cattle spread that G. W. Miller operated for a short time with Texan Lee Kokernut, on Quapaw lands in Indian Territory, south of Baxter Springs, Kansas. The second Miller ranch consisted of two separate grazing pastures established in 1879–1880 in the Cherokee Outlet. One was named Deer Creek Ranch, south of Hunnewell, Kansas, and the other was Salt Fork Ranch, near present Lamont, Oklahoma. The fabled 101 Ranch was founded along the Salt Fork River on Ponca Indian lands in 1893.
3. 101 Ranch Collection, OU.
4. *Brand Book* (Caldwell, Kansas: Cherokee Strip Live Stock Association, 1882), p. 21.
5. Ibid. Note: "N O on left side of cattle and 101 and brass knob on either horn. Also J Y on left side; T cross T left side; I C left loin; connected L K lying down on left loin; circle bar on both jaws; X on left side; and L K on right side. Horse brand connected L K on left shoulder, I I on left side; X left hip and dewlapped," p. 21.
6. Information provided to the author by Kansas historian Richard Kay Wortman, Arkansas City, Kansas, 22 September 1995.
7. Attributed to W. A. Brooks, a Miller cousin, and used in Ellsworth Collings and Alma Miller England, *The 101 Ranch* (Norman: University of Oklahoma Press, 1937, 1971), p. 17.
8. Ibid.
9. This anecdote was included in Oklahoma Historical Society files and records provided to the author in 1994 by the Pioneer Woman Museum, Ponca City. Note: A rank tenderfoot to ranch life, Brooks first came to visit his uncle, G. W. Miller, in about 1887. He become familiar with the family's cattle operations and later served for several years as mayor of Marland, Oklahoma, across the Salt Fork River from the 101 Ranch headquarters. By the time of his death at age sixty-nine, Brooks knew the Miller family and 101 Ranch history backward and forward.
10. Ibid.
11. W. T. Melton, interview by Lillian M. Gassaway, Anadarko, Oklahoma, 2 June 1937, Oklahoma Historical Society files, Interview 4261, IPH vol. 36, p. 37. Provided to the author in August 1994. Note: Melton was a former Texas Ranger who became a Chisholm Trail cowboy.
12. Collings and England, p. 16. Note: "At first the brand was not burned into the steer's hide, but consisted of a small brand burned in its horns. John Hiatt of Hunnewell, Kansas, reports he helped to build the first fire in 1881 to burn the 101 on the horns of the steers."
13. Fred and Velma Strickland, interviews by author, Ponca City, Oklahoma, 2 October 1994, South Haven and Hunnewell, Kansas, 30 October 1994. Note: Strickland, a local historian and farmer-rancher, and his wife, Velma, were particularly helpful to the author because of their collection of historical files, photographs, and records from the Hunnewell area. Fred Strickland's maternal great-aunt, Ella B. Hollingsworth (October 24, 1867–September 30, 1896), was John Hiatt's wife. "It was common knowledge that John Hiatt was the nephew of G. W. Miller and his wife," said Strickland, "and that he built that very first branding fire when they first used the 101 iron."
14. Howard Kennedy Gaines, interview by Pendleton Woods, Oklahoma City, 1974, Oklahoma Historical Society files, Living Legend Library, Oklahoma Christian College–Oklahoma Historical Society. Note: Born in Texas in 1889, Gaines was a line rider and cowboy who eventually became an accountant.
15. Note: Usually served breaded and fried, calf testicles, or "prairie oysters," also were called

"Rocky Mountain oysters." The "calf fry" was a revered tradition in the high days of cattle roundups. On some cattle outfits, it still is.

16. Note: According to Fred Strickland, the first fire built by Hiatt in 1881 was by no means the cowboy's last branding session. Hiatt (March 22, 1862–April 19, 1947) worked for the Millers for several years and went on many cattle drives for the family. "I recall him [Hiatt] being a tough and mean old man," said Strickland. "He was a bit unscrupulous and was sure a rough nut. By the time he died, he had done it all." Hiatt passed away in 1947, one month after his eighty-fifth birthday. He was laid to rest next to his first wife, Ella, in Rosehill Cemetery, near South Haven, Kansas.
17. Red Steagall, *Ride for the Brand: A Collection of Original Cowboy Poetry* (Fort Worth: RS Records), audiocassette of ten original cowboy poems, 1990. Note: "Some of them were inspired by other folks and some of them just came out of nowhere," Steagall said of the poems.
18. Laban Samuel Records, *Cherokee Outlet Cowboy: Recollections of Laban S. Records*, ed. Ellen Jayne Maris Wheeler (Norman: University of Oklahoma Press, 1995), p. 293. Note: This is an excellent account of a cowpuncher's life in the Cherokee Outlet, written by Laban Samuel Records (1856–1940), the youngest of twelve children, who moved with his family from Indiana to Kansas. When he was an old man, Records scribbled on Big Chief tablets his memories of experiences in the outlet. His granddaughter, Ellen Jayne Maris Wheeler, organized and edited his colorful stories and helped to produce this entertaining book.
19. Ibid.
20. Joseph B. Thoburn and Muriel H. Wright, *Oklahoma: A History of the State and Its People*, vol. 2 (New York: Lewis Historical Publishing Company, Inc., 1929), p. 502.
21. Ibid.
22. Ibid.
23. Ibid., p. 503.
24. Ibid.
25. Tim Zwink and Donovan Reichenberger, *Ranchlands to Railroads* (Alva, Oklahoma: Alva Centennial Commission, 1986), p. 10.
26. Ibid.
27. W. J. Nicholson, interview by Effie S. Jackson, Tulsa, Oklahoma, 26 January 1938, Oklahoma Historical Society files, Interview 12886, IPH vol. 81, p. 220. Provided to the author in August 1994. Note: Nicholson described himself "as a cowpuncher who lived it."
28. Irene Sturm Lefebvre, *Cherokee Strip in Transition* (Enid, Oklahoma: Cherokee Strip Centennial Foundation, Inc., 1993), p. 51.
29. Ibid.
30. Ibid.
31. Ibid. Note: "Again in March, 1882, their second meeting did not result in the perfection of an organization. However, the ranchers ordered wire and built fences."
32. William W. Savage Jr., *The Cherokee Strip Live Stock Association* (Norman: University of Oklahoma Press, 1990), p. 35.
33. Ibid.
34. Zwink and Reichenberger, pp. 11–12.
35. Ibid., p. 12. Note: "Drumm moved his ranching operation to the Cherokee Outlet in 1874 and established the 'U' ranch . . . one of the earliest range cattle enterprises to be established in the Outlet. Moreover, Drumm was the first cattleman to turn his cattle loose in the Outlet, depending entirely on grazing for feed."
36. Savage, pp. 37–38. Note: "Clearly, Cherokees were in tacit agreement on the value of enclosures, viewing them as a means of facilitating tax collections."
37. Ibid., pp. 40, 42. Note: "The cattlemen cited the $100,000 they had invested in fencing, and they demanded a fair hearing before their investment should be destroyed."
38. Ibid., p. 47. Note: The first directors of the Cherokee Strip Live Stock Association were Andrew Drumm, Ben S. Miller, E. W. Hewins, J. J. Hamilton, A. J. Day, S. Tuttle, M. H. Bennett, E. W. Payne, and Charles H. Eldred.

39. Lefebvre, p. 51.
40. Zwink and Reichenberger, pp. 10–11.
41. Ibid., p. 11.
42. Lefebvre, p. 52.

Ride 'em, Cowboy

1. Zack Miller Jr., interview by author, 12 October 1988.
2. Ellsworth Collings and Alma Miller England, *The 101 Ranch* (Norman: University of Oklahoma Press, 1937, 1971), p. 142. Note: The word *rodeo* was not commonly used until after World War I. Pronounced *roh*-dee-oh and not roh-*day*-oh among trail hands, the word *rodeo* came from the Spanish verb *rodear*, meaning "to encircle, to surround, to round up." The word first was used in certain regions of cow country to describe a gathering or rounding up of cattle, not the modern entertainment spectacle made up of seven standard events—bulldogging, saddle-bronc riding, bareback-bronc riding, bull riding, calf roping, steer roping, and team roping.
3. Harry E. Chrisman, *1001 Most-asked Questions about the American West* (Athens, Ohio: Swallow Press/Ohio University Press, 1982), p. 85.
4. Frank W. Jennings, "Did San Antonio Lasso Texas' First Rodeo?," *Texas Highways*, August 1994, pp. 38–39. Note Author J. C. Duval, who in 1844 was working as a surveyor in San Antonio, described the rodeolike event in *Early Times in Texas*, published serially beginning in 1867 and as a book in 1892. Duval became known as "the first Texas man of letters" for describing his and others' adventures in vivid detail.
5. Ibid. Note: In his account of that early contest, Duval wrote that "a great many other extraordinary feats were performed such as hanging by one leg to the horn of the saddle, in such a way that the rider could not be seen by those he was supposed to be charging, and whilst in that position, discharging pistols or shooting arrows at an imaginary foe under the horse's neck; jumping from the horse when at a gallop, running a few steps by his side, and springing into the saddle again without checking him for a moment; passing under the horse's neck, and coming up into the saddle again from the opposite side, etc.—all performed while the horse was running."
6. See "P. T. Barnum Invents the Wild West," earlier in this book.
7. Jack Weston, *The Real American Cowboy* (New York: New Amsterdam Books, 1985), p. 196.
8. Bailey C. Hanes, *Bill Pickett, Bulldogger* (Norman: University of Oklahoma Press, 1977), pp. 6–7.
9. Ibid., p. 7.
10. Ibid., pp. 7–8.
11. Ibid., p. 8. Note: "The wild west show helped to establish rodeo and whet the public's appetite for cowboy sports. It was the brainchild of William F. Cody."
12. Jon E. Lewis, *The Mammoth Book of the West* (New York: Carroll & Graf Publishers, Inc., 1996), pp. 488–489. Note: "So successful was North Platte's 'Old Glory Blowout' that Cody took it on the road the next year, only on a bigger scale. When he advertised for cowpunchers to join his show as 'actors' so many applied that he had to arrange competitions to select the best. His first full-scale version of the 'Wild West' (he thought the term 'show' lacked dignity) took place at the Omaha Fair Grounds on 19 May 1883. The event was billed as 'The Wild West, Hon. W. F. Cody and Dr. W. F. Carver's Mountain and Prairie Exhibition.' "
13. Barbara Williams Roth, "The 101 Ranch Wild West Show, 1904–1932," *The Chronicles of Oklahoma*, winter 1965–66, p. 417. Note: "The Winfield Roundup was also the first commercial rodeo in the midwest, and fittingly the exhibition was presented by Colonel George W. Miller, father of the Miller Brothers."
14. Sally Wilcox, *Winfield and the Walnut Valley* (Arkansas City, Kansas: Gilliland's Publishing, 1975), p. 16.
15. Ibid.
16. Ibid., pp. 23–24. Note: "Among other things these hard times had a definite impact on

romance, for there were few weddings reported during these lean months. On March 11, 1875, the *Courier* reported '. . . the young fellows seem perfectly willing that the old folks should winter the girls once more. Hard times, girls, hard times. Wait 'til the grass comes.' " In her county history book, Wilcox further details the horrors of the grasshopper plague of 1874 and writes of another infestation, in 1877. "Recalling the previous attack and determined to drive the hungry horde away, two hundred citizens gathered with a brass band in an outlying wheatfield. The group, led by Trustee Hunt brandishing a drawn sword and Marshal Cochran carrying the starspangled [sic] banner, converged on the insects. In a couple of hours, vast numbers of grasshoppers were destroyed."

17. *Winfield* (Kansas) *Courier*, supplemental edition, 14 March 1901, reprinted by Cowley County (Kansas) Historical Society, p. 25. Note: "Since 1882 the county has shown a constant and substantial gain. Farming has become more diversified. On most every farm one now finds herds of cattle and swine. The raising of hogs has been largely stimulated by the introduction of alfalfa, upon which they feed and which has proven to be fattening and healthy. There have been no severe droughts nor pests during these later years, and Cowley county is today one of the most fertile and prosperous spots in the world."
18. Collings and England, p. 142.
19. Ibid.
20. Ibid.
21. Corb Sarchet's memoirs, written for an article titled "Here's How All the Rodeos Got Started" and published 5 June 1949 in the *Daily Oklahoman*, Oklahoma City, were provided by the Pioneer Woman Museum, Ponca City, Oklahoma.
22. Ibid.
23. Ibid.
24. From the Murphey Collection, records and documents contained in the 101 Ranch Collection of Jerry and Ruth Murphey, Corpus Christi, Texas.

CHAPTER 16: RIDING THE HOME RANGE

1. From a Miller Brothers' 101 Ranch Wild West Show promotional booklet, circa 1907. The quote was contained in a feature story in the booklet, "The Most Famous Ranch in the World."
2. Irwin R. Blacker, ed., *The Old West in Fact* (New York: Ivan Obolensky, Inc., 1962), p. 265. Note: After 1884, cattle drives declined markedly. In the winter of 1884–1885, Kansas passed a quarantine statute against Texas cattle because of the threat of the disease known as "Texas fever." In 1886, devastating blizzards that led to the so-called Big Die-Up took the heart out of much of the cattle industry. Thus, 1883 and 1884 were considered the biggest years ever on Texas cattle trails.
3. Ellsworth Collings and Alma Miller England, *The 101 Ranch* (Norman: University of Oklahoma Press, 1937, 1971), p. 136.
4. Ibid.
5. Alice Miller Harth, "What Goes Up," a family memoir. Note: No other records could be located to document this early episode in Joe Miller's life. Family members speculate that the youngster no doubt was guided by older cowboys and trail foremen who worked for Colonel George W. Miller.
6. From a feature story, "Indian Chief Blocked Traffic in Birmingham Talk," *Daily Oklahoman*, Oklahoma City, 6 February 1927.
7. Ibid.
8. Ibid. Note: Joe Miller is quoted in the *Daily Oklahoman*, 6 February 1927. This article was one of a series of feature stories about the Miller Brothers 101 Ranch. Joe Miller died on October 21, 1927.
9. Ibid. Note: White Eagle originally had selected Peter Mitchell, a Ponca, to interpret for him.
10. Ibid.
11. Ibid.
12. *Daily Oklahoman*, 6 February 1927.

13. Archival records of Central University, supplied by Charles C. Hay III, archivist, Eastern Kentucky University, Richmond, Kentucky.
14. Ibid.
15. Madison County (Kentucky) Historical Society records, supplied by Becca Palmer of the Richmond Chamber of Commerce, Richmond, Kentucky. Note: In 1769, Daniel Boone entered the southern part of what became Madison County, along creeks that flow northward to the Kentucky River. "Kit" Carson was born in Madison County in 1809.
16. Ninth Annual Catalogue of Central University, Richmond, Kentucky, for the session 1882–83; Central University archival records, supplied by Charles C. Hay III. Note: Central University was founded as the result of a split of the Presbyterian Church in Kentucky into northern and southern branches. Although the Presbyterian Church had divided into two branches in 1861, principally over the issue of slavery, the church did not split in Kentucky until 1867. The branches both claimed control of Centre College in Danville, and it finally took a federal court in 1871 to determine that the northern branch controlled the institution. A group of concerned members of the Southern Synod met in 1872 and formed the Alumni Association of Central University. Members included alumni of Centre College as well as other prominent leaders of the movement. The alumni association offered to cooperate with the synod in establishing a university. The legislature chartered Central University on March 3, 1873.
17. Ibid.
18. Ibid.
19. Ibid. Note: The only other person from Kansas enrolled at Central University for the academic year 1882–1883 was James E. Stewart, a student in the College of Medicine, in Louisville.
20. Ninth Annual Catalog of Central University, 1882–83.
21. Ibid.
22. Ibid.
23. Ibid.
24. Ibid.
25. Ibid.
26. Tenth Annual Catalogue of Central University, Richmond, Kentucky, for the session 1883–1884.
27. Note: Although some references, including Collings and England, *The 101 Ranch*, pp. 30–31, claim Joe Miller attended Central University for three years, a thorough examination of archival records indicates that Joe attended the university for only two academic years.
28. Note: In her memoirs, Alice Miller Harth, Joe Miller's daughter, stated, "I never heard anyone say when Papa quit school. I'm sure he never graduated from anything, having very early started to help his father in the cattle business."
29. Joseph B. Thoburn and Muriel H. Wright, *Oklahoma: A History of the State and Its People*, vol. 3 (New York: Lewis Historical Publishing Company, Inc., 1929), p. 344.
30. From the 101 Ranch records and collection of Jerry and Ruth Murphey, Corpus Christi, Texas.
31. Ibid.
32. Collings and England, p. 31.
33. Ibid.; material provided by the State Department of Highways and Public Transportation, Travel and Information Division, Austin, Texas.
34. Fred Tarpley, *1001 Texas Place Names* (Austin: University of Texas Press, 1980), p. 7.
35. Ibid. Note: A group of local citizens led by Walter Garnett and C. E. Way met in the rear of a drugstore to come up with an alternative name for Murphyville. Garnett supposedly thumbed through a postal directory and found the name of Alpine, Alabama, which the group decided was suitable because their town was in the mountains, at an altitude of 4,481 feet. After citizens circulated a petition to change the name, an election was held on February 3, 1888, in which ninety-two votes were cast and the name Alpine was adopted.
36. Ibid.

37. Collings and England, pp. 31–32.
38. Ibid., p. 32.
39. Ibid.
40. Ibid.
41. Ibid. Note: Prior to this time, the herds that young Joe Miller had helped lead up the cattle trails had belonged to his father. Joe bought and paid for this herd with his grubstake money.
42. Ibid.
43. Ibid.
44. From records and archives of Cowley County Historical Society, Winfield, Kansas.
45. From materials compiled and produced in 1993 by the Winfield Convention and Tourism Committee, chaired by Nancy Tredway, owner of the former Miller residence at 508 West Ninth.
46. Ibid.
47. Ibid.
48. Ibid.
49. Ibid.
50. Collings and England, p. 15.
51. Ibid.
52. Various Miller family records provided to the author. Note: The statistic concerning the ratio of African-American cowboys to whites appeared in a *U.S. News & World Report* article of 8 August 1994, "The Forgotten Pioneers," which discussed new scholarship revealing the major role African-Americans played on the frontier. However, other sources claim the ratio is lower.
53. Judy Welch, "101 Ranch Dream Actually Began in Winfield," *Arkansas City* (Kansas) *Traveler*, September 1976.
54. Ibid. Note: Jim North's remarks appeared in a two-part series about the 101 Ranch and the Millers. North worked for the Millers when he was "12 or 13 years old" and later was one of many witnesses in a 1902 murder case involving G. W. Miller and several members of the Miller family and their employees.
55. Angela Bates, "The Kansas African American History Trail," a publication guide of the Kansas Department of Commerce and Housing, Travel and Tourism Development Division, Topeka.
56. Ibid. Note: At least a half-dozen all-black settlements were in Kansas, but little is known about their short-lived histories. The Graham County town of Nicodemus, on the high plains of northeastern Kansas, survived, however.
57. John Rydjord, *Kansas Place-Names* (Norman: University of Oklahoma Press, 1972), pp. 201–202. Note: Although many people thought the name Nicodemus was of biblical origin, the town was named for an escaped slave. It commonly was distorted to "Demus."
58. Collings and England, p. 29.
59. Fred Gipson, *Fabulous Empire* (Boston: Houghton Mifflin Company, 1946), p. 6. Note: "Zack's booklearning, he got from the Limerick girls, whom G.W. had hired to tutor him, his older sister Alma, and his younger brother George. Joe, his older brother, was already too old for apron-string teaching by this time."

The Big Die-Up

1. Harry E. Chrisman, *1001 Most-asked Questions About the American West* (Athens, Ohio: Swallow Press/Ohio University Press, 1982), p. 63. Note: "The actual cowboy of the cattle range, those men who lived with their herds and knew no other life, were a breed apart from the heroic figures we fictionalize on the screen or in the 'Western' novel. . . . They smelled of cow and horse dung, and seldom bathed. They wore beards that easily became nests for lice, fleas, or other vermin and provided secure foci of infection for barber's itch."
2. Everett Rich, ed., *The Heritage of Kansas: Selected Commentaries on Past Times*

(Lawrence: University of Kansas Press, 1960), p. 195. Note: "Much glamour and romance have been thrown around the figure of the cow-boy. . . . The cow-boy lived a hard life. For months he never saw a bed, nor slept beneath a roof," quoting Charles M. Harger in chapter 6, "End of the Cattle Trail."

3. William H. Forbis, *The Cowboys* (New York: Time-Life Books, 1973), p. 162.
4. Ibid.
5. Ramon F. Adams, *The Cowboy Dictionary* (Norman: University of Oklahoma Press, 1968), pp. 207–208. Note: According to Adams, what is called "a *blizzard* in the rest of the West is called a *norther* in Texas and the Southwest."
6. Ramon F. Adams, *The Old-time Cowhand* (New York: The MacMillan Company, 1948), p. 218. Note: According to Adams, the blizzards affected cattle much the same as cowboys. Horses, he pointed out, usually survived severe storms because they sought shelter and pawed down to grass. That constant movement seemed to keep them warmer.
7. Winfred Blevins, *Dictionary of the American West* (New York: Facts on File, Inc., 1993), p. 303. Note: Blevins explains that the name "sawbones" likely arose because the treatment of wounds and injuries often required amputating limbs, which necessitated sawing through bones.
8. Tom B. White, interview by Augusta H. Custer, Geary, Oklahoma, 31 July 1937, Oklahoma Historical Society files, Interview 4942, IPH vol. 67, p. 243. Note: Tom White started to work for the Millers in 1885.
9. Terry Hall with Gregg Stebben, *Cowboy Wisdom* (New York: Warner Books, Inc., 1995), pp. 31, 34. Note: Another anonymous trail remedy for pneumonia called for wilting large cabbage leaves over a fire and placing them on the sick person's chest, sides, and back. A thin cloth wrap was used to hold the leaves in place, and hot vinegar was poured over the dressing. This caused the patient to sweat profusely and supposedly broke up the pneumonia.
10. Mrs. John A. Logan, *The Home Manual* (Chicago: H. J. Smith & Co., 1889), p. 189. Note: The use of "stimulants" was suggested widely in several other remedies, including those for snakebite ("whisky [sic] regarded as one of the best remedies for rattlesnake bites"), gunshot wounds ("give doses of whisky, wine, or brandy"), shock ("give a teaspoonful of brandy or whisky in a tablespoon of hot water, every ten minutes, for several hours"), and lightning stroke.
11. John S. Bowman, ed., *The World Almanac of the American West* (New York: World Almanac, an imprint of Pharos Books, 1986), p. 225.
12. Ibid.
13. Ibid.; Blevins, p. 111. Note: The term *die-up* developed because of the substantial numbers of livestock that perished during blizzards and droughts throughout the West.
14. Blevins, p. 111.
15. *101 Magazine*, May 1927. Note: The name Tulsa is said to be a variant spelling of a Creek tribal settlement in Alabama called Tallasi, which probably translates as "Old Town." Early spellings of Tulsa included Tulsee and Tulsey, most often followed with the word *Town*. In 1879, when the first mail service arrived, the name was listed simply as Tulsa.
16. Ibid.
17. Ibid.
18. Ibid.
19. Manfred R. Wolfenstine, *The Manual of Brands and Marks* (Norman: University of Oklahoma Press, 1970), p. 9.
20. Ibid. Note: The decline in cattle prices lasted until 1893, and at one point became so serious that a U.S. Senate panel was formed to probe the cattle industry.
21. Robert West Howard, ed., *This Is the West* (New York: Rand McNally & Company, 1957), p. 169.
22. Laurence Ivan Seidman, *Once in the Saddle: The Cowboy's Frontier, 1866–1896* (New York: Alfred A. Knopf, Inc., 1973), p. 137.
23. Ibid.

24. Clyde A. Milner II, Carol A. O'Connor, and Martha A. Sandweiss, eds., *The Oxford History of the American West* (New York: Oxford University Press, 1994), p. 266.
25. Ibid.
26. Ibid.; Roberta Conlan, ed., *The Wild West* (New York: Time-Life Books, 1993), p. 117. Note: Stuart, who had come to Montana in 1858 as a gold prospector, gave up his ranch holdings in 1894 to serve as United States minister to Uruguay and Paraguay.
27. E. C. Abbott and Helena Huntington Smith, *We Pointed Them North: Recollections of a Cowpuncher* (Norman: University of Oklahoma Press, 1955), p. 176.
28. Robert W. DeMoss, *A Look at the History of Nowata, Oklahoma* (Nowata: Nowata County Historical Museum, 1976), p. 3.
29. Mari Sandoz, *The Cattlemen* (New York: Hastings House, 1958), p. 261. Note: Chapter 3 of this book, "The Big Die-Ups," is perhaps one of the most complete descriptions of the crippling storms that shocked the cattle industry.
30. Ibid.
31. Evan G. Barnard, *A Rider of the Cherokee Strip* (Boston: Houghton Mifflin Company, 1936), p. 126.

CHAPTER 17: LAND OF THE FAIR GOD

1. Fred Gipson, *Fabulous Empire* (Boston: Houghton Mifflin Company), 1946, p. 60.
2. Zack Miller Jr., interview by author, 12 October 1988.
3. Laurence Ivan Seidman, *Once in the Saddle: The Cowboy's Frontier, 1866–1896* (New York: Alfred A. Knopf, Inc., 1973), p. 187.
4. William H. Forbis, *The Cowboys* (New York: Time-Life Books, 1973), p. 89.
5. Note: This attitude did not diminish. Even today, roaming dogs and other animals are casually dumped, shot, and otherwise disposed of throughout rural America.
6. Forbis, p. 89.
7. Ibid.
8. Jack Weston, *The Real American Cowboy* (New York: New Amsterdam Books, 1985), p. 45. Note: One Texas cowboy stated that "no insurance company would in those days insure the life of a cowboy. . . ."
9. Forbis, p. 29.
10. Deborah Clow and Donald Snow, eds., *Northern Lights: A Selection of New Writings from the American West* (New York: Vintage Books, 1994), p. 156.
11. Weston, pp. 82–83, quoting J. Frank Dobie, *A Vaquero of the Brush Country* (1929).
12. Donald E. Green, ed., *Rural Oklahoma* (Oklahoma City: Oklahoma Historical Society, 1977), p. 56. Note: Milton W. Reynolds, who settled at Edmond soon after the land run of April 22, 1889, called Oklahoma the "Land of the Fair God."
13. Ellsworth Collings and Alma Miller England, *The 101 Ranch* (Norman: University of Oklahoma Press, 1937, 1971), p. 66. Note: Collings and England gleaned much of their information about this period from old-time Cherokee Outlet cowboys such as Hugo Milde and others. Milde provided some of this material to Collings during an interview, 5 March 1936.
14. Ibid. Note: Milde was a charter member of the Cherokee Strip Cow-Punchers Association (CSCPA) and the Old Trail Drivers Association of Texas; ibid., p. 157. Note: The name of the CSCPA has appeared in various forms during the years.
15. From interviews and historical records provided by Fred and Velma Strickland, Ponca City, Oklahoma, 2 October 1994, South Haven and Hunnewell, Kansas, 30 October 1994.
16. Ibid. Note: A remuda (from the Spanish word meaning "replacement") was the herd of extra saddle horses, most always geldings, kept by every cattle outfit.
17. Ibid. Note: The town was named for H. H. Hunnewell, a director of the Atchison, Topeka, and Santa Fe Railway, and former president of the Saint Louis and Southwestern Railroad. According to Fred Strickland, before a post office was established at Hunnewell, on August 20, 1880, the mail was brought from nearby South Haven and deposited on a desk at the depot, where people picked out their own letters.

18. James A. Browning, *Violence Was No Stranger: A Guide to Grave Sites of Famous Westerners* (Stillwater, Oklahoma: Barbed Wire Press, 1993), p. 133. Note: A typical incident from the untamed years in Hunnewell was the case of Fred Kuhlman. He was murdered in the Red Light on June 23, 1881, after an argument over one of the working girls. Buried at Caldwell, Kansas, Kuhlman shares a massive granite headstone with George Woods, owner of the Red Light, who also was murdered there.
19. From Strickland interviews and historical records.
20. Ibid. Note: From "The Old Cimarron," a song by H. H. Halsell, provided by the Stricklands.
21. Ibid.
22. From Oklahoma Historical Society records and files provided to the author in 1994 by the Pioneer Woman Museum, Ponca City. Oklahoma.
23. Ibid.
24. Ibid.
25. Gipson, p. 22.
26. Ibid., p. 23.
27. Joe Colby, interview by author, 1 October 1994.
28. Ibid.
29. Gipson, p. 25.
30. Ibid., pp. 28–29.
31. Ibid., p. 31.
32. Zack Miller Jr., interview by author, 9 September 1988.
33. Ibid. Note: Cowboys coming up the cattle trails enjoyed pausing at those towns "with the hair on"—rough-and-tumble places with little law and order. A cowboy who showed that he could take care of himself was said to be a man "with the hair on." According to lexicographer Ramon Adams, another popular cowboy expression to describe someone with experience was to say that he had the "hair off the dog."
34. Ibid.
35. From records and documents in the 101 Ranch Collection of John Cooper of Stroud, Oklahoma.
36. Ibid.
37. Ibid.; Collings and England, p. 63.
38. From the Cooper collection, especially an undated account of the interview between Oscar Brewster and J. Frank Dobie, "Cusey of the Chuck Wagon." The interview took place at Crescent, Oklahoma, where Brewster was operating a leather shop. Note: *Cusey*, sometimes spelled *coosie*, was one of the many names used for range cooks. Other common names included bean master, belly cheater, biscuit roller, cookie, dough-puncher, gut burglar, hash slinger, lizard scorcher, Miss Sally, stew builder, and swamper.
39. Ibid. Note: Brewster told Dobie, "Whenever a chance came, I generally made pie or duff or some kind of sweetening." Brewster also described how he took care of a cowboy bully by smacking the horse wrangler over the head with his trusty rolling pin.
40. Ibid. Note: According to Brewster, many of "those Texas fellers would drink coffee boiling off the fire. They never mixed their whiskey either, and a man had to drink when he ran with cowboys in those days."
41. Collings and England, p. 64. Note: ". . . Colonel Joe Miller was the best round-up boss I ever worked for during all my time on the ranges," Brewster told Collings on 21 July 1936.
42. Ibid., p. 63. Note: The Millers operated three divisions during the general roundups—eastern, southwestern, and western.
43. Ibid., p. 64.
44. Bonnie Speer, *Moments in Oklahoma History* (Norman, Oklahoma: Reliance Press, 1988), pp. 15–17. Note: Boomer leader David L. Payne had died while eating breakfast in Wellington, Kansas, on November 27, 1884, but the Boomer invasions continued.
45. Angie Debo and John M. Oskison, eds., *Oklahoma: A Guide to the Sooner State* (Norman: University of Oklahoma Press, 1941), p. 28.

46. Ibid. Note: The Five Tribes are the Cherokees, Choctaws, Chickasaws, Creeks, and Seminoles. Some whites and, ironically, even some Native Americans continue to use the offensive term *Five Civilized Tribes.*
47. W. David Baird and Danney Goble, *The Story of Oklahoma* (Norman: University of Oklahoma Press, 1994), p. 297. Note: Indiana's William Springer wrote the authorizing amendment.
48. Edwin C. McReynolds, *Oklahoma: A History of the Sooner State* (Norman: University of Oklahoma Press, 1954), p. 288.
49. D. Earl Newsom, *The Cherokee Strip: Its History and Grand Opening* (Stillwater, Oklahoma: New Forums Press, Inc., 1992), pp. 26–27.
50. Howard F. Stein and Robert F. Hill, eds., *The Culture of Oklahoma* (Norman: University of Oklahoma Press, 1993), pp. 31–32.
51. Arrell M. Gibson, *The Oklahoma Story* (Norman: University of Oklahoma Press, 1978), p. 155.
52. Ibid.

Shanghai Pierce

1. Zack Miller Jr., interview by author, 12 October 1988.
2. Ibid.
3. Ibid.
4. William H. Forbis, *The Cowboys* (New York: Time-Life Books, 1973), p. 49. Note: "By 1885 beef cattle represented by far the biggest business in all of the Old West. And by that time . . . no more than perhaps three dozen rangeland rajahs controlled more than 20 million acres of United States soil, private and public, and owned at least one third of the beeves that grazed the Western prairie."
5. Lewis Atherton, *The Cattle Kings* (Lincoln: University of Nebraska Press, 1961), p. 197.
6. Michele Morris, *The Cowboy Life* (New York: A Fireside Book, published by Simon & Shuster, 1993), pp. 34–36.
7. Jimmy M. Skaggs, *The Cattle-Trailing Industry* (Norman: University of Oklahoma Press, 1991), p. 63.
8. Fred Gipson, *The Fabulous Empire* (Boston: Houghton Mifflin Company, 1946), pp. 66–67.
9. Denis McLoughlin, *Wild and Woolly: An Encyclopedia of the Old West* (New York: Barnes & Noble Books, 1975), p. 406.
10. Ibid.
11. Ibid.
12. Ibid.
13. Ibid., p. 331.
14. Jack Weston, *The Real American Cowboy* (New York: New Amsterdam Books, 1985), p. 83.
15. Ibid.
16. Thomas W. Knowles and Joe R. Lansdale, eds., *The West That Was* (New York: Wing Books, 1993), p. 299.
17. Ramon F. Adams, *The Cowboy Dictionary* (New York: Perigee Books, published by the Putnam Publishing Group, 1993), p. 270.
18. Skaggs, p. 63; Knowles and Lansdale, p. 299.
19. Chris Emmett, *Shanghai Pierce: A Fair Likeness* (Norman: University of Oklahoma Press, 1953), p. 217.
20. Ibid., pp. 217–218.
21. Ibid.
22. Based on documents and notations supplied by Oklahoma Historical Society from the files of the Pioneer Woman Museum, Ponca City, Oklahoma, including a feature story, "The Fabulous Empire," written by Connie Cronley and published in the October 1977 edition of *Oklahoma Monthly.*

23. Gipson, pp. 66–68.
24. Emmett, p. 238.

CHAPTER 18: THE RUN OF '93

1. Zack T. Miller Jr., interview by author, 9 September 1988.
2. Edwin C. McReynolds, *Oklahoma: A History of the Sooner State* (Norman: University of Oklahoma Press, 1954), p. 292.
3. H. Wayne Morgan and Anne Hodges Morgan, *Oklahoma: A History* (New York and London: W. W. Norton & Company, 1977), p. 55.
4. Joseph Miller Jr., interview by author, 3 October 1994.
5. Zack T. Miller Jr., interview, 9 September 1988. Note: These are opinions based on stories passed on by his father, Zack Miller, and others, including some of the old-time 101 cowboys.
6. Irene Sturm Lefebvre, *Cherokee Strip in Transition* (Enid, Oklahoma: Cherokee Strip Centennial Foundation, Inc., 1993), pp. 52–53.
7. Ibid.
8. Ibid., p. 53.
9. Ibid., p. 54.
10. Ibid., pp. 53–54.
11. Ibid., p. 55.
12. Fred Gipson, *Fabulous Empire* (Boston: Houghton Mifflin Company, 1946), p. 61.
13. Ibid.
14. Ibid., pp. 61–66. Note: Based on Zack Miller's recollections, Gipson offers one of the more colorful accounts of an encounter between Miller cowhands and buffalo soldiers in the Cherokee Outlet.
15. Ibid., p. 61.
16. Ibid.
17. William W. Savage Jr., *The Cherokee Strip Live Stock Association* (Columbia: University of Missouri Press, 1973), pp. 122–123.
18. Ibid., p. 123. Note: In 1961, after decades of litigation, the federal government gave the Cherokee Nation of Oklahoma an additional $14,789,000 for the outlet lands.
19. Ellsworth Collings and Alma Miller England, *The 101 Ranch* (Norman: University of Oklahoma Press, 1937, 1971), pp. 44–45.
20. Gipson, p. 82. Note: Indian lands in Oklahoma are not designated as reservations.
21. Ibid.
22. Lefebre, p. 65.
23. Ibid.
24. Ibid.
25. Ibid., p. 66.
26. Copy of the August 23, 1893, letter from J. C. Miller, provided to the author by Terry Whitehead, of Blackwell, Oklahoma, a grandson of John Thomas Whitehead.
27. D. Earl Newsom, *The Cherokee Strip: Its History & Grand Opening* (Stillwater, Oklahoma: New Forums Press, Inc., 1992), pp. 41–42.
28. Ibid. Note: "Rumors spread that Sooners or those with fast horses might rush into the Strip [sic] and blow up railroad bridges. As the day of the run neared, most men in the camps were wearing guns," p. 39.
29. *101 Ranch, The Most Famous Ranch in the World*, promotional magazine published by the Miller family in 1908.
30. Ibid.
31. Newsom, p. 42.
32. *101 Ranch*, Miller promotional brochure, 1908.
33. Ibid.
34. Ibid. Note: Many horses reportedly dropped dead in the heat of the race into the Cherokee Outlet, and many others had to be destroyed after they broke their legs stepping into holes.

35. Ibid. Note: According to family records, September 16, 1893, always was considered the official birthdate of the 101 Ranch.

The Great White City

1. George Miller England, "The Great Ranches," in *The Last Run, Kay County, Oklahoma, 1893*, stories assembled by the Ponca City Chapter of the Daughters of the American Revolution (Ponca City, Oklahoma: The Courier Printing Company, 1939), p. 261.
2. John S. Bowman, gen. ed., *The World Almanac of the American West* (New York: World Almanac, an imprint of Pharos Books, 1986), p. 240.
3. Ibid.
4. Donald L. Miller, "The White City," *American Heritage*, July–August 1993, p. 71.
5. Ibid.
6. Jamie Kageleiry, "One Day at the Chicago World's Fair," *The Old Farmer's Almanac 1993* (Dublin, New Hampshire: Yankee Publishing Incorporated, 1992), p. 163.
7. Ibid., p. 165. Note: As many as seventeen thousand people could dine at one time in the various eating establishments on the fairgrounds.
8. Ibid., p. 168; *Portfolio of Photographs of the World's Fair*, art series no. 9 (Chicago: The Werner Company, 1893), p. 5.; *Portfolio of Photographs of the World's Fair*, art series no. 7 (Chicago: The Werner Company, 1893), p. 13.
9. Miller, p. 85; Kageleiry, p. 164.
10. Miller, p. 80.
11. Andrea Oppenheimer Dean, "Revisiting the White City," *Historic Preservation*, March–April 1993, p. 42.
12. Phil Patton, "Sell the Cookstove if Necessary, but Come to the Fair," *Smithsonian*, June 1993, pp. 46, 48.
13. Ibid., p. 48.
14. Kageleiry, p. 166.
15. Patton, p. 48.
16. Ibid.
17. Dean, p. 42.
18. Zack Miller Jr., interview by author, 9 September 1988.
19. Richard White, "Frederick Jackson Turner and Buffalo Bill," in *The Frontier in American Culture*, ed. James R. Grossman (Berkeley: University of California Press, 1994), p. 7.
20. Ibid.
21. Ibid.
22. Wilbur R. Jacobs, foreword to *The Frontier in American History*, by Frederick Jackson Turner (Tucson: University of Arizona Press, 1986), p. ix.
23. Ibid; White, pp. 7–8.
24. Irwin R. Blacker, ed., *The Old West in Fact* (New York: Ivan Obolensky, Inc., 1962), p. 425.
25. Ibid.
26. Ibid., p. 427. Note: In 1910, Turner joined the faculty at Harvard University, where he trained an untold number of historians before he retired in 1924. Among his disciples at Harvard was Edward Everett Dale, who for many years was head of the history department at the University of Oklahoma. Turner died in 1932.
27. Richard Slotkin, "The Wild West," in *Buffalo Bill and the Wild West* (Brooklyn, New York: The Brooklyn Museum, 1981), p. 27. Note: This work was published for the exhibition *Buffalo Bill and the Wild West*, a joint project of the Brooklyn Museum; the Museum of Art, Carnegie Institute; and the Buffalo Bill Historical Center.
28. Ibid., p. 28.
29. Miller, p. 86.
30. Ephraim Katz, *The Film Encyclopedia* (New York: Perigee Books, 1979), p. 374.
31. Ibid.
32. Ibid.
33. William Judson, "The Movies," in *Buffalo Bill and the Wild West*, p. 68.

34. Ibid., p. 76.
35. Kevin Brownlow, *The War, the West, and the Wilderness* (New York: Alfred A. Knopf, Inc., 1978), pp. 253–254.
36. Ibid.

PART FOUR: THE REAL THING

1. From the Murphey Collection, records and documents contained in the 101 Ranch Collection of Jerry and Ruth Murphey, Corpus Christi, Texas.

CHAPTER 19: SHADES OF GRAY

1. James H. Thomas, "The 101 Ranch: A Matter of Style," *Ranch and Range in Oklahoma*, ed. Jimmy K. Skaggs (Oklahoma City: Oklahoma Historical Society, 1978), p. 77.
2. United States District Court records furnished by Steve H. Bunch, Perry, Oklahoma; documents from the Fred Barde Collection, scrapbook vol. 10, Oklahoma Historical Society, Oklahoma City, including *Kansas City Star*, 25 April 1903.
3. *Winfield* (Kansas) *Courier*, 14 January 1893, from the collection of Richard Kay Wortman, Arkansas City, Kansas.
4. Zack Miller Jr., interview by author, 9 September 1988. Note: Zack Jr. also related that there was a definite benefit for corporal punishment and that once he had relied on a bullwhip for settling a dispute with a rival over a woman.
5. Ibid.
6. Marc McCutcheon, *The Writer's Guide to Everyday Life in the 1800s* (Cincinnati: Writer's Digest Books, 1993), p. 246. Note: According to the *Chicago Tribune*, between 1882 and 1903 (the year G. W. Miller died) more than thirty-three hundred people were lynched in the United States. In the vast majority of these cases, no arrests were made.
7. Sally Wilcox, *Winfield and the Walnut Valley* (Arkansas City, Kansas: Gilliland's Publishing, 1975) pp. 27, 30, 31, 40, 42. Note: By 1900, the Winfield Reds were declared the Kansas champions and won a gourd trophy "three feet long, representing a bat, neatly lettered and accompanied by the badge of the old Reds."
8. Ibid., pp. 9, 11.
9. Ibid., p. 36. Note: The Winfield Chautauqua was organized in 1886 as part of the national circuit which had begun in New York in 1874.
10. Ibid., p. 48.
11. Ibid.
12. Ellsworth Collings and Alma Miller England, *The 101 Ranch* (Norman: University of Oklahoma Press, 1937, 1971), pp. 25–26.
13. Ibid., p. 26.
14. *Time*, 11 February 1929, p. 63.
15. Worth Robert Miller, *Oklahoma Populism: A History of the People's Party in the Oklahoma Territory* (Norman: University of Oklahoma Press, 1987), p. 85.
16. Ibid., pp. 90–91.
17. Alvin O. Turner, "Order and Disorder: The Opening of the Cherokee Outlet," *The Chronicles of Oklahoma*, summer 1993, p. 161.
18. Fred Gipson, *Fabulous Empire* (Boston: Houghton Mifflin Company, 1946), pp. 86–87.
19. Ibid., p. 87.
20. Ibid.
21. Thomas, p. 80.
22. Ibid.
23. Ibid.
24. Gipson, p. 87.
25. Ibid., p. 88.
26. Ibid., pp. 88–89.
27. Ibid.
28. Thomas, p. 80.

29. Ibid.
30. Charles Lane Callen, "The Story of the Great 101 Ranch," *American Magazine*, July 1928, p. 149.
31. Gipson, p. 95.
32. Ibid., pp. 95–96.
33. Ibid., p. 96.
34. Ibid.
35. Ibid.
36. Ibid.
37. Ibid, p. 99.
38. W. H. Day, interview by Merrill A. Nelson, Enid, Oklahoma, 13 October 1937, Oklahoma Historical Society files, Interview 1392, IPH vol. 83, pp. 140–141.
39. Callen, p. 149.
40. Ibid.
41. Ibid.
42. Ibid.
43. Gipson, pp. 99–100.
44. Collings and England, p. 68.
45. W. A. West, interview by Robert W. Small, Tonkawa, Oklahoma, 28 October 1937, Oklahoma Historical Society files, Interview 9101, IPH vol. 53, p. 465.
46. Callen, p. 149.
47. Ibid., p. 150.

"56"

1. Charles Lane Callen, "The Story of the Great 101 Ranch," *American Magazine*, July 1928, p. 149.
2. Zack Miller Jr., interview by author, 12 October 1988.
3. Fred Gipson, *Fabulous Empire* (Boston: Houghton Mifflin Company, 1946), p. 37.
4. Ibid., pp. 7–10.
5. Ibid., pp. 99–100.
6. Ibid., p. 104.
7. Joseph B. Thoburn and Muriel H. Wright, *Oklahoma: A History of the State and Its People*, vol. 3 (New York: Lewis Historical Publishing Company, Inc., 1929), p. 345.
8. Gipson, p. 59.
9. Thoburn and Wright, p. 345.
10. From the 101 Ranch Collection of Jerry and Ruth Murphey, Corpus Christi, Texas.
11. Roy Meador, "The 101 Line Rider Known As Fifty-Six," *Good Old Days*, January 1987, p. 42.
12. Ibid., p. 43.
13. Ibid., pp. 42–43.
14. Ibid., p. 43.
15. Ibid., pp. 43, 58.
16. Ibid., p. 58.

CHAPTER 20: LORDS OF THE PRAIRIE

1. W. A. Vines, interview by Johnston H. Hampton, Snow, Oklahoma, 12 October 1937, Oklahoma Historical Society files, Interview 7837, IPH vol. 48, p. 173.
2. Charles Lane Callen, "The Story of the Great 101 Ranch," *American Magazine*, July 1928, p. 149.
3. Fred Gipson, *Fabulous Empire* (Boston: Houghton Mifflin Company, 1946), p. 106.
4. James H. Thomas, "The 101 Ranch: A Matter of Style," *Ranch and Range in Oklahoma*, ed. Jimmy M. Skaggs (Oklahoma City: Oklahoma Historical Society, 1978), p. 80.
5. From documents in the 101 Ranch collection of John Cooper, Stroud, Oklahoma.
6. Gipson, pp. 106–107.

7. Ibid., p. 107.
8. Ibid.
9. Cooper Collection.
10. Ibid.
11. Ibid.
12. Edward Everett Dale, *American Hereford Journal*, 15 December 1936, p. 6, quoted in Ellsworth Collings and Alma Miller England, *The 101 Ranch* (Norman: University of Press, 1937, 1971), p. 69.
13. Lizzie T. Miller, "Early Days at the 101 Ranch and Ponca City," in *The Last Run: Kay County, Oklahoma, 1893*, stories Assembled by the Ponca City Chapter of the Daughters of the American Revolution, (Ponca City: The Courier Printing Company, 1939), p. 265.
14. Note: Cowboys and others used *girling* as a term for courting or chasing women.
15. Miller, p. 265.
16. From the undated and unpublished memoirs of Alice Miller Harth, daughter of Joseph C. Miller.
17. Ibid.
18. Unpublished manuscript of J. M. Trosper, North Central Oklahoma Historical Association, Inc., Ponca City, Oklahoma.
19. Harth memoirs.
20. Ibid.
21. Ibid.
22. Ibid.
23. Harth memoirs.
24. Ibid.
25. Joseph B. Thoburn and Muriel H. Wright, *Oklahoma: A History of the State and Its People*, vol. 3 (New York: Lewis Historical Publishing Company, Inc., 1929), p. 344.
26. Ibid.
27. Ibid.
28. J. C. Murphy, interview by W. T. Holland, Tulsa, Oklahoma, 30 March 1938, Oklahoma Historical Society files, IPH vol. 81, p. 164. Note: Murphy served as a justice of the peace for seven years.
29. *Ponca City* (Oklahoma Territory) *Courier*, 11 March 1897.
30. Ibid.
31. Ibid.
32. Ibid.
33. Berlin Basil Chapman, *The Otoes and Missourias: A Study of Indian Removal and the Legal Aftermath* (Oklahoma City: Times Journal Publishing Co., 1965), p. 338. Note: Few federal prisons existed at the time, so some federal prisoners were sent to state prisons.
34. Joe and Lizzie's first child, a daughter, was buried in Winfield; records supplied by Richard Kay Wortman, regional historian, Arkansas City, Kansas, 1994. Note: According to Wortman, the Miller family purchased a lot in Graham-Union Cemetery in Winfield. The legal description is block 2, lot 29. Besides the infant daughter of Joe and Lizzie Miller, several 101 cowboys, including Jimmy Moore, also were supposedly buried in this graveyard.
35. *Ponca City* (Oklahoma Territory) *Courier*, 15 October 1897.
36. *Ponca City* (Oklahoma Territory) *Democrat*, 13 November 1897.
37. Ibid.
38. Ibid.
39. *Ponca City* (Oklahoma Territory) *Courier*, 17 June 1897; 27 August 1897, concerning the Millers' wheat crop; 9 December 1897, concerning G. W. Miller's conviction for cattle theft.
40. *Ponca City* (Oklahoma Territory) *Courier*, 9 December 1897.
41. Chapman, p. 337.
42. Gipson, pp. 146–147.
43. Ibid., p. 152.

44. Kenny A. Franks and Paul F. Lambert, *Pawnee Pride* (Oklahoma City: Oklahoma Heritage Association, 1994), p. 79.
45. Ibid., pp. 79–80.
46. Chapman, p. 338. Note: The case was *George W. Miller v United States,* 8 Okla. 315 (1899).
47. Donald E. Green, "Beginnings of Wheat Culture in Oklahoma," in *Rural Oklahoma*, ed. Donald E. Green (Oklahoma City: Oklahoma Historical Society, 1977), p. 59.
48. Ibid., p. 60.
49. Harth memoirs.
50. Ibid.
51. Miller, pp. 265–266.
52. Harth memoirs.
53. Ibid.
54. Ibid.
55. Ibid.
56. Ibid.
57. Ibid.
58. Ibid.
59. Quoting Corb Sarchet, from records of Oklahoma Historical Society, Pioneer Woman Museum, Ponca City, Oklahoma.

Buffalo Man

1. Kent Ruth, *Oklahoma Travel Handbook* (Norman: University of Oklahoma Press, 1977), pp. 148–149.
2. Records supplied by Richard Kay Wortman, regional historian, Arkansas City, Kansas, 1994. Note: Wortman provided extensive documentation about the Millers and their ongoing feud with the railroad and with George C. Montgomery, a Santa Fe Railway detective.
3. Ibid.
4. Fred Gipson, *Fabulous Empire* (Boston: Houghton Mifflin Company, 1946), p. 148.
5. Wortman records.
6. Ibid.
7. Ibid.
8. Ibid.
9. Ibid.
10. Ibid.
11. *Arkansas City* (Kansas) *Traveler*, 18 July 1901.
12. Ibid.
13. Ibid.
14. Wortman records.
15. Ibid. Note: *Rub someone out*, a term commonly used in the West, originated in Plains Indian sign language, which used a rubbing motion to symbolize killing someone.
16. Ibid.
17. Ibid.
18. Ibid.; *Perry* (Oklahoma Territory) *Enterprise Times*, 7 October 1901, provided by Steve H. Bunch, Perry, Oklahoma.
19. Wortman records.
20. *Perry* (Oklahoma Territory) *Enterprise Times*, 4 November 1901; 15 November 1901.
21. *Perry* (Oklahoma Territory) *Republican*, 3 January 1902.
22. Ibid.
23. Reprinted in the *Perry* (Oklahoma Territory) *Enterprise Times*, 7 February 1902.
24. Ibid.
25. Wortman records.
26. *Perry* (Oklahoma Territory) *Enterprise Times*, 20 May 1902.

27. Wortman records.
28. Ibid.
29. *Perry* (Oklahoma Territory) *Republican*, 13 June 1902.
30. Wortman records.
31. Ibid.
32. Ibid.
33. Ibid.
34. Joe Colby, interview by author, 1 October 1994. Note: Joe Colby, the son of Bert Colby, maintains the family ranch.
35. *Morrison* (Oklahoma) *Transcript*, 16 March 1949.
36. From the 101 Ranch Collection of John Cooper, Stroud, Oklahoma.

CHAPTER 21: FULL CIRCLE

1. William Shakespeare, *King Lear*, 5.3.176. Note: The tragedy of Lear, king of Britain, is the story of a ruler who prepares to divide his kingdom among his three children. In Lear's case, the children are daughters and not sons.
2. Chris Emmett, *Shanghai Pierce: A Fair Likeness* (Norman: University of Oklahoma Press, 1953), pp. 232–233.
3. Ibid., p. 238.
4. Ibid.
5. Ibid., p. 270.
6. Ibid., pp. 297–298.
7. Joe Colby, interview by author, 1 October 1994.
8. Alice Miller Harth, "What Goes Up," a family memoir.
9. From the 101 Ranch Collection of John Cooper, Stroud, Oklahoma.
10. Ibid.
11. *Ponca City* (Oklahoma Territory) *Courier*, 27 April 1903.
12. Ibid.
13. George England Miller, "The Great Ranches: The Millers and the 101 Ranch," in *The Last Run: Kay County, Oklahoma, 1893*, stories assembled by the Ponca City Chapter of the Daughters of the American Revolution, (Ponca City: The Courier Printing Company, 1939), p. 262.
14. Ibid.
15. Memoirs of Alice Miller Harth.
16. Records from the Pioneer Woman Museum, Oklahoma Historical Society, Ponca City, including the National Register of Historic Places Inventory-Nomination Form, 11 April 1973.
17. Sally Wilcox, *Winfield and the Walnut Valley* (Arkansas City, Kansas: Gilliland's Publishing, 1975), pp. 20–21.
18. *Ponca City* (Oklahoma) News, 16 September 1960.
19. District Court of Noble County, Oklahoma Territory, March Term, 1903. *The United States v George W. Miller of Noble County*. Records provided to the author by Steve H. Bunch, Perry, Oklahoma.
20. Fred Gipson, *Fabulous Empire* (Boston: Houghton Mifflin Company, 1946), p. 181.
21. Harth memoirs.
22. *Kansas City* (Missouri) *Star*, 27 April 1903.
23. *Perry* (Oklahoma Territory) *Republican*, 1 May 1903. Note: Miller's obituary in the *Kansas City Star*, on April 27, 1903, discussed the fact that he was under bond at the time of his death "for alleged connection with the murder of George C. Montgomery, a Santa Fe detective."
24. *Kansas City Star*, 27 April 1903.
25. Ibid.
26. Ibid.
27. Zack Miller Jr., interview by author, 12 October 1988.

The Yaller Dog

1. Edward Buscombe, ed., *The BFI Companion to the Western* (New York: Da Capo Press, Inc., 1988), p. 214.
2. Ibid., pp. 177, 130.
3. Ibid., p. 146.
4. Bruce Watson, "If His Life Were A Short Story, Who'd Ever Believe It?," *Smithsonian*, January 1997, p. 97.
5. Lee Schultz, "Owen Wister: 'Smile!,' " in *Wild West Show!*, ed. Thomas W. Knowles and Joe R. Lansdale (New York: Wings Books, 1994), p. 66.
6. Ibid.
7. George N. Fenin and William K. Everson, *The Western: From Silents to Cinerama* (New York: The Orion Press, 1962), p. 47.
8. Ibid.
9. Buscombe, p. 265.
10. Ibid.
11. Fenin and Everson, p. 52.
12. Ibid.
13. Clifton Daniel, ed., *Chronicle of the 20th Century* (Mount Kisco, New York: Chronicle Publications, Inc., 1988), p. 55.
14. From the 101 Ranch Collection of John Cooper, Stroud, Oklahoma.
15. Ibid.
16. Ibid.
17. Ibid. Note: According to John Cooper's undated records, Ernest Jones, a former Noble County judge, wrote the poem about Buck Eldridge and the "yaller dog."

CHAPTER 22: THE MILLER BROTHERS

1. John Thompson, *Closing the Frontier* (Norman: University of Oklahoma Press, 1986), p. 122. Note: According to Thompson, the second key to the success of the 101 Ranch was the discovery of oil on the ranch, an event that will be discussed in detail later in this book.
2. Mack Wafer, interview by Ruby Wolfenbarger, Sentinel, Oklahoma, 23 March 1938, Oklahoma Historical Society files, Interview 10300, IPH vol. 95, p. 202.
3. From obituary of George Washington Miller, *Kansas City Star*, 27 April 1903, vertical files at the Oklahoma Historical Society Library, Oklahoma City.
4. From the Alma Miller England files of Oklahoma Historical Society, Pioneer Woman Museum, Ponca City, Oklahoma.
5. Ibid.
6. Ibid.
7. Ibid.
8. Ibid.; Fred Gipson, *Fabulous Empire* (Boston: Houghton Mifflin Company, 1946), p. 184.
9. Alice Miller Harth, "What Goes Up," a family memoir.
10. Alice Miller Harth memoirs, 1983.
11. Ibid.
12. Ibid.
13. Ibid.
14. Harth, "What Goes Up."
15. Ibid.
16. Ibid.
17. From the 101 Ranch collection of Jerry and Ruth Murphey, Corpus Christi, Texas.
18. Ibid.
19. Corb Sarchet, "Roundup Started on 101 Ranch," *The 101 Magazine*, September 1926, p. 10.
20. Howard F. Stein and Robert F. Hill, eds., *The Culture of Oklahoma* (Norman: University

of Oklahoma Press, 1993), p. 181. Note: After statehood in 1907, Greer became involved in a major dispute with the Democratic leadership of the new state. As a result, the seat of government was shifted from Guthrie to Oklahoma City, leading to the collapse of Greer's publishing company.

21. Glenn Shirley, foreword to *The 101 Ranch*, by Ellsworth Collings and Alma Miller England (Norman: University of Oklahoma Press, 1937, 1971), p. xii.
22. Ibid.
23. William Wirt Mills, *St. Louis: The Central Great City of the Union* (New York: Moses King, 1909), p. 4. Note: This booklet, from the author's collection, was distributed by J. S. Merrell Drug Company, Saint Louis, Missouri.
24. Margaret Johanson Witherspoon, *Remembering the St. Louis World's Fair* (Saint Louis: Comfort Printing Company, 1973), pp. 10–12.
25. W. W. Ellis, *World's Fair Handy Guide for Tourists* (Saint Louis: National Publishing Company, 1904), p. 27. Note: From the author's collection.
26. Ibid., p. 33.
27. Ibid., p. 34.
28. Gipson, p. 227.
29. Ibid.
30. Sarchet, p. 10
31. Glass cane in the 101 Ranch Collection of Jerry and Ruth Murphey.
32. From documents in the 101 Collection of John Cooper, Stroud, Oklahoma.
33. Ibid.
34. Sarchet, p. 10.
35. Ibid.

The World's First Cowgirl Meets the Cherokee Kid

1. Vincent dePaul Lupriano and Ken W. Sayers, *It Was a Very Good Year: A Cultural History of the United States from 1776 to the Present* (Holbrook, Massachusetts: Bob Adams, Inc., 1994), p. 215. Note: On November 8, 1904, Theodore Roosevelt, who had succeeded to the presidency in 1901 after McKinley's assassination, won a full four-year term of office by a margin of almost two million votes, the largest number ever received by any candidate up to that time.
2. Ibid. Note: The Russo-Japanese War (1904–1905) ended with the signing of a peace treaty on September 5, 1905, at Portsmouth, New Hampshire. President Roosevelt mediated and played a key role in arranging the treaty. He received the Nobel Peace Prize for his efforts.
3. Ibid.
4. Alice Miller Harth, "What Goes Up," a family memoir.
5. Ibid.
6. Don Russell, *The Wild West: A History of the Wild West Shows* (Fort Worth: Amon Carter Museum of Western Art, 1970), p. 79.
7. Paul O'Neil, *The End and the Myth* (Alexandria, Virginia: Time-Life Books Inc., 1979), p. 103.
8. Russell, p. 79, quoting from the *New York World*, 7 July 1900.
9. Ibid.
10. Kathryn Stansbury, *Lucille Mulhall: Wild West Cowgirl* (Mulhall, Oklahoma: Homestead Heirlooms Publishing Company, 1985), p. v of prologue. Note: This well-researched book is the definitive work on the life and times of the Mulhall family. Stansbury also wrote a history of Mulhall, Oklahoma.
11. Ibid., pp. v–vi of prologue.
12. Ibid. Note: No evidence has been found that the Joseph Mulhalls ever legally adopted Zack. It is believed that Zack was born in Cooper County, Missouri, although he sometimes said he was a native Texan. Both Zack and Mary Agnes were related through marriage or blood to the Joseph Mulhall family.
13. Ibid., p. vi of prologue.

14. Ibid.
15. Ibid., p. vii of prologue.
16. Ibid.
17. Ibid., p. 2.
18. Ibid., pp. 4–5.
19. Russell, p. 79.
20. Glenda Carlile, *Buckskin, Calico, and Lace* (Oklahoma City: Southern Hills Publishing Company, 1990), pp. 89–90.
21. Ibid., p. 90.
22. Stansbury, p. 7.
23. Carlile, p. 89.
24. Ibid., p. 90; Stansbury, p. 11.
25. Ibid., both references above.
26. Stansbury, p. 13.
27. Ibid.
28. David Randolph Milsten, *Will Rogers: The Cherokee Kid* (West Chicago, Illinois: Glean-heath Publishers, 1987), p. 21.
29. Ibid., pp. 23, 37.
30. Joseph H. Carter, *Never Met A Man I Didn't Like: The Life and Writings of Will Rogers* (New York: Avon Books, 1991), p. 34. Note: In an introductory note in David Randolph Milsten's *Will Rogers: The Cherokee Kid*, the author states that "Cherokee Kid" was Rogers' favorite nickname.
31. Stansbury, p. 13. Note: This column was published in its entirety in October 1931 by the McNaught Syndicate.
32. Ibid., pp. 13–15. Note: Stansbury points out in her accompanying text notes that Lucille Mulhall was indeed the "first cowgirl" because, at the time, other female performers in Wild West shows did not rope steers or compete directly with male riders. Most of them were specialists, such as sharpshooters Annie Oakley and May Lillie, wife of famed showman Pawnee Bill.

CHAPTER 23: A STATE OF MIND

1. Gerald D. Nash, *Creating the West: Historical Interpretations, 1890–1990* (Albuquerque: University of New Mexico Press, 1991), p. 220.
2. From a review of the Articles of Incorporation and the Book of By-Laws of "The 101 Ranch," April 1905; transcripts of the official minutes of stockholders' meetings, June 1905. Copies from the 101 Ranch Collection of Jerry and Ruth Murphey, Corpus Christi, Texas.
3. Ibid.
4. Ibid. Note: According to the corporation by-laws, both Joe and George Miller received an annual sum of fifteen hundred dollars as compensation for their services.
5. Ibid.
6. Brian Lee Smith, "Theodore Roosevelt Visits Oklahoma," *The Chronicles of Oklahoma*, fall 1973, p. 268.
7. Ibid., pp. 268, 270, 271.
8. Robert B. Jackson, *The Remarkable Ride of the Abernathy Boys* (Norman: Transcript Press, originally published by Henry Z. Walck, Inc., 1967; reprinted by Levite of Apache, 1988, copyright 1993 by Robert B. Jackson), p. 12. Note: Quanah Parker was the son of Cynthia Ann Parker, a white woman taken captive by Indians when she was a girl, and Peta Nacona, a prominent Comanche chief.
9. Theodore Roosevelt, "A Wolf Hunt in Oklahoma," *Scribner's Magazine*, November 1905, p. 513.
10. *Daily Oklahoman*, Oklahoma City, 1 July 1900.
11. Ibid.
12. Kathryn Stansbury, *Lucille Mulhall: Wild West Cowgirl* (Mulhall, Oklahoma: Homestead Heirlooms Publishing Company, 1985), pp. 17, 33. Note: The Frisco Railroad considered

Zack Mulhall's band good advertising. Although Mulhall managed the musicians, the Frisco furnished the cowboy costumes and paid all travel expenses. Charles Seymour served as bandleader.

13. Ben Yagoda, *Will Rogers: A Biography* (New York: Alfred A. Knopf, Inc., 1993), p. 46. Note: "When Will joined up, he was given a trombone and told to mime playing it between ropings."
14. Smith, p. 267.
15. *Daily Oklahoman*, Oklahoma City, 4 July 1900, p. 2.
16. Ibid.
17. La-Vere S. Anderson, "Original Cowgirl Still Lives on Ranch," *Tulsa World*, 28 June 1931, p. 11.
18. Ibid.
19. Ibid.
20. Stansbury, p. 19.
21. Ibid., pp. 19, 21.
22. Note: Another version of the wolf story suggested that Lucille tracked down a killer lobo that had devoured several of her father's calves. She shot the wolf through the heart with her trusty Winchester, and the pelt was stretched across a wall in her mother's drawing room.
23. Daniel, p. 31.
24. Arrell Morgan Gibson, *Oklahoma: A History of Five Centuries*, 2nd ed. (Norman: University of Oklahoma Press, 1981), pp. 188–189.
25. Sam Henderson, "Show Biz Western Style," *Wild West*, October 1994, p. 36.
26. Ibid.
27. Gibson, p. 189.
28. Stansbury, pp. 23, 25.
29. Ibid., p. 47; Anderson, p. 11.
30. Ibid.
31. Glenda Carlile, *Buckskin, Calico, and Lace* (Oklahoma City: Southern Hills Publishing Company, 1990), pp. 95.
32. David Randolph Milsten, *Will Rogers: The Cherokee Kid* (West Chicago, Illinois: Gleanheath Publishers, 1987), p. 45.
33. Yagoda, p. 75.
34. Ibid., pp. 70–71.
35. Ibid., p. 71.
36. Ibid.
37. Ibid.
38. Ibid., p. 72.
39. Ibid., pp. 72–73. Note: The venerable *New York Times*, in reporting the shooting incident, made factual errors, including the bold headline, "President's Friend Slays," when, in fact, no fatalities occurred.
40. Ibid., p. 73.
41. Stansbury, pp. 56–57.
42. Ibid., p. 58.
43. Ibid., p. 61.
44. Ibid., pp. 61, 63.
45. Ibid., p. 65.
46. Ibid., pp. 65, 81. Note: "There was a great friendship between these two wild west show families. Both Joe and Zack Miller were with the Mulhalls at Madison Square Garden. . . ."
47. Robert G. Athearn, *The Mythic West in Twentieth Century America* (Lawrence: University of Kansas Press, 1986), p. 274.

King of the Cowboys

1. Kathryn Stansbury, *Lucille Mulhall: Wild West Cowgirl* (Mulhall, Oklahoma: Homestead Heirlooms Publishing Company, 1985), p. 65.

2. Paul E. Mix, *The Life and Legend of Tom Mix* (Cranbury, New Jersey: A. S. Barnes and Co., Inc., 1972), pp. 16–17. Note: The Reverend Thomas Hollen married the widowed grandmother of Elizabeth Smith, Tom Mix's mother. Hollen later performed the wedding ceremony uniting Elizabeth and Edwin Mix.
3. Ben Yagoda, *Will Rogers: A Biography* (New York: Alfred A. Knopf, Inc., 1993), pp. 82–83. Note: Some sources add an extra letter *i* and spell the stage name Mixico.
4. Mix, p. 30. Note: When he enlisted in the army, Tom Mix changed not only his middle name but also lied about his date and place of birth.
5. Ibid., p. 43; files of Oklahoma Tourism and Recreation Department, Travel and Tourism Division, Oklahoma City. Note: Some sources claim Mix also tended bar in Oklahoma City and worked briefly as a barkeep in the saloon of the Royal Hotel and Opera House in Guthrie.
6. Howard F. Stein and Robert F. Hill, eds., *The Culture of Oklahoma* (Norman: University of Oklahoma Press, 1993), p. 174. Note: A second-floor plan of the Blue Belle Saloon appears on page 175 of Stein and Hill's book.
7. Ibid.
8. Fred Gipson, *Fabulous Empire* (Boston: Houghton Mifflin Company, 1946), p. 233. Note: "Tom [Mix] was shoving drinks across the mahogany in an Oklahoma City [sic] bar when Zack blew into town for a cowman's convention in 1902 and ran into him. They got into a conversation and Tom let it be known that he would admire to be a cowhand."
9. M. G. "Bud" Norris, *The Tom Mix Book* (Waynesville, North Carolina: The World of Yesterday, 1989), p. 13.
10. Mix, pp. 16–17.
11. Ibid., p. 18.
12. Ibid., pp. 18, 20.
13. John. H. Nicholas, *Tom Mix: Riding up to Glory* (Kansas City: Lowell Press, 1980), p. 3.
14. Ibid., pp. 3–4.
15. Ibid., p. 5.
16. Mix, pp. 30–31. Note: According to National Archives records, Mix was first assigned to Battery M, Fourth Regiment, United States Artillery. The battery guarded the powder mills against the possibility of sabotage.
17. Ibid., pp. 34–37.
18. Ibid., p. 37. Note: Mix was promoted to first sergeant at Fort Hancock, New Jersey, on November 13, 1900.
19. Ibid., pp. 37–38.
20. Ibid., pp. 38–39.
21. Ibid., pp. 39–40.
22. Ibid., p. 43.
23. Ibid.
24. Ibid.
25. Ibid.
26. Ibid., p. 45.
27. Ibid.
28. Ibid.
29. Robert Heide and John Gilman, *Cowboy Collectibles* (New York: Harper & Row, Publishers, Inc., 1982), p. 44.

CHAPTER 24: OKLAHOMA'S GALA DAY

1. Don Russell, *The Wild West: A History of the Wild West Shows* (Fort Worth: Amon Carter Museum of Western Art, 1970), pp. 76, 78.
2. Kathryn Stansbury, *Lucille Mulhall: Wild West Cowgirl* (Mulhall, Oklahoma: Homestead Heirlooms Publishing Company, 1992), p. 65; records from the 101 Ranch Collection of Ruth and Jerry Murphey, Corpus Christi, Texas.
3. La-Vere S. Anderson, "Original Cowgirl Still Lives on Ranch," *Tulsa World*, 28 June 1931, p. 11.

4. Ibid.
5. Fred Gipson, *Fabulous Empire* (Boston: Houghton Mifflin Company, 1946), pp. 232, 233.
6. Ibid., p. 234.
7. Ibid., p. 235.
8. Ibid.
9. *The WPA Guide to New York City* (New York: Random House, 1939), pp. 204–205. Note: Originally named the Fuller Building but called the "Flatiron" because of its distinctive shape, the early skyscraper was built at the intersection of Broadway and Fifth Avenue, at Twenty-third Street. According to the WPA Guide editors, "policemen used to shoo loungers away from the Twenty-third Street corner, and the expression 'twenty-three skidoo' is supposed to have originated from this association."
10. Ibid., pp. 330–331.
11. Nathan Silver, *Lost New York* (New York: American Legacy Press, 1967), p. 51. Note: On June 16, 1890, the completed Madison Square Garden opened to a crowd of seventeen thousand people.
12. Ibid., pp. 51–52. Note: Irish-born Saint-Gaudens dressed his goddess statue with drapery, which was soon torn away by the winds that blew the ladies' skirts on the avenues below.
13. Stansbury, p. 65.
14. Ibid., pp. 65, 67.
15. Ben Yagoda, *Will Rogers: A Biography* (New York: Alfred A. Knopf, Inc., 1993), pp. 82–83.
16. *New York Times*, 23 April 1905.
17. Yagoda, p. 84; Stansbury, p. 71.
18. Stansbury, p. 75.
19. David Randolph Milsten, *Will Rogers: The Cherokee Kid* (West Chicago: Gleanheath Publishers, 1987), p. 51.
20. Stansbury, pp. 72–73.
21. Ibid. Note: There were several versions of this story, including one account that suggested that Tom Mix helped Rogers rope the wayward steer.
22. Yagoda, pp. 85–86, 89.
23. Ibid., p. 87. Note: Prior to opening at Keith's Union Square, Rogers did rope tricks at Shanley's, a popular Manhattan burlesque house, and appeared as a roper and clown during a three-day horse show in East Orange, New Jersey.
24. Ibid., p. 90. Note: Oscar Hammerstein's namesake grandson, Oscar II, a ten-year-old boy when the Hammerstein family hired Will Rogers, became a noted lyricist and librettist. His large body of work included the 1943 musical *Oklahoma!*, inspired by the musical play *Green Grow the Lilacs*, by Lynn Riggs, famed poet and playwright from Claremore, Oklahoma.
25. *Bliss, Oklahoma, In the Heart of the Rich Ponca Reservation*, promotional publication produced and distributed by the Miller family in 1911, from the 101 Ranch Collection of Ruth and Jerry Murphey, Corpus Christi, Texas. Note: As was often the case, the attendance number was exaggerated. Most credible sources state that approximately sixty-five thousand persons, not one hundred thousand, attended the June 11, 1905, event at the 101 Ranch.
26. From an undated 1905 editorial in the *Lawton* (Oklahoma Territory) *State Democrat*; records in the 101 Ranch Collection of John Cooper, Stroud, Oklahoma.
27. *Lawton State Democrat.*
28. *Lawton State Democrat.*
29. Ibid. Note: The *Lawton State Democrat* editorial was reprinted by the *Okmulgee* (Indian Territory) *Capital News*, one of three newspapers published in Okmulgee at that time.
30. May 1905 correspondence, from the 101 Ranch Collection of Jack Keathly, Ponca City, Oklahoma.
31. *Bliss* (Oklahoma Territory) *Breeze*, May 1905.
32. Ibid.
33. Ibid.

34. Ibid.
35. 1907 promotional publication for the 101 Ranch, from the 101 Ranch Collection of Ruth and Jerry Murphey, Corpus Christi, Texas.
36. Gipson, p. 229.
37. *Bliss Breeze*, May 1905.
38. Gipson, p. 229. Note: The international Boy Scout movement, started in 1908 by Sir Robert Stephenson Smyth Baden-Powell of England, had been patterned partly on an earlier American group which Dan Beard had led.
39. Ibid.
40. Ellsworth Collings and Alma Miller England, *The 101 Ranch* (Norman: University of Oklahoma Press, 1937, 1971), p. 144.
41. Gipson, pp. 228–229; documents in the Murphey Collection and Keathly Collection.
42. Keathly Collection.
43. *Lamont* (Oklahoma Territory) *Valley News*, 14 April 1905.
44. Ibid.
45. The *Bliss Breeze*, May 1905.
46. Ibid.
47. Gipson, p. 228.
48. *Bliss, Oklahoma*, 1911 promotional publication.
49. From the Oklahoma Historical Society's 101 Ranch files, Pioneer Woman Museum, Ponca City, Oklahoma.
50. Lizzie T. Miller, "Early Days at the 101 Ranch and Ponca City," in *The Last Run: Kay County, Oklahoma, 1893*, stories assembled by the Ponca City Chapter, Daughters of the American Revolution (Ponca City: The Courier Printing Company, 1939), p. 269.
51. Note: Most credible sources stress that only one automobile appeared at the 101 Ranch on the date of the buffalo chase.
52. Pioneer Woman Museum records.
53. Ibid.
54. Ibid. Note: Crowd estimates range from thirty thousand to one hundred thousand. The sixty-five thousand figure appears to be the most accurate.
55. 101 Ranch guest badge from the Murphey Collection.
56. 101 Ranch souvenir program and other material from the Murphey Collection.
57. Ibid.
58. Ivy Coffey, "Former Hands of 101 Ranch Reminisce at Reunion," *Daily Oklahoman*, Oklahoma City, 29 August 1969; Fred Davis, "Guarding Geronimo—A Thrill Tulsan Will Never Forget," *Tulsa World*, 19 July 1971.
59. Ibid.
60. 101 Ranch souvenir program.
61. Ibid.
62. David Roberts, "The Last Warrior," *Oklahoma Today*, May–June 1993, p. 34.
63. Ibid.
64. Gipson, pp. 229–230; Roberts, pp. 32–34. Note: Geronimo rode the range for the Millers in a Locomobile, although some sources claim the vehicle was a White Steamer.
65. Ibid.
66. 101 Ranch souvenir program.
67. Gipson, pp. 230–231; Pioneer Woman Museum files.
68. Gibson, p. 231.
69. Ibid.

Bill Pickett: The Dusky Demon

1. Note: Part of the text for this portrait, "Bill Pickett: The Dusky Demon," has been adapted from "101 Ranch," a story in *Songdog Diary: 66 Stories from the Road*, by Michael Wallis and Suzanne Fitzgerald Wallis (Tulsa: Council Oak Publishing, 1996), pp. 131–135.
2. Bailey C. Hanes, *Bill Pickett, Bulldogger* (Norman: University of Oklahoma Press, 1977), pp. 16, 21. Note: This biography is considered the definitive work about Pickett. The

author states that according to family tradition, the Pickett ancestors "were of mixed Negro, Caucasian, and Cherokee Indian blood." Pickett's mother was from a family of "Negro, Mexican, Caucasian, and Indian extraction."

3. Ibid. pp. 20–21, 29, 13. Note: Pickett's parents, Thomas Jefferson Pickett and Mary Virginia Elizabeth Gilbert, married in 1870. The eldest of their thirteen children, Willie M. Pickett, known as Bill, was born in Travis County, Texas, in 1871.
4. Elizabeth Atwood Lawrence, *Rodeo: An Anthropologist Looks at the Wild and the Tame* (Chicago and London: University of Chicago Press, 1984), p. 34.
5. Ibid.
6. Ibid, p. 25. Note: The competitive events in a modern rodeo program are divided into the rough-stock and the timed events. Standard rough-stock events are saddle-bronc riding, bareback-bronc riding, and bull riding. The timed events are calf roping, steer wrestling, team roping, and steer roping.
7. Ibid., p. 34.
8. David Dary, *Cowboy Culture: A Saga of Five Centuries* (Lawrence: University of Kansas Press, 1981, 1989), p. 333.
9. Hanes, pp. 25–27.
10. Ibid., p. 33. Note: Maggie, a native of Palestine, Texas, was the daughter of Sherman Turner, a white plantation owner. According to Hanes, Bill and Maggie's marriage license erroneously listed her surname as Williams, the name of her stepfather.
11. Ibid., pp. 34–36.
12. Bill O'Neal, "Bulldoggin' Bill Pickett," in *The West That Was*, Thomas W. Knowles and Joe R. Lansdale, (New York: Wings Books, 1993), p. 310.
13. Ibid.
14. Hanes, p. 40.
15. Ibid., pp. 45–46.
16. Ibid., pp. 53–54.
17. Ibid. Note: Weadick, who put up twenty thousand dollars for the Calgary Stampede, was one of the first show promoters to offer substantial money prizes.
18. Ibid., p. 59.
19. Ibid.
20. Ibid.
21. Fred Gipson, *Fabulous Empire* (Boston: Houghton Mifflin Company, 1946), p. 226. Note: According to Zack, "when they turned Bill Pickett out, they broke the mold."

CHAPTER 25: SHOW TIME

1. Ellsworth Collings and Alma Miller England, *The 101 Ranch* (Norman: University of Oklahoma Press, 1937, 1971), p. 161.
2. J. B. Kent, *Official Souvenir: The 101 Ranch, Bliss, Oklahoma* (Chandler, Oklahoma Territory: J. B. Kent, 1905), from the 101 Ranch Collection of Jerry and Ruth Murphey, Corpus Christi, Texas.
3. Ibid.
4. Ibid.
5. Ibid.
6. James H. Thomas, "The 101 Ranch: A Matter of Style," in *Ranch and Range in Oklahoma*, ed. Jimmy M. Skaggs (Oklahoma City: Oklahoma Historical Society, 1978), pp. 77–78.
7. Writings of Corb Sarchet of the 101 Ranch Collection of Jack Keathly, Ponca City, Oklahoma. Note: According to Sarchet, writing in *The 101 Magazine*, September 1926, "The Millers brothers frown upon the use of 'rodeo' and other such appellations . . . and remain true to 'roundup' as the best and most typical name for these wild west sports."
8. "Covington Diner Advance Publicity Car for Famous 101 Ranch Show," *Enid* (Oklahoma) *Morning News*, 29 July 1971; files of Oklahoma Historical Society, Pioneer Woman Museum, Ponca City, Oklahoma.
9. 101 Ranch Wild West show promotional materials from the 101 Ranch Collection of Jerry and Ruth Murphey, Corpus Christi, Texas.

10. Ibid.
11. William C. Davis and Joseph G. Rosa, eds., *The West* (New York: Smithmark Publishers, Inc., 1994), p. 170.
12. Ibid., pp. 170–171.
13. Undated and untitled Wild West show records, from the Murphey Collection.
14. Ibid. Note: Several of the Wild West shows survived only a single season and some failed in midseason.
15. Ibid.
16. Ibid.; *Anderson* (Missouri) *Argus*, 20 February 1903.
17. *Anderson* (Missouri) *Argus*. Note: Some sources on the James and Younger brothers, including Homer Croy, *Jesse James Was My Neighbor* (New York: Duell, Sloan, and Pearce, 1949), pp. 212–214, claim that the Cole Younger–Frank James Wild West returned to Maryville, Missouri, in 1908, but most authorities state that the show was finished after a single season.
18. Allen L. Farnum, *Pawnee Bill's Historic Wild West* (West Chester, Pennsylvania: Schiffer Publishing, Ltd., 1992), p. 11.
19. "The Editor's Corral," *Real West*, March 1967, p. 6.
20. Zack Miller Jr., interview by author, 12 October 1988.
21. Kathryn B. Stansbury, *Lucille Mulhall: Wild West Cowgirl* (Mulhall, Oklahoma: Homestead Heirlooms Publishing Co., 1985), p. 81.
22. Ibid., p. 83.
23. Ibid.
24. Ibid., pp. 83, 85.
25. Ibid., p. 85.
26. Ibid.
27. Ibid., pp. 85–86.
28. Ibid., p. 86.
29. Ibid.
30. *Ponca City* (Oklahoma Territory) *Daily Courier*, 2 November 1905, from the 101 Ranch vertical files at Ponca City (Oklahoma) Public Library. Note: The headline of this news story read, "Miller's Proposition."
31. From records, including documents from Oklahoma Historical Society, supplied by Lance A. Millis, Oklahoma State University, Stillwater.
32. Ibid.; data gleaned from Frank Eaton, *Pistol Pete: Veteran of the Old West* (Boston: Little, Brown and Company, 1952), the folksy story of Eaton's early life.
33. Eaton, p. 127.
34. Ibid.
35. Ibid.
36. Ibid. Note: In 1997, the National Cowboy Hall of Fame, Oklahoma City, posthumously honored Frank "Pistol Pete" Eaton with a Director's Award.
37. Arthur Lamb, *Tragedies of the Osage Hills* (Pawhusk, Oklahoma: Red Corn Publishing, 1964), pp. 122–124; documents from the 101 Ranch Collection of Jack Keathly, Ponca City, Oklahoma.
38. Keathly Collection.
39. Bailey C. Hanes, *Bill Pickett, Bulldogger* (Norman: University of Oklahoma Press, 1977), p. 58.
40. Lamb, p. 123.
41. Ibid., pp. 122, 124.
42. Kenny A. Franks, *The Osage Oil Boom* (Oklahoma City: Oklahoma Heritage Association, 1989), p. 119. Note: By 1926, as many as seventeen Osage men and women had been murdered in what investigators suspected was a conspiracy to steal the Indians' oil wealth.
43. Ibid., p. 122.
44. Nema Anderson, "Jim Collier—101 Ranch Showman," *Frontier Times*, April–May 1980, pp. 12–13.
45. Ibid.
46. Ibid., p. 13.

47. Ibid.
48. Ibid., pp. 13–15.

Pawnee Bill

1. From Oklahoma Historical Society documents and files at Pawnee Bill Mansion and Museum, Pawnee, Oklahoma.
2. Zack Miller Jr., interview by author, 12 October 1988.
3. Edward T. James, ed., *Dictionary of American Biography*, supplement 3, 1941–1945 (New York: Charles Scribner's Sons), p. 459.
4. Ibid.
5. Glenn Shirley, *Pawnee Bill: A Biography of Major Gordon W. Lillie* (Stillwater, Oklahoma: Western Publications, 1993), p. 17.
6. Ibid., p. 16.
7. Ibid., p. 19.
8. Ibid., p. 13.
9. Ibid., p. 19.
10. Edward Curtis, "Pawnee Bill—Ace Showman Looks Back over the Trail as He Nears his 80th Birthday," *Tulsa World*, 11 February 1940. Note: This feature story, carried by the Associated Press, was published a few days before Lillie's birthday celebration in Pawnee, Oklahoma.
11. Ibid.
12. Ibid.
13. Shirley, p. 21.
14. Ibid., p. 25.
15. Ibid., pp. 32–33.
16. Ibid., pp. 34–38.
17. Allen L. Farnum, *Pawnee Bill's Historic Wild West* (West Chester, Pennsylvania: Schiffer Publishing, Ltd., 1992), p. 7. Note: Lillie had many names. His family always called him Gordon, the old buffalo hunters knew him as Bill Lillie, the Pawnees named him Little Bear, and the Boomer settlers gave him the title "The Little Giant of Oklahoma."
18. Ibid., p. 8.
19. Shirley, p. 101.
20. Farnum, p. 8.
21. Shirley, p. 107.
22. Ibid.
23. Ibid., pp. 115–116.
24. Ibid., p. 116.
25. Ibid., pp. 116–117.
26. Ibid., p. 117.
27. Ibid., p. 118.
28. Ibid., pp. 120–121.
29. Farnum, p. 8.
30. Ibid.
31. Ibid., p. 9.
32. Kenny A. Franks and Paul F. Lambert, *Pawnee Pride* (Oklahoma City: Oklahoma Heritage Association, 1994), p. 107.
33. Ibid.
34. Shirley, p. 159.

CHAPTER 26: "GOING UP"

1. Attributed to Charles Cowskin, of the Cheyenne tribe, and excerpted from a 1908 courier for the 101 Ranch show.

2. Note: On June 16, 1906, President Roosevelt signed the Enabling Act, which provided for a state constitutional convention.
3. Barbara Williams Roth, "The 101 Ranch Wild West Show, 1904–1932," *The Chronicles of Oklahoma*, winter 1965–1966, pp. 419–420.
4. Ibid., p. 420.
5. 1906 program from the 101 Ranch Collection of Jerry and Ruth Murphey, Corpus Christi, Texas.
6. Ibid.
7. Ibid.
8. Ibid.
9. Ellsworth Collings and Alma Miller England, *The 101 Ranch* (Norman: University of Oklahoma Press, 1937, 1971), p. 146.
10. Ibid.
11. 1906 program from the Murphey Collection.
12. Collings and England, p. 148.
13. 1906 program from the Murphey Collection.
14. Bailey C. Hanes, *Bill Pickett, Bulldogger* (Norman: University of Oklahoma Press, 1977), p. 63. Note: Viewing the devastation caused by the 1906 earthquake in San Francisco so affected Pickett that it remained one of his favorite topics of discussion for many years.
15. 1906 program from the Murphey Collection.
16. Ibid.
17. Robert E. Cunningham, *Perry: Pride of the Prairie* (Stillwater, Oklahoma: Frontier Printers, Inc., n.d.), p. 84.
18. Ibid.; 101 Ranch records from the Murphey Collection.
19. Note: For a compelling perspective on Native American issues and images as projected by the media and the entertainment industry, read *The American Indian and the Media*, published in 1991 by the National Conference. Of particular interest is an essay by Paul O. Sand, "Cowboys and Indians."
20. Francis Paul Prucha, ed., *Americanizing the American Indians* (Lincoln: University of Nebraska Press, First Bison Book printing, 1978,) p. 311. Excerpted from report of 5 September 1890 in House Executive Document No. 1, part 5, vol. 2, 51st Cong., 2d sess., serial 2841, pp. lvii–lix.
21. Ibid., pp. 306–307. Excerpted from "Instructions to Agents in Regard to Manner of Issuing Beef," 21 July 1890, in House Executive Document No. 1, part 5, vol. 2, 51st Cong., 2d sess., serial 2841, pg. clxvi.
22. Ibid.
23. Rennard Strickland, *The Indians in Oklahoma* (Norman: University of Oklahoma Press, 1980), p. 109.
24. The 1915 "Miller Bros. & Arlington 101 Ranch Real Wild West Magazine and Daily Review," from the Murphey Collection.
25. Ibid.
26. Ibid.
27. Ibid.
28. Ibid.
29. Ibid.
30. Ibid.
31. Excerpted from an early Miller Brothers' 101 Ranch Wild West Show courier in the Murphey Collection.
32. Fred Gipson, *Fabulous Empire* (Boston: Houghton Mifflin Company, 1946), pp. 243–244; Don Russell, *The Wild West: A History of the Wild West Shows* (Fort Worth: Amon Carter Museum of Western Art, 1970), p. 78.
33. Gipson, p. 244. Note: The old Kansas City Convention Hall, at 220 West Thirteenth Street, was destroyed by fire on April 4, 1900, ninety days before the Democratic National Convention opened there. By the time the Democrats gathered in Kansas City on July 3, the building had been rebuilt.

Jane Woodend: Fence Rider

1. Lizzie T. Miller, "Early Days at the 101 Ranch And Ponca City," in *The Last Run: Kay County, Oklahoma, 1893*, stories assembled by the Ponca City Chapter, Daughters of the American Revolution (Ponca City: The Courier Printing Company, 1939), p. 267.
2. Note: According to Lizzie Miller, most of these guests were "Young men from the east, who aspired to play cowboy. . . ."
3. From the 101 Ranch Collection of Jerry and Ruth Murphey, Corpus Christi, Texas. Note: According to most authorities, the word *dude* can be traced to the British word for a fop, or dandy, derived from the German *dudendop*, or *dudenkop*, "a lazy fellow."
4. Excerpted from an article, "The Most Famous Ranch in the World," published in a courier for the 101 Ranch show of 1908, from the Murphey Collection.
5. Ibid.; "A Different Vacation on the Big 101 Ranch," a feature article in the same 1908 courier.
6. "A Different Vacation," 1908.
7. Ibid.
8. Ibid.
9. Ibid.
10. Quoted in Ellsworth Collings and Alma Miller England, *The 101 Ranch* (Norman: University of Oklahoma Press, 1937, 1971) p. 158.
11. Paul E. Mix, *The Life and Legend of Tom Mix* (Cranbury, New Jersey: A. S. Barnes and Co., Inc., 1972), p. 47.
12. Ibid.
13. Ibid., pp. 46–47.
14. Ibid., p. 47.
15. Excerpted from material in the 101 Ranch Collection of John Cooper, Stroud, Oklahoma. Note: Lew Stockdale, at age one hundred, could still recall having shaken hands with Abraham Lincoln. Stockdale claimed to have brought the first threshing machine to Kay County, prior to moving to Bliss.
16. Fred Gipson, *Fabulous Empire* (Boston: Houghton Mifflin Company, 1946), p. 234.
17. Excerpted from a feature article, "Life Took Her New York Riches, But Repays with the West's Joys," *Kansas City Star*, 29 October 1922, from the Murphey Collection.
18. Ibid.
19. Ibid.
20. Ibid.; a feature article, "Former Wealthy Society Woman Now Cowgirl on Ranch in Okla.," *Kansas City Journal-Post*, 1 October 1922, from the Murphey Collection.
21. Ibid.; an article by Ray Ditson, "Mrs. W. E. Woodend—'Fence Rider,'" *The World Magazine*, *New York World*, 22 October 1922, from the Murphey Collection.
22. *New York World*, 22 October 1922.
23. Excerpted from a feature article, "Dr. Woodend's Stable of Show Horses," *The Horseman*, 21 July 1903, from the Murphey Collection.
24. Vincent dePaul Lupiano and Ken W. Sayers, *It Was a Very Good Year* (Holbrook, Massachusetts: Bob Adams, Inc., 1994), p. 215. Note: This economic depression—the United States' nineteenth financial setback since 1790—lasted one year.
25. *Daily Oklahoman*, Oklahoma City, 12 November 1922, from the Murphey Collection.
26. Ibid.
27. Ibid.
28. Ibid.
29. Ibid.
30. Ibid.
31. Ibid. Note: According to the feature story which tells of the first encounter between Jennie Woodend and Tom Mix, the incident supposedly took place in 1906 at a Cummings Wild West Show performance in New Rochelle, New York, just north of New York City. Although the Millers had employed Mix as early as 1905, he may have been on temporary leave at the time of the meeting with Woodend. It should also be noted that in *Fabulous Empire*, pp. 240–241, reference is made to Dr. Woodend meeting Zack

Miller and Will Rogers in 1905 when they played Madison Square Garden with the Mulhalls.

32. Ibid.
33. Ibid.
34. Ibid; additional 101 Ranch files from the Murphey Collection.
35. Ibid. Note: Jennie Woodend sometimes was called Jane as a young woman and Howard was, of course, her maiden name.
36. Ibid.
37. Ibid. Stories about Jane Woodend's accident in the arena appeared in several New York newspapers including the *Sun,* the *World*, and the *Journal.*
38. Ibid.
39. Ibid.
40. Ibid.
41. Ibid.; *New York World*, 22 October 1922.
42. *New York World*, 22 October 1922.
43. Ibid.
44. *Daily Oklahoman*, 12 November 1922.
45. *New York World*, 22 October 1922.
46. Joe Miller Jr., interview by author, 3 October 1994.

CHAPTER 27: SPINNING WHEELS

1. Barbara Williams Roth, "The 101 Ranch Wild West Show, 1904–1932," *The Chronicles of Oklahoma*, winter 1965–1966, pp. 416, 418.
2. Miller family records from the 101 Ranch Collection of Jerry and Ruth Murphey, Corpus Christi, Texas.
3. Fred Gipson, *Fabulous Empire* (Boston: Houghton Mifflin Company, 1946), p. 1.
4. Memoirs of Alice Miller Harth, June 1983.
5. Ibid.
6. Ibid.
7. The *Ponca City* (Oklahoma Territory) *Daily Courier*, 5 January 1906.
8. Ibid.
9. Ibid.
10. Joe Miller Jr., interview by author, 3 October 1994.
11. Ibid.; Joe Miller Jr., interview by Neil Tuhoy, Ponca City, Oklahoma, 16 March 1972, Oklahoma Historical Society files, Living Legend Library, Oklahoma Christian College–Oklahoma Historical Society. Note: Although eighteen years apart, Miller stressed in both interviews that he liked his Ponca name. "It was so appropriate to be named 'Morning Star,' because I really am very bright in the morning, and tend to fade as the day goes on."
12. Alice Miller Harth, "What Goes Up," a family memoir.
13. Ibid.
14. Lizzie T. Miller, "Early Days at the 101 Ranch And Ponca City," in *The Last Run: Kay County, Oklahoma, 1893*, stories assembled by the Ponca City Chapter, Daughters of the American Revolution (Ponca City: The Courier Printing Company, 1939), pp. 267, 173.
15. Ibid.
16. Alice M. Allen, "The 'Big V' Ranch," in *The Last Run: Kay County, Oklahoma, 1893*, pp. 270, 271, 273, 275. Note: George L. Miller declared, "Vanselous is the best actual farmer in Oklahoma."
17. Memoirs of Alice Miller Harth, 1983.
18. Lizzie T. Miller, pp. 267, 269.
19. Harth memoirs, 1983.
20. Note: On November 16, 1907, Oklahoma and Indian Territories joined the Union as Oklahoma, the forty-sixth state.
21. Roth, p. 420. Note: Jamestown was officially founded on May 13, 1607, on the James

River in Virginia. The Jamestown Tercentenary Exposition opened on May 20, 1907, at Norfolk, Virginia.

22. Zack Miller Jr., interview by author, 9 September 1988.
23. Don Russell, *The Wild West: A History of the Wild West Shows* (Fort Worth: Amon Carter Museum of Western Art, 1970), p. 78.
24. 101 Ranch Wild West show records for 1907, from the 101 Ranch Collection of Jerry and Ruth Murphey, Corpus Christi, Texas.
25. Michael Wallis, *Oil Man: The Story of Frank Phillips and the Birth of Phillips Petroleum* (New York: Doubleday, 1988), p. 42.
26. Ibid., pp. 42–43. Note: The Ringling Brothers Circus of Baraboo, Wisconsin, was booked to open the Chicago Coliseum and inaugurate the first season. Frank Phillips was placed in charge of ticket sales for this event.
27. Show records from the Murphey Collection.
28. Chang Reynolds, "101 Ranch Wild West Show, 1907–1916," *Bandwagon*, January–February 1969, p. 6.
29. Bailey C. Hanes, *Bill Pickett, Bulldogger* (Norman: University of Oklahoma Press, 1977), pp. 66–67.
30. Reynolds, p. 6.
31. Ibid.
32. Ibid.
33. Ibid.
34. From records in the Murphey Collection, including a reference to Starr working for the Millers, in a "Picked up in the Rodeo Arena" column by Jerry Armstrong in the June 1971 edition of *The Western Horseman*, p. 74. Note: Henry Starr was one of the first loan customers to borrow money from Frank and L. E. Phillips after they established Citizens Bank & Trust in Bartlesville, Indian Territory, in late 1905. Starr borrowed five hundred dollars in cash and paid the note in full by the due date. He never robbed the Phillips brothers' bank.
35. Hanes, pp. 65–67.
36. Reynolds, p. 7.
37. Ibid.
38. Ibid.
39. Ibid.
40. Ibid.
41. Hanes, pp. 65, 68.
42. Lizzie T. Miller, p. 269.
43. Harth memoirs, 1983.
44. Ibid.
45. Hanes, p. 69. Note: Injuries were so commonplace during the shows that the Millers maintained their own on-site emergency hospital wherever they traveled.
46. Ibid., pp. 69–70.
47. Ibid., p. 65; records from the Murphey Collection.
48. Murphey Collection.
49. From the 101 Ranch Collection of Colonel Frank S. Giles, Oklahoma Historical Society, Pioneer Woman Museum, Ponca City. Note: A native of New York, Giles came to Oklahoma as a boy in the early 1900s and eventually settled at Bliss, where he became acquainted with the Millers and several of the principal figures associated with the 101 Ranch. In 1969, Giles presented his "scrapbook" of 101 Ranch memories and material to the Pioneer Woman Museum in Ponca City, Oklahoma.
50. Ibid. Note: Edward Milhau's grandfather, Count John de Milhau, fled Santo Domingo with others of the French aristocracy during the French Revolution, in 1789. He moved to Philadelphia and became a United States citizen. In 1813, he went to Baltimore and started a drug business which he moved to New York City in 1830. Milhau's father, Edward J. Milhau, died in 1891, and his son took over the business and remained active until 1907, when he joined the Millers at Norfolk.

51. Ibid.
52. Ibid.

The Band Played On

1. Jerry Armstrong, "Picked Up in the Rodeo Arena," *The Western Horseman* (Colorado Springs: Western Horseman, Inc., June 1971), p. 117.
2. Ibid.
3. Ibid.; Don Russell, *The Wild West: A History of the Wild West Shows* (Fort Worth: Amon Carter Museum of Western Art, 1970), pp. 27, 29, 47, 90.
4. Ibid., p. 90.
5. La Banca family records provided to the author by Jean La Banca Cox, great-granddaughter of Donato La Banca.
6. La Banca obituary, *St. Louis Globe Democrat*, 23 November 1942.
7. Thelma Peters, "The Music Man of St. Charles," *St. Charles Banner-News*, 20 February 1974.
8. *Miller Brothers & Arlington 101 Ranch Real Wild West Magazine and Daily Review*, 1915, from the 101 Ranch Collection of Jerry and Ruth Murphey, Corpus Christi, Texas.
9. La Banca family records.
10. Ibid.
11. Ibid.
12. Ibid.
13. Fred and Velma Strickland, interviews by author, Ponca City, Oklahoma, and South Haven, Kansas, October 1994.
14. Ibid; records provided by the Stricklands.
15. Ibid.
16. Ibid.
17. Ibid.
18. Ibid.
19. Ibid.
20. Ibid.
21. Ibid.
22. Ibid.
23. Ibid.
24. Ibid.
25. Ibid.

CHAPTER 28: HARD KNOCKS

1. Excerpt from letter from the Miller Brothers 101 Ranch Collection, the Wild West Show, University of Oklahoma Library, Manuscripts Division, Western History Collections, Norman, Oklahoma, hereafter referred to as 101 Ranch Collection, OU. Note: This letter, dated September 17, 1912, was one of innumerable job requests sent to the Millers through the years by young men and women from across the nation. On September 28, 1912, a response letter was sent to Queen Hovermale, the eager aspirant. Despite the candidate's obvious enthusiasm and the fact that she hailed from the Millers' ancestral stomping grounds of eastern Kentucky, the application was politely refused.
2. Ibid. Note: A notice for cornhuskers posted by the Miller brothers on October 3, 1911, seeking "a large number of men," offered to pay each laborer "three cents per bushel and board, or four cents per bushel where parties board themselves."
3. Ibid.
4. Ibid.
5. Chang Reynolds, "101 Ranch Wild West Show, 1907–1916," *Bandwagon*, January–February 1969, p. 7.
6. Terry Whitehead, "John Cudahy's Big Adventure," *Country Gazette*, Blackwell, Oklahoma,

March 1992, pp. 1–2. Note: Whitehead is a regional historian whose kinsmen were friends of the Miller family prior to the opening of the Cherokee Outlet, in 1893.

7. Ibid.
8. Ibid.
9. Ibid.
10. Ibid.
11. Frank Eagle, "Ponca Indian Chieftain," in *The Last Run: Kay County, Oklahoma, 1893*, stories assembled by the Ponca City Chapter, Daughters of the American Revolution (Ponca City: The Courier Printing Company, 1939), p. 338. Note: The author of this article was one of White Eagle's sons and the brother of Horse Chief Eagle. White Eagle died in 1914 and Horse Chief Eagle became the new chief.
12. Tom Mix, "Happy Days on the 101 Ranch," *101 Magazine*, March 1926, p. 3.
13. Glenn Shirley, *Pawnee Bill: A Biography of Major Gordon W. Lillie* (Stillwater, Oklahoma: Western Publications, 1993), p. 176.
14. Ibid., pp. 176–177.
15. Ibid., pp. 176–179. Note: Cody served as president of the new show and Lillie was vice president and general manager.
16. Ibid., p. 180; Kenny A. Franks and Paul F. Lambert, *Pawnee Pride* (Oklahoma City: Oklahoma Heritage Association, Inc., 1994), pp. 107–108.
17. Reynolds, pp. 7–8.
18. Ibid.; Miller-Arlington contract, 1909–1901, from the 101 Ranch Collection, OU.
19. 101 Ranch Collection, OU, correspondence of William H. England to Joseph Miller, 15 July 1913.
20. Ibid.
21. Reynolds, pp. 8–9.
22. Ibid., p. 8.
23. Don Russell, *The Wild West: A History of the Wild West Shows* (Fort Worth: Amon Carter Museum of Western Art, 1970), p. 82.
24. Ellsworth Collings and Alma Miller England, *The 101 Ranch* (Norman: University of Oklahoma Press, 1937, 1971), p. 162.
25. Ibid.
26. Ibid.
27. From a 1908 courier in the 101 Ranch Collection of Jerry and Ruth Murphey, Corpus Christi, Texas.
28. Ibid.
29. Ibid.
30. Ibid.
31. Ibid.
32. Ibid. Note: Historic sources offer varying opinions about this incident. Some Oklahoma historians blamed the attack on Kiowa warriors, but several others presumed that Cheyennes were responsible, although no absolute proof was ever established. Still another theory, mentioned by the Millers in their 1908 courier, was that the slaughter was carried out by white men disguised as Indians.
33. Ibid.
34. Memoirs of Alice Miller Harth, 1983.
35. Russell, p. 82.
36. Roth, pp. 420–421.
37. Ibid.
38. Reynolds, pp. 9–10.
39. Ibid.
40. Edith and D. Vernon Tantlinger Collection, University of Oklahoma Library, Manuscripts Division, Western History Collection, Norman, Oklahoma. Note: The Tantlinger Collection includes manuscripts, photographs, and postcards dealing with the couple's respective careers as show people from 1896 to the 1930s. The main body of material concentrates on the Miller Brothers 101 Ranch Wild West Show.
41. Ibid.

42. Ibid.
43. Ibid.
44. Ibid.
45. Ibid. Note: The Tantlinger Collection includes five scrapbooks and four diaries.
46. Ibid.
47. Ibid.
48. Ibid.
49. Reynolds, p. 10.
50. Ibid.

Princess Wenona: The California Girl

1. From the Lillian Smith files in the 101 Ranch Collection of Jerry and Ruth Murphey, Corpus Christi, Texas. Note: Jerry Murphey's grandmother was a 101 Ranch Indian dancer at the time Princess Wenona appeared with the Millers' early Wild West shows. Murphey and his wife are considered the definitive 101 Ranch collectors and preservationists, and he has developed a special interest in Princess Wenona. The Murphey Collection includes many of her personal items, correspondence, photographs, and other related documents and records.
2. Ibid. Note: According to many records and newspaper reports in the Murpheys' vast collection, considerable feeling existed among show people that Princess Wenona was a much better shot than Annie Oakley but never received the credit and critical acclaim she deserved.
3. Ibid.
4. Ibid. Note: The Murphey Collection includes the United States Census Report, Schedule 1, inhabitants in Tuolumne County, California, June 11, 1880. This county neighbors Mono County, Lillian Smith's birthplace.
5. Ibid.
6. Ibid.
7. Ibid.; Shirl Kasper, *Annie Oakley* (Norman: University of Oklahoma Press, 1992), p. 60; many other sources, including the leading biographies of Buffalo Bill Cody. Note: Kasper's comprehensive biography of Annie Oakley provides a compelling portrait of the woman who was a true American original. Kasper discusses at length the nature of the running feud between Oakley and Lillian Smith.
8. Murphey Collection; Kasper, p. 60.
9. Kasper, p. 60.
10. Ibid.
11. Murphey Collection; Glenn Shirley, "Four Lives of Princess Wenona," *Old West*, spring 1991, p. 14.
12. Joseph G. Rosa and Robin May, *Buffalo Bill and His Wild West* (Lawrence: University of Kansas Press, 1989), p. 91. Note: The popular Staten Island resort was named for its founder, Erastus Wiman.
13. Undated press accounts and records from the Murphey Collection.
14. Ibid.
15. Rosa and May, p. 91.
16. Don Russell, *The Lives and Legends of Buffalo Bill* (Norman: University of Oklahoma Press, 1960), p. 318. Note: Some authorities, including Russell, believe it was Annie Oakley who coached Baker and taught him to shoot marbles in the air.
17. Kasper, p. 61. Note: Oakley was born Phoebe Ann Moses on August 13, 1860, in Ohio.
18. Ibid., pp. 61–62.
19. Russell, p. 323; Rosa and May, pp. 94–95. Note: During the journey to England aboard the ship *State of Nebraska*, when many of Cody's company suffered from severe seasickness, some of the ninety-seven Indian performers believed the end was near and sang their death songs, although Cody tried to convince them the condition would pass.
20. Kasper, pp. 89–90.
21. Russell, p. 323. Note: The command performance took place on May 11, 1887. Besides

Lillian Smith and Annie Oakley, others presented to Queen Victoria included Nate Salsbury, an Oglala Sioux named Red Shirt, two Indian women with their babies in cradleboards and, of course, Buffalo Bill Cody.
22. Ibid.
23. Rosa and May, p. 119. Note: The historic event was recorded in the *Illustrated London News* of 21 May 1887.
24. Kasper, p. 89.
25. Ibid.
26. Ibid., p. 91.
27. Isabelle S. Sayers, *Annie Oakley and Buffalo Bill's Wild West* (New York: Dover Publications, Inc., 1981), p. 34, quoting Buffalo Bill Cody's *Story of the Wild West and Camp-Fire Chats*, published in 1888, p. 41.
28. Records and unidentified newspaper reports from the Murphey Collection.
29. Ibid.
30. Ibid.
31. Ibid. Note: The Murphey Collection includes examples of these cards, complete with bullet holes from Lillian Smith's repeating rifle.
32. Ibid.
33. Ibid.
34. Ibid. Note: Bob Johnson, of Meadville, Pennsylvania, provided *The Frontier Guide* of 1904 to the Murpheys.
35. Ibid.
36. Princess Wynona [sic], "Wintering at Malden," *101 Magazine*, May 1926, p. 4.
37. Ibid.
38. Undated newspaper reports from the Murphey Collection.
39. Murphey Collection, quoting the *Ponca City* (Oklahoma) *Democrat*, 21 September 1911,
40. Murphey Collection.
41. Ibid.
42. Joan Carpenter Troccoli, "The Sketchbooks of Emil Lenders: Down to the Soles of the Moccasins," *Gilcrease Journal*, spring 1993, p. 35. Note: Troccoli, former director of Gilcrease Museum in Tulsa, wrote this extensive feature story about Lenders for the inaugural issue of the *Gilcrease Journal*, published biannually.
43. Murphey Collection.
44. Ibid. Note: Lenders appeared in the 1924 film *Trail Dust*.
45. Ibid.
46. Ibid.; Troccoli, p. 35. Note: The reported size of the Thunderbird Ranch varies from twenty to forty acres.
47. Murphey Collection.
48. Ibid. Note: Lenders later lived in Tulsa and then spent his final years in Oklahoma City, where he died in 1934.
49. "Princess Wenona to Write her Memories," *Ponca City* (Oklahoma) *News*, 27 October 1927; "Princess Wenona's Pony 'Piebald' Dies at Age 25, *Ponca City News*, 28 October 1928.
50. Murphey Collection.
51. Ibid; *Ponca City News*, 3 February 1930.
52. Elston Brooks, *I've Heard Those Songs Before* (Fort Worth: The Summit Group, 1991), p. 2.
53. *Ponca City News*, 4 February 1930, p. 1.
54. Murphey Collection.

CHAPTER 29: SOUTH OF THE BORDER

1. Excerpted from a 1908 101 Ranch courier, from the 101 Ranch Collection of Jerry and Ruth Murphey, Corpus Christi, Texas.
2. From newspaper and correspondence files in the Murphey Collection.

3. Lesley Byrd Simpson, *Many Mexicos* (Berkeley: University of California Press, 1941), pp. 287, 293, 294; Nicholas Cheetham, *Mexico: A Short History* (New York: Thomas Y. Crowell Company, 1970), pp. 210–212.
4. Records and news accounts from the Murphey Collection.
5. Fred Gipson, *Fabulous Empire* (Boston: Houghton Mifflin Company, 1946), p. 259.
6. Murphey Collection.
7. Ibid.
8. Ibid.; James Norman, *Terry's Guide to Mexico* (New York: Doubleday & Company, Inc., 1965), pp. 240–241.
9. Norman, pp. 237–238. Note: The street was called *Paseo de Hombres Illustres* (Illustrious Men) but was renamed after the Reform Laws of 1861, following the removal of Emperor Maximilian and Empress Carlotta.
10. Ibid.
11. Bailey C. Hanes, *Bill Pickett, Bulldogger* (Norman: University of Oklahoma Press, 1977), p. 87.
12. Ibid.
13. Ibid. Note: Pickett was working on the Bailey Carson farm, where it was said he could pick as much as five hundred pounds of cotton a day.
14. Ibid.
15. Ibid., pp. 87–88.
16. Ibid., p. 88.
17. Ibid.
18. Ibid.
19. Ibid., pp. 88–89.
20. *New York Herald* story reprinted in a 1913 Miller Brothers & Arlington 101 Ranch Real Wild West courier from the Murphey Collection.
21. Ibid.
22. Ibid.
23. Ibid.
24. Ibid.
25. Ibid.
26. Ibid.
27. Ibid.
28. From newspapers and files in the Murphey Collection. Note: Pickett was first scheduled to bulldog a fighting bull named Bonito, a renowned beast that had so impressed the aficionados in a traditional bullfighting contest that his life had been spared in tribute to his courage. Many of the posters and handbills for the December 23, 1908, contest advertised Bonito—"The Bull of the most power and bravery that has trod the bull rings of the Republic." For a variety of reasons, bullring officials canceled Bonito's appearance at the last minute and decided to substitute Frijoles Chiquitos, an equally fierce bull. Some matadors believed Frijoles Chiquitos was an even stronger and more formidable opponent for the American bulldogger than Bonito.
29. Ibid.
30. Ibid.
31. Ibid.
32. Hanes, pp. 95–96.
33. Ibid., p. 97.
34. Murphey Collection newspaper files, especially courier reprint of the *New York Herald* story of 1913.
35. Ibid.
36. Ibid.
37. Ibid.
38. Ibid.
39. Ibid.
40. Ibid.
41. Ibid. Note: In some accounts of the famous bullring incident, 101 Ranch cowboy Stack

Lee was reported to have been the one who rescued Pickett. Still other reports credited an unnamed young matador with distracting the bull to give Pickett a chance to leave the ring. However, the *New York Herald* account, which states that Vester Pegg rescued Pickett, appears to be the most credible.

42. Ibid. Note: All published accounts of this escapade were in agreement concerning the amount of time Pickett stayed on the bull and in the arena.
43. Ibid.
44. Hanes, p. 103.
45. Ibid., pp. 103–104.
46. Ibid., p. 106.
47. Murphey Collection.
48. Ibid.

Willie-Cries-for-War

1. "The Story of Ernest W. Marland," in *The Last Run: Kay County, Oklahoma, 1893*, stories assembled by the Ponca City Chapter, Daughters of the American Revolution (Ponca City: The Courier Printing Company, 1939), p. 218.
2. Vincent dePaul Lupriano and Ken W. Sayers, *It Was a Very Good Year* (Holbrook, Massachusetts: Bob Adams, Inc., 1994, pp. 225–226. Note: Taft, whom outgoing President Theodore Roosevelt had endorsed, won the electoral college vote 314–169 and captured the popular vote with a majority of more than a million to become the twenty-seventh president of the United States.
3. *The Last Run*, p. 218.
4. Ibid., p. 216. Note: This profile of E. W. Marland is based on excerpts taken from a biography written for the *Oklahoma City Times* by Harold E. Mueller.
5. Ibid.
6. Ibid.
7. Ibid.
8. John Joseph Mathews, *Life and Death of an Oilman* (Norman: University of Oklahoma Press, 1951), p. 8. Note: This biography, considered the definitive work on the life and times of E. W. Marland, is by Osage historian John Joseph Mathews.
9. Ibid., p. 18.
10. *The Last Run,* pp. 216–217.
11. Mathews, p. 47. Note: The two were married on November 5, 1903.
12. *The Last Run,* p. 218.
13. Ibid.
14. Ellsworth Collings and Alma Miller England, *The 101 Ranch* (Norman: University of Oklahoma Press, 1937, 1971), p. 102.
15. Ibid., pp. 102–103.
16. Mathews, p. 77.
17. Ibid., p. 78.
18. Ibid., p. 79.
19. Ibid., p. 80.
20. Ibid., p. 79. Note: W. H. McFadden had left Pennsylvania for Hot Springs, Arkansas, to regain his health when George Miller and E. W. Marland approached him for his support. McFadden agreed to finance the drilling operations.
21. Collings and England, p. 104.
22. Ibid.
23. Ibid., pp. 104–105.
24. Mathews, p. 80.
25. E. W. Marland, quoted in the *Oklahoma City Times*, 20 July 1934.
26. Mathews, p. 80.
27. Kenny A. Franks, Paul F. Lambert, and Carl N. Tyson, *Early Oklahoma Oil: A Photographic History, 1859–1936* (College Station: Texas A & M University Press, 1981), p. 146.

28. Ibid.
29. Ibid.
30. Ibid.

PART FIVE: GALLOPING GHOSTS

1. Stan Hoig, *The Humor of the American Cowboy* (Lincoln: University of Nebraska Press, 1958), pp. 17–18.

CHAPTER 30: CREATING THE WEST

1. Kevin Brownlow, *The War, the West, and the Wilderness* (New York: Alfred A. Knopf, Inc., 1978), p. 254.
2. Joe Miller Jr., interview by author, 3 October 1994.
3. Chang Reynolds, "101 Ranch Wild West Show 1907–1916," *Bandwagon*, January–February 1969, p. 15.
4. The *Bliss* (Oklahoma) *Breeze*, 14 January 1909; *Ponca City* (Oklahoma) *Courier*, 14 January 1909.
5. Ellsworth Collings and Alma Miller England, *The 101 Ranch* (Norman: University of Oklahoma Press, 1937, 1971), p. 36.
6. Based on undated files and personal accounts in the 101 Ranch Collection of Jerry and Ruth Murphey, Corpus Christi, Texas.
7. Ibid.
8. Ibid.
9. Memoirs of Alice Miller Harth, 1983.
10. *Bliss* (Oklahoma) *Breeze*, 14 January 1909.
11. Ibid.
12. Ibid.
13. Ibid.
14. Harth memoirs.
15. Ibid.
16. James A. Browning, *Violence Was No Stranger* (Stillwater, Oklahoma: Barbed Wire Press, 1933), p. 94. Note: Geronimo, who had become a celebrity and a symbol of the American Indian, was buried beneath a stone pyramid in the Apache cemetery a few miles from the Fort Sill post cemetery.
17. Records of National Register of Historic Places, U.S. Department of the Interior, National Park Service, April 1973. Note: Kent Ruth of Oklahoma Historical Society prepared a National Register nomination form and subsequent documentation for the 101 Ranch in August 1972. Some of the data was taken from an Oklahoma Historic Site Survey conducted in 1958.
18. Ibid.
19. Ibid.
20. Ibid.
21. Ibid. Note: One of the Miller family's primary suppliers was Ranney-Davis Mercantile Company, wholesale grocers from Arkansas City, Kansas.
22. Ibid.
23. John S. Bowman, ed., *The World Almanac of the American West* (New York: Pharos Books, 1986), p. 264.
24. Clifton Daniel, ed., *Chronicle of the 20th Century* (Mount Kisco, New York: Chronicle Publications, 1987), p. 130. Note: The U.S. secretary of agriculture's thirteenth annual report, released in 1909, placed the corn-crop value at $1.7 billion.
25. From records and press clippings in the Collection.
26. Ibid.
27. Reynolds, p. 11.
28. Ibid.
29. Ibid., p. 14.

30. Ibid., pp. 13–14.
31. Ibid., p. 11.
32. Ibid., p. 14.
33. From ranch documents in the 101 Ranch files of the Western History Collections, University of Oklahoma, Norman, Oklahoma.
34. Ibid.
35. Bailey C. Hanes, *Bill Pickett, Bulldogger* (Norman: University of Oklahoma Press, 1977), p. 113.
36. Ibid., p. 117.
37. Ibid., p. 121.
38. Ibid., p. 108.
39. Murphey Collection; Ephraim Katz, *The Film Encyclopedia* (New York: Perigee Books, The Putnam Publishing Group, 1982), p. 1037. Note: William Selig was born March 14, 1864, in Chicago. He died in 1948.
40. Katz, p. 1037.
41. Ibid.
42. Ibid.
43. Ibid.
44. Reynolds, p. 15; Hanes, p. 113.
45. Reynolds, p. 15.
46. Ibid.
47. Paul E. Mix, *The Life and Legend of Tom Mix* (Cranbury, New Jersey: A. S. Barnes and Co., Inc., 1972), p. 50.
48. Ibid. Note: Olive bore Tom a daughter, named Ruth, in 1912. As stormy as all of Mix's marriages, the union lasted until 1917.
49. Ibid.
50. Buck Rainey, *Saddle Aces of the Cinema* (San Diego: A. S. Barnes & Company, Inc., 1980), p. 60.
51. Ibid. Note: Several sources stated that *Ranch Life in the Great Southwest* was filmed on a small spread owned by Tom Mix and his wife, Olive.
52. John Baxter, *Sixty Years of Hollywood* (Cranbury, New Jersey: A. S. Barnes and Company, 1973), p. 14.
53. Rainey, pp. 60–61.

Coney Island

1. Chang Reynolds, "101 Ranch Wild West Show 1907–1916," *Bandwagon*, January–February 1969, p. 18.
2. Ibid., p. 17.
3. Ibid.
4. Ibid.
5. Ibid., pp. 17–18.
6. Ibid., p. 18.
7. From May 1910 newspaper files of the 101 Ranch Collection of Jerry and Ruth Murphey, Corpus Christi, Texas.
8. Jerry Armstrong, "The Day the 101 Ranch Invaded Coney Island," *The Western Horseman*, March 1962, p. 60.
9. Ibid.
10. Ibid.
11. Ibid.
12. Lou Gody, ed., *The WPA Guide to New York City* (New York: Pantheon Books, 1939), pp. 471–472.
13. Ibid., p. 472.
14. Ibid., pp. 474–475.
15. Armstrong, p. 60.
16. Ibid.

17. Ibid.
18. Ibid.
19. Ibid.
20. Ibid.
21. Ibid.
22. Ibid.
23. Reynolds, p. 18. Note: The Miller-Arlington show closed its 1910 season at West Point, Mississippi, on November 19.

CHAPTER 31: CALIFORNIA DREAMING

1. Richard Griffith and Arthur Mayer, *The Movies* (New York: Bonanza Books, 1957), p. 88.
2. Zack Miller Jr., interview by author, 9 September 1988.
3. Ibid. Note: In this interview and in subsequent conversations, Zack Miller Jr. expressed his frustration with film historians and others who he insisted had failed to recognize the Miller family's many contributions to western motion pictures.
4. Ibid.
5. Kevin Brownlow, *The War, the West, and the Wilderness* (New York: Alfred A. Knopf, 1978), p. 223.
6. Ibid.
7. From the *Billboard* issue of 15 August 1911. Note: The magazine described Pickett as "... the modern Urus, in a demonstration of courage, nerve, strength, and agility in which he duplicated his feat conquering a Spanish fighting bull, unarmed and unaided, by forcing the largest of bulls to the tanbark of sheer strength." It is not known if the publication intended to compare Pickett to urus, an extinct bovine mammal believed to have been a forerunner of domestic cattle, or if it really meant to compare the cowboy to Uranus, the oldest god in Greek mythology.
8. Paul E. Mix, *The Life and Legend of Tom Mix* (Cranbury, New Jersey: A. S. Barnes and Co., Inc., 1972), p. 70.
9. Ibid., p. 51.
10. Ibid.
11. Bailey C. Hanes, *Bill Pickett, Bulldogger* (Norman: University of Oklahoma Press, 1977), p. 123.
12. Mix, pp. 51–52.
13. Ibid. Note: One story suggested that the Millers won fifty-three thousand dollars in the wager and that Mix and the others received hefty cash bonuses.
14. Ibid., p. 52; Fred Gipson, *Fabulous Empire* (Boston: Houghton Mifflin Company, 1946), p. 306.
15. Mix, p. 52.
16. Gipson, p. 306.
17. Ibid. Note: Gipson, among others, referred to the Mexican boy as Zack's adoptive son.
18. Ibid.
19. Ibid, pp. 306–307.
20. Ibid, pp. 307–309.
21. Mix, p. 51.
22. Ibid.
23. The 101 Ranch Collection of Ruth and Jerry Murphey, Corpus Christi, Texas; *Ponca City* (Oklahoma) *News* centennial edition, 12 September 1993.
24. Ibid., both references above.
25. Ibid., both references above.
26. Ibid., both references above.
27. Tom Mix, "Happy Days on the 101 Ranch," *The 101 Magazine*, March 1926, p. 3.
28. From the 1910 correspondence and media files in the Murphey Collection.
29. Ibid.
30. Ibid.
31. James A. Nottage, "Authenticity and Western Film," *Gilcrease Journal*, spring 1993, p. 57.

32. Chang Reynolds, "101 Ranch Wild West Show 1907–1916," *Bandwagon*, January–February 1969, p. 18; 1911 files in the Murphey Collection.
33. Murphey Collection.
34. Ibid.
35. Ibid.
36. Reynolds, p. 18.
37. Ibid., p. 18–19.
38. Ibid., p. 18.
39. Ibid.; Murphey Collection.
40. Murphey Collection; Reynolds, p. 19.
41. Reynolds, p. 19.
42. Murphey Collection.
43. Art Seidenbaum, *Los Angeles 200: A Bicentennial Celebration* (New York: Harry N. Abrams, Inc., 1980), pp. 16, 202.
44. Murphey Collection.
45. Ibid.
46. Ibid.
47. Carolyn Elayne Alexander, *Abbot Kinney's Venice-of-America,* vol. 1, *The Golden Years: 1905–1920* (Los Angeles Westside Genealogical Society, 1991), p. 60.
48. Ibid.
49. Tom Moran and Tom Sewell, *Fantasy by the Sea: A Visual History of the American Venice* (Culver City, California: Peace Press, Inc., 1979, 1980), p. 7. Note: The Kinney family's tobacco firm blended Virginia tobacco with imported Turkish varieties. It marketed Egyptian, Cleopatra, Flowers, and Sweet Caporal cigarettes.
50. Ibid., pp. 11–12. Note: Besides writing several books and pamphlets on social, scientific, and political topics, Kinney published a weekly newspaper, the *Los Angeles Post.* He also coauthored a report which recommended solutions and reforms for the treatment of Indians in California.
51. Ibid., pp. 15, 17.
52. Ibid., pp. 25–31. Note: Sarah Bernhardt's two days of performances in Venice, in May 1906, came during what was billed as her "Farewell America Tour." Although the aging actress received mixed reviews, she played to full houses and was summoned back to the stage for twenty curtain calls. Bernhardt returned to Venice seven years later as part of a vaudeville tour, but her engagement was cut short after two weeks when she was injured in an automobile accident.
53. Ibid., p. 29.
54. Alexander, p. 60.
55. Ibid.
56. Ibid., p. 61.
57. Ibid.
58. Ibid.
59. Ibid.
60. Ibid.

Bison 101

1. Ellsworth Collings and Alma Miller England, *The 101 Ranch* (Norman: University of Oklahoma Press, 1937, 1971), pp. 211–212.
2. An October 3, 1911, job posting typed on ranch letterhead and signed by the Miller Brothers, 101 Ranch, Bliss, Oklahoma. From the 101 Ranch Collection of John Cooper, Stroud, Oklahoma. Note: The letterhead states that the 101 Ranch is the largest diversified farm and ranch in the United States, boasting the largest herd of Hampshire hogs in the world, pedigreed seed corn of all varieties, and mixed carloads of alfalfa meal, corn chop, and seed corn. The last sentence of the advertisement states: "Come at once if you want work."

3. The Miller Brothers 101 Ranch Collection, University of Oklahoma Library, Manuscripts Division, Western History Collections, Norman, Oklahoma. Note: Unsigned letter believed to have been written by Joe Miller, January 8, 1911, Bliss, Oklahoma, during his holiday visit to Oklahoma after setting up winter headquarters for the Wild West show at Venice, California.
4. Ibid.
5. Paul O'Neil, *The End and the Myth* (Alexandria, Virginia: Time-Life Books, 1979), p. 7.
6. Vincent dePaul Lupiano and Ken. W. Sayers, *It Was a Very Good Year* (Holbrook, Massachusetts: Bob Adams, Inc., 1994), p. 237. Note: Just a short time after his triumphant return to the United States, Jim Thorpe was stripped of his amateur athletic honors, including his Olympic medals, when it was discovered that he had played semiprofessional baseball in 1909. On April 15, 1912, the *Titanic* struck an iceberg off the coast of Newfoundland and sank.
7. Fred J. Balshofer and Arthur C. Miller, *One Reel a Week* (Berkeley: University of California Press, 1967), p. 22.
8. Notes provided to the author from the files and exhibits of the American Museum of the Moving Image, Astoria, New York.
9. Balshofer and Miller, p. 24.
10. Ibid., pp. 25, 30, 31.
11. Ibid., pp. 24–25, 54. Note: According to Balshofer, "After a long weary ride of four nights and five days our small company, consisting of Evelyn Graham, Charles French and his wife, Charles Inslee, J. Barney Sherry, Young Deer and his wife Red Wing, Bill Edwards (the prop man), Maxwell Smith, who came in Arthur Miller's place, and I, arrived in Los Angeles the day after Thanksgiving, 1909."
12. Joseph Dispenza, "On Location in New Mexico," *New Mexico Magazine*, November 1984, p. 75.
13. Ibid.
14. Anthony Slide, *Early American Cinema* (New York: A. S. Barnes & Co., 1970), p. 81.
15. John Baxter, *Sixty Years of Hollywood* (Cranbury, New Jersey: A. S. Barnes and Co., Inc., 1973), p. 16.
16. Lewis Jacobs, *The Rise of the American Film* (New York: Harcourt, Brace, 1939), pp. 81–86.
17. Balshofer and Miller, pp. 54–55. Note: Two brothers—David and William Horsley—are reputed to have been the first film producers to settle in Hollywood. They leased the Blondeau Tavern and barn, at Sunset Boulevard and Gower Street, in October 1911, converted them into a studio, and made the first Hollywood film, *The Law of the Range*.
18. Ibid., pp. 63–64.
19. Ibid., p. 74.
20. Ibid., p. 76.
21. Edward Buscombe, ed., *The BFI Companion to the Western* (New York: Da Capo Press, 1988), pp. 26–27.

CHAPTER 32: INCEVILLE

1. Quote attributed to 101 Ranch cowboy and movie star Hoot Gibson from his Associated Press obituary, 23 August 1962.
2. Anthony Slide, *Early American Cinema* (New York: A. S. Barnes & Co., 1970), p. 81.
3. Kevin Brownlow, *The War, the West, and the Wilderness* (New York: Alfred A. Knopf, Inc., 1978), p. 237.
4. Ibid. Note: Born in Toronto in 1885, Allan Dwan played football at the University of Notre Dame before entering the film business in the early 1900s. From 1911 to 1913, Dwan made hundreds of films, mostly split-reel westerns, at American Film Company. He acknowledged that the prominent director D. W. Griffith was a major influence. Later, Dwan worked under Griffith at Triangle, where he directed Lillian and Dorothy Gish and formed a long working association with Douglas Fairbanks Sr.

5. Zack Miller Jr., interview by author, 9 September 1988.
6. L. G. Moses, *Wild West Shows and the Images of American Indians, 1883–1933* (Albuquerque: University of New Mexico Press, 1996), p. 227.
7. Brownlow, pp. 253, 256.
8. Ibid., p. 254.
9. Edward Buscombe, ed., *The BFI Companion to the Western* (New York: Da Capo Press, Inc., 1988), p. 355.
10. Ephraim Katz, *The Film Encyclopedia* (New York: Perigee Books, 1979), p. 597. Note: Thomas Ince's brothers—John and Ralph—also worked as actors and directors in the film business but did not enjoy the same fame as Thomas.
11. Ibid., pp. 596–597, 677.
12. Fred J. Balshofer and Arthur C. Miller, *One Reel a Week* (Berkeley: University of California Press, 1967), pp. 75–76.
13. Brownlow pp. 254, 256.
14. Ibid., p. 256.
15. Balshofer and Miller, p. 78.
16. Ibid., pp. 78–80.
17. Ibid., p. 80.
18. Ellsworth Collings and Alma Miller England, *The 101 Ranch* (Norman: University of Oklahoma Press, 1937, 1971), p. 119. Note: Will Brooks related this story to Ellsworth Collings on April 10, 1936, less than eight months before Brooks' death, on December 1, 1936.
19. Brownlow, p. 260.
20. Ibid., p. 256, quoting *Motion Picture World*, 27 January 1912.
21. Ibid.
22. Ibid., pp. 253, 257.
23. William H. Goetzmann and William N. Goetzmann, *The West of the Imagination* (New York: W. W. Norton & Company, 1986), p. 306.
24. Brownlow, p. 256.
25. John Baxter, *Sixty Years of Hollywood* (Cranbury, New Jersey: A. S. Barnes and Co., Inc., 1973), p. 19, quoting the November 1929 issue of *Photoplay*.
26. Goetzmann and Goetzmann, p. 307.
27. Ibid. Note: David Belasco (1859–1931), a famed American producer, director, and dramatist, was one of the most popular figures in drama at the time the article about Thomas Ince and the Bison 101 movies appeared in the 24 February 1912 issue of *Film Fancies*.
28. Brownlow, p. 261.
29. Collings and England, p. 119.
30. Carolyn Elayne Alexander, *Abbot Kinney's Venice-of-American*, vol. 1, *The Golden Years: 1905–1920* (Los Angeles Westside Genealogical Society, 1991), pp. 61–62.
31. Ibid.
32. Ibid.
33. "Standing Bear, The Friend of His Race," *The 101 Magazine*, July 1925, p. 6.
34. William J. Ehrheart, "Chief Luther Standing Bear II: Activist, Author, Historian," *Persimmon Hill*, autumn 1997, p. 44.
35. Balshofer and Miller, pp. 28–29.
36. Moses, p. 227.
37. Brownlow, p. 261.
38. Ibid.
39. Ibid.
40. Moses, p. 227.
41. Ibid. Note: Born in Japan in 1889, Sessue Hayakawa gave up a naval career for the stage. After playing various roles in Thomas Ince's films, Hayakawa worked with a variety of directors, including Cecil B. DeMille. Hayakawa left Hollywood in 1923 and continued his acting career in Europe and Japan. In the late 1940s, he made a comeback in Hollywood. He was nominated for an Oscar in 1957 for his portrayal of a Japanese army officer in *The Bridge on the River Kwai*. Hayakawa died in 1973.

42. Ehrheart, p. 45. Note: Despite his failure to convince Thomas Ince of the contributions of Indians to movies, Luther Standing Bear kept his ties to the film industry. He also remained in California for the rest of his life. Standing Bear went on to teach sign language at the University of California at Los Angeles and at the Southwest Indian Museum, and he helped form the first Native American branch of the Screen Actors Guild. He appeared in many silent and sound motion pictures and continued to fight for government reforms in Indian affairs. He died in 1939 and was laid to rest in Hollywood.
43. Balshofer and Miller, pp. 76–77.
44. Ibid., pp. 77, 80. Note: Henry Lehrman, born in Vienna in 1886, moved to America and was working as a trolley conductor when he launched his film career in 1909 by falsely presenting himself as an agent for the French Pathé company. As a result of this ploy, he earned his colorful nickname. Lehrman went on to become Mack Sennett's right-hand man in Hollywood. In the early 1920s, Lehrman's name was connected with the scandal involving Fatty Arbuckle in the mysterious death of starlet Virginia Rappe, who was Lehrman's fiancée.
45. Ibid., pp. 80–81.
46. Ibid., p. 81.

Hollywood-on-the-Arkansas

1. Ellsworth Collings and Alma Miller England, *The 101 Ranch* (Norman: University of Oklahoma Press, 1937, 1971), p. 119.
2. Ibid.
3. Ibid., p. 115.
4. Jack Spears, "Hollywood's Oklahoma," *The Chronicles of Oklahoma*, winter 1989–1990, p. 341.
5. Ibid.
6. Ibid., p. 342.
7. Kevin Brownlow, *The War, the West, and the Wilderness* (New York: Alfred A. Knopf, Inc., 1978), p. 281.
8. Spears, p. 342.
9. Ibid.
10. Brownlow, p. 282.
11. Spears, pp. 343–344.
12. From Fred Phillips' letter and Geronimo Film Co. promotional material sent to Waite Phillips, postmarked Lawton, Oklahoma, March 25, 1915, in the collection of the author.
13. Ibid.
14. Spears, p. 342.
15. Ibid., p. 344.
16. Ibid., p. 345.
17. Ibid.
18. Ibid.
19. Ibid., p. 346.
20. Paul I. Wellman, *A Dynasty of Western Outlaws* (New York: Bonanza Books, 1961), p. 293.
21. Ibid.
22. Ibid., p. 295.
23. Brownlow, p. 278.
24. Ibid., p. 275.
25. Wellman, p. 288.
26. Ibid., p. 289. Note: Some accounts, including the *Tulsa Democrat* of March 27, 1914, put Curry's age at sixteen at the time of the Stroud incident.
27. C. W. "Dub" West, *Outlaws and Peace Officers of Indian Territory* (Muskogee, Oklahoma: Muscogee Publishing Company, 1987), p. 127.
28. Brownlow, pp. 275, 277. Note: Henry Starr had worked on Zack Mulhall's ranch as well as on the 101 Ranch.

29. West, p. 127.
30. Ibid., p. 128; Spears, p. 347.
31. Ronald L. Trekell, *History of the Tulsa Police Department, 1882–1990* (Tulsa: Ronald L. Trekell, 1990), p. 15. Note: "The outlaws always pulled their crimes outside of Tulsa but lived near Tulsa and often walked the streets of Tulsa."
32. Danney Goble, *Tulsa! Biography of the American City* (Tulsa: Council Oak Books, 1997), pp. 39–40.
33. Richard Patterson, *Historical Atlas of the Outlaw West* (Boulder, Colorado: Johnson Books, 1985), p. 147. Note: Emmett Dalton served on the Tulsa police force as a special officer in 1911–1912.
34. Spears, p. 347. Note: Emmett Dalton moved to Los Angeles in 1920. He sold real estate, appeared in bit parts in movies, and wrote a popular book, *When the Daltons Rode*, which was made into a film. He died in Los Angeles in 1937.
35. Patterson, p. 147.
36. Ibid., p. 146.
37. Spears, pp. 347–348.
38. Patterson, p. 146.
39. West, p. 128.
40. Fred Gipson, *Fabulous Empire* (Boston: Houghton Mifflin Company, 1946), p. 140.
41. Patterson, p. 147.
42. From correspondence and media files in the 101 Ranch Collection of Ruth and Jerry Murphey, Corpus Christi, Texas.
43. Ibid.
44. Wellman, p. 290.
45. Ibid., p. 291. Note: Some accounts of the robbery erroneously report that W. J. Meyers used a shotgun.
46. West, pp. 128–129; Don Cusic, *Cowboys and the Wild West: An A-Z Guide from the Chisholm Trail to the Silver Screen* (New York: Facts on File, Inc., 1994), p. 273.
47. West, pp. 122, 128.
48. Wellman, p. 291.
49. From diary notations kept by a local person who attended Henry Starr's funeral and from other records in the collection of Washington County Historical Society, Bartlesville, Oklahoma.
50. Gipson, p. 140.
51. Gerald Lindemann, "Gunfighters and Lawmen," *Wild West*, June 1997, p. 75.

CHAPTER 33: A VANISHING BREED

1. Thomas McGuane, foreword in *Vanishing Breed: Photographs of the Cowboy and the West* by William Albert Allard (Boston: Little, Brown and Company, 1982), p. 6.
2. Vincent dePaul Lupiano and Ken W. Sayers, *It Was a Very Good Year: A Cultural History of the United States from 1776 to the Present* (Holbrook, Massachusetts: Bob Adams, Inc., 1994), pp. 238–239.
3. Miller Brothers Collection, Western History Collections, University of Oklahoma Library, Norman, Oklahoma, hereafter referred to as Miller Brothers Collection, OU. Note: In correspondence from this file addressed to George Miller and dated February 1, 1912, performer G. W. Edwards, of Des Moines, Iowa, noted that he had seen the Millers' advertisement in *Billboard*. Edwards, who had ridden with Buffalo Bill Cody's show for four years, was hired for the Millers' 1912 season.
4. Ibid.
5. Ibid. Note: According to records provided by Arkansas City, Kansas, historian Richard Kay Wortman, Walter T. "Uncle Doc" Miller died in St. Mary's Hospital in Winfield, Kansas, after five years' hospitalization.
6. Miller Brothers Collection, OU.
7. Ibid.
8. Ronald L. Trekell, *History of the Tulsa Police Department, 1882–1990* (Tulsa: Ronald

L. Trekell, 1990), p. 39. Note: Four Harry Steges have worked in the Tulsa Police department—"Harry Edward Stege, 1913–1916; Harry Leroy Stege, 1930–1961; Harry William Stege, 1955–1983; and Harry Gerard Stege, 1987–current. This is the only four-generation family to work for the Tulsa Police Department," p. 39.

9. Miller Brothers Collection, OU. Note: Correspondence dated December 28, 1911, on Dyer-Stege Detective Agency letterhead.
10. Ibid. Note: Correspondence dated January 2, 1912, on Dyer-Stege Detective Agency letterhead.
11. Ibid.
12. Chang Reynolds, "101 Ranch Wild West Show, 1907–1916," *Bandwagon*, January-February 1969, p. 19.
13. Ibid.
14. William Bryant Logan and Susan Ochshorn, *The Smithsonian Guide to Historic America: The Pacific States* (New York: Stewart, Tabori & Chang, 1989), p. 64.
15. Ibid.
16. Reynolds, p. 19.
17. March 30, 1962, Hazel King letter to George Virgines, from the 101 Ranch Collection of Ruth and Jerry Murphey, Corpus Christi, Texas.
18. Carolyn Elayne Alexander, *Abbot Kinney's Venice-of-America*, vol. 1, *The Golden Years: 1905–1920* (Los Angeles Westside Genealogical Society, 1991), p. 62.
19. Reynolds, p. 19.
20. Ibid.
21. Ibid.
22. Ibid.
23. 1912 records from the Murphey Collection.
24. Ibid.
25. Ibid.
26. Ibid.
27. Jerry Armstrong, "Picked up in the Rodeo Arena," *The Western Horseman*, March 1963, p. 45.
28. Ibid.
29. Ibid.; "Wild West in Bad Wreck," *Platteville* (Wisconsin) *Witness*, 14 August 1912.
30. Armstrong, p. 45.
31. Ibid.
32. *Creek County Republican*, Sapulpa, Oklahoma, 27 September 1912, p. 1; *Tulsa Daily World*, 25 September 1912, p. 8; *Daily Oklahoman*, Oklahoma City, 25 September 1912, p. 5.
33. Miller Brothers Collection, OU. Note: For example, on September 28, 1912, James T. Lloyd, chairman of the Democratic National Congressional Committee, wrote to George Miller at the ranch, soliciting information about the congressional races in Miller's district. Under separate cover, Lloyd also sent to Miller copies of several political speeches which he asked Miller to examine and circulate in the community. "How are the Republicans divided?" asked Lloyd. "Will any of them support the Democratic candidate? . . . Please give us any information you have with reference to conditions in the district, and incidentally what you think of the outlook for your State?"
34. Armstrong, p. 45.
35. Alexander, p. 64, quoting the *Venice* (California) *Vanguard* of 22 November 1912.
36. Miller Brothers Collection, OU.
37. Ibid. Note: Quoting from 7 December 1912 letter from Joe Miller to Dan Dix at Wisner, Louisiana.
38. Anthony Slide, *Early American Cinema* (New York: A. S. Barnes & Co., 1970), p. 99.
39. Ibid. Note: Universal Film Manufacturing Company was officially formed on June 8, 1912.
40. Kevin Brownlow, *The War, the West, and the Wilderness* (New York: Alfred A. Knopf, Inc., 1978), p. 257.
41. Fred J. Balshofer and Arthur C. Miller, *One Reel a Week* (Berkeley: University of California Press, 1967), pp. 84–85.

42. Ibid., p. 85.
43. Ibid.
44. Balshofer and Miller, pp. 85–88. Note: Carl Laemmle was elected president of Universal in July 1912. He remained president until 1936, when he sold his interest in the firm and retired. Laemmle died in September 1939, at age seventy-two.
45. Ibid., p. 89.
46. Ibid.
47. Brownlow, p. 257.
48. Balshofer and Miller, p. 91.
49. Miller Brothers Collection, OU, 7 December 1912 letter from Joe Miller to Dan Dix.
50. Ibid. Note: The letter from Mrs. Anson Yeager to the Miller brothers was written January 27, 1913, but was erroneously dated January 27, 1912.
51. Ibid.
52. Ibid. Note: Quoting from 31 January 1913 letter from George L. Miller to Mrs. Anson Yeager at Moline, Illinois.
53. Bailey C. Hanes, *Bill Pickett, Bulldogger* (Norman: University of Oklahoma Press, 1977), p. 127.
54. Ibid.
55. Murphey Collection.
56. Ibid.
57. Ibid.
58. Ibid.; Harry E. Chrisman, *1001 Most-asked Questions about the American West* (Athens, Ohio: Swallow Press/University of Ohio Press, 1982), p. 158. Note: According to James Earle Fraser, the image on the nickel was a composite likeness of three Indians. He recalled the names of two—Iron Tail and Two Moons, a hereditary chief of the Montana Cheyennes. Several people claimed to have been the third model, including John Big Trees, a Seneca, and George Squires, a Sioux. The bison depicted on the other side of the coin was modeled after Black Diamond, born in New York's Central Park Zoo.
59. Miller Brothers Collection, OU; Murphey Collection. Note: S. D. Myres manufactured high-quality saddles and cowboy supplies, including spurs, bridles, and blankets. The firm's slogan was "Ride Myres' Saddles and You Ride the Best."
60. Ibid. Note: The Millers claimed that Joe's saddle was the finest in the world and even issued postcards depicting it. The caption erroneously lists the manufacturer as S. D. Myers instead of Myres.
61. "101 Wild West Opens Season," *Ponca City* (Oklahoma) *Courier*, 5 April 1913, p. 1.
62. Ibid.
63. Ibid.
64. Miller Brothers Collection, OU; L. G. Moses, *Wild West Shows and the Images of American Indians, 1883–1933* (Albuquerque: University of New Mexico Press, 1996), p. 183.
65. Moses, p. 184.
66. Miller Brothers Collection, OU. Note: Joe Miller also sent complimentary watch fobs to Oliver Lone Bear and some of the other Indians who worked as movie extras under the direction of Will Brooks, at Venice, California.
67. Ibid. Note: Quoting from 19 July 1913 letter from Joe Miller to Major John R. Brennan at Pine Ridge agency.
68. Ibid. Note: Quoting from 24 July 1913 letter from Wayne Beasley to Joe Miller, on the road with the 101 Ranch show.
69. Ibid.
70. Ibid.
71. Ibid.
72. Ibid.
73. Ibid. Note: Quoting from 31 July 1913 letter from Joe Miller to J. S. Johnson, care of H. B. Marinelli, Ltd., Berlin, Germany.
74. Ibid. Note: Quoting from 25 August 1913 letter from Joe Miller to William E. Hawks at Bennington, Vermont.

75. Ibid. Note: Quoting from 25, 1913, letter from Joe Miller to William A. Bell at Sigourney, Iowa.
76. Ibid.
77. Hanes, p. 128.
78. Reynolds, pp. 19–20.
79. Hanes, pp. 129.
80. Ibid.
81. Ibid., p. 130.
82. 1913 records from the Murphey Collection.
83. Ibid.
84. Ibid.
85. Ibid.

Hollywood Buckaroos and the Gower Gulch Gang

1. From various files in the 101 Ranch Collection of Jerry and Ruth Murphey, Corpus Christi, Texas.
2. Ibid.
3. John Baxter, *Sixty Years of Hollywood* (Cranbury, New Jersey: A. S. Barnes and Company, 1973), p. 21.
4. Ray Riegert, *Hidden Southern California* (Berkeley, California: Ulysses Press, 1988, 1990, 1992), pps. 75–76.
5. Ibid., p. 76.
6. Carey McWilliams, *Southern California Country* (New York: Duell, Sloan & Pearce, 1946), p. 332.
7. Ibid.
8. Baxter, pp. 21–22. Note: DeMille not only directed *Squaw Man* but also coauthored the script. He remade the film in 1918 and 1930. No print of the original film exists.
9. Walton Bean, *California: An Interpretive History* (New York: McGraw-Hill Book Company, 1978, 1973, 1968), p. 319.
10. Diana Serra Cary, *The Hollywood Posse* (Boston: Houghton Mifflin, 1975; Norman: University of Oklahoma Press, 1996), p. 37. Note: Known in silent films as Baby Peggy, Diana Cary, daughter of movie cowboy Jack Montgomery, provides a rich medley of movie and Hollywood lore in this revealing book.
11. Ibid.
12. McWilliams, p. 332.
13. Cary, p. xiii.
14. Ibid., p. 47. Note: Hart's "Blue Streak" serials won him the title "America's Pal."
15. Miller Brothers Collection, Western History Collections, University of Oklahoma Library, Norman, Oklahoma.
16. Ibid. Note: From correspondence between Jane Bernoudy and the Millers, including a February 2, 1912, letter from Bernoudy which included her photograph on horseback and a list of her qualifications.
17. Zack Miller Jr., interview by author, 12 October 1988.
18. Ephraim Katz, *The Film Encyclopedia* (New York: Perigee Books, 1979), p. 1213.
19. Ibid., p. 435.
20. Ibid. Note: John Ford discussed with film director Peter Bogdanovich his role as an extra in *The Birth of a Nation.*
21. Bertrand Tavernier, "Notes of a Press Attaché: John Ford in Paris, 1966," *Film Comment*, July–August 1994, excerpted from a collection of interviews with American directors and screenwriters, originally published in France in 1993.
22. Katz, p. 237. Note: Marguerite Churchill and George O'Brien, star of many John Ford films, were married from 1933 to 1948. Their son, Darcy O'Brien (1939–1998), became a best-selling author who lived in Oklahoma at the time of his death.
23. Ibid., pp. 1213–1214.

24. Ibid., p. 203.
25. Ibid.
26. Yakima Canutt, *Stunt Man: The Autobiography of Yakima Canutt,* with Oliver Drake (Norman: University of Oklahoma Press, 1997), pp. 43–45.
27. W. David Baird and Danney Goble, *The Story of Oklahoma* (Norman: University of Oklahoma Press, 1994), p. 361.
28. Murphey Collection, including material from John W. Dunn, "Fabulous Empire and Its Money," *Numismatic Scrapbook Magazine*, March 1968, pp. 359–364.
29. Ibid.
30. Deborah Lightfoot Sizemore, "Cowboy Stuntman Yakima Canutt," *Persimmon Hill*, autumn 1988, p. 33.
31. Ibid., pp. 34–37. Note: Some of Canutt's major nonwestern film credits include *Gone with the Wind, Ivanhoe, Ben Hur*, and *Spartacus*.
32. Baird and Goble, p. 361.
33. Betty White Smith, ed., *Osage County Profiles* (Pawhuska, Oklahoma: Osage County Historical Society, Inc., 1964), p. 178.
34. From the private collection at Mohawk Trading Post, Clinton, Oklahoma.
35. Smith, pp. 178–179.
36. Ibid.
37. Katz, p. 621.
38. David G. Brown, "Last of a Breed," *American Cowboy*, September–October 1995, p. 43.
39. Ibid.
40. Ibid., p. 44.
41. "Actor Buried Near Pawhuska," Associated Press story, *Tulsa World*, 15 April 1996.
42. Alexander Walker, *Elizabeth* (New York: Grove Weidenfeld, 1990), pp. 4–5.
43. Ibid., p. 6.
44. From the 101 Ranch files of Richard Kay Wortman, Arkansas City, Kansas, including the *Arkansas City Daily Traveler*, 16 July 1921.
45. Walker, pp. 6–7.
46. Ibid., p. 7.
47. Ibid., pp. 8–9.
48. Ibid., p. 23.
49. Ibid., p. 25; Elizabeth Taylor, *Elizabeth Taylor* (New York: Harper & Row, Publishers, Inc., 1964, 1965), p. 4.
50. Walker, p. 6.
51. William Bryant Logan and Susan Ochshorn, *The Smithsonian Guide to Historic America: The Pacific States* (New York: Stewart, Tabori & Chang, 1989), pp. 39, 41. Note: The famous sign cost $21,000 to erect in 1923. In 1974, concerned celebrities restored the sign at a cost of $27,500 per letter.

CHAPTER 34: WHERE THE WEST COMMENCES

1. Jack Weston, *The Real American Cowboy* (New York: New Amsterdam Books, 1985), p. 209. Note: These are supposedly the last words Mix uttered to movie mogul William Fox.
2. Note: The line "where the West commences" is from "Don't Fence Me In," the nation's top song for eight consecutive weeks in late 1944 and early 1945.
3. Joe Colby, interview by author, 1 October 1994.
4. Ibid.
5. The 1914 files from the 101 Ranch Collection of Jerry and Ruth Murphey, Corpus Christi, Texas; Zack Miller Jr., interviews by author and various correspondence and conversations between Miller and the author throughout August and October 1988.
6. Ibid., both references above.
7. Ibid., both references above.
8. Ibid., both references above.
9. Murphey Collection; Ephraim Katz, *The Film Encyclopedia* (New York: Perigee Books,

1979), p. 844. Note: Mutual Film Corporation subsidiaries included Keystone, the production company founded by Charles Bauman and Adam Kessel with Mack Sennett as director and Mabel Normand as a major star. Eventually, Mutual was absorbed by Film Booking Offices of America (FBO), which evolved into Radio-Keith-Orpheum, or RKO.

10. Martín Luis Guzmán, *Memoirs of Pancho Villa* (Austin: University of Texas Press, 1965), pp. 129–130. Note: Guzmán, an eminent historian, traveled with Pancho Villa at various times throughout the revolution. Villa's *Memoirs* were first published in Mexico in 1951.
11. Guzmán, pp. 130–131.
12. Ibid, p. 132. Note: Pancho Villa, not in the habit of capturing prisoners, was known to take lives casually.
13. Fred Gipson, *Fabulous Empire* (Boston: Houghton Mifflin Company, 1946), p. 315. Note: Gipson devoted an entire chapter, "The Army That Zack Bought," to Miller's adventure on the Mexican border.
14. Ibid.
15. Ibid., p. 316.
16. Murphey Collection.
17. Gipson, p. 317.
18. Ibid.
19. Ibid., p. 318.
20. Murphey Collection.
21. Ibid. Note: Eyewitness accounts portrayed the exodus of refugees as an "inhuman, sinful spectacle." General Mercado and his family eventually settled in Las Cruces, New Mexico.
22. Ibid. Note: As secretary of state, William Jennings Bryan tried to preserve U.S. interests in Latin America. Concerned about President Woodrow Wilson's belligerent response to Germany after the sinking of the *Lusitania*, Bryan resigned in 1915.
23. Gipson, p. 332. Note: The Millers shipped the arms and equipment to Brownsville, Texas, for delivery to the Mexican government.
24. Ibid., pp. 334–335.
25. Ibid., p. 335; Murphey Collection.
26. Ellsworth Collings and Alma Miller England, *The 101 Ranch* (Norman: University of Oklahoma Press, 1937, 1971), p. 140.
27. Murphey Collection.
28. Gipson, pp. 287–288.
29. Muriel H. Wright, *A Guide to the Indian Tribes of Oklahoma* (Norman: University of Oklahoma Press, 1951, 1986), p. 213. Note: In *Fabulous Empire*, author Fred Gipson made the case that White Eagle's horse was killed by Zack Miller, who reluctantly agreed to take part in the old chief's burial ritual at the request of his brother Joe Miller. No evidence could be found to substantiate this questionable claim.
30. Ibid.
31. Paula Carmack Denson, ed., *North Central Oklahoma: Rooted in the Past—Growing for the Future*, vol. 2 (Ponca City: North Central Oklahoma Historical Association, Inc., 1995), p. 776.
32. Ibid.
33. Ibid.
34. Murphey Collection.
35. Ibid. Note: All dates for the 1914 season are listed in the official route book for the Miller Brothers & Arlington 101 Ranch Real Wild West Show.
36. Buck Rainey, *The Life and Films of Buck Jones* (Waynesville, North Carolina: The World of Yesterday, 1988), p. 15.
37. Ibid., p. 19.
38. Murphey Collection.
39. Ibid.
40. Ibid; *SideSaddle Magazine* (published annually by the National Cowgirl Hall of Fame and Western Heritage Center), 1989, p. 24.
41. *SideSaddle Magazine*; Judy Crandall, *Cowgirls: Early Images and Collectibles* (Atglen, Pennsylvania; Schiffer Publishing Ltd., 1994), pp. 23–25. Note: "Prairie Rose" Hender-

son, as most rodeo fans knew her, was born Ann Robbins. Her exact birthdate is unknown. During her many years on the rodeo circuit, Rose was known for bronc riding and prowess as a flat racer. During a severe blizzard in the 1930s, she left her ranch headquarters to tend to some livestock and became lost. Many years later, her remains were reportedly identified only by a large championship belt buckle.

42. Murphey Collection. Note: Ruth Roach won several world-championship titles in bronc, fancy, and trick riding during her long and colorful career. Although her ten-year marriage to Bryan Roach ended in divorce, Ruth kept his surname even after her marriages to Ambrose Richardson, a famous bronc rider better known as "Nowata Slim"; Fred Alvord, a rodeo arena director and champion cowboy; and Fred "Dick" Salmon, a rancher from Nocona, Texas. Ruth Scantlin Roach Salmon, remembered as "America's Rodeo Sweetheart," died on June 26, 1986.
43. From the 6 December 1990 editions of the *Ponca City* (Oklahoma) *News* and the Jackie McFarlin Laird files at Oklahoma Historical Society, Pioneer Woman Museum, Ponca City, Oklahoma.
44. Ibid. Note: Some sources, including newspaper articles about Jackie McFarlin Laird, erroneously listed the Populist activist as Mary Ellen Lease instead of her true name, Mary Elizabeth Clyens Lease. Born in western Pennsylvania in 1853, the agrarian reformer was a lifelong radical. She wrote and lectured for many causes, including birth control, woman's suffrage, evolution, and Roosevelt Progressivism.
45. Ibid.
46. Ibid.
47. Ibid.
48. Murphey Collection.
49. Ibid.
50. Bailey C. Hanes, *Bill Pickett, Bulldogger* (Norman: University of Oklahoma Press, 1977), p. 132.
51. Ibid.
52. Ibid.
53. Murphey Collection. Note: Shapiro, Bernstein & Co., Inc., 224 West 47th Street, New York, published the song in 1914.
54. Ibid.
55. Ibid. Note: Much of the Murphey Collection file material pertaining to the Miller show's appearances in London is based on feature stories contained in various editions of the *White City Herald*, published in summer 1914 in London during the Anglo-American Exposition, Shepherd's Bush, as well as the 1914 show courier published for the Miller Brothers & Arlington 101 Ranch Real Wild West.
56. Ibid.
57. Ibid.
58. Ibid. Note: Sir Thomas Johnstone Lipton competed for the America's Cup, the award given for the international championship in yachting, five times—in 1899, 1901, 1903, 1920, and finally in 1930, when he was presented with a "loser's cup." Lipton died the next year.
59. Hanes, p. 133.
60. Ibid.
61. Ibid., pp. 133–134.
62. Murphey Collection.
63. Ibid.
64. Gipson, p. 341. Note: After young Virginia Miller saw Queen Mary slap her husband's hands, the little girl supposedly remarked: "I didn't think that *anybody* could slap a king!"
65. Ibid.
66. From the *Daily Chronicle*, London, 26 June 1914. Note: The daughter of King Christian IX of Denmark, Alexandra, born in 1844, married the prince of Wales in 1863, the year her brother ascended the Greek throne as George I. Renowned for her youthful beauty and natural dignity, she died in 1925.
67. *White City Herald*, 27 June 1914.

68. *Daily Chronicle*, 26 June 1914.
69. Clifton Daniel, ed., *Chronicle of the 20th Century* (Mount Kisco, New York: Chronicle Publications, 1988), p. 183.
70. Ibid.
71. Murphey Collection.
72. Daniel, p. 185.
73. Gipson, p. 345.
74. Ibid.
75. Quote from the *Ponca City* (Oklahoma) *Courier*, 18 March 1915.
76. Gipson, p. 345.
77. Joe Miller Jr., interview by author, 3 October 1994.
78. Ibid.
79. Gipson, p. 350.
80. Ibid., pp. 350–351.
81. L. G. Moses, *Wild West Shows and the Images of American Indians, 1883–1933* (Albuquerque: University of New Mexico Press, 1996), pp. 186–187.
82. Note: By late autumn of 1914, the Germans had increased their submarine warfare, although orders during the first year of the conflict were for German U-boats to attack only warships.
83. Ibid., p. 186.
84. Ibid.
85. Ibid., p. 188.
86. Ibid.
87. Gipson, p. 355.
88. Note: It has been reported in a variety of books and publications that the 101 Ranch Show folded when the British government confiscated the show stock at the outbreak of World War I. Although it was true that the show in England did terminate, it should be noted that the overseas company was a second unit. The main Miller show continued to tour the United States for two more years.
89. From the 1915 files of the 101 Ranch Collection of John D. Cooper, Stroud, Oklahoma.
90. Ibid.
91. Ibid.
92. Ibid.
93. Ibid.
94. Ibid.
95. Charlsie Poe, *Booger Red: World Champion Cowboy* (Winters, Texas: Quality Publications, 1991), p. 2.
96. Ibid., p. 55.
97. Ibid., p. 56.
98. Ibid. Note: Quoting from "Ella Privett: Sensation of Day," *San Francisco Chronicle*, 30 May 1915.
99. Ibid., pp. 56–57.
100. Ibid., p. 58.
101. Ibid., pp. 77, 110. Note: "Booger Red" Privett died on March 25, 1925, a victim of Bright's disease. He was buried at Miami, Oklahoma.
102. From the Bessie Herberg correspondence and newspaper files in the 101 Ranch Collection of Jack Keathly, Ponca City, Oklahoma.
103. Ibid.
104. Cooper Collection.
105. Keathly Collection.
106. Joe Miller Jr., interview by author, 3 October 1994.
107. Memoirs of Alice Miller Harth, 1983; Harth, "What Goes Up," a family memoir.
108. Cooper Collection.
109. *Ponca City* (Oklahoma) *Courier*, 18 March 1915.
110. Ibid.
111. Ibid.

112. Ibid.
113. Ibid.
114. Lupiano and Sayers, p. 247.
115. Ibid., p. 248.
116. Note: Jack Dempsey dethroned Willard in 1919. After only three rounds, Willard threw a towel into the boxing ring to signify defeat.
117. Bob Tabor, "Jess Willard: Prize Fighter—Wild West Attraction—Circus Owner," *The White Tops*, March–April 1965, p. 4.
118. Ibid.
119. Cooper Collection.
120. Ibid. Note: Outlaw Butch Cassidy, born Robert Leroy Parker, and his sidekick, Harry Longbaugh, "the Sundance Kid," were reportedly shot to death by Bolivian troops after a bank robbery. The year of their demise is variously given as 1908, 1909, or 1911. Some people believed the two survived and Cassidy actually died in Washington state in 1937, a dubious claim.
121. Ibid.
122. Ibid.; Murphey Collection.

Saturday's Heroes and Heroines

1. George N. Fenin and William K. Everson, *The Western: From Silents to Cinerama* (New York: The Orion Press, 1962), p. 25.
2. Ibid.
3. "Movies Killed the Wild West Shows," no date or source given, Edith and Vern Tantlinger newspaper interview by C. E. Clark, explaining the demise of Wild West shows and providing historical background of their careers, Tantlinger Collection, Western History Collections, the University of Oklahoma, Norman.
4. Ibid.
5. Jesse L. Lasky Jr., *Whatever Happened to Hollywood?* (New York: Funk & Wagnalls, 1973, 1975), p. 8.
6. Carey McWilliams, *Southern California Country* (New York: Duell, Sloan & Pearce, 1946), pp. 332–333.
7. Kevin Brownlow, *The War, the West, and the Wilderness* (New York: Alfred A. Knopf, Inc., 1978), p. 243. Note: Zack Miller hired A. D. Kean for the ranch film operation after viewing a widely distributed film the cowboy filmmaker had shot with his high-speed Graflex camera at the 1912 Calgary Stampede. Kean later established his own film company and, during World War I, he documented the British Columbian battalions in action on the western front.
8. Ken Schessler, *This Is Hollywood* (Redlands, California: Ken Schessler Publishing, 1978), p. 28. Note: The mansion at 7269 Hollywood Boulevard, where John Cudahy took his life, became known as Hollywood's "Jinx Mansion," thanks to Louella Parsons, the gossip writer who was syndicated in Hearst newspapers. The mansion was torn down in 1940.
9. Terry Whitehead, "John Cudahy's Big Adventure." *Country Gazette*, Blackwell, Oklahoma, March 1992, pp. 1–2.
10. From the 101 Ranch Collection of Jerry and Ruth Murphey, Corpus Christi, Texas. Note: Many recorded instances of deadly duels involved Miller employees. For example, at Atlantic City, New Jersey, in 1915, a quarrel between one of the Millers' former cooks, Charles Greathouse, and Jack Egan, a sideshow snake handler, erupted into gunplay which left young Egan mortally wounded.
11. Anthony Slide, *Early American Cinema* (New York: A. S. Barnes & Co., 1970), pp. 146–147.
12. Ibid., p. 147. Note: Kenneth Anger, an underground filmmaker and writer known for scathing accounts of the seamy side of celebrity life, wrote of Mabel Normand's supposed narcotics addiction in *Hollywood Babylon* (New York: Dell Publishing, 1975). Although

he offered no credible proof, Anger alleged that Mack Sennett "first put Mabel Normand, Juanita Hansen, Barbara La Marr and Alma Rubens on the junk."

13. Ibid. Note: William Desmond Taylor (his real name was William Cunningham Dean Tanner) should not be confused with William Desmond, an actor in some of the silent films involving the Millers.
14. Ibid. Note: No arrests were ever made in the murder of William Desmond Taylor. The homicide shattered many lives, including those of two of his young girlfriends, Mabel Normand and Mary Miles Minter. The well-publicized crime, along with the Fatty Arbuckle sex scandal, resulted in increased pressure on the film industry by a variety of citizen watch groups and film censorship advocates. Eventually, the studios established the Motion Picture Producers and Distributors of America, Inc. (MPPDA), to combat widely publicized scandals. By 1930, the year Mabel Normand died, the MPPDA had become known as the Hays Office after director Will H. Hays, former chairman of the Republican National Committee and member of Warren G. Harding's cabinet. The Motion Picture Production Code, a set of strict regulations better known as the Hays Code, allowed the narrow-minded Hays and his cronies to influence the image and content of motion pictures for many years.
15. Ibid.
16. *Ponca City* (Oklahoma) *News*, 4 February 1936.
17. Zack Miller Jr., interview by author, 12 October 1988.
18. Brownlow, pp. 263–264.
19. Ronald L. Davis, *John Ford: Hollywood's Old Master* (Norman: University of Oklahoma Press, 1995), p. 32.
20. Brownlow, p. 265.
21. Ibid., pp. 261–262, 264.
22. Ibid., p. 260.
23. Ibid., p. 262. Note: It was said that next to Rudolph Valentino, John Gilbert was the most widely admired screen lover of the time.
24. Ibid., pp. 261–262.
25. Ephraim Katz, *The Film Encyclopedia* (New York: Perigee Books, 1979), p. 598.
26. Otto Friedrich, *City of Nets: A Portrait of Hollywood in the 1940s* (New York: Harper & Row Publishers, 1986), pp. 92–93.
27. Ibid. Note: In his telling portrait of Hollywood, Friedrich related another popular theory of the time which maintained that gossip columnist Louella Parsons owed her job to Thomas Ince's death. Parsons supposedly witnessed Ince's shooting aboard the yacht but kept silent, thus securing forever a position with Hearst's chain of newspapers. But as Friedrich further states, "Ince seems actually to have died of too much food and liquor, and Mrs. Parsons seems to have been in New York at the time. Her chief appeal to Hearst was her gushing enthusiasm for the movies, and specifically for all movies featuring Marion Davies."
28. Katz, pp. 333, 410, 562, 572; Ellsworth Collings and Alma Miller England, *The 101 Ranch* (Norman: University of Oklahoma Press, 1937, 1971), pp 116–118.
29. Katz, pp. 880–881.
30. Ibid., p. 7.
31. Ibid.
32. Ibid., p. 583; Leo Kelley, " 'Reel' Oklahoma Cowboys," *The Chronicles of Oklahoma*, spring 1996, p. 13.
33. Kelley, pp. 13–14.
34. Elmer Kelton, "A Novelist's Recollections on the West," *Persimmon Hill*, spring 1996, pp. 15–17. Note: A highly acclaimed western novelist, Kelton has authored many best-selling books and has received several prestigious prizes.
35. Ibid.
36. Katz, pp. 792–793. Note: According to studio publicity and several movie almanacs, Ken Maynard was born in Mission, Texas. However, several years before his death, it was confirmed that Maynard was born at Vevay, Indiana, as was his younger brother, Kermit (1902–1971).

37. *Ponca City* (Oklahoma) *News*, 9 September 1973.
38. *Tulsa Daily World*, 4 April 1969.
39. Ibid.
40. Don Cusic, *Cowboys and the Wild West: An A-Z Guide from the Chisholm Trail to the Silver Screen* (New York: Facts on File, 1994), pp. 187–188.
41. Ibid., pp. 19, 188.
42. *Tulsa Daily World*, 4 April 1969.
43. Ibid.
44. Kelton, p. 15.
45. Buck Rainey, *The Life and Films of Buck Jones: The Silent Era* (Waynesville, North Carolina: The World of Yesterday, 1988), p. 22.
46. Ibid., pp. 17–18, 22.
47. Ibid., p. 19.
48. Ibid., p. 15. Note: The popular yarn that Buck Jones, as a young boy, moved with his family to a cattle ranch near Red Rock, Oklahoma, not far from the Millers was a fabrication of the Fox studio's publicity department.
49. Ibid., p. 21.
50. Ibid.
51. Ibid., pp. 21–22.
52. Thomas W. Knowles and Joe R. Lansdale, eds., *Wild West Show!* (New York and Avenel, New Jersey: Wings Books, 1994), p. 146. Note: In 1940, Maxine wed Noah Beery Jr., a character actor from the famous movie family.
53. Brownlow, p. 323.
54. Paul O'Neil, *The End and the Myth* (Chicago: Time-Life Books, Inc., 1979), p. 220.
55. M. J. Van Deventer, "Buck Jones, the Screen's Greatest Outdoor Star," *Cowboys Country*, spring–summer 1996, p. 29.
56. Ibid., p. 31.
57. Ibid., pp. 31–32. Note: Buck Rainey, author of the three books on Jones, has stated, "We all want to believe that legend. But all evidence is against it."
58. Cusic, p. 117.
59. Buck Rainey, *Saddle Aces of the Cinema* (San Diego and New York: A. S. Barnes & Company, Inc., 1980), p. 218. Note: Some sources claim the nickname came from Gibson's penchant for hunting owls as a boy in Nebraska.
60. Ibid.
61. Ibid.
62. Brownlow, p. 297.
63. Slide, p. 165. Note: Born Rose Helen Wenger in Cleveland in 1894, Hoot Gibson's first wife enjoyed perhaps the longest film career of any actress in Hollywood. Starting with her early work with Tom Ince for Bison 101, she remained in films until her retirement, in 1960.
64. Katz, p. 480.
65. Associated Press obituary in the *Tulsa World*, 23 August 1962.
66. Ibid.
67. Ibid.
68. Ibid.
69. Paul E. Mix, *The Life and Legend of Tom Mix* (Cranbury, New Jersey: A. S. Barnes and Company, 1972), p. 151.
70. Ibid.
71. Mix, p. 59. Note: Paul Mix found documentary evidence proving that Tom Mix did briefly serve as a deputy sheriff and night marshal in Dewey, Oklahoma, the home of Olive Stokes, one of Mix's five wives.
72. Knowles and Lansdale, p. 131.
73. Brownlow, p. 309.
74. Katz, p. 816.
75. Brownlow, pp. 309, 312.
76. Ibid.

77. Ibid., p. 312.
78. Mix, p. 151.
79. Walt Coburn, "Tom Mix's Last Sundown," *Frontier Times*, August–September 1968, pp. 8, 10.
80. Ibid., p. 10.
81. John H. Nicholas, *Tom Mix: Riding up to Glory* (Oklahoma City: National Cowboy Hall of Fame and Western Heritage Center, 1978), p. 88.
82. Mix, p. 151.
83. Brownlow, p. 312.
84. Ibid., p. 304.
85. Mix, p. 152.
86. Friedrich, p. 255.
87. Mix, p. 154.

CHAPTER 35: TRAIL'S END

1. Note: "Caught in his own loop" was a common cowboy expression for one who had failed through some fault of his own.
2. Bill Yenne, *The Encyclopedia of North American Indian Tribes* (New York: Crescent Books, 1986), p. 129.
3. James H. Howard, *The Ponca Tribe* (Lincoln: University of Nebraska Press, 1995), p. 154.
4. Ibid., pp. 154–155.
5. Ray and Wilma Falconer, interview by author, 1 October 1994.
6. Kenney A. Franks, Paul F. Lambert, and Carl N. Tyson, *Early Oklahoma Oil: A Photographic History, 1859–1936* (College Station: Texas A & M University Press, 1981), p. 146.
7. E. W. Marland, quoted in *Oklahoma City Times*, 21 July 1934.
8. Ruth and Jerry Murphey, interview by author, February 1998.
9. Howard, p. 6. Note: Some sources state that the Ponca name means "sacred head."
10. Ibid., p. 138.
11. Barbara Williams Roth, "101 Ranch Wild West Show," *The Chronicles of Oklahoma*, winter 1965–1966, p. 422.
12. Ibid.
13. Don Russell, *The Wild West: A History of the Wild West Shows* (Fort Worth: The Amon Carter Museum, 1970), p. 90.
14. Don Russell, *The Lives and Legends of Buffalo Bill* (Norman: University of Oklahoma Press, 1960), pp. 452–456. Note: Henry H. Tammen started his business career at age seven as a helper in a beer garden before becoming a bartender at the Palmer House in Chicago. In 1894, Tammen and his partner, Frederick G. Bonfils, purchased the *Denver Post*. They then acquired a dog-and-pony show which they renamed the Sells-Floto Circus.
15. Ibid., p. 456.
16. Ibid., p. 463.
17. Ibid., p. 464.
18. Ibid., pp. 463–464; 1916 show couriers and programs from the 101 Ranch Collection of Jerry and Ruth Murphey, Corpus Christi, Texas.
19. Murphey Collection.
20. Ibid.; Russell, p. 90.
21. Murphey Collection.
22. Ibid.
23. Ibid. Note: Johnny Baker received General Scott's letter, dated March 10, 1916, at his address in New Rochelle, New York.
24. Ibid. Note: Details concerning the specific military units were included in the *Buffalo Bill (Himself) and 101 Ranch Wild West Combined, Magazine and Daily Review*, which sold for ten cents per copy at all performances.

25. Ibid.
26. Russell, pp. 88, 90.
27. Ibid., pp. 90–91.
28. Murphey Collection.
29. Bailey C. Hanes, *Bill Pickett, Bulldogger* (Norman: University of Oklahoma Press, 1977), pp. 141–143.
30. *Chicago Shan-Kive and Round-Up Official Souvenir Program*, August 19–27, 1916. Note: In 1916, Chicago boasted of being "the sixth [largest] German city in the world."
31. Ibid.
32. Nellie Snyder Yost, *Buffalo Bill, His Family, Friends, Fame, Failures, and Fortunes* (Chicago: The Swallow Press, Inc., 1979), p. 399.
33. Joseph G. Rosa and Robin May, *Buffalo Bill and His Wild West* (Lawrence: University of Kansas Press, 1989), p. 215.
34. Ibid.
35. Ibid., p. 217. Note: Johnny Baker, who kept Cody's memory before the public for many years, died in Denver in 1931.
36. Ibid.
37. From various publications and research material provided by Oklahoma Historical Society, Oklahoma City.
38. *Tulsa World*, 11 January 1917.
39. Memoirs of Alice Miller Harth, 1983.
40. Ibid.
41. Bob Tabor, "Jess Willard: Prize Fighter—Wild West Attraction—Circus Owner," *The White Tops*, March–April 1965, pp. 3–8.
42. Ibid.
43. From the Bess Herberg-Joe Miller correspondence files in the 101 Ranch Collection of Jack Keathly, Ponca City, Oklahoma.
44. Ibid.
45. Ibid
46. Ibid.
47. Clifton Daniel, ed., *Chronicle of the 20th Century* (Mount Kisco, New York: Chronicle Publications, 1988), p. 253.
48. Keathly Collection.
49. Ellsworth Collings and Alma Miller England, *The 101 Ranch* (Norman: University of Oklahoma Press, 1937, 1971), p. 47.
50. Ibid., p. 105.
51. *Ponca City* (Oklahoma) *Democrat*, 15 August 1912.
52. Ibid.
53. Joe Miller Jr., interview by author, 3 October 1994.
54. Ibid.
55. *Ponca City* (Oklahoma) *Courier*, 1 August 1918.
56. "Final decree in the Matter of the Estate of Mollie A. Miller, County Court, Kay County, Oklahoma, October 17, 1919."
57. Ibid.
58. Collings and England, p. 47.
59. Keathly Collection. Note: This collection contains a variety of documents and other correspondence supporting the ongoing relationship between Joe Miller and Bess Herberg, such as an oil and gas mining-lease agreement with Gypsy Oil Company, dated September 10, 1921, two days before the formal execution of the Miller Brothers 101 Ranch Trust Agreement. The Keathly Collection also includes tax receipts from the Noble County treasurer for the tract of land owned jointly by Joe and Bessie.
60. Ibid.
61. Ibid.
62. Ibid. Note: According to some newspaper reports, the fire at the store ignited during a severe electrical storm. Some Ponca Indians, however, claimed that lightning did not cause the blaze. Local authorities found that the fire was accidental and of unknown origin.

63. "Final decree of Estate of Mollie A. Miller, 1919."
64. Miller Brothers 101 Ranch Trust Agreement, September 12, 1921. Note: England drew up a corporate form of organization known as a "Massachusetts common-law trust," under which the ranch would continue to operate as a unit after the deaths of the three brothers.
65. Ibid.
66. Murphey Collection.
67. Joe Miller Jr., interview by author, 3 October 1994.
68. Ibid.
69. Ibid.; Murphey Collection.
70. Murphey Collection.
71. Ibid.
72. Ibid.
73. Advertisement in *The 101 Magazine,* Official Publication, Cherokee Strip Cow Punchers' Association, November 1925.
74. Notes and recollections of David Buffalo Head, December 1987, in the 101 Ranch Collection of Oklahoma Historical Society, Pioneer Woman Museum, Ponca City.
75. Ibid. Note: During both world wars, Indian people from throughout Oklahoma served with distinction in the armed forces. Many other Indians invested heavily in war bonds or donated time and service to the Red Cross and various war organizations.
76. Murphey Collection, quoting from a letter written by Jack McCracken, 16 August 1967. Note: A credible and prolific source of information concerning the 101 Ranch, McCracken died after a heart attack on September 4, 1972.
77. Fred Gipson, *Fabulous Empire* (Boston: Houghton Mifflin Company, 1946), p. 279.
78. Ibid., pp. 277–278.
79. Collings and England, p. 129.
80. Ibid., p. 131.
81. Note: Lew Wentz moved from Pittsburgh, Pennsylvania, to Ponca City in 1911 and became known not only as a successful oil operator but also as a major philanthropist. One of his closest friends was George L. Miller.
82. Kenny A. Franks, *The Osage Oil Boom* (Oklahoma City: Oklahoma Heritage Association, 1989), pp. 128–129.
83. Ibid., p. 129.
84. Paula Carmack Denson, ed., *North Central Oklahoma: Rooted in the Past—Growing for the Future* (Ponca City, Oklahoma: North Central Oklahoma Historical Association, Inc., 1995), p. 129H.
85. *Oklahoma's Oil & Gas Centennial*, April 1995, p. 21, in the 101 Ranch Collection of John Cooper, Stroud, Oklahoma.
86. Ibid.
87. Ibid.
88. Collings and England, p. 109.
89. Ibid., pp. 110–111, quoting 101 Ranch records, 1 November 1931.
90. Note: By the late 1920s, Lew Wentz had become one of the wealthiest people in the United States.
91. Memorandum dated 26 November 1982, from Ferdie J. Deering to Roberta E. Newman, curator, Pioneer Woman Museum, Ponca City. Note: Deering, a native of Ada, Oklahoma, wrote columns and editorials for the *Daily Oklahoman*, the state's largest daily newspaper, for many years. He also served as editor of *Farmer-Stockman Magazine* for more than forty years. After his retirement in 1975, he continued to contribute articles to the monthly publication. Deering died in 1993 at age eighty-three.
92. "Tape Transcript of Major Herbert Peck, Special Counselor appointed to prosecute the Miller Brothers for defrauding the Indians," recorded by Ferdie J. Deering.
93. Samuel Hopkins Adams, *Incredible Era: The Life and Times of Warren Gamaliel Harding* (Boston: Houghton Mifflin Company, 1939), p. 325.
94. Ferdie J. Deering, "Here's a 101 Ranch Story You Probably Haven't Heard," *Farmer-Stockman Magazine*, February 1980, pp. 16–17.
95. Peck tape transcript.

96. Daniel, p. 262.
97. Peck tape transcript. Note: Peck's investigators came from the Indian Bureau and the Secret Service.
98. Ibid.
99. Ibid.
100. Ibid.
101. Ibid.
102. Ibid.
103. Adams, p. 325.
104. Ibid, p. 326.
105. Peck tape transcript.
106. Ibid.
107. Ibid.
108. Ibid.
109. Ibid.
110. Ibid.
111. Daniel, p. 313.
112. Deering, p. 17.
113. *Daily Oklahoman*, Oklahoma City, 27 May 1927.
114. Files from the 101 Ranch Collection, Oklahoma Historical Society, Pioneer Woman Museum, Ponca City.
115. *Kansas City Star*, 18 October 1932.
116. Collings and England, p. 49.

Nothing But Cowboys, Cowgirls, and Indians

1. Final verse from the three-verse poem "Lamentations," printed in its entirety on the back of a 101 Ranch photo postcard of Joe Miller, Gilcrease Museum Collections and photographic files, Tulsa, Oklahoma.
2. Note: Many of the old-school ranchers and cattlemen such as G. W. Miller, Lee Kokernut, and Ike Pryor commonly used the term *cow-fever*.
3. *New York Times*, 7 July 1998. Note: This quote is excerpted from an editorial, "A Cowboy's Trail," on the death of cowboy motion-picture and television star Roy Rogers.
4. Note: During interviews with the author, several former 101 Ranch cowhands and performers privately admitted that they believed E. W. Marland and the Millers had been cursed after they coaxed tribal leaders into allowing oil and gas exploration on sacred Indian lands.
5. Correspondence from May and June 1923 from the Miller Brothers 101 Ranch Collection, Western History Collections, University of Oklahoma, Norman, Oklahoma. Note: In a May 28 letter to Ray Archer, Jess Willard's manager, Joe Miller wrote: "We have decided on Sunday, June 10, as the date for the show. I am sure we can have a good crowd on that day. I had figured that in addition to the exhibition bout of Jess and one of his trainers, we would put on a six or eight-round go between two fairly good boys we may be able to date out of Oklahoma City or Tulsa; then a little of the usual round-up attractions, including roping and riding steers."
6. Ibid.
7. Ibid.
8. *Ponca City* (Oklahoma) *News*, 9 September 1973. Note: Clair Nickles, a prominent Ponca City businessman, was born in Nebraska in 1887. One of his grandsons—Don Nickles, an ultraconservative Oklahoma politician—became the youngest Republican ever to serve in the United States Senate at the time of his first election, in 1980.
9. Miller correspondence, OU.
10. *Ponca City News*, 9 September 1973.
11. Ibid.
12. Arthur "Capper" Newton, interview by author, 1 October 1994.

13. Fred Gipson, *Fabulous Empire* (Boston: Houghton Mifflin Company, 1946), p. 358.
14. Newspaper and periodical files in the 101 Ranch Collection of Jerry and Ruth Murphey, Corpus Christi, Texas.
15. Gipson, pp. 361–362.
16. *Ponca City* (Oklahoma) *News*, 26 August 1924.
17. 101 Ranch Collection of John Cooper, Stroud, Oklahoma.
18. Notes and recollections of David Buffalo Head, December 1987, in the 101 Ranch Collection of the Pioneer Woman Museum, Oklahoma Historical Society, Ponca City.
19. Cooper Collection. Note: Although his horse escaped from the submerged fence and swam to safety, Rhoades' body was never recovered.
20. Letter dated 7 August 1923, from Joe Miller to Vern Tantlinger.
21. Note: William England and Alma Miller England had six children: William Henry Jr., born in 1906; George Miller, 1907; Mary Ann, 1910; Eleanor, 1911; Louise, 1913; and Victor, 1919.
22. 101 Ranch Collection, Pioneer Woman Museum.
23. Ellsworth Collings and Alma Miller England, *The 101 Ranch* (Norman: University of Oklahoma Press, 1937, 1971), pp. 30, 34, 35. Note: In 1929, Oklahoma Governor W. J. Holloway also appointed Zack as an honorary colonel on his personal staff, along with Will Rogers and E. W. Marland.
24. Edwin C. McReynolds, *Oklahoma: A History of the Sooner State* (Norman: University of Oklahoma Press, 1954), pp. 339–349.
25. From memoirs of Alice Miller Harth, 1983. Note: Harth stated that "Mama [Lizzie Miller] said Zack was lazy but she may have been repeating Papa's [Joe Miller's] opinion."
26. Ibid.
27. Zack Miller correspondence from 1923, Miller Brothers Collection, OU.
28. Harth memoir, 1983.
29. Miller legal papers, H. J. Johnston Collection, Western History Collections, OU.
30. Ibid.
31. Ibid.
32. Ibid.
33. Harth memoir, 1983.
34. Letter dated 17 January 1924, from George Miller to Zack Miller, in the Cooper Collection.
35. Ibid.
36. *Daily Oklahoman*, Oklahoma City, 6 February 1927.
37. Jimmy M. Skaggs, ed., *Ranch and Range in Oklahoma* (Oklahoma City: Oklahoma Historical Society, 1978), p. 84.
38. Cooper Collection; D. Earl Newsom, *The Cherokee Strip: Its History & Grand Opening* (Stillwater, Oklahoma: New Forums Press, Inc., 1992), p. 119.
39. Cooper Collection.
40. Ibid.
41. Arthur "Capper" Newton, interview by author, 1 October 1994.
42. Ibid.
43. *Daily Oklahoman*, Oklahoma City, 6 February 1927.
44. Ibid.
45. Charles Lane Cullen, "The Story of the Great 101 Ranch," *American Magazine*, July 1928, p. 54.
46. Ibid.
47. Ibid.
48. Cooper Collection.
49. Ibid.
50. Ibid.
51. Reminiscences of George W. Miller, one of Joe Miller's sons, in the *Ponca City* (Oklahoma) *News*, 9 September 1973.
52. W. David Baird and Danney Goble, *The Story of Oklahoma* (Norman: University of Oklahoma Press, 1994), pp. 359–360.

53. *The Daily Oklahoman*, Oklahoma City, 23 April 1939.
54. Ibid.
55. Ibid.
56. Ibid.
57. John Gibson Phillips Jr., interview by author, 12 February 1987.
58. *The Daily Oklahoman*, Oklahoma City, 23 April 1939.
59. *The Daily Oklahoman*, Oklahoma City, 6 February 1927.
60. *Tulsa Tribune*, 9 September 1970.
61. *Tulsa World*, 28 July 1974.
62. *Ponca City* (Oklahoma) *News*, 14 September 1949. Note: Unfortunately, the Millers did not heed all the advice Ezra Meeker offered in his recipe for longevity: "Eat to live, not to eat. Be temperate in all things. Live the simple life. Work."
63. Gipson, p. 249.
64. E. W. Long, interview by author, 23 September 1993. Note: When Bill McFadden joined E. W. Marland in the search for oil in 1909, he lived in a tent near the Millers' White House. McFarland kept his money in a pillowcase and carried two derringer pistols for protection. For a short time, the Millers had Tom Mix pitch a tent alongside McFadden's to guard him and his grubstake. McFadden later served as mayor of Ponca City for seven years and died in Fort Worth in 1956 at age eighty-seven.
65. Ibid.
66. *Ponca City* (Oklahoma) *News*, 15 September 1968.
67. Bailey C. Hanes, *Bill Pickett, Bulldogger* (Norman: University of Oklahoma Press, 1977), pp. 160–161.
68. Taped recollections of Melvon Lewis, provided to the author October 1994.
69. Cherokee Strip Cow-Punchers Association records from the Murphey Collection.
70. Ibid.
71. Collings and England, p. 157.
72. Ibid.
73. Cooper Collection.
74. Ibid.
75. Ibid.
76. *Tulsa World*, 10 July 1955.
77. Ibid.
78. Cooper Collection; Murphey Collection.
79. Ibid., both references above.
80. *Ponca City* (Oklahoma) *News*, 9 September 1972.
81. Ibid.
82. Chang Reynolds, "Miller Brothers 101 Ranch Real Wild West Show, Part One, 1925 & 1926," *Bandwagon*, March–April 1975, pp. 3–13.
83. Ibid.
84. Ibid.
85. Cooper Collection.
86. Ibid.
87. Joe Miller letter to Edward Arlington, 8 October 1925, Miller Brothers Collection, OU.
88. Reynolds, p. 8; Cooper Collection.
89. Reynolds, pp. 10–11.
90. Winifred Johnston, "Passing of the Wild West: A Chapter in the History of American Entertainment," *Southwest Review*, October 1935, pp. 33–51.
91. Reynolds, p. 12.
92. Cooper Collection.
93. Reynolds, quoting Collings and England.
94. Cooper Collection; Harth memoir, 1983.
95. Cooper Collection; 101 Ranch Collection, Pioneer Woman Museum.
96. Cooper Collection.
97. 101 Ranch Collection, Pioneer Woman Museum.
98. Ibid.

99. *Tulsa World*, 2 May 1976.
100. Alice Miller Harth, "What Goes Up," a family memoir.
101. *101 Magazine*, Official Publication of the Cherokee Strip Cow Punchers' Association, November 1927. Note: Later, the name of Joe Miller's youngest son was changed again, to William Joseph Miller.
102. Ibid.
103. Ibid.
104. Ibid. Note: There was no indication of foul play or suicide. Joe Miller's death was ruled accidental.
105. Zack Miller, letter to John Wright, inmate at the federal prison, Atlanta, Georgia, 29 October 1927.
106. Murphey Collection; *Ponca City* (Oklahoma) *News*, 23–24–25 October 1927.
107. Murphey Collection.
108. Ibid.
109. Harth, "What Goes Up."
110. Gipson, p. 366.
111. Harth, "What Goes Up."
112. Ibid.
113. Ibid.
114. Harth memoir, 1983.
115. Ibid.
116. Collings and England, p. 192.
117. Chang Reynolds, "Miller Brothers 101 Ranch, Part Two, 1927 to 1931," *Bandwagon*, pp. 3–14.
118. Ibid, p. 7.
119. Baird and Goble, p. 390.
120. Ibid.
121. Ibid., p. 389.
122. Ibid., p. 399. Note: E. W. Marland changed political parties and won Oklahoma's Eighth Congressional District seat, the first Democrat ever to do so. He ran on the campaign slogan "Bring the New Deal to Oklahoma."
123. John Joseph Mathews, *Life and Death of an Oilman: The Career of E. W. Marland* (Norman: University of Oklahoma Press, 1951), p. 105. Note: E. W. Marland's father, Alfred Marland, died in 1914 at the Arcade Hotel in Ponca City. E. W. was always sorry that his father did not live to see the riches he gathered from the oil fields. Lydie Marland never recovered from E. W.'s death in 1941. A recluse for many years, she received national publicity when she mysteriously disappeared in 1953. Lydie returned to Ponca City twenty-two years later and lived in a small stone house on the old Marland estate until her death, in 1987.
124. Collings and England, p. 191.
125. Fred D. Pfening III, "Al G. Barnes Circus, Season of 1929, Part One," *Bandwagon*. November–December 1991, pp. 4–6.
126. Ibid.
127. Ibid.
128. Pat Redmond, "Ponca City's Arcade, Home of Instant Millionaires," *Frontier Times*, August–September, 1975, p. 40.
129. Ibid.
130. Ibid.; Cooper Collection.
131. *Ponca City* (Oklahoma) *News*, 9 February 1929.
132. Cooper Collection.
133. Murphey Collection.
134. Collings and England, p. 212.
135. Ibid, p. 192.
136. Ibid.
137. *Ponca City* (Oklahoma) *News*, 9 September 1973.
138. *Ponca City* (Oklahoma) *News*, 18 March 1931.

139. Reynolds, "Miller Brothers 101 Ranch, Part Two, 1927 to 1931," p. 12.
140. Jack Quait, interview by author, 31 August 1995.
141. Reynolds, p. 13.
142. Ibid.
143. *Daily Oklahoman*, Oklahoma City, 25 March 1932.
144. Hanes, pp. 173–175.
145. Ibid., pp. 176–177.
146. Ibid., pp. 178–179.
147. Bill Snodgrass, "The Vanishing of the Fabulous Empire: The '101' Ranch," *The Journal of the Cherokee Strip*, September 1971, p. 13; Gipson, pp. 393–397.
148. Gibson, pp. 393–397.
149. *Guthrie* (Oklahoma) *Daily Leader*, 18 July 1932.
150. Ibid.
151. Ibid.
152. Zack Miller, letter to Louis "Diamond Jack" Alterie, 11 July 1932.
153. *Blackwell (Oklahoma) Morning Tribune*, 27 July 1932.
154. Reynolds, "Miller Brothers 101 Ranch, Part Two, 1927 to 1931," p. 13.
155. Collings and England, p. 201.
156. Ibid., pp. 201–202.
157. *Ponca City* (Oklahoma) *News*, 29 November 1932.
158. *Ponca City* (Oklahoma) *News*, 28 February 1933.
159. Reynolds, "Miller Brothers 101 Ranch, Part Two, 1927–1931," p. 13; Collings and England, p. 206.
160. *Tulsa World*, 10 February 1935.
161. Ibid.
162. *Daily Oklahoman*, Oklahoma City, 26 July 1936.
163. Reynolds, "Miller Brothers 101 Ranch, Part Two, 1927–1931," p. 13.
164. *Ponca City* (Oklahoma) *News*, 17 August 1988.
165. Ibid.
166. Don Russell, *The Wild West: A History of the Wild West Shows* (Fort Worth: Amon Carter Museum of Western Art, 1970), p. 109.
167. *Tulsa World*, 4 January 1952.
168. *Chicago Daily Tribune*, 4 January 1952.
169. *Ponca City* (Oklahoma) *News*, 8 January 1952.
170. *Ponca City* (Oklahoma) *News*, 4 June 1986.
171. *Tulsa Tribune*, 22 September 1987; *Ponca City* (Oklahoma) *News*, 17 July 1963.

EPILOGUE

1. Kenneth S. Clark, ed., *The Cowboy Sings* (New York: Paull-Pioneer Music Corp., 1932), p. 85.

BIBLIOGRAPHY

PRIVATE COLLECTIONS

101 Ranch Collection of John Cooper, Stroud, Oklahoma.
101 Ranch Collection of Jack Keathly, Ponca City, Oklahoma.
101 Ranch Collection of Jerry and Ruth Murphey, Corpus Christi, Texas.
101 Ranch Collection of Ken Theobald, Danville, Kentucky.
101 Ranch Collection of Fred and Velma Strickland, South Haven, Kansas.
101 Ranch Collection of Michael Wallis, Tulsa, Oklahoma.
101 Ranch Collection of Richard Kay Wortman, Arkansas City, Kansas.

ARCHIVES, MUSEUMS, LIBRARIES, AND HISTORICAL SOCIETIES

American Film Institute Library, Kennedy Center, Washington, D. C.
American Museum of the Moving Image, Astoria, New York.
Baxter Springs (Kansas) Heritage Center and Museum.
Baxter Springs (Kansas) Historical Society.
Central University archives, Eastern Kentucky University, Richmond.
Cherokee Strip Museum, Oklahoma Historical Society, Perry.
Circus World Museum, Baraboo, Wisconsin.
Cowley County Historical Society, Winfield, Kansas.
Cultural Center and Indian Museum, Ponca City, Oklahoma.
Devil's Rope Museum, McLean, Texas.
Federal Archives, Fort Worth, Texas.
Gilcrease Museum, Tulsa, Oklahoma.
Harvey Helm Memorial Library, Stanford, Kentucky.
Margaret Herrick Library, Beverly Hills, California.
Kansas State Historical Society, Topeka.
Kentucky Historical Society, Frankfort.
Lexington (Kentucky) Public Library.
Lincoln County (Kentucky) Historical Society.
Madison County Historical Society, Richmond, Kentucky.
Menard (Texas) Historical Society.
Miami (Oklahoma) Public Library.
Missouri Historical Society, Saint Louis.
Tom Mix Museum, Dewey, Oklahoma.
Museum of the Cherokee Strip, Oklahoma Historical Society, Enid.
National Cowboy Hall of Fame and Western Heritage Center, Oklahoma City.
Newton County Historical Society, Neosho, Missouri.
North Central Oklahoma Historical Association, Inc., Ponca City.
Oklahoma Historical Society, Oklahoma City.

Okmulgee (Oklahoma) Historical Society.
Osage County Historical Society, Pawhuska, Oklahoma.
Pawnee Bill Ranch, Oklahoma Historical Society, Pawnee.
Perry (Oklahoma) Carnegie Library.
Pioneer Woman Museum, Oklahoma Historical Society, Ponca City.
Ponca City (Oklahoma) Public Library.
Rockcastle County Historical Society, Inc., Mount Vernon, Kentucky.
Will Rogers Memorial, Claremore, Oklahoma.
Rylander Memorial Library, San Saba, Texas.
St. Louis Mercantile Library.
San Antonio Museum Association.
Top of Oklahoma Museum, Blackwell.
Tulsa City-County Library System.
The Institute of Texan Cultures, University of Texas, San Antonio.
McFarlin Library, the University of Tulsa.
Venice (California) Historical Society.
Washington County Historical Society, Bartlesville, Oklahoma.
Western History Collections, the University of Oklahoma, Norman.
Woolaroc Museum, Bartlesville, Oklahoma.

MEMOIRS

Harth, Alice Miller. "What Goes Up," a family memoir (undated).
———. Memoir. 1983.
Lewis, Melvon. Audiotaped recollections.
Rainwater, James. Diary, 1871–1872.

INTERVIEWS

Colby, Joe.
Day, W. H.
Falconer, Ray and Wilma.
Gaines, Howard Kennedy.
Hale, Clarence B.
Long, E. W.
Melton, W. T.
Miller, Joe Jr.
Miller, Zack Jr.
Murphey, J. C.
Murphey, Ruth and Jerry.
Newton, Arthur "Capper."
Nicholson, W. J.
Phillips, John Gibson Jr.
Quait, Jack.
Strickland, Fred and Velma.
Vines, W. A.
Wafer, Mack.
West, W. A.
White, Tom B.

LEGAL DOCUMENTS

Miller, George W., v United States, 8 Okla. 315 (1899).
Miller, Mollie A., Final decree in the Matter of the Estate of, County Court, Kay County, Oklahoma, October 17, 1919.

"Tape Transcript of Major Herbert Peck, Special Counselor appointed to prosecute the Miller Brothers for defrauding the Indians," recorded by Ferdie J. Deering.

The United States v George W. Miller of Noble County, District Court of Noble County, Oklahoma Territory (March term 1903).

GOVERNMENT DOCUMENTS

U.S. House Executive Document. Report of September 5, 1890, no. 1, part 5, vol. II, 51st Cong., 2nd sess., 1890, serial 2841, lvii–lix.

U.S. House Executive Document. "Instructions to Agents in Regard to Manner of Issuing Beef," July 21, 1890, no. 1, part 5, vol. II, 51st Cong., 2nd sess., serial 2841, clxvi.

Sherman, General W. T., to Leslie Combs, August 11, 1864, in *The War of the Rebellion: A Compilation of the Official Records of the Union and Confederate Armies*, 129 vols. Washington, D.C.: U.S. Government Printing Office, 1880–1901, ser. 1, 39, pt. 2:241.

SOUND RECORDING

Steagall, Red, *Ride for the Brand: A Collection of Original Cowboy Poetry*. Fort Worth: RS Records, 1991.

ELECTRONIC DOCUMENTS

The 1995 Grolier Multimedia Encyclopedia Version 7.0.2, Grolier Electronic Publishing, Inc., 1995.

NEWSPAPERS

Anderson (Missouri) *Argus*.
Arkansas City (Kansas) *Daily Traveler*.
Blackwell (Oklahoma) *Morning Tribune*.
Bliss (Oklahoma Territory) *Breeze*.
Chicago Daily Tribune.
Creek County (Oklahoma) *Republican*.
Daily Chronicle, London.
Daily Oklahoman, Oklahoma City.
El Imparcial.
Enid (Oklahoma) *Morning News*.
Guthrie (Oklahoma) *Daily Leader*.
Illustrated London News.
Joplin (Missouri) *Globe*.
Kansas City Journal-Post.
Kansas City Star.
Lamont (Oklahoma Territory) *Valley News*.
Lawton (Oklahoma Territory) *State Democrat*.
Lincoln Ledger, Stanford, Kentucky.
Morrison (Oklahoma) *Transcript*.
Neosho (Missouri) *Daily News*.
New York Herald.
New York Journal.
New York Sun.
New York Times.
New York World.
Oklahoma City Times.
Perry (Oklahoma) *Enterprise Times*.
Perry (Oklahoma) *Republican*.

Platteville (Wisconsin) *Witness.*
Ponca City (Oklahoma) *Courier.*
Ponca City (Oklahoma) *Daily Courier.*
Ponca City (Oklahoma) *Democrat.*
Ponca City (Oklahoma) *News.*
St. Charles (Missouri) *Banner News.*
St. Louis Globe-Democrat.
Tulsa Tribune.
Tulsa World.
Weekly Elevator, Fort Smith, Arkansas.
White City Herald.
Winfield (Kansas) *Courier.*

PERIODICALS

Anderson, Nema. "Jim Collier—101 Ranch Showman," *Frontier Times* 54:3 (April–May 1980): 12–13.

Armstrong, Jerry. "Picked Up in the Rodeo Arena," *The Western Horseman* (March 1963): 44.

——. "The Day the 101 Ranch Invaded Coney Island," *The Western Horseman* (March 1962): 60.

Bearss, Edwin C. "The Army of the Frontier's First Campaign: The Confederates Win at Newtonia," *Missouri Historical Review* (April 1966): 311.

Brown, David G. "Last of a Breed," *American Cowboy* (September–October 1995): 43.

Brown, Opal Hartsell. "Penal Institutions and Punishment in Indian Territory," Western Publications, Inc. 57:2 (April 1985): 44–48.

Callen, Charles Lane. "The Story of the Great 101 Ranch," *The American Magazine* (July 1928): 148. This same feature story was published in the August 4, 1928, edition of *Literary Digest.*

Castel, Albert E. "A New View of the Battle of Pea Ridge," *Missouri Historical Review* 62: 2 (January 1968): 136–151.

——. *The Guerrilla War, 1861–1865*, A special issue of *Civil War Times Illustrated, Historical Times* (1974): 30.

Coburn, Walt. "Tom Mix's Last Sundown," *Frontier Times* 42:5 (August–September 1968): 8, 10.

Dale, Edward Everett. *American Hereford Journal* (1936): 6.

Dean, Andrea Oppenheimer. "Revisiting the White City," *Historic Preservation* (March–April 1993): 42.

Deering, Ferdie J. "Here's a 101 Ranch Story You Probably Haven't Heard," *Farmer-Stockman Magazine* (February 1980): 16–17.

Dispenza, Joseph. "On Location in New Mexico," *New Mexico Magazine* (November 1984): 75.

Dunn, John W. "Fabulous Empire and its Money," *The Numismatic Scrapbook Magazine* (March 1968): 359–364.

"The Editor's Corral," *Real West* 10:52, (March 1967): 6.

Ehrheart, William J. "Chief Luther Standing Bear II: Activist, Author, Historian," *Persimmon Hill* 25:3 (Autumn 1997): 44.

Faragher, John Mack. "But a Common Man," *American History Illustrated*, p. 31 of an article based on Faragher's research for *Daniel Boone: The Life and Legend of an American Pioneer* (1992).

Fetterman, John. "The People of Cumberland Gap," *National Geographic* 140:5 (November 1971): 594.

"The Forgotten Pioneers," *U.S. News & World Report* (8 August 1994): 53–55.

Hale, Douglas. "Rehearsal for Civil War: The Texas Cavalry in the Indian Territory, 1861," *The Chronicles of Oklahoma* 68:3 (fall 1990): 255.

Henderson, Sam. "Show Biz Western Style," *Wild West* (October 1994): 36.
Hollingsworth, Gerelyn. "Legitimate Theater in St. Louis, 1870–1879," *Missouri Historical Review* 69:3 (April 1975): 267.
101 Magazine 1:9 (November 1925).
101 Magazine 2:12 (November 1927).
101 Ranch, Miller promotional brochure (1908).
Jennings, Frank W. "Did San Antonio Lasso Texas' First Rodeo?" *Texas Highways* (1994): 38–39.
Johnston, Winifred. "Passing of the Wild West: A Chapter in the History of American Entertainment," *Southwest Review* 21 (October 1935): 33–51.
Kageleiry, Jamie. "One Day at the Chicago World's Fair," *The Old Farmer's Almanac 1993* (1992): 162–168.
Kelley, Leo. " 'Reel' Oklahoma Cowboys," *The Chronicles of Oklahoma* 74:1 (spring 1996): 13.
Kelton, Elmer. "A Novelist's Recollections on the West," *Persimmon Hill* 24:1 (spring 1996): 15–17.
Kentucky Historical Society, "The Battle of Perryville," *The Bulletin of the Kentucky Historical Society* 5:5 (October 1979): 55.
La Fay, Howard. "Texas!" *National Geographic* (April 1980): 444.
Lancaster, Bob. "Bare Feet and Slow Trains," *Arkansas Times* (June 1987): 88.
Lindemann, Gerald. "Gunfighters and Lawmen," *Wild West* 10:1 (June 1997): 75.
March, David D. "Sobriquets of Missouri and Missourians," *Missouri Historical Review* 72: 3 (April 1978): 252.
Meador, Roy. "The 101 Line Rider Known As Fifty-Six," *Good Old Days* 23:7 (January 1987): 42.
Meredith, Paul W. *Violent Kin!* 20 (October 1993).
Miller Brothers & Arlington 101 Ranch Real Wild West Magazine and Daily Review (1915).
Miller, C. H. "George Miller As I Knew Him," *101 Magazine* (January 1926): 7–8.
——. "Newtonia's Most Beautiful Woman," *101 Magazine* (March 1926): 11.
Miller, Donald L. "The White City," *American Heritage* (July–August 1993): 71–93.
Mix, Tom. "Happy Days on the 101 Ranch," *101 Magazine* 2:1 (March 1926): 3.
Moize, Elizabeth A. "Daniel Boone: First Hero of the Frontier," *National Geographic* 168:6 (December 1985).
Motion Picture World (1912).
Nichols, Claude H. "Hard Times in Baxter Springs," *History of Baxter Springs* (1958): 9–10.
Nottage, James A. "Authenticity and Western Film," *Gilcrease Journal* 1:1 (spring 1993): 57.
Oklahoma's Oil & Gas Centennial (April 1995).
Patton, Phil. "Sell the Cookstove if Necessary, but Come to the Fair," *Smithsonian* (June 1993): 46, 48.
Pfening, Fred D. III. "Al G. Barnes Circus, Season of 1929, Part One," *Bandwagon* 35:6 (November–December 1991): 4–6.
Princess Wynona [sic]. "Wintering at Malden," *101 Magazine* 2:3 (May 1926): 4.
Redmond, Pat. "Ponca City's Arcade: Home of Instant Millionaires," *Frontier Times* (August–September 1975): 40.
Reynolds, Chang. "101 Ranch Wild West Show 1907–1916," *Bandwagon* 13:1 (January–February 1969): 18.
——. "Miller Brothers 101 Ranch Real Wild West Show, Part One, 1925 & 1926," *Bandwagon* 19:2 (March–April 1975): 3–13.
——. "Miller Brothers 101 Ranch, Part Two, 1927 to 1931," *Bandwagon* 19:3, (May–June 1975): 3–14.
Roberts, David. "The Last Warrior," *Oklahoma Today* 43:3 (May–June 1993): 34.
Roosevelt, Theodore. "A Wolf Hunt in Oklahoma," *Scribner's Magazine* 38:5 (November 1905): 513.
Roth, Barbara Williams. "The 101 Ranch Wild West Show, 1904–1932," *The Chronicles of Oklahoma* 43:4 (winter 1965–66): 417.

Sarchet, Corb. "Necrology: Col. George L. Miller," *The Chronicles of Oklahoma* 7:2 (June 1929): 194.
——. "Roundup Started on 101 Ranch," *101 Magazine* 2:7 (September 1926): 10.
Savage, William W. Jr. "Of Cattle and Corporations: The Rise, Progress, and Termination of the Cherokee Strip Live Stock Association," *The Chronicles of Oklahoma* 71:2 (summer 1993): 139.
Shirley, Glenn. "Four Lives of Princess Wenona," *Old West* (spring 1991): 14–19.
SideSaddle Magazine (1989).
Sizemore, Deborah Lightfoot. "Cowboy Stuntman Yakima Canutt," *Persimmon Hill* (autumn 1988): 33.
Smith, Brian Lee. "Theodore Roosevelt Visits Oklahoma," *The Chronicles of Oklahoma* 51: 3 (fall 1973): 268.
Snodgrass, Bill. "The Vanishing of the Fabulous Empire: The '101' Ranch," *The Journal of the Cherokee Strip* 13, (September 1971): 13.
Spears, Jack. "Hollywood's Oklahoma," *The Chronicles of Oklahoma* 67:4 (winter 1989–90): 341.
"Standing Bear, the Friend of His Race," *101 Magazine* 1:5 (July 1925): 6.
Tabor, Bob. "Jess Willard: Prize Fighter—Wild West Attraction—Circus Owner," *The White Tops* 38:2, (March–April 1965): 3–8.
Tavernier, Bertrand. "Notes of a Press Attaché: John Ford in Paris, 1966," *Film Comment* (July–August 1994).
Troccoli, Joan Carpenter. "The Sketchbooks of Emil Lenders: Down to the Soles of the Moccasins," *Gilcrease Journal* 1:1 (spring 1993): 32.
Turner, Alvin O. "Order and Disorder: The Opening of the Cherokee Outlet," *The Chronicles of Oklahoma* 71:2 (summer 1993): 161.
Van Deventer, M. J. "Buck Jones, The Screen's Greatest Outdoor Star," *Cowboys Country* 3 (spring–summer 1996): 29.
Watson, Bruce. "If His Life Were a Short Story, Who'd Ever Believe It?," *Smithsonian* (January 1997) 27:10): 97.
Whitehead, Terry. "John Cudahy's Big Adventure," *Country Gazette* 1:4 (March 1992): 1–2.

BOOKS

Abbott, E. C., and Helena Huntington Smith. *We Pointed Them North: Recollections of a Cowpuncher*. Norman: University of Oklahoma Press, 1955.
Adams, Ramon F. *The Cowboy Dictionary*. Norman: University of Oklahoma Press, 1968; New York: Perigee Books, 1993.
——. *The Old-Time Cowhand*. New York: The Macmillan Company, 1948.
Adams, Samuel Hopkins. *Incredible Era: The Life and Times of Warren Gamaliel Harding*. Boston: Houghton Mifflin Company, 1939.
Alexander, Carolyn Elayne. *Abbot Kinney's Venice-of-America,* Vol. 1, *The Golden Years: 1905–1920*. Los Angeles Westside Genealogical Society, 1991.
Allard, William Albert. *Vanishing Breed: Photographs of the Cowboy and the West*. Boston: Little, Brown and Company, 1982.
Allen, Alice M. "The 'Big V' Ranch," *The Last Run, Kay County, Oklahoma, 1893*. Ponca City, Oklahoma: The Courier Printing Company, stories assembled by the Ponca City Chapter of the Daughters of the American Revolution, 1939.
Argo, Burnis, and Ruth Kent. *Oklahoma: Historical Tour Guide*. Carpentersville, Illinois: Crossroads Communications, 1992.
Athearn, Robert G. *The Mythic West in Twentieth Century America*. Lawrence: University of Kansas Press, 1986.
Atherton, Lewis. *The Cattle Kings*. Lincoln: University of Nebraska Press, 1961.
Baird, W. David, and Danney Goble. *The Story of Oklahoma*. Norman: University of Oklahoma Press, 1994.
Balshofer, Fred J., and Arthur C. Miller. *One Reel a Week*. Berkeley: University of California Press, 1967.

Barnard, Evan G. *A Rider of the Cherokee Strip*. Boston: Houghton Mifflin Company, 1936.
Bates, Angela. "The Kansas African American History Trail." Topeka: Kansas Department of Commerce and Housing, Travel and Tourism Development Division, n.d.
Baxter, John. *Sixty Years of Hollywood*. Cranbury, New Jersey: A. S. Barnes and Co., Inc., 1973.
The Baxter Springs Story, 1858–1958. Baxter Springs, Kansas: Centennial Historical Committee, 1958.
Bean, Walton. *California: An Interpretive History*. New York: McGraw-Hill Book Company, 1978.
Blacker, Irwin R., ed. *The Old West In Fact*. New York: Ivan Obolensky, Inc., 1962.
Blevins, Winfred. *Dictionary of the American West*. New York: Facts on File, Inc., 1993.
Bolté, Mary. *Dark and Bloodied Ground*. Riverside, Connecticut: The Chatham Press, Inc., 1973.
Bowman, John S., gen. ed. *The World Almanac of the American West*. New York: Pharos Books, 1986.
Brand Book. Caldwell, Kansas: Cherokee Strip Live Stock Association, 1882.
Brooks, Elston. *I've Heard Those Songs Before*. Fort Worth: The Summit Group, 1991.
Brown, Dee. *The Gentle Tamers: Women of the Old Wild West*. Lincoln: University of Nebraska Press, 1968.
Browning, James A. *Violence Was No Stranger: A Guide to Grave Sites of Famous Westerners*. Stillwater, Oklahoma: Barbed Wire Press, 1993.
Brownlow, Kevin. *The War, the West, and the Wilderness*. New York: Alfred A. Knopf, Inc., 1978.
Buffalo Bill and 101 Ranch Wild West Combined. Philadelphia: The Harrison Press, 1916.
Burroughs, John Rolfe. *Where the Old West Stayed Young*. New York: Bonanza Books, 1962.
Buscombe, Edward, ed. *The BFI Companion to the Western*. New York: Da Capo Press, Inc., 1988.
Butler, Anne M. *Daughters of Joy, Sisters of Misery: Prostitutes in the American West, 1865–1890*. Urbana: University of Illinois Press, 1985.
Butler, William J. *Fort Smith, Past and Present: A Historical Summary*. Fort Smith, Arkansas: The First National Bank of Fort Smith, 1972.
Canutt, Yakima, with Oliver Drake. *Stunt Man: The Autobiography of Yakima Canutt*. Norman: University of Oklahoma Press, 1997.
Cargill, O. A. *My First 80 Years*. Oklahoma City: Banner Book Co., 1965.
Carlile, Glenda. *Buckskin, Calico, and Lace*. Oklahoma City: Southern Hills Publishing Company, 1990.
Carter, Joseph H. *Never Met A Man I Didn't Like: The Life and Writings of Will Rogers*. New York: Avon Books, 1991.
Cary, Diana Serra. *The Hollywood Posse*. Boston: Houghton Mifflin, 1975; Norman: University of Oklahoma Press, 1996.
Central University, Richmond, Kentucky. Ninth Annual Catalogue for the session 1882–1883.
Central University, Richmond, Kentucky. Tenth Annual Catalogue for the session 1883–1884.
Channing, Steven A. *Kentucky: A Bicentennial History*. New York: W. W. Norton & Company, Inc., 1977.
Chapman, Berlin Basil. *The Otoes and Missourias: A Study of Indian Removal and the Legal Aftermath*. Oklahoma City: Times Journal Publishing Co., 1965.
Cheetham, Nicholas. *Mexico: A Short History*. New York: Thomas Y. Crowell Company, 1970.
Chicago Shan-Kive and Round-Up Official Souvenir Program. 1916.
Chrisman, Harry E. *1001 Most-Asked Questions about the American West*. Athens, Ohio: Swallow Press Books, Ohio University Press, 1982.
Clark, Kenneth S., ed. *The Cowboy Sings*. Paull-Pioneer Music Corp., New York, 1932.
Clow, Deborah, and Donald Snow, eds. *Northern Lights: A Selection of New Writing from the American West*. New York: Vintage Books, 1994.
Collings, Ellsworth, and Alma Miller England. *The 101 Ranch*. Norman: University of Oklahoma Press, 1937, 1971.

Collins, Lewis. *History of Kentucky*. Vol. 2. 1877; Reprint, Frankfort: Kentucky Historical Society, 1966.

Conlan, Roberta, ed. *The Wild West*. New York: Time-Life Books, 1993.

Conrad, Howard L., ed. *Encyclopedia of the History of Missouri*. Vol. 4. New York: The Southern History Company, 1901.

Constable, George, ed. *The Old West*. New York: Time-Life Books, 1990.

Cunningham, Robert E. *Perry, Pride of the Prairie*. Stillwater, Oklahoma: Perry Chamber of Commerce, n.d.

Cusic, Don. *Cowboys and the Wild West: An A-Z Guide from the Chisholm Trail to the Silver Screen*. New York: Facts on File, Inc., 1994.

Daniel, Clifton, ed. in chief. *Chronicle of the 20th Century*. Mount Kisco, New York: Chronicle Publications, 1987.

Dary, David. *Cowboy Culture: A Saga of Five Centuries*. New York: Alfred A. Knopf, Inc., 1981; Lawrence: University of Kansas Press, 1981, 1989.

Davis, Burke. *The Civil War: Strange and Fascinating Facts*. New York: The Fairfax Press, 1982.

Davis, Ronald L. *John Ford: Hollywood's Old Master*. Norman: University of Oklahoma Press, 1995.

Davis, William C., and Joseph G. Rosa, cons. eds. *The West*. New York: Smithmark Publishers, Inc., 1994.

Debo, Angie, and John M. Oskison, eds. *Oklahoma: A Guide to the Sooner State*. Norman: University of Oklahoma Press, 1941.

Debo, Angie. *A History of the Indians of the United States*. Norman: University of Oklahoma Press, 1970.

DeMoss, Robert W. *A Look at the History of Nowata, Oklahoma*. Nowata: Nowata County Historical Museum, 1976.

Denson, Paula Carmack, ed. *North Central Oklahoma: Rooted In the Past—Growing for the Future*. Ponca City: North Central Oklahoma Historical Association, Inc., 1995.

Dobie, J. Frank. *A Vaquero of the Brush Country*. 1929.

Dunn, Mrs. M. H. *Early Lincoln County History*. Stanford, Kentucky: Lincoln County Historical Society, n.d.

Eagle, Frank. "Ponca Indian Chieftain," *The Last Run: Kay County, Oklahoma, 1893*. Ponca City, Oklahoma: The Courier Printing Company, stories assembled by the Ponca City Chapter of the Daughters of the American Revolution, 1939.

Eaton, Frank. *Pistol Pete: Veteran of the Old West*. Boston: Little, Brown and Company, 1952.

Edwards, Don. *Classic Cowboy Songs*. Layton, Utah: A Peregrine Smith Book, 1994.

Ellis, W. W. *World's Fair Handy Guide for Tourists*. Saint Louis: National Publishing Company, 1904.

Emmett, Chris. *Shanghai Pierce: A Fair Likeness*. Norman: University of Oklahoma Press, 1953.

England, George Miller. "The Great Ranches," *The Last Run: Kay County, Oklahoma, 1893*. Ponca City, Oklahoma: The Courier Printing Company, stories assembled by the Ponca City Chapter of the Daughters of the American Revolution, 1939.

Evans, Harold C., chief ed. *Kansas: A Guide to the Sunflower State*. New York: Viking Press, 1939.

Farnum, Allen L. *Pawnee Bill's Historic Wild West*. West Chester, Pennsylvania: Schiffer Publishing, Ltd., 1992.

Fenin, George N., and William K. Everson. *The Western: From Silents to Cinerama*. New York: The Orion Press, 1962.

Fitzgerald, David. *Portrait of the Ozarks*. Portland, Oregon: Graphic Arts Center Publishing Company, 1995.

Foner, Eric, and John A. Garraty. *The Reader's Companion to American History*. Boston: Houghton Mifflin Company, 1991.

Forbis, William H. *The Cowboys*. New York: Time-Life Books, 1973.

Franks, Kenny A., Paul F. Lambert, and Carl N. Tyson. *Early Oklahoma Oil: A Photographic History, 1859–1936*. College Station: Texas A & M University Press, 1981.

Franks, Kenny A., and Paul F. Lambert. *Pawnee Pride.* Oklahoma City: Oklahoma Heritage Association, Inc., 1994.
Franks, Kenny A. *The Osage Oil Boom.* Oklahoma City: Oklahoma Heritage Association, 1989.
Friedrich, Otto. *City of Nets: A Portrait of Hollywood in the 1940s.* New York: Harper & Row Publishers, 1986.
Fugate, Francis L., and Roberta B. Fugate. *Roadside History of Oklahoma.* Missoula, Montana: Mountain Press Publishing Company, 1991.
Gaddy, Jerry J. *Obituaries of the Gunfighters: Dust to Dust.* Fort Collins, Colorado: The Old Army Press, 1977.
Gibson, Arrell M. *The Oklahoma Story.* Norman: University of Oklahoma Press, 1978.
———. *Oklahoma: A History of Five Centuries.* 2nd ed. Norman: University of Oklahoma Press, 1981.
Gipson, Fred. *Fabulous Empire: Colonel Zack Miller's Story.* Boston: Houghton Mifflin Company, 1946.
Goble, Danney. *Tulsa! Biography of the American City.* Tulsa: Council Oak Books, 1997.
Goetzmann, William H., and William N. Goetzmann. *The West of the Imagination.* New York: W. W. Norton & Company, Inc., 1986.
Gould, David B. *Gould's St. Louis Directory for 1874.* Saint Louis: David B. Gould Publishers, 1874.
Gragg, Rod. *The Old West Quiz & Fact Book.* New York: Promontory Press, 1986.
Green, Donald E., ed. *Rural Oklahoma.* Oklahoma City: Oklahoma Historical Society, 1977.
Griffith, Richard, and Arthur Mayer. *The Movies.* New York: Bonanza Books, 1957.
Guzmán, Martín Luis. *Memoirs of Pancho Villa.* Austin: University of Texas Press, 1965.
Hall, Terry, with Gregg Stebben. *Cowboy Wisdom.* New York: Warner Books, Inc., 1995.
Hamrick, Alma Ward. *The Call of the San Saba: A History of San Saba County.* Austin: San Felipe Press, Jenkins Publishing Company, 1969.
Hanes, Bailey C. *Bill Pickett, Bulldogger.* Norman: University of Oklahoma Press, 1977.
Harlow, Victor E. *Oklahoma.* Oklahoma City: Harlow Publishing Co., 1949.
Hartman, Mary, and Elmo Ingenthron. *Bald Knobbers: Vigilantes on the Ozark Frontier.* Gretna, Louisiana: Pelican Publishing Company, 1988.
Heide, Robert, and John Gilman. *Cowboy Collectibles.* New York: Harper & Row Publishers, Inc., 1892.
History of Newton, Lawrence, Barry and McDonald Counties, Missouri. Chicago: Goodspeed Publishing Company, 1888.
Hoig, Stan. *Jesse Chisholm: Ambassador of the Plains.* Niwot: University Press of Colorado, 1991.
Horan, James D. *The Great American West.* New York: Crown Publishers, 1959.
Hough, Emerson. *The Passing of the Frontier.* New Haven: Yale University Press, 1921.
Howard, James H. *The Ponca Tribe.* Lincoln: University of Nebraska Press, 1995.
Howard, Robert West. *This Is the West.* New York: Rand McNally & Company, 1957.
Hoy, Jim. *Cowboys and Kansas: Stories from the Tallgrass Prairie.* Norman: University of Oklahoma Press, 1995.
Hunter, J. Marvin, ed. *The Trail Drivers of Texas.* Austin: University of Texas Press, 1985.
Jackson, A. P., and E. C. Cole. *Oklahoma! Politically and Topographically Described, History and Guide to Indian Territory.* Kansas City: Ramsey, Millett and Hudson, 1885.
Jackson, Robert B. *The Remarkable Ride of the Abernathy Boys.* Norman, Oklahoma: Transcript Press, 1993; Henry Z. Walck, Inc., 1967; Levite of Apache, 1988.
Jacobs, Lewis. *The Rise of the American Film.* New York: Harcourt, Brace, 1939.
James, Edward T., ed. *Dictionary of American Biography.* Supplement 3, 1941–1945. New York: Charles Scribner's Sons.
Jordan, H. Glenn, and Thomas M. Holm, eds. *Indian Leaders: Oklahoma's First Statesmen.* Oklahoma City: Oklahoma Historical Society, 1979.
Judson, William. "The Movies," *Buffalo Bill and the Wild West.* Brooklyn, New York: The Brooklyn Museum, 1981.

Kasper, Shirl. *Annie Oakley*. Norman: University of Oklahoma Press, 1992.
Katz, Ephraim. *The Film Encyclopedia*. New York: Perigee Books, 1979.
Kent, J. B. *Official Souvenir: The 101 Ranch, Bliss, Oklahoma*. Chandler, Oklahoma Territory: J. B. Kent, 1905.
Ketchum, Richard M. *Will Rogers: The Man and his Times*. New York: Simon and Shuster, 1973.
Knowles, Thomas W., and Joe R. Lansdale, eds. *The West That Was*. New York: Wings Books, 1993.
——, and ——, eds. *Wild West Show!* New York: Wings Books, 1994.
Kolatch, Alfred J. *Dictionary of First Names*. New York: Perigee Books, Putnam Publishing Group, 1990.
Kooistra, Paul. *Criminals as Heroes: Structure, Power & Identity*. Bowling Green, Ohio: Bowling Green State University Popular Press, 1989.
Lamb, Arthur. *Tragedies of the Osage Hills*. Pawhuska, Oklahoma: Red Corn Publishing, 1964.
Lasky, Jesse L. Jr. *Whatever Happened to Hollywood?* New York: Funk & Wagnalls, 1973, 1975.
Lawrence, Elizabeth Atwood. *Rodeo: An Anthropologist Looks at the Wild and the Tame*. Chicago: University of Chicago Press, 1982.
Lefebvre, Irene Sturm. *Cherokee Strip in Transition*. Enid, Oklahoma: Cherokee Strip Centennial Foundation, Inc., 1993.
Lewis, Jon. E. *The Mammoth Book of the West*. New York: Carroll & Graf Publishers, Inc., 1996.
Logan, Mrs. John A. *The Home Manual*. Chicago: H. J. Smith & Co., 1889.
Logan, William Bryant, and Susan Ochshorn. *The Smithsonian Guide to Historic America: The Pacific States*. New York: Stewart, Tabori & Chang, 1989.
Logue, Roscoe. *Under Texas and Border Skies*. Amarillo, Texas; Russell Stationery Co., 1935.
Luchetti, Cathy. *Home on the Range : A Culinary History of the American West*. New York: Villard Books, 1993.
Lupiano, Vincent dePaul, and Ken W. Sayers. *It Was a Very Good Year: A Cultural History of the United States from 1776 to the Present*. Holbrook, Massachusetts: Bob Adams, Inc., 1994.
Marcy, Randolph B. *The Prairie Traveler*. By authority of the U. S. War Department, 1859. Reprint, Bedford, Massachusetts: Applewood Books, 1993.
Marquart, John. *Six Hundred Receipts Worth their Weight in Gold*. Philadelphia: John E. Potter and Company, 1867.
Mathews, John Joseph. *Life and Death of an Oilman: The Career of E. W. Marland*. Norman: University of Oklahoma Press, 1951.
McCallum, Henry D., and Frances T. *The Wire That Fenced the West*. Norman: University of Oklahoma Press, 1965.
McCutcheon, Marc. *The Writer's Guide to Everyday Life in the 1800s*. Cincinnati: Writer's Digest Books, 1993.
McLoughlin, Denis. *Wild and Woolly: An Encyclopedia of the Old West*. New York: Barnes & Noble Books, 1975.
McReynolds, Edwin C. *Oklahoma: A History of the Sooner State*. Norman: University of Oklahoma Press, 1954.
McWilliams, Carey. *Southern California Country*. New York: Duell, Sloan & Pearce, 1946.
Miller, Lizzie T. "Early Days at the 101 Ranch and Ponca City," *The Last Run, Kay County Oklahoma 1893*. Ponca City: The Courier Printing Company, stories assembled by the Ponca City Chapter of the Daughters of the American Revolution, 1939.
Miller, Worth Robert. *Oklahoma Populism: A History of the People's Party in the Oklahoma Territory*. Norman: University of Oklahoma Press, 1987.
Mills, William Wirt. *St. Louis: The Central Great City of the Union*. New York: Moses King, 1909.
Milner II, Clyde A., Carol A. O'Connor, and Martha A. Sandweiss, eds. *The Oxford History of the American West*. New York: Oxford University Press, 1994.

Milsten, David Randolph. *Will Rogers: The Cherokee Kid.* West Chicago, Illinois: Gleanheath Publishers, 1987.

Mix, Paul E. *The Life and Legend of Tom Mix.* Cranbury, New Jersey: A. S. Barnes and Co., Inc., 1972.

Moran, Tom, and Tom Sewell. *Fantasy by the Sea: A Visual History of the American Venice.* Culver City, California: Peace Press, Inc., 1979.

Morgan, H. Wayne, and Anne Hodges Morgan. *Oklahoma: A History.* New York: W. W. Norton & Company, 1977.

Morris, Michele. *The Cowboy Life.* New York: Simon & Shuster, 1993.

Moses, L. G. *Wild West Shows and the Images of American Indians, 1883–1933.* Albuquerque: University of New Mexico Press, 1996.

Myres, Sandra L. *Westering Women and the Frontier Experience 1800–1915.* Albuquerque: University of New Mexico Press, 1982.

Nash, Gerald D. *Creating the West: Historical Interpretations 1890–1990.* Albuquerque: University of New Mexico Press, 1991.

Nash, Jay Robert. *Bloodletters and Badmen: A Narrative Encyclopedia of American Criminals from the Pilgrims to the Present.* New York: M. Evans and Company, Inc., 1973.

Newsom, D. Earl. *The Cherokee Strip: Its History & Grand Opening.* Stillwater, Oklahoma: New Forums Press, Inc., 1992.

Nicholas, John. H. *Tom Mix: Riding up to Glory.* Kansas City: Lowell Press, 1980.

Norman, James. *Terry's Guide to Mexico.* New York: Doubleday & Company, Inc., 1965.

Norris, M. G. "Bud." *The Tom Mix Book.* Waynesville, North Carolina: The World of Yesterday, 1989.

O'Brien, Darcy. *A Dark and Bloody Ground.* New York: HarperCollins Publishers, Inc., 1993.

O'Neal, Bill. "Bulldoggin' Bill Pickett," *The West That Was.* Edited by Thomas W. Knowles and Joe R. Lansdale. New York: Wings Books, 1993.

O'Neil, Paul. *The End and the Myth.* Chicago: Time-Life Books, Inc., 1979.

Official Review and History of the Great Wild West, Miller Bros. 101 Ranch Wild West. New York: M. Southern & Co. Publishers, 1910.

Okmulgee Historical Society and the Heritage Society of America, *History of Okmulgee County.* Tulsa: Historical Enterprises, Inc., 1985.

Parker, Nathan H. *Missouri as It Is in 1867.* Philadelphia: J. B. Lippincott & Co., 1867.

Parton, James. *Life of Horace Greeley.* 1855.

Peirce, Neal R., and Jerry Hagstrom. *The Book of America: Inside 50 States Today.* New York: W. W. Norton & Company, 1983.

Poe, Charlsie. *Booger Red: World Champion Cowboy.* Winters, Texas: Quality Publications, 1991.

Portfolio of Photographs of the World's Fair, art series no. 7. Chicago: The Werner Company, 1893.

Portfolio of Photographs of the World's Fair, art series no. 9. Chicago: The Werner Company, 1893.

Prucha, Francis Paul, ed. *Americanizing the American Indians.* Lincoln: University of Nebraska Press, 1978.

Quantrill's Raid at Baxter Springs, official reenactment program, 1985.

Rainey, Buck. *Saddle Aces of the Cinema.* San Diego: A. S. Barnes & Company, Inc., 1980.

——. *The Life and Films of Buck Jones: The Silent Era.* Waynesville, North Carolina: The World of Yesterday, 1988.

Records, Laban Samuel. *Cherokee Outlet Cowboy: Recollections of Laban S. Records.* Edited by Ellen Jayne Maris Wheeler. Norman: University of Oklahoma Press, 1995.

Report of the Adjutant General of the State of Kentucky, Confederate Kentucky Volunteers, War 1861–65. Vol. 2. Utica, Kentucky: Cook and McDowell Publications, 1980.

Rich, Everett, ed. *The Heritage of Kansas: Selected Commentaries on Past Times.* Lawrence: University of Kansas Press, 1960.

Riegert, Ray. *Hidden Southern California.* Berkeley: Ulysses Press, 1992.

Rosa, Joseph G., and Robin May. *Buffalo Bill and his Wild West.* Lawrence: University of Kansas Press, 1989.

Russell, Don. *The Lives and Legends of Buffalo Bill.* Norman: University of Oklahoma Press, 1960.

Russell, Don. *The Wild West: A History of the Wild West Shows.* Fort Worth: Amon Carter Museum of Western Art, 1970.

Ruth, Kent, and Jim Argo. *Windows on the Past: Historic Places in Oklahoma.* Oklahoma City: Oklahoma Historical Society, 1984.

Ruth, Kent. *Oklahoma Travel Handbook.* Norman: University of Oklahoma Press, 1977.

Rydjord, John. *Kansas Place-Names.* Norman: University of Oklahoma Press, 1972.

Sadler, Francis Hurd. *St. Louis Day by Day.* Saint Louis: Patrice Press, 1989.

San Saba County History, 1856–1983. San Saba, Texas: San Saba County Historical Commission, 1983.

Sandoz, Mari. *The Cattlemen.* New York: Hastings House, 1958.

Savage, William W. Jr. *The Cherokee Strip Live Stock Association: Federal Regulation and the Cattleman's Last Frontier.* Columbia: University of Missouri Press, 1973.

Sayers, Isabelle S. *Annie Oakley and Buffalo Bill's Wild West.* New York: Dover Publications, Inc., 1981, quoting Buffalo Bill Cody's *Story of the Wild West and Camp-Fire Chats*, 1888.

Scenes Near Baxter Springs. Chicago: J. M. W. Jones Stationery & Printing Co., 1888.

Schessler, Ken. *This Is Hollywood.* Redlands, California: Ken Schessler Publishing, 1978.

Seidenbaum, Art. *Los Angeles 200: A Bicentennial Celebration.* New York: Harry N. Abrams, Inc., 1980.

Seidman, Laurence Ivan. *Once in the Saddle: The Cowboy's Frontier 1866–1896.* New York: Alfred A. Knopf, Inc., 1973.

Shirley, Glenn. *Pawnee Bill: A Biography of Major Gordon W. Lillie.* Stillwater, Oklahoma: Western Publications, 1993.

Shoemaker, Floyd C. *Missouri: Heir of Southern Tradition and Individuality.* Columbia: State Historical Society of Missouri, 1942.

Silver, Nathan. *Lost New York.* New York: American Legacy Press, 1967.

Simpson, Lesley Byrd. *Many Mexicos.* Berkeley: University of California Press, 1941.

Skaggs, Jimmy M., ed., *Ranch and Range in Oklahoma.* Oklahoma City: Oklahoma Historical Society, 1978.

Skaggs, Jimmy M. *The Cattle-Trailing Industry.* Norman: University of Oklahoma Press, 1991.

Slatta, Richard W. *Cowboys of the Americas.* New Haven: Yale University Press, 1990.

Slide, Anthony. *Early American Cinema.* New York: A. S. Barnes & Co., 1970.

Sloan, Jym A. *Old Timers of Wallace Creek.* San Saba, Texas: The *San Saba News*, 1958.

Slotkin, Richard. "The Wild West," *Buffalo Bill and the Wild West.* Brooklyn, New York: The Brooklyn Museum, 1981.

Smith, Betty White, ed. *Osage County Profiles.* Pawhuska, Oklahoma: Osage County Historical Society, Inc., 1964.

Sonnichsen, C. L. *I'll Die Before I'll Run.* New York: Harper & Brothers, 1951.

Speer, Bonnie. *Moments in Oklahoma History.* Norman: Reliance Press, 1988.

Stansbury, Kathryn. *Lucille Mulhall: Wild West Cowgirl.* Mulhall, Oklahoma: Homestead Heirlooms Publishing Company, 1985.

Steele, William O. *The Old Wilderness Road: An American Journey.* New York: Harcourt, Brace & World, Inc., 1968.

Stein, Howard F., and Robert F. Hill, eds. *The Culture of Oklahoma.* Norman: University of Oklahoma Press, 1993.

Steiner, Stan. *The Waning of the West.* New York: St. Martin's Press, 1989.

Steinfeldt, Cecilia. *San Antonio Was: Seen Through a Magic Lantern.* San Antonio: San Antonio Museum Association.

"The Story of Ernest W. Marland," *The Last Run, Kay County, Oklahoma, 1893.* Ponca City, Oklahoma: The Courier Printing Company, stories assembled by the Ponca City Chapter of the Daughters of the American Revolution, 1939.

Strickland, Rennard. *The Indians in Oklahoma.* Norman: University of Oklahoma Press, 1980.

Tarpley, Fred. *1001 Texas Place Names.* Austin: University of Texas Press, 1980.

Taylor, Elizabeth. *Elizabeth Taylor.* New York: Harper & Row, Publishers, Inc., 1965.
Third Annual Report of the Denver Board of Trade, 1872, quoted in Ernest Staples Osgood. *The Day of the Cattleman.* Chicago: University of Chicago Press, 1929.
Thoburn, Joseph B., and Muriel H. Wright. *Oklahoma: A History of the State and its People.* Vol. 3. New York: Lewis Historical Publishing Company, Inc., 1929.
Thomas, Dianne Stine, ed. *The Old West.* New York: Prentice Hall Press, Time-Life Books, Inc., 1990.
Thomas, James H. "The 101 Ranch: A Matter of Style," *Ranch and Range in Oklahoma.* Edited by Jimmy K. Skaggs. Oklahoma City: Oklahoma Historical Society, 1978.
Thompson, John. *Closing the Frontier: Radical Response in Oklahoma, 1889–1923.* Norman: University of Oklahoma Press, 1986.
Thorp, N. Howard (Jack). *Songs of the Cowboys.* Lincoln: University of Nebraska Press, 1984.
Tibbles, Henry. *The Ponca Chief.* Boston: Lockwood, Brooks, 1880.
Tibbles, Thomas Henry. *Standing Bear and the Ponca Chiefs.* Lincoln: University of Nebraska Press, 1972.
Trachtman, Paul. *The Gunfighters.* New York: Time-Life Books, 1974.
Trekell, Ronald L. *History of the Tulsa Police Department, 1882–1990.* Tulsa: Ronald L. Trekell, 1990.
Turner, Frederick Jackson. *The Frontier in American History.* Tucson: University of Arizona Press, 1986.
Walker, Alexander. *Elizabeth.* New York: Grove Weidenfeld, 1990.
Wallis, Michael. *Oil Man: The Story of Frank Phillips and the Birth of Phillips Petroleum.* New York: Doubleday, 1988.
———. *Pretty Boy: The Life and Times of Charles Arthur Floyd.* New York: St. Martin's Press, Inc., 1992.
Wallis, Michael, and Suzanne Fitzgerald Wallis. *Songdog Diary: 66 Stories from the Road.* Tulsa: Council Oak Publishing, 1996.
Watts, Peter. *A Dictionary of the Old West.* New York: Promontory Press, 1977.
Webb, Walter Prescott. *The Great Plains.* Boston: Ginn and Co., 1931, quoting Edwin Ford Piper's *Barbed Wire and Wayfarers*, Macmillan Company.
Wellman, Paul I. *A Dynasty of Western Outlaws.* New York: Bonanza Books, 1961.
Werner, M. R. *Barnum.* New York: Harcourt, Brace and Company, Inc., 1923.
West, C. W. "Dub." *Outlaws and Peace Officers of Indian Territory.* Muskogee, Oklahoma: Muscogee Publishing Company, 1987.
Weston, Jack. *The Real American Cowboy.* New York: New Amsterdam Books, 1985.
White, Richard, "Frederick Jackson Turner and Buffalo Bill," *The Frontier In American Culture.* Edited by James R. Grossman. Berkeley: University of California Press, 1994.
Wilcox, Sally. *Winfield and the Walnut Valley.* Arkansas City, Kansas: Gilliland's Publishing, 1975.
Wise, Lu Celia. *Indian Cultures of Oklahoma.* Oklahoma City: Oklahoma State Department of Education, 1978.
Wister, Owen. *The Virginian.* New York: The Macmillan Company, 1902.
Witherspoon, Margaret Johanson. *Remembering the St. Louis World's Fair.* Saint Louis: Comfort Printing Company, 1973.
Wolfenstine, Manfred R. *The Manual of Brands and Marks.* Norman: University of Oklahoma Press, 1970.
Woolford, Sam, and Bess Woolford. *The San Antonio Story.* Austin: The Steck Co., 1950.
Worcester, Don. *The Chisholm Trail: High Road of the Cattle Kingdom.* New York: Indian Head Books, a division of Barnes & Noble, Inc., by arrangement with the University of Nebraska Press, 1980.
The WPA Guide to 1930s Missouri. Lawrence: University Press of Kansas, 1986; originally published by Duell, Sloan and Pearce as *Missouri: A Guide to the "Show Me" State*, 1941.
The WPA Guide to 1930s Oklahoma. Lawrence: University Press of Kansas, 1986; originally published by the University of Oklahoma Press as *Oklahoma: A Guide to the Sooner State*, 1941.

The WPA Guide to New York City. New York: Random House, 1939; Pantheon Books, 1982.
Wright, Muriel H. *A Guide to the Indian Tribes of Oklahoma*. Norman and London: University of Oklahoma Press, 1951, 1986.
Wyatt, Frank S., and George Rainey. *Brief History of Oklahoma*. Oklahoma City: Webb Publishing Company, 1919.
Yagoda, Ben. *Will Rogers: A Biography*. New York: Alfred A. Knopf, Inc., 1993.
Yenne, Bill. *The Encyclopedia of North American Indian Tribes*. New York: Crescent Books, 1986.
Yost, Nellie Snyder. *Buffalo Bill: His Family, Friends, Fame, Failures, and Fortunes*. Chicago: The Swallow Press, Inc., 1979.
Zwink, Tim, and Donovan Reichenberger. *Ranchlands to Railroads*. Alva, Oklahoma: Alva Centennial Commission, 1986.

ACKNOWLEDGMENTS

Thank God for the guardians of the Hundred and One.

From the moment I decided to tell the complete story of the Miller family and its empire, I was fortunate to find diligent sentinels of history dedicated to keeping alive the legacy of the 101 Ranch—a truly significant icon of the American West.

Throughout the many years of research and development required to write this book, this posse of wisdom keepers who came to my rescue did everything humanly possible to make the process easier. Literally hundreds of individuals—including former 101 Ranch employees and performers, Miller family members, collectors, researchers, historians, teachers, authors, journalists, and friends—assisted me. I will be forever in their debt, and I unconditionally concede that many of their names should rightfully be listed as coauthors of this work along with mine.

Most of those who helped me are mentioned in the text itself or in the accompanying endnotes and bibliography. Many of those names also appear in these acknowledgments. Some of them deserve special mention.

At the top of my long list are the many members of the extended Miller family and their descendants. I was delighted to have been able to spend significant amounts of time with the late Zack Miller Jr. and with Joe C. Miller Jr. Their help was limitless. I consider myself a lucky man to have had their enormous storehouse of memories at my disposal.

The unpublished diaries and memoirs of Alice Miller Harth, daughter of Joseph Carson Miller, greatly augmented this book. Her remarkable papers were made available to me through her daughters—Elizabeth Harth Wyman, of Rogers, Arkansas, and Virginia Harth Richards, of Fort Worth, Texas. Thank you, ladies, for granting me permission to excerpt the exquisite writings of your late mother.

It was not until almost seventy years after the death of Joseph C. Miller that surviving Miller family members learned his youngest son, Will Brooks Miller, had grown to manhood and changed his name yet again. He became William Joseph Miller and raised a family, including a son named Joseph in honor of the famous father Will never knew.

A tip of my author's hat goes to this part of the Miller family, especially Joseph B. Miller, Jim Miller, and Jeff Miller, the sons of the late William Joseph Miller and Joyce M. Miller. These lively grandsons of Joe C. Miller and his second wife, Mary Verlin Miller, have become active in the 101 Ranch Old Timers Association, Inc., and 101 Ranch Collectors Association and are obviously proud of their rich heritage. It is my constant pleasure to observe this new generation of Millers connect with other family members during the various events held at the site of the 101 Ranch headquarters.

My gratitude also goes to the family of Alma Miller England—the lone Miller sister—including Marianne England Mann; Bess and Arthur Mann; Victoria England Quinn and Elizabeth England Neunuebel, daughters of the late George England.

There can be no question that this book would never have been published without my wife and life partner, Suzanne Fitzgerald Wallis. Readers need to know that Suzanne not only served as the book's architect but also enhanced every word and photograph. Her personal sacrifice, attention to detail, and unflagging encouragement fueled my creative spirit and inspired me, especially on those dark days when all looked hopeless. Suzanne—aided by her constant companions and our feline muses, Beatrice and Molly—waved her magic wand over every paragraph and image. My appreciation is as everlasting as my love for this remarkable woman.

There is no way I can ever repay Jerry and Ruth Murphey for all the help and guidance they unselfishly provided me as I put this book together. As I enjoy saying, the Murpheys are blessed with the intestinal fortitude of seasoned bronc busters, the diligence of Texas Rangers in pursuit, and the stamina of a herd of longhorns.

No two people have done more than this dedicated duo when it comes to guarding the 101 Ranch image and ensuring that the Millers' incredible story remains in the public eye. Their magnificent obsession with the Hundred and One and their maintenance of the most extensive collection of 101 Ranch artifacts stand as prime illustrations of resourcefulness and hard work for all those interested in historical preservation. My heartfelt thanks go to Jerry and Ruth and the entire Murphey clan, especially their daughter, Karen Murphey Terry. Bravo, Jerry and Ruth! Bravo, my dear friends!

I was indeed blessed to have been able to spend considerable amounts of time with some of the men and women who worked for the 101 Ranch and others who had direct ties to the Millers and their sprawling ranch empire. I will be forever grateful for all the help I received from Bethel Freeman, Lloyd F. "Sam" Hill, Jack Quait, Kenneth and Opal Goodeagle, Joe Colby, Cecil Cornish, Buddy Kemp, Hilde Workman, Lee H. Cornell, Rex and Maude Spangler, Arthur "Capper" Newton, Della May Loving Hand, Art Loving, Vernon Vance, Melvon Lewis, and so many others. Although some of them have not lived to see the completion of this work, their contributions and insight remain invaluable.

At the Pioneer Woman Museum in Ponca City, Oklahoma, the late Laura Mae McDonagh Streich, one of the most dedicated historians I have ever met, and Jan Prough, hardworking curator, went above and beyond in their efforts to help me track down useful and critical facets of the Millers' story. Laura was taken from us far too soon, but her incredible effort to preserve the history of the 101 Ranch will never be forgotten.

Robert Weil, former executive editor of St. Martin's Press, was a diligent and faithful guide throughout the development of this book. Bob served as the editor of several of my books, and in each instance his intelligence and love of history—especially the history of the American West—proved invaluable.

I was also fortunate to have the creative input and editing skills of Andrew Miller, a fine associate editor at St. Martin's Press. With Bob Weil's support and guidance, Andrew deftly shaped the manuscript and provided me with a steady flow of sage advice. I am proud that the prints of Bob Weil and Andrew Miller can be found throughout my book.

Others at St. Martin's Press who deserve recognition are Mara Lurie, production editor; Curt Alliaume, production manager; Rob Belshe, publicist; Gretchen Achilles, design director; and Steve Snider, creative director.

As she has done with several of my previously published books, Hazel Rowena Mills once again provided her superb editorial expertise to this effort. She was deeply involved in every aspect of the book's development from the research stage all the way through copy editing. Many thanks to you, dear Rowena.

Allen "Storm" Strider was another good friend who was always there for me, acting as a researcher, sounding board, and counselor, particularly when the going got rough, as it does at some point in every book's evolution. Allen spent countless hours probing various files at the Western History Collections at the University of Oklahoma. My gratitude to you, Allen.

I relied greatly on *Fabulous Empire*, by Fred Gipson, and *The 101 Ranch*, by Ellsworth Collings and Alma Miller England, the two previously published works about the 101 Ranch. Both of these books and many other important sources are discussed in the text, endnotes, and bibliography.

I also gleaned excellent tidbits of information about the Millers from the late Mike Sokoll's self-published works, *101 Ranch Stars I Have Known* and *Roping the 101 Ranch*. Mike truly was "the man who put it all back together" when it came to salvaging memories of the Hundred and One. The 101 Ranch collections of Jack Keathly and John D. Cooper also were important, providing much detail which had never before been revealed. I appreciate the generosity of John Larbus, of Mount Blanchard, Ohio, who furnished one of the historic 101 Ranch Show posters used in this book. And thanks to Kristin Peterson, a fine Saint Louis photographer who went out of her way to help obtain a copy of a rare photograph of Donata La Banca.

Velma and Ray Falconer, owners of The Glass Negative in Ponca City, Oklahoma, generously shared with me their extensive collection of 101 Ranch photographs, including many rare images. Many thanks to both of you for your support and assistance.

Jean Webb Evans, president of the 101 Ranch Old Timers Association, and Linda Rennie, secretary-treasurer, were godsends to me. Jeannie, many thanks for your patience and trust. Linda, I am particularly indebted to you for everything you did for me during my frequent trips to Ponca City. I am pleased that I was able to spend time with your parents, Rex and Maude Spangler, at their home in Marland. I also appreciate all the officers and members of the 101 Ranch Collectors Association.

My profound thanks go to the skilled professionals at the Wallis Group, Inc., the advertising, public relations, and marketing firm headed by my wife, Suzanne Fitzgerald Wallis. I am forever grateful to Suzanne and her staff, especially Lynne Henson, Linda Adams, Stacy Ryle, Debra Silkman, and Lynn Adair. Lynne Henson, vice president, helped keep me on track every single day and inspired me with her optimistic approach to everything she does. An extra round of applause goes to Linda Adams for all the time and energy she devoted to the development of this book. Linda, I am in your debt—*muchas gracias.*

Thanks go to Carol Mann, the primary literary agent for this book. She handled the initial negotiations for the book and continued as a wise emissary throughout its lengthy gestation period. Michael Carlisle, of Carlisle & Company, and Amy Schiffman, of the William Morris Agency, also rate kudos for their considerable contributions and assistance.

I am most grateful for all the invaluable assistance I received from the management and staff of the Frank Phillips Foundation, Inc. In particular, I wish to thank the foundation's general manager, Richard T. Miller, and, at Woolaroc Museum, Robert Lansdown, director; Kenneth D. Meek, curator of collections; and Linda Stone Laws, curator of art. Kenneth and Linda were especially helpful in the selection of photographs from the museum collection.

My gratitude goes to the late Gene Autry and to Larry McMurtry and Jim Lehrer for reading early chapters of this book and providing me with their comments and insight. I am proud that the quotes of this diverse trio grace the cover of my book.

Others whom I thank for all their help and contributions include the following:

Kentucky: Ron D. Bryant, curator of rare books and director of reading rooms, Kentucky Historical Society, Frankfort; Birney Fish; Greater Lexington Convention & Visitors Bureau; Charles C. Hay III, archivist, Eastern Kentucky University, Richmond; Harvey Helm Memorial Library, Stanford; T. J. and Nancy Miller Hill; Kentucky Department of Travel Development; Allan R. Leach; Lexington Public Library; Lincoln County Historical Society; the *Lincoln County Post*, Stanford; Glennis Miller; David Newcomb, mayor, Crab Orchard; Rockcastle County Historical Society, Inc., Mount Vernon; Martha Wallace Scott; Ray W. and Mae Margaret Fish Settle; Kenneth Theobald; Juanita Witt.

Missouri: Charles E. Brown, manager, information services, St. Louis Mercantile Library; Steven Call, assistant curator, photographs and prints, and Dennis Northcott, archivist, Missouri Historical Society, Saint Louis; Carthage Chamber of Commerce; Jean La Banca Cox; Timothy Darch; Richard E. Dillon, postmaster, Newtonia; Charles and Carolyn Dunlap; Historic Daniel Boone Home & Boonesfield Village, Inc., Defiance; Helen La Banca; Sue Navratil, Newton County Historical Society, Neosho; David Weems.

Texas: Christine Bessent, librarian, Rylander Memorial Library, San Saba, Texas; the Devil's Rope Museum, McLean; Sammy Gold; Meg Hacker and Barbara Rust, Federal Archives, Fort Worth; San Antonio Convention & Visitors Bureau; Zigy Kaluzny; Jo Linzey, San Saba Chamber of Commerce; Teresa Maskunas, secretary, county attorney's office, and David M. Williams, county attorney, San Saba County; Menard Historical Society; the Menger Hotel, San Antonio; Frances Williams Robinson; San Antonio Museum Association; Tom Shelton, library department, Institute of Texan Cultures, the University of Texas at San Antonio; Violet D. Smith; Red Steagall.

Kansas: Phyllis Abbott, president, and Joan Martin, Baxter Springs Heritage Center and Museum; Bill Balcer; Baxter Springs Historical Society; Leslie A. Cade, reference archivist, Larry Jochims, director of historical research, and Christie K. Stanley, registrar, Center for Historical Research, Kansas State Historical Society, Topeka; Frankie S. Cullison, Cowley County Historical Society, Winfield; Jolene McCallister, Baxter Springs Chamber of Commerce, Inc.; Scott Nelson; Barbara Rice, city clerk, Baxter Springs; Fred G. Sprang; Fred and Velma Strickland; Dean Walker; Winfield Area Chamber of Commerce; Winfield Convention and Tourism Committee; Mary Ann and Richard Kay Wortman.

Oklahoma: Louise Abercrombie and Kathy Zehr, *Ponca City News*; Marilyn Andrews; Alfred Arkeketa; Rosetta "Muffin" Arkeketa; Fred Beers; Karen Bigbee, Perry Carnegie Library; Keith Binning, World Publishing Company Library, Tulsa; Loyd Bishop, genealogy librarian, Ponca City Public Library; Carol Bryant Bluethman; Quay Bonfy; Jean and Jerry Brace, Brace Books & More, Ponca City; Bettie Brown; Steve Bunch, former sheriff, Noble County; Pat Cain; Joseph H. Carter, director, Will Rogers Memorial and Birthplace, Claremore; Mary Elizabeth Hodges Case; W. J. "Bill" Casto; Bob Clark; Kenny Coldiron; Lee H. Cornell; Robert Cotton; Sharon Courtright, *Perry Daily Journal*; the *Daily Oklahoman*, Oklahoma City; Linda Strickland Day; Dixie Haas Dooley; Frederick F. Drummond; John Dunning; Sarah Erwin, curator of archival collections, Gilcrease Museum, Tulsa; Lieutenant Governor Mary Fallin; Scott Fitzgerald; Kenny Franks; Lawanda French, Cultural Center and Indian Museum, Ponca City; Charles Edward Garrott; Mary Thompson Garrott; Joanna Gary; Ronnie Goodeagle; Terry Griffith.

Rodger G. Harris, oral historian, and Judith Michener, historian and archivist, Archives and Manuscripts Division, Chester Cowan, photo archivist, and William D. Welge, archivist, Oklahoma Historical Society,

Oklahoma City; Harold Hiatt; Luvina M. Hill; Sammy Hill; Bobby Joe Howe; Bill Howell; Martha Jones; David W. Keathly; Lou and Jack Keathly; Bud Kemp; Bob Kerr; Paul Lambert; Ervin and Mary Grace Lebeda; Antonine E. T. Le Clair; Rosetta Le Clair; Melvon and Grace Lewis; Dr. Guy Logsdon; John R. Lovett, photographic archivist, and Kristina L. Southwell, graduate research assistant, Western History Collections, University of Oklahoma, Norman; John Maker; Louisa McCune, editor, *Oklahoma Today*; Glen V. McIntyre, site attendant, Museum of the Cherokee Strip, Oklahoma Historical Society, Enid; Liz Medley; Lance A. Millis; Tom Mix Museum, Dewey; National Cowboy Hall of Fame and Western Heritage Center, Oklahoma City; David Mills, president, First National Bank, Ponca City; Pat Muchmore.

Oklahoma Bankers Association, Oklahoma City; Okmulgee Historical Society; Osage County Historical Society, Pawhuska; J. W. "Jim" Parker; Pawnee Bill Ranch, Oklahoma Historical Society, Pawnee; Vic and Pearl Lewis Peri; Frank Phillips Jr.; Paul Prather; Jeanne Ronda; Elden G. Roscher; Lavaughn Howell Roth; Michael Roughface; Randy Roughface; Vinnie Scott; Wilma F. Sokoll; Clyde Speer, site attendant, Cherokee Strip Museum, Oklahoma Historical Society, Perry; Sean StandingBear; Chris Stansberry; Susan Stansberry, Frontier School Media Department, Red Rock; Miller Story, U.S. Court, Western District, Oklahoma City; Guy Strong; Bob Teichmer; Top of Oklahoma Museum, Blackwell; Mark Talbert; Eddie Trumbla; Tulsa City-County Library System; Marjorie Turk; McFarlin Library, University of Tulsa; Washington County Historical Society, Inc., Bartlesville; Frances Webb, Miami Public Library; John Welch, superintendent, Chickasaw National Recreational Area, Sulphur; Maxine and J. D. Welch; Bob Westmoreland; Terry Whitehead; Joyce Woodruff.

California: Carolyn Elayne Alexander; Château Marmont, Los Angeles; Bill Ehrheart; Sam Gill, archivist, Special Collections, Margaret Herrick Library, Beverly Hills; Betsy Goldman, Santa Monica Convention & Visitors' Bureau; Linda and Christopher Lewis, the Entertainment Group; Special Collections, University of California at Los Angeles; Venice Chamber of Commerce; Venice Historical Society; Will Rogers State Historic Park.

Others: American Museum of the Moving Image, Astoria, New York; Tim Brookes, East Liverpool, Ohio; Phillip Capritto, court clerk's office, U.S. Court, Eastern District, New Orleans, Louisiana; Circus World Museum, Baraboo, Wisconsin; Roger M. Crowley, general manager, the Old

West Shop, Vienna, West Virginia; Susan Dalton, American Film Institute Library, Kennedy Center, Washington, D.C.; Louis DeCarlo, Buffalo, New York; Larry D. Griffin, dean, Arts and Sciences, Dyersburg (Tennessee) State Community College; Carol Haralson, Sedona, Arizona; Dr. William McRae, Baltimore; National Park Service, Preservation Assistance Division, Washington, D.C.; Terrence Moore, Tucson, Arizona; Michael Martin Murphey, Taos, New Mexico; Stephen Skidmore, Chicago, Illinois; George Virgines, Albuquerque, New Mexico; Charles Wade III, Benton, Louisiana.

INDEX

ABOUT THE AUTHOR

MICHAEL WALLIS, a native of Missouri, has lived and worked throughout the West. His writing has been published in hundreds of newspapers and magazines, and he has written ten books. Wallis has received numerous honors, including the first Steinbeck Award, the Lynn Riggs Award, and the Arrell Gibson Lifetime Achievement Award. He was inducted into the Oklahoma Professional Writers' Hall of Fame and was the first inductee of the Oklahoma Route 66 Hall of Fame. Wallis and his wife, Suzanne Fitzgerald Wallis, have lived in Oklahoma since 1982 and maintain a hideout in northern New Mexico.